TAILOR-MADE POLYSACCHARIDES IN DRUG DELIVERY

TAILOR-MADE POLYSACCHARIDES IN DRUG DELIVERY

Edited by

AMIT KUMAR NAYAK

Professor, Department of Pharmaceutics, Seemanta Institute of Pharmaceutical Sciences, Jharpokharia, Mayurbhanj, Odisha, India

MD SAQUIB HASNAIN

Professor, Department of Pharmacy, Palamau Institute of Pharmacy, Daltonganj, Jharkhand, India

ELSEVIER

ACADEMIC PRESS

An imprint of Elsevier

Academic Press is an imprint of Elsevier
125 London Wall, London EC2Y 5AS, United Kingdom
525 B Street, Suite 1650, San Diego, CA 92101, United States
50 Hampshire Street, 5th Floor, Cambridge, MA 02139, United States
The Boulevard, Langford Lane, Kidlington, Oxford OX5 1GB, United Kingdom

ISBN 978-0-12-821286-8

For information on all Academic Press publications
visit our website at https://www.elsevier.com/books-and-journals

Publisher: Stacy Masucci
Acquisitions Editor: Andre G. Wolff
Editorial Project Manager: Kristi L. Anderson
Production Project Manager: Omer Mukthar
Cover Designer: Greg Harris

Typeset by STRAIVE, India

Contents

8. Polysaccharide-based polyelectrolyte complex systems in drug delivery

Gouranga Nandi, Md Saquib Hasnain, and Amit Kumar Nayak

9. Polysaccharide-based interpenetrating polymeric network systems in drug delivery

Sudipta Das, Arnab Samanta, Md Saquib Hasnain, and Amit Kumar Nayak

10. Polysaccharide nanoconjugates in drug delivery

Mohammed Tahir Ansari, Farheen Sami, Md Saquib Hasnain, Mohd Usman Mohd Siddique, and Amit Kumar Nayak,

11. Functionalized chitosan in drug delivery

Zahra Shariatinia

12. Modified alginates in drug delivery

Nandan Sarkar and Arindam Maity

13. Uses of tailor-made plant starches in drug delivery

Md Saquib Hasnain, Mohd Usman Mohd Siddique, Manoj M. Gadewar, Mohammed Tahir Ansari, Mohd Neyaz Ahsan, Gouranga Nandi, and Amit Kumar Nayak

14. Cancer targeting by tailor-made polysaccharides

Azim Ansari, Abdullah Sheriker, Mohd Usman Mohd Siddique, Mrunali Patil, Sameer N. Goyal, Sheikh Murtuja, Mohd Neyaz Ahsan, Md Saquib Hasnain, and Amit Kumar Nayak

Contributors

Syed Anees Ahmed Department of Pharmacology, Hygia Institute of Pharmaceutical Application and Research, Lucknow, Uttar Pradesh, India

Mohd Neyaz Ahsan Department of Medical Laboratory Technology, University Polytechnic, Birla Institute of Technology, Ranchi, Jharkhand, India

Muhanna K. Al-Muhanna The National Center for Composite and High Performances Materials, King Abdulaziz City for Science and Technology (KACST), Riyadh, Saudi Arabia

Azim Ansari Department of Pharmaceutical Chemistry, Shri Vile Parle Kelavani Mandal's Institute of Pharmacy, Dhule, Maharashtra, India

Mohammed Tahir Ansari School of Pharmacy, Faculty of Science and Engineering, University of Nottingham Malaysia, Semenyih, Selangor, Malaysia

Naushad Anwar Department of Chemistry, Aligarh Muslim University, Aligarh, Uttar Pradesh, India

Pranab Kumar Bandyopadhyay Department of Pharmaceutics, Seemanta Institute of Pharmaceutical Sciences, Jharpokharia, Mayurbhanj, Odisha, India

Sudipta Das Department of Pharmaceutics, Netaji Subhas Chandra Bose Institute of Pharmacy, Nadia, West Bengal, India

Rimi Dey Department of Pharmaceutics, Netaji Subhas Chandra Bose Institute of Pharmacy, Nadia, West Bengal, India

Manoj M. Gadewar Dept of Pharmacology, School of Medical and Allied Sciences, K.R. Mangalam University, Gurgaon, (Haryana), India

Mohammad Reza Ganjali Center of Excellence in Electrochemistry, School of Chemistry, College of Science, University of Tehran; Biosensor Research Center, Endocrinology and Metabolism Molecular-Cellular Sciences Institute, Tehran University of Medical Sciences, Tehran, Iran

Sameer N. Goyal Department of Pharmacology, Shri Vile Parle Kelavani Mandal's Institute of Pharmacy, Dhule, Maharashtra, India

Sajjad Habibzadeh Department of Chemical Engineering, Amirkabir University of Technology (Tehran Polytechnic), Tehran, Iran

Md Saquib Hasnain Department of Pharmacy, Palamau Institute of Pharmacy, Daltonganj, Jharkhand, India

Ali Khodadadi Department of Internal Medicine, School of Medicine, Gonabad University of Medical Sciences, Gonabad, Iran

Arindam Maity Department of Pharmaceutical Technology, JIS University, Kolkata, West Bengal, India

Amin Hamed Mashhadzadeh Department of Mechanical and Aerospace Engineering, School of Engineering and Digital Sciences, Nazarbayev University, Nur-Sultan, Kazakhstan

Mohd Usman Mohd Siddique Department of Pharmaceutical Chemistry, Shri Vile Parle Kelavani Mandal's Institute of Pharmacy, Dhule, Maharashtra, India

Muhammad Tajammal Munir College of Engineering and Technology, American University of the Middle East, Egaila, Kuwait; Department of Chemical and Materials Engineering, The University of Auckland, Auckland, New Zealand

Sheikh Murtuja Department of Pharmaceutical Science and Technology, Birla Institute of Technology, Mesra, Jharkhand, India

Gouranga Nandi Division of Pharmaceutics, Department of Pharmaceutical Technology, University of North Bengal, Raja Rammohunpur, Darjeeling, West Bengal, India

Amit Kumar Nayak Department of Pharmaceutics, Seemanta Institute of Pharmaceutical Sciences, Jharpokharia, Mayurbhanj, Odisha, India

Mrunali Patil Department of Pharmaceutical Chemistry, Shri Vile Parle Kelavani Mandal's Institute of Pharmacy, Dhule, Maharashtra, India

Morteza Rezapour IP Department, Research Institute of Petroleum Industry (RIPI), Tehran, Iran

Mohammad Reza Saeb Department of Polymer Technology, Faculty of Chemistry, Gdańsk University of Technology, Gdańsk, Poland

Foad Salehnia Center of Excellence in Electrochemistry, School of Chemistry, College of Science, University of Tehran, Tehran, Iran

Azam Salmankhani Faculty of Mechanical Engineering, K. N. Toosi University of Technology, Tehran, Iran

Arnab Samanta Department of Pharmaceutics, Netaji Subhas Chandra Bose Institute of Pharmacy, Nadia, West Bengal, India

Farheen Sami Department of Pharmaceutics, Hygia Institute of Pharmaceutical Education and Research, Lucknow, India

Nandan Sarkar Department of Pharmaceutical Technology, School of Medical Science, Adamas University, Kolkata, West Bengal, India

Farzad Seidi Jiangsu Co-Innovation Center of Efficient Processing and Utilization of Forest Resources and International Innovation Center for Forest Chemicals and Materials, Nanjing Forestry University, Nanjing, China

Zahra Shariatinia Department of Chemistry, Amirkabir University of Technology (Tehran Polytechnic), Tehran, Iran

Abdullah Sheriker Department of Pharmacology, Shri Vile Parle Kelavani Mandal's Institute of Pharmacy, Dhule, Maharashtra, India

Mohsen Khodadadi Yazdi Center of Excellence in Electrochemistry, School of Chemistry, College of Science, University of Tehran, Tehran, Iran

Payam Zarrintaj School of Chemical Engineering, Oklahoma State University, Stillwater, OK, United States

About the editors

Amit Kumar Nayak, PhD
Professor, Department of Pharmaceutics, Seemanta Institute of Pharmaceutical Sciences, Jharpokharia, Mayurbhanj, Odisha, India

Prof. (Dr.) Amit Kumar Nayak is currently working as a professor in Seemanta Institute of Pharmaceutical Sciences, Odisha, India. He earned his PhD in Pharmaceutical Sciences from IFTM University, India. He worked as a senior project associate at IIT Kanpur in a CSIR-sponsored project. Dr. Nayak has over 13 years of research experience in the field of pharmaceutics, especially in the development and characterization of novel biopolymeric and nanostructured drug delivery systems made of natural biopolymers. He has authored over 130 research and review articles in various high-impact peer-reviewed journals and 108 book chapters in various international books. In addition, he has authored 2 books and edited 17 books published by international publishers. He received the University Foundation Day Research Award-2019 from Biju Patnaik University of Technology, Odisha. He serves as a reviewer for several reputed journals and is a life member of the Association of Pharmaceutical Teachers of India (APTI).

Md Saquib Hasnain, PhD
Professor, Department of Pharmacy, Palamau Institute of Pharmacy, Daltonganj, Jharkhand, India

Prof. (Dr.) Md Saquib Hasnain is currently working as a Professor in the Department of Pharmacy, Palamau Institute of Pharmacy, Jharkhand, India and has over 10 years of research experience in the field of drug delivery and pharmaceutical formulation analyses, especially systematic development and characterization of diverse nanostructured drug delivery systems, controlled release drug delivery systems, bioenhanced drug delivery systems, nanomaterials, and nanocomposites employing "Quality by Design" approaches and many more. To date, he has authored over 70 publications in various high-impact peer-reviewed journals, more than 100 book chapters, and has 16 books to his credit. He also serves as reviewer for several prestigious journals. He has participated and presented his research work at over 10 conferences in India and abroad. He was also a member of scientific societies such as the Royal Society of Chemistry, United Kingdom; the International Association of Environmental and Analytical Chemistry, Switzerland; and the Swiss Chemical Society, Switzerland.

Preface

The application of natural polysaccharides as biomaterials in place of synthetic biopolymers can be attributed to some of their potential advantages such as ready availability from natural resources, cost-effective extraction/production, biocompatibility, and biodegradability. For a long time, polysaccharides have been employed as drug delivery excipient biomaterials in various kinds of drug delivery formulations such as powders, granules, gels, hydrogels, beads, pellets, capsules, tablets, microparticles, nanoparticles, membranes, films, implants, and scaffolds. The reality behind the escalating use of different polysaccharides as drug delivery excipient biomaterials is that the raw material resources are renewable and suitable for sustainable extraction/production of polysaccharides. However, native polysaccharides exhibit some functional disadvantages for their use as excipient biomaterials such as uncontrolled hydration rate, inconsistent aqueous solubility, viscosity fall during storage, and the presence of microbial load. To instill various potential and desired functional properties, polysaccharides can be tailored chemically by the introduction of different functional groups in the polysaccharide structures. The wide variety of polysaccharide structures allows tailoring of their structures via different chemical reactions, such as oxidation, esterification, carboxymethylation, thiolation, cross-linking, grafting copolymerization, formation of polyelectrolyte complexes (PECs), and interpenetrating polymer networks (IPNs), to improve the functional properties of polysaccharides. These tailor-made polysaccharides not only curtail the potential drawbacks of native forms, but also facilitate their utilization prospects as improved drug delivery excipient biomaterials in various kinds of drug delivery formulations. In this context, *Tailor-Made Polysaccharides in Drug Delivery* aims to present a thorough insight into the comprehensive discussions about the synthesis of various tailor-made polysaccharides and their usefulness in drug delivery fields. The book has a collection of *15 chapters* presenting different key topics related to the synthesis of various tailor-made polysaccharides emphasizing their drug delivery applications by the leading experts. A concise account of the contents of each chapter follows to provide a glimpse of the book to the readers.

Chapter 1 entitled "Synthesis of tailor-made polysaccharides: An overview" describes various chemical reactions and mechanisms of tailoring of polysaccharides through derivatization of various functional groups (such as oxidation, phosphorylation, sulfation, thiolation, amidation, esterification, carboxymethylation, carbamoylethylation, etc.) in the polysaccharide structure, grafting with polysaccharides (i.e., graft copolymerization), cross-linking of polysaccharides, etc.

Chapter 2 entitled "Drug delivery dosage forms made of tailor-made natural polysaccharides" deals with a comprehensive discussion about various drug delivery dosage forms composed of tailor-made natural polysaccharides.

Chapter 3 entitled "Carboxymethylated polysaccharides in drug delivery" is focused on the principles and applications of drug delivery platforms based on carboxymethylated polysaccharides. In addition, this chapter provides an overview of various drug carriers obtained from ionically cross-linked carboxymethylated polysaccharides for delivery of various drugs.

Chapter 4 entitled "Thiolated polysaccharides in drug delivery" envisages summarizing the syntheses of various thiolated natural polysaccharides and their potential uses in drug delivery application.

Chapter 5 entitled "Cross-linked polysaccharides in drug delivery" addresses the importance of cross-linking on the drug loading and release behavior of polysaccharides. Furthermore, various physical and chemical cross-linking methods used in cross-linking of polysaccharides have been comprehensively overviewed in high-level depth.

Chapter 6 entitled "Graft copolymers of polysaccharides: Synthesis techniques and pharmaceutical applications" contends with a variety of techniques engaged in the synthesis of grafted polysaccharides in addition to the up-to-date developments for the designing of novel drug delivery systems.

Chapter 7 entitled "Grafted polysaccharides in drug delivery" presents an overview of recent grafted polysaccharide-based drug delivery systems. The advantages and drawbacks of using grafted polysaccharides have also been discussed.

Chapter 8 entitled "Polysaccharide-based polyelectrolyte complex systems in drug delivery" discusses about various novel approaches of drug delivery with PECs.

Chapter 9 entitled "Polysaccharide-based interpenetrating polymeric network systems in drug delivery" deals with an inclusive discussion on IPNs/semi-IPNs as drug delivery carriers prepared using different polysaccharides.

Chapter 10 entitled "Polysaccharide nanoconjugates in drug delivery" presents an overview of nanoconjugates formulated using polysaccharide for precise diagnosis, mitigation, and treatment of diseases.

Chapter 11 entitled "Functionalized chitosan in drug delivery" summarizes most recent investigations accomplished on the applications of functionalized chitosan materials in drug delivery.

Chapter 12 entitled "Modified alginates in drug delivery" discusses various approaches and applications of different alginate modifications as a tool in drug delivery.

Chapter 13 entitled "Uses of tailor-made plant starches in drug delivery" presents various chemical modifications of starches and the uses of chemically modified starch materials as pharmaceutical excipients in various drug delivery formulations.

Chapter 14 entitled "Cancer targeting by tailor-made polysaccharides" summarizes various tailor-made polysaccharide-based targeted cancer drug therapy and their effectiveness.

Chapter 15 entitled "Delivery of genes and growth factors using tailor-made polysaccharides" describes the uses of various tailor-made polysaccharides as carrier materials for delivery of gene and growth factors.

We, the editors, express our heartfelt gratitude to all eminent writers of the chapters for providing us with their invaluable contributions in a timely manner, which helped us publish this book. We thank *Elsevier Inc.'s Erin Hill-Parks* and *Andre Gerhard Wolff* in particular for their invaluable assistance with the editing process. We also express our heartfelt gratitude to *Mona Zahir* and *Kristi L. Anderson* (Editorial Project Managers) for their invaluable assistance during the book's development. We gratefully acknowledge *Kavitha Balasundaram* (Copyright Coordinator) for her invaluable assistance in acquiring clearances, as well as *Omer Mukthar* (Production Project Manager) for helping us complete the production of this book. All permits for reprinting copyright content from various copyright sources have been gratefully acknowledged. Finally, we must acknowledge our family members' efforts and contributions to the development of the book. All our friends, colleagues, and students who assisted in the development of this book are deserving of our gratitude. We, along with our contributing writers and publishers, will be ecstatic if our efforts meet the demands of students, academicians, researchers, drug delivery formulators, pharmaceutical specialists, polymer engineers, biological experts, and others.

Amit Kumar Nayak
Seemanta Institute of Pharmaceutical Sciences, Jharpokharia, India

Md Saquib Hasnain
Palamau Institute of Pharmacy, Daltonganj, India

CHAPTER

1

Synthesis of tailor-made polysaccharides: An overview

Muhanna K. Al-Muhanna[a], *Naushad Anwar*[b], *Md Saquib Hasnain*[c], *and Amit Kumar Nayak*[d]

[a]The National Center for Composite and High Performances Materials, King Abdulaziz City for Science and Technology (KACST), Riyadh, Saudi Arabia, [b]Department of Chemistry, Aligarh Muslim University, Aligarh, Uttar Pradesh, India, [c]Department of Pharmacy, Palamau Institute of Pharmacy, Daltonganj, Jharkhand, India, [d]Department of Pharmaceutics, Seemanta Institute of Pharmaceutical Sciences, Jharpokharia, Mayurbhanj, Odisha, India

1 Introduction

Polysaccharides are the polymeric carbohydrates (e.g., starches, cellulose, pectins, etc.) composed of repeating monosaccharide units joined by the glycosidic bonds (a covalent bond that joins a sugar molecule to another group, which may or may not be another sugar) to create a large molecular framework [1–4]. They are heterogeneous in composition, which yields simple sugar units, viz.; arabinose, galactose, glucose, mannose, xylose, or uronic acids and so upon hydrolysis [4,5]. The naturally occurring polysaccharides are involved in various purposes such as [1,3,6,7]: (i) mechanical role by cellulose and chitin, (ii) starch as storage material, (iii) glycogen synthesis, and (iv) formation of gel network by mucopolysaccharides (glycosaminoglycans), agar, pectins, etc.

A number of polysaccharides are being economically and abundantly produced to be used as raw materials/excipients in many industrial applications since the industrial applications of various polysaccharides have been growing because of their sustainability, safety, biodegradability, and biocompatibility [8–16]. Sometimes various native polysaccharides are suffering from some shortcomings of material properties like low solubility,

https://doi.org/10.1016/B978-0-12-821286-8.00013-6

low swelling or high swelling, instability, etc. [17–20]. Therefore, these are sometimes not suitable to compete with already available synthetic excipients to meet the material properties for many industrial applications [18]. In general, polysaccharides are highly soluble aqueous media due to the presence of multihydroxyl groups in the polysaccharide structures, which involve several hydrogen bonding with water molecules [9,21]. These hydroxyl groups are ubiquitous in the polysaccharide structures and are involved in many chemical modifications [17]. Polysaccharides can be easily modified by physical or chemical processes to improve physicochemical properties [22]. In addition, the chemical modifications of polysaccharides further enhance their mechanical and functional behaviors [19,22–24]. The chemical modification procedures are allowing the synthesis of many tailor-made polysaccharides and the most useful functional moieties/groups for tailoring/modifying the polysaccharide structures are ester, ether, amide, amine, and alkyl groups [17,22,25,26]. For the synthesis of tailor-made polysaccharides, the starting materials are polysaccharides, and the reaction for tailoring/modifying the polysaccharide structures is usually considered with a regioselective point of view (preference of one direction of chemical bond making or breaking over all other possible directions) [17,27]. Therefore, there is a need to explore different kinds of natural polysaccharides with different modification techniques. In this context, the current chapter deals with various chemical reactions and mechanisms of tailoring (modification) of polysaccharides through derivatization of various functional groups (such as oxidation, phosphorylation, sulfation, thiolation, amidation, esterification, carboxymethylation, carbamoylethylation, etc.) in the polysaccharide structure, grafting with polysaccharides (i.e., graft copolymerization), and cross-linking of polysaccharides.

2 Syntheses of tailor-made polysaccharides

There is a rapid demand for the development of new materials, especially from renewable resources and this trend influences to synthesize various tailor-made polysaccharides with improved physicochemical and functional material properties via different chemical modification procedures [17,19,20]. Different polysaccharides are being tailored by modifying their functional group(s) occurring in their molecular structures, via oxidation [28,29], phosphorylation [30], sulfation [31], thiolation [32], amidation [33], esterification [34,35], carboxymethylation [36], carbamoylethylation [37], graft copolymerization [38], and cross-linking [17]. The chemical reactions, methodologies, and mechanisms of tailoring (modification) of polysaccharides are discussed in the following section.

2.1 Oxidation

The oxidation of polysaccharides results in changes in physicochemical properties, which usually depends upon the nature of polysaccharides (e.g., the perfect change has been observed in tamarind xyloglucan, which is capable to produce a gel after its oxidation) [39]. Various approaches to oxidation of polysaccharides are as follows [28,39–41]: oxidative glycol cleavage, chemical oxidation of primary alcohols to carboxylic acids, enzymatic oxidation of primary alcohols to aldehydes, etc. The oxidation of polysaccharides takes place in a different way to produce different structures. The free primary alcohol available at C–6 in cellulose or amylose undergoes oxidation to produce the aldehyde or further to the carboxylic acid [42]. Oxidation of the carboxylic acid gives natural polyuronic acids, such as pectin or alginates [40]. Chemical and enzymatic procedures are being used for the oxidation of primary alcohols of polysaccharides [43,44]. The presence of C–2 and C–3 in cellulose, amylose, or xylose of polysaccharides undergoes the oxidative C–C bond cleavage to produce dicarbonyl compounds via a ring-opening procedure [40,42]. When the primary alcohols are oxidized, it may also be anticipated to circumvent possible oxidation of unprotected secondary alcohols to produce ketones. The periodate oxidation of polysaccharides and the oxidation of cellulose have recently been in many researches [41,45]. The treatment with oxygen has been applied over a heterogeneous platinum metal surface as a catalyst in a method, which has been employed for the oxidation of C–6 of monosaccharide glycosides to the uronic acid level [46]. However, oxidation of primary alcohols has a significant disadvantage: the degree of oxidation (DS_{ox}) can be quite low as a heterogeneous catalyst is required [47]. Though, inulin with a degree of polymerization of *ca* 30 has been oxidized to the uronic acid level at the primary positions (C–6) with a DS_{ox} of c. 0.20 under such conditions [48], and C–6 oxidation of a galactan over platinum to the uronic acid level with a DS_{ox} of c. 0.15 has also been achieved [47,49].

Recently, Freitas et al., found that a homogeneous catalyst, (2,2,6,6-tetramethyl-piperidin-1-yl) oxyl (i.e., TEMPO) for oxidation of polysaccharide through automatic continuous online monitoring of polymerization reactions (ACOMP) [50]. The obtained products were different at various pH values (pH 5, 7, and 9) and concentrations of catalyst were assessed by automatic continuous mixing (ACM) and size exclusion chromatography (SEC). The degree of oxidation was found to be higher at pH 9 but was much higher without catalyst TEMPO. The rate constant (k) was dependent on reaction pH and TEMPO concentration. At pH 9, the amount of –COOH per g of polysaccharide, in the presence and absence of TEMPO was different, 0.215 and 0.395 mM/g, respectively. This suggested secondary and nonselective polysaccharide oxidation occurring at a lower rate in the absence of catalyst [50]. The enzymatic oxidation of polysaccharides is carried out using a galactose-6-oxidase catalyst, followed by C–6 oxidation of galactose to the aldehyde level (using oxygen as the oxidant and liberating hydrogen peroxide as the reduced by-product). The reactions are carried out in an aqueous solution. Thus, the reaction is complementary to the TEMPO oxidation, where the product of C–6 oxidation is the carboxylic acid rather than the aldehyde. Xyloglucan was the most efficiently oxidized (up to DS_{ox} 0.8 based on the galactose residues), followed by galactoglucomannan (DS_{ox} c. 0.65) and guar gum (DS_{ox} c. 0.4) [39]. In a research, Sorokina et al., studied a novel clean catalytic method by single-step oxidative modification of polysaccharides by H_2O_2 catalyzation by water-soluble iron phthalocyanine and permitted the quantitative synthesis of a wide range of tailor-made polysaccharides without generating any waste [51]. In this experiment, the active species were found to be competent to cleave the C_2–C_3 bond of an anhydroglucose unit of carbohydrate (AGU) having adjacent hydroxyl functions to form aldehyde and carboxyl groups.

In a work by Gupta et al. (2013), periodate oxidation of pectin was carried out using Malaprade mechanism to synthesize a dialdehyde structure [52]. In this synthesis, the aldehyde content in the synthesized product was found to increase as the reaction time was increased. The intrinsic viscosity of the synthesized product was found to be reduced (indicative of oxidation). The quantity of aldehyde produced was found to increase with the increment of periodic acid concentration used in the synthesis reaction as well as reaction temperature. Because of the polyanionic behavior of pectin, higher aldehyde contents were achieved at a lesser pH. A higher amount of aldehyde was reported to be produced with the increment of ethanol content. In another work, Gomez et al. investigated the periodate oxidation of alginate, using sodium periodate in an aqueous solution at room temperature for 24h in the dark [53]. The reactions on the –OH groups at C-2 and C-3 positions of the uronic units of sodium alginate structure took place, which led by the rupture of carbon-carbon bond, to the arrangement of two aldehyde groups in each oxidized monomeric unit (Fig. 1). The influences of the degree of oxidation on the

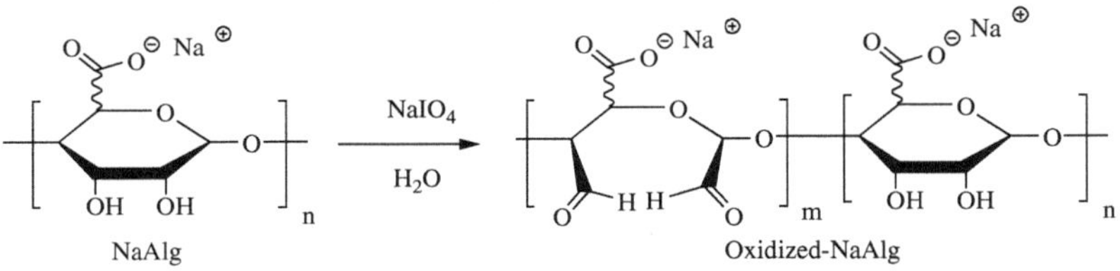

FIG. 1 Oxidation of sodium alginate and formation of aldehyde groups on main chain (NaAlg: sodium alginate, oxidized-NaAlg: oxidized sodium alginate) [53]. *Copyright © 2006 with permission from Elsevier Ltd.*

physical properties of these periodate oxidized alginate derivatives were characterized. The molar mass was decreased speedily until the oxidation of 10 M% and afterward, remained almost constant. From the results of this investigation, it was revealed that oxidized alginate derivatives with a degree of oxidation higher than 10 M% were not capable of forming gels with divalent calcium ions. Both the elastic modulus and degree of swelling of the alginate gels were found to be reduced with the increment of the degree of oxidation. It was reported that the new active functional groups on the structure of periodate oxidized alginate derivatives made them a high-quality functional polymer.

2.2 Phosphorylation

Due to the limited number and types of natural phosphate monosaccharides and polysaccharides, few studies are accessible on their biological studies [30,54]. Phosphorylation modification induces the natural bioactivities in fructose, glucose, and a few other monosaccharides [55]. Therefore, additional emphasis has been given to the synthesis of phosphated polysaccharides. A lot of previous reports have shown that the phosphorylated polysaccharides exhibited particular medicinal importance, due to the presence of phosphate groups, which can enhance the aqueous solubility, variation of molecular weight, and alter chain conformation [54,56]. Generally, strong acid as a catalyst is needed to perform the phosphorylation, which often leads to the cleavage of the polysaccharide and complex compositions [55]. For example, attachment of phosphoric acid groups of sugar units in polysaccharides at 2nd, 3rd, and/or 4th positions are responsible for phosphorylation. For this purpose, firstly, phosphoric acid is added to dimethyl sulfoxide (DMSO) solution of polysaccharide samples and the solution is heated in a water bath with temperature and time-controlled conditions based on the nature of different polysaccharides. However, the primary disadvantage associated with this technique is the more chance of polysaccharide hydrolysis. The regioselective synthesis of non-C–6 phosphorylated guar gum was achieved by using formamide pyridine and triph-enylchloromethane via triphenylmethylation process, which exhibited a degree of substitution (DS) 0.34 [57]. Furthermore, anhydrous pyridine and $POCl_3$ were used to esterify the guar gum. Phosphorylated reaction was carried out by suspending guar gum in anhydrous formamide with simultaneous addition of esterification reagents. The crude product was purified by dialysis and the calculated DS was found to be 0.42. The synthetic procedure for regioselective phosphorylation of guar gum is shown in Fig. 2 [57]. The second method of phosphorylation is to use phosphates without any degradation of polysaccharides. Various sodium hydrogen phosphate derivatives (such as sodium dihydrogen phosphate, sodium tripolyphosphate, sodium

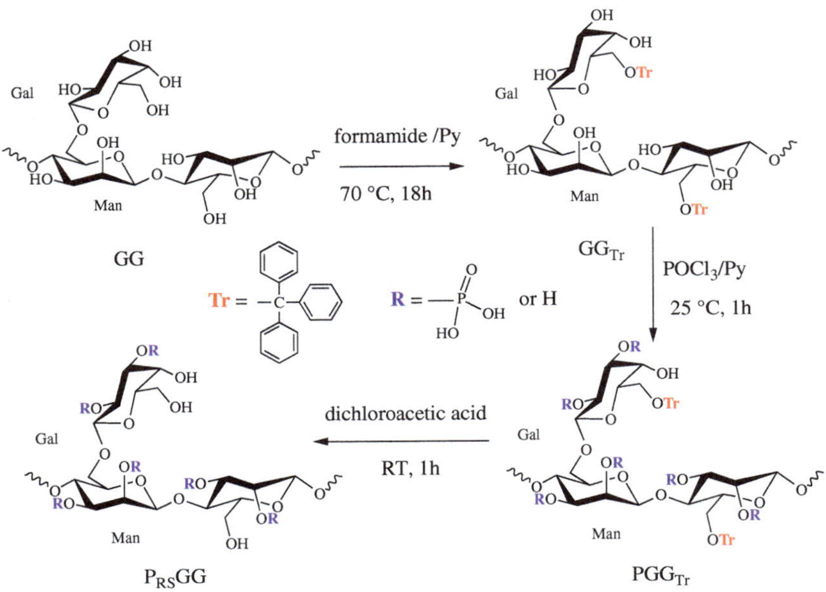

FIG. 2 Regioselective phosphorylation of guar gum (GG$_{Tr}$: 6-*O*-trityl-guar gum; PGG$_{Tr}$: phosphorylated 6-*O*-trityl-guar gum; P$_{RS}$GG: phosphorylated guar gum) [57]. *Crown copyright © 2013 with permission from Elsevier B.V.*

hexametaphosphate, etc.) or their mixed salts are constantly being used for the phosphorylation of polysaccharides [58,59]. However, it is hard to get products with a high DS and high reaction activity [60]. This method requires a certain amount of aqueous solution of phosphate in a beaker and stirring of the solution is operated until complete dissolution. Then, the pH of the solution is required to be adjusted by acid while stirring and heating are followed by addition of polysaccharides. Modification of starch can be achieved by using this method. Another method of phosphorylation is to use phosphorus oxychloride [61]. Because of high reactivity and intense reaction, it produces low product yield and high incidences of side effects. These limit the use of phosphorus oxychloride for the synthesis of simple phosphoryl esters [61]. To stimulate the possibility and application of this method, it is essential to select phosphorus oxychloride as acylation reagent, and pyridine is used to generate pyridinium salt with hydrochloric acid. This process is supportive to avoid the hydrolysis of polysaccharides [61]. Simultaneously, the addition of trimethyl phosphate decreases the reaction activity of phosphorus oxychloride, and hence, it increases the solubility of reactants [54]. Previous studies also revealed that the free hydroxyl groups of carbohydrates can be phosphorylated via heating the mixture of moistened polysaccharide and orthophosphate salts [62,63]. The reaction mechanism may be described as [55,64]:

(a) sodium dihydrogen phosphate reacts with disodium monohydrogen phosphate at high temperature to produce sodium tripolyphosphate, and (b) sodium tripolyphosphate reacts with the hydroxyls of polysaccharides to obtain orthophosphate ester.

2.3 Sulfation

Sulfation is a chemical process by which polysaccharides can be modified/tailored by attaching a sulfate group to the saccharide hydroxyl group [65]. Mizumoto et al. recognized the attachment of sulfate moieties to the polysaccharide structures via the substitution of hydroxyl moieties and reported that the sulfated polysaccharides could prevent T lymphocyte virus, and thus, played a very important role in structural modification of a polysaccharide [66]. The reactants for sulfation of polysaccharides are chlorosulfonic acid in pyridine, piperidine *N*-sulfonic acid, or sulfur trioxide complexes with pyridine, etc., were used for sulfate derivitization (i.e., sulfation) in presence of following solvents systems, such as formamide, dimethylformamide (DMF), DMSO, and pyridine [65,67].

In an investigation, sulfation of bael (*Aegle marmelos*) fruit gum was carried out using 200 mg bael fruit gum suspended in 20 mL of anhydrous DMF [68]. In the synthesis (sulfation reaction), chlorosulfonic acid and pyridine were used as sulfation reagents. Chlorosulfonic acid to pyridine was 1:4. The mixture was processed under different conditions. However, the sulfation reaction carried out at 70°C for 2 h yielded maximum sulfated bael fruit gum (138 mg) with a DS of 3.68. Recently, Wang et al. carried out the sulfation of guar gum by suspending it in anhydrous formamide and using chlorosulfonic acid-pyridine (1:4) as sulfating reagents and 4-dimethylaminopyridine (DMAP)/dimethylcyclohexylcarbodiimide (DCC) as a catalyst in homogeneous conditions [69]. The mixture was processed for 3 h at 40°C temperature. The DS for the synthesized sulfated guar gum was found to be 0.989. The sulphated derivative of guar gum showed a sharp decrease in molecular weight, due to degradation of polysaccharides throughout the sulfation process. It was concluded that low molecular weight sulfated polysaccharides could stimulate antioxidant activities. In addition, the same research group synthesized the sulfated guar gum employing Box-Behnken design using drop-wise addition of anhydrous formamide and the sulfating reagents (chlorosulfuric acid-pyridine complex). The reaction was optimized for the ratio of chlorosulfuric acid to pyridine, reaction time, and/or temperatures as intended by Box-Behnken design [70]. It was determined that the optimal reaction condition of guar gum were: ratio of chlorosulfuric acid to pyridine of 1.86, reaction temperature of 59.5°C, and reaction time of 128 min. Following this method, several sulfated guar gum derivatives with different DS (0.61–0.99) were synthesized. In another study, Bo et al. investigated the

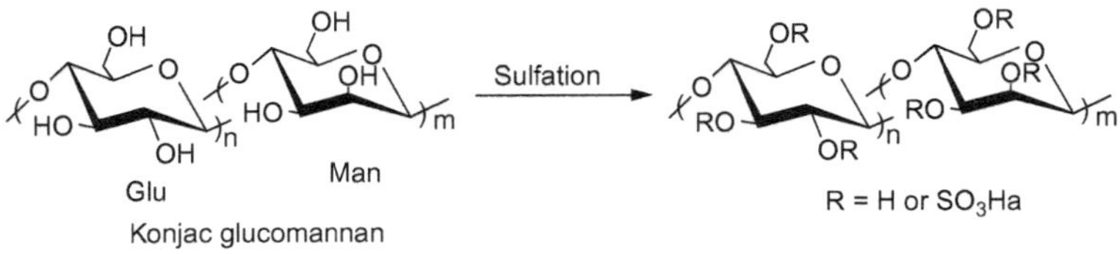

FIG. 3 Sulfation of konjac glucomannan using piperidine-*N*-sulfonic acid or SO_3-pyridine solvents complex [71]. *Copyright © 2013 with permission from Elsevier Ltd.*

sulfation of konjac glucomannan using piperidine-*N*-sulfonic acid or SO_3-pyridine solvents complex of different molecular weights (Fig. 3) [71]. Konjac glucomannan has low water solubility with high viscosity at lower concentrations. Hydrolysis of konjac glucomannan was performed before sulfation using dilute sulfuric acid to reduce the molecular weights ($M_n = 19.2 \times 10^4 - 0.2 \times 10^4$). In the sulfation process by piperidine-*N*-sulfonic acid, konjac glucomannan (0.25 g, $M_n = 0.8 \times 10^4$) was dissolved in anhydrous DMSO solution at 85°C and then, piperidine-*N*-sulfonic acid was added and reflux the mixture for 2 h. The synthesized sulfated konjac glucomannan was isolated in a good yield (0.26 g) and the number average molecular weight of $M_n = 0.7 \times 10^4$. Similarly, in the sulfation by SO_3-pyridine complex, konjac glucomannan (0.25 g, $M_n = 0.8 \times 10^4$) was dissolved in anhydrous DMSO followed by the addition of SO_3-pyridine complex. The reaction yielded 0.57 g of sulfated glucomannan with the number average molecular weight of $M_n = 0.8 \times 10^4$ [71].

2.4 Thiolation

The thiolation (or thiol-modification) of polysaccharides is carried out to enhance the mucoadhesion characteristic through the intra- and/or intermolecular cross-linking interactions between the mucin and the thiolated polysaccharides [72]. In a work, Yadav et al. synthesized gellan gum-thioglycolic acid conjugate by reacting gallan gum with thioglycolic acid in the presence of hydrochloric acid [73]. The aqueous solution (50 mL) of gellan gum (1 g) was added thioglycolic acid (0.3 mL) and hydrochloric acid (0.3 mL, 7 N) and allowed to be kept at stirring for 3 h at 80°C under reflux conditions. The reaction mixture was precipitated with methanol (100 mL) and further washing was done with methanol. The resulting precipitate was kept at −80°C for 4 h, and further dried by a lypophilizer for 24 h at −90°C, at 0.0010 mbar [73]. In another work, Esmaeilzadeh et al. synthesized the thiolated chondroitin sulfate. The synthesis was carried out through partial thiolation (~25% representing 0.25 equivalents of the available –COOH groups) [74]. It has also been investigated that the polysaccharides treatment can be achieved by the treatment with thioglycolic acid or l-cysteine [75–77]. These thiolated polysaccharides presented enhanced mucoadhesivity and permeation properties [77]. Solution of chitosan in acetic acid was treated with 2-iminothiolane hydrochloride at pH 7 [78]. The modification of chitosan using 2-iminothiolane led to producing excellent in situ gelling properties with enhanced mucoadhesive properties. In another report, thiolated pectin was produced by employing a reaction with thioglycolic acid in the presence of hydrochloric acid [79]. The optimum conditions for thiolation of pectin were as follows: pectin (16 g), 80% thioglycolic acid (7.59 g) in acidic conditions for 150 min at 80°C. The synthesized thiolated pectin was found to have 0.60 ± 0.04 mM of thiol groups/g. Mahajan et al. optimized the thiolation of xyloglucan using thioglycolic acid (0.223 mL), xyloglucan (1 g), and hydrochloride acid (1 mL, 7N) at 80°C for 150 min [80]. The researcher reported that the covalent attachment of xyloglucan to thioglycolic acid was formed via the formation of ester bonds in between –OH groups of xyloglucan (beta-galactose moieties) and $-COO^-$ group of thioglycolic acid (Fig. 4). The synthesized thiolated xyloglucan showed improved mucoadhesive property as compared with pure xyloglucan.

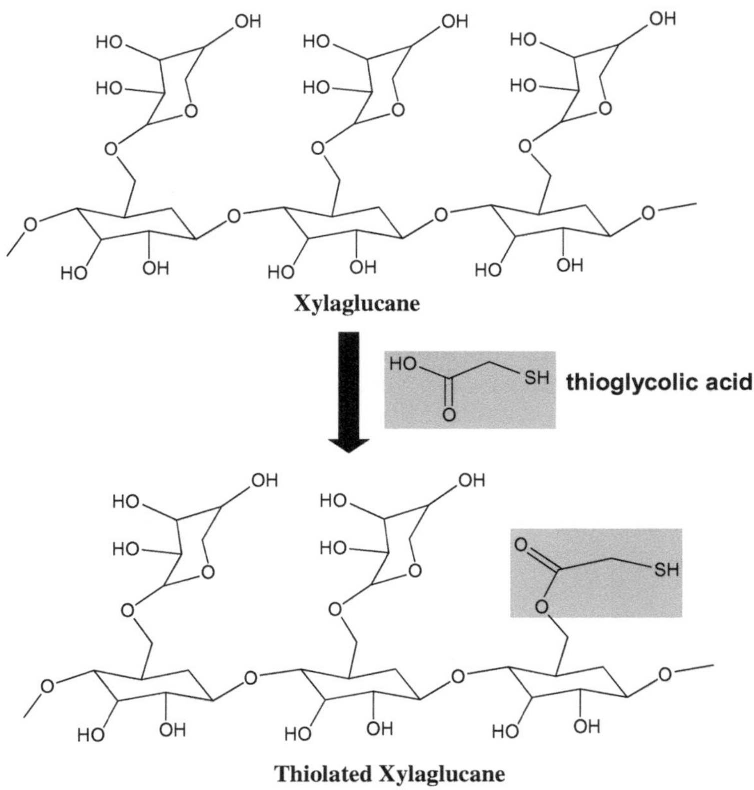

FIG. 4 Thiolation of xyloglucan using thioglycolic acid [80]. *Copyright © 2012 with permission from Elsevier Ltd.*

2.5 Amidation

The presence of the carboxylic group on the polysaccharide chain promotes the amidation of polysaccharide [33]. In a work, Mishra and coworkers synthesized amidated pectin using ethanolamine in different proportions [81]. Methanolic solution (50 mL) of pectin (0.2 M) was transferred to a 250 mL three-necked flask and then, methanolic solution of ethanolamine (0.08 M) was gradually added and stirred continuously at room temperature to achieve the final product. The product was washed with 0.1 M HCl in ethanol–water mixture (1: 1 ratio, v/v) for the conversion of free carboxylic group into protonated form. Final washing was done using 40% ethanol (v/v) until the negative reaction to chloride was appeared and left the product for drying at 60°C. The highest degree of amidation (D_A) was found in case of 0.02 M pectin and 0.32 M ethanolamine used for synthesis. Vallee et al. reported new amphiphilic derivatives of alginates by covalent bonding of dodecylamine onto the polysaccharide chain [82]. Rowley et al. synthesized alginate derivatives containing cell-adhesive peptides by coupling the terminal amine of the peptide with the carboxyl group of the polysaccharide chain, using activators as 1-ethyl (dimethylaminopropyl) carbodiimide and *N*-hydroxy-sulfosuccinimide [83]. In another research, Huerta-Angeles et al. synthesized highly substituted amide hyaluronan derivatives (propargylamido-substituted-hyaluronan and 3-azidopropyl amido substituted-hyaluronan) and their crosslinking was accomplished via click chemistry [84]. The elevated degree of substitution of hyaluronic acid was achieved after activation of the $-COO^-$ group with ethyl chloroformate and subsequent functionalization of the carboxylic group with primary amine containing either a terminal azido or alkynyl groups (Fig. 5). The chemical modification of hyaluronic acid to synthesize amide hyaluronan derivatives was investigated to be highly chemoselective facilitating only amide-modified hyaluronan derivates, which exhibited high resistance toward the thermal degradation in comparison with that of the pure and unmodified hyaluronic acid.

2.6 Esterification

Esterification of polysaccharides exemplifies the utmost flexible changes as they offer informal access to an array of bio-based resources with important properties [17]. It gives broad spectrum of polysaccharide derivatives with a good yield. General procedure for the acylation method of polysaccharides is the reaction with carboxylic acid together with anhydride in a heterogeneous phase [85–87]. Carboxylic acid containing cellulose acetate is the most important polysaccharide ester prepared industrially by transformation of cellulose with acetic

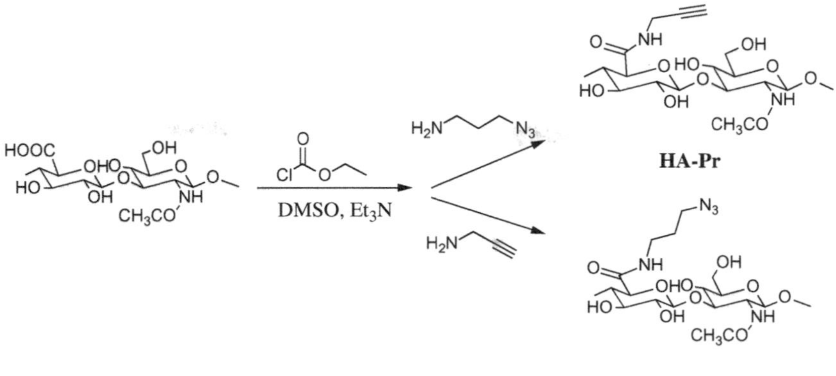

FIG. 5 Amidation of hyaluronic acid with primary amines via click chemistry (HA-Pr: propargylamido-substituted-hyaluronan and HA-APA: 3-azidopropyl amido substituted-hyaluronan) [84]. *Copyright © 2011 with permission from Elsevier Ltd.*

acid and acetic anhydride using catalyst amount of sulphuric acid (up to 15%, w/w). During the process of conversion, mixed sulphuric acid-acetic acid anhydride is formed as an intermediate, leads to the generation an acetyl cation [87,88]. Hence, a partial sulphation suppresses the production of cellulose triacetate. Nonetheless, many of the sulfate moieties presented are switched by acetyl functions throughout the reaction.

Hamcerencu et al. investigated the chemical modification of xanthan gum via unsaturated esterification using acrylic acid or with other reactive acid derivatives, viz., acryloyl chloride and maleic anhydride [89]. Strategies for esterification of xanthan gum using acrylic acid, acryloyl chloride, and maleic anhydride are presented in Fig. 6. Furthermore, water-swollen hydrogels with interpenetrating-polymer networks (IPN) were obtained after copolymerization of maleate polysaccharides (here xanthan gum maleates) with *N*-isopropylacrylamide (NIPAm) [90]. The hydrogels showed different response rates to the external stimuli depending upon composition. Microparticles with hydrogel character based on these xanthan gum maleates/NIPAm were synthesized by a grafting-crosslinking reaction with either *N,N′*-methylenebisacrylamide (BIS) or cyclodextrin acrylate as crosslinking agent [91]. These particles were found to be capable to swell in aqueous medium and included (and release) water-soluble drugs and organo-soluble ones in case of cross-linking with cyclodextrin acrylate. The presence of PNIPAm within the hydrogel microparticles imparts a thermosensitive character, which, in combination with the capacity to load drugs, opens interesting prospects in ophthalmic applications.

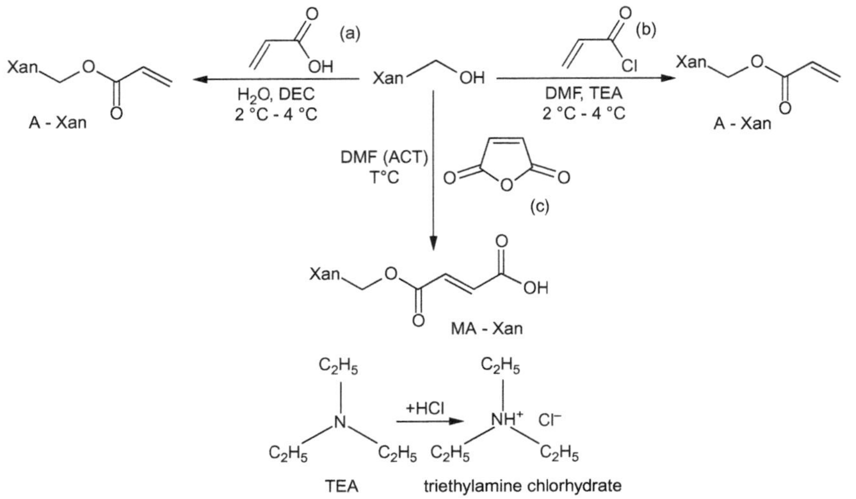

FIG. 6 Esterification of xanthan gum using (A) acrylic acid, (B) acryloyl chloride, and (C) maleic anhydride (Xan: xanthan gum, TEA: triethylamine) [89]. *Copyright © 2007 with permission from Elsevier Ltd.*

2.7 Carboxymethylation

Carboxymethylation of polysaccharides was performed with an aim to increase aqueous solubility, hydrophilicity, and solution clarity through covalent attachment of $-CH_2COOH$ moieties at 6th position of hexose substituting –OH moieties [36]. It is well known that the production of carboxymethyl polysaccharides achieved by the Williamson ether synthesis, followed by the conversion of aqueous solution of sodium hydroxide to its sodium salt monochloroacetic acid [17]. The process of carboxymethylation reaction needs two steps (Fig. 7) [92]. Firstly, sodium hydroxide responded with the –OH groups of the polymer to yield alkoxides groups. Secondly, the carboxymethyl groups formed between the polymer alkoxide and monochloroacetic acid via SN^2 reaction mechanism [17,93]. The carboxymethylation *Auricularia auricula* polysaccharide [94], tamarind kernel powder [93], cashew tree exudate polysaccharide [92,95], gum kondagogu [96], chitosan [97], etc., have already been reported. Carboxymethylation reaction can easily be altered by the use of different amounts of sodium hydroxide and monochloroacetic acid because they act as a key role in DS [36]. For example, amount of alkali required to produce alkoxides was 80 mL of 45% w/v for gum kondagogu (1 g), 2.7 mL, 10 M for cashew gum, and 0.158 M for tamarind kernel powder (0.05 M) to achieve DS of 0.2, 2.21, and 0.649, respectively [92,93,96]. Similarly, DS of carboxymethylated polysaccharides can be influenced by monochloroacetic acid. For example, the

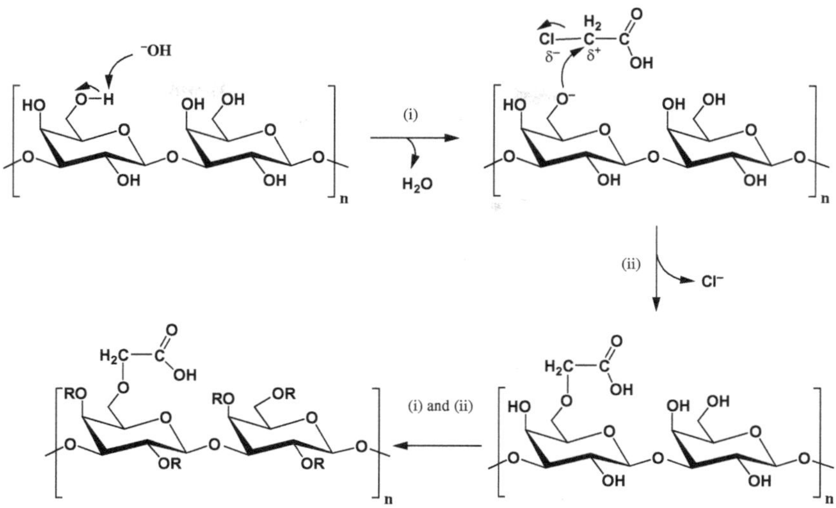

FIG. 7 Carboxymethylation reaction for polysaccharide (R could be H or CH_2COOH group, if the carboxymethylation progresses) [92]. *Copyright © 2004 with permission from Elsevier Ltd.*

addition of monochloroacetic acid 10 mL (75%, w/v), 10 mL (26%, w/v), and 0.09 M, respectively, for the carboxymethylation of tamarind kernel powder, cashew gum, and gum kondagogu.

2.8 Carbamoylethylation

Carbamoylethylation process involves the covalent attachment of $-CH_2CH_2COOH$ group at 6th position of sugar units present within the polysaccharides through the replacement of −OH group [17]. The alkaline solution of polysaccharides using sodium hydroxide was added to the acrylamide under optimized temperature and time yielded carbamoylethylation of polysaccharides [17,98]. For illustration, the optimum conditions for formulating carbamoylethyl guar gum comprised acrylamide (1 M), sodium hydroxide (0.75 M), and guar gum (0.061 M) at 30°C for 2 h [98]. The optimal conditions for the syntheses of carbamoylethylated derivative of *Cassia tora* gum were achieved through: acrylamide (1.12 M), sodium hydroxide (1.25 M) and cassia tora gum (0.197 M) at 30°C for 2 h [99]. Similar results were found in the synthesis of carbamoylethyled *Cassia occidentalis* seed gum [100]. The ideal condition for synthesis of carbamoylethyled *Cassia occidentalis* seed gum comprised concentration of acrylamide (0.070 M), sodium hydroxide (0.125 M), and *Cassia occidentalis* seed gum (0.03 M) at 30°C for 3 h.

2.9 Cross-linking

Cross-linking is the process of forming 3-D networks by linking two polysaccharide chains by covalent or noncovalent bonds [17]. The cross-linking technique was found useful for modifying physicochemical, electrical, rheological, and mechanical performances of polysaccharides.

2.9.1 *Cross-linking by metallic cations*

Different divalent cations form gels with pectin through cross-linking with various metal ions; however, magnesium cations does not form gels or dimers [101]. Calcium chloride, barium chloride, aluminium chloride, etc., are important metallic cations ions that form bridges with the anionic polysaccharide chains to form ionotropically cross-linked structure via ionic interaction in between divalent/trivalent metal ions and caroboxyl groups of polysaccharides [102–104]. The divalent/trivalent metal ions-induced ionotropic gelation method was generally used to produce gelled ionic polysaccharide-based beads, microspheres, nanoparticles, etc. [105,106]. For example, sodium alginate experiences ionotropic gelation in aqueous solution in the presence of various metallic cations, such as Ca^{2+}, Cd^{2+}, Ba^{2+}, Zn^{2+}, Al^{3+}, etc., fit into electronegative cavities of the sodium alginate like eggs in an "Egg Box model" model to form calcium alginate due to ionic interaction between $-COO^{-}$ group of sodium alginate and metallic cations present in the cross-linking solution [101,107–113]. Low methoxy pectin can form gel structures by ionotropic gelation with various metallic cations (such as calcium, zinc) for the use as effective vehicles in drug delivery applications [114–122]. The interactions of the carboxyl groups of low methoxy pectin backbone with cross-linking metallic cations induce the formation of the so-called "egg-box" structure, even though it slightly differs from the "egg-box" model originally defined for alginates [116]. Deacetylated gellan gum undergoes ionotropic-gelation in the presence of various metallic cations [117–128]. The mechanism of ionotropic-gelation property of gellan gum in presence of multivalent metal cations involves the formation of double helical junction zones followed by aggregation of double helical segments to form three-dimensional network by complexation with metallic cations and hydrogen bonding with water [102,117,129].

2.9.2 *Cross-linking by glutaraldehyde*

Glutaraldehyde is generally used for the cross-linking polymers having hydroxyl groups. It was perceived that on increasing the glutaraldehyde amount, there was an increase in the cross-link density [17]. Hydrogel changes irreversibly on drying of hydrogel form the discs formed by physical enlargements in the polymer network, caused in a change in the amount of swelling. However, this process of cross-linking reactions required higher concentration of glutaraldehyde suggesting the lesser efficacy of cross-linking [17]. In a work, to prepare chitosan nanoparticles using glutaraldehyde cross-linking process, amino groups of chitosan structure formed covalent bond with aldehyde groups of glutaraldehyde (Fig. 8) [130]. Alginate-guar gum hydrogel were prepared with distinct alginate chain to guar gum percentage weight ratios [131]. A cross-linking bridge in between alginate chains and guar gum were formed using glutaraldehyde as a covalent cross-linker. To the prepared guar gum solution, sufficient amount of sodium alginate was added and the mixture was stirred to obtain a uniform solution of sodium alginate-guar gum. After that, glutaraldehyde was added to the final concentration of 0.2% (v/v), blended, and precipitated (in 0.5% w/w calcium chloride) to form beads.

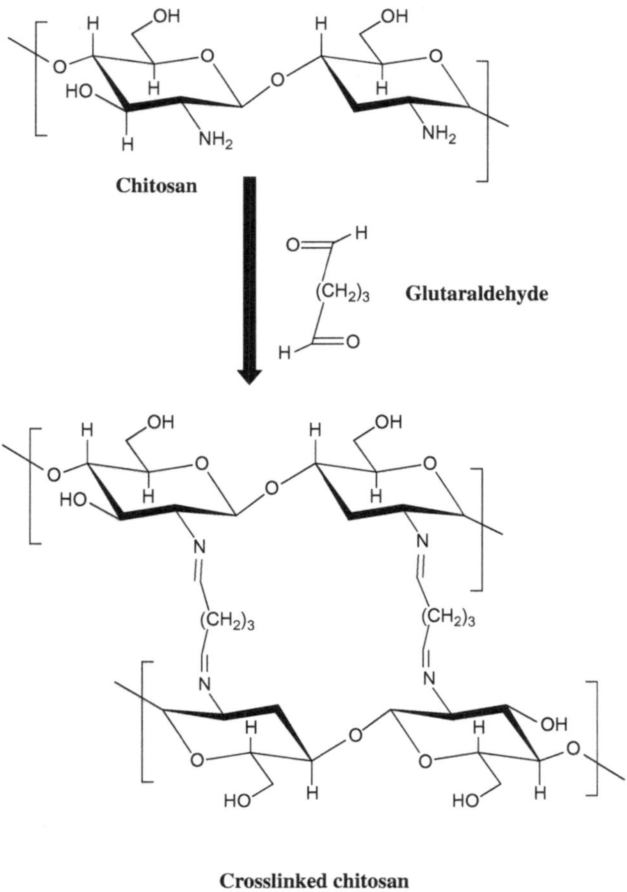

FIG. 8 Crosslinking of chitosan by glutaraldehyde [130]. *Copyright © 2018 with permission from Elsevier B.V.*

The beads were washed with distilled water to remove residual glutaraldehyde and calcium chloride, and lyophilized [131]. Kaity et al. investigated the formation of glutaraldehyde cross-linked locust bean gum-poly(vinyl alcohol) IPN composed of for controlled release drug delivery [132]. They have reported that the acetal ring was formed between the –OH groups of locust bean gum-poly(vinyl alcohol) strands and aldehyde groups of glutaraldehyde to form the IPN matrix network microsphere of rigid nature.

2.9.3 Cross-linking by epichlorohydrin

Cross-linking of polymer can be carried out by using epichlorohydrin as cross-linker [17]. In a work, the alkaline paste of cashew gum was cross-linked employing epichlorohydrin followed by heating at different temperature to provide cross-linked gel [133]. The reaction yielded cross-linked cashew gum with high degree of cross-linking, which was reported to be increased with the increasing amount of epichlorohydrin to guar gum molar ratio up to 0.17 and then, decreased. The swelling degree of cashew gum gels was revealed to be decreased with increment epichlorohydrin to guar gum molar ratio due to the increase of cross-linking density.

2.9.4 Cross-linking by genipin

Genipin, extracted from gardenia fruits, is an aqueous soluble and bi-functional cross-linking reagent [134]. Generally, it gives blue-color fluorescent hydrogels when reacted with chitosan and proteins as cross-linking reagent. Muzzarelli et al. studied the biomedical and pharmaceutical applications of genipin cross-linked chitosan hydrogels [135]. The genipin plays a pivotal role in the encapsulations and controlled releasing of numerous drugs, biological materials, living cells, etc. It was shown that the mechanisms for cross-linking of chitosan with genipin are different at different pH. A nucleophilic attack at C3 position of chitosan molecular structure by the amino functionality caused the opening of the dihydropyran ring and attacked by the secondary amino group on the newly formed aldehyde group when the reaction took place under acidic and neutral conditions. The intermediate aldehyde group was formed during the ring-opening reaction of genipin, which subsequently experienced aldol condensation under basic conditions. Schiff reaction occurred in between aldehyde group of genipin and amino groups of chitosan to produce cross-linked networks [136]. However, it was also established that the genipin cross-linked products are found to be less toxic as shown by food and forensic science. Borza et al. investigated the genipin-induced cross-linking of gelatin-maltodextrin for microencapsulation process, which improved the survival of *Bifidobacterium adolescentis* for the duration of exposure to gastrointestinal conditions, in vitro [137]. The physical stability of microencapsulated formulations in the simulated gastric juice was noticed without affecting the cell viability, which was found to be improved by genipin-induced cross-linking. Increasing genipin concentration from 10 to 24 mM significantly ($P<.05$) increased the physical stability of genipin-induced cross-linked gelatin-maltodextrin microencapsulated formulations.

2.9.5 *Phosphate cross-linking*

Phosphate cross-linking has been employed to prevent the swelling characteristic of natural polysaccharides, which is highly useful in the delivering of drugs to distal parts of the gut [138,139]. Gliko-Kabir et al. investigated the synthesis of phosphated cross-linked guar gum for colon-specific drug delivery [138]. In this work, the cross-linking of guar gum was carried out using 30% (w/v) sodium trimetaphosphate supposing that each mole of sodium trimetaphosphate could react with three pairs of hydroxyl groups of guar gum [140]. In another study by Shalviri et al., starch and xanthan gum was cross-linked using sodium trimetaphosphate [141]. Starch and xanthan gum was dissolved using vigorous mixing and the mixture was then boiled. Followed by addition of sodium hydroxide, the cross-linking was then initiated by adding different amounts of sodium trimetaphosphate and sodium sulfate. It was recognized that the swelling ratio of the films was found to be increased on increasing sodium trimetaphosphate and xanthan levels. The penetrability of various anionic molecules (namely, pyrogallol red, methylene blue, sodium salt of ibuprofen, caffeine, sodium salicylate, and vitamin B12) through the polymeric films was found to be considerably lower than their neutral form mainly because of electrostatic repulsion in between the negatively charged polymer materials. Therefore, sodium trimetaphosphate-induced cross-linked starch-xanthan gum can be possibly used as a film-forming substance in the formulations of controlled release.

2.10 Graft copolymerization

Graft copolymerization is the cross-linking reaction, where two or more different kinds of polymers are cross-linked in a single unit [20,23,38]. The macromolecular-chain of these copolymeric structures is connected to the main polymeric chain(s) with one or more species of block(s) [38]. Graft copolymers comprise of a backbone and two or more branches, which differ chemically from the backbone [20,142]. Within the graft copolymer structure, branches are usually distributed randomly along the backbone, although recent advances in synthetic methods have allowed for the preparation of better-defined structures. Comb-shaped graft copolymers can be prepared by three general synthetic methods: "grafting onto," "grafting from," and "grafting through." The term "grafting" can be described as the covalent attachment process and irreversible [142]. The chemical and structural properties of these graft copolymers are the basic parameters to reveal various important performances [20,38]. Owing to their excellent mechanical and swelling properties, graft copolymers are extensively investigated for their valuable uses in many fields, such as drug delivery, tissue engineering, wound dressing, coagulants, paper additives, film coatings, chelating resins, etc. [20,23,38].

In an investigation, Mundargi et al. investigated the graft modification of xanthan gum, where acrylamide grafted xanthan gum copolymer was synthesized by free radical polymerization in presence of ceric ammonium nitrate [143]. The synthesized acrylamide grafted xanthan gum copolymer was used to formulate matrix tablets for controlling release of carvedilol and atenolol (antihypertensive drugs). Toti et al. synthesized polyacrylamide-*grafted*-guar gum copolymer and the synthesized grafted copolymer was used to formulate matrix tablets of diltiazem HCl [144]. Huang et al. synthesized the multifunctional nanoparticles, intended by hyaluronic acid grafted polycaprolactone (PCL) nanoparticles (hyaluronic acid-*g*-PCL NPs) coated with chitosan [145]. The experimental investigation revealed that the nanoparticles were found suitable for the oral delivery of lipophilic anticancer drugs (paclitaxel and doxorubicin). AL-Kahtani and Sherigara (2014) synthesized acrylamide-*grafted*-sodium alginate by free-radical graft polymerization process in presence of initiator ceric ammonium nitrate at various acrylamide concentrations with monomer to polymer ratio of 1:1, 2:1 and 3:1, respectively [146]. The synthesized acrylamide-*grafted*-sodium alginate was used to prepare semi-interpenetrating network microspheres of diclofenac sodium for controlled release using glutaraldehyde as cross-linking agent. Proposed reaction mechanism for grafting of acrylamide onto sodium alginate using ceric ion initiation is presented in Fig. 9.

3 Conclusion

The current chapter enlightened the recent approaches for tailoring various polysaccharides via derivatization of various functional groups (such as oxidation, phosphorylation, sulfation, thiolation, amidation, esterification, carboxymethylation, carbamoylethylation, etc.) in the polysaccharide structure, grafting with polysaccharides (i.e., graft copolymerization), cross-linking of polysaccharides, etc. The tailoring of polysaccharides has already been found to be beneficial technique to alter physicochemical as well as functional properties of the native polysaccharides. The native polysaccharides are suffering from some shortcomings of material properties like low solubility, low swelling or high swelling, instability, etc. Therefore, these are sometimes not suitable to compete with already available synthetic excipients to meet the material properties for many industrial applications. The tailoring of polysaccharides leads to improvement

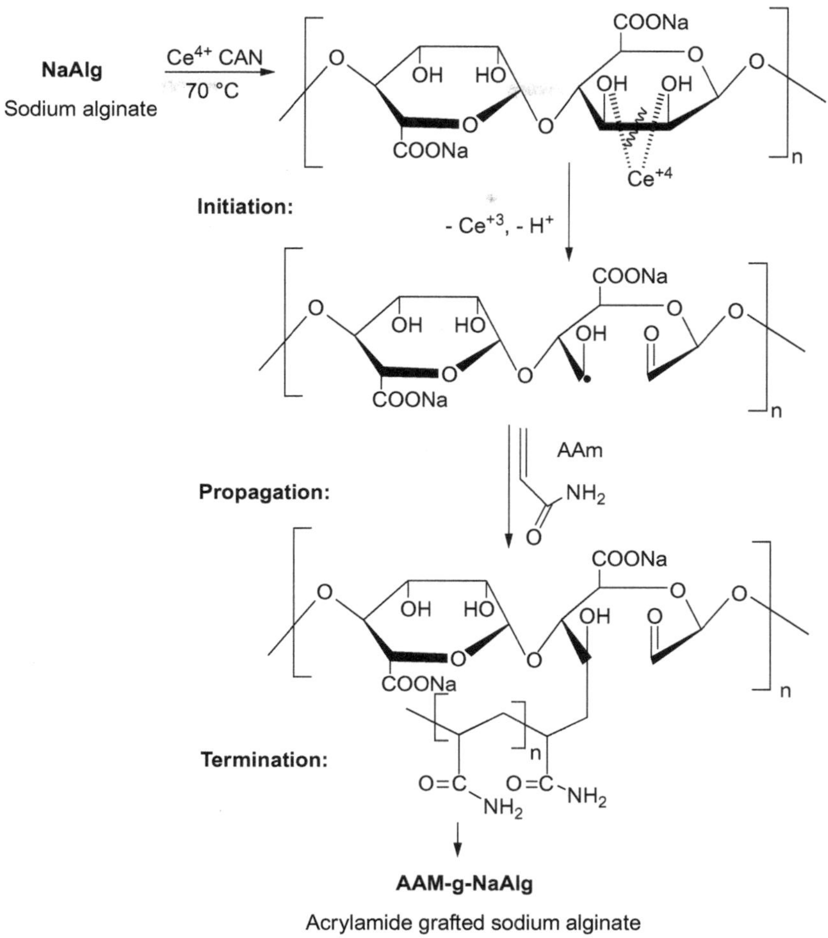

FIG. 9 Proposed reaction mechanism for grafting of acrylamide onto sodium alginate using ceric ion initiation (AAm: acrylamide; NaAlg: sodium alginate; AAm-*g*-NaAlg: acrylamide grafted sodium alginate) [146]. *Copyright © 2013 with permission from Elsevier B.V.*

of physicochemical, mechanical as well as functional performances as these can be used for many industrial applications. For examples, carboxymethylation increases the gelation behavior and solubility of polysaccharides, thiolation of increases the mucoadhesion of polysaccharides, sulfation increases the anticoagulant activity, and graft copolymerization increases the mechanical behavior of polysaccharides. In addition, the cross-linking provides a major platform to enhance the matrix properties including mechanical behavior of polysaccharides. Interestingly, the graft copolymerization and cross-linking of polysaccharides are being used in the preparation of hydrogels for many industrial applications.

References

[1] Lovegrove A, Edwards CH, De Noni I, Patel H, El SN, Grassby T, Zielke C, Ulmius M, Nilsson L, Butterworth PJ, Ellis PR, Shewry PR. Role of polysaccharides in food, digestion, and health. Crit Rev Food Sci Nutr 2017;57(2):237–53.

[2] Hasnain SMM, Hasnain MS, Nayak AK. Natural polysaccharides: sources and extraction methodologies. In: Hasnain MS, Nayak AK, editors. Natural polysaccharides in drug delivery and biomedical applications. United States: Academic Press, Elsevier Inc.; 2019. p. 1–14.

[3] Maity M, Hasnain MS, Nayak AK, Aminabavi TM. Biomedical applications of polysaccharides. In: Nayak AK, Hasnain MS, Aminabhavi TM, editors. Tailor-made polysaccharides in biomedical applications. USA: Academic Press, Elsevier Inc.; 2021. p. 1–34.

[4] Slavin JL. Structure, nomenclature, and properties of carbohydrates. In: Stipanuk MH, Caudill MA, editors. Biochemical, physiological, and molecular aspects of human nutrition. St. Louis: Elsevier, Inc.; 2013. p. 50–68.

[5] Navarro DMDL, Abelilla JJ, Stein HH. Structures and characteristics of carbohydrates in diets fed to pigs: a review. J Anim Sci Biotechnol 2019;10:39.

[6] Posocco B, Dreussi E, de Santa J, et al. Polysaccharides for the delivery of antitumor drugs. Materials (Basel) 2015;8(5):2569–615.

[7] Mizrahy S, Peer D. Polysaccharides as building blocks for nanotherapeutics. Chem Soc Rev 2012;41:2623–40.

[8] Ferreira AR, Alves VD, Coelhoso IM. Polysaccharide-based membranes in food packaging applications. Membranes (Basel) 2016;6(2):22.

[9] Paul F, Morin A, Monsan P. Microbial polysaccharides with actual potential industrial applications. Biotechnol Adv 1986;4(2):245–59.

[10] Franz G. Polysaccharides in pharmacy: current applications and future concepts. Planta Med 1989;55(6):493–7.

[11] He X, Wang X, Fang J, Chang Y, Ning N, Guo H, Huang L, Huang X, Zhao Z. Structures, biological activities, and industrial applications of the polysaccharides from *Hericium erinaceus* (Lion's mane) mushroom: a review. Int J Biol Macromol 2017;97:228–37.

[12] Nayak AK, Hasnain MS, Dhara AK, Pal D. Plant polysaccharides in pharmaceutical applications. In: Pal D, Nayak AK, editors. Bioactive natural products for pharmaceutical applications. Advanced Structured Materials, vol. 140. Cham: Springer; 2021. p. 93–125.

[13] Nayak AK, Hasnain MS. Plant polysaccharides in drug delivery applications. In: Nayak AK, Hasnain MS, editors. Plant polysaccharides-based multiple-unit systems for oral drug delivery. Singapore: Springer; 2019. p. 19–23.

[14] Nayak AK, Hasnain MS. Some other plant polysaccharide based multiple units for oral drug delivery. In: Nayak AK, Hasnain MS, editors. Plant polysaccharides-based multiple-unit systems for oral drug delivery. Singapore: Springer; 2019. p. 123–1128.

[15] Ullah S, Khalil AA, Shaukat F, Song Y. Sources, extraction and biomedical properties of polysaccharides. Foods 2019;8(8):304.

[16] Nayak AK, Pal D, Santra K. Screening of polysaccharides from tamarind, fenugreek and jackfruit seeds as pharmaceutical excipients. Int J Biol Macromol 2015;79:756–60.

[17] Rana V, Rai P, Tiwary AK, Singh RS, Kennedy JF, Knill Charles J. Modified gums: approaches and applications in drug delivery. Carbohydr Polym 2011;83:1031–47.

[18] Xiao C, Gao SJ, Li GR, Zhang QC. Preparation of konjac glucomannan and acrylamide grafted konjac glucomannan. J Nat Sci 1999;4:459–62.

[19] Nayak AK, Pal D. Functionalization of tamarind gum for drug delivery. In: Thakur VK, Thakur MK, editors. Functional biopolymers. Cham: Springer; 2018. p. 35–56.

[20] Nayak AK, Bera H, Hasnain MS, Pal D. Synthesis and characterization of graft-copolymers of plant polysaccharides. In: Thakur VK, editor. Biopolymer grafting, synthesis and properties. Netherlands: Elsevier Inc.; 2018. p. 1–62.

[21] Rinaudo M. Non-covalent interactions in polysaccharide systems. Macromol Biosci 2006;6(8):590–610.

[22] Xu Y, Wu YJ, Sun PL, Zhang FM, Linhardt RJ, Zhang AQ. Chemically modified polysaccharides: synthesis, characterization, structure activity relationships of action. Int J Biol Macromol 2019;132:970–7.

[23] Dey S, Roy S, Hasnain MS, Nayak AK. Grafted alginates in drug delivery. In: Nayak AK, Hasnain MS, editors. Alginates in drug delivery. United States: Academic Press, Elsevier Inc.; 2020. p. 71–100.

[24] Hasnain MS, Ray P, Nayak AK. Alginate-based interpenetrating polymer networks for sustained drug release. In: Nayak AK, Hasnain MS, editors. Alginates in drug delivery. United States: Academic Press, Elsevier Inc.; 2020. p. 101–28.

[25] Alkahtani S, Hasnain MS, Nayak AK, Aminabhavi TM. Polysaccharide-based polyelectrolyte complex systems for biomedical uses. In: Nayak AK, Hasnain MS, Aminabhavi TM, editors. Tailor-made polysaccharides in biomedical applications. USA: Academic Press, Elsevier Inc.; 2021. p. 151–74.

[26] Nayak AK, Hasnain MS, Tabis M, Aminabhavi TM. Use of tailored polysaccharides in dentistry. In: Nayak AK, Hasnain MS, Aminabhavi TM, editors. Tailor-made polysaccharides in biomedical applications. USA: Academic Press, Elsevier Inc.; 2021. p. 287–304.

[27] Senf D, Ruprecht C, Kishani S, Matic A, Toriz G, Gatenholm P, Wågberg L, Pfrengle F. Tailormade polysaccharides with defined branching patterns: enzymatic polymerization of arabinoxylan oligosaccharides. Angew Chem Int Ed Engl 2018;57(37):11987–92.

[28] Sen SO, Nayak AK, Devbhuti P, Ghosh A. Modification of gums by periodate oxidation: a natural cross-linker. Int J Pharm Pharm Sci 2019;11:1–6.

[29] da Silva LM, Araújo LFS, Alvez RC, Ono L, Sá DAT, da Cunha PLR, Monteiro de Paula RC, Maciel JS. Promising alternative gum: extraction, characterization, and oxidation of the galactomannan of *Cassia fistula*. Int J Biol Macromol 2020;165(Pt A):436–44.

[30] Bombaldi de Souza RF, Bombaldi de Souza FC, Thorpe A, Mantovani D, Popat KC, Moraes ÂM. Phosphorylation of chitosan to improve osteoinduction of chitosan/xanthan-based scaffolds for periosteal tissue engineering. Int J Biol Macromol 2020;143:619–32.

[31] Nagpal M, Kaur M, Sharma D, Baldi A, Chandra R, Madan J. Optimization of sulfation of okra fruit gum for improved rheological and pharmacological properties. Int J Biol Macromol 2019;122:1–9.

[32] Grewal P, Mundlia J, Ahuja M. Thiol modified Moringa gum—a potential bioadhesive polymer. Carbohydr Polym 2019;209:400–8.

[33] Chen J, Niu X, Dai T, Hua H, Feng S, Liu C, McClements DJ, Liang R. Amino acid-amidated pectin: preparation and characterization. Food Chem 2020;309, 125768.

[34] Zuo Y, Gu J, Yang L, Qiao Z, Tan H, Zhang Y. Synthesis and characterization of maleic anhydride esterified corn starch by the dry method. Int J Biol Macromol 2013;62:241–7.

[35] Meng R, Wu Z, Xie HQ, Xu GX, Cheng JS, Zhang B. Preparation, characterization, and encapsulation capability of the hydrogel cross-linked by esterified tapioca starch. Int J Biol Macromol 2020;155:1–5.

[36] Chakka VP, Zhou T. Carboxymethylation of polysaccharides: synthesis and bioactivities. Int J Biol Macromol 2020;165(Pt B):2425–31.

[37] Singh RS, Kaur N, Rana V, Singla RK, Kang N, Kaur G, Kaur H, Kennedy JF. Carbamoylethyl locust bean gum: synthesis, characterization and evaluation of its film forming potential. Int J Biol Macromol 2020;149:348–58.

[38] Cheng H, Zhang X, Cui Z, Mao S. Grafted polysaccharides as advanced pharmaceutical excipients. In: Nayak AK, Pal K, Banerjee I, Maji S, Nanda U, editors. Advances and challenges in pharmaceutical technology: materials, process development and drug delivery strategies. USA: Academic Press, Elsevier Inc.; 2021. p. 75–129.

[39] Parikka K, Leppänen AS, Pitkänen L, Reunanen M, Willför S, Tenkanen M. Oxidation of polysaccharides by galactose oxidase. J Agric Food Chem 2010;58(1):262–71.
[40] Parikka K, Master E, Tenkanen M. Oxidation with galactose oxidase: multifunctional enzymatic catalysis. J Mol Catal B: Enzym 2015;120:47–59.
[41] Kristiansen KA, Potthast A, Christensen BE. Periodate oxidation of polysaccharides for modification of chemical and physical properties. Carbohydr Res 2010;345:1264–71.
[42] Cumpstey I. Chemical modification of polysaccharides. ISRN Org Chem 2013;2013, 417672.
[43] Park K-M, Kim YN, Choi SJ, Park J-H, Chang P-S. Chemoselective oxidation of C6 primary hydroxyl groups of polysaccharides in rice bran for the application as a novel water-soluble dietary fiber. Int J Food Prop 2013;18(8):1664–76.
[44] Chen J, Guo X, Zhu M, et al. Polysaccharide monooxygenase-catalyzed oxidation of cellulose to glucuronic acid-containing cello-oligosaccharides. Biotechnol Biofuels 2019;12:42.
[45] Coseri S, Biliuta G, Simionescu BC, Stana-Kleinschek K, Ribitsch V, Harabagiu V. Oxidized cellulose—survey of the most recent achievements. Carbohydr Polym 2013;93(1):207–15.
[46] Dirkx JMH, van der Baan HS. The oxidation of carbohydrates with platinum on carbon as catalyst. J Catal 1981;67:1–13.
[47] Aspinall GO, Nicolson A. The catalytic oxidation of European larch ε-galactan. J Chem Soc 1960;505:2503–7.
[48] Verraest DL, Peters JA, Van Bekkum H. The platinum catalyzed oxidation of insulin. Carbohydr Res 1998;306:197–203.
[49] Aspinall GO. Reduction of uronic acids in polysaccharides. In: Whistler RL, editor. Methods in carbohydrate chemistry: general polysaccharides, 5. New York, NY, USA: Academic Press; 1963. p. 397.
[50] Spier VC, Sierakowski MR, Reed WF, Freitas RA. Polysaccharide depolymerization from TEMPO-catalysis: effect of TEMPO concentration. Carbohydr Polym 2017;170:140–7.
[51] Kachkarova-Sorokina SL, Gallezot P, Sorokin AB. A novel clean catalytic method for waste-free modification of polysaccharides by oxidation. Chem Commun 2004;2844–5.
[52] Gupta B, Tummalapalli M, Deopura BL, Alam MS. Functionalization of pectin by periodate oxidation. Carbohydr Polym 2013;98(1):1160–5.
[53] Gomez C, Rinaudo M, Villar M. Oxidation of sodium alginate and characterization of the oxidized derivatives. Carbohydr Polym 2007;67:296–304.
[54] Liu X, Wan Z, Shi L, Lu X. Preparation and antiherpetic activities of chemically modified polysaccharides from *Polygonatum cyrtonema* Hua. Carbohydr Polym 2011;83:737–42.
[55] Li S, Xiong Q, Lai X, Li X, Wan M, Zhang J, Yan Y, Cao M, Lu L, Guan J, Zhang D, Lin Y. Molecular modification of polysaccharides and resulting bioactivities. Compr Rev Food Sci Food Saf 2016;15:237–50.
[56] Wang JL, Yang T, Tian J, Zeng T, Wang XF, Yao J, Zhang J, Lei ZQ. Synthesis and characterization of phosphorylated galactomannan: the effect of DS on solution conformation and antioxidant activities. Carbohydr Polym 2014;113:325–35.
[57] Niu S, Wang J, Zhao B, Zhao M, Nie M, Wang X, Yao J, Zhang J. Regioselective synthesis and antioxidant activities of phosphorylated guar gum. Int J Biol Macromol 2013;62:741–7.
[58] Liu H, Li F, Luo P. Effect of carboxymethylation and phosphorylation on the properties of polysaccharides from *Sepia esculenta* ink: Antioxidation and anticoagulation *in vitro*. Mar Drugs 2019;17(11):626.
[59] Rao MR, Warrier DU, Gaikwad SR, Shevate PM. Phosphorylation of psyllium seed polysaccharide and its characterization. Int J Biol Macromol 2016;85:317–26.
[60] Ciric J, Loos K. Synthesis of branched polysaccharides with tunable degree of branching. Carbohydr Polym 2013;93:31–7.

[61] Illy N, Fache M, Ménard R, Negrell C, Caillol S, et al. Phosphorylation of bio-based compounds: the state of the art. Polym Chem R Soc Chem 2015;6(35):6257–91.
[62] Riverside RWK, Cleveland FC. Orthophosphate esters of starch; 1959. U.S. patent; 2-884-413.
[63] Tienfenthaler KHO, Nittner EWK. Phosphated locust bean gums; 1979. U.S. patent; 4-162-925.
[64] El-Thalouth IA, Rekaby M, Abdel-Rahman A, Sh A. Preparation and characterization of phosphorylated sesbania galactomannan gum derivatives and their applications in textile printing. Res J Text Apparel 2012;16:68–76.
[65] Jiao G, Yu G, Zhang J, Ewart HS. Chemical structures and bioactivities of sulfated polysaccharides from marine algae. Mar Drugs 2011;9(2):196–223.
[66] Mizumoto K, Sugawara IW, Kodama T, Hayami M, Mori S. Sulfated homopolysaccharides with immunomodulating activities are more potent anti-HTLV-III agents than sulfated heteropolysaccharides. Jap J Exp Med 1988;58:145–51.
[67] Muthukumar J, Chidambaram R, Sukumaran S. Sulfated polysaccharides and its commercial applications in food industries—a review. J Food Sci Technol 2021;58:2453–66.
[68] Jindal M, Rana V, Kumar V, Singh RS, Kennedy JF, Tiwary AK. Sulfation of *Aegle marmelos* gum: synthesis, physico-chemical and functional characterization. Carbohydr Polym 2013;92:1660–8.
[69] Wang J, Zhao B, Wang X, Yao J, Zhang J. Structure and antioxidant activities of sulfated guar gum: homogeneous reaction using DMAP/DCC catalyst. Int J Biol Macromol 2012;50:1201–6.
[70] Wang J, Zhao B, Wang X, Zhang J. Preparation and characterization of sulfated galactomannan from guar gum: optimization of reaction conditions by BBD and molecule conformational studies. J Taiwan Inst Chem Eng 2012;43:889–96.
[71] Bo S, Muschin T, Kanamoto T, Nakashima H, Yoshida T. Sulfation and biological activities of konjac glucomannan. Carbohydr Polym 2013;94:899–903.
[72] Naveen N, Gopinath C, Rao D. A spotlight on thiolated natural polymers and their relevance in mucoadhesive drug delivery system. Futur J Pharm Sci 2018;4:47–52.
[73] Yadav S, Ahuja M, Kumar A, Kaur H. Gellan-thioglycolic acid conjugate: synthesis, characterization and evaluation as mucoadhesive polymer. Carbohydr Polym 2014;99:601–7.
[74] Esmaeilzadeh P, Kowitsch A, Heyroth F, Schmidt G, Fischer S, Ritchter K, Groth T. Synthesis of thiolated polysaccharides for formation of polyelectrolyte multilayers with improved cellular adhesion. Carbohydr Polym 2017;157:1205–14.
[75] Bernkop-Schnürch A, Brandt U, Clausen A. Synthesis and *in vitro* evaluation of chitosan-cysteine conjugates. Sci Pharm 1999;67:196–208.
[76] Bernkop-Schnurchand A, Hopf TE. Synthesis and in vitro evaluation of chitosan-thioglycolic acid conjugates. Sci Pharm 2001;69:109–18.
[77] Bernkop-Schnürch A, Kast CE, Richter MF. Improvement in the mucoadhesive properties of alginate by the covalent attachment of cysteine. J Control Release 2001;71:277–85.
[78] Bernkop-Schnürch A, Hornof M, Zoidl T. Thiolated polymers-thiomers: synthesis and *in vitro* evaluation of chitosan-2-iminothiolane conjugates. Int J Pharm 2003;260:229–37.
[79] Sharmaand R, Ahuja M. Thiolated pectin: synthesis, characterization and evaluation as a mucoadhesive polymer. Carbohydr Polym 2011;85:658–63.
[80] Mahajan HS, Tyagi VK, Patil RR, Dusunge SB. Thiolated xyloglucan: synthesis, characterization and evaluation as mucoadhesive in situ gelling agent. Carbohydr Polym 2013;91:618–25.
[81] Mishra RK, Datt M, Pal K, Banthia AK. Preparation and characterization of amidated pectin based hydrogels for drug delivery system. J Mater Sci Mater Med 2008;19:2275–80.
[82] Vallee F, Muller C, Durand A. Synthesis and rheological properties of hydrogels based on amphiphilic alginate-amide derivatives. Carbohydr Res 2009;344:223–8.

[83] Rowley JA, Madlambayan G, Mooney DJ. Alginate hydrogels as synthetic extracellular matrix materials. Biomaterials 1999;20:45–53.
[84] Huerta-Angeles G, Smejkalova D, Chladkova D, Ehlova T, Buffa R, Velebny V. Synthesis of highly substituted amide hyaluronan derivatives with tailored degree of substitution and their crosslinking via click chemistry. Carbohydr Res 2011;84:1293–300.
[85] Bogan RT, Brewer RJ. Cellulose esters, organic, survey. In: Mark HF, Bikales NM, Overberger CG, Menges G, Kroshwitz JI, editors. Encyclopedia of polymer science and engineering. New York: Wiley; 1985. p. 158.
[86] Serad GA. Cellulose esters, organic, fibres. In: Mark HF, Bikales NM, Overberger CG, Menges G, Kroshwitz JI, editors. Encyclopedia of polymer science and engineering. New York: Wiley; 1985. p. 200.
[87] Müller F, Leuschke C. Organic cellulose esters, thermoplastic molding compounds. In: Bottenbruch L, editor. Engineering thermoplastics: polycarbonates-polyacetals-polyesters-cellulose esters. Munich: Hanser; 1996. p. 385.
[88] March J. Advanced organic chemistry: reactions, mechanisms, and structure. 4th ed. New York: Wiley; 1992. p. 170.
[89] Hamcerencu M, Desbrieres J, Popa M. New unsaturated derivatives of xanthan gum: synthesis and characterization. Polymer 2007;48:1921–9.
[90] Hamcerencu M, Desbrieres J, Popa M. Stimuli-sensitive xanthan derivatives/N-isopropylacrylamide hydrogels: influence of crosslinking agent on interpenetrating polymer networks properties. Biomacromolecules 2009;10:1911–22.
[91] Hamcerencu M, Desbrieres J, Popa M. Thermosensitive microparticles based on unsaturated esters of some poly- and oligosaccharides: preparation, characterization, drug inclusion and release. Macromol Symp 2010;297:114–25.
[92] Silva DA, de Paula R, Feitosa J, de Brito AC, Maciel JS, Paula HC. Carboxymethylation of cashew tree exudate polysaccharide. Carbohydr Polym 2004;58:163–71.
[93] Goyal P, Kumar V, Sharma P. Carboxymethylation of tamarind kernel powder. Carbohydr Polym 2007;69:251–5.
[94] Yang L, Zhao T, Wei H, Zhang M, Zou Y, Mao G, Wu X. Carboxymethylation of polysaccharides from *Auricularia auricula* and their antioxidant activities *in vitro*. Int J Biol Macromol 2011;49:1124–30.
[95] Das B, Dutta S, Nayak AK, Nanda U. Zinc alginate-carboxymethyl cashew gum microbeads for prolonged drug release: development and optimization. Int J Biol Macromol 2014;70:505–15.
[96] Kumar A, Ahuja M. Carboxymethyl gum kondagogu: synthesis, characterization and evaluation as mucoadhesive polymer. Carbohydr Polym 2012;90:637–43.
[97] Bidgoli H, Zamani A, Taherzadeh MJ. Effect of carboxymethylation conditions on the water-binding capacity of chitosan-based superabsorbents. Carbohydr Res 2010;345:2683–9.
[98] Sharma BR, Kumar V, Soni P. Carbamoylethylation of guar gum. Carbohydr Polym 2004;58:449–53.
[99] Sharma BR, Kumar V, Soni P. Carbamoylethylation of *Cassia tora* gum. Carbohydr Polym 2003;54:143–7.
[100] Gupta S, Sharma P, Soni P. Chemical modification of *Cassia occidentalis* seed gum: carbamoylethylation. Carbohydr Polym 2005;59:501–6.
[101] Racovita S, Vasilu S, Popa M, Luca C. Polysaccharides based micro- and nanoparticles obtained by ionic gelation and their applications as drug delivery systems. Rev Rom de Chim 2009;54:709–18.
[102] Nayak AK, Pal D. Plant-derived polymers: ionically gelled sustained drug release systems. In: Mishra M, editor. Encyclopedia of biomedical polymers and polymeric biomaterials, vol. VIII. New York: Taylor and Francis; 2016. p. 6002–17.
[103] Nayak AK, Pal D. Natural starches-blended ionotropically-gelled micrparticles/beads for sustained drug release. In: Thakur VK, Thakur MK, Kessler MR, editors. Handbook

of composites from renewable materials, vol. 8, nanocomposites: advanced applications. USA: WILEY-Scrivener; 2017. p. 527–60.
[104] Pal D, Nayak AK. Plant polysaccharides-blended ionotropically-gelled alginate multiple-unit systems for sustained drug release. In: Thakur VK, Thakur MK, Kessler MR, editors. Handbook of composites from renewable materials, vol. 6, polymeric composites. USA: WILEY-Scrivener; 2017. p. 399–400.
[105] Nayak AK, Bera H, Hasnain MS. Particulate matrices of ionotropically gelled alginate- and plant-derived starches for sustained drug release. In: Nayak AK, Hasnain MS, editors. Alginates in drug delivery. United States: Academic Press, Elsevier Inc.; 2020. p. 257–95.
[106] Nayak AK, Hasnain MS. Ionotropically gelled alginate particles in sustained drug release. In: Nayak AK, Hasnain MS, editors. Alginates in drug delivery. United States: Academic Press, Elsevier Inc.; 2020. p. 203–30.
[107] Hasnain MS, Jameel E, Mohanta B, Dhara AK, Alkahtani S, Nayak AK. Alginates: sources, structure, and properties. In: Nayak AK, Hasnain MS, editors. Alginates in drug delivery. United States: Academic Press, Elsevier Inc.; 2020. p. 1–17.
[108] Hasnain MS, Rishishwar P, Rishishwar S, Ali S, Nayak AK. Isolation and characterization of *Linum usitatisimum* polysaccharide to prepare mucoadhesive beads of diclofenac sodium. Int J Biol Macromol 2018;116:162–72.
[109] Nayak AK, Pal D, Santra K. Swelling and drug release behavior of metformin HCl-loaded tamarind seed polysaccharide-alginate beads. Int J Biol Macromol 2016;82:1023–7.
[110] Sinha P, Ubaidulla U, Hasnain MS, Nayak AK, Rama B. Alginate-okra gum blend beads of diclofenac sodium from aqueous template using $ZnSO_4$ as a cross-linker. Int J Biol Macromol 2015;79:555–63.
[111] Jana S, Gangopadhaya A, Bhowmik BB, Nayak AK, Mukhrjee A. Pharmacokinetic evaluation of testosterone-loaded nanocapsules in rats. Int J Biol Macromol 2015;72:28–30.
[112] Nayak AK, Pal D. Ionotropically-gelled mucoadhesive beads for oral metformin HCl delivery: formulation, optimization and antidiabetic evaluation. J Sci Ind Res 2013;72:15–22.
[113] Pal D, Nayak AK. Alginates, blends and microspheres: controlled drug delivery. In: Mishra M, editor. Encyclopedia of biomedical polymers and polymeric biomaterials, vol. I. New York: Taylor and Francis; 2015. p. 89–98.
[114] Sriamornsak P, Nunthanid J, Cheewatanakornkool K, Manchun S. Effect of drug loading method on drug content and drug release from calcium pectinate gel beads. AAPS PharmSciTech 2010;11:1315–9.
[115] Das S, Ng K-Y, Ho PC. Formulation and optimization of zinc-pectinate beads for the controlled delivery of resveratrol. AAPS PharmSciTech 2010;11:729–42.
[116] Munarin F, Tanzi MC, Petrini P. Advances in biomedical applications of pectin gels. Int J Biol Macromol 2012;51:681–9.
[117] Guru PR, Bera H, Das M, Hasnain MS, Nayak AK. Aceclofenac-loaded *Plantago ovata* F. husk mucilage-Zn^{+2}-pectinate controlled-release matrices. Starch-Stärke 2018;70, 1700136.
[118] Nayak AK, Pal D, Santra K. Development of pectinate-ispagula mucilage mucoadhesive beads of metformin HCl by central composite design. Int J Biol Macromol 2014;66:203–21.
[119] Nayak AK, Pal D, Santra K. Development of calcium pectinate-tamarind seed polysaccharide mucoadhesive beads containing metformin HCl. Carbohydr Polym 2014;101:220–30.
[120] Nayak AK, Pal D, Das S. Calcium pectinate-fenugreek seed mucilage mucoadhesive beads for controlled delivery of metformin HCl. Carbohydr Polym 2013;96:349–57.
[121] Nayak AK, Kalia S, Hasnain MS. Optimization of aceclofenac-loaded pectinate-poly (vinyl pyrrolidone) beads by response surface methodology. Int J Biol Macromol 2013;62:194–202.

[122] Nayak AK, Pal D. Blends of jackfruit seed starch-pectin in the development of mucoadhesive beads containing metformin HCl. Int J Biol Macromol 2013;62:137–45.
[123] Nayak AK, Bera H, Hasnain MS, De A, Pal D, Samanta A. Gellan gum-based nanomaterials in drug delivery applications. In: Bera H, Hossain CM, Saha S, editors. Biopolymer-based nanomaterials in drug delivery and biomedical applications. United States: Academic Press, Elsevier Inc.; 2021. p. 313–31.
[124] Ali SA, Nayak AK, Sen KK, Prabhakar T. Preparation and characterization of vetiver oil encapsulated polymeric microcapsules for sedative and hypnotic activity. Int J Res Pharm Sci 2019;10(4):3616–25.
[125] Nayak AK, Pal D, Santra K. Ispaghula mucilage-gellan mucoadhesive beads of metformin HCl: development by response surface methodology. Carbohydr Polym 2014;107:41–50.
[126] Nayak AK, Pal D. *Trigonella foenum-graecum* L. seed mucilage-gellan mucoadhesive beads for controlled release of metformin HCl. Carbohydr Polym 2014;107:31–40.
[127] Nayak AK, Pal D, Santra K. *Artocarpus heterophyllus* L. seed starch-blended gellan gum mucoadhesive beads of metformin HCl. Int J Biol Macromol 2014;65:329–39.
[128] Nayak AK, Pal D, Santra K. Tamarind seed polysaccharide-gellan mucoadhesive beads for controlled release of metformin HCl. Carbohydr Polym 2014;103:154–63.
[129] Milivojevic M, Pajic-Lijakovic I, Bugarski B, Nayak AK, Hasnain MS. Gellan gum in drug delivery applications. In: Hasnain MS, Nayak AK, editors. Natural polysaccharides in drug delivery and biomedical applications. United States: Academic Press, Elsevier Inc.; 2019. p. 145–86.
[130] Ray S, Sinha P, Laha B, Maiti S, Bhattacharyya UK, Nayak AK. Polysorbate 80 coated crosslinked chitosan nanoparticles of ropinirole hydrochloride for brain targeting. J Drug Delivery Sci Technol 2018;48:21–9.
[131] Geaorge M, Abraham TE. pH sensitive alginate-guar gum hydrogel for the controlled delivery of protein drugs. Int J Pharm 2007;335:123–9.
[132] Kaity S, Isaac J, Ghosh A. Interpenetrating polymer network of locust bean gumpoly(vinyl alcohol) for controlled release drug delivery. Carbohydr Polym 2013;94:456–67.
[133] Silva DA, Feitosa J, Maciel JS, Paula HC, de Paula R. Characterization of crosslinked cashew gum derivatives. Carbohydr Polym 2006;66:16–26.
[134] Xu M, Sun Q, Su J, Wang J, Xu C, Zhang T, Sun Q. Microbial transformation of geniposide of *Gardenia jasminoides* Ellis into genipin by *Penicillium nigricans*. Enzyme Microb Technol 2008;42:440–4.
[135] Muzzarelli RAA. Genipin-crosslinked chitosan hydrogels as biomedical and pharmaceutical aids. Carbohydr Polym 2009;77:1–9.
[136] Mi FL, Shyu SS, Peng CK. Characterization of ring-opening polymerization of genipin and pH-dependent crosslinking reactions between chitosan and genipin. J Polym Sci A Polym Chem 2005;43:1985–2000.
[137] Borza AD, Annan NT, Moreau DL, Allan-Wojtas PM, Ghanem A, Rousseau D, Paulson AT, Hansen LT. Microencapsulation in genipin cross-linked gelatin-maltodextrin improves survival of *Bifidobacterium adolescentis* during exposure to *in vitro* gastrointestinal conditions. J Microencapsul 2010;27:387–99.
[138] Gliko-Kabir I, Yagen B, Baluom M, Rubinstein A. Phosphated crosslinked guar for colon-specifi c drug delivery: II. *In vitro* and *in vivo* evaluation in the rat. J Control Release 2000;63:129–34.
[139] Dulong V, Lack S, Le Cerf D, Picton L, Vannier J, Muller G. Hyaluronan-based hydrogels particles prepared by crosslinking with trisodium trimetaphosphate: synthesis and characterization. Carbohydr Polym 2004;57:1–6.
[140] Gliko-Kabir I, Yagen B, Penhasi A, Rubinstein A. Phosphated crosslinked guar for colon-specific drug delivery: I. preparation and physicochemical characterization. J Control Release 2000;63:121–7.

[141] Shalviri A, Liu Q, Abdekhodaie MJ, Wu XY. Novel modified starch–xanthan gum hydrogels for controlled drug delivery: synthesis and characterization. Carbohydr Polym 2010;79:898–907.
[142] Antanase LI, Desbrieres J, Riess G. Micellization of synthetic and polysaccharides-based graft copolymers in aqueous media. Prog Polym Sci 2017;73:32–60.
[143] Mundargi RC, Patil SA, Aminabhavi TM. Evaluation of acrylamide-grafted-xanthan gum copolymer matrix tablets for oral controlled delivery of antihypertensive drugs. Carbohydr Polym 2007;69:130–41.
[144] Toti US, Aminabhavi TM. Modified guar gum matrix tablet for controlled release of diltiazem hydrochloride. J Control Release 2004;95:567–77.
[145] Huang P, Yang C, Liu J, Wang W, Guo S, Li J, Sun Y, Dong H, Deng L, Zhang J, Liu J, Dong A. Improving the oral delivery efficiency of anticancer drugs by chitosan coated polycaprolactone grafted hyaluronic acid nanoparticles. J Mater Chem B 2014;2:4021.
[146] AA AL-K, Sherigara B. Semi-interpenetrating network of acrylamide-grafted sodium alginate microspheres for controlled release of diclofenac sodium, preparation and characterization. Colloids Surf B Biointerfaces 2014;115:132–8.

CHAPTER

2

Drug delivery dosage forms made of tailor-made natural polysaccharides

Md Saquib Hasnain[a], *Muhanna K. Al-Muhanna*[b], *Naushad Anwar*[c], *Mohd Usman Mohd Siddique*[d], *Mohd Neyaz Ahsan*[e], *Syed Anees Ahmed*[f], *Mohammad Tahir Ansari*[g], *and Amit Kumar Nayak*[h]

[a]Department of Pharmacy, Palamau Institute of Pharmacy, Daltonganj, Jharkhand, India, [b]The National Center for Composite and High Performances Materials, King Abdulaziz City for Science and Technology (KACST), Riyadh, Saudi Arabia, [c]Department of Chemistry, Aligarh Muslim University, Aligarh, Uttar Pradesh, India, [d]Department of Pharmaceutical Chemistry, Shri Vile Parle Kelavani Mandal's Institute of Pharmacy, Dhule, Maharashtra, India, [e]Department of Medical Laboratory Technology, University Polytechnic, Birla Institute of Technology, Ranchi, Jharkhand, India, [f]Department of Pharmacology, Hygia Institute of Pharmaceutical Application and Research, Lucknow, Uttar Pradesh, India, [g]School of Pharmacy, Faculty of Science and Engineering, University of Nottingham Malaysia, Semenyih, Selangor, Malaysia, [h]Department of Pharmaceutics, Seemanta Institute of Pharmaceutical Sciences, Jharpokharia, Mayurbhanj, Odisha, India

1 Introduction

Natural polysaccharides are naturally derived carbohydrate biopolymers, which are molecularly composed of repeating units of monosaccharide(s) and joined by glycosidic linkages to form a macromolecular structure [1,2]. In polysaccharide molecules, glycosidic linkages are covalent bonds, which join a monosaccharide unit to another unit/group, which may or may not be another

Tailor-Made Polysaccharides in Drug Delivery
https://doi.org/10.1016/B978-0-12-821286-8.00003-3

monosaccharide unit [2]. Since long, a number of polysaccharides are being economically extracted from various natural resources like plants, algae, fungi, microbes, animals, etc. [3–9]. Natural polysaccharides are favored over the synthetic raw materials because of their nontoxicity and high biosafety [2,10]. Recent years, the uses of natural polysaccharides as raw materials in various biomedical applications including drug delivery, wound management, tissue regeneration, etc., have been growing [10–16]. It is well established that polysaccharides are widely used biopolymeric materials for biomedical uses due to the facts that: (i) they can be found in reproducible way from the natural resources [17]; (ii) they can experience a wide variety of chemical and enzymatic responses due to occurring of various functional groups [18]; (iii) they have high biodegradability, good biocompatibility, low immunogenic property, and excellent mucoadhesivity [19–21]; (iv) ionic polysaccharides have ability to overcome the drawbacks of synthetic polymers in the strategy of stimuli responsiveness [22]; and (v) they are capable of producing conjugates with proteins and other biomacromolecules for the application in conjugate-based delivery [20,23,24]. Since long, natural polysaccharides are being used as drug delivery excipients, such as thickening agents, gelling agents, emulsifying agents, binding agents, disintegrating agents, swelling agents, encapsulating agents, matrix-formers, foam stabilizers, etc., in the formulations of many kinds of dosage forms [2,10,25–40]. Natural polysaccharides are highly water soluble because of the occurrence of multiple number hydroxyl groups, which usually form hydrogen bonding with water molecules and these hydroxyl groups are ubiquitous in structures of polysaccharides and involved in many chemical modifications [41,42]. Interestingly, the hydroxyl groups are unable to form strong ionic interactions with counter ions, and hence, these natural polysaccharides cannot be used for controlling drug release over a longer period [43]. To improve the physicochemical and functional properties of natural polysaccharides, they are being tailor-made via chemical derivatization of various functional groups (such as oxidation, phosphorylation, sulfation, thiolation, carboxymethylation, amidation, esterification, etc.), graft copolymerization, and crosslinking (using different crosslinkers) [23,44–48]. The synthesized tailor-made natural polysaccharides are being used as high-quality excipients to formulate various drug delivery dosage forms, such as tablets, beads, microparticles, nanoparticles, gels and hydrogels, films and patches, scaffolds, etc. [46–54]. The current chapter deals with a comprehensive discussion about the drug delivery dosage forms, which have been reported to be composed of tailor-made natural polysaccharides.

2 Tablets made of tailor-made natural polysaccharides

Natural polysaccharides and their tailor-made forms have been much explored as pharmaceutical excipients for the formulations of tablets containing various drugs [55–57]. Among various dosage forms, tablets are widely accepted for oral administration [58]. Formulations of tablets are simple and easy. Besides conventional immediate releasing tablets, matrix tablets are also widely being investigated for their sustained drug releasing potential [55,56]. A number of tailor-made natural polysaccharides are also being used as release modifiers as well as controlled release drug delivery dosage forms [57,59–61].

In an investigation, acrylamide (Am)-grafted xanthan gum (XG) as a copolymer (PAAm-*g*-XG) was synthesized by free radical polymerization in the presence of ceric ammonium nitrate employing XG and Am [59]. For the purpose of investigating the control drug releasing potential of drug, PAAm-*g*-XG matrix tablets were prepared. In this investigation, two antihypertensive drugs, such as carvedilol and atenolol were evaluated as model drugs. The result, of in vitro dissolution, showed that the releasing of atenolol from these PAAm-*g*-XG and XG matrix tablets was continued up to 24 and 12h, respectively. PAAm-*g*-XG matrix tablets of atenolol showed 85% release in both simulated gastric fluid (acidic pH) and simulated intestinal fluid (alkaline pH); however, XG matrix tablets of atenolol showed 99% release. On the other hand, there was no substantial difference in the release rate of PAAm-*g*-XG matrix tablets and XG matrix tablets of carvedilol. The release rate of PAAm-*g*-XG matrix tablets was found to be followed non-Fickian behavior. The overall results of this study indicated that the PAAm-*g*-XG can be used as a promising hydrophilic drug carrier in matrix tablets systems for antihypertensive drugs [59]. A similar formulation of matrix tablets of metronidazole was formulated using a derivative of guar gum (GG), that is, partially carboxymethylated guar gum (PCMGG) [60]. In this work, PCMGG was ionically crosslinked with Ca^{2+} ions. By changing the concentration of Ca^{2+} ions, the drug release from the ionically crosslinked PCMGG matrix tablets can be controlled. In a work, Toti et al. (2004) synthesized polyacrylamide-*grafted*-guar gum (PAAm-*g*-GG) and the synthesized grafted copolymer (i.e., PAAm-*g*-GG) was used to formulate matrix tablets for diltiazem HCl releasing [61]. Matrix tablets of PAAm-*g*-GG and hydrolyzed PAAm-*g*-GG copolymers exhibited sustained release of diltiazem HCl up to 8 and 12h, respectively. Unhydrolyzed copolymer released the drug in a dissolution-controlled manner (pH7.4), while hydrolyzed copolymers released the drug in a swelling-controlled manner (0.1N HCl). It was establish that hydrolyzed PAAm-*g*-GG matrix tablets were of pH sensitive and can be applicable for intestinal drug delivery. Photographs of PAAm-*g*-GG matrix tablets and hydrolyzed PAAm-*g*-GG matrix tablets in 0.1N HCl and pH7.4 phosphate buffer after 1h are shown in Figs. 1 and 2, respectively.

In a work, interpolymer complexes (IPC) of crosslinked chitosan and carboxymethyl guar gum (CMGG) as coating agent was investigated as fluticasone tablets for colon-specific drug release [62]. In vitro studies

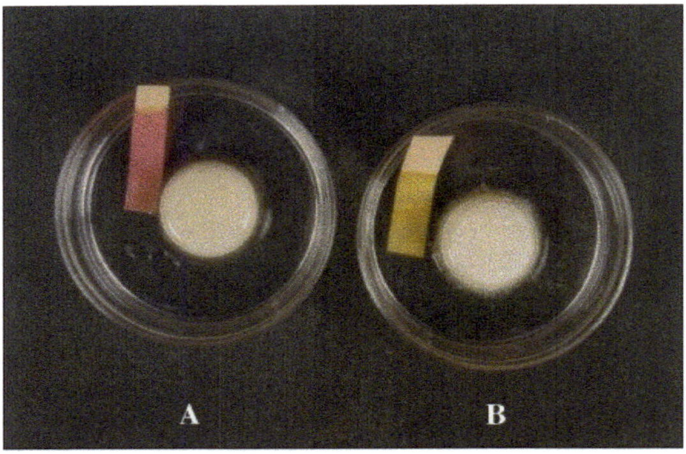

FIG. 1 Photographs of PAAm-*g*-GG matrix tablets in (A) 0.1 N HCl and (B) pH 7.4 phosphate buffer after 1 h. *From Toti US, Aminabhavi TM. Modified guar gum matrix tablet for controlled release of diltiazem hydrochloride. J Control Release 2004;95:567–577. Copyright © 2004 with permission from Elsevier B.V.*

FIG. 2 Photographs of hydrolyzed PAAm-*g*-GG matrix tablets in (A) 0.1 N HCl and (B) pH 7.4 phosphate buffer after 1 h [61]. *From Toti US, Aminabhavi TM. Modified guar gum matrix tablet for controlled release of diltiazem hydrochloride. J Control Release 2004;95:567–577. Copyright © 2004 with permission from Elsevier B.V.*

showed that uncoated tablets started releasing fluticasone within 1 h at pH 1.2; however, the amount of drug release from uncoated tablets was found to be only 10% after 2 h, limited its use for colon targeting. Once, the tablets coated with different ratios of chitosan to CMMG (60:40, 50:50, or 40:60), the release of fluticasone was varied as 5.60 ± 0.29, 2.34 ± 0.14, and $5.05 \pm 0.25\%$, respectively, at pH 1.2. The results demonstrated that the

< 10% drug releases in acidic media. However, the coated tablets released 15.11 ± 0.58%, 8.01 ± 0.17%, and 13.08 ± 0.021% fluticasone in pH 7.4 after 5 h. Upon increasing pH to 6.8, the release rate increased to 53.87 ± 0.33%, 37.86 ± 0.42% and 49.63 ± 0.61% after 24 h. In terms of pharmacodynamics estimation, the tablets coated with the IPC film coat showed significantly greater reduction in TNBS-induced ulcerative colitis than uncoated tablets. Some recently developed tablets made of tailor-made polysaccharides are listed in Table 1.

TABLE 1 Some recently developed tablets made of tailor-made polysaccharides.

Tablets made of tailor-made polysaccharides	Drugs released	References
Sodium carboxymethyl okra gum-*graft*-polymethacrylamide sustained release tablets	Diclofenac sodium	Patra et al. [63]
GG-*graft*-2-hydroxyl ethyl methacrylate tablets	5-Amino salicylic acid	Mahto and Mishra [64]
Jhingan gum-*graft*-PAAm matrix tablets	5-Amino salicylic acid	Mate et al. [65]
Carboxymethyl XG-*graft*-PAAm matrix tablets of	Diltiazem HCl	Badwaik et al. [66]
Carboxymethylated locust bean gum matrix tablets	Ibuprofen and metronidazole	Chakravorty et al. [67]
Tablets prepared using hydrolyzed *Cordia myxa* gum as a binder	Paracetamol	Tahir et al. [68]
Microwave-modified *Terminalia mantaly* gum-based sustained release tablets	Naproxen sodium	Odeniyi et al. [69]
Crosslinked pregelatinized potato starch matrix-based controlled release tablets	Diprophylline, theophylline, and diltiazem HCl	Elgaied-Lamouchi et al. [70]
AAm-*graft*-neem (*Azadirachta indica*) gum sustained release tablets	Propranolol HCl	Bhagwat et al. [71]
Buoyant tablets using PAAm-*graft*-corn fiber gum	Cinnarizine	Sethi et al. [72]
Carboxymethylated *Tamarindus indica* and *Cassia fistula* gum-based controlled release tablets	Diclofenac sodium	Huanbutta and Sittikijyothin [73]
Sustained release gastroretentive tablets based on PAAm-*graft*-gellan gum	Metformin HCl	Sarkar et al. [74]
Gastroretentive extended tablets prepared using methacrylamide-*graft*-gellan gum and tamarind seed gum composite matrix	Metformin HCl	Priyadarshini et al. [75]

3 Nanoparticles made of tailor-made natural polysaccharides

Since past few years, natural polysaccharides-based nanoparticles are of prime importance for the delivery of drugs to their intended target owing to their biodegradability [76–80]. Moreover, the preparation of natural polysaccharides-based nanoparticles is found advantageous for easily handling in aqueous solutions. Thus the avoidance of the involvement of environmentally hazardous organic solvents is possible.

Ray et al. (2018) formulated polysorbate 80-coated ropinirole HCl-loaded chitosan nanoparticles by emulsification crosslinking using glutaraldehyde [81]. The uncoated ropinirole HCl-loaded chitosan nanoparticles and polysorbate 80-coated ropinirole HCl-loaded chitosan nanoparticles (in scanning electron microscopy) are shown in Fig. 3. The in vitro release of ropinirole HCl from uncoated and coated glutaraldehyde-crosslinked chitosan nanoparticles demonstrated a preliminary burst release of drug followed by a sustained release pattern over 10h (Fig. 4). In vivo biodistribution of ropinirole HCl in Wistar rats demonstrated an increased concentration of ropinirole HCl in the brain with lower ropinirole HCl concentrations in the kidney, liver, and spleen after 1h of intravenous (i.v.) administration for polysorbate 80-coated ropinirole HCl-loaded glutaraldehyde-crosslinked chitosan nanoparticles as compared to uncoated nanoparticles (Fig. 5). Overall results suggested that these nanoparticles could be used in treatment of Parkinson's disease. Jana et al. (2013) developed chitosan-egg albumin-PEG 400 nanoparticles

FIG. 3 Uncoated ropinirole HCl-loaded chitosan nanoparticles and polysorbate 80-coated ropinirole HCl-loaded chitosan nanoparticles (in scanning electron microscopy) [81]. *From Ray S, Sinha P, Laha B, Maiti S, Bhattacharyya UK, Nayak AK. Polysorbate 80 coated crosslinked chitosan nanoparticles of ropinirole hydrochloride for brain targeting. J Drug Delivery Sci Technol 2018;48:21–29. Copyright © 2018 with permission from Elsevier B.V.*

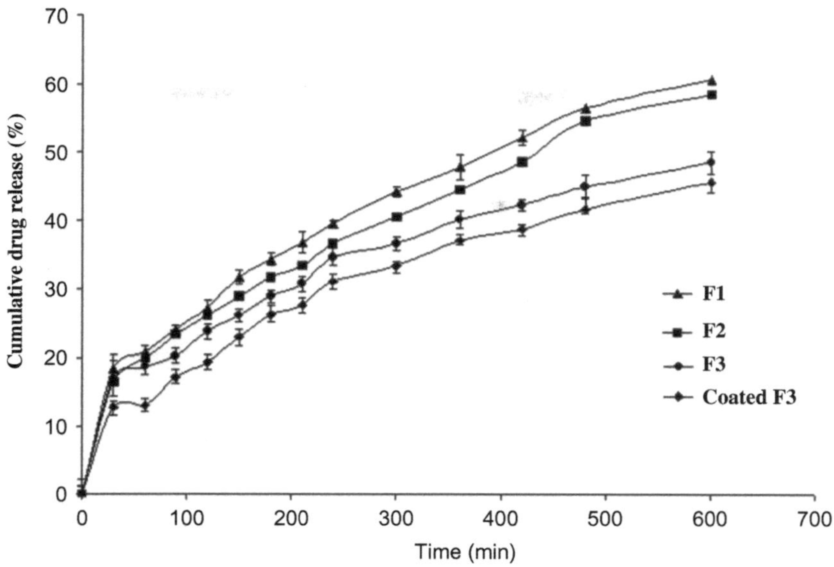

FIG. 4 In vitro release of ropinirole HCl from uncoated and coated glutaraldehyde-crosslinked chitosan nanoparticles [mean ± S.D., $n = 3$]. *From Ray S, Sinha P, Laha B, Maiti S, Bhattacharyya UK, Nayak AK. Polysorbate 80 coated crosslinked chitosan nanoparticles of ropinirole hydrochloride for brain targeting. J Drug Delivery Sci Technol 2018;48:21–29. Copyright © 2018 with permission from Elsevier B.V.*

of alprazolam via heat coagulation procedure, where interpolymeric complexation was occurred in-between negatively modified egg albumin and positively charged chitosan at 80°C and pH 5 [82]. In the preparation of these chitosan-based nanoparticles of alprazolam, PEG 400 was used as stabilizing agent. The field emission-scanning electron microscopy image of lyophilized chitosan-egg albumin-PEG 400 nanoparticles of alprazolam indicated nanoscale range and spherical nanoparticles. In vitro alprazolam releasing from these chitosan-based nanoparticles of alprazolam demonstrated a sustained release pattern over 24 h (Fig. 6). In another research, the same research group formulated aceclofenac-loaded chitosan-egg albumin nanoparticles using 2% w/v sodium tripolyphosphate (crosslinker) [83]. The in vitro aceclofenac release from nanoparticles was measured to be sustained over 8 h.

In a work, glutaraldehyde-crosslinked GG nanoparticles were synthesized to load tamoxifen citrate (a nonsteroidal antiestrogenic drug) for the treatment of breast cancer [84]. These tamoxifen citrate-loaded nanoparticles were prepared by using oil in the aqueous emulsion method. The time dependent releasing of tamoxifen citrate from glutaraldehyde-crosslinked GG nanoparticles influenced by GG (polymer) and glutaraldehyde (crosslinker) concentrations. Furthermore, the results of in vivo

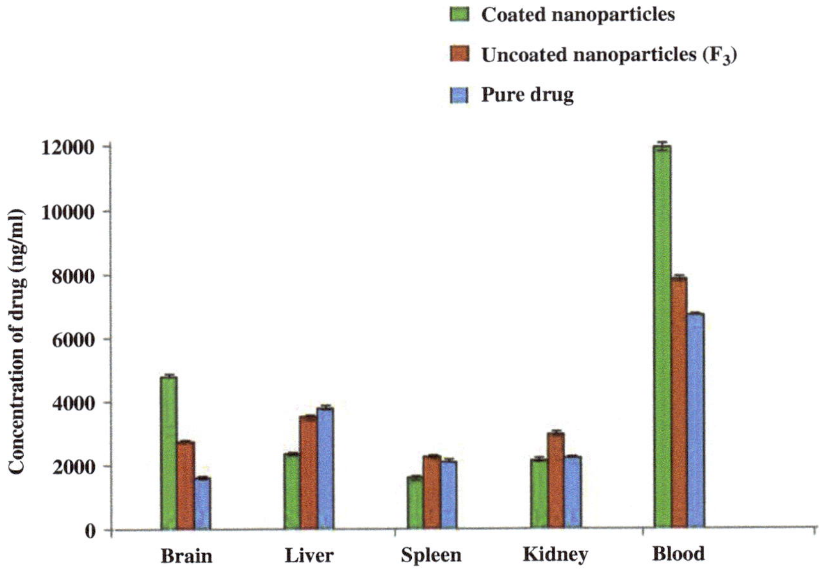

FIG. 5 In vivo biodistribution in the brain, liver, spleen, kidney, and blood after 1 h of dose administration (i.v.) of pure drug (ropinirole HCl), uncoated ropinirole HCl-loaded chitosan nanoparticles (F3), and polysorbate 80-coated ropinirole HCl-loaded chitosan nanoparticles in Wistar rats [mean ± S.D., $n=6$] [81]. *From Ray S, Sinha P, Laha B, Maiti S, Bhattacharyya UK, Nayak AK. Polysorbate 80 coated crosslinked chitosan nanoparticles of ropinirole hydrochloride for brain targeting. J Drug Delivery Sci Technol 2018;48:21–29. Copyright © 2018 with permission from Elsevier B.V.*

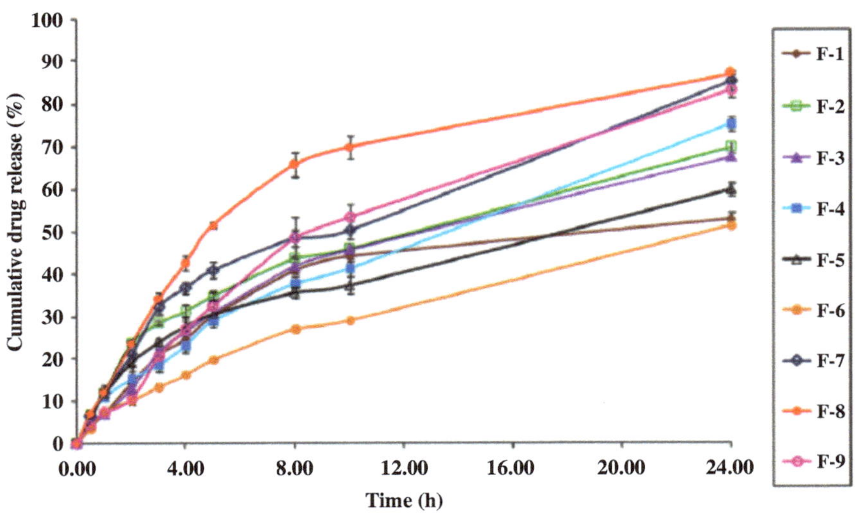

FIG. 6 In vitro drug release from alprazolam-loaded nanoparticles in phosphate buffer, pH7.4 (mean ± S.D.; $n=3$) [82]. *From Jana S, Maji N, Nayak AK, Sen KK, Basu SK, Development of chitosan-based nanoparticles through inter-polymeric complexation for oral drug delivery. Carbohydr Polym 2013;870–876. Copyright © 2013 with permission from Elsevier Ltd.*

studies established that maximum uptake of tamoxifen by mammillary tissue of albino female mice after 24h of administration with tamoxifen citrate-loaded glutaraldehyde crosslinked GG nanoparticles than tamoxifen citrate tablets. Further, it was found that the process to the encapsulation process by GG was depended upon the uses of dichloromethane as a drug loading solvent. In another report, lipase-functionalized GG nanoparticles having size ranges from 19 to 32nm were synthesized by nanoprecipitation and the crosslinking technique for the purpose of drug delivery applications [85]. It was perceived that the development of nanoparticles was depended upon the mass of GG, solvent, surfactant, crosslinker, and agitation. The release of crystal violet proved the efficacy of drug release by the GG nanocarrier. The time-dependent kinetic studies showed that the release was faster up to 24h, and thereafter, the release was very gentle, suggested that lipase-functionalized GG nanoparticles might be possibly used as a carrier for drug delivery [85]. In another research, Huang et al. (2014) prepared hyaluronic acid-*grafted*-polycaprolactone nanoparticles coated with chitosan for the oral delivery of paclitaxel and doxorubicin (anticancer drugs) [86]. Some recently developed nanoparticles made of tailor-made polysaccharides are listed in Table 2.

4 Microparticles made of tailor-made natural polysaccharides

Microparticles are small spherical particles having diameters range around 1–1000μm [101]. Drug-loaded biodegradable microparticles composed of tailor-made natural polysaccharides have already gained much attention for their potential uses in drug delivery as because of the facts that natural polysaccharides are biodegradable and biocompatible [102,103]. Moreover, these microparticles exhibit sustain release of loaded drugs.

In a work, Das et al. (2014) formulated carboxymethyl cashew gum-based microbeads of isoxsuprine HCl [104]. They employed sodium alginate-carboxymethyl cashew gum blends and zinc sulfate to prepare spherical shaped microbeads of isoxsuprine HCl (Fig. 7). These carboxymethyl cashew gum-alginate microbeads demonstrated the sustained releasing of loaded isoxsuprine HCl over a prolonged period, in vitro (Fig. 8). Jana et al. (2013) formulated tamarind seed polysaccharide-chitosan interpenetrating polymeric network microparticles of aceclofenac using glutaraldehyde as crosslinker [105]. These glutaraldehyde-crosslinked microparticles demonstrated sustained releasing of aceclofenac over 8h, in vitro and in vivo antiinflammatory action was found in the carrageenan-induced rats after oral intake. In a work, glutaraldehyde-crosslinked GG microspheres of ornidazole were formulated for colon-specific delivery [106]. These GG microspheres of ornidazole showed slower drug release and increased drug release at the colonic

TABLE 2 Some recently developed nanoparticles made of tailor-made polysaccharides.

Nanoparticles made of tailor-made polysaccharides	Drugs released	References
Phthalated cashew gum nanoparticles	Benznidazole	Oliveira et al. [87]
Acetylated cashew gum nanoparticles	Insulin	Vasconcelos et al. [88]
Self-assembled nanoparticles of acetylated cashew gum	Indomethacin	Pitombeira et al. [89]
Phenylboronic acid-conjugated chitosan nanoparticles	Curcumin	Wang et al. [90]
Octenylsuccinic anhydride-modified pH-sensitive chitosan nanoparticles	Curcumin and quercetin	Yu et al. [91]
Alginate-chitosan nanoparticles	Amygdalin	Sohail and Abbas [92]
Poly(ε-caprolactone)-*graft*-cashew gum nanoparticles	Epirubicin	Ribeiro et al. [93]
Chitosan-tamarind gum polyelectrolyte complex-stabilized nanoparticles	Simvastatin	Malviya et al. [94]
Zein/carboxymethyl dextrin nanoparticles	Curcumin	Meng et al. [95]
Carboxymethyl moringa gum-chitosan nanoparticles	Ofloxacin	Rimpy et al. [96]
Colon specific enzyme responsive oligoester crosslinked dextran nanoparticles	5-Fluorouracil	Abid et al. [97]
Thiolated alginate nanoparticles	Budesonide	Arif et al. [98]
Disulfide crosslinked sodium alginate derivative nanoparticles	Paclitaxel	Ayub et al. [99]
Disulfide crosslinked thiolated sodium alginate nanoparticles	Docetaxel	Chiu et al. [100]

pH [107]. Similar kind of GG microspheres of metronidazole was formulated using glutaraldehyde as a crosslinking agent. The in vitro release of loaded metronidazole was found to be dependent on the GG concentration and glutaraldehyde concentration and pH of the release medium. In another work, microspheres of chitosan/carboxymethyl cashew gum loaded with bovine serum albumin (BSA) were prepared and investigated for delivery of protein drugs [108]. The in vitro release of BSA from these chitosan/carboxymethyl cashew gum microspheres followed the non-Fickian BSA release mechanism.

Al-Kahtani et al. (2014) formulated semiinterpenetrating network microspheres of acrylamide-*grafted*-sodium alginate (AAm-*g*-NaAlg) for controlled release of diclofenac sodium [109]. These diclofenac sodium–loaded

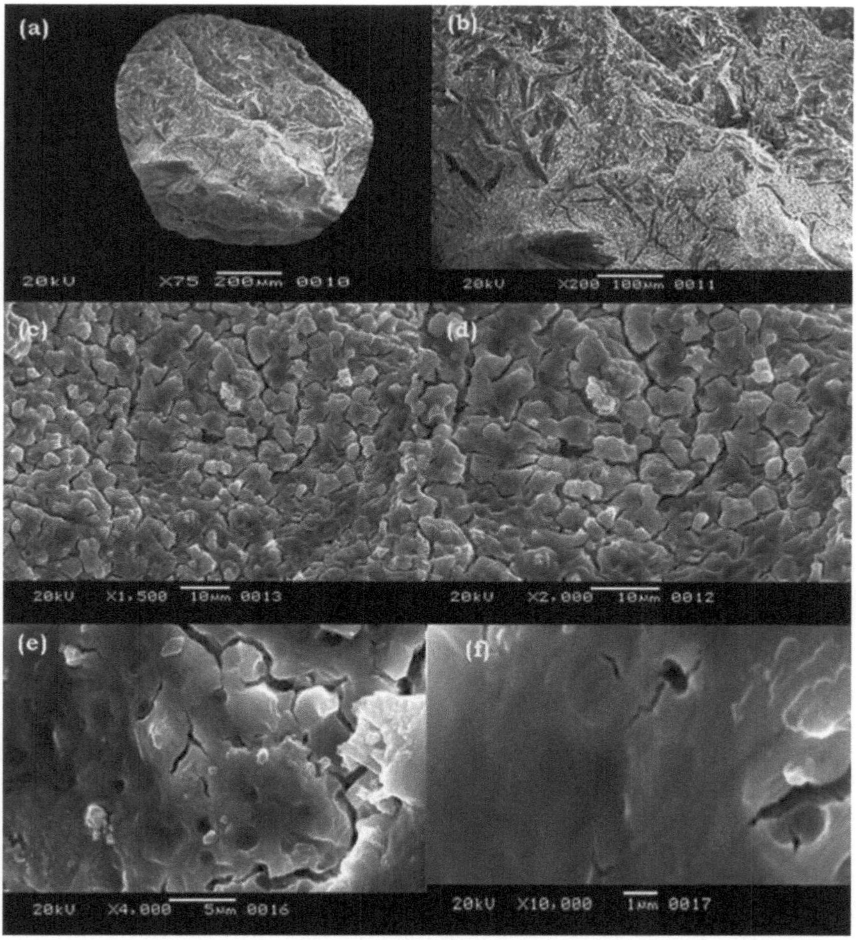

FIG. 7 Scanning electron microscopy photograph of optimized carboxymethyl cashew gum-based microbeads of isoxsuprine HCl at different magnifications (75 ×, 200 ×, 1500 ×, 2000 ×, 4000 ×, and 10,000 ×) [104]. *From Das B, Dutta S, Nayak AK, Nanda U. Zinc alginate-carboxymethyl cashew gum microbeads for prolonged drug release: development and optimization. Int J Biol Macromol 2014;70:505–515. Copyright © 2014 with permission from Elsevier B.V.*

microspheres were prepared by the emulsion-crosslinking method using glutaraldehyde as a crosslinking agent. The acrylamide grafting onto the sodium alginate (NaAlg) was synthesized by the free-radical graft polymerization process in the presence of initiator ceric ammonium nitrate at various Am concentrations with monomer to polymer ratio of 1:1, 2:1, and 3:1, respectively. The drug release rate (in vitro) was found to be controlled by glutaraldehyde, Am to NaAlg grafting ratio in microspheres. In vitro drug release followed the super case II transport. Jana et al. (2013) formulated

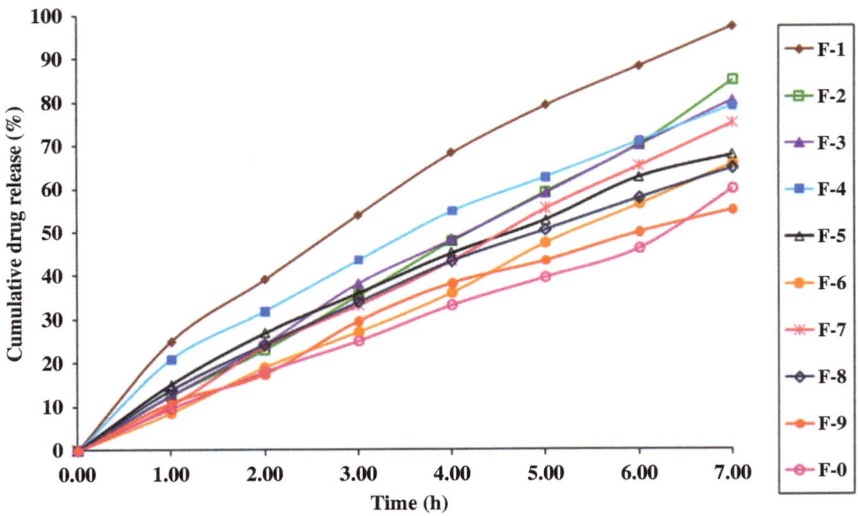

FIG. 8 In vitro drug release from various carboxymethyl cashew gum-based microbeads of isoxsuprine HCl [104]. *From Das B, Dutta S, Nayak AK, Nanda U. Zinc alginate-carboxymethyl cashew gum microbeads for prolonged drug release: development and optimization. Int J Biol Macromol 2014;70:505–515. Copyright © 2014 with permission from Elsevier B.V.*

alginate/gellan gum microspheres of aceclofenac by maleic anhydride–induced unsaturated esterification [110]. These unsaturated esterified alginate/gellan gum microspheres were found almost spherical shaped with rough surface, and elongated tails were noticed when the polymer concentration was increased (Fig. 9). The in vitro aceclofenac releasing results demonstrated a sustained release pattern over 6h. The unsaturated esterified alginate/gellan gum microspheres formulated using 3% (w/v) maleic anhydride and 3% (w/v) aluminum chloride produced comparatively slower drug release than other formulations (Fig. 10). The in vivo results in rabbits and in carrageenan-induced rats (using the paw edema model) exhibited sustained systemic absorption of aceclofenac (pharmacokinetic) and antiinflammatory action (pharmacodynamic) after oral administration of the prepared unsaturated esterified alginate/gellan gum microspheres of aceclofenac. Some recently developed microparticles made of tailor-made polysaccharides are listed in Table 3.

5 Beads made of tailor-made natural polysaccharides

Beads are the multiparticulate system, and in comparison to single-unit systems, they facilitate some potential benefits, namely, increased bioavailability, reduced risk of systemic toxicity, reduced risk of local irritation, and so on [122–125].

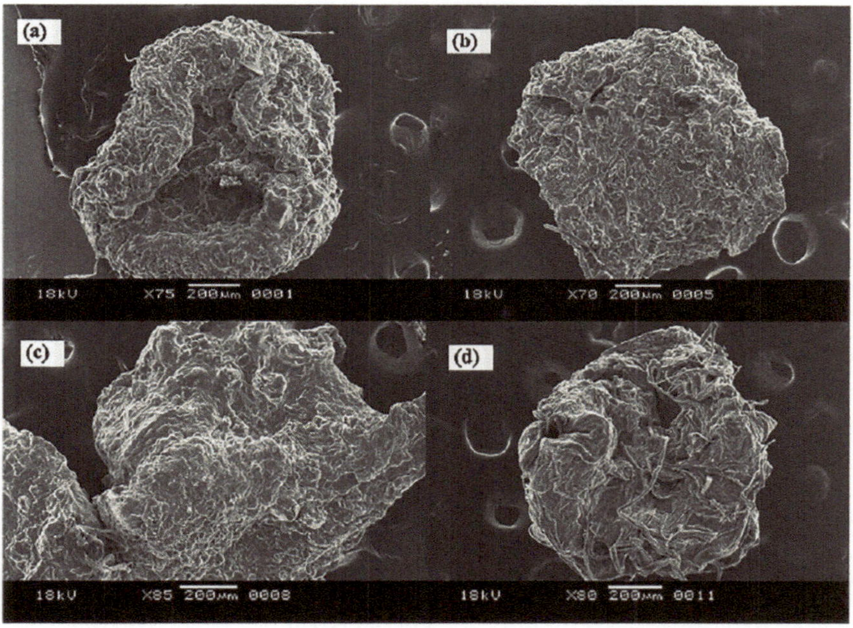

FIG. 9 Scanning electron microscopy photograph of alginate/gellan gum microspheres: (A) aceclofenac-loaded alginate/gellan gum microspheres prepared using 3% (w/v) maleic anhydride; (B) aceclofenac-loaded alginate/gellan gum microspheres prepared using 3% (w/v) maleic anhydride and 3% (w/v) aluminum chloride; (C) aceclofenac-loaded alginate/gellan gum microspheres prepared using 3% (w/v) aluminum chloride; and (D) alginate/gellan gum microspheres without drug prepared using 3% (w/v) maleic anhydride [110]. *From Jana S, Das A, Nayak AK, Sen KK, Basu SK, Aceclofenac-loaded unsaturated esterified alginate/gellan gum microspheres: in vitro and in vivo assessment. Int J Biol Macromol 2013;129–137. Copyright © 2013 with permission from Elsevier B.V.*

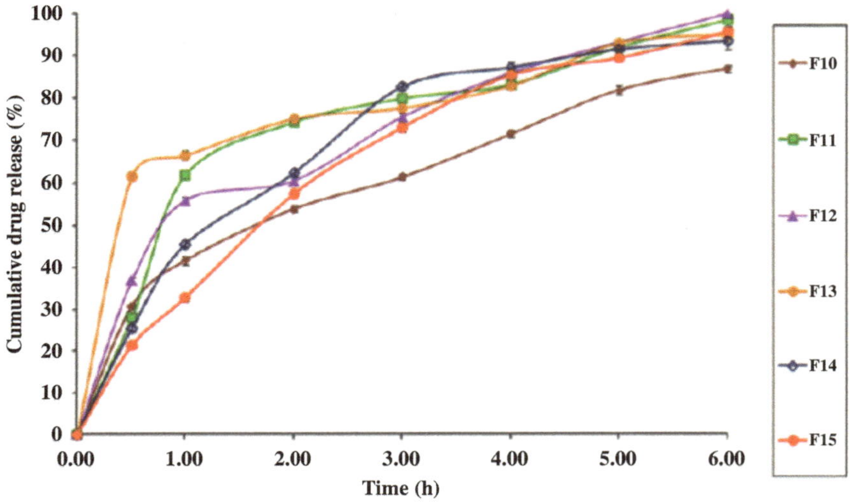

FIG. 10 In vitro drug release from aceclofenac-loaded microspheres prepared using 3% (w/v) maleic anhydride and 3% (w/v) aluminum chloride [110]. *From Jana S, Das A, Nayak AK, Sen KK, Basu SK, Aceclofenac-loaded unsaturated esterified alginate/gellan gum microspheres: in vitro and in vivo assessment. Int J Biol Macromol 2013;129–137. Copyright © 2013 with permission from Elsevier B.V.*

TABLE 3 Some recently developed microparticles made of tailor-made polysaccharides.

Microparticles made of tailor-made polysaccharides	Drugs released	References
Crosslinked xylan microparticles	Mesalamine	Urtiga et al. [111]
Thiolated sodium alginate mucoadhesive microspheres	Metformin HCl	Khalid et al. [112]
Citric acid-crosslinked chitosan microparticles	Bovine serum albumin	Sedyakina et al. [113]
Porous crosslinked microparticles based on glycidyl methacrylate and XG	Theophylline	Lungan et al. [114]
Carboxymethyl chitosan/poly(γ-glutamic acid) composite microparticles	Levofloxacin	Yan et al. [115]
Genipin crosslinked gum Arabic/*O*-carboxymethyl chitosan-coated layer-by-layer microcapsules	Omeprazole	Huang et al. [116]
Genipin crosslinked *O*-carboxymethyl chitosan/gum Arabic coacervate microcapsules	Bovine serum albumin	Xiao et al. [117]
PAAm-*graft*-gum karaya pH-sensitive spray dried microspheres	Capecitabine	Alange et al. [118]
Glutaraldehyde crosslinked interpenetrating network microspheres of gum ghatti and poly vinyl alcohol	Glipizide	Ray et al. [119]
Microbeads containing thiolated pectin	Doxorubicin	Cheewatanakornkool et al. [120]
Mucoadhesive microspheres of glutaraldehyde-crosslinked mucilage of Isabgol husk	Gliclazide	Sharma et al. [121]

Bera et al. (2015) prepared ziprasidone HCl-loaded interpenetrating polymer network beads of sterculia gum (SG) and low methoxy pectin by simultaneous ionotropic crosslinking (using zinc acetate as ionotropic crosslinker) and covalent crosslinking (using glutaraldehyde as covalent crosslinker) [126]. These ziprasidone HCl–loaded simultaneous ionotropic-covalent crosslinked beads were of spherical-shaped with rough surface morphology (Fig. 11). In addition, typical wrinkles and cracks were seen on the surface of these crosslinked SG-pectin beads. These ziprasidone HCl-loaded beads presented a controlled releasing pattern of the loaded drug (here ziprasidone HCl) over 8h (Fig. 12) with excellent buoyancy and mucoadhesivity. A work by Agarwal et al. (2015) developed and evaluated CMC-calcium alginate (CaAlg) beads for colon-targeted delivery of

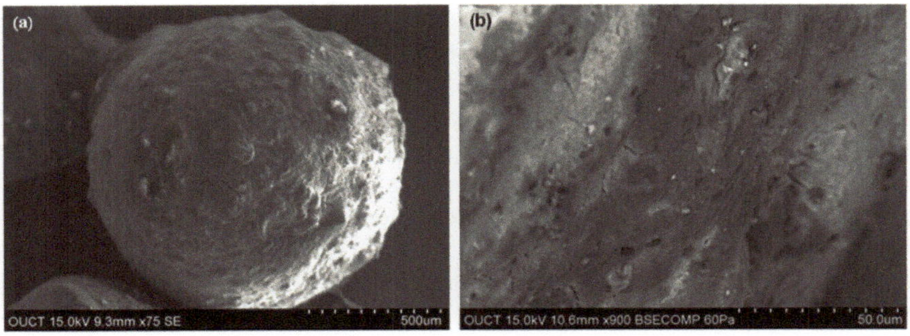

FIG. 11 Scanning electron microphotograph of ziprasidone HCl-loaded crosslinked sterculia gum-pectin beads showing rough surface with less zoom (75 ×) (A) and presence of pores and channels with high zoom (900 ×) (B) [126]. *From Bera H, Boddupalli S, Nayak AK, Mucoadhesive-floating zinc-pectinate-sterculia gum interpenetrating polymer network beads encapsulating ziprasidone HCl. Carbohydr Polym 2015;108–118. Copyright © 2015 with permission from Elsevier Ltd.*

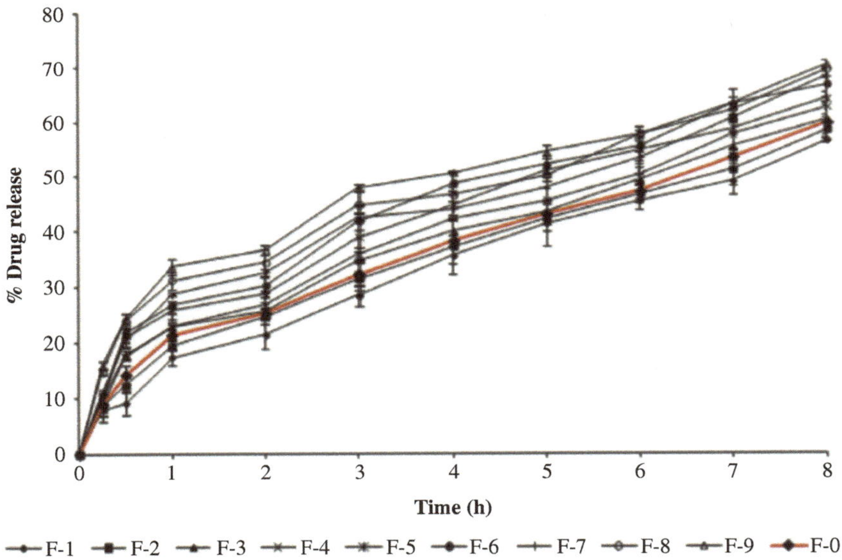

FIG. 12 In vitro drug release profiles of ziprasidone HCl-loaded crosslinked sterculia gum-pectin beads (A) [126]. *From Bera H, Boddupalli S, Nayak AK, Mucoadhesive-floating zinc-pectinate-sterculia gum interpenetrating polymer network beads encapsulating ziprasidone HCl. Carbohydr Polym 2015;108–118. Copyright © 2015 with permission from Elsevier Ltd.*

an anticancer drug, 5-fluorouracil [127]. These 5-fluorouracil-loaded CMC-CaAlg beads were prepared by the ionic gelation technique. The ionically crosslinked beads exhibited mucoadhesivity and noticeable pH-dependent release of loaded 5-fluorouracil at the colonic atmosphere. Carboxymethyl gum kondagogu (CMGK) was synthesized by the reaction between gum kondagogu and monochloroacetic acid at a higher pH value [128]. The synthesized CMGK was used to formulate mucoadhesive ionotropically gelled beads of metformin using calcium chloride. The mucoadhesion studies of CMGK beads were performed by wash off analysis using isolated chick ileum, which exhibited bioadhesion greater than 80% over a period of 24h. It was clearly noticed that upon increasing the crosslinking concentration, percent drug entrapment was increased and, thereby, reduced the drug releasing from CMGK beads. The same research group formulated ionotropically gelled beads of carboxymethyl gellan gum [129]. The carboxymethyl gellan gum exhibited 2.71-fold higher mucoadhesive potential than the native gellan gum. The formulated carboxymethyl gellan gum beads of metformin HCl showed ex vivo bioadhesion of 100% over 24h and a sustained pattern of drug releasing over a longer period. In a work, modified starch (cationized)-alginate beads containing aceclofenac were formulated [130]. The instrumental analysis suggested the formation of polyelectrolyte complexation in-between two polymers used in the formulation of such beads. These modified starch (cationized)-alginate beads of aceclofenac exhibited a sustained drug releasing pattern over a longer period. Some recently developed beads made of tailor-made polysaccharides are listed in Table 4.

6 Hydrogels made of tailor-made natural polysaccharides

The swollen nature of polymer networks with water is usually referred to as "hydrogels," which are 3-D, hydrophilic, crosslinked water-soluble polymers networks [42,147]. Sometimes, hydrogels are very sensitive toward the different stimuli, such as changing adjacent pH, temperature, ionic strength, and electrical stimuli [42,148–151]. These stimuli cause swelling of hydrogels and make them potential candidates for drug delivery devices [152,153]. Because of this property, hydrogels (specially based on tailor-made natural polysaccharides) have attracted immense consideration as an outstanding applicant for the controlled delivery of therapeutic agents to their target site of action [152,154].

In a work, a pH sensitive polyacrylamide (PAm)-*grafted*-pectin hydrogel was synthesized [155]. It was observed that the crosslinked polyacrylamide grafted pectin with varying amount of glutaraldehyde showed better hydrogel forming property and gelling property than pectin. The synthesized hydrogel exhibited pH-dependent release of salicylic acid. A polyelectrolyte complex-based hydrogel of cationic GG and poly (acrylic acid) (PAA) induced by photoinitiated free radical polymerization was synthesized by Huang et al. (2007) [156]. Within the synthesized cationic GG/PAA hydrogel, ketoprofen was loaded as model drug. The progress of the hydrogel could be attributed to the strong electrostatic interaction between cationic GG and anionic-natured PAA. Their swelling characteristics

TABLE 4 Some recently developed beads made of tailor-made polysaccharides.

Beads made of tailor-made polysaccharides	Drugs released	References
Carboxymethyl *Cassia obtusifolia* galactomannan beads	Diclofenac sodium	Verma et al. [131]
Tamarind seed gum-hydrolyzed polymethacrylamide-*graft*-gellan beads for extended release	Diclofenac sodium	Nandi et al. [132]
Silica coated carboxymethyl tamarind kernel polysaccharide beads	Ibuprofen	Kumar et al. [133]
Pectin/carboxymethyl tamarind seed polysaccharide beads	Moxifloxacin	Pandit et al. [134]
GG succinate-sodium alginate beads	Ibuprofen	Seeli et al. [135]
Interpenetrating polymer network beads using alginate, polyvinyl alcohol, and methylcellulose	Flurbiprofen	Bulut [136]
Covalent semiinterpenetrating polymer network beads using chitosan and sodium carboxylated agarose	Azithromycin	Rajesh and Popat [137]
Carboxymethyl fenugreek galactomannan-gellan gum-calcium silicate composite beads	Glimepiride	Bera et al. [138]
Self-mineralizing calcium-enriched methacrylated gellan gum beads	Dexamethasone 21-phosphate	Vieira et al. [139]
Glutaraldehyde crosslinked alginate-gelatin beads	Gliclazide	Elsayed et al. [140]
Glycopolymeric gel–stabilized N-succinyl chitosan beads	Doxorubicin	Ajish et al. [141]
Dual cross linked sodium alginate/montmorillonite polymeric composite beads	Curcumin	Sreekanth Reddy et al. [142]
Chitosan/K-carrageenan polyelectrolyte complex beads	Verapamil HCl	Yousry et al. [143]
Modified alginate beads using gelatinized and ungelatinized arrowroot (*Tacca leontopetaloides* L. Kuntze) starch	Diclofenac sodium	Khlibsuwan et al. [144]
Dual crosslinked pectin-alginate network beads	Repaglinide	Awasthi et al. [145]
Covalent crosslinked sericin/alginate beads	Naproxen	Freitas et al. [146]

were found to be highly influenced by pH. Ketoprofen-loaded cationic GG–PAA hydrogel confirmed the release of drug in buffer of pH7.4, followed by the non-Fickian diffusion method. Hydrogel was synthesized using SG and methacrylic acid (MAA) [157]. Ranitidine HCl was loaded within these SG/MAA hydrogel, which displayed the quantitative release of loaded ranitidine HCl from per gram of the gel is higher in acidic pH (2.2) as compared to alkaline pH (7.4) and neutral pH (7). This hydrogels synthesis was found to be dependent upon the concentration of monomer, initiator, crosslinker, and extent of SG used. In another work, crosslinked PAAm-*g*-GG microgels were synthesized by the emulsification technique, which involved the conversion of $-CONH_2$ group to $-COOH$ group (saponification) [158]. The derivatized microgels were revealed very much sensitive toward the pH and ionic strength of the surrounding environment. At higher pH, the in vitro swelling of the microgels was found to be increased. The crosslinked PAAm-*g*-GG microgels were loaded with diltiazem HCl and nifedipine, which showed pH-sensitive releasing. The same research group formulated PAAm-*g*-GG hydrogel microspheres for controlled release of verapamil HCl and nifedipine [159]. In a work, glutaraldehyde-crosslinked GG-based hydrogel discs were formulated for colon-specific delivery of ibuprofen by Das et al. (2006) [160]. These tailored GG hydrogel discs experienced the significant reduction in the in vitro swelling due to glutaraldehyde-induced crosslinking. The percentage release of ibuprofen from these hydrogel discs was found to be controlled by glutaraldehyde concentration. In another work, pH-sensitive hydrogels were formulated using methacrylated and succinated derivatives of dextran [161]. The potentials of these tailored dextran-based hydrogels for colon-specific drug delivery were investigated using 2-methoxyestradiaol as a model drug. In vitro cell compatibility studies were carried out to analyze the mucoadhesive behavior of hydrogel. The experiential results designated that the hydrogel promoted the release of drug at the colonic site for prolonged period without any toxic effects. Some recently developed hydrogels made of tailor-made polysaccharides are listed in Table 5.

7 Miscellaneous

In an investigation, gellan gum-thioglycollic acid conjugate was synthesized by functionalization of gellan gum with thiol group [181]. Metronidazole gels were formulated using gellan gum-thioglycollic acid conjugate, which displayed a 1.82-fold higher mucoadhesive strength than the gels prepared using gellan gum alone. In vitro release of metronidazole from various gel formulations was evaluated by the dialysis sac method. Drug release rate from gels followed first-order and Higuchi square roof release kinetics. Overall, the observations pointed toward the potential of gellan gum-thioglycollic acid conjugate as bioadhesive agent in pharmaceutical formulations. In another work, thiolation of deacetylated gellan gum was done by the cysteine conjugation process and the synthesized material was used in the preparation of in situ nasal gel [182]. The thiolation of deacetylated gellan gum was found to enhance

TABLE 5 Some recently developed hydrogels made of tailor-made polysaccharides.

Hydrogels made of tailor-made polysaccharides	Drugs released	References
Self-crosslinked chitosan/dialdehyde XG-blended hypromellose hydrogel	Ampicillin, minocycline and rifampicin	Ngwabebhoh et al. [162]
Hydrogel of N-trimethyl chitosan/sodium carboxymethyl xanthan gum (CMXG)	Ciprofloxacin	Hanna and Saad [163]
Furfurylamine-functionalized alginate hydrogels	Vanillin	García-Astrain et al. [164]
Furan modified chitosan hydrogels crosslinked with polyetheramine-derived bismaleimide	Chloramphenicol	Guaresti et al. [165]
De-esterified gum tragacanth-chitosan nanohydrogel	Methotrexate	Sadrjavadi et al. [166]
Injectable tyramine-modified gellan gum/silk fibroin hydrogels	Betamethasone	Oliveira et al. [167]
Tyramine-modified gellan gum hydrogels (horseradish peroxidase crosslinking)	Betamethasone	Oliveira et al. [168]
XG/poly (*N*-vinyl imidazole) hydrogel	Bovine serum albumin	Sabaa et al. [169]
Tragacanth gum crosslinked poly(lactic acid-*co*-itaconic acid) hydrogel	Amoxicillin	Gupta et al. [170]
Hydrogel network of moringa gum by radiation-induced crosslinking	Ciprofloxacin HCl	Singh and Kumar [171]
Hydrogel prepared by radiation induced crosslinked copolymerization of AAm onto moringa gum	Levofloxacin	Singh and Kumar [172]
Hydrogel prepared by graft copolymerization of polyvinylpyrollidone onto *A. indica* gum	Methyl prednisolone	Singh and Singh [173]
Highly elastic galactomannan-poly(acrylamide-*N*,*N*-bis (acryloyl) cysteamine) hydrogel	Doxorubicin HCl	Gao et al. [174]
Gum acacia-crosslinked-poly (2-hydroxyethyl methacrylate)-carbopol-based hydrogels	Lidocaine	Singh and Dhiman [175]
GG oleate-*graft*-poly(methacrylic acid) hydrogel	Ibuprofen	Seeli and Prabaharan [176]
Tragacanth gum-crosslinked-poly (lactic acid-co-itaconic acid) hydrogel	Amoxicillin	Gupta et al. [177]
Injectable and self-healing hydrogel composed of carboxyethyl-modified chitosan and aldehyde-modified hyaluronic acid	Doxorubicin	Qian et al. [178]
Periodate-modified gum Arabic crosslinked polyvinyl alcohol hydrogels	Folic acid	Pandit et al. [179]
Oxidized gellan gum/resistant starch hydrogel beads	Resveratrol	Wang et al. [180]

the viscoelastic property of in situ nasal gel, on account of the further intra- and intermolecular crosslinking interactions among the amino acid and the thiolated deacetylated gellan gum. The in situ gelling property of the thiolated material was improved, even at the physiological milieu, improving the residency time of nasal gel on the nasal mucosa. A similar work was reported by Mahajan et al. (2013), where the thiolation of xyloglucan by the cysteine conjugation was carried out and investigated the improvement of mucoadhesive property of the in situ nasal gels, after the thiolation of xyloglucan [183]. The thiol-modified xyloglucan-based in situ nasal gels of ondansetron exhibited a sol–gel transition temperature within the range 25–30°C and produced enhanced mucoadhesivity. Ex vivo permeation of ondansetron across the nasal mucosal membrane of sheep exhibited significantly improved ondansetron permeability devoid of any toxic effect was revealed after the exposure to the nasal epithelium.

In a recent investigation, polysaccharide extracted from the achenes of jelly fig (*Ficus pumila* var. *awkeotsang*) was blended with commercial high methoxyl pectin in film casting to assess the appropriateness for colon target drug delivery [184]. Among all tested blending ratios, the film derived from pure jelly fig polysaccharide had higher tensile strength and improved role in simulated gastrointestinal fluids. The results displayed that the jelly fig polysaccharide composite capsules were stable without notable deformation and releasing of encapsulated substance in gastrointestinal fluids. The degradation of capsules was took place within 2h in operational colonic fluid and the rate of release was increases from 15% to 90%. Therefore, pectic polysaccharide extracted from jelly fig could be a useful material for the preparation of a colon-targeted capsule. The aceclofenac-loaded chitosan-egg albumin nanoparticles were incorporated within Carbopol 940 gel for transdermal application [83]. The prepared gel demonstrated sustained ex vivo aceclofenac permeation across the excised mouse skin over 8h (Fig. 13A). In vivo antiinflammatory action in carrageenan-induced rats after topical use of the prepared gel inhibited the swelling of rat paw edema more effectively than the marketed aceclofenac gel over 4h (Fig. 13B).

8 Conclusion

The current chapter deals with a comprehensive discussion about different drug delivery dosage forms, such as tablets, beads, microparticles, nanoparticles, gels and hydrogels, films and patches, scaffolds, etc., wherein various synthesized tailor-made natural polysaccharides have been used as thickening agents, gelling agents, emulsifying agents, binding agents, disintegrating agents, swelling agents, encapsulating agents, matrix-formers, foam stabilizers, etc. These tailor-made natural polysaccharides have been

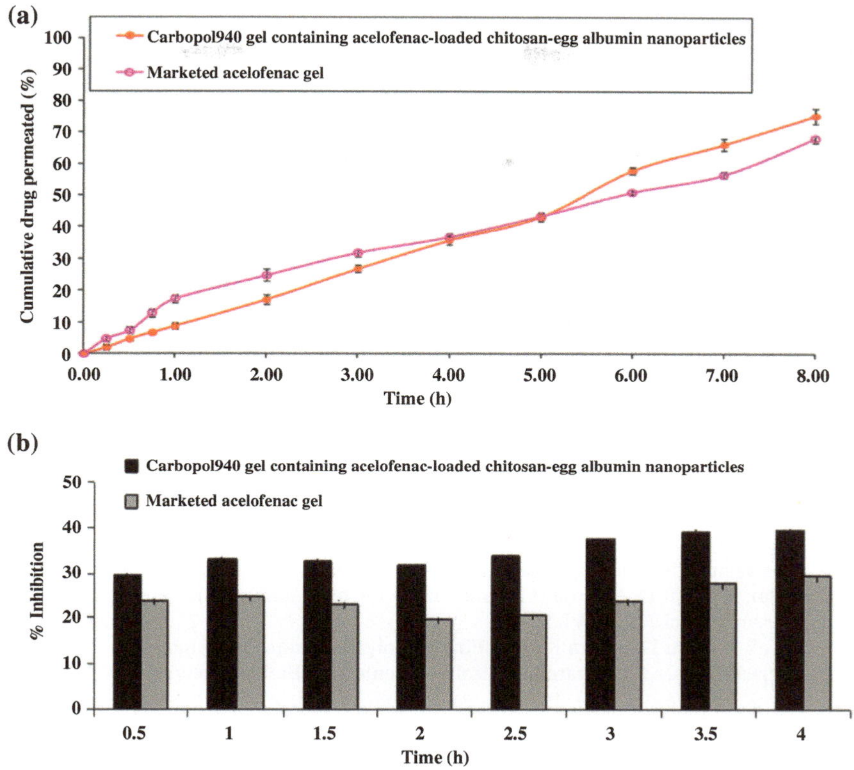

FIG. 13 (A) The comparative ex vivo drug permeation from Carbopol 940 gel containing aceclofenac-loaded chitosan-egg albumin nanoparticles and a marketed aceclofenac gel through excised mouse skin (mean ± S.D.; $n=3$); (B) comparative percentage inhibition profile of paw edema for Carbopol 940 gel containing aceclofenac-loaded nanoparticles and marketed aceclofenac gel at various time intervals in the carrageenan-induced rat model for antiinflammatory activity evaluation [83]. *From Jana S, Manna S, Nayak AK, Sen KK, Basu SK, Carbopol gel containing chitosan-egg albumin nanoparticles for transdermal aceclofenac delivery. Colloids Surf B Biointerfaces 2014;6–44. Copyright © 2013 with permission from Elsevier B.V.*

synthesized via chemical derivatization of various functional groups (such as oxidation, phosphorylation, sulfation, thiolation, carboxymethylation, amidation, esterification, etc.), graft copolymerization, and crosslinking (using different crosslinkers). The tailoring of natural polysaccharides leads to the improvement of their physicochemical performance such that they are made suitable to be used as desirable quality drug delivery excipients. The abundance of natural polysaccharides, their economic extraction, and biodegradability are forcing the formulation scientists to use various tailor-made natural polysaccharides for modifying the drug release by the dosage forms. Unlike the oral dosage forms formulated using synthetic polymers, the oral dosage forms formulated using tailor-made natural polysaccharides do not experience the disadvantages of dose dumping or incomplete drug release. This might be due to their susceptibility to degradation by colonic microflora. In nutshell, the tailoring of natural polysaccharides is helpful in modifying the drug releasing, adhesion, disintegration, gelation, etc. The future of formulation design using natural polysaccharides and their tailor-made forms is in a strong position as the scientists are continuing their valued researches to explore the new natural polysaccharides as well as to tailor them to be used as high-quality drug delivery excipients.

References

[1] Niu W, Chen X, Xu R, Dong H, Yang F, Wang Y, Zhang Z, Ju J. Polysaccharides from natural resources exhibit great potential in the treatment of ulcerative colitis: a review. Carbohydr Polym 2021;254:117189.
[2] Maity M, Hasnain MS, Nayak AK, Aminabavi TM. Biomedical applications of polysaccharides. In: Nayak AK, Hasnain MS, Aminabhavi TM, editors. Tailor-made polysaccharides in biomedical applications. USA: Academic Press, Elsevier Inc.; 2021. p. 1–34.
[3] Rehman A, Jafari SM, Tong Q, Riaz T, Assadpour E, Aadil RM, Niazi S, Khan IM, Shehzad Q, Ali A, Khan S. Drug nanodelivery systems based on natural polysaccharides against different diseases. Adv Colloid Interface Sci 2020;284:102251.
[4] Nayak AK, Pal D. Natural polysaccharides for drug delivery in tissue engineering. Everyman's Sci 2012;XLVI:347–52.
[5] Nayak AK, Pal D, Santra K. Screening of polysaccharides from tamarind, fenugreek and jackfruit seeds as pharmaceutical excipients. Int J Biol Macromol 2015;79:756–60.
[6] Nayak AK, Hasnain MS, Tabis M, Aminabhavi TM. Use of tailored polysaccharides in dentistry. In: Nayak AK, Hasnain MS, Aminabhavi TM, editors. Tailor-made polysaccharides in biomedical applications. USA: Academic Press, Elsevier Inc.; 2021. p. 287–304.
[7] Kandar CC, Hasnain MS, Nayak AK. Natural polymers as useful pharmaceutical excipients. In: Nayak AK, Pal K, Banerjee I, Maji S, Nanda U, editors. Advances and challenges in pharmaceutical technology: materials, process development and drug delivery strategies. USA: Academic Press, Elsevier Inc.; 2021. p. 1–44.
[8] Hasnain MS, Ahmed SA, Alkahtani S, Milivojevic M, Kandar CC, Dhara AK, Nayak AK. Biopolymers for drug delivery. In: Nayak AK, Hasnain MS, editors. Advanced biopolymeric systems for drug delivery. Switzerland: Springer; 2020. p. 1–29.
[9] Hasnain SMM, Hasnain MS, Nayak AK. Natural polysaccharides: sources and extraction methodologies. In: Hasnain MS, Nayak AK, editors. Natural polysaccharides in drug delivery and biomedical applications. United States: Academic Press, Elsevier Inc.; 2019. p. 1–14.
[10] Liu ZH, Jiao YP, Wang YF, Zhou CR, Zhang ZY. Polysaccharides-based nanoparticles as drug delivery systems. Adv Drug Deliv Rev 2008;60:1650–62.
[11] Nayak AK, Hasnain MS. Some other plant polysaccharide based multiple units for oral drug delivery. In: Nayak AK, Hasnain MS, editors. Plant polysaccharides-based multiple-unit systems for oral drug delivery. Singapore: Springer; 2019. p. 123–1128.
[12] Nayak AK, Hasnain MS. Plant polysaccharides in drug delivery applications. In: Nayak AK, Hasnain MS, editors. Plant polysaccharides-based multiple-unit systems for oral drug delivery. Singapore: Springer; 2019. p. 19–23.
[13] Hasnain MS, Rishishwar P, Rishishwar S, Ali S, Nayak AK. Isolation and characterization of Linum usitatisimum polysaccharide to prepare mucoadhesive beads of diclofenac sodium. Int J Biol Macromol 2018;116:162–72.

[14] Nayak AK, Ahmed SA, Tabish M, Hasnain MS. Natural polysaccharides in tissue engineering application. In: Hasnain MS, Nayak AK, editors. Natural polysaccharides in drug delivery and biomedical applications. United States: Academic Press, Elsevier Inc.; 2019. p. 531–48.
[15] Hasnain MS, Ahmad SA, Chaudhary N, Hoda MN, Nayak AK. Biodegradable polymer matrix nanocomposites for bone tissue engineering. In: Inamuddin AAM, Mohammad A, editors. Applications of nanocomposite materials in orthopedics. Woodhead publishing series in biomaterials. United States: Elsevier Inc.; 2019. p. 1–37.
[16] Pal D, Nayak AK. Plant polysaccharides-blended ionotropically-gelled alginate multiple-unit systems for sustained drug release. In: Thakur VK, Thakur MK, Kessler MR, editors. Handbook of composites from renewable materials, volume 6, polymeric composites. USA: Wiley-Scrivener; 2017. p. 399–400.
[17] Lapasin R, Pricl S. Rheology of industrial polysaccharides: theory and applications. London, UK: Blackie Academic and Professional: Chapman and Hall; 1995.
[18] Buschmann MD, Merzouki A, Lavertu M, Thibault M, Jean M, Darras V. Chitosans for delivery of nucleic acids. Adv Drug Deliv Rev 2013;65:1234–70.
[19] Chen MC, Mi FL, Liao ZX, Hsiao CW, Sonaje K, Chung MF, Hsu LW, Sung HW. Recent advances in chitosan-based nanoparticles for oral delivery of macromolecules. Adv Drug Deliv Rev 2013;65:865–79.
[20] Ganguly K, Chaturvedi K, More UA, Nadagouda MN, Aminabhavi TM. Polysaccharide-based micro/nanohydrogels for delivering macromolecular therapeutics. J Control Release 2014;193:162–73.
[21] Hasnain MS, Rishishwar P, Rishishwar S, Ali S, Nayak AK. Extraction and characterization of cashew tree (*Anacardium occidentale*) gum; use in aceclofenac dental pastes. Int J Biol Macromol 2018;116:1074–81.
[22] Hasnain MS, Nayak AK. Chitosan as responsive polymer for drug delivery applications. In: Makhlouf ASH, Abu-Thabit NY, editors. Stimuli responsive polymeric nanocarriers for drug delivery applications, volume 1, types and triggers. Woodhead publishing series in biomaterials. United States: Elsevier Ltd.; 2018. p. 581–605.
[23] Ranaa V, Rai P, Tiwary AK, Singh RS, Kennedy JF, Knill Charles J. Modified gums: approaches and applications in drug delivery. Carbohydr Polym 2011;83:1031–47.
[24] Martinez-Robinson KG. Polymer conjugates in biomedical applications. In: Nayak AK, Hasnain MS, Aminabhavi TM, editors. Tailor-made polysaccharides in biomedical applications. USA: Academic Press Elsevier Inc.; 2021. p. 175–96.
[25] Nayak AK, Hasnain MS, Dhara AK, Pal D. Plant polysaccharides in pharmaceutical applications. In: Pal D, Nayak AK, editors. Bioactive natural products for pharmaceutical applications, Advanced Structured Materials, vol. 140. Cham: Springer; 2021. p. 93–125.
[26] Hasnain MS, Rishishwar P, Ali S, Alkahtani S, Tabish M, Milivojevic M, Ansari MT, Nayak AK. Formulation and ex vivo skin permeation of lidocaine HCl topical gels using dillenia (*Dillenia indica* L.) fruit gum. Rev Mex Ing Quim 2020;19:1465–76.
[27] Hasnain MS, Rishishwar P, Ali S. Use of cashew bark exudate gum in the preparation of 4% lidocaine HCL topical gels. Int J Pharm Pharm Sci 2017;9(8):146–50.
[28] Hasnain MS, Rishishwar P, Ali S. Floating-bioadhesive matrix tablets of hydralazine HCL made of cashew gum and HPMC K4M. Int J Pharm Pharm Sci 2017;9(7):124–9.
[29] Hasnain MS, Guru PR, Rishishwar P, Ali S, Ansari MT, Nayak AK. Atenolol-releasing buccal patches made of *Dillenia indica* L fruit gum: preparation and ex vivo evaluations. SN Appl Sci 2020;2:57.
[30] Hasnain MS, Rishishwar P, Ali S, Nayak AK. Preparation and evaluation of aceclofenac dental pastes using dillenia fruit gum for periodontitis treatment. SN Appl Sci 2020;2(3):1–8.
[31] Nayak AK, Pal D. Tamarind seed polysaccharide: an emerging excipient for pharmaceutical use. Indian J Pharm Educ Res 2017;51:S136–46.

[32] Nayak AK, Pal D. Plant-derived polymers: ionically gelled sustained drug release systems. In: Mishra M, editor. Encyclopedia of Biomedical Polymers and Polymeric Biomaterials, vol. VIII. New York: Taylor and Francis; 2016. p. 6002–17.
[33] Nayak AK. Tamarind seed polysaccharide-based multiple-unit systems for sustained drug release. In: Kalia S, Averous L, editors. Biodegradable and bio-based polymers: Environmental and biomedical applications. USA: Wiley-Scrivener; 2016. p. 471–94.
[34] Verma A, Dubey J, Verma N, Nayak AK. Chitosan-hydroxypropyl methylcellulose matrices as carriers for hydrodynamically balanced capsules of moxifloxacin HCl. Curr Drug Deliv 2017;14:83–90.
[35] Milivojevic M, Pajic-Lijakovic I, Bugarski B, Nayak AK, Hasnain MS. Gellan gum in drug delivery applications. In: Hasnain MS, Nayak AK, editors. Natural polysaccharides in drug delivery and biomedical applications. United States: Academic Press, Elsevier Inc.; 2019. p. 145–86.
[36] Nayak AK, Kalia S, Hasnain MS. Optimization of aceclofenac-loaded pectinate-poly (vinyl pyrrolidone) beads by response surface methodology. Int J Biol Macromol 2013;62:194–202.
[37] Bera H, Abbasi YF, Hasnain MS, Nayak AK. Sterculia gum in drug delivery applications. In: Hasnain MS, Nayak AK, editors. Natural polysaccharides in drug delivery and biomedical applications. United States: Academic Press, Elsevier Inc.; 2019. p. 223–47.
[38] Nayak AK, Pal D, Das S. Calcium pectinate-fenugreek seed mucilage mucoadhesive beads for controlled delivery of metformin HCl. Carbohydr Polym 2013;96:349–57.
[39] Nayak AK, Ansari MT, Sami F, Bera H, Hasnain MS. Cashew gum in drug delivery applications. In: Hasnain MS, Nayak AK, editors. Natural polysaccharides in drug delivery and biomedical applications. United States: Academic Press, Elsevier Inc.; 2019. p. 263–83.
[40] Dey S, Nandy BC, De JN, Hasnain MS, Nayak AK. Tamarind gum in drug delivery applications. In: Hasnain MS, Nayak AK, editors. Natural polysaccharides in drug delivery and biomedical applications. United States: Academic Press, Elsevier Inc.; 2019. p. 285–306.
[41] Alkahtani S, Hasnain MS, Nayak AK, Aminabhavi TM. Polysaccharide-based polyelectrolyte complex systems for biomedical uses. In: Nayak AK, Hasnain MS, Aminabhavi TM, editors. Tailor-made polysaccharides in biomedical applications. USA: Academic Press, Elsevier Inc.; 2021. p. 151–74.
[42] Nayak AK, Pal D. Sterculia gum-based hydrogels for drug delivery applications. In: Kalia S, editor. Polymeric hydrogels as smart biomaterials. Springer series on polymer and composite materials. Switzerland: Springer International Publishing; 2016. p. 105–51.
[43] Ostmark E, Nystrom D, Malmstrom E. Unimolecular nanocontainers prepared by ROP and subsequent ATRP from hydroxypropylcellulose. Macromolecules 2008;41:4405–15.
[44] Metaxa AF, Vrontaki E, Efthimiadou EK, Mavromoustakos T. Drug delivery systems based on modified polysaccharides: synthesis and characterization. Methods Mol Biol 2021;2207:151–61.
[45] Sen SO, Nayak AK, Devbhuti P, Ghosh A. Modification of gums by periodate oxidation: a natural cross-linker. Int J Pharm Pharm Sci 2019;11:1–6.
[46] Nayak AK, Bera H, Hasnain MS, Pal D. Synthesis and characterization of graft-copolymers of plant polysaccharides. In: Thakur VK, editor. Biopolymer grafting, synthesis and properties. Netherlands: Elsevier Inc.; 2018. p. 1–62.
[47] Nayak AK, Pal D, Thakur VK, Thakur MK. Functionalization of tamarind gum for drug delivery. In: Functional biopolymers. Cham: Springer; 2018. p. 35–56.
[48] Raj V, Lee JH, Shim JJ, Lee J. Recent findings and future directions of grafted gum karaya polysaccharides and their various applications: a review. Carbohydr Polym 2021;258:117687.

[49] Dey S, Roy S, Hasnain MS, Nayak AK. Grafted alginates in drug delivery. In: Nayak AK, Hasnain MS, editors. Alginates in drug delivery. United States: Academic Press, Elsevier Inc.; 2020. p. 71–100.
[50] Hasnain MS, Ray P, Nayak AK. Alginate-based interpenetrating polymer networks for sustained drug release. In: Nayak AK, Hasnain MS, editors. Alginates in drug delivery. United States: Academic Press, Elsevier Inc.; 2020. p. 101–28.
[51] Ribeiro AJ, de Souza FRL, Bezerra JMNA, Oliveira C, Nadvorny D, de La Roca Soares MF, Nunes LCC, Silva-Filho EC, Veiga F, Soares Sobrinho JL. Gums' based delivery systems: review on cashew gum and its derivatives. Carbohydr Polym 2016;147:188–200.
[52] Mohanta BC, Javed MN, Hasnain MS, Nayak AK. Polyelectrolyte complexes of alginate for controlling drug release. In: Nayak AK, Hasnain MS, editors. Alginates in drug delivery. United States: Academic Press, Elsevier Inc.; 2020. p. 297–321.
[53] Bostanudin MF, Lalatsa A, Górecki DC, Barbu E. Engineering butylglyceryl-modified polysaccharides towards nanomedicines for brain drug delivery. Carbohydr Polym 2020;236:116060.
[54] Nayak AK, Mohanta BC, Hasnain MS, Hoda MN, Tripathi G. Alginate-based scaffolds for drug delivery in tissue engineering. In: Nayak AK, Hasnain MS, editors. Alginates in drug delivery. United States: Academic Press, Elsevier Inc.; 2020. p. 359–86.
[55] Malakar J, Das K, Nayak AK. In situ cross-linked matrix tablets for sustained salbutamol sulfate release - formulation development by statistical optimization. Polym Med 2014;44:221–30.
[56] Malakar J, Nayak AK. Floating bioadhesive matrix tablets of ondansetron HCl: optimization of hydrophilic polymer-blends. Asian J Pharm 2013;7:174–83.
[57] Naga Durga DH, Lohithasu D, Ramana Murthy Kolapalli V. Araucaria gum: novel natural polymer for controlled drug delivery. Development, in vitro and in vivo evaluation of araucaria gum based matrix tablets for controlled release. Curr Drug Deliv 2017;14(7):955–67.
[58] Nayak AK, Ahmad SA, Beg S, Ara TJ, Hasnain MS. Drug delivery: Present, past and-future of medicine. In: Inamuddin, Asiri AM, Mohammad A, editors. Applications of nanocomposite materials in drug delivery. Woodhead publishing series in biomaterials. United States: Elsevier Inc.; 2018. p. 255–82.
[59] Mundargi RC, Patil SA, Aminabhavi TM. Evaluation of acrylamide-grafted-xanthan gum copolymer matrix tablets for oral controlled delivery of antihypertensive drugs. Carbohydr Polym 2007;69:130–41.
[60] Singh R, Maity S, Sa B. Effect of ionic crosslink on the release of metronidazole from partially carboxymethylated guar gum tablet. Carbohydr Polym 2014;106:414–21.
[61] Toti US, Aminabhavi TM. Modified guar gum matrix tablet for controlled release of diltiazem hydrochloride. J Control Release 2004;95:567–77.
[62] Kumar V, Tiwary A, Kaur G. Investigations on chitosan-carboxymethyl guar gum complexes interpolymer complexes for colon delivery of fluticasone. Inter J Drug Deliv 2010;2:242–50.
[63] Patra S, Bala NN, Nandi G. Synthesis, characterization and fabrication of sodium carboxymethyl-okra-gum-grafted-polymethacrylamide into sustained release tablet matrix. Int J Biol Macromol 2020;164:3885–900.
[64] Mahto A, Mishra S. Design, development and validation of guar gum based pH sensitive drug delivery carrier via graft copolymerization reaction using microwave irradiations. Int J Biol Macromol 2019;138:278–91.
[65] Mate CJ, Mishra S, Srivastava PK. In vitro release kinetics of graft matrices from *Lannea coromandelica* (Houtt) gum for treatment of colonic diseases by 5-ASA. Int J Biol Macromol 2020;149:908–20.

[66] Badwaik HR, Sakure K, Nakhate KT, Kashayap P, Dhongade H, Alexander A, Ajazuddin, Tripathi DK. Effect of Ca^{+2} ion on the release of diltiazem hydrochloride from matrix tablets of carboxymethyl xanthan gum graft polyacrylamide. Int J Biol Macromol 2017;94(Pt A):691–7.
[67] Chakravorty A, Barman G, Mukherjee S, Sa B. Effect of carboxymethylation on rheological and drug release characteristics of locust bean gum matrix tablets. Carbohydr Polym 2016;144:50–8.
[68] Tahir MF, Bukhari SA, Anjum F, Qasim M, Anwar H, Naqvi SAR. Purification and modification of *Cordia myxa* gum to enhance its nutraceutical attribute as binding agent. Pak J Pharm Sci 2019;32(5(Supplementary)):2245–50.
[69] Odeniyi MA, Oyedokun BM, Bamiro OA. Native and microwave-modified *Terminalia mantaly* gums as sustained-release and bioadhesive excipients in naproxen matrix tablet formulations. Polim Med 2017;47(1):35–42.
[70] Elgaied-Lamouchi D, Descamps N, Lefèvre P, Mackin-Mohamour AR, Neut C, Siepmann F, Siepmann J, Muschert S. Robustness of controlled release tablets based on a cross-linked pregelatinized potato starch matrix. AAPS PharmSciTech 2020;21(5):148.
[71] Bhagwat DA, Kolekar VR, Nadaf SJ, Choudhari PB, More HN, Killedar SG. Acrylamide grafted neem (*Azadirachta indica*) gum polymer: screening and exploration as a drug release retardant for tablet formulation. Carbohydr Polym 2020;229:115357.
[72] Sethi S, Mangla B, Kamboj S, Rana V. A QbD approach for the fabrication of immediate and prolong buoyant cinnarizine tablet using polyacrylamide-g-corn fibre gum. Int J Biol Macromol 2018;117:350–61.
[73] Huanbutta K, Sittikijyothin W. Use of seed gums from *Tamarindus indica* and *Cassia fistula* as controlled-release agents. Asian J Pharm Sci 2018;13(5):398–408.
[74] Sarkar D, Nandi G, Changder A, Hudati P, Sarkar S, Ghosh LK. Sustained release gastroretentive tablet of metformin hydrochloride based on poly (acrylic acid)-grafted-gellan. Int J Biol Macromol 2017;96:137–48.
[75] Priyadarshini R, Nandi G, Changder A, Chowdhury S, Chakraborty S, Ghosh LK. Gastroretentive extended release of metformin from methacrylamide-g-gellan and tamarind seed gum composite matrix. Carbohydr Polym 2016;137:100–10.
[76] De Anda-Flores Y, Rascón-Chu A, Campa-Mada AC, Lizardi-Mendoza J, Tanori-Cordova J, Carvajal-Millan E. Polysaccharides nanoparticles as oral drug delivery systems. In: Hasnain MS, Nayak AK, editors. Natural polysaccharides in drug delivery and biomedical applications. United States: Academic Press, Elsevier Inc.; 2019. p. 399–417.
[77] Nayak AK, Bera H, Hasnain MS, De A, Pal D, Samanta A. Gellan gum-based nanomaterials in drug delivery applications. In: Bera H, Hossain CM, Saha S, editors. Biopolymer-based nanomaterials in drug delivery and biomedical applications. United States: Academic Press, Elsevier Inc.; 2021. p. 313–31.
[78] De A, Nayak AK, Kundu A, Das B, Samanta A. Gum arabic-based nanomaterials in drug delivery and biomedical applications. In: Bera H, Hossain CM, Saha S, editors. Biopolymer-based nanomaterials in drug delivery and biomedical applications. United States: Academic Press, Elsevier Inc.; 2021. p. 165–77.
[79] Singh V, Malviya T, Shehala, Gupta S, Dwivedi LM, Baranwal K, Prabha M, Aayushee. Polysaccharide-based nanoparticles: nanocarriers for sustained delivery of drugs. In: Nayak AK, Hasnain MS, editors. Advanced biopolymeric systems for drug delivery. Switzerland: Springer; 2020. p. 151–81.
[80] Kumar A, Gupta S, Vasanth D. Polysaccharide-based nanocarriers for oral delivery of insulin in diabetes. In: Nayak AK, Hasnain MS, editors. Advanced biopolymeric systems for drug delivery. Switzerland: Springer; 2020. p. 183–93.
[81] Ray S, Sinha P, Laha B, Maiti S, Bhattacharyya UK, Nayak AK. Polysorbate 80 coated crosslinked chitosan nanoparticles of ropinirole hydrochloride for brain targeting. J Drug Delivery Sci Technol 2018;48:21–9.

[82] Jana S, Maji N, Nayak AK, Sen KK, Basu SK. Development of chitosan-based nanoparticles through inter-polymeric complexation for oral drug delivery. Carbohydr Polym 2013;98:870–6.

[83] Jana S, Manna S, Nayak AK, Sen KK, Basu SK. Carbopol gel containing chitosan-egg albumin nanoparticles for transdermal aceclofenac delivery. Colloids Surf B Biointerfaces 2014;114:36–44.

[84] Sarmah JK, Mahanta R, Bhattacharjee SK, Mahanta R, Biswas A. Controlled release of tamoxifen citrate encapsulated in cross-linked guar gum nanoparticles. Int J Biol Macromol 2011;49:390–6.

[85] Soumya RS, Ghosh S, Abraham ET. Preparation and characterization of guar gum nanoparticles. Int J Biol Macromol 2010;46:267–9.

[86] Huang P, Yang C, Liu J, Wang W, Guo S, Li J, Sun Y, Dong H, Deng L, Zhang J, Liu J, Dong A. Improving the oral delivery efficiency of anticancer drugs by chitosan coated polycaprolactonegrafted hyaluronic acid nanoparticles. J Mater Chem B 2014;2:4021.

[87] Oliveira ACJ, Chaves LL, Ribeiro FOS, de Lima LRM, Oliveira TC, García-Villén F, Viseras C, de Paula RCM, Rolim-Neto PJ, Hallwass F, Silva-Filho EC, Alves da Silva D, Soares-Sobrinho JLS. MFR Microwave-initiated rapid synthesis of phthalated cashew gum for drug delivery systems. Carbohydr Polym 2021;254:117226.

[88] Vasconcelos Silva EL, Oliveira ACJ, Patriota YBG, Ribeiro AJ, Veiga F, Hallwass F, Silva-Filho EC, da Silva DA, Soares MFR, Wanderley AG, Soares-Sobrinho JL. Solvent-free synthesis of acetylated cashew gum for oral delivery system of insulin. Carbohydr Polym 2019;207:601–8.

[89] Pitombeira NAO, Veras Neto JG, Silva DA, Feitosa JPA, Paula HCB, dePaula RCM. Self-assembled nanoparticles of acetylated cashew gum: characterization and evaluation as potential drug carrier. Carbohydr Polym 2015;117:610–5.

[90] Wang J, Liu LG, Jiao WQ, Yang H, Liu J, Liu D. Phenylboronic acid-conjugated chitosan nanoparticles for high loading and efficient delivery of curcumin. Carbohydr Polym 2021;256:117497.

[91] Yu Z, Ma L, Ye S, Li G, Zhang M. Construction of an environmentally friendly octenylsuccinic anhydride modified pH-sensitive chitosan nanoparticle drug delivery system to alleviate inflammation and oxidative stress. Carbohydr Polym 2020;236:115972.

[92] Sohail R, Abbas SR. Evaluation of amygdalin-loaded alginate-chitosan nanoparticles as biocompatible drug delivery carriers for anticancerous efficacy. Int J Biol Macromol 2020;153:36–45.

[93] Ribeiro IS, Pontes FJG, Carneiro MJM, Sousa NA, Pinto VPT, Ribeiro FOS, Silva DA, Araújo GS, Marinho Filho JDB, Araújo AJ, Paula HCB, Feitosa JPA, de Paula RCM. Poly(ε-caprolactone) grafted cashew gum nanoparticles as an epirubicin delivery system. Int J Biol Macromol 2021;179:314–23.

[94] Malviya R, Raj S, Fuloria S, Subramaniyan V, Sathasivam K, Kumari U, Unnikrishnan Meenakshi D, Porwal O, Hari Kumar D, Singh A, Chakravarthi S, Kumar FN. Evaluation of antitumor efficacy of chitosan-tamarind gum polysaccharide polyelectrolyte complex stabilized nanoparticles of simvastatin. Int J Nanomedicine 2021;16:2533–53.

[95] Meng R, Wu Z, Xie QT, Cheng JS, Zhang B. Preparation and characterization of zein/carboxymethyl dextrin nanoparticles to encapsulate curcumin: physicochemical stability, antioxidant activity and controlled release properties. Food Chem 2021;340:127893.

[96] Rimpy, Abhishek, Ahuja M. Evaluation of carboxymethyl moringa gum as nanometric carrier. Carbohydr Polym 2017;174:896–903.

[97] Abid M, Naveed M, Azeem I, Faisal A, Faizan Nazar M, Yameen B. Colon specific enzyme responsive oligoester crosslinked dextran nanoparticles for controlled release of 5-fluorouracil. Int J Pharm 2020;586:119605.

[98] Arif M, Chi Z, Liu YJ, Liu CG. Preparation, characterization, and in vitro drug release behavior of thiolated alginate nanoparticles loaded budesonide as a potential drug delivery system toward inflammatory bowel diseases. J Biomater Sci Polym Ed 2020;31(18):2299–317.
[99] Ayub AD, Chiu HI, Mat Yusuf SNA, Abd Kadir E, Ngalim SH, Lim V. Biocompatible disulphide cross-linked sodium alginate derivative nanoparticles for oral colon-targeted drug delivery. Artif Cells Nanomed Biotechnol 2019;47(1):353–69.
[100] Chiu HI, Ayub AD, Mat Yusuf SNA, Yahaya N, Abbd Kadir E, Lim V. Docetaxel-loaded disulfide cross-linked nanoparticles derived from thiolated sodium alginate for colon cancer drug delivery. Pharmaceutics 2020;12(1):38.
[101] Maji R, Das B, Nayak AK, Ray S. Ethyl cellulose microparticles containing metformin HCl by emulsification-solvent evaporation technique: effect of formulation variables. ISRN Polym Sci 2012;, 801827.
[102] Pal D, Nayak AK. Novel tamarind seed polysaccharide-alginate mucoadhesive microspheres for oral gliclazide delivery. Drug Deliv 2012;19:123–31.
[103] Pal D, Nayak AK. Development, optimization and anti-diabetic activity of gliclazide-loaded alginate-methyl cellulose mucoadhesive microcapsules. AAPS PharmSciTech 2011;12(4):1431–41.
[104] Das B, Dutta S, Nayak AK, Nanda U. Zinc alginate-carboxymethyl cashew gum microbeads for prolonged drug release: development and optimization. Int J Biol Macromol 2014;70:505–15.
[105] Jana S, Saha A, Nayak AK, Sen KK, Basu SK. Aceclofenac-loaded chitosan-tamarind seed polysaccharide interpenetrating polymeric network microparticles. Colloids Surf B Biointerfaces 2013;105:303–9.
[106] Kumar SR, Piyush T, Suman R, Akanksha T. Preparation and characterization of cross-linked guar gum microspheres: optimization using factorial design. Chem Pharm Bull(Tokyo) 2011;59:185.
[107] Chourasia M, Jain S. Design and development of multiparticulate system for targeted drug delivery to colon. Drug Deliv 2004;11:201–7.
[108] Magalhães Jr GA, Santos CM, Silva DA, Maciel JS, Feitosa J, Paula HC, de Paula R. Microspheres of chitosan/carboxymethyl cashew gum (CH/CMCG): effect of chitosan molar mass and CMCG degree of substitution on the swelling and BSA release. Carbohydr Polym 2009;77:217–22.
[109] Al-Kahtani AA, Sherigara B. Semi-interpenetrating network of acrylamide-grafted sodium alginate microspheres for controlled release of diclofenac sodium, preparation and characterization. Colloids Surf B Biointerfaces 2014;115:132–8.
[110] Jana S, Das A, Nayak AK, Sen KK, Basu SK. Aceclofenac-loaded unsaturated esterified alginate/gellan gum microspheres: in vitro and in vivo assessment. Int J Biol Macromol 2013;57:129–37.
[111] Urtiga SCDC, Alves VMO, Melo CO, Lima MN, Souza E, Cunha AP, Ricardo NMPS, Oliveira EE, Egito ESTD. Xylan microparticles for controlled release of mesalamine: production and physicochemical characterization. Carbohydr Polym 2020;250:116929.
[112] Khalid S, Abbas G, Hanif M, Shah S, Shah SNH, Jalil A, Yaqoob M, Ameer N, Anum A. Thiolated sodium alginate conjugates for mucoadhesive and controlled release behavior of metformin microspheres. Int J Biol Macromol 2020;164:2691–700.
[113] Sedyakina N, Kuskov A, Velonia K, Feldman N, Lutsenko S, Avramenko G. Modulation of entrapment efficiency and in vitro release properties of BSA-loaded chitosan microparticles cross-linked with citric acid as a potential protein-drug delivery system. Materials (Basel) 2020;13(8):1989.
[114] Lungan MA, Popa M, Racovita S, Hitruc G, Doroftei F, Desbrieres J, Vasiliu S. Surface characterization and drug release from porous microparticles based on methacrylic monomers and xanthan. Carbohydr Polym 2015;125:323–33.

[115] Yan X, Tong Z, Chen Y, Mo Y, Feng H, Li P, Qu X, Jin S. Bioresponsive materials for drug delivery based on carboxymethyl chitosan/poly(γ-glutamic acid) composite microparticles. Mar Drugs 2017;15(5):127.

[116] Huang GQ, Zhang ZK, Cheng LY, Xiao JX. Intestine-targeted delivery potency of O-carboxymethyl chitosan-coated layer-by-layer microcapsules: an in vitro and in vivo evaluation. Korean J Couns Psychother 2019;105:110129.

[117] Xiao JX, Zhu CP, Cheng LY, Yang J, Huang GQ. pH-dependent intestine-targeted delivery potency of the O-carboxymethyl chitosan-gum Arabic coacervates. Int J Biol Macromol 2018;117:315–22.

[118] Alange VV, Birajdar RP, Kulkarni RV. Functionally modified polyacrylamide-graft-gum karaya pH-sensitive spray dried microspheres for colon targeting of an anti-cancer drug. Int J Biol Macromol 2017;102:829–39.

[119] Ray S, Bera M, Bhattacharyya UK, Das S, Seth S, Pal PK, Aziz A. pH sensitive interpenetrating network bio containers of gum ghatti for sustained release of glipizide. Curr Drug Deliv 2019;16(9):849–61.

[120] Cheewatanakornkool K, Niratisai S, Manchun S, Dass CR, Sriamornsak P. Characterization and in vitro release studies of oral microbeads containing thiolated pectin-doxorubicin conjugates for colorectal cancer treatment. Asian J Pharm Sci 2017;12(6):509–20.

[121] Sharma VK, Sharma PP, Mazumder B, Bhatnagar A, Subramaniyan V, Fuloria S, Fuloria NK. Mucoadhesive microspheres of glutaraldehyde crosslinked mucilage of Isabgol husk for sustained release of gliclazide. J Biomater Sci Polym Ed 2021;1–30.

[122] Pal D, Nayak AK. Alginates, blends and microspheres: controlled drug delivery. In: Mishra M, editor. Encyclopedia of biomedical polymers and polymeric biomaterials, vol. I. New York: Taylor and Francis; 2015. p. 89–98.

[123] Guru PR, Nayak AK, Sahu RK. Oil-entrapped sterculia gum-alginate buoyant systems of aceclofenac: development and in vitro evaluation. Colloids Surf B Biointerfaces 2013;104:268–75.

[124] Malakar J, Nayak AK, Jana P, Pal D. Potato starch-blended alginate beads for prolonged release of tolbutamide: development by statistical optimization and in vitro characterization. Asian J Pharm 2013;7:43–51.

[125] Nayak AK, Das B, Maji R. Calcium alginate/gum Arabic beads containing glibenclamide: development and in vitro characterization. Int J Biol Macromol 2012;51:1070–8.

[126] Bera H, Boddupalli S, Nayak AK. Mucoadhesive-floating zinc-pectinate-sterculia gum interpenetrating polymer network beads encapsulating ziprasidone HCl. Carbohydr Polym 2015;131:108–18.

[127] Agarwal T, Narayana SNGH, Pal K, Pramanik K, Giri S, Banerjee I. Calcium alginate-carboxymethyl cellulose beads for colon-targeted drug delivery. Int J Biol Macromol 2015;75:409–17.

[128] Kumar A, Ahuja M. Carboxymethyl gum kondagogu: synthesis, characterization and evaluation as mucoadhesive polymer. Carbohydr Polym 2012;90:637–43.

[129] Ahuja M, Singh S, Kumar A. Evaluation of carboxymethyl gellan gum as a mucoadhesive polymer. Int J Biol Macromol 2013;53:114–21.

[130] Malakar J, Nayak AK, Das A. Modified starch (cationized)-alginate beads containing aceclofenac: formulation optimization using central composite design. Starch-Starke 2013;65:603–12.

[131] Verma S, Rimpy, Ahuja M. Carboxymethyl modification of *Cassia obtusifolia* galactomannan and its evaluation as sustained release carrier. Int J Biol Macromol 2020;164:3823–34.

[132] Nandi G, Nandi AK, Khan NS, Pal S, Dey S. Tamarind seed gum-hydrolyzed polymethacrylamide-g-gellan beads for extended release of diclofenac sodium using 3^2 full factorial design. Int J Biol Macromol 2018;114:214–25.

[133] Kumar D, Mundlia J, Kumar T, Ahuja M. Silica coating of carboxymethyl tamarind kernel polysaccharide beads to modify the release characteristics. Int J Biol Macromol 2020;146:1040–9.
[134] Pandit AP, Koyate KR, Kedar AS, Mute VM. Spongy wound dressing of pectin/carboxymethyl tamarind seed polysaccharide loaded with moxifloxacin beads for effective wound heal. Int J Biol Macromol 2019;140:1106–15.
[135] Seeli DS, Dhivya S, Selvamurugan N, Prabaharan M. Guar gum succinate-sodium alginate beads as a pH-sensitive carrier for colon-specific drug delivery. Int J Biol Macromol 2016;91:45–50.
[136] Bulut E. Flurbiprofen-loaded interpenetrating polymer network beads based on alginate, polyvinyl alcohol and methylcellulose: design, characterization and in-vitro evaluation. J Biomater Sci Polym Ed 2020;31(13):1671–88.
[137] Rajesh AM, Popat KM. Taste masking of azithromycin by resin complex and sustained release through interpenetrating polymer network with functionalized biopolymers. Drug Dev Ind Pharm 2017;43(5):732–41.
[138] Bera H, Mothe S, Maiti S, Vanga S. Carboxymethyl fenugreek galactomannan-gellan gum-calcium silicate composite beads for glimepiride delivery. Int J Biol Macromol 2018;107(Pt A):604–14.
[139] Vieira S, da Silva MA, Garet E, Silva-Correia J, Reis RL, González-Fernández Á, Miguel OJ. Self-mineralizing Ca-enriched methacrylated gellan gum beads for bone tissue engineering. Acta Biomater 2019;93:74–85.
[140] Elsayed EW, El-Ashmawy AA, Mursi NM, Emara LH. Optimization of gliclazide loaded alginate-gelatin beads employing central composite design. Drug Dev Ind Pharm 2019;45(12):1959–72.
[141] Ajish JK, Ajish Kumar KS, Chattopadhyay S, Kumar M. Glycopolymeric gel stabilized N-succinyl chitosan beads for controlled doxorubicin delivery. Carbohydr Polym 2016;144:98–105.
[142] Sreekanth Reddy O, Subha MCS, Jithendra T, Madhavi C, Chowdoji Rao K. Curcumin encapsulated dual cross linked sodium alginate/montmorillonite polymeric composite beads for controlled drug delivery. J Pharm Anal 2021;11(2):191–9.
[143] Yousry C, Ahmed IS, Amin MM, El Gazayerly ON. Superhydrophobic substrates for ultrahigh encapsulation of hydrophilic drug into controlled-release polyelectrolyte complex beads: statistical optimization and in vivo evaluation. Pharmaceutics 2019;11(6):257.
[144] Khlibsuwan R, Tansena W, Pongjanyakul T. Modification of alginate beads using gelatinized and ungelatinized arrowroot (*Tacca leontopetaloides* L. Kuntze) starch for drug delivery. Int J Biol Macromol 2018;118(Pt. A):683–92.
[145] Awasthi R, Kulkarni GT, Ramana MV, de Jesus Andreoli Pinto T, Kikuchi IS, Molim Ghisleni DD, de Souza Braga M, De Bank P, Dua K. Dual crosslinked pectin-alginate network as sustained release hydrophilic matrix for repaglinide. Int J Biol Macromol 2017;97:721–32.
[146] Freitas ED, Freitas VMS, Rosa PCP, da Silva MGC, Vieira MGA. Development and evaluation of naproxen-loaded sericin/alginate beads for delayed and extended drug release using different covalent crosslinking agents. Korean J Couns Psychother 2021;118:111412.
[147] Nayak AK, Hasnain MS, Pal K, Banerjee I, Pal D. Gum-based hydrogels in drug delivery. In: Pal K, Banerjee I, Sarkar P, Kim D, Deng W-P, Dubey NK, Majumder K, editors. Biopolymer-based formulations, biomedical and food applications. United States: Elsevier Inc.; 2020. p. 605–45.
[148] Koetting MC, Peters JT, Steichen SD, Peppas NA. Stimulus-responsive hydrogels: theory, modern advances, and applications. Mater Sci Eng R Rep 2015;93:1–49.
[149] Bedoya DA, Figueroa FN, Macchione MA, Strumia MC. Stimuli-responsive polymeric systems for smart drug delivery. In: Nayak AK, Hasnain MS, editors. Advanced biopolymeric systems for drug delivery. Switzerland: Springer; 2020. p. 115–34.

[150] Prabaharan M, Mano JF. Stimuli-responsive hydrogels based on polysaccharides incorporated with thermo-responsive polymers as novel biomaterials. Macromol Biosci 2006;6(12):991–1008.
[151] Jiang Y, Wang Y, Li Q, Yu C, Chu W. Natural polymer-based stimuli-responsive hydrogels. Curr Med Chem 2020;27(16):2631–57.
[152] Figueroa-Pizano MD, Carvajal-Millan E. Tailor-made polysaccharide-based hydrogels for biomedical applications. In: Nayak AK, Hasnain MS, Aminabhavi TM, editors. Tailor-made polysaccharides in biomedical applications. USA: Academic Press, Elsevier Inc.; 2021. p. 101–32.
[153] Wei W, Li J, Qi X, Zhong Y, Zuo G, Pan X, Su T, Zhang J, Dong W. Synthesis and characterization of a multi-sensitive polysaccharide hydrogel for drug delivery. Carbohydr Polym 2017;177:275–83.
[154] Iresha H, Kobayashi T. Smart polysaccharide hydrogels in drug delivery and release. In: Nayak AK, Hasnain MS, editors. Advanced biopolymeric systems for drug delivery. Switzerland: Springer; 2020. p. 135–49.
[155] Sutar PB, Mishra RK, Pal K, Banthia AK. Development of pH sensitive polyacrylamide grafted pectin hydrogel for controlled drug delivery system. J Mater Sci Mater Med 2008;19:2247–53.
[156] Huang Y, Yu H, Xiao C. pH-sensitive cationic guar gum/poly (acrylic acid) polyelectrolyte hydrogels: swelling and in vitro drug release. Carbohydr Polym 2007;69:774–83.
[157] Singh B, Sharma N. Modification of sterculia gum with methacrylic acid to prepare a novel drug delivery system. Int J Biol Macromol 2008;43:142–50.
[158] Soppimath KS, Kulkarni AR, Aminabhavi TM. Chemically modified polyacrylamide-g-guar gum-based crosslinked anionic microgels as pH-sensitive drug delivery systems: preparation and characterization. J Control Release 2001;75:331–45.
[159] Soppirnath KS, Aminabhavi TM. Water transport and drug release study from crosslinked polyacrylamide grafted guar gum hydrogel microspheres for the controlled release application. Eur J Pharm Biopharm 2002;53:87–98.
[160] Das A, Wadhwa S, Srivastava A. Cross-linked guar gum hydrogel discs for colon-specific delivery of ibuprofen: formulation and in vitro evaluation. Drug Deliv 2006;13:139–42.
[161] Casadei MA, Pitarresi G, Calabrese R, Paolicelli P, Giammona G. Biodegradable and pH-sensitive hydrogels for potential colon-specific drug delivery: characterization and in vitro release studies. Biomacromolecules 2007;9:43–9.
[162] Ngwabebhoh FA, Zandraa O, Patwa R, Saha N, Capáková Z, Saha P. Self-crosslinked chitosan/dialdehyde xanthan gum blended hypromellose hydrogel for the controlled delivery of ampicillin, minocycline and rifampicin. Int J Biol Macromol 2021;167:1468–78.
[163] Hanna DH, Saad GR. Encapsulation of ciprofloxacin within modified xanthan gum-chitosan based hydrogel for drug delivery. Bioorg Chem 2019;84:115–24.
[164] García-Astrain C, Avérous L. Synthesis and evaluation of functional alginate hydrogels based on click chemistry for drug delivery applications. Carbohydr Polym 2018;190:271–80.
[165] Guaresti O, García-Astrain C, Aguirresarobe RH, Eceiza A, Gabilondo N. Synthesis of stimuli-responsive chitosan-based hydrogels by Diels-Alder cross-linking 'click' reaction as potential carriers for drug administration. Carbohydr Polym 2018;183:278–86.
[166] Sadrjavadi K, Shahbazi B, Fattahi A. De-esterified tragacanth-chitosan nano-hydrogel for methotrexate delivery; optimization of the formulation by Taguchi design. Artif Cells Nanomed Biotechnol 2018;46(sup2):883–93.
[167] Oliveira IM, Gonçalves C, Shin ME, Lee S, Reis RL, Khang G, Oliveira JM. Anti-inflammatory properties of injectable betamethasone-loaded tyramine-modified gellan gum/silk fibroin hydrogels. Biomolecules 2020;10(10):1456.

[168] Oliveira IM, Gonçalves C, Shin ME, Lee S, Reis RL, Khang G, Oliveira JM. Enzymatically crosslinked tyramine-gellan gum hydrogels as drug delivery system for rheumatoid arthritis treatment. Drug Deliv Transl Res 2021;11(3):1288–300.
[169] Sabaa MW, Hanna DH, Abu Elella MH, Mohamed RR. Encapsulation of bovine serum albumin within novel xanthan gum based hydrogel for protein delivery. Korean J Couns Psychother 2019;94:1044–55.
[170] Gupta VK, Sood S, Agarwal S, Saini AK, Pathania D. Antioxidant activity and controlled drug delivery potential of tragacanth gum-cl-poly (lactic acid-co-itaconic acid) hydrogel. Int J Biol Macromol 2018;107:2534–43.
[171] Singh B, Kumar A. Network formation of Moringa oleifera gum by radiation induced crosslinking: evaluation of drug delivery, network parameters and biomedical properties. Int J Biol Macromol 2018;108:477–88.
[172] Singh B, Kumar A. Hydrogel formation by radiation induced crosslinked copolymerization of acrylamide onto moringa gum for use in drug delivery applications. Carbohydr Polym 2018;200:262–70.
[173] Singh B, Singh B. Graft copolymerization of polyvinylpyrollidone onto *Azadirachta indica* gum polysaccharide in the presence of crosslinker to develop hydrogels for drug delivery applications. Int J Biol Macromol 2020;159:264–75.
[174] Gao Y, Zong S, Huang Y, Yang N, Wen H, Jiang J, Duan J. Preparation and properties of a highly elastic galactomannan-poly(acrylamide-N,N-bis (acryloyl) cysteamine) hydrogel with reductive stimuli-responsive degradable properties. Carbohydr Polym 2020;231:115690.
[175] Singh B, Dhiman A. Evaluation of gentamicin and lidocaine release profile from gum Acacia-crosslinked-poly(2-hydroxyethylmethacrylate)-carbopol based hydrogels. Curr Drug Deliv 2017;14(7):981–91.
[176] Seeli DS, Prabaharan M. Guar gum oleate-graft-poly(methacrylic acid) hydrogel as a colon-specific controlled drug delivery carrier. Carbohydr Polym 2017;158:51–7.
[177] Gupta VK, Sood S, Agarwal S, Saini AK, Pathania D. Antioxidant activity and controlled drug delivery potential of tragacanth gum-cl-poly (lactic acid-co-itaconic acid) hydrogel. Int J Biol Macromol 2018;107(Pt B):2534–43.
[178] Qian C, Zhang T, Gravesande J, Baysah C, Song X, Xing J. Injectable and self-healing polysaccharide-based hydrogel for pH-responsive drug release. Int J Biol Macromol 2019;123:140–8.
[179] Pandit AH, Mazumdar N, Imtiyaz K, Rizvi MMA, Ahmad S. Periodate-modified gum Arabic cross-linked PVA hydrogels: a promising approach toward photoprotection and sustained delivery of folic acid. ACS Omega 2019;4(14):16026–36.
[180] Wang P, Luo ZG, Xiao ZG. Preparation, physicochemical characterization and in vitro release behavior of resveratrol-loaded oxidized gellan gum/resistant starch hydrogel beads. Carbohydr Polym 2021;260:117794.
[181] Yadav S, Ahuja M, Kumar A, Kaur H. Gellan–thioglycolic acid conjugate: synthesis, characterization and evaluation as mucoadhesive polymer. Carbohydr Polym 2014;99:601–7.
[182] Krauland AH, Leitner VM, Bernkop-Schnürch A. Improvement in the in situ gelling properties of deacetylated gellan gum by the immobilization of thiol groups. J Pharm Sci 2003;92:1234–41.
[183] Mahajan HS, Tyagi VK, Patil RR, Dusunge SB. Thiolated xyloglucan: synthesis, characterization and evaluation as mucoadhesive in situ gelling agent. Carbohydr Polym 2013;91:618–25.

[184] Ponrasu T, Gu J-S, Wu J-J, Cheng Y-S. Evaluation of jelly fig polysaccharide as a shell composite ingredient of colon-specific drug delivery. J Drug Delivery Sci Technol 2021;61:10169.

Further reading

Nayak AK, Pal D. Chitosan-based interpenetrating polymeric network systems for sustained drug release. In: Tiwari A, Patra HK, Choi J-W, editors. Advanced theranostics materials. USA: Wiley-Scrivener; 2015. p. 183–208.

CHAPTER

3

Carboxymethylated polysaccharides in drug delivery

Payam Zarrintaj[a], *Mohammad Reza Ganjali*[b,c], *Azam Salmankhani*[d], *Amin Hamed Mashhadzadeh*[e], *Muhammad Tajammal Munir*[f,g], *Foad Salehnia*[b], *Morteza Rezapour*[h], *Sajjad Habibzadeh*[i], *and Mohammad Reza Saeb*[j]

[a]School of Chemical Engineering, Oklahoma State University, Stillwater, OK, United States, [b]Center of Excellence in Electrochemistry, School of Chemistry, College of Science, University of Tehran, Tehran, Iran, [c]Biosensor Research Center, Endocrinology and Metabolism Molecular-Cellular Sciences Institute, Tehran University of Medical Sciences, Tehran, Iran, [d]Faculty of Mechanical Engineering, K. N. Toosi University of Technology, Tehran, Iran, [e]Department of Mechanical and Aerospace Engineering, School of Engineering and Digital Sciences, Nazarbayev University, Nur-Sultan, Kazakhstan, [f]College of Engineering and Technology, American University of the Middle East, Egaila, Kuwait, [g]Department of Chemical and Materials Engineering, The University of Auckland, Auckland, New Zealand, [h]IP Department, Research Institute of Petroleum Industry (RIPI), Tehran, Iran, [i]Department of Chemical Engineering, Amirkabir University of Technology (Tehran Polytechnic), Tehran, Iran, [j]Department of Polymer Technology, Faculty of Chemistry, Gdańsk University of Technology, Gdańsk, Poland

1 Introduction

Terminologically, "drug delivery" consists of all procedures, technologies, formulations, and systems that work under a disciplined manner so as to transport a pharmaceutical compound to the body by the use of some biomaterials like polymers, nanoparticles, or a combination of several kinds

Tailor-Made Polysaccharides in Drug Delivery
https://doi.org/10.1016/B978-0-12-821286-8.00012-4

of materials, with the aim of achieving a desired therapeutic effect after a roughly specified estimated time [1]. Regardless of the way the drug is delivered to the body (classically through targeting at specified tissues within the body or by facilitating the pharmacokinetics under which drug can affect the target), the effectiveness of drug delivery can be adjusted by the simultaneous control over the quantity and the duration of drug presence in the body [2]. Moreover, the success of drug delivery depends largely on the chemical interaction of the drug with the target, which is always a function of chemical formulation as well as the device by which the drug is delivered to the body. In this regard, the short-term and long-term effects and side effects of a drug should additionally be taken into account in designing highly efficient drug delivery systems (DDSs). Following the emergence of the pioneering work performed on DDSs in the early 1950s [3], drug delivery and controlled release strategies have become hot fields of research over the half century to heal wounds, treat cancers, make vaccines, and avoid classical treatment methods with serious drawbacks. In the meantime, big companies have started commercializing their drugs and drug delivery devices, and also new legislations and standards have continuously been defined and implemented by the Food and Drug Administration (FDA or USFDA) agency so as to give rise to advanced treatment to a wide variety of diseases. Following such administration and legislations, the DDSs liberated the active ingredients, and accordingly they made it possible to facilitate transporting bioactive molecules across various biological barriers toward target by reaching the exact site of action [4].

In conventional DDSs, which are mainly based on the oral and transdermal administration, there are some limitations concerning the rate of release, the rate of adsorption of drug onto the target site, and limitations with drug loading capacity [5,6]. In addition, these kinds of delivery usually had to be checked repeatedly as a consequence of they were being developed for short-time deliveries; moreover, the fluctuations that could occur during their releasing process might increase the level of toxicity in the organ or lead to an insufficient uptake [7,8]. However, the increasing demand from the medical science investigators for the highly efficient therapeutic materials and systems has opened a new perspective yet multidimensional challenges over drug delivery methods and formulations with the main focus being placed on the delivery platforms so as to provide slower, safer, more controllable, continuous, and more stable release behavior compared with the old-fashion medical approaches. In this sense, various platforms including biomaterials [9–12], polymers [13–16], nanomaterials [17–19], metal-organic frameworks [20–23], and zeolites [24–26] have been introduced and examined as potential candidates to develop novel DDSs and; consequently, more fascinating outcomes have been achieved regarding targeted [27], controlled [28], repeatable [29], and low toxic drug release strategies [30]. For example, a new branch of medicine, denoted as nanomedicine, has been identified and materialized, which was based on the application of nanotechnology in the medicine, mainly grounded on the use of nanoparticles as the therapeutic carriers [31]. For example, despite the fact that delivery of drug to the solid regions was less than 1%, some promising angles were opened in using nanoparticles in diagnosis and therapy of cancerous tumors as a general concept [32].

Among the materials examined for drug delivery, polymers have captured considerable attention due to their biocompatibility with the blood and the tissue fueled by their promising characteristics such as surface energy, lubricity, and smoothness along with their physical characteristics such as degradability, durability, and permeability [33–36]. Because of the inherent characteristics of polymers such as long entangled chains and glass transition temperature, which gives polymers a dual temperature-dependent behavior, controlled drug delivery and drug release from macromolecules has become an advanced area of research, where chemical engineers, chemists, and polymerization reaction engineers contributed to human healthcare by designing advanced materials [37]. However, difficulties have always been associated with designing DDSs based on polymers in view of the fact that mainly synthetic polymers could meet controlled release requirements. Natural polymers, alone or together with the synthetic polymers in the form of blend or composite, have also been known as the most appropriate candidates for drug delivery purpose. Recently, theranostic platforms, with the ability to combine both therapy and diagnosis in one system, have been found worthy of usage as highly efficient cancer treatment systems [38,39]. Synthetic polymers have attracted the interests of tissue engineers and researchers working in the field of drug delivery in recent years due to their exceptional chemistry, tunable properties, and the reproducibility [40,41]. For instance, biodegradable synthetic polymers, which mainly include aliphatic polyesters such as poly(glycolic acid) (PGA) [42], poly(lactic acid) (PLA) [43], poly (lactic-*co*-glycolic acid) (PLGA) [44], poly(δ-decalactone) (PLD) [45], and poly(ε-caprolactone) (PCL) [46] have widely been considered for DDS purposes, among which the PLGA has gained the greatest attention for a number of reasons. For PLGAs, degradation time could be adjustable on the basis of tuning (or selecting polymers having) appropriate characteristics considering the molecular weight of the polymer, the degree of crystallinity, and the ratio of lactic acid (LA) to the glycolic acid (GA) [47]. Furthermore, PLGAs could be hydrolyzed to lactic acid and glycolic acid, as the monomers that could simply be metabolized by the human body [48]. Therefore, the ability of PLGAs to minimize the toxicity in the course of the drug release has extended their applications in DDSs [49,50]. In addition, other kinds of degradable and nondegradable synthetic polymers such as polyvinyl alcohol (PVA) [51,52], ethylene vinyl acetate copolymers (EVA) [53], polyvinylpyrrolidone (PVP) [54], and polyurethane (PU) [55] have been examined as drug carriers with their own beneficial and limited potentials [56,57].

A promising class of polymers applied for delivery purposes are polymer hydrogels. Their biocompatibility and the resemblance between their structure and native extracellular matrices have made them potential candidates for the regenerative applications over decades [58]. Although hydrogels were initially implanted outside the patients' body via invasive surgical techniques, development of materials with tailored microstructure made possible effective delivery of hydrogels inside the human body without the need for implantation. By manipulating, adjusting, and prolonging the release kinetics of drugs from the hydrogels, the degree of control over targeted and controlled release of drugs on the predetermined sites, tissues, and organs was enhanced considerably by the use of architecturally tailored polymer hydrogels [59]. A particular class of hydrogels widely used as DDS are the hydrogel nanoparticles. In such systems, the very small size of nanoparticles that provides a huge surface area from one side and the hydrophilicity of hydrogels from the other side are combined in one material, where both natural and synthetic polymers evoked promising outcomes in controlled delivery [60].

Natural biomaterials have also received a considerable attention in recent years. Self-assembly of peptides, as the building blocks of proteins, have shown extraordinary features for drug and vaccine delivery targeting [61]. The ability of peptide and its oligomers to self-assembly was used as a basis for designing and implementing DDSs working with proteins, where high sensitivity to any changes into the environment including the temperature, the pH, the ionic strength, and the interactions between the drug as the host and the guest molecules should be tailored [62]. Inspired by such investigations that consider drug delivery of a natural polymer as molecules from which they are made, one can give a bright view of delivery behavior of natural polymers. Overall, polysaccharides (e.g., chitosan, dextran and pectin) and proteins (e.g., collagen, gelatin and silk fibroin) have been the most commonly used ones in DSSs [63]. For example, nanocelluloses "nanocellulose-only" and "nanocellulose-containing" hydrogels have increasingly been used as DDSs [64].

Natural polymers can be extracted from a variety of the materials found in nature, i.e., from plants or can be formed by living organisms like animals and microbes that benefit from the biocompatibility, hydrophilicity, biodegradation, and tissue-like structure [65–67]. Natural polymers are superior to their synthetic counterparts, for drug delivery applications, in view of the fact that they can be simply modified due to their nature, they are abundant, and because of their low-cost extraction [68]. Although proteins have abundantly been found in animal bodies serving as enzymes, hormones, antibodies, receptors, and structural species, polysaccharides have been found in both animals and plants. Due to being easily modified on demand, owing to their derivable groups such as amino groups and the carboxyl functional groups, polysaccharides exhibit high stability in biological fluids, they are degradable and also nontoxic [69]. Furthermore, these polymers have diverse structures and properties because of being rich in the functional groups as well as the wide range of molecular weight they have [70]. Starch, glycogen, and cellulose are the most abundant polysaccharides in the nature. Glycogen and starch function as food storage in the plants and animals, respectively, whereas cellulose is the main component of the plant structure. Polysaccharides that are the product of natural carbon dioxide capturing using photosynthesis and biosynthesis processes are composed of the repeating units called monosaccharides (or simple sugars). These building blocks of polysaccharides can be found in the glucose, fructose, and galactose as the monosaccharide units that assist in formation of the main building blocks of different polysaccharides [71]. On the other hand, hetero-polysaccharides, also known as heteroglycans, are made of two or more different monosaccharide units [72]. They have properties quite often different from monosaccharide, e.g., they are hardly water soluble. Other types of polysaccharides can be extracted from the species such as seaweeds and crab shells. Indeed, in this class, some of the hydroxyl groups of the abundant polysaccharides are substituted by the carboxyl groups (e.g., in the pectin and agarose), amino groups (e.g., in the chitosan), or other chemical functionalities [73,74]. Although some of the polysaccharides have only the hydroxyl functional groups in their chemical structure as pendant groups (e.g., cellulose, dextran, guar gum, and pullulan), others contain uronic acids (e.g., alginate and pectin) or nitrogen-included functional groups (e.g., chitosan and chitin) [75,76]. Studies prove that the role of such functional groups on the solubility and physiochemical properties of the polysaccharides should be taken seriously.

In addition to the nature-based biosynthesis processes, polysaccharides can also be artificially modified using various physical, chemical, and biological routes to be endowed with new physical and chemical properties as well as improved bioactivities [58]. Although physical and biological modifications can only adjust polysaccharides' molecular weight, chemical modifications can significantly affect their physicochemical behavior. It was reported that acetylation, sulfation, carboxymethylation, and alkylation are the main chemical strategies used for the chemical modification of polysaccharides [77]. In carboxymethylation, which is a common modification technique adapted for various polysaccharides such as the cellulose, chitin, and dextran [78,79], carboxymethyl groups are introduced to the polymer chains of polysaccharide so as to effectively improve its water solubility. For instance, the modified carboxymethyl cellulose (CMC) is highly water-soluble, whereas the pure naturally available cellulose is not soluble in water or in organic solvents [80]. Furthermore, it is possible by using the carboxymethyl functional groups bearing negative charges form polyelectrolyte complexes (PEC) to modify the positively charged polymers such as chitosan (as the only positively charged natural polysaccharide available) [81–83]. Electrostatic interactions between the polymer chains bearing opposite charges leads to complexation of the drug delivery mechanism of polysaccharides. Besides, small molecules or metal ions could interact electrostatically with the negatively charged polymers. Such electrostatic interactions are useful to develop polymer nanoparticles for the drug carriers or theranostic platforms [84]. The discussed methods are the subgroups of cross-linking strategies that will be explained in the following section.

Overall, the number of publications on polysaccharides over the past decade followed as ascending trend (Fig. 1A and B). It can be seen that carboxymethylated polysaccharides contributed considerable to the publications on this family of carbohydrate polymers. Moreover, applications of polysaccharides and carboxymethylated polysaccharides in drug delivery have similarly followed an increasing trend from 2010 to 2020. The contribution of drug delivery to the number of publications on the carboxymethylated polysaccharide is also noticeable (Fig. 1B). Moreover, according to the diagrams, the importance of the topic and doing research in the filed in the future can be easily understood.

2 Carboxymethylation process

Chemical modification has been frequently employed to boost the solubility of polymers, in particular in the case of polysaccharides. Some of the polysaccharides such as the cellulose are poorly (limitedly) soluble in water and also in the organic solvents. Therefore, by overcoming this limitation it would definitely be possible to broaden the application interval of polysaccharides, especially for the drug delivery purposes. Carboxymethylation is a robust strategy by which one can develop water-soluble polysaccharide derivatives like carboxymethyl cellulose (CMC) [85]. The CMC benefit from the biocompatibility, bioadhesive characteristics, and the biodegradability [86]. Furthermore, carboxymethylation has been utilized to develop carboxymethyl derivatives from the other types of polysaccharides [87]. It has been reported that multivalent metal cations and polycationic species can be used to make cross-linked the carboxymethyl polysaccharides so as to produce novel hydrogels. For instance, CMC/bentonite composite hydrogels have been used to control the release of herbicide using Fe^{3+} ions to the cross-linked CMC [88].

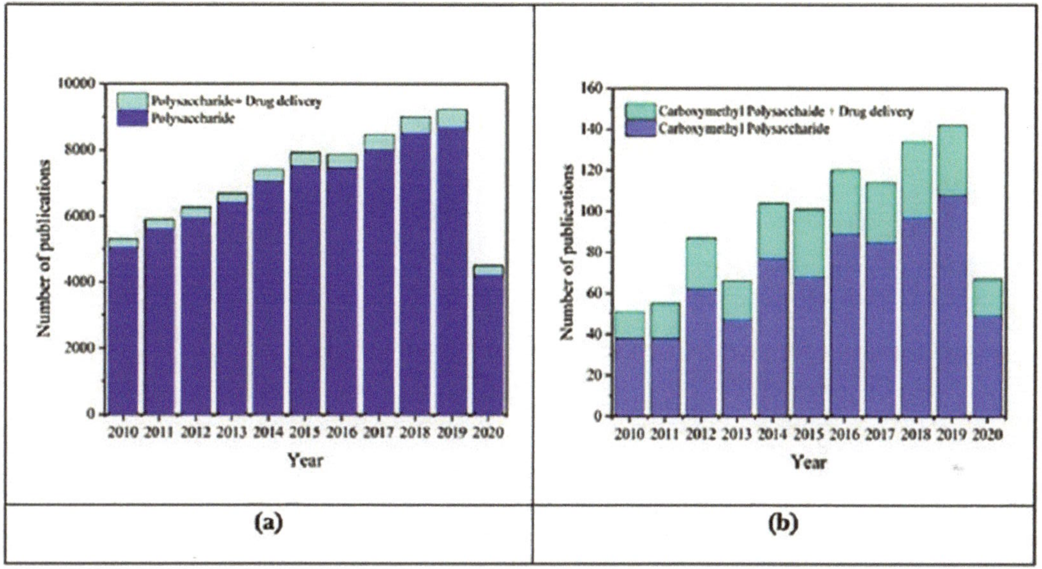

FIG. 1 The number of publications on polysaccharides, carboxymethylated polysaccharides, and their contribution to drug delivery applications (based on polysaccharide, polysaccharides, carboxymethylated polysaccharide, carboxymethylated polysaccharides, drug, drug delivery, and drug release keywords). Data are collected from the Scopus Web of Science on June, 6, 2020. The ongoing data on publications in 2020 should be considered in the present form of bar diagrams.

3 Carboxymethyl polysaccharides in drug delivery

3.1 Carboxymethyl cellulose (CMC)

Synthesis of CMC and its derivative like CMC-*g*-polyacrylamide varying the operating and materials parameters [89], its rheological properties when used as solution including shear thinning parameters, creep, frequency-sweep and viscoelastic behavior [90,91], its preparation from wastes [92], corrosion protection potential for mild steel in H_2SO_4 solution at 30–60°C, and also structure-property relationships of CMC blends with other polymers [93] have been the subject of variety of reports. The use of the CMC and its blends with other water-soluble polymers have also been proved to be a potential way for developing a series of drug delivery devices for various therapeutic agents [94–96]. In this regard, metal ions like the Fe^{3+} ions have been used as ionic cross-linking agents and an improved CMC integrity was achieved. However, the efficiency of Fe^{3+}-cross-linked CMC carriers reduces to withstand acidic conditions (e.g., gastric pH), which considerably limits the oral administration of the CMC-based DDSs. Blending and coating the CMC with other polymers have been suggested to overcome this issue [97]. Bulut used the blend of chitosan-coated sodium CMC (NaCMC) and polyvinyl alcohol (PVA) to make flurbiprofen (FBP)-loaded microsphere for the controlled release applications [98]. FBP is known as an almost insoluble, nonsteroidal, antiinflammatory drug suitable for the arthritic disorder treatments. In their article, they used Fe^{3+} chelation to prepare (NaCMC)/PVA microspheres (~ 3.8 to 9 μm), and chitosan coating was applied to enhance the mechanical integrity of the microparticles as well as preventing the burst release of the FBP. It was observed that a relatively high drug loading capacity of the microparticles (c. 22%–40%, depending on the used method) was achieved, and also it was found that chitosan coating could provide slow and continuous release of FBP from the microspheres [98].

In another study performed by Bulut et al., sodium alginate (SA)/NaCMC microspheres were used to keep the release of donepezil hydrochloride (DP) under control in the treatment of Alzheimer's disease [99]. They used a water-in-oil (w/o) emulsion cross-linking method to prepare microspheres for the oral administration of DP by conducting in vitro release experiments in the gastrointestinal tract pH values. Their results showed that by increasing SA in the polymer blends, the release rate of DP was increased while it has decreased by increasing the cross-linking degree. The DP release of the microspheres was classically explained following the Fickian transport below a value of $n < 0.5$ while anomalous transport was detected above such critical value ($n = 0.5–1.0$). Kim et al. used Fe^{3+} cross-linked SA/CMC beads as the carrier of protein-based therapeutic agents [100]. They showed that the electrostatic interactions between the CMC and the Fe^{3+} resulted in polymer chain collapse and the formation of beads. Furthermore, the pore size of the beads increased by the CMC loading in the hydrogel beads. In the albumin release process from hydrogel beads in gastrointestinal, the pH values revealed a pH-dependent protein release behavior [100]. $FeCl_3$ was utilized by Akalin et al. as an ionic cross-linkers for the fabrication of pH sensitive NaCMC hydrogel beads [101]. They suggested these nanoporous beads as the potential drug delivery vehicles due to the high stability obtained. Samrot et al. emphasized the effect of chelator on the synthesis and drug delivery performance of the chitosan-CMC composite microparticles using barium chloride and sodium tripolyphosphate as chelating agents [102]. The so-called curcuminoid isolated from the rhizome of *Curcuma longa* L. (CUR) as a hydrophobic drug was synthesized in the form of microparticles and its drug release kinetics against *Pseudomonas aeruginosa* was investigated. Assessments based on antimicrobial activity analyses revealed that all drug-encapsulated microcarriers had acceptable activity regardless of drug concentration using acetic acid as solvent. The maximum drug delivery took place at 0.6% concentration of barium chloride. Elsewhere, alginate-CMC composites were cross-linked using barium chloride for cancer treatment by the delivery of methotrexate (MTX) [103]. In vitro release assessments in phosphate-buffered saline (PBS) (conditioned at 37°C, and pH of 7.4) showed that c. 98% of MTX was released within just 5h with a significant burst release. Al^{3+} cations were used by Dye et al. to carboxymethyl locust bean gum (CMLBG)/alginate hydrogels for the oral delivery antidiabetic glipizide medication [104] and high loading capacity (93%–98%) was obtained for the glipizide. In addition, they generated in vivo experiments on rats and obtained a remarkable hypoglycemic activity.

3.2 Carboxymethyl chitosan/chitin (CMCS/CMCN)

Chitosan as a natural cationic polysaccharide can be cross-linked by the use of chemical agents such as glutaraldehyde or can be physically cross-linked with the aid of anions and anionic molecules such as tripolyphosphate (TPP) or the polyanions like polyphosphates [105,106]. In contrast to chitosan that bears positive charges, carboxymethyl chitosan (CMCS) is negatively charged. Therefore, cationic species such as multivalent metal ions can induce ionic cross-linking in the CMCS structure. For instance, Ca^{2+} ions have a key role in cross-linking CMCS and the formation of nanoparticles [107]. These pH-sensitive nanoparticles can be effectively used to prepare DDSs. By embedding Cu nanoparticles into the alginate-CMCS mixture, Lu et al. (Fig. 2) investigated the gradual release behavior of the Cu^{2+} ions from nanoparticles that led to ionic cross-linking of these polyanions. In addition, alginate-CMCS/Cu scaffolds exhibited

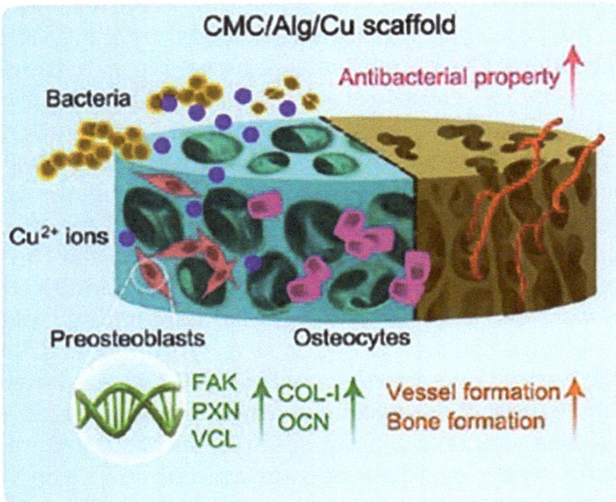

FIG. 2 The schematic illustration of the CMC/alginate (nominated and abbreviated as Alg in the illustration)/Cu scaffolds with enhanced antibacterial effect and improved osteogenesis, developed by Lu et al. [108]. In vivo investigations made possible to present further evidence for the performance of the CMC/alginate/Cu scaffolds that effectively assisted in the formation of vascularized new bone tissue within one month. They also prevented infection caused by the clinical bacterial, quite interestingly even when the implantation sites were exposed to the clinically collected *Staphylococcus aureus* bacteria. The result approved that the facile and innovative approach used in this work make possible fabrication of Cu containing polymer scaffolds to be intended to repair infected bone defects.

an enhanced antibacterial effect as well as an improved osteogenesis, which both were interesting for the bone tissue engineering applications [108]. There is an agreement that the controlled release of metal cations not only induces the cross-linking but also improves the antibacterial characteristics. Mi et al. prepared microspheres using Fe^{+3} cations for cross-linking carboxymethylchitin (CMCN) using in-liquid curing method and proposed the microspheres as an appropriate pH-sensitive vehicle for the 6-mercaptopurine delivery [109]. They reported that elution of Fe^{+3} cations from the CMCN complex was decreased from pH1.2 to pH7.5 because of the complex formed being unstable in acidic solution. The relaxation of macromolecular chains was speculated to be the additional reason besides diffusion of drug that controlled kinetics of drug release.

3.3 Other kinds of polysaccharides

By chemical modification of starch, it is possible to prepare various cheap biopolymers for a wide range of biomedical applications [110].

Carboxymethyl starch (CMST) has been used as another polysaccharide-based biomaterial to develop drug delivery systems and theranostic platforms [111–113]. CMST can be synthesized under heterogeneous condition through the reaction between starch and monochloroacetic acid in the presence of sodium hydroxide [114]. It was reported that the properties of CMST and its derivatives like sodium CMST are significantly under the influence of the degree of substitution of the carboxymethyl starch and the reaction efficiency of carboxymethylation variables, and also the functionalization method [115–118]. In some research reports, sodium trimetaphosphate (STMP) has been named and used as a chemical cross-linker for synthesis of CMST microgels [119,120] and in most of the drug-delivery-related experimental research, complex coacervation (i.e., the electrostatic interactions between two oppositely charged ionic polymers) was considered as the physical cross-linking strategy suitable for the CMST [121,122]. Nagasawa et al. used irradiation under highly concentrated solution, or so-called paste-like condition, as a source of cross-linking in development of biodegradable CMST hydrogels [123]. the effect of the concentration of the prepared paste on the cross-linking efficiency of CMST as well as the properties of the resulting three dimensional hydrogel network was then investigated. It was observed that cross-linking was severely induced by the irradiation at concentration range of 20%–50%. Biodegradability of the cross-linked CMST at given irradiation dosage was monitored over a period of 2 weeks, which happened faster than the standard cellulose powder as the control system.

Carboxymethyl dextran (CMD) have been widely studied and applied in different filed such as sensor for the analysis and detection of biospecific interaction by using surface plasmon resonance [124,125] and to inhibit corneal epithelial tissue outgrowth and bovine corneal epithelial cell attachment and growth [126]. It has particularly suggested for making various drug delivery platforms [127,128]. This chemically modified polysaccharide with its several functional groups such as hydroxyl, carboxyl, and aldehyde groups possesses the potential of interaction with drug molecules, polymers, and ionic species [129]. When used as drug carrier, the loaded drug can be released through the polymer degradation process [128]. In most of the research studies regarding CMD, cationic polymers, especially chitosan, have been used in electrostatical cross-linking of CMD and developing new drug delivery platforms. For example, Lin et al. used chitosan to coacervate CMD and prepare 5-fluorouracil (5-FU)- or indocyanine green (ICG)-loaded chitosan-CMD nanoparticles [130]. Drug-loaded CMD nanoparticles were prepared by embedding 5-FU and absorption of ICG, such that the particle size rose with drug association efficiency increase, particularly at lower contents of amino group attached to the surface of CMD.

Hyaluronic acid (HA) or also known as hyaluronan is an important naturally forming high molecular weight polysaccharide discovered in 1934, by Karl Meyer with biocompatibility and biodegradability performance [131,132]. Both HA and its derivatives have been widely used in biomedical applications [133], especially in preparation of targeted drug delivery platforms for cancer therapy [134,135]. Carboxymethyl hyaluronic acid (CMHA) has also been used to coat and stabilize calcium phosphate nanoparticles [136], which appeared suitable for the development of DDSs [137]. If chemotherapeutic agents are loaded in CMHA-coated calcium phosphate nanoparticles they can effectively target human breast cancer cells [136].

Synthesis, characterization, and properties of carboxymethyl guar gum (CMGG) beads have been the subjects of continued research programs [138,139]. They have been used as drug vehicle of bovine serum albumin (BSA, model drug) through gastrointestinal tract [140], where divalent barium (Ba^{2+}) and calcium (Ca^{2+}) were used as ionic cross-linking agents. Minimal drug release was observed in simulated gastric pH within 6h while almost all encapsulated drug was released in the simulated intestinal fluid (SIF) [140]. Carboxymethyl xanthan gum (CMXG) have also been employed to make drug carriers by introducing $CaCl_2$ solution to cross-link CMXG [141].

4 Conclusion

Synthetic and natural polymers are emerging elements of advanced delivery and controlled release systems. Natural polymers, especially polysaccharides, are superior to synthetic ones due to their abundance, low-cost extraction, biodegradability, biocompatibility, and also their tailorable microstructure and properties. In this sense, according to the open literature, polysaccharides have been in the core of attention of researchers for drug delivery uses. Moreover, a considerable contribution has been made in developing functionalized polysaccharides so as to optimize and trigger exactly the sites of tissues in the body for an efficient drug delivery. Chemical modification of polysaccharides has been considered as an effective strategy to improve the properties of this class of macromolecules, and has been extensively suggested for controlling and improving the properties of polysaccharides. By recent advancements of the drug delivery science, carboxymethylation, as a subgroup of the chemical modification techniques, has been frequently recommended to alter the drug delivery features of polysaccharides. Overall, carboxymethylated polysaccharides make possible bearing negative charges to polysaccharides for making them (more) soluble in water and organic solvents compared with the pristine polysaccharides. Such feature can provide the polysaccharide with an ability to slow down the transfer of drug from polymer and controlling the release rate in oral administration. Therefore, chemically modified carboxymethylated polysaccharides with their interesting drug delivery performance play a prominent role in targeted cancer therapy and exciting prospects are considerable for them for developing future drug delivery systems.

References

[1] Anselmo AC, Mitragotri S. Impact of particle elasticity on particle-based drug delivery systems. Adv Drug Deliv Rev 2017;108:51–67.
[2] Pattni BS, Torchilin VP. Targeted drug delivery systems: strategies and challenges. In: Targeted drug delivery: concepts and design. Springer; 2015. p. 3–38.
[3] Yun YH, Lee BK, Park K. Controlled drug delivery: historical perspective for the next generation. J Control Release 2015;219:2–7.
[4] Maiti S, Sen KK. Introductory chapter: drug delivery concepts. Adv Technol Deliv Ther 2017;1–12.
[5] Tibbitt MW, Dahlman JE, Langer R. Emerging frontiers in drug delivery. J Am Chem Soc 2016;138(3):704–17.
[6] Abu-Thabit N, Makhlouf ASH. Historical development of drug delivery systems: from conventional macroscale to controlled, targeted, and responsive nanoscale systems. Elsevier; 2018. p. 3–41.
[7] Hossain S, Chowdhury EH, Akaike T. Nanoparticles and toxicity in therapeutic delivery: the ongoing debate. Ther Deliv 2011;2(2):125–32.
[8] Din FU, Aman W, Ullah I, Qureshi OS, Mustapha O, Shafique S, Zeb A. Effective use of nanocarriers as drug delivery systems for the treatment of selected tumors. Int J Nanomedicine 2017;12:7291–309.
[9] Langer R. Biomaterials in drug delivery and tissue engineering: one laboratory's experience. Acc Chem Res 2000;33(2):94–101.
[10] Fenton OS, Olafson KN, Pillai PS, Mitchell MJ, Langer R. Advances in biomaterials for drug delivery. Adv Mater 2018;30(29):1705328.
[11] Dhayani A, Kalita S, Mahato M, Srinath P, Vemula PK. Biomaterials for topical and transdermal drug delivery in reconstructive transplantation. Nanomedicine (Lond) 2019;14(20):2713–33.
[12] Hossen S, Hossain MK, Basher MK, Mia MNH, Rahman MT, Uddin MJ. Smart nanocarrier-based drug delivery systems for cancer therapy and toxicity studies: a review. J Adv Res 2019;15:1–18.
[13] Langer R. Polymer-controlled drug delivery systems. Acc Chem Res 1993;26(10):537–42.
[14] Bagheri B, Zarrintaj P, Surwase SS, Baheiraei N, Saeb MR, Mozafari M, Kim YC, Park OOJC, Biointerfaces SB. Self-gelling electroactive hydrogels based on chitosan–aniline oligomers/agarose for neural tissue engineering with on-demand drug release. Colloids Surf B Biointerfaces 2019;184, 110549.
[15] Joralemon MJ, McRae S, Emrick T. PEGylated polymers for medicine: from conjugation to self-assembled systems. Chem Commun 2010;46(9):1377–93.
[16] Rohani Rad E, Vahabi H, Formela K, Saeb MR, Thomas S. Injectable poloxamer/graphene oxide hydrogels with well-controlled mechanical and rheological properties. Polym Adv Technol 2019;30(9):2250–60.
[17] Farokhzad OC, Langer R. Impact of nanotechnology on drug delivery. ACS Nano 2009;3(1):16–20.
[18] Vega-Vásquez P, Mosier NS, Irudayaraj J. Nanoscale drug delivery systems: from medicine to agriculture. Front Bioeng Biotechnol 2020;8:79.

[19] Tariverdian T, Zarintaj P, Milan PB, Saeb MR, Kargozar S, Sefat F, Samadikuchaksaraei A, Mozafari M. Nanoengineered biomaterials for kidney regeneration. In: Nanoengineered biomaterials for regenerative medicine. Elsevier; 2019. p. 325–44.
[20] Horcajada P, Chalati T, Serre C, Gillet B, Sébrié C, Baati T, Eubank J, Heurtaux D, Clayette P, Kreuz C, Chang J-S, Lee KY, Marsaud V, Bories P-N, Cynober L, Gil S, Férey G, Couvreur P, Gref R. Porous metal-organic-framework nanoscale carriers as a potential platform for drug delivery and imaging. Nat Mater 2009;9:172–8.
[21] Tamames-Tabar C, Cunha D, Imbuluzqueta E, Ragon F, Serre C, Blanco-Prieto MJ, Horcajada P. Cytotoxicity of nanoscaled metal–organic frameworks. J Mater Chem B 2014;2(3):262–71.
[22] Cai W, Wang J, Chu C, Chen W, Wu C, Liu G. Metal–organic framework-based stimuli-responsive systems for drug delivery. Adv Sci 2019;6(1):1801526.
[23] Jouyandeh M, Tikhani F, Shabanian M, Movahedi F, Moghari S, Akbari V, Gabrion X, Laheurte P, Vahabi H, Saeb MR. Synthesis, characterization, and high potential of 3D metal–organic framework (MOF) nanoparticles for curing with epoxy. J Alloys Compd 2020;, 154547.
[24] Servatan M, Zarrintaj P, Mahmodi G, Kim S-J, Ganjali MR, Saeb MR, Mozafari M. Zeolites in drug delivery: progress, challenges and opportunities. Drug Discov Today 2020.
[25] Mahmodi G, Dangwal S, Zarrintaj P, Zhu M, Mao Y, McIlroy DN, Saeb MR, Vatanpour V, Ramsey JD, Kim S-J. NaA zeolite-coated meshes with tunable hydrophilicity for oil-water separation. Sep Purif Technol 2020;240, 116630.
[26] Mahmodi G, Zarrintaj P, Taghizadeh A, Taghizadeh M, Manouchehri S, Dangwal S, Ronte A, Ganjali MR, Ramsey JD, Kim S-J. From microporous to mesoporous mineral frameworks: an alliance between zeolite and chitosan. Carbohydr Res 2020;489, 107930.
[27] Langer R. Drug delivery. Drugs on target. Science 2001;293(5527):58–9.
[28] Mura S, Nicolas J, Couvreur P. Stimuli-responsive nanocarriers for drug delivery. Nat Mater 2013;12(11):991–1003.
[29] Rwei AY, Lee J-J, Zhan C, Liu Q, Ok MT, Shankarappa SA, Langer R, Kohane DS. Repeatable and adjustable on-demand sciatic nerve block with phototriggerable liposomes. Proc Natl Acad Sci U S A 2015;112(51):15719–24.
[30] Bharti C, Nagaich U, Pal AK, Gulati N. Mesoporous silica nanoparticles in target drug delivery system: a review. Int J Pharm Investig 2015;5(3):124–33.
[31] Wang AZ, Langer R, Farokhzad OC. Nanoparticle delivery of cancer drugs. Annu Rev Med 2012;63:185–98.
[32] Wilhelm S, Tavares AJ, Dai Q, Ohta S, Audet J, Dvorak HF, Chan WC. Analysis of nanoparticle delivery to tumours. Nat Rev Mater 2016;1(5):1–12.
[33] Pillai O, Panchagnula R. Polymers in drug delivery. Curr Opin Chem Biol 2001;5(4):447–51.
[34] Zarrintaj P, Ahmadi Z, Saeb MR, Mozafari M. Poloxamer-based stimuli-responsive biomaterials. Mater Today: Proc 2018;5(7):15516–23.
[35] Farokhi M, Mottaghitalab F, Fatahi Y, Saeb MR, Zarrintaj P, Kundu SC, Khademhosseini A. Silk fibroin scaffolds for common cartilage injuries: possibilities for future clinical applications. Eur Polym J 2019;115:251–67.
[36] Zarrintaj P, Saeb MR, Ramakrishna S, Mozafari M. Biomaterials selection for neuroprosthetics. Curr Opin Biomed Eng 2018;6:99–109.
[37] Uhrich KE, Cannizzaro SM, Langer RS, Shakesheff KM. Polymeric systems for controlled drug release. Chem Rev 1999;99(11):3181–98.
[38] Sharma R, Mody N, Agrawal U, Vyas S. Theranostic nanomedicine; a next generation platform for cancer diagnosis and therapy. Mini Rev Med Chem 2017;17(18):1746–57.
[39] Farokhi M, Mottaghitalab F, Saeb MR, Thomas S. Functionalized theranostic nanocarriers with bio-inspired polydopamine for tumor imaging and chemo-photothermal therapy. J Control Release 2019;309:203–19.

[40] Guo B, Ma PX. Synthetic biodegradable functional polymers for tissue engineering: a brief review. Sci China: Chem 2014;57(4):490–500.

[41] Li J, Mooney DJ. Designing hydrogels for controlled drug delivery. Nat Rev Mater 2016;1(12):16071.

[42] Grayson ACR, Voskerician G, Lynn A, Anderson JM, Cima MJ, Langer R. Differential degradation rates in vivo and in vitro of biocompatible poly(lactic acid) and poly(glycolic acid) homo- and co-polymers for a polymeric drug-delivery microchip. J Biomater Sci Polym Ed 2004;15(10):1281–304.

[43] Tyler B, Gullotti D, Mangraviti A, Utsuki T, Brem H. Polylactic acid (PLA) controlled delivery carriers for biomedical applications. Adv Drug Deliv Rev 2016;107:163–75.

[44] Ding D, Qingdi Z. Recent advances of PLGA micro/nanoparticles for the delivery of biomacromolecular therapeutics. Mater Sci Eng C 2018;92:1041–60.

[45] Bansal KK, Gupta J, Rosling A, Rosenholm JM. Renewable poly(δ-decalactone) based block copolymer micelles as drug delivery vehicle: in vitro and in vivo evaluation. Saudi Pharm J 2018;26(3):358–68.

[46] Espinoza SM, Patil HI, Martinez ESM, Pimentel RC, Ige PP. Poly-ε-caprolactone (PCL), a promising polymer for pharmaceutical and biomedical applications: focus on nanomedicine in cancer. Int J Polym Mater Polym Biomater 2020;69(2):85–126.

[47] Makadia HK, Siegel SJ. Poly lactic-co-glycolic acid (PLGA) as biodegradable controlled drug delivery carrier. Polymers 2011;3(3):1377–97.

[48] Baghaei B, Jafari SH, Khonakdar HA, Saeb MR, Wagenknecht U, Heinrich G. A multi-optimization approach to assessment of drug delivery of PLGA nanoparticles: simultaneous control of particle size and release behavior. Int J Polym Mater Polym Biomater 2015;64(12):641–52.

[49] Mir M, Ahmed N, Rehman AU. Recent applications of PLGA based nanostructures in drug delivery. Colloids Surf B Biointerfaces 2017;159:217–31.

[50] Baghaei B, Saeb MR, Jafari SH, Khonakdar HA, Rezaee B, Goodarzi V, Mohammadi Y. Modeling and closed-loop control of particle size and initial burst of PLGA biodegradable nanoparticles for targeted drug delivery. J Appl Polym Sci 2017;134(33):45145.

[51] Shojaie S, Rostamian M, Samadi A, Alvani MAS, Khonakdar HA, Goodarzi V, Zarrintaj R, Servatan M, Asefnejad A, Baheiraei N, Saeb MR. Electrospun electroactive nanofibers of gelatin-oligoaniline/poly (vinyl alcohol) templates for architecting of cardiac tissue with on-demand drug release. Polym Adv Technol 2019;30(6):1473–83.

[52] Sargazi G, Afzali D, Mostafavi A, Shadman A, Rezaee B, Zarrintaj P, Saeb MR, Ramakrishna S, Mozafari M. Chitosan/polyvinyl alcohol nanofibrous membranes: towards green super-adsorbents for toxic gases. Heliyon 2019;5(4), e01527.

[53] Koutsamanis I, Paudel A, Nickisch K, Eggenreich K, Roblegg E, Eder S. Controlled-release from high-loaded reservoir-type systems—a case study of ethylene-vinyl acetate and progesterone. Pharmaceutics 2020;12(2):103.

[54] Anwar M, Pervaiz F, Shoukat H, Noreen S, Shabbir K, Majeed A, Ijaz S. Formulation and evaluation of interpenetrating network of xanthan gum and polyvinylpyrrolidone as a hydrophilic matrix for controlled drug delivery system. Polym Bull 2020;78:59–80.

[55] Lowinger MB, Barrett SE, Zhang F, Williams 3rd RO. Sustained release drug delivery applications of polyurethanes. Pharmaceutics 2018;10(2):55.

[56] Schneider C, Langer R, Loveday D, Hair D. Applications of ethylene vinyl acetate copolymers (EVA) in drug delivery systems. J Control Release 2017;262:284–95.

[57] Jensen BE, Dávila I, Zelikin AN. Poly (vinyl alcohol) physical hydrogels: matrix-mediated drug delivery using spontaneously eroding substrate. J Phys Chem B 2016;120(26):5916–26.

[58] Dimatteo R, Darling NJ, Segura T. In situ forming injectable hydrogels for drug delivery and wound repair. Adv Drug Deliv Rev 2018;127:167–84.

[59] Hoare TR, Kohane DS. Hydrogels in drug delivery: progress and challenges. Polymer 2008;49(8):1993–2007.

[60] Hamidi M, Azadi A, Rafiei P. Hydrogel nanoparticles in drug delivery. Adv Drug Deliv Rev 2008;60(15):1638–49.
[61] Gombotz WR, Pettit DK. Biodegradable polymers for protein and peptide drug delivery. Bioconjug Chem 1995;6(4):332–51.
[62] Eskandari S, Guerin T, Toth I, Stephenson RJ. Recent advances in self-assembled peptides: implications for targeted drug delivery and vaccine engineering. Adv Drug Deliv Rev 2017;110:169–87.
[63] Doppalapudi S, Katiyar S, Domb AJ, Khan W. Biodegradable natural polymers. In: Advanced polymers in medicine. Springer; 2015. p. 33–66.
[64] De France KJ, Hoare T, Cranston ED. Review of hydrogels and aerogels containing nanocellulose. Chem Mater 2017;29(11):4609–31.
[65] Bassas-Galia M, Follonier S, Pusnik M, Zinn M. 2—Natural polymers: a source of inspiration. In: Perale G, Hilborn J, editors. Bioresorbable polymers for biomedical applications. Woodhead Publishing; 2017. p. 31–64.
[66] Vahabi H, Michely L, Moradkhani G, Akbari V, Cochez M, Vagner C, Renard E, Saeb MR, Langlois V. Thermal stability and flammability behavior of poly (3-hydroxybutyrate) (PHB) based composites. Materials 2019;12(14):2239.
[67] Vahabi H, Rad ER, Parpaite T, Langlois V, Saeb MR. Biodegradable polyester thin films and coatings in the line of fire: the time of polyhydroxyalkanoate (PHA)? Prog Org Coat 2019;133:85–9.
[68] Hamid Akash MS, Rehman K, Chen S. Natural and synthetic polymers as drug carriers for delivery of therapeutic proteins. Polym Rev 2015;55(3):371–406.
[69] Sonam, Chaudhary H, Arora V, Kholi K, Kumar V. Effect of physicochemical properties of biodegradable polymers on nano drug delivery. Polym Rev 2013;53:546–67.
[70] Zhang N, Wardwell PR, Bader RA. Polysaccharide-based micelles for drug delivery. Pharmaceutics 2013;5(2):329–52.
[71] Lovegrove A, Edwards C, De Noni I, Patel H, El S, Grassby T, Zielke C, Ulmius M, Nilsson L, Butterworth P. Role of polysaccharides in food, digestion, and health. Crit Rev Food Sci Nutr 2017;57(2):237–53.
[72] Ruthes AC, Smiderle FR, Iacomini M. Mushroom heteropolysaccharides: a review on their sources, structure and biological effects. Carbohydr Polym 2016;136:358–75.
[73] Sambrook J, Russell DW. Agarose gel electrophoresis. vol. 2006. Cold Spring Harbor Protocols; 2006. (1): p. pdb. prot4020.
[74] Zarrintaj P, Manouchehri S, Ahmadi Z, Saeb MR, Urbanska AM, Kaplan DL, Mozafari MJCP. Agarose-based biomaterials for tissue engineering. Carbohydr Polym 2018;187:66–84.
[75] Cumpstey I. Chemical modification of polysaccharides. ISRN Org Chem 2013;2013:1–27.
[76] Bagheri B, Zarrintaj P, Samadi A, Zarrintaj R, Ganjali MR, Saeb MR, Mozafari M, Park OO, Kim YCJIJOBM. Tissue engineering with electrospun electro-responsive chitosan-aniline oligomer/polyvinyl alcohol. Int J Biol Macromol 2020;147:160–9.
[77] Li S, Xiong Q, Lai X, Li X, Wan M, Zhang J, Yan Y, Cao M, Lu L, Guan J. Molecular modification of polysaccharides and resulting bioactivities. Compr Rev Food Sci Food Saf 2016;15(2):237–50.
[78] Zeller SG, Greisgraber GW, Gray GR. Analysis of positions of substitution of O-carboxymethyl groups in partially O-carboxymethylated cellulose by the reductive-cleavage method. Carbohydr Res 1991;211(1):41–5.
[79] Machová E, Kvapilová K, Kogan G, Šandula J. Effect of ultrasonic treatment on the molecular weight of carboxymethylated chitin–glucan complex from *Aspergillus niger*. Ultrason Sonochem 1999;5(4):169–72.
[80] Sroková I, Tomanová V, Ebringerová A, Malovíková A, Heinze T. Water-soluble amphiphilic O-(carboxymethyl)cellulose derivatives—synthesis and properties. Macromol Mater Eng 2004;289(1):63–9.

[81] Maciel J, Silva D, Paula HC, De Paula R. Chitosan/carboxymethyl cashew gum polyelectrolyte complex: synthesis and thermal stability. Eur Polym J 2005;41(11):2726–33.
[82] Assaad E, Wang YJ, Zhu XX, Mateescu MA. Polyelectrolyte complex of carboxymethyl starch and chitosan as drug carrier for oral administration. Carbohydr Polym 2011;84(4):1399–407.
[83] Mejía EH, Contreras H, Delgado E, Quintana G. Effect of experimental parameters on the formation of hydrogels by polyelectrolyte complexation of carboxymethylcellulose, carboxymethyl starch, and alginic acid with chitosan. Int J Chem Eng 2019;2019.
[84] Mizrahy S, Peer D. Polysaccharides as building blocks for nanotherapeutics. Chem Soc Rev 2012;41(7):2623–40.
[85] Li Y-Y, Wang B, Ma M-G, Wang B. Review of recent development on preparation, properties, and applications of cellulose-based functional materials. Int J Polym Sci 2018;2018.
[86] Wang G, Miao F, Dong F, Li Q, Guo Z, Guo Z. Synthesis of carboxymethyl polysaccharides and their moisture absorption and retention abilities. Asian J Chem 2014;26:5239–41.
[87] Mocanu G, Souguir Z, Picton L, Le Cerf D. Multi-responsive carboxymethyl polysaccharide crosslinked hydrogels containing Jeffamine side-chains. Carbohydr Polym 2012;89(2):578–85.
[88] Li J, Lu J, Li Y. Carboxylmethylcellulose/bentonite composite gels: water sorption behavior and controlled release of herbicide. J Appl Polym Sci 2009;112(1):261–8.
[89] Biswal D, Singh R. Characterisation of carboxymethyl cellulose and polyacrylamide graft copolymer. Carbohydr Polym 2004;57(4):379–87.
[90] Toğrul H, Arslan N. Production of carboxymethyl cellulose from sugar beet pulp cellulose and rheological behaviour of carboxymethyl cellulose. Carbohydr Polym 2003;54(1):73–82.
[91] Benchabane A, Bekkour K. Rheological properties of carboxymethyl cellulose (CMC) solutions. Colloid Polym Sci 2008;286(10):1173.
[92] Pushpamalar V, Langford SJ, Ahmad M, Lim YY. Optimization of reaction conditions for preparing carboxymethyl cellulose from sago waste. Carbohydr Polym 2006;64(2):312–8.
[93] Su J-F, Huang Z, Yuan X-Y, Wang X-Y, Li M. Structure and properties of carboxymethyl cellulose/soy protein isolate blend edible films crosslinked by Maillard reactions. Carbohydr Polym 2010;79(1):145–53.
[94] Butun S, Ince FG, Erdugan H, Sahiner N. One-step fabrication of biocompatible carboxymethyl cellulose polymeric particles for drug delivery systems. Carbohydr Polym 2011;86(2):636–43.
[95] Kadry G. Comparison between gelatin/carboxymethyl cellulose and gelatin/carboxymethyl nanocellulose in tramadol drug loaded capsule. Heliyon 2019;5(9), e02404.
[96] El-Hag Ali A, El-Rehim HAA, Kamal H, Hegazy DESA. Synthesis of carboxymethyl cellulose based drug carrier hydrogel using ionizing radiation for possible use as site specific delivery system. J Macromol Sci, Part A: Pure Appl Chem 2008;45(8):628–34.
[97] Hosny EA, Al-Helw AA-RM. Effect of coating of aluminum carboxymethylcellulose beads on the release and bioavailability of diclofenac sodium. Pharm Acta Helv 1998;72(5):255–61.
[98] Bulut E. Chitosan coated-and uncoated-microspheres of sodium carboxymethyl cellulose/polyvinyl alcohol crosslinked with ferric ion: flurbiprofen loading and in vitro drug release study. J Macromol Sci A 2020;57(1):72–82.
[99] Bulut E, Şanli O. Optimization of release conditions of Alzheimer's drug donepezil hydrochloride from sodium alginate/sodium carboxymethyl cellulose blend microspheres. J Macromol Sci, Part B 2014;53(5):902–17.
[100] Kim MS, Park SJ, Gu BK, Kim C-H. Ionically crosslinked alginate–carboxymethyl cellulose beads for the delivery of protein therapeutics. Appl Surf Sci 2012;262:28–33.

[101] Akalin GO, Pulat M. Preparation and characterization of nanoporous sodium carboxymethyl cellulose hydrogel beads. J Nanomater 2018;2018, 9676949.
[102] Samrot AV, Jahnavi T, Padmanaban S, Philip S-A, Burman U, Rabel AM. Chelators influenced synthesis of chitosan–carboxymethyl cellulose microparticles for controlled drug delivery. Appl Nanosci 2016;6(8):1219–31.
[103] Kahya N, Gölcü A, Erim FB. Barium ion cross-linked alginate-carboxymethyl cellulose composites for controlled release of anticancer drug methotrexate. J Drug Delivery Sci Technol 2019;54, 101324.
[104] Dey P, Maiti S, Sa B. Gastrointestinal delivery of glipizide from carboxymethyl locust bean gum–Al3+–alginate hydrogel network: in vitro and in vivo performance. J Appl Polym Sci 2013;128(3):2063–72.
[105] Abdelgawad A, Hudson S. Chitosan nanoparticles: polyphosphates cross-linking and protein delivery properties. Int J Biol Macromol 2019;136:133–42.
[106] Quiñones JP, Peniche H, Peniche C. Chitosan based self-assembled nanoparticles in drug delivery. Polymers 2018;10(3):235.
[107] Kalliola S, Repo E, Srivastava V, Heiskanen JP, Sirviö JA, Liimatainen H, Sillanpää M. The pH sensitive properties of carboxymethyl chitosan nanoparticles cross-linked with calcium ions. Colloids Surf B Biointerfaces 2017;153:229–36.
[108] Lu Y, Li L, Zhu Y, Wang X, Li M, Lin Z, Hu X, Zhang Y, Yin Q, Xia H. Multifunctional copper-containing carboxymethyl chitosan/alginate scaffolds for eradicating clinical bacterial infection and promoting bone formation. ACS Appl Mater Interfaces 2017;10(1):127–38.
[109] Mi F-L, Chen C-T, Tseng Y-C, Kuan C-Y, Shyu S-S. Iron (III)-carboxymethylchitin microsphere for the pH-sensitive release of 6-mercaptopurine. J Control Release 1997;44(1):19–32.
[110] Haroon M, Wang L, Yu H, Abbasi NM, Saleem M, Khan RU, Ullah RS, Chen Q, Wu J. Chemical modification of starch and its application as an adsorbent material. RSC Adv 2016;6(82):78264–85.
[111] Saikia C, Hussain A, Ramteke A, Sharma HK, Deb P, Maji TK. Carboxymethyl starch-coated iron oxide magnetic nanoparticles: a potential drug delivery system for isoniazid. Iran Polym J 2015;24(10):815–28.
[112] Ispas-Szabo P, De Koninck P, Calinescu C, Mateescu MA. Carboxymethyl starch excipients for drug chronodelivery. AAPS PharmSciTech 2017;18(5):1673–82.
[113] Mohapatra S, Asfer M, Anwar M, Sharma K, Akhter M, Ahmad FJ, Siddiqui AA. Doxorubicin loaded carboxymethyl Assam bora rice starch coated superparamagnetic iron oxide nanoparticles as potential antitumor cargo. Heliyon 2019;5(6), e01955.
[114] Stojanović Ž, Jeremić K, Jovanović S. Synthesis of carboxymethyl starch. Starch-Stärke 2000;52(11):413–9.
[115] Hebeish A, Khalil M. Chemical factors affecting preparation of carboxymethyl starch. Starch-Stärke 1988;40(4):147–50.
[116] Stojanović Ž, Jeremić K, Jovanović S, Lechner MD. A comparison of some methods for the determination of the degree of substitution of carboxymethyl starch. Starch-Stärke 2005;57(2):79–83.
[117] Heinze T, Liebert T, Heinze U, Schwikal K. Starch derivatives of high degree of functionalization 9: carboxymethyl starches. Cellul 2004;11(2):239–45.
[118] Spychaj T, Wilpiszewska K, Zdanowicz M. Medium and high substituted carboxymethyl starch: synthesis, characterization and application. Starch-Stärke 2013;65(1–2):22–33.
[119] Zhang B, Tao H, Wei B, Jin Z, Xu X, Tian Y. Characterization of different substituted carboxymethyl starch microgels and their interactions with lysozyme. PLoS ONE 2014;9(12), e114634.
[120] Zhang B, Wei B, Hu X, Jin Z, Xu X, Tian Y. Preparation and characterization of carboxymethyl starch microgel with different crosslinking densities. Carbohydr Polym 2015;124:245–53.

[121] Saboktakin MR, Tabatabaie RM, Maharramov A, Ramazanov MA. Synthesis and in vitro evaluation of carboxymethyl starch–chitosan nanoparticles as drug delivery system to the colon. Int J Biol Macromol 2011;48(3):381–5.

[122] Quadrado RF, Fajardo AR. Microparticles based on carboxymethyl starch/chitosan polyelectrolyte complex as vehicles for drug delivery systems. Arab J Chem 2018;13:2183–94.

[123] Nagasawa N, Yagi T, Kume T, Yoshii F. Radiation crosslinking of carboxymethyl starch. Carbohydr Polym 2004;58(2):109–13.

[124] Johnsson B, Löfås S, Lindquist G, Edström Å, Hillgren RMM, Hansson A. Comparison of methods for immobilization to carboxymethyl dextran sensor surfaces by analysis of the specific activity of monoclonal antibodies. J Mol Recognit 1995;8(1–2):125–31.

[125] Löfås S, Johnsson B, Edström Å, Hansson A, Lindquist G, Hillgren R-MM, Stigh L. Methods for site controlled coupling to carboxymethyldextran surfaces in surface plasmon resonance sensors. Biosens Bioelectron 1995;10(9–10):813–22.

[126] McLean KM, Johnson G, Chatelier RC, Beumer GJ, Steele JG, Griesser HJ. Method of immobilization of carboxymethyl-dextran affects resistance to tissue and cell colonization. Colloids Surf B Biointerfaces 2000;18(3–4):221–34.

[127] Ning S, Huang Q, Sun X, Li C, Zhang Y, Li J, Liu Y-N. Carboxymethyl dextran-coated liposomes: toward a robust drug delivery platform. Soft Matter 2011;7(19):9394–401.

[128] Thambi T, You DG, Han HS, Deepagan V, Jeon SM, Suh YD, Choi KY, Kim K, Kwon IC, Yi GR. Bioreducible carboxymethyl dextran nanoparticles for tumor-targeted drug delivery. Adv Healthc Mater 2014;3(11):1829–38.

[129] Goodarzi N, Varshochian R, Kamalinia G, Atyabi F, Dinarvand R. A review of polysaccharide cytotoxic drug conjugates for cancer therapy. Carbohydr Polym 2013;92(2):1280–93.

[130] Lin Y, Radzi R, Morimoto M, Saimoto H, Okamoto Y, Minami S. Characterization of chitosan-carboxymethyl dextran nanoparticles as a drug carrier and as a stimulator of mouse splenocytes. J Biomater Sci Polym Ed 2012;23(11):1401–20.

[131] Collins MN, Birkinshaw C. Hyaluronic acid based scaffolds for tissue engineering—a review. Carbohydr Polym 2013;92(2):1262–79.

[132] Necas J, Bartosikova L, Brauner P, Kolar J. Hyaluronic acid (hyaluronan): a review. Vet Med 2008;53(8):397–411.

[133] Tiwari S, Bahadur P. Modified hyaluronic acid based materials for biomedical applications. Int J Biol Macromol 2019;121:556–71.

[134] Huang G, Huang H. Application of hyaluronic acid as carriers in drug delivery. Drug Deliv 2018;25(1):766–72.

[135] Kim K, Choi H, Choi ES, Park M-H, Ryu J-H. Hyaluronic acid-coated nanomedicine for targeted cancer therapy. Pharmaceutics 2019;11(7):301.

[136] Woodman JL, Suh MS, Zhang J, Kondaveeti Y, Burgess DJ, White BA, Prestwich GD, Kuhn LT. Carboxymethyl hyaluronan-stabilized nanoparticles for anticancer drug delivery. Int J Cell Biol 2015;**2015**, 249573.

[137] Jun W, Lin L, Yurong C, Juming Y. Recent advances of calcium phosphate nanoparticles for controlled drug delivery. Mini Rev Med Chem 2013;13(10):1501–7.

[138] Pal S, Ghorai S, Dash M, Ghosh S, Udayabhanu G. Flocculation properties of polyacrylamide grafted carboxymethyl guar gum (CMG-g-PAM) synthesised by conventional and microwave assisted method. J Hazard Mater 2011;192(3):1580–8.

[139] Gong H, Liu M, Chen J, Han F, Gao C, Zhang B. Synthesis and characterization of carboxymethyl guar gum and rheological properties of its solutions. Carbohydr Polym 2012;88(3):1015–22.

[140] Thimma RT, Tammishetti S. Barium chloride crosslinked carboxymethyl guar gum beads for gastrointestinal drug delivery. J Appl Polym Sci 2001;82(12):3084–90.

[141] Maity S, Sa B. Ca-carboxymethyl xanthan gum mini-matrices: swelling, erosion and their impact on drug release mechanism. Int J Biol Macromol 2014;68:78–85.

CHAPTER

4

Thiolated polysaccharides in drug delivery

Pranab Kumar Bandyopadhyay[a], *Md Saquib Hasnain*[b], *and Amit Kumar Nayak*[a]

[a]**Department of Pharmaceutics, Seemanta Institute of Pharmaceutical Sciences, Jharpokharia, Mayurbhanj, Odisha, India,** [b]**Department of Pharmacy, Palamau Institute of Pharmacy, Daltonganj, Jharkhand, India**

1 Introduction

Natural polysaccharides have extensively been employed in several industrial applications including food [1,2], biomedical [3], pharmaceutical [4], water purification [5], electronics [6], etc. In view of the potential advantages related to easy availability, sustainable production from natural resources, biocompatibility, and biodegradability, natural polysaccharides are extensively accepted in drug delivery, tissue engineering, wound management, etc. [7–16]. Unfortunately, there are a number of disadvantages with the use of natural polysaccharides in the abovementioned fields. These disadvantages comprise uncontrolled aqueous solubility and degree of hydration, viscosity drop-off in prolonged storage, probability of microbial attack-related contaminations, etc. [17]. The usefulness of the natural polysaccharides can further be improved via physical or chemical modifications of these to their tailor-made forms (physically or chemically modified derivatives of polysaccharides) [18,19]. Many useful modification approaches (physical or chemical) for natural polysaccharides have already been explored and exploited to meet the tailor-made specifications, including physical or chemical cross-linking [20], oxidation [21], sulfation [22], phosphorylation [23], carboxymethylation [24], carbamoylethylation [25], esterification [26], thiolation [27], graft copolymerization [28], interpenetrating polymer network (IPN) [29,30], polyelectrolyte complex (PEC) formations [31,32], etc. Among these tailor-made

Tailor-Made Polysaccharides in Drug Delivery
https://doi.org/10.1016/B978-0-12-821286-8.00008-2

approaches, thiolation is well-known as potential polymer modification approach imparting the mucoadhesive properties on the tailored (modified) derivatives of polymers [33]. The mucoadhesive properties of polymers are, in general, based on the noncovalent interactions/bondings, for example, hydrogen bonding, ionic interactions, and van der Waals forces [34]. These (hydrogen bonding, ionic interactions, and van der Waals forces) are known as weaker and accordingly, are unable to show satisfactory biomucoadhesive residence period at the desired sites [35]. However, the tailoring of polymers via the introduction of thiol groups (–SH) to the polymers usually presents elevated biomucoadhesive characteristics when applied to the biological system. Actually, the thiol groups occurred in the thiol-modified (thiolated) polymers structure disulfide linkage in between the thiolated polymer(s) and the mucus lining of the biological surfaces improving its biomucoadhesion [36].

A new era of the use of thiolated polymers (polymeric thiomers) bearing thiol side chain in their structures has already been proven to be potential polymeric mucoadhesive excipients [37]. Thiolated polymers are capable of structuring stronger covalent natured bond(s) via the reactions of thiol-disulfide exchanging with cysteine-rich subdomains of mucosal layers [35,38]. Thiolated polymers form intra- and interchain disulfide bondings, which facilitate the stronger biomucoadhesive features. The cross-linking characteristics of thiolated polymers are corresponding to the degree of intra- and interchain disulfide bondings formed [39]. As necessitates be, thiolated polymers guarantee the satisfactory localization of the dosage forms with a higher biomucoadhesive residence period at the desired sites. Thiolated polymers inhibit the efflux pump and furthermore, perform as a defensive shield mainly for proteins and peptides from the enzymatic attack [40–42]. Apart from biomucoadhesion, thiolated polymers have been reported to improve the oral permeation of protein and peptide drugs [43]. Thiolated polymers were also reported to exhibit good in situ gelling characteristics [44].

Improvement of mucoadhesion of natural polysaccharides by derivatizations with chemical reagents possessing thiol (–SH) functional groups have been employed [35]. During the past few years, several natural polysaccharides, such as chitosan [45], alginate [46], pectin [27], xanthan gum [47], moringa gum [48], tamarind seed polysaccharide [49], xyloglucan [50], Psyllium husk [51], etc., have been thiolated to improve their biomucoadhesivity for use in mucoadhesive drug delivery. The higher biomucoadhesive residence period at the desired sites by mucoadhesive dosage forms made of thiolated polysaccharides may produce better control in drug releasing as well as permeation [52]. Considering the applicability and usefulness of thiolated polysaccharides, the current chapter envisages summarizing the synthesis of various thiolated natural polysaccharides and their potential uses in drug delivery applications.

2 Various thiolated polysaccharides used in drug delivery formulations

2.1 Thiolated chitosan

Thiolated chitosan is being synthesized via the chemical derivatization of the primary amino groups present in the glucosamine units of the chitosan molecular structure utilizing thiol group containing reagents [53,54]. Since the past few years, a number of thiolated chitosan-based materials, such as chitosan-cysteine conjugate [55], chitosan-*N*-acetyl cysteine conjugate [56], chitosan-thioglycolic acid conjugate [53], chitosan-6-mercaptonicotinic acid [57], chitosan-4-mercaptobenzoic acid [58], etc., have already been chemically synthesized. Millotti et al. developed mucoadhesive tablets using thiolated chitosan material (i.e., chitosan-6-mercaptonicotinic acid) and evaluated the in vivo effectiveness of these mucoadhesive tablets after oral administration [58]. These chitosan-6-mercaptonicotinic acid mucoadhesive tablets showed higher mucoadhesivity even with pH-independent characteristics. After oral administration of these chitosan-6-mercaptonicotinic acid mucoadhesive tablets, the obtained in vivo results exhibited significant influences on insulin absorption. From the obtained in vivo results, it was also obvious that these chitosan-6-mercaptonicotinic acid mucoadhesive tablets can be beneficial to help in target-specific drug releasing. In addition, it will be also beneficial to attain a prolonged intestinal residence period for absorption of proteins and peptides drugs. In a recent research, Sudhakar et al. reported the use of thiolated chitosan to prepare insulin-loaded nanoparticles for oral delivery [59]. In this work, thiolated chitosan was synthesized from chitosan and pentaerythritol tetrakis (3-mercaptopropionate). Insulin-loaded thiolated chitosan nanoparticles were prepared using chitosan and pentaerythritol tetrakis (3-mercaptopropionate) at the ratio of 4:1 exhibited 220 ± 4 nm particle size, 2.3 ± 1 mV particle charge, and 119 ± 4 μM/g sulfhydryl content, correspondingly. The in vitro release of insulin from insulin-loaded thiolated chitosan nanoparticles was tested at pH 2 and pH 5.3. The in vitro insulin release result exhibited approximately 96% of insulin release from insulin-loaded thiolated chitosan nanoparticles within a period of 12 h at pH 2, whereas 92% of insulin release was estimated within a period of 24 h at pH 5.3 (Fig. 1). At pH 5.3, a sustained pattern of insulin releasing from insulin-loaded thiolated chitosan nanoparticles was noticed. Cytotoxicity (in vitro) of the prepared thiolated chitosan nanoparticles was carried out by MTT [3-(4,5-dimethylthiazol-2-yl)-2,5-diphenyltetrazolium bromide] assay testing using human intestinal Caco-2 cells. The results of in vitro cytotoxicity suggested no alteration of cell viability (in vitro). In the in vivo evaluation, the oral administration of thiolated chitosan nanoparticles was attained over the tip of the

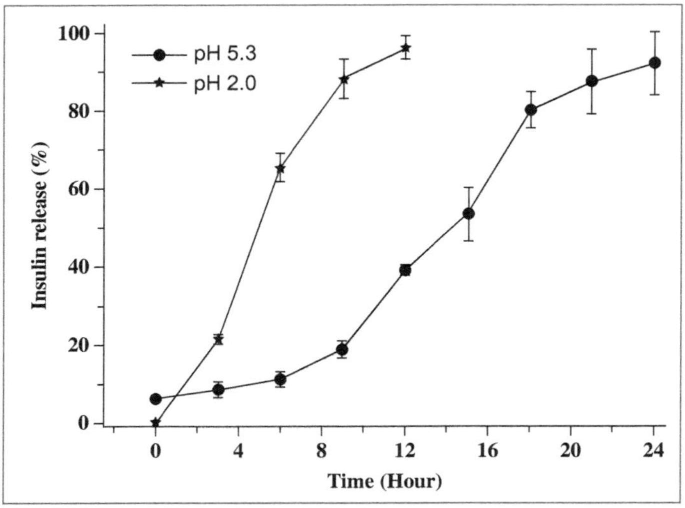

FIG. 1 In vitro release of insulin releasing from insulin-loaded thiolated chitosan nanoparticles at pH 2 and pH 5.3 [59]. *Copyright © 2020, with permission from Elsevier B.V.*

microvilli near the intestinal mucosa, in vivo. There were improved and reduced insulin as well as glucose levels in the blood, respectively, when the insulin-loaded thiolated chitosan nanoparticles were administered to the diabetic rats via the oral route.

Sakloetsakun et al. synthesized thiolated chitosan-based nanoparticles and evaluated the distribution of these nanoparticles in the gastrointestinal tract [60]. The obtained results exhibited that the dried thiolated chitosan-based nanoparticles demonstrated higher mucoadhesivity than that of the nanoparticles suspended in the medium containing miglyol, PEG 300, and 100 mM phosphate buffer. These dried nanoparticles made of thiolated chitosan-thiobutyric acid when enclosed within capsules showed gastrointestinal residence prolongation of 3.6-folds after 3 h in case of oral intake.

In another work, Mahmood et al. chemically synthesized chitosan-stearic acid-thioglycolic acid conjugate by stearic acid linking to chitosan molecules, where thioglycolic acid was covalently linked to the amphiphilic chitosan-stearic acid [45]. Free thiol groups and the degree of amine substitutions within the synthesized chitosan-stearic acid-thioglycolic acid conjugate were estimated. The obtained results showed that 41.73% amine groups of substituted chitosan and the thiol groups used for immobilization on chitosan molecules were measured $471.01 \pm 109.37\,\mu M/g$ of the total polymer content. In addition, it was also estimated that more than 80% of amine groups were free. Employing the amphiphilic thiolated chitosan (here chitosan-stearic acid-thioglycolic acid conjugate),

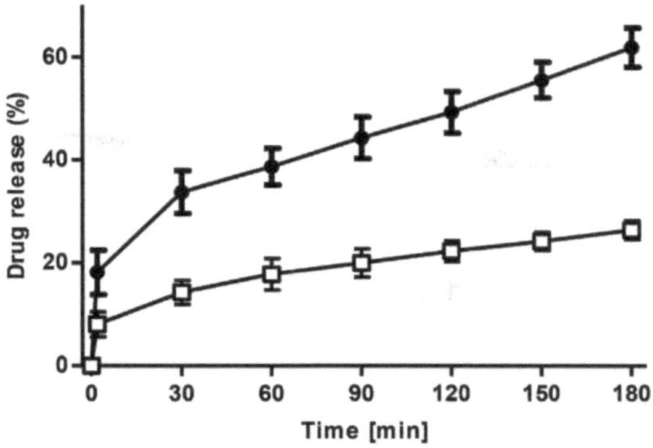

FIG. 2 Percentage of curcumin release from chitosan-stearic acid micelles (●) and chitosan-stearic acid-thioglycolic acid micelles (□) applied to an excised porcine intestinal mucosa over a period of 3h [45]. *Copyright © 2017, with permission from Elsevier Ltd.*

Mahmood et al. developed polymeric micelles for curcumin releasing [45]. The sizes of developed polymeric micelles containing curcumin made of chitosan-stearic acid and chitosan-stearic acid-thioglycolic acid were estimated 13.40 ± 9.38 nm and 26.30 ± 26.86 nm, respectively; whereas, the zeta potentials were measured as 0.01 and 0.03 mV, respectively. The results of in vitro drug release demonstrated that loaded curcumin of 18% (approximately) was found released from the polymeric micelles containing curcumin made of chitosan-stearic acid-thioglycolic acid within 3h, as compared with that from the polymeric micelles containing curcumin made of chitosan-stearic acid (approximately 44%) (Fig. 2). In this study, the mucoadhesive nature of polymeric micelles containing curcumin was also evaluated. The polymeric micelles containing curcumin made of chitosan-stearic acid-thioglycolic acid exhibited increments of dynamic viscosity (1.80-folds), elastic modulus (2.12-folds) and viscous modulus (1.72-folds) when tested mucoadhesion with the porcine mucus membrane. The polymeric micelles containing curcumin made of chitosan-stearic acid-thioglycolic acid exhibited a higher degree of mucoadhesion on the intestinal mucosa and vaginal mucosa up to 56.10-folds and 28.60-folds increments, respectively, in comparison with the polymeric micelles containing curcumin made of chitosan-stearic acid. The obtained results of this research suggested the prospective uses of thiolated chitosan to prepare polymeric micelles containing curcumin [45].

2.2 Thiolated sodium alginate

Recently, Khalid et al. synthesized thiolated sodium alginate via esterification using thioglycolic acid with a percentage yield of 60.8%–73.2% [61]. The thiol contact was estimated $320 \pm 3.232\,\mu M/g$ when the 1:1 M ratio of sodium alginate was treated with thioglycolic acid. An increment in thiolation up to 750 ± 4.234 μM/g was measured when the molar concentration of thioglycolic acid was doubled to the molar concentration of sodium alginate. The sulfur contact of thiolated sodium alginate was measured at 7%, whereas the degree of thiol substitution in the thiolated sodium alginate was measured as 0.9869. Mucoadhesion (ex vivo) of thiolated sodium alginate was evaluated with the preparation of compressed tablets using the rabbit intestine. Increasing mucoadhesion of thiolated sodium alginate was found with an increasing degree of thiol substitution with sodium alginate. The equilibrium was attained after a maximum of 40% mucoadhesion of the compressed tablets made of sodium alginate at 40 min as compared with that of compressed tablets made of thiolated sodium alginate showing 80% mucoadhesion to the rabbit mucosal membrane (Fig. 3). The in vitro swelling of thiolated sodium alginate was evaluated using 0.1 N HCl (acidic medium) and phosphate buffer pH 6.8 (alkaline medium) at 37°C temperature. The results of in vitro swelling demonstrated lesser swelling capacity of thiolated sodium alginate in both acidic medium as well as alkaline medium than that of sodium alginate (Fig. 3). The synthesized thiolated sodium alginate was employed for the formulation of mucoadhesive microspheres for controlled release of metformin. The particle sizes of microspheres made of thiolated sodium alginate were 2–7 μm. The in vitro metformin release from mucoadhesive microspheres made of thiolated sodium alginate was evaluated in phosphate buffer of

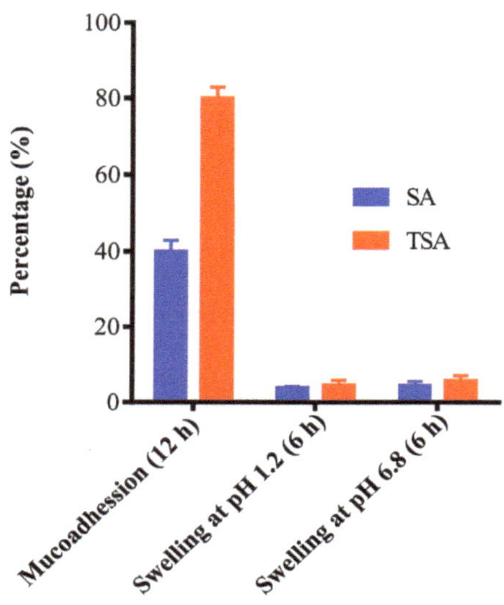

FIG. 3 Percent ex vivo mucoadhesion and percentage in vitro swelling of sodium alginate and thiolated sodium alginate at different times [61]. *Copyright © 2020, with permission from Elsevier B.V.*

pH 6.8 and the results demonstrated a sustained pattern of metformin release over a period of 12 h. The in vitro metformin release was followed the non-Fickian mechanism of drug release behavior. Schematic diagram for thiolation of sodium alginate and conversion into mucoadhesive microspheres and compressed tablets made of thiolated sodium alginate for drug release and mucoadhesive studies is presented in Fig. 4.

In a research, Kassem et al. developed mucoadhesive microbeads using thiolated sodium alginate containing resveratrol to treat periodontitis, locally [46]. In this work, thiolated sodium alginate was chemically synthesized via the conjugation of sodium alginate using thioglycolic acid. The mucoadhesive microbeads using thiolated sodium alginate containing resveratrol were formulated by ionotropic gelation technique. The selected formulation was evaluated for ex vivo mucoadhesion by wash-off method, which demonstrated good mucoadhesion. The resveratrol entrapment efficiency of these beads was ranged within 83.72%–104.54%. The in vitro resveratrol release from these mucoadhesive microbeads demonstrated a slower resveratrol release rate with zero-order kinetics. In another research, the same research group developed mucoadhesive films containing metformin using thiolated sodium alginate to treat moderate chronic periodontitis [62]. These mucoadhesive films were prepared by double casting technique followed by compression technique, where either 6% sodium alginate or sodium carboxymethylcellulose formed the inner drug-loaded (0.6%) layer and thiolated sodium alginate formed the outer drug-free layer. The prepared films were uniform and found mechanically hard enough. The optimized multiple-layer mucoadhesive films containing metformin exhibited improved mucoadhesion and controlled in vitro release of metformin over a period of 12 h. The controlled in vitro release of metformin from optimized multiple-layer mucoadhesive films containing metformin was estimated at 83.73% over 12 h.

In a recent work, Chiu et al. developed docetaxel (DTX)-loaded nanoparticles using thiolated sodium alginate for use in the treatment of colon cancer [63]. In this research, thiolated sodium alginate was synthesized using 3-mercaptopropionic acid. The synthesized thiolated sodium alginate was self-assembled and air-oxidized to produce nanoparticles under sonication via the disulfide cross-linking. The nanoparticles showing the highest DTX loading efficiency (17.80%) were selected for fluorescein-labeled wheat germ agglutinin surface conjugation to produce fluorescein-labeled wheat germ agglutinin-conjugated disulfide cross-linked nanoparticles with 14.10% conjugation efficiency. The results of in vitro drug release from these nanoparticles demonstrated a cumulative drug release of 48.6%. HT-29 human colon cancer cells treated with fluorescein-labeled wheat germ agglutinin-conjugated disulfide cross-linked nanoparticles containing DTX exhibited lower viability as compared with that of L929 mouse fibroblast cells. The obtained results clearly indicated that these

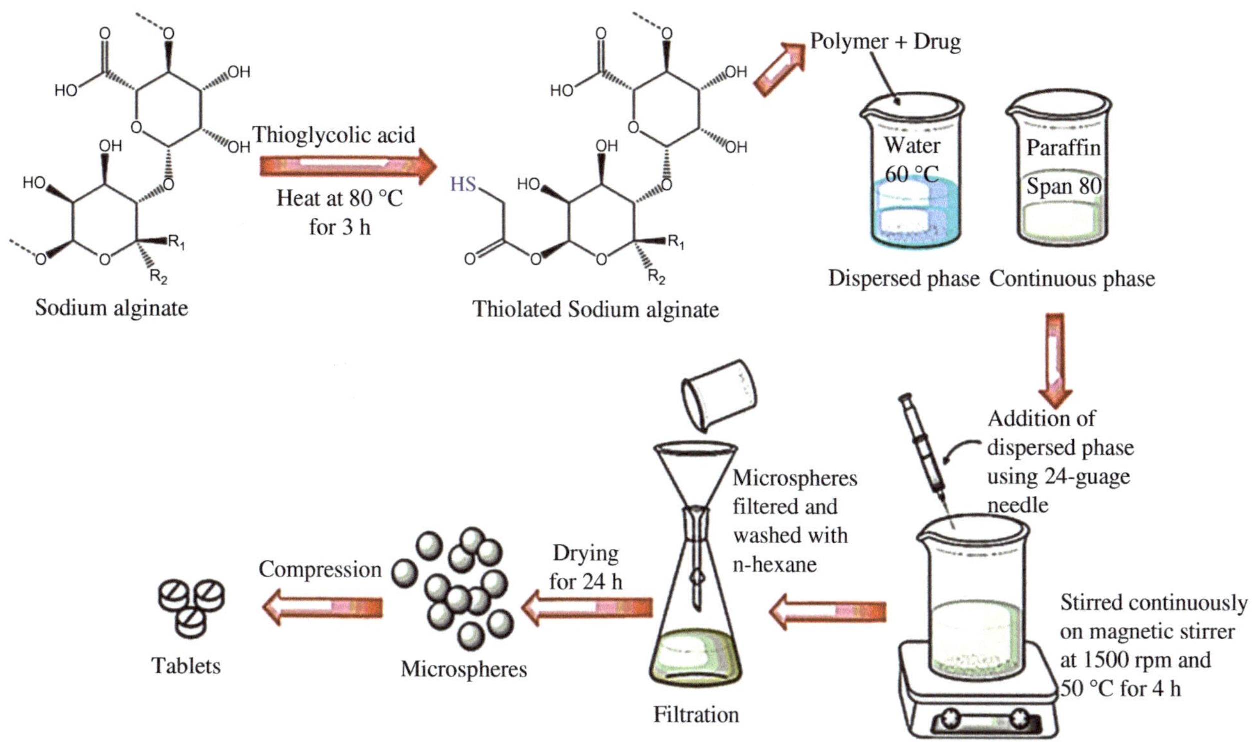

FIG. 4 Schematic diagram for thiolation of sodium alginate and conversion into mucoadhesive microspheres and compressed tablets made of thiolated sodium alginate for drug release and mucoadhesive studies [61]. *Copyright © 2020, with permission from Elsevier B.V.*

fluorescein-labeled wheat germ agglutinin-conjugated disulfide cross-linked nanoparticles containing DTX were competently taken up by HT-29 human colon cancer cells (29.90%).

Arif et al. developed thiolated alginate nanoparticles loaded budesonide for colon-specific delivery to treat inflammatory bowel diseases [64]. In this research, these nanoparticles of budesonide were formulated via the self-assembly of amphiphilic thiolated sodium alginate (sodium alginate-cysteine) and subsequently cross-linking of disulfide bonds. Transmission electron microscopy (TEM) image of these nanoparticles demonstrated a spherical core-shell configuration with approximately 430 nm sizing. The results of cytotoxicity study indicated that there was no evidence of cell inhibition by these thiolated alginate nanoparticles loaded budesonide. There was a significant augmentation in budesonide releasing in pH 7.4 buffer with glutathione from thiolated alginate nanoparticles loaded budesonide as compared with that in glutathione-free buffer, suggesting that these nanoparticles of budesonide can be useful for colon-specific delivery.

2.3 Thiolated pectin

Thiolation of pectin was carried out via esterification using thioglycolic acid [27]. Thiol substitution in the synthesized thiolated pectin was measured by Ellman's method and it was measured as 0.60 ± 0.04 mM of thiol group substitution per gram of polymer. The mechanism of thiolation reaction for pectin by using thioglycolic acid can be described by the formation of ester bonds in between hydroxyl group of galacturonic acid moieties that occurred in the pectin molecules and carboxyl group of thioglycolic acid. The mucoadhesive potential of synthesized thiolated pectin was investigated via the formulation of metformin-loaded ionotropically gelled beads of pectin and thiolated pectin. The surface morphology of these metformin-loaded beads of thiolated pectin was examined by scanning electron microscopy (SEM) observation (Fig. 5). SEM image showed spherically shaped beads with rough and grooved surface. A comparative mucoadhesivity evaluation of metformin-loaded ionotropically gelled beads of pectin and thiolated pectin was carried out by ex vivo wash-off test using goat intestinal mucosa as a mucosal membrane. The result of ex vivo mucoadhesivity evaluation demonstrated a higher ex vivo bioadhesion time for metformin-loaded beads of thiolated pectin as compared with that of metformin-loaded beads of pectin. It was seen that metformin-loaded beads of thiolated pectin showed adhesion until 5 h of the experiment while metformin-loaded beads of non-thiolated pectin were washed away within 2.5 h. In vitro release study of these metformin-loaded beads was conducted in phosphate buffer (pH 6.8) using a United States Pharmacopeia (USP) type II dissolution apparatus and the obtained results demonstrated an almost similar pattern of motorman

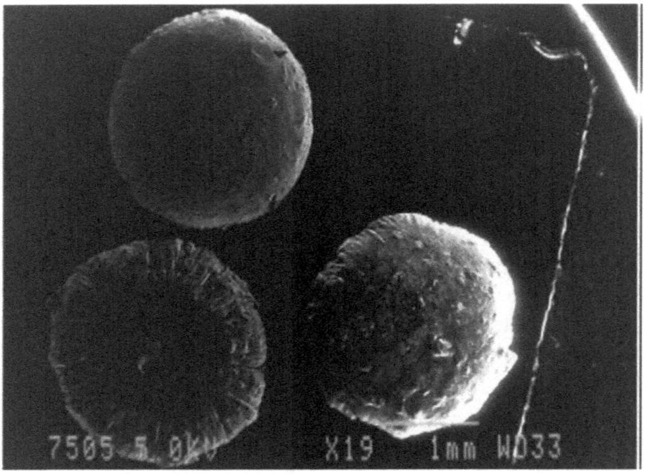

FIG. 5 SEM image of metformin-loaded ionotropically gelled beads of thiolated pectin [27]. *Copyright © 2011, with permission from Elsevier Ltd.*

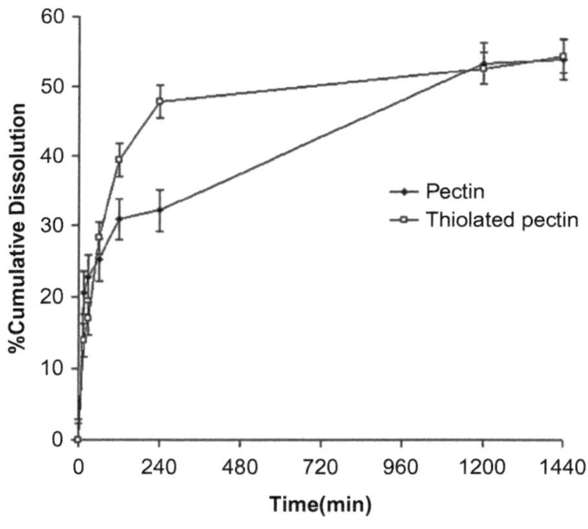

FIG. 6 In vitro release profile of metformin from metformin-loaded ionotropically gelled beads of thiolated pectin in phosphate buffer (pH 6.8) at different time intervals [27]. *Copyright © 2011, with permission from Elsevier Ltd.*

releasing from these metformin-loaded beads of pectin and thiolated pectin (Fig. 6). The overall results of this study indicated the improvement of the viscosity via thiolation of pectin with affecting drug-releasing pattern.

Cheewatanakornkool et al. developed microbeads based on thiolated pectin-doxorubicin (DOX) conjugates for oral delivery to treat colorectal cancer [65]. In this work, the thiolated pectin-DOX conjugates were formed via reducible disulfide bonds and oral microbeads were formulated using thiolated pectin-DOX conjugates via ionotropic gelation method (where Al^{3+}, Ca^{2+}, and Zn^{2+} cations were used in ionotropic cross-linking). The obtained results demonstrated that comparatively strongest microbeads with spherical shape when Zn^{2+} cations were used to prepare oral microbeads made of thiolated pectin-DOX conjugates than other cations used (Al^{3+} and Ca^{2+}). To prepare stronger as well as spherical microbeads, the native pectin was then added to the formula of these microbeads. The sizing of these microbeads made of thiolated pectin-DOX conjugates was within the range of 0.87–1.14 mm. The results of powder X-ray diffractometry demonstrated that DOX was present in the crystalline form within these microbeads. In drug release study, these microbeads made of thiolated pectin-DOX conjugates demonstrated reduction-responsive behavior. This occurrence could be attributed to the fact that the thiolated pectin-DOX conjugate could uncouple, which might be resulting from a disulfide linker-cleavage in reducing environments. These microbeads followed a zero-order release model as the best-fit model for DOX releasing in the reducing agent contained medium; whereas, these followed Korsmeyer-Peppas model as the best-fit model for DOX releasing in the medium without reducing agent. Thus, the overall results of the study indicated that these oral microbeads made of thiolated pectin-DOX conjugates can be used for the treatment of colorectal cancer. In another research, the same research group investigated the in vitro toxicity and in vivo anticancer activity of redox-responsive microbeads made of thiolated pectin-DOX conjugates [66]. These microbeads were coated by an enteric polymer for efficient colon-targeted delivery of DOX. The in vitro cytotoxicity of these coated microbeads was evaluated on mouse colon carcinoma, human bone osteosarcoma, and human colorectal adenocarcinoma cells. The results of in vitro cytotoxicity of these coated microbeads inhibited the growth of all these cell lines, significantly. The in vivo anticancer activity of these coated microbeads was evaluated in BALB/c mice with murine colon carcinoma and the results demonstrated the releasing of DOX at the colorectal tumor-site, redox-responsiveness, and anticancer efficiency of coated thiolated pectin-DOX conjugates-based microbeads. In addition, these coated microbeads were found to be inhibited primary tumor growth and suppressed the tumor metastases devoid of gross toxicity to the healthy tissues. Besides these results, any kind of noticeable damage was not found in the mouse gastrointestinal tissues, suggesting the lacking of DOX toxicity (Fig. 7).

2.4 Thiolated xanthan gum

Thiolation of xanthan gum was carried out by esterification with thioglycolic acid and mercaptopropionic acid [47]. The synthesized thiolated xanthan gum samples (xanthan-thioglycolic acid conjugate and xanthan-mercaptopropionic acid conjugate) were evaluated for its

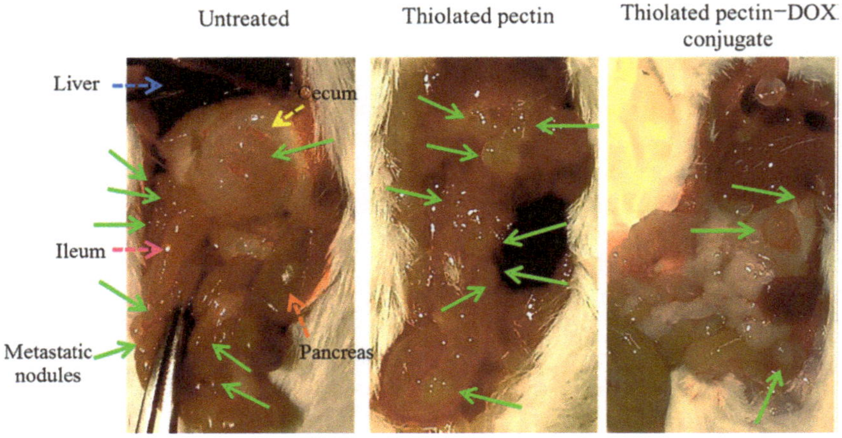

FIG. 7 Images of CT26 murine colon carcinoma bearing BALB/c mice after treating for 15 days with microbeads containing thiolated pectin and microbeads containing thiolated pectin-DOX conjugate. Untreated group was used as control. Arrows indicate the organs and metastatic nodules [66]. *Copyright © 2018, with permission from Elsevier B.V.*

mucoadhesive potential via the formulation of metronidazole-loaded buccal pellets. Thiol substitutions in the synthesized xanthan-thioglycolic acid conjugate and xanthan-mercaptopropionic acid conjugate were found to possess 432.68 and 465.02 mM of thiol groups substitutions per gram of polymer, respectively, when measured by Ellman's method. The ex vivo mucoadhesive testing using chicken buccal pouch membrane demonstrated an enhanced bioadhesion period for metronidazole-loaded buccal pellets made of thiolated xanthan gum samples as compared with that of buccal pellets made of nonthiolated xanthan gum. In addition, metronidazole-loaded buccal pellets made of xanthan-mercaptopropionic acid conjugate and xanthan–thioglycolic acid conjugate showed threefold and fivefold increments of bioadhesion periods, respectively. The enhanced ex vivo bioadhesion shown by buccal pellets made of thiolated xanthan gum samples can be attributed by the fact of the formation of disulfide bond in between thiolated xanthan gum and mucus. The results of in vitro drug release study in phosphate buffer (pH 6.8) demonstrated a sustained release profile by metronidazole-loaded buccal pellets made of thiolated xanthan gum samples as compared with that of buccal pellets made of nonthiolated xanthan gum. In addition, metronidazole-loaded buccal pellets made of xanthan-mercaptopropionic acid conjugate and xanthan-thioglycolic acid conjugate showed sustained release profiles over 5 h and 8 h, respectively. Therefore, the synthesized xanthan-mercaptopropionic acid conjugate and xanthan-thioglycolic acid conjugate can be employed as competent bioadhesive agents in sustained drug-releasing formulations.

2.5 Thiolated xyloglucan

Xyloglucan was thiolated and thiolated xyloglucan was used in formulation of various drug-delivery dosage forms. In a work, thiolated xyloglucan was synthesized via the esterification using thioglycolic acid and evaluated for its mucoadhesivity potential as gelling agent through the formulation of in situ nasal gels [67]. Thiol substitution in the synthesized thiolated xyloglucan was measured by Ellman's method and it was measured that 4 mM of thiol group substitution per gram of polymer. The synthesized thiolated xyloglucan was used as gelling agent to formulate ondansetron containing in situ gel and compared with gel prepared using pure xyloglucan. The mucoadhesivity of both the nasal gels was tested using sheep nasal mucosal tissue, ex vivo. The results of ex vivo mucoadhesivity testing revealed higher ex vivo bioadhesion time for ondansetron containing in situ gel prepared using thiolated xyloglucan as compared with ondansetron containing in situ gel prepared using xyloglucan. This result can be attributed to the fact of disulfide bond formation in between thiolated xyloglucan and mucus. Ex vivo permeation study of these ondansetron-containing in situ gels was performed using sheep nasal mucosal tissue in Franz diffusion cells and the result of this study indicated enhanced drug (ondansetron) permeation for ondansetron-containing in situ gel prepared using thiolated xyloglucan as compared with ondansetron-containing in situ gel prepared using xyloglucan. In mucosal toxicity study, the photomicrographs of sheep nasal mucosa after ex vivo permeation study of ondansetron-containing in situ gels were observed for histopathological changes (if any) with reference to the untreated sheep nasal mucosa. The mucosal section treated with ondansetron-containing in situ gels prepared using thiolated xyloglucan exhibited a very minor degeneration of nasal epithelium without any sign of erosion. Therefore, the mucosal toxicity study result clearly suggested the absence of any sign of significant destructive effect by the formulated ondansetron-containing mucoadhesive in situ gels on the treated nasal mucosa. The overall results of this work suggested that the use of thiolated xyloglucan as mucoadhesive agent in gel systems can improve the bioadhesion and drug permeation without affecting the resultant gel characteristics.

In a research, Madgulkar et al. developed thiolated xyloglucan nanoparticles loaded with antiviral drug, acyclovir, to increase its oral bioavailability [50]. These thiolated xyloglucan nanoparticles of acyclovir were lyophilized by using a cryoprotectant. The formulation optimization of these nanoparticles was carried out by using Box Behnken Design. The thiolated xyloglucan nanoparticles of acyclovir exhibited 474.40 ± 2.01 nm particle size and 81.57% acyclovir entrapment efficiency. In mucoadhesion study, a noticeable improvement of mucoadhesion was recorded by these thiolated xyloglucan nanoparticles of acyclovir. The in vivo evaluation of these thiolated xyloglucan nanoparticles of acyclovir in a rat model demonstrated an improvement of relative bioavailability of acyclovir (~ 2.575-fold) as compared with that of the marketed suspension of acyclovir. In another work, the same research group formulated the microspheres of lopinavir using thiolated xyloglucan to improve the oral bioavailability of lopinavir without coadministration of ritonavir [68]. These thiolated xyloglucan microspheres were formulated by ionotropic gelation using alginic acid and calcium ions. The formulation optimization of these microspheres was carried out by using 3^2 Factorial designs. The optimized formulation revealed 93.12% lopinavir entrapment efficiency and time for 80% drug release was estimated at 358.10 min. The optimized microspheres showed 88% mucoadhesion after a period of 1 h in in vitro wash-off test. The ex vivo permeation of lopinavir from optimized thiolated xyloglucan microspheres was found to be improved 3.15 times when tested using everted chick intestine. The in vivo evaluation in a rat model demonstrated an increment of relative bioavailability over 3.22-fold over the combination of lopinavir and ritonavir.

In another work, xyloglucan was thiolated by using cysteine and the mucoadhesive potential of the thiolated xyloglucan was investigated by formulation of glipizide-loaded microspheres using sodium trimetaphosphate as crosslinking agent [69]. The mucoadhesivity and drug-releasing potentials of glipizide-loaded thiolated xyloglucan microspheres were compared with those of the glipizide-loaded xyloglucan microspheres. The surface morphologies of these glipizide-loaded xyloglucans and thiolated xyloglucan microspheres were examined by SEM observation and results presented in Fig. 8. Glipizide-loaded thiolated xyloglucan microspheres were found very close to spherical-shape morphology with a rougher surface, which might be due to aggregation of microspheres and faster gelation of thiomer. On the other hand, glipizide-loaded xyloglucan microspheres were also very close to spherical-shape with slightly rough surface morphology than that of thiolated xyloglucan microspheres. In

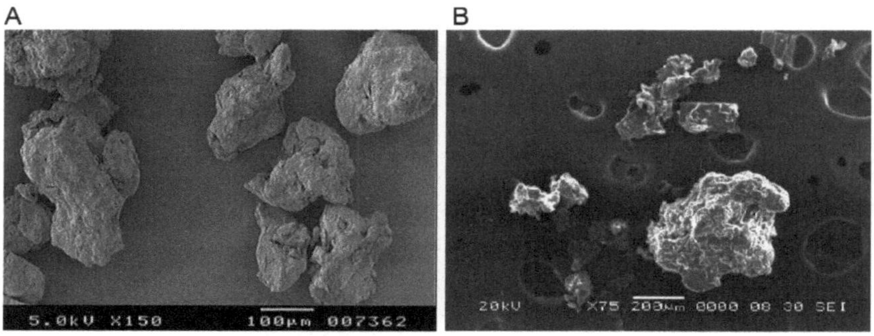

FIG. 8 Scanning electron microscopy of (A) xyloglucan microspheres and (B) thiolated xyloglucan microspheres [69]. *Copyright © 2014, with permission from Elsevier B.V.*

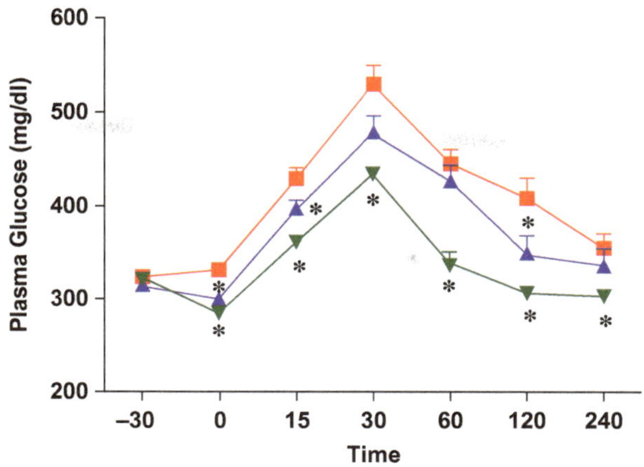

FIG. 9 Results of oral glucose tolerance test: (■) diabetic control, (▲) xyloglucan microspheres, and (▼) thiolated xyloglucan microspheres. *$P < .05$ vs. diabetic control [69]. *Copyright © 2014, with permission from Elsevier B.V.*

oral glucose tolerance test using alloxan-induced diabetic Wistar albino rats, glipizide-loaded thiolated xyloglucan microspheres exhibited better control with a significant reduction ($P < .05$) in blood glucose levels as compared with glipizide-loaded xyloglucan microspheres (Fig. 9).

2.6 Thiolated karaya gum

Thiolated karaya gum was synthesized to explore its mucoadhesivity and sustained drug releasing via the formulation of directly compressible tablets containing metoprolol succinate [70]. In this work, the thiolation of karaya gum was carried out by using 80% thioglycolic acid and 7N HCl via the formation of ester bonding in between –OH groups of karaya gum –COOH groups of thioglycolic acid. The yield (avg.) of thiolated karaya gum was estimated 45% and its color was white to buff. In cytotoxixity study (in vitro) using HepG2 cell line, thiolated karaya gum exhibited almost similar result of cell viability as compared with that of unmodified karaya gum. In the whole, the results of in vitro cytotoxicity study indicated the biocompatibility of synthesized thiolated karaya gum. In this work, unmodified karaya gum and thiolated karaya gum were compressed using a rotary compression machine to prepare metoprolol succinate tablets. The results of disintegration test demonstrated that the compressed tablets made of unmodified karaya gum disintegrated within 30 and 45 min in 0.1 N HCl and pH 6.8 phosphate buffer, respectively; whereas, compressed tablets made of thiolated karaya gum remained stable for more than a period of 10 h in both the media. In swelling (in vitro) study, maximum swelling was noticed after 24 h as 88.76% and 89.24% in

0.1 N HCl and pH 6.8 phosphate buffer, respectively. Ex vivo mucoadhesion study on the metoprolol succinate compressed tablets was carried out using freshly excised goat gastric and intestinal mucosa in acidic pH (0.1 N HCl) and alkaline pH (pH 6.8 phosphate buffer), respectively. Ex vivo residence time of metoprolol succinate compressed tablets made of thiolated karaya gum was found to be increased by sevenfold and 15-fold in acidic pH and in alkaline pH, respectively, as compared with metoprolol succinate compressed tablets made of unmodified karaya gum. In vitro drug release from metoprolol succinate compressed tablets made of unmodified and thiolated karaya gum was evaluated in acidic pH (0.1 N HCl) and alkaline pH (pH 6.8 phosphate buffer). Metoprolol succinate compressed tablets made of thiolated karaya gum showed 76.2% drug release in acidic pH and 46.14% drug release in alkaline pH media even after 24 h. Overall, the in vitro drug release results indicated a sustained pattern of drug releasing from the compressed tablets made of thiolated karaya gum.

2.7 Thiolated tamarind seed polysaccharide

In a work, tamarind seed polysaccharide was thiolated employing thioglycolic acid with HCl (at 80°C for 180 min) to explore the potential of thiolated tamarind seed polysaccharide as mucoadhesive agent [49]. In the thiolation process employing thioglycolic acid with HCl, the reaction occurs between hydroxyl group of galactoxylan (present in tamarind seed polysaccharide) and carboxyl group (present in thioglycolic acid). The synthesized thiolated tamarind seed polysaccharide was found to be water-soluble and off-white in color. Thiol group content in the synthesized thiolated product was estimated by Ellman's method and 104.5 mM thiol groups were estimated to be present per gram of polymer. Mucoadhesive potential was estimated by preparing compact of both thiolated and nonthiolated tamarind seed polysaccharide by compression method and subsequently, evaluated by texture analysis and mucin dispersion study. The thiolated tamarind seed polysaccharide exhibited a 6.85-fold stronger mucoadhesive potential than that of the nonthiolated tamarind seed polysaccharide. Mucoadhesive gels were prepared using thiolated and nonthiolated tamarind seed polysaccharide, in which metronidazole was used as a model drug and Carbopol 974P was used as a gelling agent. Mucoadhesive potential of these metronidazole gels was determined using a modified pan analytical balance and fresh chicken intestinal mucosa. Maximum mucoadhesive strength was noticed in case of metronidazole gel prepared using thiolated tamarind seed polysaccharide. A dissolution apparatus was used to study in vitro drug release from these metronidazole gels by dialysis bag method. The test gels were taken individually in a dialysis bag and attached to the paddle of dissolution apparatus. A phosphate buffer of pH 6.8 was used at 37°C for this purpose at a rotation speed of 100 rpm. The metronidazole gel prepared using thiolated tamarind seed polysaccharide followed Higuchi's square root release kinetics, whereas metronidazole gel prepared using nonthiolated polysaccharide followed first-order release kinetics. These metronidazole gels (prepared using thiolated and nonthiolated tamarind seed polysaccharide) were compared with available marketed gel preparations of metronidazole and showed promising mucoadhesive potential for the thiolated tamarind seed polysaccharide. From the results of in vitro drug release, it was found that marketed gel preparations of metronidazole (i.e., Metrogyl) exhibited the slowest metronidazole releasing followed by metronidazole gels prepared using thiolated tamarind seed polysaccharide and the fastest release of drug occurred from metronidazole gels prepared using nonthiolated tamarind seed polysaccharide (Fig. 10).

2.8 Thiolated psyllium husk mucilage and arabinoxylan

Psyllium husk mucilage was thiolated by Bhatia and Ahuja using thioglycolic acid to explore mucoadhesive potential of the synthesized thiolated psyllium husk mucilage [51]. In this work, 2M thioglycolic acid in

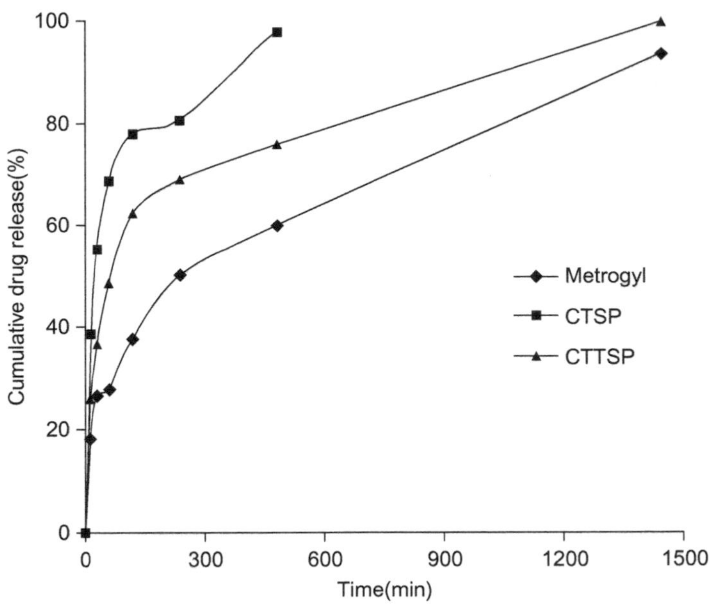

FIG. 10 In vitro release profile of metronidazole from various gel formulations (Key: CTSP = metronidazole gels prepared using nonthiolated tamarind seed polysaccharide; CTTSP = metronidazole gels prepared using thiolated tamarind seed polysaccharide; Metrogyl = marketed gel preparations of metronidazole) [49]. *Copyright © 2012, with permission from Elsevier Ltd.*

presence of HCl was used for every mole of hydroxyl group in psyllium husk. Reaction was allowed for 90 min at 70°C. Yield percentage of synthesized thiolated psyllium husk mucilage was 91.80%. Thiol group content was estimated to be 3.282 ± 1.051 mM/g. Ellman's method was used for the estimation of thiol substitution in the newly synthesized thiolated psyllium husk mucilage. Thiolation has changed the morphological properties of the psyllium as it was observed that fibrous nature of the material changed to granular one with enhanced swelling capacity and crystallinity. Scanning electron microscopic image revealed that particles of both thiolated and nonthiolated materials were polyhedral. Thiolated material was amorphous and nonthiolated material was granular. In this work, mucoadhesive gels were formulated by dispersing 2% of thiolated and nonthiolated psyllium husk mucilage, in which metronidazole was used drug to explore the mucoadhesive capacity of the thiolated psyllium husk mucilage. A modified balance was used to determine mucoadhesive strength in which fresh chicken buccal mucosa was attached to a glass slide at the bottom of one pan and the base. Gel was applied in the middle. There was threefold increase in mucoadhesive potential of the psyllium husk mucilage as compared with nonthiolated psyllium husk mucilage. In the in vitro drug release study results, the release time of the metronidazole from the gel prepared by thiolated psyllium husk mucilage was found to be increased. The in vitro drug release from these metronidazole gels made of thiolated psyllium husk mucilage was found to follow the first-order kinetics with the mechanism of diffusion and polymer relaxation through the gel-matrix.

In another research, Hanif and Zaman synthesized thiolated arabinoxylan to explore mucoadhesive and controlled release potential via the formulation of oral films [71]. In this work, thiolated arabinoxylan was synthesized by esterification of thiol group of thioglycolic acid with arabinoxylan extracted from psyllium (ispaghula) husk in presence of a catalytic quantity of HCl. Oral mucoadhesive film was prepared by mixing solution of thiolated arabinoxylan, glycerin, HPMC, and tizanidine (as test drug) in a magnetic stirrer with a hot plate. The mixture was then poured into a Petri dish and dried to form thin film. The prepared polymeric film showed good folding endurance and uniformity in weight and thickness. A modified "two pan" analytical balance was used for ex vivo mucoadhesive evaluation of the film. Fresh buccal mucosa of goat was used for this purpose. The study revealed an enhanced ex vivo mucoadhesion due to covalent bond formation in between the polymer and the mucus membrane. It was found that ex vivo mucoadhesion capacity increased with the increasing polymer concentration used in the formulation of oral film. Franz diffusion cell was used to determine ex vivo permeation rate, where phosphate buffer pH 6.8 was utilized as a medium. Fresh goat mucosa was placed in between the receptor and donor cell in which a film strip was mounted. From the results of ex vivo permeation, it was noticed that the percentage of permeated drug was decreased with the increase of polymer concentration used in the formulation of oral film.

2.9 Thiolated moringa gum

In a work, moringa gum (obtained from *Moringa olifera* tree) was treated using thioglycolic acid in the presence of 7N HCl for 150 min at 80°C to synthesize thiolated moringa gum [72]. The obtained thiolated material was odorless white powder and the yield percentage was estimated at 83%. Thiol substitution in the synthesized thiolated moringa gum was measured by Ellman's method and it was measured that 0.956 ± 0.024 mM of thiol group substitution per gram of gum. Biocompatibility study revealed that both thiolated and nonthiolated moringa gum form less blood clots compared with a positive control. Percentages of thrombose formation for thiolated and unthiolated gum were 78.47% and 50.91%, respectively. The synthesized thiolated moringa gum was tested as a bioadhesive polymer through the formulation of mucoadhesive buccal tablets. These tablets were prepared in several batches with variable amount of thiolated and nonthiolated polymers using polyethylene glycol 4000 (PEG 4000) and variable amount of lactose. Metronidazole benzoate was used as a test drug in these mucoadhesive buccal tablets. Study of compression behavior revealed that both thiolated and nonthiolated moringa gum possessed plastic behavior as bending strength increased with the dwell time and decreased with the blending time. It was observed that drug content, average weight, thickness, etc., of these tablets were within the standard range. Adhesion property was determined by a texture profile analyzer. It was observed that detachment force of tablets prepared by thiolated moringa gum was found much more than the tablets prepared by nonthiolated moringa gum. Thus, the result suggested the mucoadhesive nature of the thiolated moringa gum. Fresh buccal pouch of a chick was attached to the side paddle of a dissolution apparatus in which Mcllvaine buffer of pH 6.8 was used at 37°C to determine ex vivo bioadhesion time. Tablets were pasted into the inner side of the pouch with application of little pressure and paddle was allowed to rotate at 50 rpm. Time required by the tablets to detach itself from the pouch was noted as the bioadhesion time. An increase in bioadhesion time was observed to be 1.5-fold in case of the thiolated moringa gum tablets. Dissolution apparatus was used for in vitro drug release study of buccal tablets prepared with moringa gum. Tablets were attached at the bottom of the 250 mL beaker with the help of cyanoacrylate adhesive and filled with Mcllvaine buffer of pH 6.8 and temperature was maintained at approximately 37°C with 50 rpm rotation speed. From the in vitro drug release results, it was observed that drug release rate of buccal tablets prepared using thiolated moringa gum was several times slower than the buccal tablets prepared using nonthiolated moringa gum.

Mechanism of release of drug from these buccal tablets prepared using thiolated moringa gum might be due to erosion and diffusion while release of drug from buccal tablets prepared using nonthiolated moringa gum might be due to diffusion through matrix. The overall results of this work clearly demonstrated that the thiolation of moringa gum can improve mucoadhesive property with drug release retardance property.

3 Conclusion

Thiol-modification (thiolation) of various natural polysaccharides considerably improves the biomucoadhesivity of the polysaccharides to be used as mucoadhesive excipients in the formulations of various mucoadhesive drug delivery systems. The improved efficacy of thiolated natural polysaccharides made mucoadhesive drug delivery systems have already been demonstrated by many studies, both in vitro and in vivo. On the whole, according to the reported works on the uses of thiolated natural polysaccharides in drug delivery, it has been clear that these thiolated natural polysaccharides have successfully been maintained the balance in between the excellent biomucoadhesivity with prolonged residence period at the desired sites, controlled releasing of drugs over a longer period, and acceptability as drug delivery excipients.

References

[1] Bilal M, Gul I, Basharat A, Qamar SA. Polysaccharides-based bio-nanostructures and their potential food applications. Int J Biol Macromol 2021;176:540–57.
[2] Pilnik W, Rombouts FM. Polysaccharides and food processing. Carbohydr Res 1985;142(1):93–105.
[3] Maity M, Hasnain MS, Nayak AK, Aminabavi TM. Biomedical applications of polysaccharides. In: Nayak AK, Hasnain MS, Aminabhavi TM, editors. Tailor-made polysaccharides in biomedical applications. United States: Academic Press, Elsevier Inc.; 2021. p. 1–34.
[4] Nayak AK, Hasnain MS, Dhara AK, Pal D. Plant polysaccharides in pharmaceutical applications. In: Pal D, Nayak AK, editors. Bioactive natural products for pharmaceutical applications. Advanced structured materials, vol. 140. Cham: Springer; 2021. p. 93–125.
[5] Pandey S. A comprehensive review on recent developments in bentonite-based materials used as adsorbents for waste water treatment. J Mol Liq 2017;241:1091–113.
[6] Pandey S, Ramontja J. Rapid, facile microwave-assisted synthesis of xanthan gum grafted polyaniline for chemical sensor. Int J Biol Macromol 2016;89:89–98.
[7] Pawar HA, Kamat SR, Choudhary PD. An overview of natural polysaccharides as biological macromolecules: their chemical modification and pharmaceuticals applications. Biol Med 2015;7(1):1–9.
[8] Nayak AK, Hasnain MS. Plant polysaccharides in drug delivery applications. In: Nayak AK, Hasnain MS, editors. Plant polysaccharides-based multiple-unit systems for oral drug delivery. Singapore: Springer; 2019. p. 19–23.
[9] Nayak AK, Hasnain MS. Some other plant polysaccharide based multiple units for oral drug delivery. In: Nayak AK, Hasnain MS, editors. Plant polysaccharides-based multiple-unit systems for oral drug delivery. Singapore: Springer; 2019. p. 123–1128.

[10] Milivojevic M, Pajic-Lijakovic I, Bugarski B, Nayak AK, Hasnain MS. Gellan gum in drug delivery applications. In: Hasnain MS, Nayak AK, editors. Natural polysaccharides in drug delivery and biomedical applications. United States: Academic Press, Elsevier Inc; 2019. p. 145–86.
[11] Nayak AK, Hasnain MS. Linseed polysaccharide based multiple units for oral drug delivery. In: Nayak AK, Hasnain MS, editors. Plant polysaccharides-based multiple-unit systems for oral drug delivery. Singapore: Springer; 2019. p. 117–21.
[12] Nayak AK, Ahmed SA, Tabish M, Hasnain MS. Natural polysaccharides in tissue engineering application. In: Hasnain MS, Nayak AK, editors. Natural polysaccharides in drug delivery and biomedical applications. United States: Academic Press, Elsevier Inc.; 2019. p. 531–48.
[13] Hasnain MS, Ahmad SA, Chaudhary N, Hoda MN, Nayak AK. Biodegradable polymer matrix nanocomposites for bone tissue engineering. In: Inamuddin, Asiri AM, Mohammad A, editors. Applications of nanocomposite materials in orthopedics. Woodhead publishing series in biomaterials. United States: Elsevier Inc; 2019. p. 1–37.
[14] Pal D, Nayak AK. Plant polysaccharides-blended ionotropically-gelled alginate multiple-unit systems for sustained drug release. In: Thakur VK, Thakur MK, Kessler MR, editors. Handbook of composites from renewable materials. Polymeric composites, vol. 6. USA: WILEY-Scrivener; 2017. p. 399–400.
[15] Nayak AK, Mohanta BC, Hasnain MS, Hoda MN, Tripathi G. Alginate-based scaffolds for drug delivery in tissue engineering. In: Nayak AK, Hasnain MS, editors. Alginates in drug delivery. United States: Academic Press, Elsevier Inc.; 2020. p. 359–86.
[16] Kurakula M, Rao GSNK, Kiran V, Hasnain MS, Nayak AK. Alginate-based hydrogel systems for drug releasing in wound healing. In: Nayak AK, Hasnain MS, editors. Alginates in drug delivery. United States: Academic Press, Elsevier Inc.; 2020. p. 323–58.
[17] Rana V, Rai P, Tiwary AK, Singh RS, Kennedy JF, Knill Charles J. Modified gums: approaches and applications in drug delivery. Carbohydr Polym 2011;83:1031–47.
[18] Makhado E, Pandey S, Ramontja J. Microwave assisted synthesis of xanthan gum-cl-poly (acrylic acid) based-reduced graphene oxide hydrogel composite for adsorption of methylene blue and methyl violet from aqueous solution. Int J Biol Macromol 2018;119:255–69.
[19] Makhado E, Pandey S, Nomngongo PN, Ramontja J. Preparation and characterization of xanthan gum-cl-poly(acrylic acid)/o-MWCNTs hydrogel nanocomposite as highly effective re-usable adsorbent for removal of methylene blue from aqueous solutions. J Colloid Interface Sci 2018;513:700–14.
[20] Banegas RS, Zornic CF, Borges ADMG, Porto LC, Soldi V. Preparation, characterization and properties of films obtained from cross linked guar gum. Polimeros 2013;23:182–3.
[21] Sen SO, Nayak AK, Devbhuti P, Ghosh A. Modification of gums by periodate oxidation: a natural cross-linker. Int J Pharm Pharm Sci 2019;11:1–6.
[22] Wang J, Bao A, Wang Q, Guo H, Zhang Y, Liang J, Kong W, Yao J, Zhang J. Sulfation can enhance antitumor activities of *Artemisia sphaerocephala* polysaccharide *in vitro* and *vivo*. Int J Biol Macromol 2018;107(Pt A):502–11.
[23] Rao MR, Warrier DU, Gaikwad SR, Shevate PM. Phosphorylation of psyllium seed polysaccharide and its characterization. Int J Biol Macromol 2016;85:317–26.
[24] Das B, Dutta S, Nayak AK, Nanda U. Zinc alginate-carboxymethyl cashew gum microbeads for prolonged drug release: development and optimization. Int J Biol Macromol 2014;70:505–15.
[25] Singh RS, Kaur N, Rana V, Singla RK, Kang N, Kaur G, Kaur H, Kennedy JF. Carbamoylethyl locust bean gum: synthesis, characterization and evaluation of its film forming potential. Int J Biol Macromol 2020;149:348–58.
[26] Silva SCCC, Braz EMA, Brito CARS, Alves MMM, Carvalho FAA, Barreto HM, Oliveira AL, Silva DA, Silva-Filho EC. Phthalic anhydride esterified chicha gum: characterization and antibacterial activity. Carbohydr Polym 2021;251:117077.
[27] Sharma R, Ahuja M. Thiolated pectin: synthesis, characterization and evaluation as a mucoadhesive polymer. Carbohydr Polym 2011;85:658–63.

[28] Nayak AK, Bera H, Hasnain MS, Pal D. Synthesis and characterization of graft-copolymers of plant polysaccharides. In: Thakur VK, editor. Biopolymer grafting, synthesis and properties. Netherlands: Elsevier Inc.; 2018. p. 1–62.
[29] Pal D, Nayak AK. Interpenetrating polymer networks (IPNs): natural polymeric blends for drug delivery. In: Mishra M, editor. Encyclopedia of biomedical polymers and polymeric biomaterials, vol. VI. New York: Taylor and Francis; 2015. p. 4120–30.
[30] Hasnain MS, Ray P, Nayak AK. Alginate-based interpenetrating polymer networks for sustained drug release. In: Nayak AK, Hasnain MS, editors. Alginates in drug delivery. United States: Academic Press, Elsevier Inc.; 2020. p. 101–28.
[31] Mohanta BC, Javed MN, Hasnain MS, Nayak AK. Polyelectrolyte complexes of alginate for controlling drug release. In: Nayak AK, Hasnain MS, editors. Alginates in drug delivery. United States: Academic Press, Elsevier Inc.; 2020. p. 297–321.
[32] Alkahtani S, Hasnain MS, Nayak AK, Aminabhavi TM. Polysaccharide-based polyelectrolyte complex systems for biomedical uses. In: Nayak AK, Hasnain MS, Aminabhavi TM, editors. Tailor-made polysaccharides in biomedical applications. USA: Academic Press, Elsevier Inc.; 2021. p. 151–74.
[33] Duggan S, Cummins W, O'Donovan O, Hughes H, Owens E. Thiolated polymers as mucoadhesive drug delivery systems. Eur J Pharm Sci 2017;100:64–78.
[34] Hombach J, Bernkop-Schnürch A. Mucoadhesive drug delivery systems. Handb Exp Pharmacol 2010;197:251–66.
[35] Bernkop-Schnurch A. Thiomers: a new generation of mucoadhesive polymers. Adv Drug Deliv Rev 2005;57:1569–82.
[36] Bernkop-Schnurch A, Kast CE, Richter MF. Improvement in the mucoadhesive properties of alginate by the covalent attachment of cysteine. J Control Release 2001;71:277–85.
[37] Bernkop-Schnurch A, Schwarz V, Steininger S. Polymers with thiol groups: a new generation of mucoadhesive polymers. Pharm Res 1999;16:876–81.
[38] Ijaz M, Matuszczak B, Rahmat D, Mahmood A, Bonengel S, Hussain S, Huck CW, Bernkop-Schnürch A. Synthesis and characterization of thiolated-cyclodextrin as a novel mucoadhesive excipient for intra-oral drug delivery. Carbohydr Polym 2015;132:187–95.
[39] Anitha A, Deepa N, Chennazhi KP, Nair SV, Tamura H, Jayakumar R. Development of mucoadhesive thiolated chitosan nanoparticles for biomedical applications. Carbohydr Polym 2011;83:66–73.
[40] Bernkop-Schnurch A. Polymer-inhibitor conjugates: a promising strategy to overcome the enzymatic barrier to perorally administered (poly)peptide drugs. STP Pharma Sci 1999;9:78–87.
[41] Bernkop-Schnurch A, Walker G, Zarti H. Thiolation of polycarbophil enhances its inhibition of intestinal brush border membrane bound aminopeptidase N. J Pharm Sci 2001;90(11):1907–14.
[42] Werle M, Hoffer M. Glutathione and thiolated chitosan inhibit multidrug resistance P-glycoprotein activity in excised small intestine. J Control Release 2006;111(1–2):41–6.
[43] Bernkop-Schnurch A, Kast CE, Guggi D. Permeation enhancing polymers in oral delivery of hydrophilic macromolecules: thiomer/GSH systems. J Control Release 2003;93(2):95–103.
[44] Krauland AH, Leitner VM, Bernkop-Schnurch A. Improvement in the in situ gelling properties of deacetylaed gellan gum by immobilization of thiol groups. J Pharm Sci 2003;92:1234–41.
[45] Mahmood A, Lanthaler M, Laffleur F, Huck CW, Bernkop-Schnürch A. Thiolated chitosan micelles: highly mucoadhesive drug carriers. Carbohydr Polym 2017;167:250–8.
[46] Kassem AA, Farid RM, Issa DA, Khalil DS, Abd-El-Razzak MY, Saudi HI, Eltokhey HM, El-Zamarany EA. Development of mucoadhesive microbeads using thiolated sodium alginate for intrapocket delivery of resveratrol. Int J Pharm 2015;487(1–2):305–13.
[47] Bhatia M, Ahuja M, Mehta H. Thiol derivatization of xanthan gum and its evaluation as a mucoadhesive polymer. Carbohydr Polym 2015;131:119–24.

[48] Rimpy A, Ahuja M. Evaluation of carboxymethyl Moringa gum as nanometric carrier. Carbohydr Polym 2017;174:896–903.
[49] Kaur H, Yadav S, Ahuja M, Dilbagi N. Synthesis, characterization and evaluation of thiolated tamarind seed polysaccharide as a mucoadhesive polymer. Carbohydr Polym 2012;90:1543–9.
[50] Madgulkar A, Bhalekar MR, Dikpati AA. Improving oral bioavailability of acyclovir using nanoparticulates of thiolated xyloglucan. Int J Biol Macromol 2016;89:689–99.
[51] Bhatia M, Ahuja M. Thiol modification of psyllium husk mucilage and evaluation of its mucoadhesive applications. Scientific World Journal 2013;1–7.
[52] Shahnaz G, Kremser C, Reinisch A, et al. Efficient MRI labeling of endothelial progenitor cells: design of thiolated surface stabilized superparamagnetic iron oxide nanoparticles. Eur J Pharm Biopharm 2013;85:346–55.
[53] Hornof MD, Kast CE, Bernkop-Schnürch A. *In vitro* evaluation of the viscoelastic properties of chitosan-thioglycolic acid conjugates. Eur J Pharm Biopharm 2003;55:185–90.
[54] Kafedjiiski K, Krauland AH, Hoffer MH, Bernkop-Schnürch A. Synthesis and *in vitro* evaluation of a novel thiolated chitosan. Biomaterials 2005;26:819–26.
[55] Bernkop-Schnürch A, Brandt U-M, Clausen A. Synthese und *in vitro* evaluierung von chitosan-cystein konjugaten. Sci Pharm 1999;67:197–208.
[56] Schmitz T, Hombach J, Bernkop-Schnürch A. Chitosan-N-acetyl cysteine conjugates: in vitro evaluation of permeation enhancing and P-glycoprotein inhibiting properties. Drug Deliv 2008;15:245–52.
[57] Millotti G, Samberger C, Fröhlich E, Bernkop-Schnürch A. Chitosan-graft-6-mercaptonicotinic acid: synthesis, characterization, and biocompatibility. Biomacromolecules 2009;10:3023–7.
[58] Millotti G, Samberger C, Fröhlich E, Sakloetsakun D, Bernkop-Schnürch A. Chitosan-4-mercaptobenzoic acid: synthesis and characterization of a novel thiolated chitosan. J Mater Chem 2010;20:2432–40.
[59] Sudhakar S, Chandran SV, Selvamurugan N, Nazeer RA. Biodistribution and pharmacokinetics of thiolated chitosan nanoparticles for oral delivery of insulin in vivo. Int J Biol Macromol 2020;150:281–8.
[60] Sakloetsakun D, Perera G, Hombach J, Millotti G, Bernkop-Schnürch A. The impact of vehicles on the mucoadhesive properties of orally administrated nanoparticles: a case study with chitosan-4-thiobutylamidine conjugate. AAPS PharmSciTech 2010;11:1185–92.
[61] Khalid S, Abbas G, Hanif M, Shah S, Shah SNH, Jalil A, Yaqoob M, Ameer N, Anum A. Thiolated sodium alginate conjugates for mucoadhesive and controlled release behavior of metformin microspheres. Int J Biol Macromol 2020;164:2691–700.
[62] Kassem AA, Issa DA, Kotry GS, Farid RM. Thiolated alginate-based multiple layer mucoadhesive films of metformin forintra-pocket local delivery: in vitro characterization and clinical assessment. Drug Dev Ind Pharm 2017;43(1):120–31.
[63] Chiu HI, Ayub AD, Mat Yusuf SNA, Yahaya N, Abbd Kadir E, Lim V. Docetaxel-loaded disulfide cross-linked nanoparticles derived from thiolated sodium alginate for colon cancer drug delivery. Pharmaceutics 2020;12(1):38.
[64] Arif M, Chi Z, Liu YJ, Liu CG. Preparation, characterization, and *in vitro* drug release behavior of thiolated alginate nanoparticles loaded budesonide as a potential drug delivery system toward inflammatory bowel diseases. J Biomater Sci Polym Ed 2020;31(18):2299–317.
[65] Cheewatanakornkool K, Niratisai S, Manchun S, Dass CR, Sriamornsak P. Characterization and *in vitro* release studies of oral microbeads containing thiolated pectin-doxorubicin conjugates for colorectal cancer treatment. Asian J Pharm Sci 2017;12(6):509–20.
[66] Cheewatanakornkool K, Niratisai S, Dass CR, Sriamornsak P. Redox-responsive microbeads containing thiolated pectin-doxorubicin conjugate inhibit tumor growth and metastasis: an in vitro and in vivo study. Int J Pharm 2018;545(1–2):1–9.

[67] Mahajan HS, Tyagi VK, Patil RR, Dusunge SB. Thiolated xyloglucan: synthesis, characterization and evaluation as mucoadhesive in situ gelling agent. Carbohydr Polym 2013;91(2):618–25.
[68] Madgulkar AR, Bhalekar MR, Kadam AA. Improvement of oral bioavailability of lopinavir without co-administration of ritonavir using microspheres of thiolated xyloglucan. AAPS PharmSciTech 2018;19(1):293–302.
[69] Sonawane S, Bhalekar M, Shimpi S. Preparation and evaluation of microspheres of xyloglucan and its thiolated xyloglucan derivative. Int J Biol Macromol 2014;69:499–505.
[70] Bahulkar SS, Munot NM, Surwase SS. Synthesis, characterization of thiolated karaya gum and evaluation of effect of pH on its mucoadhesive and sustained release properties. Carbohydr Polym 2015;130:183–90.
[71] Hanif M, Zaman M. Thiolation of arabinoxylan and its application in the fabrication of controlled release mucoadhesive oral films. Daru 2017;25(1):6.
[72] Grewal P, Mundlia J, Ahuja M. Thiol modified Moringa gum—a potential bioadhesive polymer. Carbohydr Polym 2019;209:400–8.

CHAPTER

5

Cross-linked polysaccharides in drug delivery

Mohsen Khodadadi Yazdi[a], *Ali Khodadadi*[b], *Payam Zarrintaj*[c], *Mohammad Reza Ganjali*[a,d], *Foad Salehnia*[a], *Morteza Rezapour*[e], *Sajjad Habibzadeh*[f], *and Mohammad Reza Saeb*[g]

[a]Center of Excellence in Electrochemistry, School of Chemistry, College of Science, University of Tehran, Tehran, Iran, [b]Department of Internal Medicine, School of Medicine, Gonabad University of Medical Sciences, Gonabad, Iran, [c]School of Chemical Engineering, Oklahoma State University, Stillwater, OK, United States, [d]Biosensor Research Center, Endocrinology and Metabolism Molecular-Cellular Sciences Institute, Tehran University of Medical Sciences, Tehran, Iran, [e]IP Department, Research Institute of Petroleum Industry (RIPI), Tehran, Iran, [f]Department of Chemical Engineering, Amirkabir University of Technology (Tehran Polytechnic), Tehran, Iran, [g]Department of Polymer Technology, Faculty of Chemistry, Gdańsk University of Technology, Gdańsk, Poland

1 Introduction

Therapeutic agents are known as the major part of the body of medicine in the realm of knowledge, so that the global market of them has reached \$1200 billion in 2018 [1]. Traditionally, many drugs have been delivered to the human body and their beneficial and hazardous features have been stressed by the specialists of the biomaterial and medicine fields. The main disadvantage of conventional drug delivery systems arises from the inability to keep the dosage of drugs under control, as well as the low possibility of drug targeting the action sites. However, modern pharmaceutical technologists benefit from biomaterials that provide the user with

Tailor-Made Polysaccharides in Drug Delivery
https://doi.org/10.1016/B978-0-12-821286-8.00005-7

an intimate and also a prolonged contact at the site of administration [2]. However, systematic delivery systems designed for drugs may result in some adverse side effects such as hair loss, vomiting, fatigue, and nausea for cancer chemotherapeutics. In addition, frequent utilization of drugs, especially for the parenterally administered drugs, is accompanied by pain and inconvenience. Accordingly, there has been a meaningful trend in the use of methods and systems working on the basis of the substitution of systemic delivery to the localized and controlled delivery systems [3,4]. Drug delivery systems (DDSs) have been widely studied in the last 70 years. In the meantime, the development of novel therapeutic agents with complex structures and unstable chemical architecture such as insulin and siRNA therapeutics has also received much attention from researchers to meet the requirements of the novel DDSs [5–7]. In this sense, effective delivery systems have been designed, and chemical modification, polymer-mediated delivery systems, and multifunctional delivery systems have experienced a new era of development toward achieving clinically safe and stable systems with high efficiency for cancer treatment based on siRNA delivery platforms [8].

Typically, modern delivery methods and strategies are seeking to facilitate the delivery of drug molecules to an especial organ, tissue, or cells [7,9,10]. These strategies have been trying to preserve the bioactivity and the stability of drugs in physiological conditions, before reaching the region of action. DDSs should isolate toxic chemotherapeutics and prevent them from attacking healthy cells. The modern systems are also designed smartly to target special cells in cancer therapy, which is known as targeted cancer therapy [11–13]. "Disruption of the normal regulation of cell cycle progression and division lies at the heart of the events leading to cancer," according to Charles Sawyers, known for pioneering works performed on the signaling pathways that drive the growth of cancer cells, from the Howard Hughes Medical Institute who holds the Marie-Josée and Henry R. Kravis Chair of the Human Oncology and Pathogenesis Program at the Memorial Sloan Kettering Cancer Center [14]. To achieve more rational and effective cancer therapy, understanding molecular changes taking place in the course of cancer evolution is of vital importance. However, designing smart delivery platforms capable of precisely detecting cancer cells, delivery of drugs into the intracellular environment, penetrating the biological barriers (e.g., blood-brain barrier), and evading the immune system are challenging issues that should be comprehensively identified for efficiency demonstration [15–18]. In this regard, nanoscale carriers constructed from various functional biomaterials are among the most promising DDSs [13,19].

Inadequate material properties have limited the manufacturing of tailor-made DDSs. Indeed, until now there is no specified strategy to make materials of desired properties to address special and narrowly determined requirements. In a classical view, based on the knowledge of materials and medicine, one may need to check a bewildering array of biomaterials with their own physical, chemical, and mechanical properties in a quite difficult way through a multistage manner that is based on selecting, screening, and modifying materials for targeting a required level of delivery. For example, toxic side effects of the traditional or naked DDSs arising from the leakage of drugs make the targeting difficult, which may be tackled by the use of nanomaterials [20]. The use of nanoparticles makes it possible to give the drug access to the cancerous cells, so that the microenvironment and the receptor sites can receive an adequate amount of drug. The effect of the nanoparticle shape and porosity on the effectiveness of drug delivery has been emphasized in cancer treatment [21,22]. It has been reported that targeted delivery of drugs with the aid of nanoparticles embedded in the drug carrier reduces the toxicity of the tissue in the course of the therapeutic period [23]. However, possible toxic side effects caused by nanoparticles in dermal and medical injectable treatments should be taken into account [24].

Although the material genome, polymer genome, and artificial intelligence concepts have recently grabbed much attention in designing new materials with desired properties for biomedical and DDS applications, it seems that there is a long way to be paved before reaching the point one may be able to find the best conditions for design and manufacture of biomaterials having predetermined specifications [25–27]. Accordingly, a combination of various materials, especially polymers and copolymers, was proposed as the most promising short-term solution for tailor-making materials of desired properties [28,29]. The applications of polymers, polymer blends, and various copolymers have recently gained much interest in biomedical applications, especially for manufacturing novel DDSs. Polymer-drug conjugates are on the road of innovations and delivery of different kinds of drugs and proteins, and targeting moieties have been comprehensively discussed in recent years [30]. Engineering polymers such as poly(ethylene glycol) (PEG) [31,32] and poly(lactide-*co*-glycolide) (PLGA) copolymers [33,34] have received credit for clinical therapies. The superiority of polymers over other materials used as DDS lies in their ability to accumulate in the solid tumor that significantly reduces the toxicity of the system [35]. The ability to degrade is a factor that affects the mode of action of polymers on the sites of administration [36]. Later, the design and development of smart multifunctional polymer-drug conjugates with the ability to respond to changes in microenvironments by the change in acidity, temperature, and cellular situation opened a new realm of research, mainly based on nanotechnology [37,38].

Polysaccharides are carbohydrate polymers composed of simple sugars as repeating units linked together by glycosidic covalent binding. They are known for their biodegradability and biocompatibility and have been widely considered in bioapplications [39]. Depending on their chemical structure, polysaccharides can be treated in homo- and hetero-polysaccharides. Homo-polysaccharides are macromolecules with one type of monosaccharide as the repeating unit in their backbone. Examples of this type of polysaccharides are cellulose, starch, and glycogen. However, hetero-polysaccharides are structures in which two or more types of monosaccharides form the backbone of the polymer [40]. Polysaccharides are abundant in nature as various parts of animals and plants, and their properties depend on their chemical structure (linearity, crystallinity, etc.). They are also known as promising candidates for making DDSs. However, due to their poor mechanical properties, they should be modified or surface-functionalized before utilization in DDSs. Some strategies such as blending with other polymers, grafting with other molecules such as oligomers and polymers, and cross-linking provide polysaccharides-based materials with diverse properties, which are not attainable with pristine naturally available polysaccharides. The chemical versatility of polysaccharides and the wide range of physicochemical properties of their derivatives and blends make them interesting materials to tailor-make DDSs [41–43]. To pattern the importance of polysaccharides in the form of pristine and functionalized structures, one can have a look at the number of publications on some of the most known members of this family of natural macromolecules (Fig. 1). It can be seen that the number of publications on polysaccharides, cross-linked polysaccharides, and some examples, including chitosan, dextran, and pectin, and also papers on their usage for drug delivery purposes are all experiencing an ascending trend over the past decade.

In this chapter, the importance and the significance of the cross-linking of polysaccharides and the cross-linked polysaccharides together with the effects of cross-linking of the polysaccharides on their properties have been discussed with an emphasis placed on the DDSs. Various types of physical and chemical cross-linking methods and their features have also been summarized and discussed. Attention was also placed on modern DDS based on cross-linked polysaccharides exhibiting smart delivery behavior.

2 Cross-linking of and the cross-linked polysaccharides

Chitosan, sodium alginate, cellulose, starch, and xanthan are the most famous polysaccharides that have been widely used in a wide variety of applications such as the food industry [44]. However, it is obvious for those working in the field that they suffer from poor mechanical properties, which has limited their applications in the biomedical field [45,46]. Cross-linking strategies make it possible to enhance the mechanical and

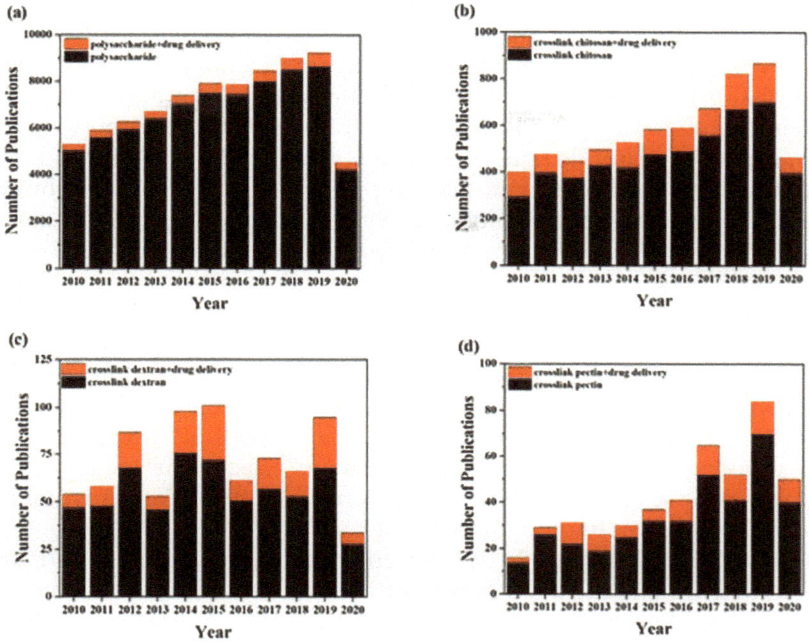

FIG. 1 The number of publications on polysaccharides and contribution of drug delivery to such papers (A), the cross-linked polysaccharides with examples, including chitosan (B), dextran (C), and pectin (D), and their contribution to drug delivery applications (data are found based on some keywords which include polysaccharide, polysaccharides, cross-linked chitosan, cross-linking chitosan, cross-link chitosan, cross-linked dextran, cross-linking dextran, cross-link dextran, cross-linked pectin, cross-link pectin, cross-linking pectin, cross-linked chitosan drug delivery, cross-linking chitosan + drug delivery, cross-link chitosan + drug delivery, cross-linked dextran + drug delivery, cross-link dextran + drug delivery, cross-linking dextran + drug delivery, cross-linked pectin + drug delivery, cross-link pectin + drug delivery, and cross-linking pectin + drug delivery). Data were collected from the Scopus Web of Science on June 8, 2020. The ongoing data devoted to the publications recorded in 2020 should be considered in the present form of bar diagrams.

other physicochemical properties of these biopolymers for worthwhile use in medicine. Because of cross-linking importance, this section would outline the concepts and methods used in cross-linking with an emphasis on well-known polysaccharides [47–49].

Cross-linking denotes the linkage of two (or more) macromolecules, especially polymers, through covalent bonding or sometimes strong physical interactions [50,51]. The chemical cross-linking may include cross-linking agents (e.g., sulfur in the vulcanization of rubbers) which create linkage between the polymer chains or may include chain scission and rebonding (e.g., cross-linked polyethylene or XLPE). However, physical cross-linking is usually created as a result of hydrogen bonding (e.g., in agarose gels) between the adjacent chains or strong electrostatic interactions between the multivalent cations or anions (e.g., Ca^{2+}, Al^{3+}, or tripolyphosphate anion) and anionic/cationic functional groups on polymer chains (e.g., carboxylic acid functional groups in alginate or amino groups on chitosan) [52–54]. Moreover, it is worth mentioning that both chemical (e.g., disulfide and isopeptide bonds in hair, cartilage, and skin) and physical (e.g., hydrogen bonding in DNA structure) cross-linking methods play vital roles in biological systems, including tissue engineering, living cell encapsulation, controlled delivery of bioactive molecules, and stimuli-responsive DDS [55]. The type and number of cross-links per unit volume, the chemical identity of cross-linking agents, and the cross-link density are the main factors significantly affecting the properties of the cross-linked polymers [56]. Chemical cross-linking is usually irreversible, while physical cross-linking constitutes reversible bonds; both have benefits for making DDSs with tailor-made properties. Furthermore, the cross-linking attributes of polymeric systems affect their transport phenomena such as mass transport characteristics, which play a pivotal role in drug release behavior of DDSs [57,58].

As illustrated in Fig. 2, diverse chemical or physical cross-linking methods have already been examined to make cross-linked polymer hydrogels [59]. Various cross-linking strategies may be used in the design of DDSs based on especial requirements such as administration route, cellular uptake, evading the immune system, and so on. For example, using physical cross-linking strategies it is possible to make nanocarriers that can disassemble reversibly as a result of an endogenous/exogenous stimulus to release the payload at desired region or internalized by especial cells [60–62]. In another case, polyethylene glycol (PEG) coating on the PEGylated nanocarriers can be detached through light-induced bond dissociation before cell internalization [63]. It was reported that the photoinduced PEG deshielding strategy applied on nanocarriers gives a wide range of therapeutic agents the possibility to be applied as anticancer drugs in on-demand delivery systems. Therefore, the diversity of cross-linking strategies can allow for manufacturing delivery platforms with tailor-made physicochemical properties and drug release behavior.

These cross-linking strategies are applicable for polysaccharides, as well. Ionic cross-linking (using divalent cations) of alginate and chemical cross-linking (using glutaraldehyde) of chitosan are well-accepted strategies to make robust hydrogels for the purpose of tissue engineering and drug delivery [64]. However, these conventional cross-linking strategies have their own limitations; for example, glutaraldehyde is a toxic chemical reagent that may cause serious problems for in vivo applications of polysaccharides. However, new discoveries and novel developments in organic chemistry allow for the making of engineered polysaccharides with nontoxic or grafted cross-linking agents. For example, natural nontoxic

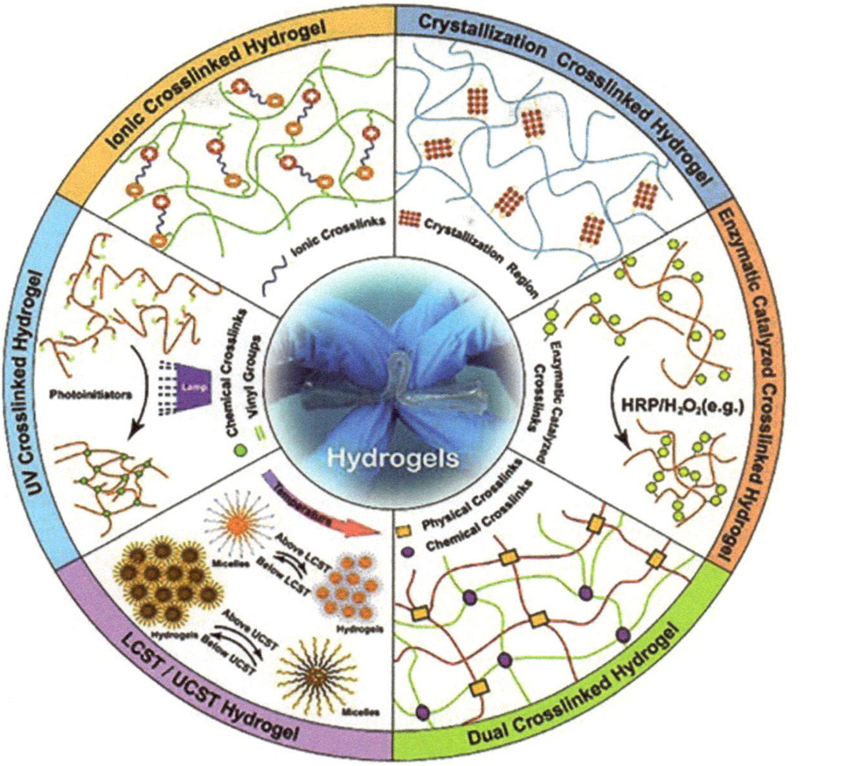

FIG. 2 Well-known cross-linking methods for making cross-linked polymer hydrogel [59]. In the illustration, LCST is the lower critical solution temperature, while UCST is the upper critical solution temperature. It can be seen that the degree of physicochemical interaction and the interfacial properties can be tailored depending on the cross-linking strategy. This makes it possible to use a wide range of drugs in DDSs.

cross-linking agents such as genipin can be used to make polysaccharides cross-linked [65]. Furthermore, diverse molecules can be grafted onto the polysaccharide chains to improve their properties and hydrophilicity, but they can also act as cross-linking agents [66,67]. However, polysaccharides can be blended with other synthetic and natural polymers, to form interpenetrating polymer networks (IPNs) or semi-IPNs [68]. For example, maleoyl-chitosan, which is a water-soluble derivative of chitosan, has been utilized to make a semi-IPN in which poly(2-dimethylaminoethyl methacrylate) was cross-linked using bisacrylamide [69]. In addition, maleoyl-chitosan interacted with the synthetic polymers through hydrogen bonding, acting as physical cross-linking.

The type of cross-linker significantly affects the release behavior of drugs. For example, Saikia studied the effect of the type of cross-linker of curcumin in the release from the iron oxide magnetic nanoparticles coated with aminated starch [70]. They used genipin, glutaraldehyde, and citric acid as three cross-linking agents, among which genipin revealed the best properties. It was also observed that drug loading and encapsulation efficiency can increase the polysaccharide cross-link density [71].

3 Cross-linked polysaccharides applied in DDSs

3.1 Chitosan

Chitosan is the most widely utilized polysaccharide in DDSs, because of its acceptable physicochemical features such as polycationic nature and abundance of the reactive hydroxyl and amino functional groups, as well as biological features like bioactivity, biocompatibility, and biodegradability [72]. To make chitosan cross-linked, glutaraldehyde has been considered the most well-known cross-linking agent [73]. Glutaraldehyde has two reactive aldehyde functional groups that react with amino functional groups adjacent to the chitosan chains, making it possible to develop a 3D hydrogel network. However, chitosan cross-linking is not limited to aldehyde-containing chemicals. For example, caseinate and chitosan were used to prepare nanoparticles for delivery of curcumin for cancer treatment in which genipin was used as a chemical cross-linker to make stable monodisperse nanoparticles [45,74–76]. However, photocleavable cross-linkers are very interesting to fabricate light-sensitive DDSs for on-demand drug release [77,78]. Such stimuli cross-linkers are known for the controlled delivery of therapeutic agents through electromagnetic radiation in a particular wavelength (normally in UV, visible, and near-infrared regions). Nisar et al. synthesized a novel photocleavable cross-linker based on orthonitrobenzyl moiety, namely 4-formylphenyl 4-((4-formylphenoxy) methyl)-3-nitrobenzoate (CHO-ONB-CHO), containing two aldehyde functional groups, similar to the glutaraldehyde (see Fig. 1) [79]. Reactive aldehyde groups can react with the amino-functional groups present on the chitosan, resulting in cross-linked chitosan hydrogels. When chitosan is cross-linked using CHO-ONB-CHO to make ONB-chitosan, a dual-responsive hydrogel would be attained for smart DDS developments. In vitro investigations revealed that doxorubicin (DOX) release is higher in an acidic medium. In addition, it was observed that the hydrogel can absorb ultraviolet (UV) irradiation in the range of 310–340 nm (Fig. 3) [79].

Because of the narrow temperature fluctuation in the human body, thermosensitive polymers have been of special interest to make DDSs [80,81]. A thermosensitive hydrogel based on chitosan and poly(*N*-isopropylacrylamide) (PNIPAAm) was made to encapsulate cyanocobalamin, as a model drug [82]. The lower critical solution temperature (LCST)

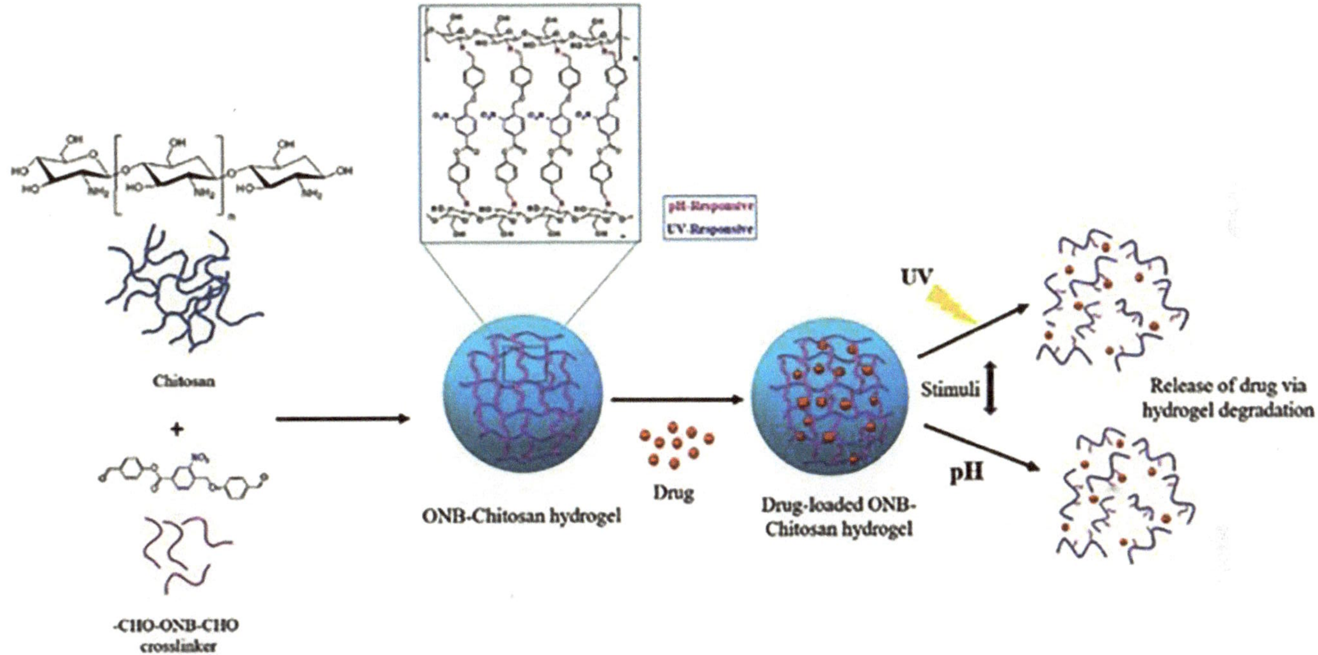

FIG. 3 Schematic illustration of a dual-responsive drug delivery system based on chitosan cross-linked by a photocleavable cross-linker. Reactive aldehyde groups present in the structure of this material make possible the reaction with the amino-functional groups present on the chitosan. As a result, a cross-linked chitosan hydrogel comes into existence. When chitosan is cross-linked using CHO-ONB-CHO in the procedure of making ONB–chitosan, a dual-responsive hydrogel can be achieved suitable for the smart DDS developments. In vitro investigations were indicative of the fact that the release of doxorubicin (DOX) is accelerated in the acidic medium. In addition, it was reported that the hydrogel can absorb ultraviolet (UV) irradiation in the range of 310–340 nm.

of the hydrogel was c. 29–32°C. Tripolyphosphate was used to ionically cross-link chitosan, making spherical particles of chitosan and PNIPAAm. It was observed that the release of encapsulated drug was accelerated beyond a fever temperature of 40°C [82].

Polycationic chitosan can form a nanoparticle complex (nominated as nanoplex) with negatively charged drug molecules such as tripolyphosphate. However, the burst release of drug molecules has been identified as a big challenge in such systems. It is well documented that very fast release of drugs in the initial stage or also known and initial burst of drug in a given drug administration system has serious side effects which are pharmacologically dangerous [83]. The utilization of a second cross-linking mechanism (or secondary cross-linking agent) has sometimes been considered as a solution to tackle this problem. For example, chitosan-curcumin nanoplex, which can ionically be cross-linked, can be further cross-linked by a secondary chemical cross-linking method to reduce the initial burst release [84]. Some researchers used amine-reactive disuccinimidyl tartrate as the cross-linking agent to impede the burst release and reduce the dissolution rate of the drug from the chitosan matrix. This highlights the importance of double cross-linked DDSs for the controlled release of therapeutic agents, which has attracted much attention in recent years [85,86].

Chitosan-based platforms can be used to deliver both small molecules and macromolecules such as proteins (e.g., insulin and growth factors) [87,88]. For example, cross-linked chitosan scaffolds were utilized to deliver stromal cell-derived factor-1 (SDF-1) to the wound area [89]. Chitosan scaffolds were cross-linked using genipin; moreover, SDF-1, which is a chemokine accelerating skin wound healing, was immobilized onto a chitosan scaffold using heparin. In vivo studies on diabetic Sprague-Dawley rats revealed better wound healing performance, improved neovascularization, and enhanced growth factors (VEGF, TGF-β) expression [89]. The wounds treated with the SDF-1 scaffolds were indicative of a higher vascular endothelial growth factor (VEGF) and transforming growth factor-beta (TGF-β) expression in Western blot assays.

3.2 Alginate

Sodium alginate is a polyanionic polysaccharide widely utilized in tissue engineering and drug delivery such as wound dressing and cancer therapy [90]. It has also some applications as a biomaterial for the encapsulation and immobilization of a wide variety of cells applied in immunoisolatory and biochemical processing uses [91]. Common cross-linking strategy used for the alginate-based systems includes ionic cross-linking using divalent cations such as Ca^{2+}. For example, Ca^{2+} ions were utilized to cross-link alginate and xanthan gum for delivery of levodopa [92].

Reports are indicative of a high potential of the resulting cross-linked network for cartilage tissue engineering in view of the fact that chondrocytes do not undergo dedifferentiation when immobilized. Additional privileges are including high processability and cell immobilization potential, which make cross-linked sodium alginate a potential candidate for DDSs. Magnetic nanoparticles have also been incorporated into such systems via in situ formation, where both the composition and the cross-linking affected drug loading and drug release behavior. In particular, it was observed that alginate-xanthan gum/magnetic nanoparticles and the neat alginate showed the highest and lowest drug loading efficiencies, respectively. These systems were served in magnetic-responsive DDSs and also as the theranostic platforms for diseases related to the central nervous system, such as Parkinson's disease [92].

A polymer blend containing linseed polysaccharide (LP) and sodium alginate was used to prepare mucoadhesive drug delivery beads for diclofenac sodium [93]. Calcium chloride was used to ionically cross-link the polysaccharides blend; the prepared beads showed pH-responsive behavior, excellent mucoadhesion on the intestinal mucosa, and a sustained drug release. Epichlorohydrin having two reactive groups of epoxy and chloride is another cross-linking agent for polysaccharides. For example, portulaca-alginate beads were double cross-linked by epichlorohydrin and Ca^{2+} ions to make targeted DDS for delivery of the anticancer drug, 5-fluorouracil (5-FU), for colon cancer [94]. Combined physical and chemical cross-linking strategy resulted in high drug encapsulation efficiency; besides, oral administration in rat models revealed sustained drug release and enhanced antitumor activity against colon cancer cells [94]. In a similar manner, a targeted DDS was made using two polysaccharides, sodium alginate and portulaca, for controlled delivery of 5-fluorouracil (5-FU) in the colon [95]. Polysaccharides were ionically cross-linked using borax to make pH-sensitive drug encapsulating beads.

3.3 Cellulose

Cellulose is a widespread polysaccharide that constitutes the structural part of plants. This biopolymer and its derivatives have been widely used to make DDSs [96,97]. For example, cellulose ester is an essential element of DDS because of providing multifarious features in view of its very low toxicity, thermal stability, high water uptake and permeability, high glass transition temperature (Tg), high strength when formed as a film, biocompatibility with a wide range of active materials, and the ability to be formed into micro- and nanoparticles [98]. Electrospun ethyl hydroxyethyl cellulose (EHEC) fibers were blended with poly(vinyl alcohol) (PVA) and cross-linked using citric acid to make a delivery platform for chlorhexidine digluconate (ChD) which is an antibacterial drug [99].

Nanogels are water-swollen cross-linked hydrophilic polymer nanoparticles or three-dimensional (3D) nanoscale hydrogels [100]. They have been vastly utilized to make DDSs because of their high loading capacity for various therapeutic agents, adjustable and stimuli-responsive release behavior, biocompatibility, and biodegradation, [101,102]. Nanogels based on polysaccharides, because of biocompatibility, biodegradability, high loading capacity, modifiable functional groups, high surface area, polyelectrolyte complexation (PEC) capability, adjustable size, and cross-linking capability, have received much attention in the delivery of therapeutics [103]. There is a belief that nanogels based on polysaccharide blends and chemically modified polysaccharides will further expand their applications in drug delivery. However, cross-linking attributes (e.g., cross-linker type and cross-linking density) have significant impact on drug loading and release behavior of nanogels. For example, a cellulose-based bionanogel was used as an intracellular stimuli-responsive DDS for delivery of DOX as anticancer drug [104]. The dual-responsive nanogel (pH- and temperature-sensitive), which benefited from colloidal stability, was manufactured with carboxymethyl cellulose (CMC) and thermoresponsive oligo (ethylene oxide)-based copolymers. Three PEG-based oligomers were copolymerized and grafted onto adjacent CMC chains to make a cross-linked polymer network, as schematically illustrated in Fig. 4. OligoPEG-based copolymer that served as a cross-linking agent is a thermosensitive polymer, while CMC responded to pH change. It was observed that an increase in temperature and a decrease in pH result in enhanced DOX release from nanogels. DOX-loaded nanogels (c. 10nm) were relatively monodisperse and can effectively be taken up by cancer cells [104].

4 Smart cross-linking strategies

As discussed earlier, polysaccharides can be cross-linked either through physical interactions or through chemical cross-linkers, as shown in Fig. 2. This enables the researcher to design versatile drug delivery platforms with tunable physicochemical properties and release behavior. For example, it is possible to make injectable thermosensitive hydrogels where physical cross-linking is formed after injection. Such structures affect the rheological behavior of the hydrogel and prevent hydrogels from flowing. These in situ cross-linking strategies have grabbed much attention for designing minimally invasive therapy [105,106]. However, mixing-induced cross-linking has emerged as an interesting strategy to design injectable hydrogels. This concept utilizes reactive functional groups, such as aldehyde and amine, to make in situ cross-linked hydrogels. For example, oxidized sodium alginate (OSA) bearing aldehyde groups can easily react with amine functional groups of gelatin, chitosan, and their derivatives

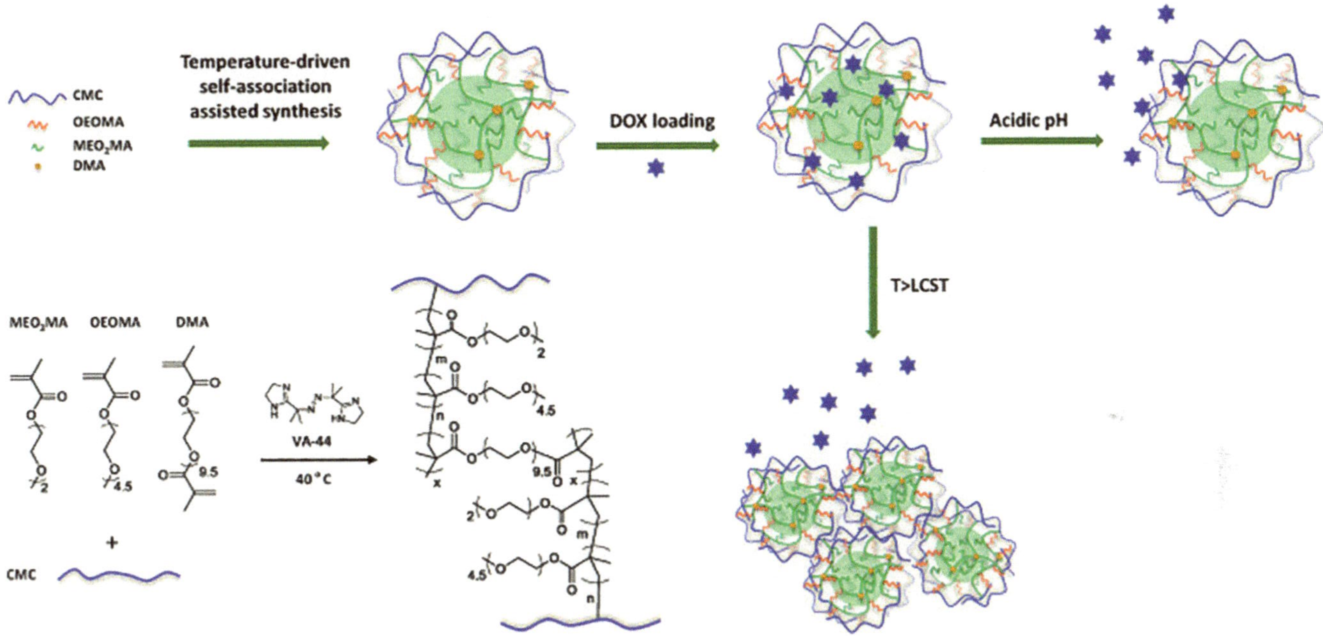

FIG. 4 Schematic representation of dual-responsive drug delivery nanogels based on CMC and oligoPEGs [104].

via Schiff base chemistry [107,108]. Cao et al. used an injectable hemostatic hydrogel based on carboxymethyl chitosan (CMCS), gelatin (Gel), and OSA for delivery of levofloxacin (an antibacterial agent) to the wound area [109]. Appropriate in situ gelation time, excellent hemostatic performance, reduced bleeding time and blood loss, and good tissue adhesive strength were observed for the rat liver injury model [109]. Polysaccharide-based tissue adhesives can be utilized as a hemostatic agent and delivery platform, which is highly interesting in biomedical applications [110].

More innovative advanced systems are usually based on mussel-inspired chemistry, which can be utilized to further modify the polysaccharides and provide them with extended functionality such as wet adhesion properties for advanced uses [111,112]. This wet adhesive characteristic can make it possible to develop long-lasting mucoadhesive DDSs for the gastrointestinal (GI) tract [112,113]. Strandman et al. fabricated hydrogels based on catechol modification of chitosan for the buccal delivery of lidocaine [114]. The hydrogel was chemically cross-linked using genipin. In vivo investigations on the rabbit buccal mucosa revealed excellent wet adhesion and sustained drug release compared to the genipin cross-linked chitosan [114]. Mussel-inspired patches based on chitosan are very promising mucosal delivery systems [115]. By contrast, their gelation time (or kinetics) alters based on the cross-linking mechanism [116]. This interesting phenomenon can be used to make DDSs with dynamic properties in which the rheological properties of the DDS change over time. This dynamic nature originates from different kinetics of chemical and/or physical cross-linking reactions/interactions, which occur in different timescales [117].

5 Conclusion

Polysaccharides are naturally abundant biopolymers with interesting biocompatibility and biodegradation properties. These carbohydrate polymers have already been used in a wide variety of biomedical applications such as tissue engineering and regenerative medicine. They are also considered as building blocks of novel drug delivery systems (DDSs). Their importance lies in the fact that they can be formed by the combination of various physical and chemical cross-linking, along with blending and chemical modifications of polysaccharides, provide a versatile playground to design and manufacture polysaccharide-based delivery systems (e.g., hydrogels, nanogels, capsules, and nanofibers) with desired mechanical properties, gelation time, biodegradation, biocompatibility, drug loading capacity, drug release kinetics, stimuli-responsiveness, and targeted delivery features that would boost their application in DDSs. The modified biopolymers are an indispensable part of novel drug delivery platforms. In this sense, cross-linking of polysaccharides has been recognized as a promising way to increase their efficiency in drug delivery systems. The functionality of polysaccharides makes their interaction with the cross-linking agents possible and widens their application range. Cross-linking methods applied in making polysaccharides improved for drug delivery purposes are studied in this chapter. DDSs based on chitosan, alginate, and cellulose are overviewed due to their importance and versatility in DDS applications. Moreover, smart cross-linking strategies are studied.

References

[1] IQVIA Institute for Human Data Science. The global use of medicine in 2019 and outlook to 2023. The IQVIA Institute; 2019.

[2] Chopra S, Mahdi S, Kaur J, Iqbal Z, Talegaonkar S, Ahmad FJ. Advances and potential applications of chitosan derivatives as mucoadhesive biomaterials in modern drug delivery. J Pharm Pharmacol 2006;58(8):1021–32.

[3] Bruck SD. Controlled drug delivery: volume 1 basic concepts. CRC Press; 2019.

[4] Nilforoushzadeh MA, Zare M, Zarrintaj P, Alizadeh E, Taghiabadi E, Heidari-Kharaji M, Amirkhani MA, Saeb MR, Mozafari M. Engineering the niche for hair regeneration—a critical review. Nanomed Nanotechnol Biol Med 2019;15(1):70–85.

[5] Chernikov IV, Vlassov VV, Chernolovskaya EL. Current development of siRNA bioconjugates: from research to the clinic. Front Pharmacol 2019;10:444.

[6] Farokhi M, Mottaghitalab F, Saeb MR, Thomas S. Functionalized theranostic nanocarriers with bio-inspired polydopamine for tumor imaging and chemo-photothermal therapy. J Control Release 2019;309:203–19.

[7] Servatan M, Zarrintaj P, Mahmodi G, Kim S-J, Ganjali MR, Saeb MR, Mozafari M. Zeolites in drug delivery: progress, challenges and opportunities. Drug Discov Today 2020;25:642–56.

[8] Xu C-F, Wang J. Delivery systems for siRNA drug development in cancer therapy. Asian J Pharm Sci 2015;10(1):1–12.

[9] Öztürk-Atar K, Eroğlu H, Çalış S. Novel advances in targeted drug delivery. J Drug Target 2018;26(8):633–42.

[10] Baghaei B, Saeb MR, Jafari SH, Khonakdar HA, Rezaee B, Goodarzi V, Mohammadi Y. Modeling and closed-loop control of particle size and initial burst of PLGA biodegradable nanoparticles for targeted drug delivery. J Appl Polym Sci 2017;134(33):45145.

[11] Aggarwal S. Targeted cancer therapies. Nature Publishing Group; 2010.

[12] Padma VV. An overview of targeted cancer therapy. Biomedicine 2015;5(4).

[13] Zarrintaj P, Mostafapoor F, Milan PB, Saeb MR. Theranostic platforms proposed for cancerous stem cells: a review. Curr Stem Cell Res Ther 2019;14(2):137–45.

[14] Sawyers C. Targeted cancer therapy. Nature 2004;432(7015):294–7.

[15] Lee Y-W, Luther DC, Kretzmann JA, Burden A, Jeon T, Zhai S, Rotello VM. Protein delivery into the cell cytosol using non-viral nanocarriers. Theranostics 2019;9(11):3280.

[16] Fadeel B. Hide and seek: nanomaterial interactions with the immune system. Front Immunol 2019;10.

[17] Laksitorini M, Prasasty VD, Kiptoo PK, Siahaan TJ. Pathways and progress in improving drug delivery through the intestinal mucosa and blood–brain barriers. Ther Deliv 2014;5(10):1143–63.

[18] Hu Q, Sun W, Wang C, Gu Z. Recent advances of cocktail chemotherapy by combination drug delivery systems. Adv Drug Deliv Rev 2016;98:19–34.

[19] Majumder J, Taratula O, Minko T. Nanocarrier-based systems for targeted and site specific therapeutic delivery. Adv Drug Deliv Rev 2019;144:57–77.
[20] He Q, Gao Y, Zhang L, Zhang Z, Gao F, Ji X, Li Y, Shi J. A pH-responsive mesoporous silica nanoparticles-based multi-drug delivery system for overcoming multi-drug resistance. Biomaterials 2011;32(30):7711–20.
[21] Truong NP, Whittaker MR, Mak CW, Davis TP. The importance of nanoparticle shape in cancer drug delivery. Expert Opin Drug Deliv 2015;12(1):129–42.
[22] Shahbazi M-A, Herranz B, Santos HA. Nanostructured porous Si-based nanoparticles for targeted drug delivery. Biomatter 2012;2(4):296–312.
[23] Haley B, Frenkel E. Nanoparticles for drug delivery in cancer treatment. In: Urologic oncology: seminars and original investigations. Elsevier; 2008.
[24] Sharifi S, Behzadi S, Laurent S, Laird Forrest M, Stroeve P, Mahmoudi M. Toxicity of nanomaterials. Chem Soc Rev 2012;41(6):2323–43.
[25] Kumar JN, Li Q, Tang KY, Buonassisi T, Gonzalez-Oyarce AL, Ye J. Machine learning enables polymer cloud-point engineering via inverse design. npj Comput Mater 2019;5(1):1–6.
[26] Ramprasad R. Polymer genome: an informatics platform for rational polymer dielectrics design and beyond. In: APS meeting abstracts; 2019.
[27] de Pablo JJ, Jackson NE, Webb MA, Chen L-Q, Moore JE, Morgan D, Jacobs R, Pollock T, Schlom DG, Toberer ES. New frontiers for the materials genome initiative. npj Comput Mater 2019;5(1):41.
[28] Zarrintaj P, Bakhshandeh B, Saeb MR, Sefat F, Rezaeian I, Ganjali MR, Ramakrishna S, Mozafari M. Oligoaniline-based conductive biomaterials for tissue engineering. Acta Biomater 2018;72:16–34.
[29] Zarrintaj P, Saeb MR, Ramakrishna S, Mozafari M. Biomaterials selection for neuroprosthetics. Curr Opin Biomed Eng 2018;6:99–109.
[30] Khandare J, Minko T. Polymer–drug conjugates: progress in polymeric prodrugs. Prog Polym Sci 2006;31(4):359–97.
[31] Zhu L, Wang T, Perche F, Taigind A, Torchilin VP. Enhanced anticancer activity of nanopreparation containing an MMP2-sensitive PEG-drug conjugate and cell-penetrating moiety. Proc Natl Acad Sci U S A 2013;110(42):17047–52.
[32] Deng H, Dong A, Song J, Chen X. Injectable thermosensitive hydrogel systems based on functional PEG/PCL block polymer for local drug delivery. J Control Release 2019;297:60–70.
[33] Rezvantalab S, Moraveji MK. Microfluidic assisted synthesis of PLGA drug delivery systems. RSC Adv 2019;9(4):2055–72.
[34] Lu B, Lv X, Le Y. Chitosan-modified PLGA nanoparticles for control-released drug delivery. Polymers 2019;11(2):304.
[35] Nishiyama N, Kataoka K. Current state, achievements, and future prospects of polymeric micelles as nanocarriers for drug and gene delivery. Pharmacol Ther 2006;112(3):630–48.
[36] Möller K, Bein T. Degradable drug carriers: vanishing mesoporous silica nanoparticles. Chem Mater 2019;31(12):4364–78.
[37] Kim S, Kim J-H, Jeon O, Kwon IC, Park K. Engineered polymers for advanced drug delivery. Eur J Pharm Biopharm 2009;71(3):420–30.
[38] Calzoni E, Cesaretti A, Polchi A, Di Michele A, Tancini B, Emiliani C. Biocompatible polymer nanoparticles for drug delivery applications in cancer and neurodegenerative disorder therapies. J Funct Biomater 2019;10(1):4.
[39] Yi Y, Xu W, Wang H-X, Huang F, Wang L-M. Natural polysaccharides experience physiochemical and functional changes during preparation: a review. Carbohydr Polym 2020;234, 115896.
[40] Naseri-Nosar M, Ziora ZM. Wound dressings from naturally-occurring polymers: a review on homopolysaccharide-based composites. Carbohydr Polym 2018;189:379–98.

[41] Zarrintaj P, Manouchehri S, Ahmadi Z, Saeb MR, Urbanska AM, Kaplan DL, Mozafari M. Agarose-based biomaterials for tissue engineering. Carbohydr Polym 2018;187:66–84.
[42] Zarrintaj P, Bakhshandeh B, Rezaeian I, Heshmatian B, Ganjali MR. A novel electroactive agarose-aniline pentamer platform as a potential candidate for neural tissue engineering. Sci Rep 2017;7(1):1–12.
[43] Atoufi Z, Zarrintaj P, Motlagh GH, Amiri A, Bagher Z, Kamrava SK. A novel bio electro active alginate-aniline tetramer/agarose scaffold for tissue engineering: synthesis, characterization, drug release and cell culture study. J Biomater Sci Polym Ed 2017;28(15):1617–38.
[44] Khosravi A, Fereidoon A, Khorasani MM, Naderi G, Ganjali MR, Zarrintaj P, Saeb MR, Gutiérrez TJ. Soft and hard sections from cellulose-reinforced poly (lactic acid)-based food packaging films: a critical review. Food Packag Shelf Life 2020;23, 100429.
[45] Alizadeh R, Zarrintaj P, Kamrava SK, Bagher Z, Farhadi M, Heidari F, Komeili A, Gutiérrez TJ, Saeb MR. Conductive hydrogels based on agarose/alginate/chitosan for neural disorder therapy. Carbohydr Polym 2019;224, 115161.
[46] Mohebbi S, Nezhad MN, Zarrintaj P, Jafari SH, Gholizadeh SS, Saeb MR, Mozafari M. Chitosan in biomedical engineering: a critical review. Curr Stem Cell Res Ther 2019;14(2):93–116.
[47] Bagheri B, Zarrintaj P, Samadi A, Zarrintaj R, Ganjali MR, Saeb MR, Mozafari M, Park OO, Kim YC. Tissue engineering with electrospun electro-responsive chitosan-aniline oligomer/polyvinyl alcohol. Int J Biol Macromol 2020;147:160–9.
[48] Bagheri B, Zarrintaj P, Surwase SS, Baheiraei N, Saeb MR, Mozafari M, Kim YC, Park OO. Self-gelling electroactive hydrogels based on chitosan–aniline oligomers/agarose for neural tissue engineering with on-demand drug release. Colloids Surf B Biointerfaces 2019;184, 110549.
[49] Khalili R, Zarrintaj P, Jafari SH, Vahabi H, Saeb MR. Electroactive poly (p-phenylene sulfide)/r-graphene oxide/chitosan as a novel potential candidate for tissue engineering. Int J Biol Macromol 2020;154:18–24.
[50] Rahmati M, Milan PB, Samadikuchaksaraei A, Goodarzi V, Saeb MR, Kargozar S, Kaplan DL, Mozafari M. Ionically crosslinked thermoresponsive chitosan hydrogels formed in situ: a conceptual basis for deeper understanding. Macromol Mater Eng 2017;302(11):1700227.
[51] Sari MG, Saeb MR, Shabanian M, Khaleghi M, Vahabi H, Vagner C, Zarrintaj P, Khalili R, Paran SMR, Ramezanzadeh B. Epoxy/starch-modified nano-zinc oxide transparent nanocomposite coatings: a showcase of superior curing behavior. Prog Org Coat 2018;115:143–50.
[52] Hecht H, Srebnik S. Structural characterization of sodium alginate and calcium alginate. Biomacromolecules 2016;17(6):2160–7.
[53] Lee KY, Mooney DJ. Alginate: properties and biomedical applications. Prog Polym Sci 2012;37(1):106–26.
[54] Sacco P, Paoletti S, Cok M, Asaro F, Abrami M, Grassi M, Donati I. Insight into the ionotropic gelation of chitosan using tripolyphosphate and pyrophosphate as cross-linkers. Int J Biol Macromol 2016;92:476–83.
[55] Friedman M. Protein crosslinking: biochemical and molecular aspects. vol. 86. Springer Science & Business Media; 2012.
[56] Aghadavoudi F, Golestanian H, Tadi Beni Y. Investigating the effects of resin crosslinking ratio on mechanical properties of epoxy-based nanocomposites using molecular dynamics. Polym Compos 2017;38:E433–42.
[57] Tronci G, Ajiro H, Russell SJ, Wood DJ, Akashi M. Tunable drug-loading capability of chitosan hydrogels with varied network architectures. Acta Biomater 2014;10(2):821–30.
[58] Teng W, Cappello J, Wu X. Physical crosslinking modulates sustained drug release from recombinant silk-elastinlike protein polymer for ophthalmic applications. J Control Release 2011;156(2):186–94.

[59] Hu W, Wang Z, Xiao Y, Zhang S, Wang J. Advances in crosslinking strategies of biomedical hydrogels. Biomater Sci 2019;7(3):843–55.
[60] Yang Y, Wang Z, Peng Y, Ding J, Zhou W. A smart pH-sensitive delivery system for enhanced anticancer efficacy via paclitaxel endosomal escape. Front Pharmacol 2019;10:10.
[61] Liu J, Huang Y, Kumar A, Tan A, Jin S, Mozhi A, Liang X-J. pH-sensitive nano-systems for drug delivery in cancer therapy. Biotechnol Adv 2014;32(4):693–710.
[62] Raza A, Rasheed T, Nabeel F, Hayat U, Bilal M, Iqbal H. Endogenous and exogenous stimuli-responsive drug delivery systems for programmed site-specific release. Molecules 2019;24(6):1117.
[63] Li J, Sun C, Tao W, Cao Z, Qian H, Yang X, Wang J. Photoinduced PEG deshielding from ROS-sensitive linkage-bridged block copolymer-based nanocarriers for on-demand drug delivery. Biomaterials 2018;170:147–55.
[64] Rohani Rad E, Vahabi H, Formela K, Saeb MR, Thomas S. Injectable poloxamer/graphene oxide hydrogels with well-controlled mechanical and rheological properties. Polym Adv Technol 2019;30(9):2250–60.
[65] Manickam B, Sreedharan R, Elumalai M. 'Genipin'—the natural water soluble cross-linking agent and its importance in the modified drug delivery systems: an overview. Curr Drug Deliv 2014;11(1):139–45.
[66] Du F, Wu Y, Du F, Zhang L, Feng W, Zhao L, Cai R, Xu L, Bian G, Li J. Construction of catechol-grafted chitosan alginate/barium sulfate microcapsules for computed tomography real-time imaging and gastroretentive drug delivery. Int J Nanomedicine 2019;14:6001.
[67] Liu J, Wang X, Bai R, Zhang N, Kan J, Jin C. Synthesis, characterization, and antioxidant activity of caffeic-acid-grafted corn starch. Starch-Stärke 2018;70(1–2):1700141.
[68] Matricardi P, Di Meo C, Coviello T, Hennink WE, Alhaique F. Interpenetrating polymer networks polysaccharide hydrogels for drug delivery and tissue engineering. Adv Drug Deliv Rev 2013;65(9):1172–87.
[69] Rusu AG, Chiriac AP, Nita LE, Bercea M, Tudorachi N, Ghilan A, Pamfil D, Rusu D, Cojocaru FD. Interpenetrated polymer network with modified chitosan in composition and self-healing properties. Int J Biol Macromol 2019;132:374–84.
[70] Saikia C, Das MK, Ramteke A, Maji TK. Effect of crosslinker on drug delivery properties of curcumin loaded starch coated iron oxide nanoparticles. Int J Biol Macromol 2016;93:1121–32.
[71] Zarrintaj P, Urbanska AM, Gholizadeh SS, Goodarzi V, Saeb MR, Mozafari M. A facile route to the synthesis of anilinic electroactive colloidal hydrogels for neural tissue engineering applications. J Colloid Interface Sci 2018;516:57–66.
[72] Denkbas EB, Ottenbrite RM. Perspectives on: chitosan drug delivery systems based on their geometries. J Bioact Compat Polym 2006;21(4):351–68.
[73] Jameela S, Jayakrishnan A. Glutaraldehyde cross-linked chitosan microspheres as a long acting biodegradable drug delivery vehicle: studies on the in vitro release of mitoxantrone and in vivo degradation of microspheres in rat muscle. Biomaterials 1995;16(10):769–75.
[74] Razi MA, Wakabayashi R, Tahara Y, Goto M, Kamiya N. Genipin-stabilized caseinate-chitosan nanoparticles for enhanced stability and anti-cancer activity of curcumin. Colloids Surf B Biointerfaces 2018;164:308–15.
[75] Bagher Z, Atoufi Z, Alizadeh R, Farhadi M, Zarrintaj P, Moroni L, Setayeshmehr M, Komeili A, Kamrava SK. Conductive hydrogel based on chitosan-aniline pentamer/gelatin/agarose significantly promoted motor neuron-like cells differentiation of human olfactory ecto-mesenchymal stem cells. Korean J Couns Psychother 2019;101:243–53.
[76] Manouchehri S, Bagheri B, Rad SH, Nezhad MN, Kim YC, Park OO, Farokhi M, Jouyandeh M, Ganjali MR, Yazdi MK. Electroactive bio-epoxy incorporated

chitosan-oligoaniline as an advanced hydrogel coating for neural interfaces. Prog Org Coat 2019;131:389–96.
[77] Jiménez-Balsa A, Pinto S, Quartin E, Lino MM, Francisco V, Ferreira L. Nanoparticles conjugated with photocleavable linkers for the intracellular delivery of biomolecules. Bioconjug Chem 2018;29(5):1485–9.
[78] Choi SK, Verma M, Silpe J, Moody RE, Tang K, Hanson JJ, Baker Jr JR. A photochemical approach for controlled drug release in targeted drug delivery. Bioorg Med Chem 2012;20(3):1281–90.
[79] Nisar S, Pandit AH, Wang L-F, Rattan S. Strategy to design a smart photocleavable and pH sensitive chitosan based hydrogel through a novel crosslinker: a potential vehicle for controlled drug delivery. RSC Adv 2020;10(25):14694–704.
[80] Sponchioni M, Palmiero UC, Moscatelli D. Thermo-responsive polymers: applications of smart materials in drug delivery and tissue engineering. Mater Sci Eng C 2019;102:589–605.
[81] Zarrintaj P, Jouyandeh M, Ganjali MR, Hadavand BS, Mozafari M, Sheiko SS, Russell AJ, Vatankhah-Varnoosfaderani M, Gutiérrez TJ, Saeb MR. Thermo-sensitive polymers in medicine: a review. Eur Polym J 2019;117:402–23.
[82] Ueoka H, Shimomura O, Ueda K, Inada K, Nomura R. Release behavior of a polyanion-crosslinked chitosan-poly (N-isopropylacrylamide) gel thermoresponsive material. J Appl Polym Sci 2018;135(41):46732.
[83] Huang X, Brazel CS. On the importance and mechanisms of burst release in matrix-controlled drug delivery systems. J Control Release 2001;73(2-3):121–36.
[84] Nguyen M-H, Tran T-T, Hadinoto K. Controlling the burst release of amorphous drug–polysaccharide nanoparticle complex via crosslinking of the polysaccharide chains. Eur J Pharm Biopharm 2016;104:156–63.
[85] Sun W, Jiang H, Wu X, Xu Z, Yao C, Wang J, Qin M, Jiang Q, Wang W, Shi D. Strong dual-crosslinked hydrogels for ultrasound-triggered drug delivery. Nano Res 2019;12(1):115–9.
[86] Thakur N, Sharma B, Bishnoi S, Jain S, Nayak D, Sarma TK. Biocompatible Fe3+ and Ca2+ dual cross-linked G-quadruplex hydrogels as effective drug delivery system for pH-responsive sustained zero-order release of doxorubicin. ACS Appl Bio Mater 2019;2(8):3300–11.
[87] Nivethaa E, Martin CA, Frank-Kamenetskaya OV, Kalkura SN. Chitosan and chitosan based nanocomposites for applications as a drug delivery carrier: a review. In: Processes and phenomena on the boundary between biogenic and abiogenic nature. Springer; 2020. p. 23–37.
[88] Qin Y, Li P, Guo Z. Cationic chitosan derivatives as potential antifungals: a review of structural optimization and applications. Carbohydr Polym 2020;116002.
[89] Yao C-H, Chen K-Y, Cheng M-H, Chen Y-S, Huang C-H. Effect of genipin crosslinked chitosan scaffolds containing SDF-1 on wound healing in a rat model. Mater Sci Eng C 2020;109, 110368.
[90] Abasalizadeh F, Moghaddam SV, Alizadeh E, Kashani E, Fazljou SMB, Torbati M, Akbarzadeh A. Alginate-based hydrogels as drug delivery vehicles in cancer treatment and their applications in wound dressing and 3D bioprinting. J Biol Eng 2020;14(1):1–22.
[91] Wang L, Shelton R, Cooper P, Lawson M, Triffitt J, Barralet J. Evaluation of sodium alginate for bone marrow cell tissue engineering. Biomaterials 2003;24(20):3475–81.
[92] Kondaveeti S, Semeano ATS, Cornejo DR, Ulrich H, Petri DFS. Magnetic hydrogels for levodopa release and cell stimulation triggered by external magnetic field. Colloids Surf B Biointerfaces 2018;167:415–24.
[93] Hasnain MS, Rishishwar P, Rishishwar S, Ali S, Nayak AK. Isolation and characterization of Linum usitatissimum polysaccharide to prepare mucoadhesive beads of diclofenac sodium. Int J Biol Macromol 2018;116:162–72.

[94] Asnani GP, Kokare CR. In vitro and in vivo evaluation of colon cancer targeted epichlorohydrin crosslinked Portulaca-alginate beads. Biomol Concepts 2018;9(1):190–9.
[95] Asnani GP, Bahekar J, Kokare CR. Development of novel pH-responsive dual cross-linked hydrogel beads based on Portulaca oleracea polysaccharide-alginate-borax for colon specific delivery of 5-fluorouracil. J Drug Delivery Sci Technol 2018;48:200–8.
[96] Sun B, Zhang M, Shen J, He Z, Fatehi P, Ni Y. Applications of cellulose-based materials in sustained drug delivery systems. Curr Med Chem 2019;26(14):2485–501.
[97] Dai L, Si C. Recent advances on cellulose-based nano-drug delivery systems: design of prodrugs and nanoparticles. Curr Med Chem 2019;26(14):2410–29.
[98] Edgar KJ. Cellulose esters in drug delivery. Cellul 2007;14(1):49–64.
[99] Wali A, Zhang Y, Sengupta P, Higaki Y, Takahara A, Badiger MV. Electrospinning of non-ionic cellulose ethers/polyvinyl alcohol nanofibers: characterization and applications. Carbohydr Polym 2018;181:175–82.
[100] Soni KS, Desale SS, Bronich TK. Nanogels: an overview of properties, biomedical applications and obstacles to clinical translation. J Control Release 2016;240:109–26.
[101] Suhail M, Rosenholm JM, Minhas MU, Badshah SF, Naeem A, Khan KU, Fahad M. Nanogels as drug-delivery systems: a comprehensive overview. Ther Deliv 2019;10(11):697–717.
[102] Zha L, Banik B, Alexis F. Stimulus responsive nanogels for drug delivery. Soft Matter 2011;7(13):5908–16.
[103] Debele TA, Mekuria SL, Tsai H-C. Polysaccharide based nanogels in the drug delivery system: application as the carrier of pharmaceutical agents. Mater Sci Eng C 2016;68:964–81.
[104] Wen Y, Oh JK. Intracellular delivery cellulose-based bionanogels with dual temperature/pH-response for cancer therapy. Colloids Surf B Biointerfaces 2015;133:246–53.
[105] Piantanida E, Alonci G, Bertucci A, De Cola L. Design of nanocomposite injectable hydrogels for minimally invasive surgery. Acc Chem Res 2019;52(8):2101–12.
[106] Lee JH. Injectable hydrogels delivering therapeutic agents for disease treatment and tissue engineering. Biomater Res 2018;22(1):1–14.
[107] Pettignano A, Häring M, Bernardi L, Tanchoux N, Quignard F, Díaz DD. Self-healing alginate–gelatin biohydrogels based on dynamic covalent chemistry: elucidation of key parameters. Mater Chem Front 2017;1(1):73–9.
[108] Pasaribu SP, Kaban J, Ginting M, Silalahi J. Preparation of in situ cross-linked N-maleoyl chitosan-oxidized sodium alginate hydrogels for drug delivery applications. Open access macedonian. J Med Sci 2019;7(21).
[109] Cao J, Xiao L, Shi X. Injectable drug-loaded polysaccharide hybrid hydrogels for hemostasis. RSC Adv 2019;9(63):36858–66.
[110] Serrero A, Trombotto S, Bayon Y, Gravagna P, Montanari S, David L. Polysaccharide-based adhesive for biomedical applications: correlation between rheological behavior and adhesion. Biomacromolecules 2011;12(5):1556–66.
[111] Scognamiglio F, Travan A, Borgogna M, Donati I, Marsich E, Bosmans J, Perge L, Foulc M, Bouvy N, Paoletti S. Enhanced bioadhesivity of dopamine-functionalized polysaccharidic membranes for general surgery applications. Acta Biomater 2016;44:232–42.
[112] Zhang W, Wang R, Sun Z, Zhu X, Zhao Q, Zhang T, Cholewinski A, Yang FK, Zhao B, Pinnaratip R. Catechol-functionalized hydrogels: biomimetic design, adhesion mechanism, and biomedical applications. Chem Soc Rev 2020;49:433–64.
[113] Narkar AR, Cannon E, Yildirim-Alicea H, Ahn K. Catechol-functionalized chitosan: optimized preparation method and its interaction with mucin. Langmuir 2019;35(48):16013–23.
[114] Xu J, Strandman S, Zhu JX, Barralet J, Cerruti M. Genipin-crosslinked catechol-chitosan mucoadhesive hydrogels for buccal drug delivery. Biomaterials 2015;37:395–404.
[115] Ryu JH, Choi JS, Park E, Eom MR, Jo S, Lee MS, Kwon SK, Lee H. Chitosan oral patches inspired by mussel adhesion. J Control Release 2020;317:57–66.

[116] Picchioni F, Muljana H. Hydrogels based on dynamic covalent and non covalent bonds: a chemistry perspective. Gels 2018;4(1):21.

[117] Perera MM, Ayres N. Dynamic covalent bonds in self-healing, shape memory, and controllable stiffness hydrogels. Polym Chem 2020;11(8):1410–23.

CHAPTER

6

Graft copolymers of polysaccharides: Synthesis techniques and pharmaceutical applications

Sudipta Das[a], *Rimi Dey*[a], *Md Saquib Hasnain*[b], *and Amit Kumar Nayak*[c]

[a]Department of Pharmaceutics, Netaji Subhas Chandra Bose Institute of Pharmacy, Nadia, West Bengal, India, [b]Department of Pharmacy, Palamau Institute of Pharmacy, Daltonganj, Jharkhand, India, [c]Department of Pharmaceutics, Seemanta Institute of Pharmaceutical Sciences, Jharpokharia, Mayurbhanj, Odisha, India

1 Introduction

Nowadays, polymers comprise a significant group of organic materials, which are known as the applicable alternative for usual resources. These materials have great importance in diversified fields of industry [1–4]. Most of the polymers cannot work under elevated temperature and pressure circumstances owing to the perception of specialty polymers came out. There are various modification techniques for improving the physicochemical and functional properties of polymeric materials under essential situations [5–8]. The newly modified polysaccharides have turned into a major vicinity of scientific study. The improved attention in polysaccharides has caused a great revolution, and such eco-friendly compounds have become on par with, and even superior to various kinds of synthetic materials. The recurrence in the utilization of natural materials as reinforcing agents has taken place in, for example, automobiles, packaging materials, building materials, etc. Innate fibers and their derivatives have been

Tailor-Made Polysaccharides in Drug Delivery
https://doi.org/10.1016/B978-0-12-821286-8.00006-9

observed to be advanced reinforcing materials for the manufacture of composites due to their ecological affability and smart mechanical properties [7,9–11]. There is a great concern for the surface morphology study of polymers, and industrially significant products are manufactured by introducing reactive sites. These reaction sites include the properties like hydrophilicity, hydrophobicity, and resistance toward acid–base attack as well as higher thermal stability [12,13].

Graft copolymerization offers a means for integrating desired characteristics (like melting point, glass transition temperature, solubility, permeability, chemical reactivity, elasticity, etc.) in backbones for specific uses with no effects on their biodegradation properties [14]. This method is used for hybridizing synthetic and natural polymers to support the primary examination of the structure–property relationship [14–16]. In recent years, graft copolymerization has increased much interest in the adjustment of chemical, physical, and functional properties of natural polymers and their derivatives [17]. Various researchers have accounted for the graft copolymerization of various vinyl monomers onto different polysaccharides. Polysaccharides occur in large quantities in nature, and this class of polymers is of particular importance for their extensive functions in the field of food, cosmetics, pharmaceuticals, etc. [18–22]. The present chapter discusses various techniques engaged in the synthesis of grafted polysaccharides in addition to up-to-date developments for the designing of novel drug delivery systems.

2 Polysaccharides

Polysaccharides molecules possess polymeric carbohydrate structures, which are arranged by repeating units attached collectively by glycosidic linkages [23]. Polysaccharides molecules are generally presented by the common formula $C_x(H_2O)_y$, where the value of y remains between 200 and 2500. Starch and glycogen are identified as storage polysaccharides, while cellulose and chitosan occur as structural materials [24]. These materials can be easily applied as fibers, films, adhesives, melt-processing plastics, hydrogels, drug delivery agents, and emulsifiers [14]. Being biobased materials, polysaccharides possess the exclusive mixture of functional characters and eco-friendly nature. In addition, these are also eco-friendly, recyclable, biocompatible, and biodegradable in nature. The physical and chemical characteristics of polysaccharides are influenced by the presence of polar functional groups, high molecular weight, and a relatively rigid backbone. Polysaccharides can be stable up to 200°C temperature for a shorter period of time. Polysaccharides also possess high melting and softening temperatures because of their severe interchain cohesive forces. They are brittle too for the rigid backbone. Natural polysaccharides possess hydroxyl groups in their molecular structures, which act as the reactive sites for various chemical modifications, such as esterification, carboxymethylation, carbamoylethylation, thiolation, cross-linking, polyelectrolyte complexes (PEC), interpenetrating polymer network (IPN), graft copolymerization, etc. [9,25–31]. Graft copolymerization of polysaccharides is a well-known technique for chemical modification of polysaccharides, where one or more side chains are chemically attached to the backbone of the polymer chain via the covalent bonds. A variety of vinyl monomers are most widely used for the grafting of various polysaccharides like cellulose, starch, chitosan, dextrin, and guar gum under diverse reaction circumstances [32–34].

3 Graft copolymers and different techniques of polymer grafting

Graft copolymers (copolymer is a polymer in which repeating units are of two unlike monomers) occupy a preformed polymeric backbone along with other polymeric chains of different chemical nature attached to it at numerous positions. Stannett described graft copolymers as "Graft copolymers consist of a polymer backbone with lateral covalently linked side chains" [24,35]. The backbone and the side chain of polymer structures can be composed of homopolymers as well as copolymers. The graft copolymer is composed of molecules with one or more blocks of species attached to the central chain. Thus, the modified polymers possess constitutional or configurational features, which are different from those in the main chain [36].

Copolymers are the kind of polymers, in which the repeating units are of two unlike monomers [14]. The relative reactivities of the monomers decide their attachment sequence in which they are connected one by one. The different types of copolymers are random, alternate, block, and graft copolymers. The sequencing patterns of monomers vary in the first three types of copolymers. In a random copolymer, monomer units are randomly arranged. In an alternate copolymer, monomer units are placed in a well-organized form. In a block copolymer, segments of dissimilar monomers are fastened simultaneously at terminals. In a graft copolymer, a preformed polymer acts as a backbone and polymeric chains are connected at various sites of it. As a consequence, a graft copolymer is composed of a polymer backbone by means of lateral covalently linked side chains [35]. Graft copolymerization of polysaccharides may also alter their physicochemical characteristics like rheological behavior, hydrophilicity, and complexing nature [14]. Consequently, the application domain of the grafted polysaccharides is being greatly extended in biomedical and environmental fields.

The two most important types of grafting are:

(i) Grafting with a single monomer.
(ii) Grafting with a blend of two (or more) monomers.

In addition, the two commonly used mechanisms for grafting of copolymers are identified as "grafting from" and "grafting onto" [14]. In the "grafting from" method, active sites are generated on the polymer backbone and monomer polymerization is initiated. In the "grafting onto" method, uniformity in composition and molecular weights distribution is found. It offers a system for including unique features in the parent backbone polymer, such as dye ability, crease resistance, moisture, and chemical resistance [37,38]. The grafting parameters, such as grafting percentage and grafting efficiency, may be influenced by some process-related parameters, such as the type and concentration of initiator, monomer concentration, reaction temperature, and time. The nature of the side chains (molecular structure, length, and number) can widely influence the characteristics of the resulting graft copolymers [39].

The different techniques of polymer grafting are as follows:

(1) Chemical grafting
   (a) Free-radical grafting
   (b) Ionic grafting
(2) Grafting through living polymerization
(3) Photochemical grafting
(4) Enzymatic grafting
(5) Plasma radiation technique
(6) Radiation grafting

3.1 Chemical grafting

In chemical grafting, the initiator plays an especially significant role since it establishes the pathway of the grafting method. In this process, chemicals are used as initiators for producing active sites on the backbone. Moreover, chemical grafting can be classified into two groups: free-radical grafting and ionization grafting.

(a) Free-radical grafting
Initiators generate free radicals, which are shifted to the substrate. Then, the free radicals react with monomers and the graft copolymers are produced. The most common initiator systems employed in free-radical grafting are [39,40]:
Ferrous ammonium sulfate (FAS)
Ceric ammonium nitrate (CAN)
Potassium diperiodatocuprate (III) (PDC)
Potassium persulfate (PPS)

Thiocarbonate potassium bromate (TCPB)
Ammonium persulfate (APS)

(b) Ionic grafting

Grafting of polymers can be stimulated in ionic surroundings going on mainly during the ionic mode. Grafting can progress through either an anionic or a cationic mechanism. The initiators employed in the anionic mechanism are alkoxide of alkali metals (such as sodium methoxide), and those in the cationic mechanism are alkaline metal salts such as alkyl aluminum (R3Al) [41].

3.2 Grafting through living polymerization

Szwarc et al. (1997) described the living polymerization as living polymer, which was found capable to proliferate for a long time and developed to a desired maximum size, whereas their degree of termination or chain transfer is still insignificant [42]. In controlled free-radical polymerizations, the features of both conventional free-radical and ionic polymerizations are merged, while in the case of living polymerization, living polymers are supplied with controlled molecular weight and low polydispersity [41]. The main drawback of conventional radical polymerization is that it cannot adjust the molecular weight, molecular weight distribution, and structural design of the polymer. Hence, its macroscopic properties become very tough to be modified, while living ionic polymerizations present a tactic for the development of copolymers with definite structures, i.e., adjusted molecular weights and contracted molecular weight distribution, distinct copolymer compositions, branching, and end-group functionalities.

(a) Stable free-radical polymerization (SFRP): A stable free radical is formed by reversible homolytic cleavage of a dormant chain end, and an active radical site was applied to the polymerization. SFRP is generally useful for styrenics, acrylates, and acrylamides; still, the main concentration in writing was on styrenic monomers [43].

(b) Reversible addition-fragmentation chain transfer (RAFT): It is attained by conducting a free-radical polymerization, where dithio compounds are employed as efficient RAFT agents [44].

(c) Atom transfer radical addition (ATRP): The halogen atoms cap the dormant chains and then reversibly shift to metal complexes during a lower oxidation state. This produces the transient growing radicals and complexes during a higher oxidation state. The activation-deactivation dynamic equilibrium process is identified as the main reaction of ATRP [44]. Sonmez et al. (2003) stated acrylamide grafting by ATRP, starting through the development of radicals in a redox reaction of *N*-chlorosulfonamide groups with CuBr [45].

All these techniques rely on the establishment of swift dynamic stability between a low concentration of active propagating chains and a predominant amount of dormant chains, which cannot propagate or terminate and are more liberal toward functional groups and impurities [46].

3.3 Photochemical grafting

Photochemical grafting can progress in two ways: (a) in the presence of a sensitizer and (b) in the absence of a sensitizer. In this method, the chromophore absorbs the light and shifts to the excited state. Therefore, dissociation of a chromophore into reactive free radicals takes place. If bond rupture does not occur to form the free radicals, the course of action is started through the accession of photosensitizers like benzoin ethyl ether, dyes, etc. Afterward, the free radicals and the monomers react together to develop grafted polymers [47–49]. The mechanism in the absence of a sensitizer occupies the production of free radicals onto the backbone, with which the monomer free radical reacts for the formation of the grafted copolymer. Alternatively, in the presence of a sensitizer, the free radicals are generated by the sensitizer and go through diffusion to take out hydrogen atoms from the base polymer, creating the radical sites necessary for grafting [41].

3.4 Enzymatic grafting

The principle of enzymatic grafting is based on the fact that the initiator used in this grafting method is an enzyme, which instigates chemical/electrochemical grafting onto the polymer backbone. It has developed interest owing to the necessity of milder reaction situation and well definite surface adaptation ensuing in nondestructive conversion of the backbone. Enzymatic grafting on natural goods has been clearly discussed for various industrialized purposes. Grafting was performed onto chitosan with a hydrophilic substance chlorogenic acid in the presence of enzyme tyrosinase to make chitosan water soluble under fundamental circumstances. Tyrosinase helps phenolic substrate to be converted into O-quinone which is capable of reacting with the amino group of chitosan to prepare graft copolymer [50]. The uses of reactive reagents in grafting techniques can be eradicated by the application of enzymes; thus, enzyme grafting proposes a green approach regarding safety, efficacy, and economy. Moreover, enzymes' specificity can precisely modify macromolecular properties to required ones [51].

3.5 Plasma radiation-induced grafting

This grafting method is set off by using plasma. The foremost incidents in this grafting technique are [52]: (a) electron-induced excitation, (b) ionization, and (c) dissociation. In the process, the high-energy accelerated electrons are moved from the plasma and those are having sufficient energy (force) to persuade cleavage of chemical bonds in the polymeric configuration. As a result, the radicals are produced and instigate the graft co-polymerization. There is no need for the addition of any kind of photosensitizer. However, there is a drawback of this method, i.e., it is limited to surface grafting [52,53]. Acrylic acid-grafted polyethylene terephthalate was applied effectively to diminish antithrombogenic nature of polyethylene terephthalate, and heparin immobilized over grafted polymer was originated to be hematocompatible [54].

3.6 Radiation grafting

In radiation grafting, the active sites of grafting (i.e., free radicals) are generated through the high-energy radiation exposure over the polymeric backbone, thus propagating side-chain grafts. These free radicals simply react with suitable functional monomers and make covalent bonds. Accordingly, macromolecular chains can develop without the application of any chemical initiators [55,56]. The rate of grafting and homopolymerization can be modified by altering various radiation parameters like radiation dose rate and total dose/time.

(a) Free-radical grafting
The homolytic cleavage of macromolecules is originated due to the irradiation, resulting in the formation of free radicals on the polymer. This technique does not involve any initiator or catalyst to start the process. The medium plays a significant role in this grafting, e.g., by using an air medium, peroxides can be generated on the polymeric structure. The life span of free radicals relies on the property of the backbone polymer. The various routes of grafting are [55]: (i) preirradiation, (ii) peroxidation, and (iii) mutual irradiation technique.

(i) Preirradiation technique:
The polymer backbone is irradiated by applying vacuum as well as inert gas for creating stable free radicals. Afterward, the irradiated polymer substrate reacts with the monomer at increased temperature. An important advantage of the preirradiation is that the homopolymer development does not happen while the monomer is not opened to radiation.

(ii) Peroxidation technique:
The polymer is exposed to high-energy radiation with the supply of air or oxygen. Then, hydroperoxides or diperoxides are produced depending upon the properties of the polymer and irradiation conditions. Thereafter, the peroxy products react with the monomer at elevated temperatures. Grafting starts at the time of decomposition of peroxides to generate radicals. An

important advantage of the peroxidation technique includes intermediate peroxy trunk polymers that can be stocked for a long duration before the ultimate grafting step.

(iii) Mutual irradiation technique:
In this method, both polymer and monomers (exist as vapor, liquid, or solutions) emit irradiation concurrently, forming free radicals and succeeding addition [56].

(b) Radiation grafting proceeding through an ionic mode
When ion formation occurs through high-energy irradiation, ionic grafting may proceed in two different ways: cationic or anionic. Irradiation of polymers results in the development of polymeric ions which react with the monomer and produce grafted copolymers. The main benefit is the fast reaction rate [41].

4 Properties of graft copolymers

The graft copolymerization method is employed to introduce required physical, chemical, and mechanical properties in polysaccharides. In addition, it also helps to make a change in the morphological structure of the end-product [14,41].

(a) Physical property:

(i) Moisture absorbance or retardance behavior
Graft copolymerization can alter the moisture absorbance or retardance nature of various backbone polysaccharides. The end-product can be made hydrophilic or hydrophobic by using different vinyl monomers with diverse chemical properties. The free hydroxyl group at C-2, C-3, C-6, and other positions of polysaccharides is replaced with hydrophilic or hydrophobic long-chain organic moieties for the alteration of morphological and moisture absorbance or retardance characteristics.

(ii) Swelling behavior
Graft copolymers show different swelling behaviors in different solvents according to the chemical nature of solvents. The absorption of water changes the hydrogen bonding of polysaccharides. The chemical affinity of the grafted polymer toward the solvent decides their swelling behavior. The greater the chemical affinity, the more will be the swelling capacity.

(iii) Salt resistance swelling behavior
Some cross-linked graft copolymers are having salt resistance swelling behavior in different conditions. Swelling is inversely proportional to the salt concentration, i.e., swelling capacity is reduced with the increase in salt concentration. Swelling

also depends on cationic charge and follows the order: $Na^{+}>NH_4^{+}>Mg^{+2}>Ca^{+2}>Ba^{+2}>Fe^{+3}$. In the case of the same valency, lesser swelling is observed for larger cation size [14,41].

(b) Chemical property:

(i) Acid resistance

Graft copolymers possess higher acid resistance than natural polysaccharides. The acid resistance enhances owing to the introduction of poly(vinyl) chains on the susceptible sites, such as –OH groups.

(ii) Base resistance

The introduction of hydrophobic moieties causes a reduction in base sensitivity of the produced graft copolymers. The greater the graft copolymerization, the more will be the alkali resistance.

(iii) Electrical stimulus sensitivity

Grafted copolymers display both AC- and DC-based electrical stimulus sensitivities in the direction of their deswelling behavior [41].

5 Pharmaceutical applications of polysaccharide graft copolymers

Polysaccharides graft copolymers obtain diverse attributes applied for a variety of functions [24]. Currently, functionalized biopolymers like graft copolymers of polysaccharides are lucrative, recyclable, eco-friendly, and proficient. After graft copolymerization and cross-linking, these tailor-made polysaccharides can be utilized in sustained-release dosage forms. Controlled release of drugs from graft copolymers of polysaccharides is the chief counteractive issue. Diffusion, degradation, or a combination of both can be the method of choice for the release process. Grafted polysaccharides-based hydrogels are widely employed in many pharmaceutical uses [14,24]. Such tailored polysaccharides possess huge importance in drug delivery, wound dressing, tissue regeneration, etc. [9,24,26]. These hydrogels are capable to entrap the colloidal particles in their folds and oblige them to settle at the base. Consequently, tailored polysaccharides possess a vital position in the elimination of colloidal particles from potable water. Being biodegradable and green in nature, these polysaccharide devices act as useful replacements for synthetic flocculants [24]. The properties of several polysaccharides (like acid–base resistance, thermal stability, and mechanical strength) can be advanced by the grafting of synthetic polymers onto the backbone. Furthermore, these grafted polysaccharides are being applied as reinforcing compounds to develop recyclable composites which show better compatibility with the matrix [57,58].

In a research, chitosan-*graft*-poly(acrylic acid-*co*-acrylamide) [chitosan-*graft*-poly(AA-*co*-AAm)] nanoparticles loaded with curcumin were developed for sustained-release drug delivery [59]. The antibacterial efficacy of curcumin-loaded chitosan-*graft*-poly(AA-*co*-AAm) nanoparticles against various bacteria was studied, which demonstrated the antibacterial effectiveness against both Gram-positive bacteria (*Staphylococcus aureus*, and *Pseudomonas aeruginosa*) and Gram-negative bacteria (*Escherichia coli*) when compared with that of tetracycline (an antibiotic) and pure chitosan. The in vitro releasing of curcumin from grafted chitosan-based nanoparticles demonstrated an enhanced release of curcumin at pH 5.4 (Fig. 1). Additionally, the curcumin released from these nanoparticles was found to be augmented with the increase in time.

In another investigation, chitosan-*graft*-poly(*N*-isopropylacrylamide) [chitosan-*graft*-poly(NIPAAm)] was synthesized [60]. The grafting ratio increment of chitosan-*graft*-poly(NIPAAm) assisted the temperature-sensitive gelation as well as pilocarpine encapsulation at the physiological pH. This grafted material was investigated for the preparation of in situ gelling systems of pilocarpine for ocular application. The grafted chitosan-based carriers demonstrated higher in vitro ocular biocompatibility, when tested in lens epithelial cells (HLE-B3 cells) cultures. In an experimental glaucoma model using rabbits, a grafted chitosan-based in situ gelling system of pilocarpine was also evaluated, in vivo. The decreasing intraocular pressure, miotic response, and corneal endothelial preservation response to pilocarpine were measured, which were found to be strongly dependent on the behavior of pilocarpine releasing. So, the developed in situ gelling system of pilocarpine made of chitosan-*graft*-poly(NIPAAm) can be used in antiglaucoma management and also can be used via intracameral injection.

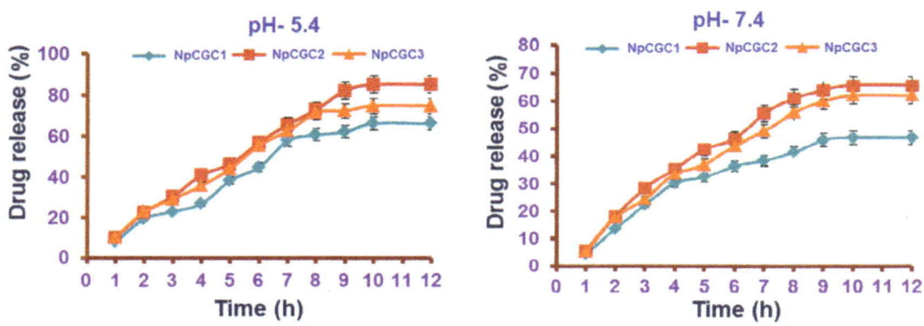

FIG. 1 In vitro release of curcumin from curcumin-loaded [chitosan-*graft*-poly(AA-*co*-AAm)] nanoparticles at pH 5.4 and pH 7.4. *From Kumar D, Raj V, Verma A, Kumar P, Pandey J. Novel binary grafted chitosan nanocarrier for sustained release of curcumin. Int J Biol Macromol 2019;131:184–191. Copyright © 2019 with permission from Elsevier B.V.*

Al-Kahtani and Sherigara synthesized acrylamide-grafted sodium alginate, where grafting of acrylamide (as monomer) onto sodium alginate backbone was performed by free-radical graft polymerization in the presence of CAN (as redox initiator) at different concentrations of acrylamide with a monomer-to-polymer ratio of 1:1, 2:1, and 3:1, respectively [61]. The synthesized grafted sodium alginate was used to develop semiinterpenetrating network-based microspheres of diclofenac sodium for controlled release applications. These grafted sodium alginate-made microspheres of diclofenac sodium were prepared by emulsion cross-linking process, where glutaraldehyde was used as a cross-linker. The in vitro diclofenac sodium release rate was found to be influenced by glutaraldehyde and acrylamide-to-sodium alginate ratio in grafted sodium alginate-made microspheres. It was also followed by the supercase II transport mechanism of diclofenac sodium release, in vitro.

In a research work, Sen et al. (2010) chemically synthesized polyacrylamide (PAm)-*graft*ed guar gum (guar gum-*graft*-PAm) via the microwave initiation grafting process varying different microwave irradiation time and microwave radiation power [62]. The synthesized guar gum-*graft*-PAm was employed in the formulation of controlled release carrier matrix for drug delivery applications. The mechanism of guar gum-*graft*-PAm synthesis was proposed as presented in Fig. 2. The irradiation time of 3 min and the irradiation power of 900 W yielded the highest grafting percentage with a desired intrinsic viscosity of synthesized guar gum-*graft*-PAm. The elemental analysis results of synthesized guar gum-*graft*-PAm demonstrated the presence of nitrogen atoms. However, the presence of nitrogen atoms was not identified in pure guar gum. Therefore, the results of elemental analyzes finally demonstrated that the PAm was graft-copolymerized on the guar gum template. The FTIR spectroscopy of guar gum-*graft*-PAm revealed some additional characteristic bands relative to guar gum, suggesting the graft copolymerization of guar gum by PAm. In the thermogravimetric analysis (TGA) graph, the occurrence of an additional zone indicated the grafting of PAm onto the guar gum backbone in the synthesized guar gum-*graft*-PAm. The results of characterization by SEM analysis demonstrated the distinguishing morphological alterations for guar gum-*graft*-PAm as compared to pure guar gum (Fig. 3). The synthesized guar gum-*graft*-PAm copolymers were found suitable as drug-eluting matrix excipients to show controlled release of drugs.

In a research work, locust bean gum was graft-modified by copolymerization process employing the microwave irradiation-initiated method using a redox initiator (CAN) [63]. The monomer used for the graft copolymerization of locust bean gum was acrylamide. The grafting procedure was statistically optimized by changing the microwave irradiation

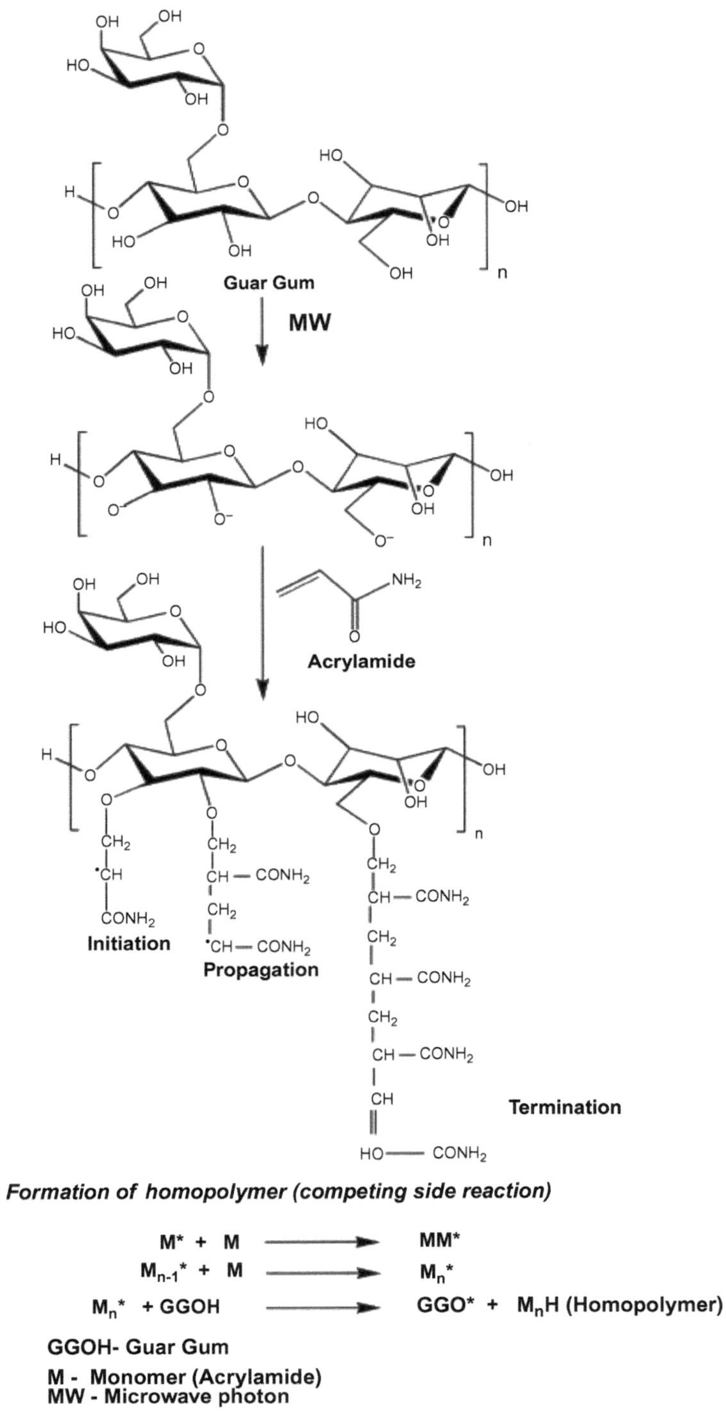

FIG. 2 The schematic presentation of the proposed mechanism for the synthesis of guar gum-*graft*-PAm by the microwave-initiated method. *From Sen G, Mishra S, Jha U, Pal S. Microwave initiated synthesis of polyacrylamide grafted guar gum (GG-g-PAM)—characterizations and application as matrix for controlled release of 5-amino salicylic acid. Int J Biol Macromol 2010;47:164–170. Copyright © 2010 Elsevier B.V.*

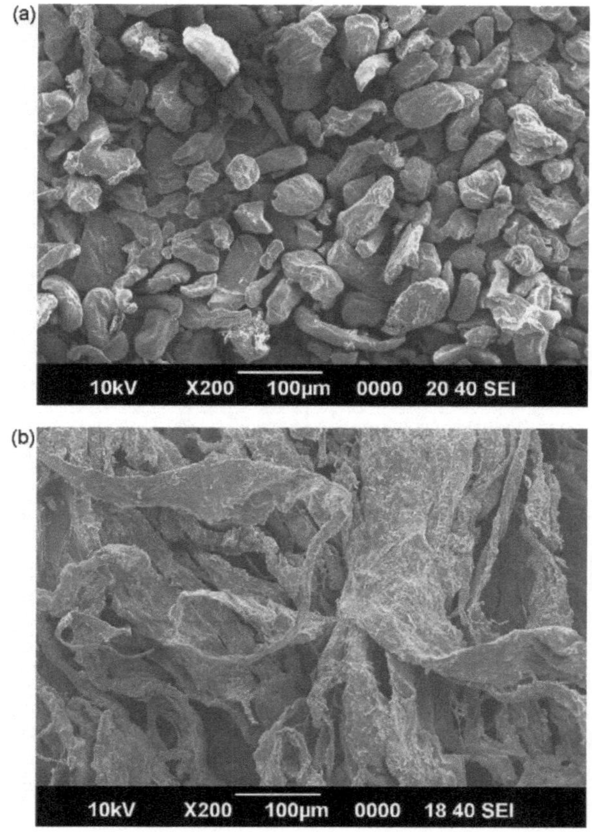

FIG. 3 SEM photograph of (A) pure guar gum and (B) guar gum-*graft*-PAm. *From Sen G, Mishra S, Jha U, Pal S. Microwave initiated synthesis of polyacrylamide grafted guar gum (GG-g-PAM)—characterizations and application as matrix for controlled release of 5-amino salicylic acid. Int J Biol Macromol 2010;47:164–170. Copyright © 2010 Elsevier B.V.*

time, concentrations of redox initiator, and acrylamide. The mechanism for the synthesis of grafted locust bean gum employing the microwave irradiation initiated method is schematically shown in Fig. 4. The grafted locust bean gum (101.083% grafting efficiency) was synthesized by optimal parameters like 1 g locust bean gum, 10 g acrylamide, 300 mg CAN, and 2.5-min irradiation time. The results of FTIR spectroscopic analyzes demonstrated that locust bean gum was successfully modified via graft polymerization to synthesize grafted locust bean gum. An extra characteristic peak at $1020\,cm^{-1}$ was found to have appeared in the FTIR spectrum of grafted locust bean gum, which might be attributed to the presence of CH-O-CH_2 group. The graft copolymerization of locust bean gum was

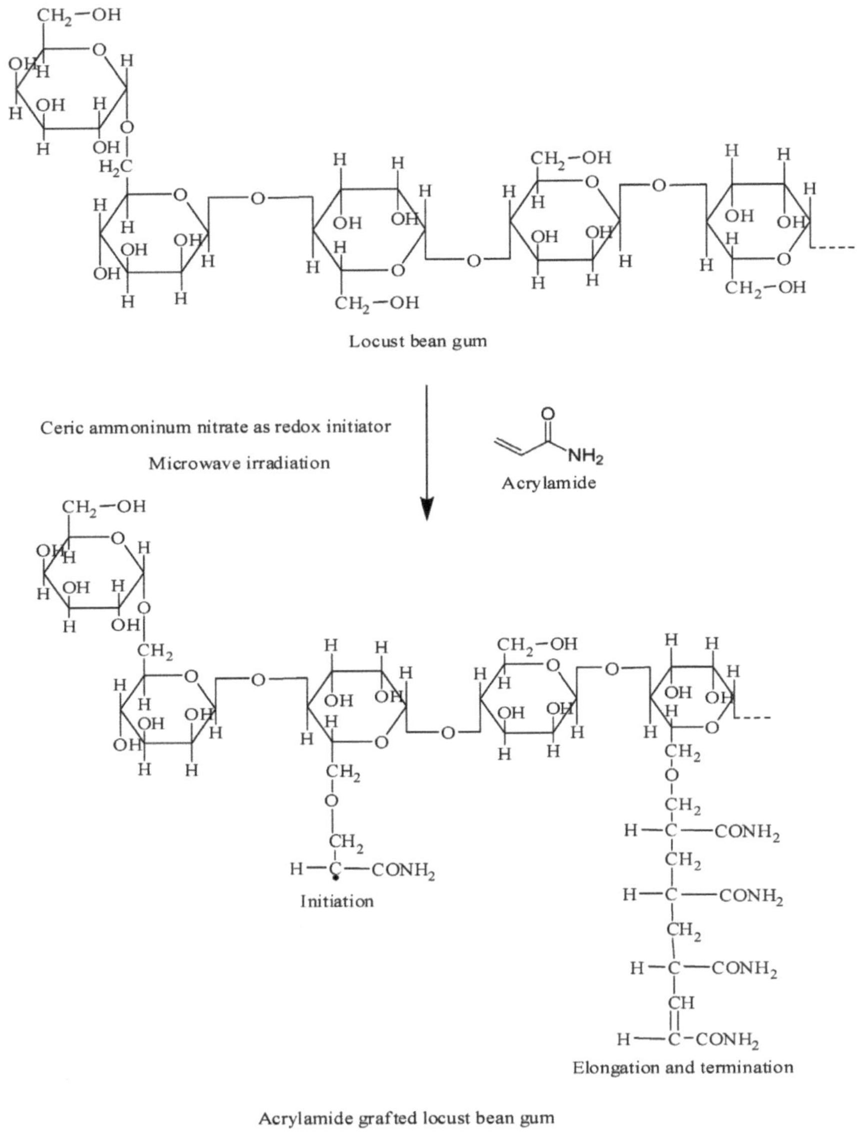

FIG. 4 The schematic presentation of the proposed mechanism for the synthesis of grafted locust bean gum by the microwave-initiated method. *From Kaity S, Isaac J, Mahesh Kumar P, Bose A, Wong TW, Ghosh A. Microwave assisted synthesis of acrylamide grafted locust bean gum and its application in drug delivery. Carbohydr Polym 2013;98:1083–1094. Copyright © 2013 Elsevier Ltd.*

also supported by the results of solid-state ^{13}C NMR analyzes, where the characteristic peak at $\delta = 41$ ppm was noticed in the ^{13}C NMR spectrum of grafted locust bean gum. This occurrence can be attributed to the fact of formation of $(–CH\text{-}CH_2\text{-}CH–)_n$ groups for the duration of the graft copolymerization reaction initiated by microwave irradiation. In addition, an intense characteristic peak at $\delta = 179$ ppm was noticed, which might be attributed to the presence of carbon atoms of $–CONH_2$ group. The results of DSC analysis showed that the heat of fusion (ΔH_m^0) for all the grafted locust bean gum was lesser in comparison with that of the native locust bean gum. The SEM photograph exhibited lumpy as well as undulant morphology with sharper breaking points for the synthesized grafted locust bean gum, which demonstrated the brittle nature (Fig. 5). In contrast, more powdery and fibrous morphology was evidenced for native locust bean gum, whereas polyhedral morphology was evidenced in the case

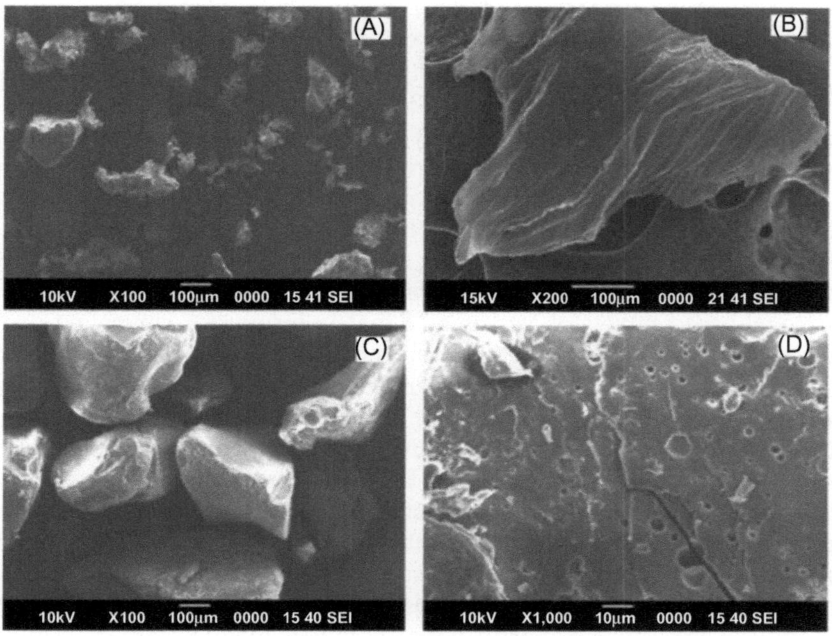

FIG. 5 SEM photographs of (A) locust bean gum, (B) acrylamide, (C) and (D) representative grafted locust bean gum by the microwave-initiated method. *From Kaity S, Isaac J, Mahesh Kumar P, Bose A, Wong TW, Ghosh A. Microwave assisted synthesis of acrylamide grafted locust bean gum and its application in drug delivery. Carbohydr Polym 2013;98:1083–1094. Copyright © 2013 Elsevier Ltd.*

of acrylamide. The granule sizes of synthesized grafted locust bean gum were bigger in comparison with that of the native locust bean gum. In addition, the grafted locust bean gum presented a sharper increment in wetting potential in the aqueous medium relative to the native locust bean gum. However, the native locust bean gum also presented a higher viscosity in comparison with that of the synthesized grafted locust bean gum. The fall in viscosity and the decreasing of molecular weight of grafted locust bean gum were attributed to the galactose branch point breakdown of native locust bean gum by microwave irradiation. Due to the introduction of free hydrophilic nature moieties via the graft copolymerization by acrylamide monomer, the swelling competence of the locust bean gum was increased. The grafted locust bean gum was found biocompatible and biodegradable in nature, which indicated the potential of the synthesized material as a biopolymer. This optimized grafted locust bean gum was investigated for the preparation of matrix tablets for controlled release of buflomedil HCl. The prepared grafted locust bean gum-based matrix tablets of buflomedil HCl showed the controlled drug releasing profile in comparison with that of HPMC K15 M.

Ghosh and Pal (2013) synthesized tamarind gum-*graft*-PAm employing acrylamide via the microwave irradiation-initiated method. As a redox initiator, CAN was used for the graft copolymerization of tamarind gum [64]. Different copolymers of tamarind gum (tamarind gum-*graft*-Pam with different grafting efficiencies) were synthesized by varying the reaction parameters. The optimized copolymerization was identified with the variation of gyration radius, grafting (%), and intrinsic viscosity. The synthesized tamarind gum-*graft*-PAm was studied to prepare pH-responsive hydrogel-based tablets of aspirin as a matrix former for controlled drug release application. To prepare aspirin matrix tablets, tamarind gum-*graft*-PAm was used as tablet binder. The results of FTIR spectroscopy clearly demonstrated the absence of chemical interaction(s) among tamarind gum-*graft*-PAm and aspirin, which might be attributed to the compatibility of tamarind gum-*graft*-PAm and aspirin in the formulations of aspirin matrix tablets. The results of SEM image analyzes demonstrated the morphological alterations indicating the physical (devoid of chemical) interaction among tamarind gum-*graft*-PAm and aspirin (Fig. 6). In a swelling study (in vitro), it was also noticed that the swelling behavior and the erosion rate of aspirin matrix tablets made of tamarind gum-*graft*-PAm were found higher and lesser with the increasing of grafting percent, respectively. In vitro aspirin-releasing pattern of these matrix tablets made of tamarind gum-*graft*-PAM was evaluated in different pHs (1.2, 6.8, and 7.4), and aspirin was found to be released completely after a duration of 24 h (Fig. 7). From the in vitro aspirin release results, it was noticed that the aspirin-releasing rate for aspirin matrix tablets made of

FIG. 6 SEM photographs of (A) tamarind gum-*graft*-PAm, (B) aspirin, and (C) aspirin matrix tablets made of tamarind gum-*graft*-PAm. *From Ghosh S, Pal S. Modified tamarind kernel polysaccharide: a novel matrix for control release of aspirin. Int J Biol Macromol 2013;58:296–300. Copyright © 2013 with permission from Elsevier B.V.*

tamarind gum-*graft*-PAm was lesser in the acidic pH (1.2), although it was noticed to be released at a higher rate in the alkaline pH (7.4) and neutral pH (6.8). In addition, it was revealed that the higher grafting percent produced a lowered rate of aspirin releasing (with a controlled releasing pattern). These aspirin matrix tablets made of tamarind gum-*graft*-PAm can be useful for lower gastrointestinal tract targeted delivery of drug via oral administration.

In another research, Ahuja et al. (2013) synthesized tamarind gum-*graft*-poly(*N*-vinyl-2-pyrrolidone) via microwave-induced graft copolymerization method employing APS as a redox initiator [65]. Aqueous solutions containing tamarind gum (10% w/v), *N*-vinyl-2-pyrrolidone (1% w/v), and APS concentration (10 mM/mL) were microwave-irradiated using a microwave oven at the microwave irradiation power of 20%–60% with microwave irradiation exposure of 60–150 s to synthesize various batches of tamarind gum-*graft*-poly(*N*-vinyl-2-pyrrolidone). The graft copolymerization method was statistically optimized by central composite design and response surface methodology, where times for microwave irradiation exposure as well as microwave irradiation power were analyzed as

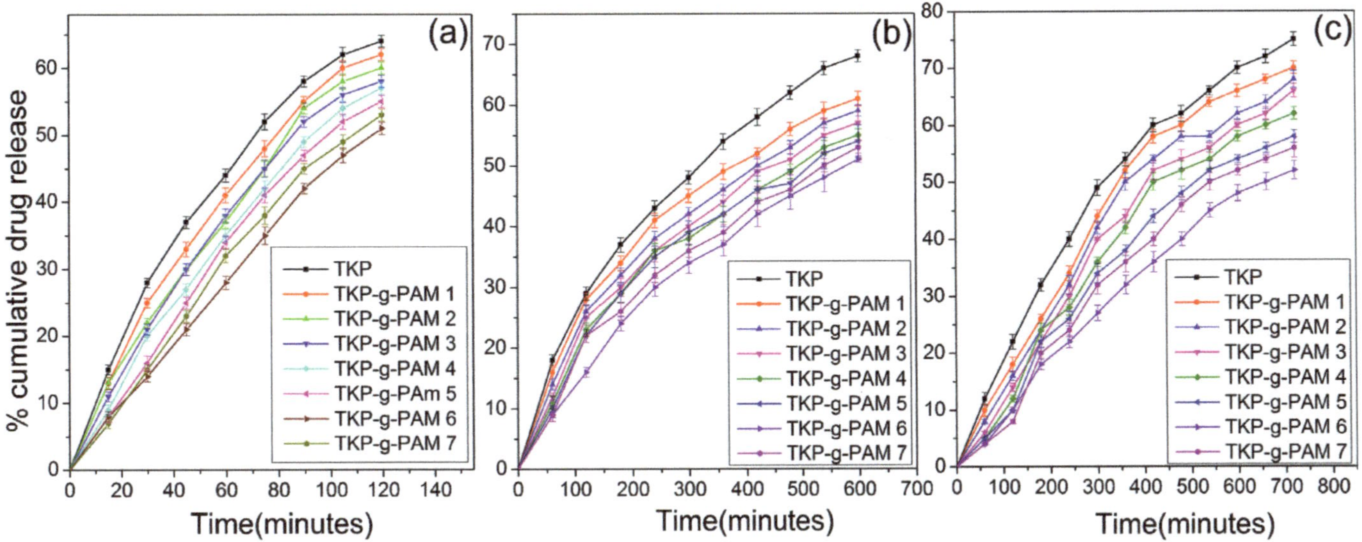

FIG. 7 Cumulative in vitro aspirin release profiles of aspirin matrix tablets made of tamarind gum-*graft*-PAM at (A) pH1.2, (B) pH6.8, and (C) pH7.4.From Ghosh S, Pal S. Modified tamarind kernel polysaccharide: a novel matrix for control release of aspirin. Int J Biol Macromol 2013;58:296–300. Copyright © 2013 with permission from Elsevier B.V.

individualized factors. As dependent responses, percent grafting efficiencies for the synthesis of tamarind gum-*graft*-poly(*N*-vinyl-2-pyrrolidone) were analyzed. The central composite design-based response surface methodology suggested a shared action of microwave irradiation power and microwave irradiation exposure on the percent grafting efficiencies. From the analysis of the graft copolymerization method, it was observed that the maximal percent grafting of *N*-vinyl-2-pyrrolidone on the tamarind gum backbone was performed at the lower microwave irradiation power for a longer microwave irradiation exposure or at higher microwave irradiation power for a shorter microwave irradiation exposure. The tamarind gum-*graft*-poly(*N*-vinyl-2-pyrrolidone) (51.6% grafting efficiency) was synthesized by optimal parameters like 20% microwave irradiation power and 132s microwave irradiation exposure. The microwave-induced synthesized graft copolymers were also characterized using XRD FTIR, DSC, and SEM analyzes, where the results suggested the formation of tamarind gum-*graft*-poly(*N*-vinyl-2-pyrrolidone). The synthesized tamarind gum-*graft*-poly(*N*-vinyl-2-pyrrolidone) was evaluated as biomucoadhesive polymeric excipient in the formulation of buccal patches containing metronidazole. The metronidazole buccal patches made of tamarind gum-*graft*-poly(*N*-vinyl-2-pyrrolidone) were found to have uniform weight (average) with uniform drug contents. The thickness and friability of these metronidazole buccal patches were in between 1.02 and 1.12mm and less than 2%, respectively. In vitro metronidazole releasing from these buccal patches exhibited a sustained pattern of drug release (>80%) and good ex vivo mucoadhesion onto the chicken pouch membrane over a longer period.

In an investigation, Hemmati and Ghaemy (2016) synthesized a novel kind of pH- and temperature-responsive gum tragacanth-based graft copolymers (amphiphilic alkyne-terminated terpolymers) to investigate their controlled drug releasing capacity [66]. The synthesized amphiphilic alkyne-terminated terpolymers were chemically synthesized via ROP and ATRP process using polycaprolactone (PCL), poly(dimethylaminoethyl methacrylate), and methylated poly(ethylene glycol) (mPEG). Then, the synthesized terpolymers were graft-copolymerized onto azide-functionalized gum tragacanth backbone via the click-chemistry-based method of graft copolymerization. Both the results of DSC and TGA analyzes suggested comparative good thermal stability of the gum tragacanth-based grafted copolymers compared to pure gum tragacanth. The results of SEM observation indicated the structural heterogeneity at the surface of the grafted copolymers; however, it was smooth and homogeneous for pure gum tragacanth. In the aqueous medium, the synthesized gum tragacanth-based grafted copolymers were self-assembled to produce single micelles, which were further assembled into micellar aggregation with the alterations of pH. These formed micelles made of gum tragacanth-based grafted copolymers were also investigated to prepare polymeric nanocarriers for drug delivery applications. These polymeric nanocarriers were loaded with quercetin using the probe sonication procedure.

Malik and Ahuja (2011) synthesized gum kondagogu-*graft*-PAm via the microwave-induced graft copolymerization of acrylamide onto gum kondagogu using ammonium persulfate (APS) as a redox initiator, where the graft copolymerization reaction condition was statistically optimized by 2^4 factorial design [67]. The microwave irradiation power, irradiation exposure time, and concentration of APS showed significant synergistic control on the grafting efficiency; while the gum kondagogu concentration did not exhibit any significant control on the grafting efficiency. The gum kondagogu-*graft*-PAm (92.35% grafting efficiency) was synthesized by optimal parameters like 40% microwave irradiation power, 120-s microwave irradiation exposure time, 10mM APS concentration, and 3% w/v gum kondagogu concentration. The FTIR spectra of gum kondagogu-*graft*-PAm demonstrated the -NH stretch band of acrylamide. The DSC thermogram of gum kondagogu-*graft*-PAm exhibited the characteristic shifting of endothermic peaks (at 95.41°C, 160.33°C, 243.95°C, and 262.29°C) of gum kondagogu-*graft*-PAm compared to gum kondagogu, and acrylamide confirmed the grafting of acrylamide chain onto gum kondagogu. The XRD profile of gum kondagogu-*graft*-PAm demonstrated the occurrence of characteristic diffraction peaks of acrylamide, implying the synthesis of graft copolymers of gum kondagogu (i.e., gum kondagogu-*graft*-PAm). SEM pictures of synthesized gum kondagogu-*graft*-PAm demonstrated an alteration of morphological features because of the grafting of acrylamide onto gum kondagogu. The particles of gum kondagogu-*graft*-PAm depicted the surface morphological features with several striations, while the surface morphological feature of pure gum kondagogu was found comparatively rough (Fig. 8). The synthesized gum kondagogu-*graft*-PAm was investigated as tableting matrix former, and the formulated matrix tablets containing diclofenac sodium showed a faster releasing of diclofenac sodium compared to pure gum kondagogu matrix-based matrix tablets.

In another investigation by Malik et al. (2012), gum kondagogu was tailored via graft copolymerization with *N*-vinyl-2-pyrrolidone [68]. The grafting of *N*-vinyl-2-pyrrolidone onto gum kondagogu employing UV-radiation-assisted procedure was statistically optimized by the response surface methodology. The concentrations of APS (as redox initiator) and *N*-vinyl-2-pyrrolidone showed a significant synergistic and antagonistic effect on the grafting efficiency, correspondingly. The gum kondagogu-*graft*-poly(*N*-vinyl-2-pyrrolidone) with 96.40% grafting efficiency was synthesized by optimal parameters like 3.95mM/L APS,

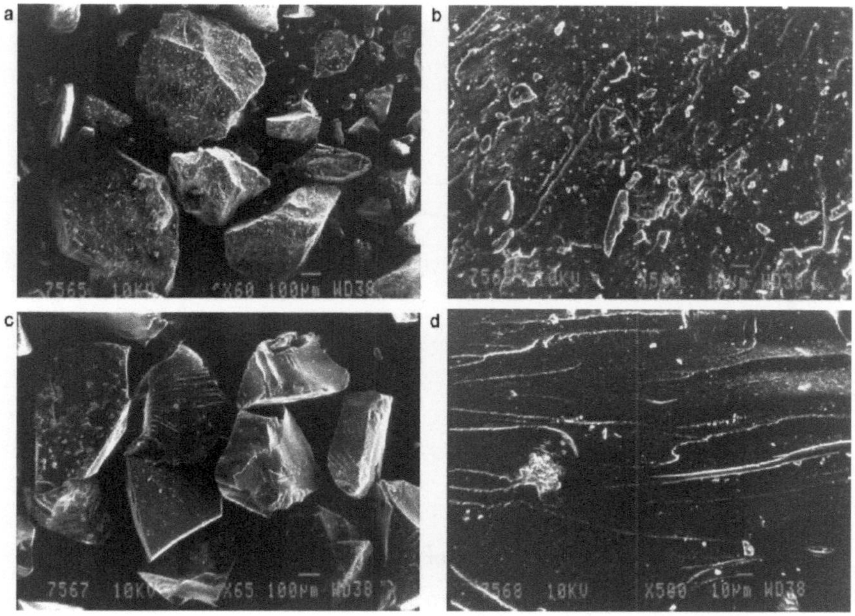

FIG. 8 SEM photographs showing (A) shape and (B) surface morphology of gum kondagogu, (C) shape and (D) surface morphology of gum kondagogu-*graft*-PAm. *From Malik S, Ahuja M. Gum kondagogu-g-poly (acrylamide): microwave-assisted synthesis, characterisation and release behaviour. Carbohydr Polym 2011;86:177–184. Copyright © 2011 Elsevier Ltd.*

1% w/v *N*-vinyl-2-pyrrolidone, and 3% w/v gum kondagogu concentration. The FTIR spectra of gum kondagogu-*graft*-poly(*N*-vinyl-2-pyrrolidone) exhibited the variation in the intensity as well as shifting of bands relative to pure gum kondagogu. The DSC thermogram of gum kondagogu-*graft*-poly(*N*-vinyl-2-pyrrolidone) showed characteristic endothermic peaks at 115.26°C, 167.34°C, and 240.25°C. The SEM photograph of synthesized grafted copolymer exhibited the morphological change because of the grafting of *N*-vinyl-2-pyrrolidone onto gum kondagogu. The surface morphology of gum kondagogu-*graft*-poly(*N*-vinyl-2-pyrrolidone) displayed the occurrence of *N*-vinyl-2-pyrrolidone fibers. The grafting copolymerization of gum kondagogu enhanced the mucoadhesiveness of gum kondagogu devoid of any significant changes in the drug-releasing potential when used as drug-releasing matrix excipient in the preparation of polymeric buccal discs containing metronidazole (an antiamoebic drug). A preliminary burst release of metronidazole was estimated with approximately 45% and 60% from gum kondagogu-*graft*-poly(*N*-vinyl-2-pyrrolidone)-based and gum kondagogu-based buccal discs, respectively (Fig. 9).

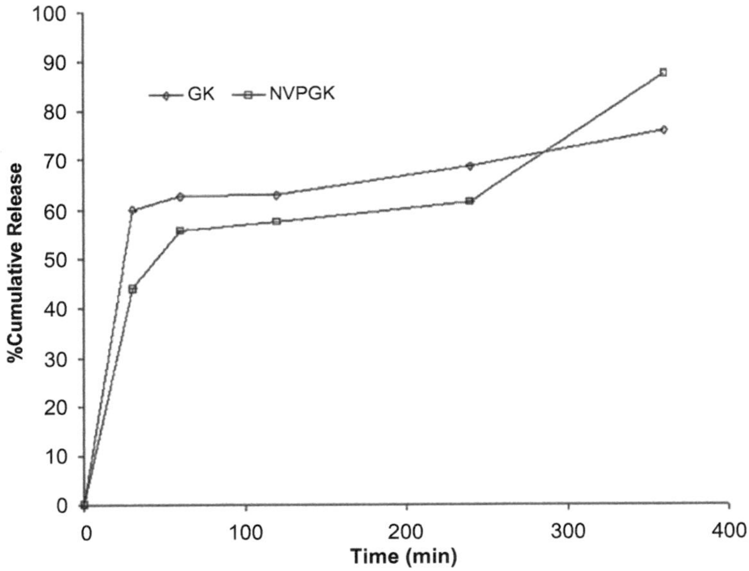

FIG. 9 In vitro release profile of metronidazole from gum kondagogu and gum kondagogu-*graft*-poly(*N*-vinyl-2-pyrrolidone)-based buccal discs. *From Malik S, Kumar A, Ahuja M. Synthesis of gum kondagogu-g-poly(N-vinyl-2-pyrrolidone) and its evaluation as a muco-adhesive polymer. Int J Biol Macromol 2012;51:756–762. Copyright © 2012 Elsevier B.V.*

Casas et al. (2010) synthesized graft copolymers of tapioca starch and hydroxypropyl tapioca starch by ethyl methacrylate by employing a free-radical copolymerization process assisted by oven-drying or freeze-drying [69]. These newly grafted copolymers were estimated with high percentages of grafting: 148.6 ± 6.2% for oven-dried tapioca starch-*graft*-ethyl methacrylate, 170.7 ± 4.5% for freeze-dried tapioca starch-*graft*-ethyl methacrylate, 213.5 ± 3.5% for oven-dried hydroxypropyl tapioca starch-*graft*-ethyl methacrylate, and 229.7 ± 6.8% for freeze-dried hydroxypropyl tapioca starch-*graft*-ethyl methacrylate. All these grafted copolymers (such as oven-dried tapioca starch-*graft*-ethyl methacrylate, freeze-dried tapioca starch-*graft*-ethyl methacrylate, oven-dried hydroxypropyl tapioca starch-*graft*-ethyl methacrylate, and freeze-dried hydroxypropyl tapioca starch-*graft*-ethyl methacrylate) were studied as matrix tablets containing theophylline for controlled releasing. The theophylline matrix tablets made of grafted copolymers of tapioca starch and hydroxypropyl tapioca starch exhibited a controlled release of theophylline, which was followed by a diffusion mechanism. However, theophylline matrix tablets made of tapioca starch-*graft*-ethyl methacrylate exhibited enhanced binding characteristics with decreased theophylline releasing pattern than that of the theophylline matrix tablets made of hydroxypropyl tapioca starch-*graft*-ethyl methacrylate. Both the drying process (oven-drying and freeze-drying) and breaking force demonstrated a significant action on the theophylline dissolution pattern of theophylline matrix tablets made of hydroxypropyl tapioca starch-*graft*-ethyl methacrylate, only. The radial theophylline releasing from matrix tablets made of tapioca starch-*graft*-ethyl methacrylate and hydroxypropyl tapioca starch-*graft*-ethyl methacrylate demonstrated that the initial amount of area provided to the dissolution medium estimated the theophylline-releasing pattern.

Some recently synthesized grafted polysaccharides used for pharmaceutical applications in drug delivery are presented in Table 1.

TABLE 1 Some recently synthesized grafted polysaccharides used for pharmaceutical applications in drug delivery.

Tailor-made polysaccharides	Drugs released	References
Sodium carboxymethyl okra gum-*graft*-polymethacrylamide sustained-release tablets	Diclofenac sodium	Patra et al. [70]
Grafted neem (*Azadirachta indica*) gum sustained-release tablets	Propranolol HCl	Bhagwat et al. [71]
Jhingan gum-*graft*-PAM matrix tablets	5-Amino salicylic acid	Mate et al. [72]
Guar gum-*graft*-2-hydroxyl ethyl methacrylate tablets	5-Amino salicylic acid	Mahto and Mishra [73]
Carboxymethyl xanthan gum-*graft*-PAm matrix tablets of	Diltiazem HCl	Badwaik et al. [74]
Buoyant tablets using grafted corn fiber gum	Cinnarizine	Sethi et al. [75]
Poly(ε-caprolactone)-*graft*-cashew gum nanoparticles	Epirubicin	Ribeiro et al. [76]
Grafted gum karaya pH-sensitive spray-dried microspheres	Capecitabine	Alange et al. [77]
Tamarind seed gum-hydrolyzed polymethacrylamide-*graft*-gellan beads for extended release	Diclofenac sodium	Nandi et al. [78]
Hydrogel prepared by graft copolymerization of polyvinylpyrrolidone onto *A. indica* gum	Methylprednisolone	Singh and Singh [79]
Gellan gum oleate-*graft*-poly(methacrylic acid) hydrogel	Ibuprofen	Seeli and Prabaharan [80]
Thermo-sensitive poly(*N*-vinyl caprolactam)-*graft*-aminated alginate hydrogels for protein release	Bovine serum albumin	Durkut and Elçin [81]
Ketoprofen-grafted alginate microcapsules in the transplantation of insulin-producing cells	Ketoprofen	Noverraz et al. [82]
Dual temperature- and pH-responsive alginate-*graft*-poly(*N*,*N*-diethyl acrylamide) microparticles	5-Fluorouracil	Işiklan et al. [83]

6 Conclusion

This chapter illustrates that grafting of the polymer unlocks a broad window of appliance in pharmaceutical industries. In this discussion, the significance of the grafting of natural polysaccharides has been pointed out. The next part of the discussion deals with the pharmaceutical applications of various grafted natural polysaccharides, more specifically in drug delivery uses. To get the customized properties of the natural polysaccharides by grafting, a variety of grafting processes are being utilized. Many grafted polysaccharides have already shown the potential with widespread pharmaceutical applications in industrial processes, more specifically in drug delivery uses. There are several freshly filed patents in the vicinity of polysaccharide grafting. The entrepreneur should have to illustrate huge attention in the field of polysaccharide grafting. In the future, polysaccharide grafting will have a wide scope in the development of various sophisticated drug delivery systems.

References

[1] Ito M, Nagai K. Degradation behaviour and application of recycled PVC sheet made of floor sheet for railway vehicle. Polym Degrad Stab 2007;92:1692–9.
[2] Makohliso SA, Giovangrandi L, Leonard D, Mathieu HJ, Ilegems M, Aebischer P. Application of teflon thin films for bio-patterning of neural cell adhesion. Biosens Bioelectron 1998;13:1227–35.
[3] Gao C, Yan D. Hyperbranched polymers: from synthesis to applications. Prog Polym Sci 2004;29:183–275.
[4] Chan HS, Ng SC. Synthesis, characterization and applications of thiophene-based functional polymers. Prog Polym Sci 1998;23:1167–231.
[5] Goddard JM, Hotchkiss JH. Polymer surface modification for the attachment of bioactive compounds. Prog Polym Sci 2007;32:698–725.
[6] Reisinger JJ, Hllmyer MA. Synthesis of fluorinated polymers by chemical modification. Prog Polym Sci 2002;27:971–1005.
[7] Marcincin A. Modification of fibre forming polymers by additives. Prog Polym Sci 2002;27:853–913.
[8] Muth O, Hirth T, Vogel H. Polymer modification by supercritical impregnation. J Supercrit Fluids 2000;17:65–72.
[9] Nayak AK, Pal D. Functionalization of tamarind gum for drug delivery. In: Thakur VK, Thakur MK, editors. Functional biopolymers. Cham: Springer; 2018. p. 35–56.
[10] Singh V, Kumara P, Sanghi R. Use of microwave irradiation in the grafting modification of the polysaccharides—a review. Prog Polym Sci 2012;37:340–64.
[11] Thakur VK, Thakur MK, Gupta RK. Graft copolymers of natural fibers for green composites. Carbohydr Polym 2014;104:87–93.
[12] Lv J, Ma J, HuangFu P, Yang S, Gong Y. Surface modification with both phosphorylcholine and stearyl groups to adjust hydrophilicity and hydrophobicity. Appl Surf Sci 2008;255:498–501.
[13] Kalia S, Kaith BS. Mechanical properties of phenolic composites reinforced with flax-g-copolymers prepared under different reaction conditions—a comparative study. E-J Chem 2008;5:177–84.
[14] Wang A, Wang W. Gum-g-copolymers: synthesis, properties and applications. In: Kalia S, Sabaa MW, editors. Polysaccharide based graft copolymers. Berlin: Springer-Verlag; 2013.

[15] Fares MM, El-faqeeh AS, Osman ME. Graft copolymerization onto starch–I. synthesis and optimization of starch grafted with N-tert-butylacrylamide copolymer and its hydrogels. J Polym Res 2003;10:119–25.
[16] Kaith BS, Kalia S. A study of crystallinity of graft copolymers of flax fiber with binary vinyl monomers. E-Polymers 2008;2:1–6.
[17] Wibowo AC, Desai SM, Mohanty AK, Drzal LT, Misra M. A solvent free graft copolymerization of maleic anhydride onto cellulose acetate butyrate bioplastic by reactive extrusion. Macromol Mater Eng 2006;291:90–5.
[18] Levis SR, Deasy PB. Pharmaceutical applications of size reduced grades of surfactant co-processed microcrystalline cellulose. Int J Pharm 2001;230:25–33.
[19] Singh J, Kaur L, McCarthy OJ. Factors influencing the physico-chemical, morphological, thermal and rheological properties of some chemically modified starches for food applications—a review. Food Hydrocoll 2007;21:1–22.
[20] Coviello T, Matricardi P, Marianecci C, Alhaique F. Polysaccharide hydrogels for modified release formulations. J Control Release 2007;119:5–24.
[21] Mehling T, Smirnova I, Guenther U, Neubert RHH. Polysaccharide-based aerogels as drug carriers. J Non Cryst Solids 2009;355:2472–9.
[22] Strickland FM. Immune regulation by polysaccharides: implications for skin cancer. J Photochem Photobiol B 2001;63:132–40.
[23] Maity M, Hasnain MS, Nayak AK, Aminabavi TM. Biomedical applications of polysaccharides. In: Nayak AK, Hasnain MS, Aminabhavi TM, editors. Tailor-made polysaccharides in biomedical applications. USA: Academic Press, Elsevier Inc.; 2021. p. 1–34.
[24] Nayak AK, Bera H, Hasnain MS, Pal D. Synthesis and characterization of graft-copolymers of plant polysaccharides. In: Thakur VK, editor. Biopolymer grafting, synthesis and properties. Netherlands: Elsevier Inc.; 2018. p. 1–62.
[25] Alkahtani S, Hasnain MS, Nayak AK, Aminabhavi TM. Polysaccharide-based polyelectrolyte complex systems for biomedical uses. In: Nayak AK, Hasnain MS, Aminabhavi TM, editors. Tailor-made polysaccharides in biomedical applications. USA: Academic Press, Elsevier Inc.; 2021. p. 151–74.
[26] Dey S, Roy S, Hasnain MS, Nayak AK. Grafted alginates in drug delivery. In: Nayak AK, Hasnain MS, editors. Alginates in drug delivery. United States: Academic Press, Elsevier Inc.; 2020. p. 71–100.
[27] Pal D, Nayak AK, Saha S. Interpenetrating polymer network hydrogels of chitosan: applications in controlling drug release. In: Mondal MIH, editor. Cellulose-based superabsorbent hydrogels. Switzerland: Springer Nature; 2019. p. 1727–68.
[28] Nayak AK, Pal D. Chitosan-based interpenetrating polymeric network systems for sustained drug release. In: Tiwari A, Patra HK, Choi J-W, editors. Advanced theranostics materials. USA: Wiley-Scrivener; 2015. p. 183–208.
[29] Pal D, Nayak AK. Interpenetrating polymer networks (IPNs): natural polymeric blends for drug delivery. In: Mishra M, editor. Encyclopedia of biomedical polymers and polymeric biomaterials, vol. VI. New York: Taylor and Francis; 2015. p. 4120–30.
[30] Ray S, Sinha P, Laha B, Maiti S, Bhattacharyya UK, Nayak AK. Polysorbate 80 coated crosslinked chitosan nanoparticles of ropinirole hydrochloride for brain targeting. J Drug Deliv Sci Technol 2018;48:21–9.
[31] Das B, Dutta S, Nayak AK, Nanda U. Zinc alginate-carboxymethyl cashew gum microbeads for prolonged drug release: development and optimization. Int J Biol Macromol 2014;70:505–15.
[32] Sun RC, Fang JM, Tomkinson J, Hill CAS. Esterification of hemicelluloses from poplar chips in homogenous solution of N,N-dimethylformamide/lithium chloride. J Wood Chem Technol 1999;19:287–306.
[33] Wan Z, Xiong Z, Ren H, Huang Y, Liu H, Xiong H, Wu Y, Han J. Graft copolymerization of methyl methacrylate onto bamboo cellulose under microwave irradiation. Carbohydr Polym 2011;83:264–9.

[34] Onishi Y, Eshita Y, Murashita A, Mizuno M, Yoshida J. Characteristics of DEAE dextran-MMA graft copolymer as a nonviral gene carrier. Nanomed Nanotechnol Biol Med 2007;3:184–91.
[35] Stannett V. Grafting. Radiat Phys Chem 1981;18:215–22.
[36] Ring W, Mita I, Jenkins AD, Bikales NM. Source-based nomenclature for copolymers (recommendations 1985). Pure Appl Chem 1985;57:1427–40.
[37] Kaith BS, Jindal R, Bhatia JK. Morphological and thermal evaluation of soy protein concentrate on graft copolymerization with ethylmethacrylate. J Appl Polym Sci 2011;120:2183–90.
[38] Mehta IK, Misra BN, Chauhan GS. Study of thermal and dyeing behavior of isotactic polypropylene fiber graft copolymerized with acrylate monomers using preirradiation method. J Appl Polym Sci 1994;54:1171–8.
[39] Alves NM, Mano JF. Chitosan derivatives obtained by chemical modifications for biomedical and environmental applications. Int J Biol Macromol 2008;43:401–14.
[40] Xie W, Xu P, Wang W, Liu Q. Preparation and antibacterial activity of a water-soluble chitosan derivative. Carbohydr Polym 2002;50(1):35–40.
[41] Bhattacharya A, Misra BN. Grafting: a versatile means to modify polymers techniques, factors and applications. Prog Polym Sci 2004;29:767–814.
[42] Szwarc M. Living polymers. Their discovery, characterization, and properties. J Polym Sci A Polym Chem 1997;36:9–15.
[43] Lizotte JR, Long TE. Stable free-radical polymerization of styrene in combination with 2-vinylnaphthalene initiation. Macromol Chem Phys 2003;4(204):570–6.
[44] Mishra V, Kumar R. Living radical polymerization: a review. J Sci Res 2012;56:141–76.
[45] Sonmez HB, Senkal BF, Sherrington DC, Bıcak N. Atom transfer radical graft polymerization of acrylamide from N-chlorosulfonamidated polystyrene resin, and use of the resin in selective mercury removal. React Funct Polym 2003;55:1–8.
[46] Arslan H. Block and graft copolymerization by controlled/living radical polymerization methods. vol. 13. InTechOpen; 2012. p. 279–320.
[47] Peng T, Cheng YL. PNIPAAm and PMAA cografted porous PE membranes: living radical co-grafting mechanism and multi-stimuli responsive permeability. Polymer 2001;42(5):2091–100.
[48] Bellobono IR, Calgari S, Leonari MC, Selli E, Paglia ED. Photochemical grafting of acrylated azo dyes onto polymeric surfaces. IV. Grafting of 4-(N-ethyl N-2-acryloxyethyl) amino-40 nitroazobenzene onto cellulose. Die Angew Makromol Chem 1981;100:135–46.
[49] Kubota H, Suka IG, Kuroda S, Kondo T. Introduction of stimuli-responsive polymers into regenerated cellulose film by means of photografting. Eur Polym J 2001;37:1367–72.
[50] Kumar G, Smith PJ, Payne GF. Enzymatic grafting of a natural product onto chitosan to confer water solubility under basic conditions. Biotechnol Bioeng 1999;63:154–65.
[51] Chen T, Kumar G, Harris MT, Smith PJ, Payne GF. Enzymatic grafting of hexyloxyphenol onto chitosan to alter surface and rheological properties. Biotechnol Bioeng 2000;70(5):564–73.
[52] Yamaguchi T, Yamahara S, Nakao S, Kimura S. Preparation of pervaporation membranes for removal of dissolved organics from water by plasma-graft filling polymerization. J Membr Sci 1994;95(94):39–49.
[53] Wenzel A, Yamgishita H, Kitamoto D, Endo A, Haraya K, Nakane T, Hanai N, Matsuda H, Kamuswetz H, Paul D. Effect of preparation condition of photoinduced graft filling polymerized membranes on pervaporation performance. J Membr Sci 2000;179:69–77.
[54] Kim YJ, Kang IK, Huh MW, Yoon SC. Surface characterization and in vitro blood compatibility of poly(ethylene terephthalate) immobilized with insulin and/or heparin using plasma glow discharge. Biomaterials 2000;21(2):121–30.
[55] Contreras-garcía A, Bucio E, Concheiro A, Alvarez-lorenzo C, Bucio E, Concheiro A, Contreras-garcı A. Surface functionalization of polypropylene devices with hemocompatible DMAAm and NIPAAm grafts for norfloxacin sustained release. J Bioact Compat Polym 2011;26(4):405–19.

[56] Koshy TM, Gowda DV, Tom S, Karunakar G, Srivastava A, Moin A. Polymer grafting—an overview. Am J PharmTech Res 2016;6(2):2249–3387.

[57] Kumar K, Kaith BS. Psyllium and acrylic acid based polymeric networks synthesized under the influence of γ-radiations for sustained release of fungicide. Fibers Polym 2010;11:147–52.

[58] Kaith BS, Mittal H, Bhatia JK, Kalia S. Polysaccharide graft copolymers–synthesis, properties and applications. In: Kalia S, Averous L, editors. Biopolymers: biomedical and environmental applications. Hoboken, NJ: Wiley; 2011.

[59] Kumar D, Raj V, Verma A, Kumar P, Pandey J. Novel binary grafted chitosan nanocarrier for sustained release of curcumin. Int J Biol Macromol 2019;131:184–91.

[60] Lai JY, Luo LJ. Chitosan-g-poly(N-isopropylacrylamide) copolymers as delivery carriers for intracameral pilocarpine administration. Eur J Pharm Biopharm 2017;113:140–8.

[61] Al-Kahtani AA, Sherigara BS. Controlled release of diclofenac sodium through acrylamide grafted hydroxyethyl cellulose and sodium alginate. Carbohydr Polym 2014;104:151–7.

[62] Sen G, Mishra S, Jha U, Pal S. Microwave initiated synthesis of polyacrylamide grafted guar gum (GG-g-PAM)—characterizations and application as matrix for controlled release of 5-amino salicylic acid. Int J Biol Macromol 2010;47:164–70.

[63] Kaity S, Isaac J, Mahesh Kumar P, Bose A, Wong TW, Ghosh A. Microwave assisted synthesis of acrylamide grafted locust bean gum and its application in drug delivery. Carbohydr Polym 2013;98:1083–94.

[64] Ghosh S, Pal S. Modified tamarind kernel polysaccharide: a novel matrix for control release of aspirin. Int J Biol Macromol 2013;58:296–300.

[65] Ahuja M, Kumar S, Kumar A. Tamarind seed polysaccharide-g-poly(N-vinyl-2-pyrrolidone): microwave-assisted synthesis, characterization and evaluation as mucoadhesive polymer. Int J Polym Mater Polym Biomater 2013;62:544–9.

[66] Hemmati K, Ghaemy M. Synthesis of new thermo/pH sensitive drug delivery systems based on tragacanth gum polysaccharide. Int J Biol Macromol 2016;87:415–25.

[67] Malik S, Ahuja M. Gum kondagogu-g-poly (acrylamide): microwave-assisted synthesis, characterisation and release behaviour. Carbohydr Polym 2011;86:177–84.

[68] Malik S, Kumar A, Ahuja M. Synthesis of gum kondagogu-g-poly(N-vinyl-2-pyrrolidone) and its evaluation as a mucoadhesive polymer. Int J Biol Macromol 2012;51:756–62.

[69] Casas M, Ferrero C, Jiménez-Castellanos MR. Graft tapioca starch copolymers as novel excipients for controlled-release matrix tablets. Carbohydr Polym 2010;80:71–7.

[70] Patra S, Bala NN, Nandi G. Synthesis, characterization and fabrication of sodium carboxymethyl-okra-gum-grafted-polymethacrylamide into sustained release tablet matrix. Int J Biol Macromol 2020;164:3885–900.

[71] Bhagwat DA, Kolekar VR, Nadaf SJ, Choudhari PB, More HN, Killedar SG. Acrylamide grafted neem (*Azadirachta indica*) gum polymer: screening and exploration as a drug release retardant for tablet formulation. Carbohydr Polym 2020;229, 115357.

[72] Mate CJ, Mishra S, Srivastava PK. *In vitro* release kinetics of graft matrices from *Lannea coromandelica* (Houtt) gum for treatment of colonic diseases by 5-ASA. Int J Biol Macromol 2020;149:908–20.

[73] Mahto A, Mishra S. Design, development and validation of guar gum based pH sensitive drug delivery carrier via graft copolymerization reaction using microwave irradiations. Int J Biol Macromol 2019;138:278–91.

[74] Badwaik HR, Sakure K, Nakhate KT, Kashayap P, Dhongade H, Alexander A, Ajazuddin, Tripathi DK. Effect of Ca^{+2} ion on the release of diltiazem hydrochloride from matrix tablets of carboxymethyl xanthan gum graft polyacrylamide. Int J Biol Macromol 2017;94(Pt A):691–7.

[75] Sethi S, Mangla B, Kamboj S, Rana V. A QbD approach for the fabrication of immediate and prolong buoyant cinnarizine tablet using polyacrylamide-g-corn fibre gum. Int J Biol Macromol 2018;117:350–61.

[76] Ribeiro IS, Pontes FJG, Carneiro MJM, Sousa NA, Pinto VPT, Ribeiro FOS, Silva DA, Araújo GS, Marinho Filho JDB, Araújo AJ, Paula HCB, Feitosa JPA, de Paula RCM. Poly(ε-caprolactone) grafted cashew gum nanoparticles as an epirubicin delivery system. Int J Biol Macromol 2021;179:314–23.
[77] Alange VV, Birajdar RP, Kulkarni RV. Functionally modified polyacrylamide-graft-gum karaya pH-sensitive spray dried microspheres for colon targeting of an anti-cancer drug. Int J Biol Macromol 2017;102:829–39.
[78] Nandi G, Nandi AK, Khan NS, Pal S, Dey S. Tamarind seed gum-hydrolyzed polymethacrylamide-g-gellan beads for extended release of diclofenac sodium using 3^2 full factorial design. Int J Biol Macromol 2018;114:214–25.
[79] Singh B, Singh B. Graft copolymerization of polyvinylpyrollidone onto *Azadirachta indica* gum polysaccharide in the presence of crosslinker to develop hydrogels for drug delivery applications. Int J Biol Macromol 2020;159:264–75.
[80] Seeli DS, Prabaharan M. Guar gum oleate-graft-poly(methacrylic acid) hydrogel as a colon-specific controlled drug delivery carrier. Carbohydr Polym 2017;158:51–7.
[81] Durkut S, Elçin YM. Synthesis and characterization of thermosensitive poly(N-vinyl caprolactam)-grafted-aminated alginate hydrogels. Macromol Chem Phys 2020;221(2), 1900412.
[82] Noverraz F, Montanari E, Pimenta J, Szabó L, Ortiz D, Gonelle-Gispert C, Bühler LH, Gerber-Lemaire S. Antifibrotic effect of ketoprofen-grafted alginate microcapsules in the transplantation of insulin producing cells. Bioconjug Chem 2018;20(29):1932–41.
[83] Işiklan N, Inal M, Kurşun F, Ercan G. pH responsive itaconic acid grafted alginate microspheres for the controlled release of nifedipine. Carbohydr Polym 2011;84(3):933–43.

CHAPTER

7

Grafted polysaccharides in drug delivery

Mohsen Khodadadi Yazdi[a], *Payam Zarrintaj*[b], *Mohammad Reza Ganjali*[a,c], *Foad Salehnia*[a], *Morteza Rezapour*[d], *Farzad Seidi*[e], *and Mohammad Reza Saeb*[f]

[a]Center of Excellence in Electrochemistry, School of Chemistry, College of Science, University of Tehran, Tehran, Iran, [b]School of Chemical Engineering, Oklahoma State University, Stillwater, OK, United States, [c]Biosensor Research Center, Endocrinology and Metabolism Molecular-Cellular Sciences Institute, Tehran University of Medical Sciences, Tehran, Iran, [d]IP Department, Research Institute of Petroleum Industry (RIPI), Tehran, Iran, [e]Jiangsu Co-Innovation Center of Efficient Processing and Utilization of Forest Resources and International Innovation Center for Forest Chemicals and Materials, Nanjing Forestry University, Nanjing, China, [f]Department of Polymer Technology, Faculty of Chemistry, Gdańsk University of Technology, Gdańsk, Poland

1 Introduction

Since its emergence in the early 1950s, the concept of drug delivery has been in the center of attention by many researchers in order to reduce the adverse side effects of medications [1,2]. Many materials as well as design strategies have correspondingly been proposed and examined over years to make a wide variety of drug delivery systems (DDSs) for different parts of the human body and various administration routes [3]. Among materials, both synthetic and natural polymers have served as essential building blocks that contributed to making highly efficient DDSs [4,5]. Natural polymers such as proteins and polysaccharides benefit from the availability, biocompatibility, biodegradation, and nontoxicity [6,7]. As a result, they have been considered

Tailor-Made Polysaccharides in Drug Delivery
https://doi.org/10.1016/B978-0-12-821286-8.00007-0

biomaterials in drug delivery and regenerative medicine [8–11]. It should be noted that synthetic polymers may provide more versatile chemistry for tailor-making DDSs. Polysaccharides, such as cellulose and starch, are abundant structural and energy storage biomaterials that constitute important various parts of animals, plants, microorganisms, and fungi [12–14]. These carbohydrate polymers have gained much interest in various biomedical applications [15–17]. Indeed, tissue-like mechanical behavior, nontoxic nature, high potential of water uptake, and biodegradability made polysaccharides promising candidates for 2D/3D cell culture, cell delivery systems, 3D/4D printing, injectable hydrogels, implantation, and drug delivery applications [18–21]. In this regard, the development of intelligent DDS based on a polysaccharide with on–off switching properties for diverse systems having various physiological conditions has become a specific branch of research of science for developing efficient delivery systems [22].

Developing novel DDSs for controlled and prolonged release of therapeutics has gained much interest in the last decade because of the high production costs and side effects caused by the conventional drugs, especially those likely to happen in chemotherapeutics [23–26]. The final goal in the DDSs is to design delivery platforms that can selectively facilitate the delivery of drugs to the diseased tissue or cells with a prescribed dosage in a definite period of time. The DDSs should not trigger any foreign body responses and be cleared out from the body, right after the delivery mission was completed. Depending on the drug features, administration route, and release duration, various DDSs may be practically utilized. In this regard, various drug delivery platforms (e.g., InPen, smart capsules, and nanobots) have been designed for various applications [27–29]. Material selection has always been a critical stage or limiting factor in manufacturing advanced DDSs. The materials should not result in foreign body responses, while they must tolerate the physiological conditions in the human body (e.g., acidic condition in the stomach), and degrade in a controlled manner [7,30,31]. The toxicity and the protein corona of degradation products should also be considered in material selection [32,33]. Novel DDSs are normally manufactured using a variety of biomaterials or multifunctional materials in which every material plays a specified role in a very special manner for a target function. For example, stimuli-responsive biomaterials can be utilized to make smart DDSs, which are triggered with various stimuli [34–37]. As another example, polyethylene glycol (PEG) coating can prevent the formation of protein corona around the superparamagnetic iron oxide nanoparticles [38]. When subjected to biological environments, a biomolecular interface will be formed onto the surface of nanoparticles. The fingerprint of protein corona can be detected by changing the coatings on the surface of monodispersed magnetic nanoparticles.

The application of polysaccharides such as cellulose, starch, chitosan, alginates, dextran, and hyaluronic acid in drug delivery systems has gained a great deal of interest over the past three decades [17,39–41]. Despite promising features such as biodegradability, biocompatibility, and non-toxicity, polysaccharides suffer from some disadvantages to pass requirements for making DDSs when they are used in the form of as-received. The main drawbacks are the lack of functionality and poor mechanical properties. Thus, they have been applied in combination with other natural or synthetic polymers to make efficient DDSs. In recent years, the grafted polysaccharides with extended functionalities and adjustable properties have gained much more interest in scientific and industrial centers for manufacturing novel and smart delivery systems.

The focus of this chapter is placed on grafter polysaccharides applied as DDS. Fig. 1 shows a general view of the importance of polysaccharides

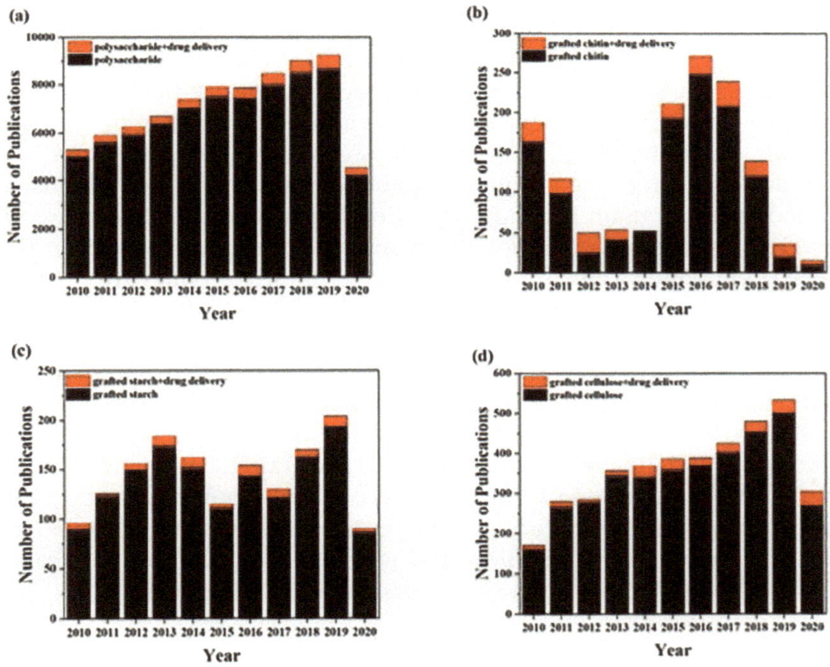

FIG. 1 The number of publications on the polysaccharides (A), grafted polysaccharides and specific polysaccharides, including chitin (B), starch (C), and cellulose (D) as the main versatile polysaccharides used in DDS, and their contribution to drug delivery applications (data are collected based on some keywords, including polysaccharide, polysaccharides, grafted chitin, grafting chitin, grafted starch, grafting starch, grafted cellulose, grafting cellulose, grafted chitin + drug delivery, grafting chitin + drug delivery, grafting starch + drug delivery, grafted starch + drug delivery, grafted cellulose + drug delivery, and grafting cellulose + drug delivery). Data were collected from the Scopus Web of Science on June 8, 2020. The ongoing data on the publications recorded in 2020 should be considered in mind in the prediction of the future trends in the present form of bar diagrams.

and grafted polysaccharides in drug delivery and controlled release applications over the past decade. It can be seen that there has been an increasing trend in the number of publications devoted to some examples of polysaccharides used as DDS. Chitin, starch, and cellulose are among the most versatile homo-polysaccharides widely used in delivery systems. Therefore, they are considered in this survey.

2 Polysaccharide-based graft copolymers

Polysaccharides are carbohydrate polymers containing sucrose or monosaccharides as the repeating unit. The backbone of polysaccharides possesses a variety of chemical functionalities such as hydroxyl, amino, and carboxyl groups, which make them favorable for being chemically modified [42–44]. In addition, they can be modified through the chain scission reactions, e.g., oxidized alginate (OA)-based hydrogels [45]. Like other natural synthetic multiblock copolymers, different monomers, oligomers, and polymers can react with carbohydrate polymers to make random, alternate, block, and graft copolymers [46–49]. In the graft copolymer structures, one or more oligomeric or polymeric side chains are grafted onto the main backbone; grafting is usually carried out through chemical reaction with chemical functionalities present on the backbone of the main polymer. The "grafting from" and "grafting onto" are the most well-known methods to make graft polymers. In the "grafting from" strategy, an active site (e.g., radicals or reactive functional groups) is created such that the polymerization of the monomer initiates and proceeds. By contrast, in the "grafting onto" method, an oligomeric or polymeric brush is attached to the main chain via covalent bonding. Condensation and ionic polymerization are usually used to make grafted copolymers [50,51]. Graft copolymerization can also be used to make polysaccharide-based graft copolymers with improved properties, including environmental stability, controlled biodegradation, and water uptake [52]. The application of grafted polysaccharides in DDS is discussed in this chapter.

3 Grafted polysaccharides in DDSs

3.1 Grafted chitosan

Chitosan is the most commonly applied polycationic biopolymer in the biomedical field [10,53–56]. It is a nontoxic biodegradable and biocompatible carbohydrate polymer that preserves promising characteristics for drug delivery purposes. Nevertheless, the limited solubility of chitosan in water and organic solvents together with its poor mechanical strength necessitates chemical modification of chitosan [57]. This polysaccharide, which is obtained through deacetylation of chitin or the reaction between β(1-4)-linked d-glucosamine and *N*-acetyl-D-glucosamine, is potent for being chemically modified to create various functionalities in its structure [10,58]. Due to the ability to grafting, chitosan has been the most utilized polysaccharide in designing DDSs with its improved interaction with drugs [59–61]. More recently, grafted copolymers based on chitosan have featured auspicious in the fabrication of advanced drug delivery platforms. For example, PEG-grafted chitosan (PEG-g-chitosan) was used as injectable thermosensitive hydrogel by grafting PEG on chitosan, and then it has been applied in vitro for the drug release assessments using a typical protein of bovine serum albumin (BSA) [62]. PEG grafting via covalent bonding was ca. 40 wt%, and a transition from fully liquid to solid-like state was observed after the hydrogel was injected into the body at 37°C. The initial burst release took about 5 h; after that, a steady-state release of BSA was achieved over a prolonged period of 3 days, followed by the prolonged quasilinear release of BSA, taking up to 40 days by in situ cross-linking of the grafted chitosan by the genipin as a cross-linking agent. Likewise, PEG-g-chitosan aggregates were found to be swelled by the uptake *N*-phenyl-1-naphthylamine (PNA) as a hydrophobic substance in the vicinity of pH = 7 [63]. The maximum release of PNA was achieved at an acidic condition.

Since many drugs are hydrophobic in nature, the hydrophobic modification of polysaccharides has been widely utilized in making efficient DDSs. Moreover, hydrophobic modification of polysaccharides could result in the formation of amphiphilic polymers with interesting self-assembly and micelle creation features. For example, N-acylation of chitosan with the aid of fatty acid chlorides of variable chain length was found to be an appropriate way to increase the hydrophobicity of chitosan [64]. Elsewhere, carbodiimide coupling chemistry was used to graft hydrophilic poly(ethylene glycol) (PEG) and hydrophobic oleic acid onto the chitosan backbone to create an amphiphilic polysaccharide [65]. Amphiphilic chitosan micelles were less than 140 nm in diameter bearing positive surface charges. A hydrophobic anticancer drug (camptothecin) was encapsulated into micelles with a high encapsulation efficiency. In vitro drug release experiments in simulated gastrointestinal fluids (SGFs) showed sustained and controlled delivery of drugs, while preserving their stability and activity. Accordingly, this DDS can be potentially used for orally administered drugs [65]. Furthermore, injectable hydrogels based on polyurethane-g-CS were used as controlled DDS for doxorubicin (DOX) and tetracycline hydrochloride (antibacterial agent) [66]. Assessment of cellular uptake behavior of drug from the chitosan hydrogel grafted with ester-diol-based polyurethane copolymer (EDPUC) has been significantly improved, which has been featured by enhanced cell killing in the developed drug-embedded hydrogel system. In vivo gelation study in an animal model proved that the EDPUC-grafted chitosan was an injectable hydrogel suitable for disease control as a well-controlled drug delivery vehicle.

In addition to the aforementioned cases in which a biodegradable polymer or copolymer was grafted onto the chitosan for achieving enhanced drug delivery, the grafting moieties can be selected among polysaccharides, leading to the polysaccharide-grafted polysaccharides like β-cyclodextrin (β-CD) with improved or expanded properties [67]. In this regard, β-CD-g-chitosan was coated onto the titanium alloy implant, through layer-by-layer assembly, and served as a biomolecular reservoir for the calcitriol (VD3, the most active form of vitamin D) and calcitonin (CT, a drug for treatment of osteoporosis) [68]. It was observed that sustained release of drugs from multilayer coating can significantly improve bone remodeling and osseointegration which is highly promising for osteoporotic fractures [68].

The harsh condition of the gastrointestinal (GI) tract makes orally administered DDSs essentially important for sensitive drugs such as peptides and insulin [69]. According to the literature, such systems should be precisely designed to be able to preserve drug stability and bioactivity through the GI tract. Insulin that bears negative charges can interact with the positively charged macromolecules via electrostatic complexation, which results in polyelectrolyte complex (PEC). Insulin complexes with oligomers and/or polymers, such as oligochitosan, were found to be able to improve the stability of insulin in harsh physiological conditions in the GI tract and, at the same time, eliminate the need for the removal of toxic cross-linking agents [70]. Sharma and Singh used a polylactic acid (PLA)-PEG–PLA thermosensitive injectable hydrogel as a delivery system for the release of insulin [71]. Chitosan was modified by the oleic acid, a hydrophobic macromolecule, to improve the dispersion of chitosan throughout the hydrophobic PLA–PEG–PLA matrix. Electrostatic interactions between the oleic acid-grafted chitosan (OA-g-CS) and the zinc-insulin hexamers resulted in the creation of a PEC. In vivo studies showed sustained release of insulin after subcutaneous injection, while preserving its biostability [71].

Gold nanoparticles (GNPs) are interesting materials for the development of DDSs [72]. Colloidal gold was also considered as a sol comprising nanoparticles of Au0, which has been considered as a therapeutic in cancer treatment and also as an indicator for immunodiagnostics [73]. They have appeared successful in photothermal therapy of the tumors because they could effectively absorb the near-infrared (NIR) light and convert it into heat [74]. Other shapes of GNPs like gold nanorods have also been used for targeting the tumor cell surface that severely damaged cancerous cells under NIR irradiation [75]. At elevated temperatures, heat buildup in the tumor microenvironment assists in killing the cancer cells. Moreover, GNPs can be used as a delivery platform for chemotherapeutic agents. However, targeted delivery of GNPs to the tumor sites and the stability issues (e.g., the aggregation of GNPs) should be tackled in designing cancer treatment systems [76]. However, thermosensitive nanocarriers are interesting materials for designing controlled drug delivery systems [77]. Poly(*N*-vinyl caprolactam) (PNVCL) is a thermoresponsive polymer that can enhance the stability of GNPs [78]. Thermoresponsive polymer coating onto GNPs not only increases the stability of GNPs, but also results in the controlled delivery of drugs [79]. Accordingly, chitosan-grafted PNVCL (CS-g-PNVCL) copolymer has the nature of a thermosensitive polymer, with a lower critical solution temperature (LCST) of around 38°C, quite close to the body temperature. In a recent research work, CS-g-PNVCL copolymer was coated onto the surface of thiol-modified GNPs as a DDS for the cisplatin anticancer drug [80]. Enhanced colloidal stability of GNPs and high drug loading efficiency (>94%) were observed for the coated GNPs. Furthermore, temperature- and pH-controlled release of the cisplatin was observed such that drug release was maximum at temperatures above 42°C and slightly acidic pH of 5 [80]. Thus, a combination of grafted chitosan and nanoparticles can lead to possible development of highly efficient DDSs.

3.2 Grafted hyaluronic acid

Hyaluronic acid (or hyaluronan), hereafter abbreviated as HA, is a high molecular weight anionic structural biopolymer, discovered in 1934, by Karl Meyer and his assistant, John Palmer, which can be found in the extracellular matrix (ECM) of connective tissues of the human body [81,82]. This polysaccharide benefits from the excellent biocompatibility, biodegradability, high water retention capacity, nontoxicity, and nonimmunogenicity, almost all reasons why this polysaccharide has been widely used in tissue engineering and drug delivery applications [83,84]. Accordingly, grafted HA that possesses extra functionalities can be utilized in a wide range of biomedical applications such as multifunctional DDSs. Some of the recent applications of grafted copolymers based on HA are summarized in this section.

Yang et al. used grafted hyaluronan copolymers as a theranostic platform for targeted delivery of the superparamagnetic iron oxide (SPIO), to be used as the contrast agent for magnetic resonance imaging (MRI), and DOX as a chemotherapeutic agent [85]. Poly-(*N*-ε-carbobenzyloxy-L-lysine) (PZLL) was grafted onto hyaluronan (HA) to make HA-g-SS-PZLL copolymer that self-assembles to make nanoparticles, as shown in Fig. 2. These redox-sensitive theranostic nanoparticles were used to deliver SPIO and DOX into the HepG2 cells, such that an improved anticancer effect was achieved [85].

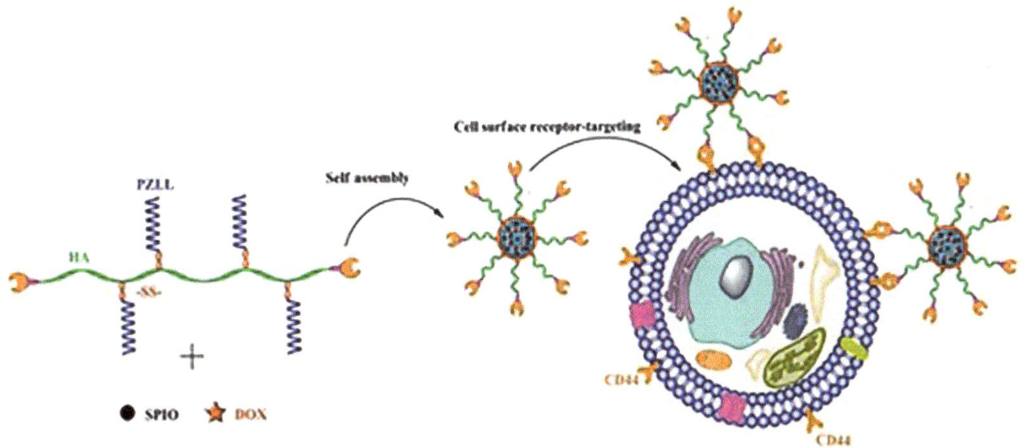

FIG. 2 Schematic representation of theranostic nanoparticles based on HA-g-SS-PZLL copolymer containing DOX and SPIO for targeted diagnosis and therapy of cancer [85]. The resulting redox-sensitive theranostic nanoparticles were served to deliver SPIO and DOX into the HepG2 cells, such that an improved anticancer effect was achieved.

HA was also been used to actively target the cluster of differentiation-44 (CD44) receptors that were overexpressed in many kinds of cancers [86]. DOX molecules can be entrapped in the porous structure of mesoporous silica nanoparticles (MSNs); however, because of the large pore diameter, DOX molecules get released rapidly, resulting in a premature release. To prevent such a premature and fast release behavior, various gatekeepers were normally tested, as a gated switch, to block the pore entrance which can be removed by diverse stimulants such as light, temperature, pH, and so on [87]. Host-guest interactions and self-assembly features made the cyclodextrins (CD) a promising gatekeeper for the MSN and metal–organic frameworks (MOFs). CD serves as a host molecule, which can be stimulated with various stimulants, based on the guest molecules (e.g., benzimidazole and ferrocene), highly interesting for designing smart DDSs [88,89]. Accordingly, Lu et al. loaded MSN with DOX and coated them with β-CD-grafted HA which was used as a dual-responsive DDS for targeted cancer therapy [90]. In the β-CD-g-HA copolymer, β-CD served as a gated switch for the MSN, which prevented the premature release of DOX molecules, while HA improved tumor cell targeting features of the nanocarriers. Benzene ring was also grafted onto the MSN via benzoic imine bond (pH-responsive) and disulfide bonds (redox-responsive). The β-CD and benzene interact via host-guest interactions, resulting in capping the MSN pores (see Fig. 3). Furthermore, entrapment efficiency (EE) and loading capacity (LC) of drugs were estimated to be 12.6% and 63.0%, respectively. The diameter of spherical particles was ca. ~100 nm, which can be internalized by cancer cells. The pH-sensitive benzoic imine bonds were hydrolyzed at the extracellular pH of solid tumors, which is slightly acidic. After cellular internalization, glutathione (GSH) molecules, in the cytosol, result in cleavage of the disulfide bond. Both bond scissions trigger DOX release, resulting in enhanced cell apoptosis [90].

Hydrophobic moieties such as fatty acids can be utilized in making graft copolymers based on polysaccharides that exhibit amphiphilic properties [91]. Grafting oleylamine, which is a fatty acid, onto the hydrophilic HA

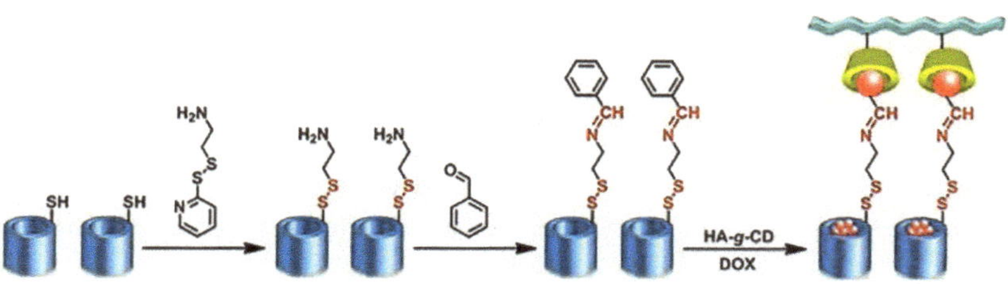

FIG. 3 Schematic illustration of the manufacturing process of dual-responsive drug delivery systems [90]. The β-CD and benzene interact via host-guest interactions resulting in capping the MSN pore.

results in oleylamine-g-HA amphilils that can be used for the delivery of various drugs. For example, oleylamine-g-HA amphilils nanoscale polymersomes have been used as a DDS for vancomycin for methicillin-resistant *Staphylococcus aureus* (MRSA) [92]. A sustained drug release was observed for the obtained nanocarriers within 72h. In addition, VCM-loaded polymersomes revealed a more profound effect on MRSA membrane compared to free VCM which uncovered its potential applications for the treatment of bacterial infections [92].

Ferrocene, also known as Ferocen (Fc), is an organometallic precursor consisting of two cyclopentadienyl rings on the opposite sides of a central iron atom. It has been reported that Fc is a redox-sensitive molecule, which has been used in making reversible self-assembly systems using β-CD that can be used in host-guest chemistry [93]. For example, HA-g-β-CD was further grafted with Fc, via host-guest interaction, for making a redox-sensitive DDS for the DOX [94]. Enhanced permeability and retention (EPR) is a well-known method used for targeted cancer therapy, which allows macromolecules to enter the tumor interstitial space, while the suppressed lymphatic filtration allows them to stay in the tumor sites [95,96]. However, the mechanism of receptor-mediated endocytosis should be taken into account and identified to enhance the efficiency of EPR in DDS. In this regard, Sang et al. used a redox-sensitive tumor-targeted delivery system, based on the EPR effect, to treat triple-negative breast cancer [97]. They designed the DDS to enhance the therapeutic effects of poorly soluble gambogic acid (GA) anticancer drugs based on magnetic-enhanced EPR effects. The DDS contained three layers, as shown in Fig. 4. The outermost layer included the mono-aminated poly(ethylene glycol)-g-HA in which PEG coating was responsible for preventing protein corona and HA targeting of CD44 receptors on the cancer cells. The core layer was composed of SPIO nanoparticles (SPION), which could improve the EPR effect through external magnetic fields, and drug molecules as well. The middle layer was also constructed from the hexadecanol (Hex)-chitosan oligosaccharide (CSO) which was a redox-sensitive copolymer due to the disulfide linkages in its structure. In in vivo investigations, tumor-bearing mice revealed effective accumulation of nanocarriers in tumors and a very promising anticancer effect [97].

3.3 Other grafted polysaccharides

There have been a number of works based on other types of grafted polysaccharides. Doosti et al. prepared a hydrogel based on the SPION and starch-grafted with fumaric acid for the delivery of quercetin as a natural flavonoid [98]. They reported that the hydrophilicity of the starch matrix was enhanced via fumaric acid grafting. In addition, electron-rich functional groups on fumaric acid chelate the ion cations, which resulted in physical cross-linking of the hydrogel. Fumaric acid-g-starch showed

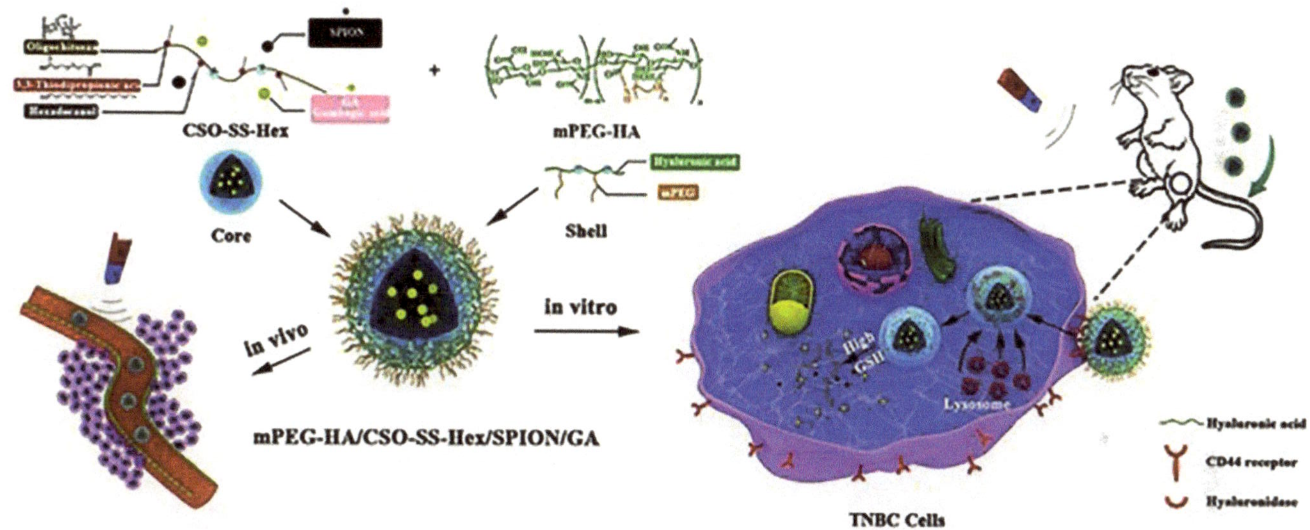

FIG. 4 Schematic representation of smart drug delivery system for delivery of anticancer drug in cancer cells [97]. The outermost layer was composed of the mono-aminated poly(ethylene glycol)-g-HA in which PEG coating was used to be responsible for preventing protein corona and HA targeting of CD44 receptors on the cancer cells. The core layer was composed of SPION, which was useful for improving the EPR effect through the external magnetic fields, and drug molecules as well. The middle layer was also constructed from the hexadecanol (Hex)-chitosan oligosaccharide (CSO) which was a redox-sensitive copolymer due to the disulfide linkages in its structure. In in vivo investigations, tumor-bearing mice revealed effective accumulation of nanocarriers in tumors and a very promising anticancer effect.

superparamagnetic properties, enhanced stability and bioavailability of the drug in plasma, and sustained release of quercetin [98]. In vitro release curve of the obtained system was appropriately fitted to the Higuchi model. In another research work, cholesterol-grafted cellulose nanocrystal (Ch-g-CNC) was used as a DDS for in vitro release of folic acid (FA) [99]. The grafting reaction was the reason for the enhanced CNC hydrophobicity; thereby, the FA uptake capacity was improved. Cellulose is a polysaccharide source known for sustainable and green chemical processing. Nevertheless, the highly ordered structure as well as the strong hydrogen bonding network made cellulose unable to be meltable and soluble in organic solvents, which severely limited its application range. It has been reported that the use of some hydrophilic ionic liquids (ILs), such as chloride-based ionic liquids, can assist in dissolving cellulose in conventional solvents [100]. Based on this capability of ILs, a silanized IL based on the 1-(trimethoxysilylpropyl)-3-methylimidazolium chloride was grafted onto the microcrystalline cellulose and subsequently has been served as DDS for the controlled release of an anionic drug, namely losartan [101]. The IL acted both as a solvent and as a surface modification agent and enhanced the drug loading capacity. In vitro studies revealed that drug release was slightly lower in the neutral pH range (pH = 7.4) compared to that of the acidic pH of 3 (stomach pH), which was anticipated to have arisen from the hydrolysis of Si–O bond in IL in the acidic medium. Thus, these IL-g-CS polymers have been used as potential pH-responsive DDSs [101].

Polyhydroxyalkanoate-type polymers such as poly(3-hydroxybutyrate-*co*-3-hydroxyvalerate) (PHBV) are biocompatible and biodegradable, for they are naturally derived polyesters that have been used in the delivery of drugs [102,103]. PHBV nanoparticles can effectively encapsulate hydrophobic drugs such as fingolimod [104]. Fingolimod, which is an immunomodulating drug for the treatment of multiple sclerosis, was loaded into the PHBV nanoparticles and was further dispersed in the oleic acid-grafted aminated alginate (OA-g-AAlg) [105]. In the assigned work, the alginate matrix was hydrophobically modified to improve the dispersion of hydrophobic PHBV nanoparticles with the aid of OA-g-AAlg. Only 47% of the fingolimod was released during 28 days of incubation in the PBS (pH 7.4, 37°C). Subcutaneous injection of the hydrogel in Wistar rats showed a significantly enhanced half-life for the drug in the DDS compared to the free drug injection method [105].

4 Conclusion

Polysaccharides have been used in many fields of biomedical applications. However, almost all polysaccharides have been relatively limited for usage in making DDSs, because of the lack of desirable properties, e.g., poor mechanical properties, very low solubility in water and organic solvents, and partial toxicity. However, recently copolymers based on the grafted polysaccharide have changed the ability of polysaccharides in DDS. In other words, in recent works, it was proved that grafted polysaccharides have been successfully applied in various advanced DDSs with multiresponsive nature, high drug loading capacity, enhanced biodegradability, and tunable mechanical properties. Hydrophobic modification of polysaccharides using small molecules or oligomers, which results in amphiphilic polymers, has been experiencing an increasing interest in recent years to utilize polysaccharides for drug delivery applications. In addition, chemical functionalization or grafting of polysaccharides via stimuli-responsive linkages has increased the application range of these carbohydrate polymers in novel DDSs. The use of grafted hyaluronan copolymers as a theranostic platform in targeted delivery of SPION was promising for the fabrication of a contrast agent needed for the magnetic resonance imaging (MRI) and also DOX as the chemotherapeutic agent. Poly-(*N*-ε-carbobenzyloxy-L-lysine) (PZLL) was elsewhere grafted onto the hyaluronan (HA) to develop HA-g-SS-PZLL copolymer with the ability of self-assembly for making smart nanoparticles. The resulting redox-sensitive theranostic nanoparticles were used to deliver SPIO and DOX into the HepG2 cells, such that an improved anticancer effect was achieved. By developing the β-CD-g-HA copolymer, researchers used β-CD as a gated switch for the MSN, which prevented the premature release of the DOX molecules, while HA improved tumor cell targeting features of the nanocarriers. Benzene ring was also grafted onto the MSN via benzoic imine bond (pH-responsive) and disulfide bonds (redox-responsive). The β-CD and the benzene interact with each other via the host-guest interactions that result in capping the MSN pores. Entrapment efficiency (EE) and loading capacity (LC) of the drug were estimated to be 12.6% and 63.0%, respectively. The diameter of spherical particles was ca. ~100 nm, which can be internalized by cancer cells. Hydrophobic moieties such as fatty acids can be utilized in making graft copolymers based on polysaccharides that exhibit amphiphilic properties. Grafting oleylamine, which is a fatty acid, onto the hydrophilic HA results in oleylamine-g-HA amphilils that can be used for the delivery of various drugs. For example, oleylamine-g-HA amphilils nanoscale polymersomes have been used as DDS for vancomycin for methicillin-resistant *S. aureus* (MRSA). A sustained drug release was observed for the obtained nanocarriers within 72 h. In addition, VCM-loaded polymersomes revealed a more profound effect on MRSA membranes compared to free VCM, which uncovered its potential applications for the treatment of bacterial infections. A redox-sensitive tumor-targeted delivery system was used based on the EPR effect, to treat triple-negative breast cancer. They designed the DDS to enhance the therapeutic effects of poorly soluble gambogic acid (GA) anticancer drugs based on magnetic-enhanced EPR effects. The DDS contained three layers. The outermost layer included the mono-aminated poly(ethylene glycol)-g-HA in which PEG coating was responsible for preventing protein corona and HA targeting of CD44 receptors on the cancer cells. The core layer was composed of SPION, which could improve the EPR effect through external magnetic fields, and drug molecules as well. The middle layer was also constructed from the hexadecanol (Hex)-chitosan oligosaccharide (CSO) which was a redox-sensitive copolymer due to the disulfide linkages in its structure. In in vivo investigations, tumor-bearing mice revealed effective accumulation of nanocarriers in tumors and a very promising anticancer effect. There have been a number of works based on other types of grafted polysaccharides. Doosti et al. prepared a hydrogel based on the SPION and starch-grafted with fumaric acid for the delivery of quercetin as a natural flavonoid. They reported that the hydrophilicity of the starch matrix was enhanced via fumaric acid grafting. In addition, electron-rich functional groups on fumaric acid chelate the ion cations, which resulted in physical cross-linking of the hydrogel. Fumaric acid-g-starch showed superparamagnetic properties, enhanced stability and bioavailability of the drug in plasma, and sustained release of quercetin. In vitro release curve of the obtained system was appropriately fitted to the Higuchi model.

References

[1] Park K. Controlled drug delivery systems: past forward and future back. J Control Release 2014;190:3–8.

[2] Langer R, Peppas NA. Present and future applications of biomaterials in controlled drug delivery systems. Biomaterials 1981;2(4):201–14.

[3] Langer R. Drug delivery and targeting. Nature 1998;5–10.

[4] Zarrintaj P, Manouchehri S, Ahmadi Z, Saeb MR, Urbanska AM, Kaplan DL, Mozafari M. Agarose-based biomaterials for tissue engineering. Carbohydr Polym 2018;187:66–84.

[5] Fenton OS, Olafson KN, Pillai PS, Mitchell MJ, Langer R. Advances in biomaterials for drug delivery. Adv Mater 2018;30(29):1705328.

[6] Zarrintaj P, Saeb MR, Ramakrishna S, Mozafari M. Biomaterials selection for neuroprosthetics. Curr Opin Biomed Eng 2018;6:99–109.

[7] Bagheri B, Zarrintaj P, Surwase SS, Baheiraei N, Saeb MR, Mozafari M, Kim YC, Park OO. Self-gelling electroactive hydrogels based on chitosan–aniline oligomers/agarose for neural tissue engineering with on-demand drug release. Colloids Surf B Biointerfaces 2019;184, 110549.

[8] Zarrintaj P, Urbanska AM, Gholizadeh SS, Goodarzi V, Saeb MR, Mozafari M. A facile route to the synthesis of anilinic electroactive colloidal hydrogels for neural tissue engineering applications. J Colloid Interface Sci 2018;516:57–66.

[9] Saberi A, Jabbari F, Zarrintaj P, Saeb MR, Mozafari M. Electrically conductive materials: opportunities and challenges in tissue engineering. Biomolecules 2019;9(9):448.

[10] Mohebbi S, Nezhad MN, Zarrintaj P, Jafari SH, Gholizadeh SS, Saeb MR, Mozafari M. Chitosan in biomedical engineering: a critical review. Curr Stem Cell Res Ther 2019;14(2):93–116.

[11] Zarrintaj P, Saeb MR, Jafari SH, Mozafari M. Application of compatibilized polymer blends in biomedical fields. In: Compatibilization of polymer blends. Elsevier; 2020. p. 511–37.
[12] Posocco B, Dreussi E, De Santa J, Toffoli G, Abrami M, Musiani F, Grassi M, Farra R, Tonon F, Grassi G. Polysaccharides for the delivery of antitumor drugs. Materials 2015;8(5):2569–615.
[13] Farokhi M, Mottaghitalab F, Fatahi Y, Saeb MR, Zarrintaj P, Kundu SC, Khademhosseini A. Silk fibroin scaffolds for common cartilage injuries: possibilities for future clinical applications. Eur Polym J 2019;115:251–67.
[14] Rohani Rad E, Vahabi H, Formela K, Saeb MR, Thomas S. Injectable poloxamer/graphene oxide hydrogels with well-controlled mechanical and rheological properties. Polym Adv Technol 2019;30(9):2250–60.
[15] Yazdi MK, Vatanpour V, Taghizadeh A, Taghizadeh M, Ganjali MR, Munir MT, Habibzadeh S, Saeb MR, Ghaedi M. Hydrogel membranes: a review. Mater Sci Eng C 2020;, 111023.
[16] Pushpamalar J, Veeramachineni AK, Owh C, Loh XJ. Biodegradable polysaccharides for controlled drug delivery. ChemPlusChem 2016;81(6):504–14.
[17] Manouchehri S, Bagheri B, Rad SH, Nezhad MN, Kim YC, Park OO, Farokhi M, Jouyandeh M, Ganjali MR, Yazdi MK. Electroactive bio-epoxy incorporated chitosan-oligoaniline as an advanced hydrogel coating for neural interfaces. Prog Org Coat 2019;131:389–96.
[18] Matsushiro Y, Kato-Negishi M, Onoe H. Differentiation of 3D-shape-controlled mouse neural stem cell to neural tissues in closed agarose microchambers. Biotechnol Bioeng 2018;115(6):1614–23.
[19] Mercey E, Obeïd P, Glaise D, Calvo-Muñoz M-L, Guguen-Guillouzo C, Fouqué B. The application of 3D micropatterning of agarose substrate for cell culture and in situ comet assays. Biomaterials 2010;31(12):3156–65.
[20] Kim C, Jeong D, Kim S, Kim Y, Jung S. Cyclodextrin functionalized agarose gel with low gelling temperature for controlled drug delivery systems. Carbohydr Polym 2019;222, 115011.
[21] Alizadeh R, Zarrintaj P, Kamrava SK, Bagher Z, Farhadi M, Heidari F, Komeili A, Gutiérrez TJ, Saeb MR. Conductive hydrogels based on agarose/alginate/chitosan for neural disorder therapy. Carbohydr Polym 2019;224, 115161.
[22] Muhammad G, Haseeb MT, Hussain MA, Ashraf MU, Farid-ul-Haq M, Zaman M. Stimuli-responsive/smart tablet formulations (under simulated physiological conditions) for oral drug delivery system based on glucuronoxylan polysaccharide. Drug Dev Ind Pharm 2020;46(1):122–34.
[23] Kato T. Encapsulated drugs in targeted cancer therapy. In: Controlled drug delivery, vol. 11. CRC Press; 2019.
[24] Sealy MJ, Dechaphunkul T, van der Schans CP, Krijnen WP, Roodenburg JL, Walker J, Jager-Wittenaar H, Baracos VE. Low muscle mass is associated with early termination of chemotherapy related to toxicity in patients with head and neck cancer. Clin Nutr 2020;39(2):501–9.
[25] Bruck S, Bruck S. Pharmacological basis of controlled drug delivery. Boca Raton, FL: CRC Press; 1983.
[26] Conklin KA. Dietary antioxidants during cancer chemotherapy: impact on chemotherapeutic effectiveness and development of side effects. Nutr Cancer 2000;37(1):1–18.
[27] Hortelão AC, Patiño T, Perez-Jiménez A, Blanco À, Sánchez S. Enzyme-powered nanobots enhance anticancer drug delivery. Adv Funct Mater 2018;28(25):1705086.
[28] Krishna G, Mary LR, Jerome K. Nanobots for biomedical applications. In: Proceedings of the 2019 9th International Conference on Biomedical Engineering and Technology; 2019.
[29] Tripathi R, Kumar A. Application of nanorobotics for cancer treatment. Maters Today: Proc 2018;5(3):9114–7.

[30] Servatan M, Zarrintaj P, Mahmodi G, Kim S-J, Ganjali MR, Saeb MR, Mozafari M. Zeolites in drug delivery: progress, challenges and opportunities. Drug Discov Today 2020;25:642–56.
[31] Farokhi M, Mottaghitalab F, Saeb MR, Thomas S. Functionalized theranostic nanocarriers with bio-inspired polydopamine for tumor imaging and chemo-photothermal therapy. J Control Release 2019;309:203–19.
[32] Berrecoso G, Crecente-Campo J, Alonso MJ. Unveiling the pitfalls of the protein corona of polymeric drug nanocarriers. Drug Deliv Transl Res 2020;1–21.
[33] Corbo C, Molinaro R, Parodi A, Toledano Furman NE, Salvatore F, Tasciotti E. The impact of nanoparticle protein corona on cytotoxicity, immunotoxicity and target drug delivery. Nanomedicine 2016;11(1):81–100.
[34] Liu L, Yao W, Rao Y, Lu X, Gao J. pH-Responsive carriers for oral drug delivery: challenges and opportunities of current platforms. Drug Deliv 2017;24(1):569–81.
[35] Bagheri B, Zarrintaj P, Samadi A, Zarrintaj R, Ganjali MR, Saeb MR, Mozafari M, Park OO, Kim YC. Tissue engineering with electrospun electro-responsive chitosan-aniline oligomer/polyvinyl alcohol. Int J Biol Macromol 2020;147:160–9.
[36] Zarrintaj P, Jouyandeh M, Ganjali MR, Hadavand BS, Mozafari M, Sheiko SS, Russell AJ, Vatankhah-Varnoosfaderani M, Gutiérrez TJ, Saeb MR. Thermo-sensitive polymers in medicine: a review. Eur Polym J 2019;117:402–23.
[37] Khalili R, Zarrintaj P, Jafari SH, Vahabi H, Saeb MR. Electroactive poly (p-phenylene sulfide)/r-graphene oxide/chitosan as a novel potential candidate for tissue engineering. Int J Biol Macromol 2020;154:18–24.
[38] Ruiz A, Alpízar A, Beola L, Rubio C, Gavilán H, Marciello M, Rodríguez-Ramiro I, Ciordia S, Morris CJ, Morales MDP. Understanding the influence of a bifunctional polyethylene glycol derivative in protein corona formation around iron oxide nanoparticles. Materials 2019;12(14):2218.
[39] Huang G, Mei X, Xiao F, Chen X, Tang Q, Peng D. Applications of important polysaccharides in drug delivery. Curr Pharm Des 2015;21(25):3692–6.
[40] Miao T, Wang J, Zeng Y, Liu G, Chen X. Polysaccharide-based controlled release systems for therapeutics delivery and tissue engineering: from bench to bedside. Adv Sci 2018;5(4):1700513.
[41] Bagher Z, Atoufi Z, Alizadeh R, Farhadi M, Zarrintaj P, Moroni L, Setayeshmehr M, Komeili A, Kamrava SK. Conductive hydrogel based on chitosan-aniline pentamer/gelatin/agarose significantly promoted motor neuron-like cells differentiation of human olfactory ecto-mesenchymal stem cells. Korean J Couns Psychother 2019;101:243–53.
[42] Cumpstey I. Chemical modification of polysaccharides. ISRN Org Chem 2013;2013.
[43] Zarrintaj P, Bakhshandeh B, Rezaeian I, Heshmatian B, Ganjali MR. A novel electroactive agarose-aniline pentamer platform as a potential candidate for neural tissue engineering. Sci Rep 2017;7(1):1–12.
[44] Atoufi Z, Zarrintaj P, Motlagh GH, Amiri A, Bagher Z, Kamrava SK. A novel bio electro active alginate-aniline tetramer/agarose scaffold for tissue engineering: synthesis, characterization, drug release and cell culture study. J Biomater Sci Polym Ed 2017;28(15):1617–38.
[45] Reakasame S, Boccaccini AR. Oxidized alginate-based hydrogels for tissue engineering applications: a review. Biomacromolecules 2018;19(1):3–21.
[46] Saeb MR, Mohammadi Y, Kermaniyan TS, Zinck P, Stadler FJ. Unspoken aspects of chain shuttling reactions: patterning the molecular landscape of olefin multi-block copolymers. Polymer 2017;116:55–75.
[47] Zarrintaj P, Ahmadi Z, Saeb MR, Mozafari M. Poloxamer-based stimuli-responsive biomaterials. Mater Today: Proc 2018;5(7):15516–23.
[48] Saeb MR, Rezaee B, Shadman A, Formela K, Ahmadi Z, Hemmati F, Kermaniyan TS, Mohammadi Y. Controlled grafting of vinylic monomers on polyolefins: a robust mathematical modeling approach. Des Monomers Polym 2017;20(1):250–68.

[49] Zarrintaj P, Ramsey JD, Samadi A, Atoufi Z, Yazdi MK, Ganjali MR, Amirabad LM, Zangene E, Farokhi M, Formela K. Poloxamer: a versatile tri-block copolymer for biomedical applications. Acta Biomater 2020;110:37–67.

[50] Penn B, Stannett V, Gilbert R. Biodegradable cellulose graft copolymers. I. Condensation-type graft reactions. J Macromol Sci—Chem 1981;16(2):473–9.

[51] Ito S, Goseki R, Ishizone T, Hirao A. Synthesis of well-controlled graft polymers by living anionic polymerization towards exact graft polymers. Polym Chem 2014;5(19):5523–34.

[52] Kalia S, Sabaa M. Polysaccharide based graft copolymers. vol. 22. Springer; 2013.

[53] Dash M, Chiellini F, Ottenbrite RM, Chiellini E. Chitosan—a versatile semi-synthetic polymer in biomedical applications. Prog Polym Sci 2011;36(8):981–1014.

[54] Mahmodi G, Zarrintaj P, Taghizadeh A, Taghizadeh M, Manouchehri S, Dangwal S, Ronte A, Ganjali MR, Ramsey JD, Kim S-J. From microporous to mesoporous mineral frameworks: an alliance between zeolite and chitosan. Carbohydr Res 2020;489, 107930.

[55] Jayakumar R, Menon D, Manzoor K, Nair SV, Tamura H. Biomedical applications of chitin and chitosan based nanomaterials—a short review. Carbohydr Polym 2010;82(2):227–32.

[56] Muzzarelli RAA, Muzzarelli C. Chitosan chemistry: relevance to the biomedical sciences. In: Heinze T, editor. Polysaccharides I: structure, characterization and use. Berlin, Heidelberg: Springer Berlin Heidelberg; 2005. p. 151–209.

[57] Riva R, Ragelle H, Rieux Ad, Duhem N, Jérôme C, Preat V. Chitosan and chitosan derivatives in drug delivery and tissue engineering. In: Chitosan for biomaterials II. Springer; 2011. p. 19–44.

[58] Ji J, Wang L, Yu H, Chen Y, Zhao Y, Zhang H, Amer WA, Sun Y, Huang L, Saleem M. Chemical modifications of chitosan and its applications. Polym-Plast Technol Eng 2014;53(14):1494–505.

[59] Li J, Cai C, Li J, Li J, Li J, Sun T, Wang L, Wu H, Yu G. Chitosan-based nanomaterials for drug delivery. Molecules 2018;23(10):2661.

[60] Ali A, Ahmed S. A review on chitosan and its nanocomposites in drug delivery. Int J Biol Macromol 2018;109:273–86.

[61] Sargazi G, Afzali D, Mostafavi A, Shadman A, Rezaee B, Zarrintaj P, Saeb MR, Ramakrishna S, Mozafari M. Chitosan/polyvinyl alcohol nanofibrous membranes: towards green super-adsorbents for toxic gases. Heliyon 2019;5(4), e01527.

[62] Bhattarai N, Ramay HR, Gunn J, Matsen FA, Zhang M. PEG-grafted chitosan as an injectable thermosensitive hydrogel for sustained protein release. J Control Release 2005;103(3):609–24.

[63] Ouchi T, Nishizawa H, Ohya Y. Aggregation phenomenon of PEG-grafted chitosan in aqueous solution. Polymer 1998;39(21):5171–5.

[64] Le Tien C, Lacroix M, Ispas-Szabo P, Mateescu M-A. N-acylated chitosan: hydrophobic matrices for controlled drug release. J Control Release 2003;93(1):1–13.

[65] Almeida A, Araújo M, Novoa-Carballal R, Andrade F, Gonçalves H, Reis RL, Lúcio M, Schwartz Jr S, Sarmento B. Novel amphiphilic chitosan micelles as carriers for hydrophobic anticancer drugs. Mater Sci Eng C 2020;, 110920.

[66] Mahanta AK, Maiti P. Injectable hydrogel through hydrophobic grafting on chitosan for controlled drug delivery. ACS Appl Bio Mater 2019;2(12):5415–26.

[67] Seidi F, Jin Y, Xiao H. Polycyclodextrins: synthesis, functionalization, and applications. Carbohydr Polym 2020;, 116277.

[68] Chen M, Huang L, Shen X, Li M, Luo Z, Cai K, Hu Y. Construction of multilayered molecular reservoirs on a titanium alloy implant for combinational drug delivery to promote osseointegration in osteoporotic conditions. Acta Biomater 2020;105:304–18.

[69] Aguirre TA, Teijeiro-Osorio D, Rosa M, Coulter I, Alonso M, Brayden D. Current status of selected oral peptide technologies in advanced preclinical development and in clinical trials. Adv Drug Deliv Rev 2016;106:223–41.

[70] Al-Kurdi ZI, Chowdhry BZ, Leharne SA, Al Omari MM, Badwan AA. Low molecular weight chitosan–insulin polyelectrolyte complex: characterization and stability studies. Mar Drugs 2015;13(4):1765–84.
[71] Sharma D, Singh J. Long-term glycemic control and prevention of diabetes complications in vivo using oleic acid-grafted-chitosanzinc-insulin complexes incorporated in thermosensitive copolymer. J Control Release 2020;323:161–78.
[72] Duncan B, Kim C, Rotello VM. Gold nanoparticle platforms as drug and biomacromolecule delivery systems. J Control Release 2010;148(1):122–7.
[73] Paciotti GF, Myer L, Weinreich D, Goia D, Pavel N, McLaughlin RE, Tamarkin L. Colloidal gold: a novel nanoparticle vector for tumor directed drug delivery. Drug Deliv 2004;11(3):169–83.
[74] Park H, Lim D-J, Vines JB, Yoon J-H, Ryu N-E. Gold nanoparticles for photothermal cancer therapy. Front Chem 2019;7:167.
[75] Tong L, Zhao Y, Huff TB, Hansen MN, Wei A, Cheng JX. Gold nanorods mediate tumor cell death by compromising membrane integrity. Adv Mater 2007;19(20):3136–41.
[76] Han G, Ghosh P, Rotello VM. Functionalized gold nanoparticles for drug delivery. Nanomedicine (Lond) 2007;2:113–23.
[77] Bordat A, Boissenot T, Nicolas J, Tsapis N. Thermoresponsive polymer nanocarriers for biomedical applications. Adv Drug Deliv Rev 2019;138:167–92.
[78] Beija M, Marty J-D, Destarac M. Thermoresponsive poly (N-vinyl caprolactam)-coated gold nanoparticles: sharp reversible response and easy tunability. Chem Commun 2011;47(10):2826–8.
[79] Vasani RB, Janardanan N, Prieto-Simón B, Cifuentes-Rius A, Bradley SJ, Moore E, Kraus T, Voelcker NH. Microwave heating of poly (N-isopropylacrylamide)-conjugated gold nanoparticles for temperature-controlled display of concanavalin A. ACS Appl Mater Interfaces 2015;7(50):27755–64.
[80] Banihashem S, Nezhati MN, Panahia HA. Synthesis of chitosan-grafted-poly (N-vinylcaprolactam) coated on the thiolated gold nanoparticles surface for controlled release of cisplatin. Carbohydr Polym 2020;227, 115333.
[81] Nusgens B. Hyaluronic acid and extracellular matrix: a primitive molecule? Ann Dermatol Venereol 2010;137 Suppl 1:S3–8.
[82] Necas J, Bartosikova L, Brauner P, Kolar J. Hyaluronic acid (hyaluronan): a review. Vet Med 2008;53(8):397–411.
[83] Huang G, Huang H. Hyaluronic acid-based biopharmaceutical delivery and tumor-targeted drug delivery system. J Control Release 2018;278:122–6.
[84] Collins MN, Birkinshaw C. Hyaluronic acid based scaffolds for tissue engineering—a review. Carbohydr Polym 2013;92(2):1262–79.
[85] Yang H, Miao Y, Chen L, Li Z, Yang R, Xu X, Liu Z, Zhang L-M, Jiang X. Redox-responsive nanoparticles from disulfide bond-linked poly-(N-ε-carbobenzyloxy-l-lysine)-grafted hyaluronan copolymers as theranostic nanoparticles for tumor-targeted MRI and chemotherapy. Int J Biol Macromol 2020;148:483–92.
[86] Mattheolabakis G, Milane L, Singh A, Amiji MM. Hyaluronic acid targeting of CD44 for cancer therapy: from receptor biology to nanomedicine. J Drug Target 2015;23(7–8):605–18.
[87] Wen J, Yang K, Liu F, Li H, Xu Y, Sun S. Diverse gatekeepers for mesoporous silica nanoparticle based drug delivery systems. Chem Soc Rev 2017;46(19):6024–45.
[88] Yi S, Zheng J, Lv P, Zhang D, Zheng X, Zhang Y, Liao R. Controlled drug release from cyclodextrin-gated mesoporous silica nanoparticles based on switchable host–guest interactions. Bioconjug Chem 2018;29(9):2884–91.
[89] Wu Y, Xu Z, Sun W, Yang Y, Jin H, Qiu L, Chen J, Chen J. Co-responsive smart cyclodextrin-gated mesoporous silica nanoparticles with ligand-receptor engagement for anti-cancer treatment. Mater Sci Eng C 2019;103, 109831.
[90] Lu J, Luo B, Chen Z, Yuan Y, Kuang Y, Wan L, Yao L, Chen X, Jiang B, Liu J. Host-guest fabrication of dual-responsive hyaluronic acid/mesoporous silica nanoparticle based drug delivery system for targeted cancer therapy. Int J Biol Macromol 2020;146:363–73.

[91] Paolino M, Licciardi M, Savoca C, Giammona G, Modica De Mohac L, Reale A, Giuliani G, Komber H, Donati A, Leone G. Hyaluronan graft copolymers bearing fatty-acid residues as self-assembling nanoparticles for olanzapine delivery. Pharmaceutics 2019;11(12):675.

[92] Walvekar P, Gannimani R, Salih M, Makhathini S, Mocktar C, Govender T. Self-assembled oleylamine grafted hyaluronic acid polymersomes for delivery of vancomycin against methicillin resistant *Staphylococcus aureus* (MRSA). Colloids Surf B Biointerfaces 2019;182, 110388.

[93] Zhao L, Hao S, Zhai Q, Guo H, Xu B, Fan H. Redox-responsive self-assembly of β-cyclodextrin and ferrocene double-headed amphiphilic molecules. Soft Matter 2017;13(17):3099–106.

[94] Lu B, Xiao Z, Wang Z, Wang B, Zhao W, Ma X, Zhang J. Redox-sensitive polymer micelles based on CD44 and folic acid receptor for intracellular drug delivery and drug controlled release in cancer therapy. ACS Appl Bio Mater 2019;2(10):4222–32.

[95] Golombek SK, May J-N, Theek B, Appold L, Drude N, Kiessling F, Lammers T. Tumor targeting via EPR: strategies to enhance patient responses. Adv Drug Deliv Rev 2018;130:17–38.

[96] Prabhakar U, Maeda H, Jain RK, Sevick-Muraca EM, Zamboni W, Farokhzad OC, Barry ST, Gabizon A, Grodzinski P, Blakey DC. Challenges and key considerations of the enhanced permeability and retention effect for nanomedicine drug delivery in oncology. Cancer Res 2013;73:2412–7. AACR.

[97] Sang M, Han L, Luo R, Qu W, Zheng F, Zhang K, Liu F, Xue J, Liu W, Feng F. CD44 targeted redox-triggered self-assembly with magnetic enhanced EPR effects for effective amplification of gambogic acid to treat triple-negative breast cancer. Biomater Sci 2020;8(1):212–23.

[98] Doosti M, Dorraji MSS, Mousavi SN, Rasoulifard MH, Hosseini SH. Enhancing quercetin bioavailability by super paramagnetic starch-based hydrogel grafted with fumaric acid: an in vitro and in vivo study. Colloids Surf B Biointerfaces 2019;183, 110487.

[99] Pourmoazzen Z, Sadeghifar H, Chen J, Yang G, Zhang K, Lucia L. The morphology, self-assembly, and host-guest properties of cellulose nanocrystals surface grafted with cholesterol. Carbohydr Polym 2020;, 115840.

[100] Zhang J, Wu J, Yu J, Zhang X, He J, Zhang J. Application of ionic liquids for dissolving cellulose and fabricating cellulose-based materials: state of the art and future trends. Mater Chem Front 2017;1(7):1273–90.

[101] de Oliveira Santos SS, Millan RDS, Speziali MG. Versatile grafted microcrystalline cellulose with ionic liquid as new losartan-controlled release material. Eur Polym J 2020;, 109490.

[102] Nigmatullin R, Thomas P, Lukasiewicz B, Puthussery H, Roy I. Polyhydroxyalkanoates, a family of natural polymers, and their applications in drug delivery. J Chem Technol Biotechnol 2015;90(7):1209–21.

[103] Radu IC, Hudita A, Zaharia C, Galateanu B, Iovu H, Tanasa E, Georgiana Nitu S, Ginghina O, Negrei C, Tsatsakis A. Poly (3-hydroxybutyrate-CO-3-hydroxyvalerate) PHBHV biocompatible nanocarriers for 5-FU delivery targeting colorectal cancer. Drug Deliv 2019;26(1):318–27.

[104] Rezaie Shirmard L, Bahari Javan N, Khoshayand MR, Kebriaee-zadeh A, Dinarvand R, Dorkoosh FA. Nanoparticulate fingolimod delivery system based on biodegradable poly (3-hydroxybutyrate-co-3-hydroxyvalerate)(PHBV): design, optimization, characterization and in-vitro evaluation. Pharm Dev Technol 2017;22(7):860–70.

[105] Rezaie Shirmard L, Ghofrani M, Bahari Javan N, Bayrami S, Tavassoli A, Rezaie A, Amini M, Kebriaee-zadeh A, Rouini M-R, Dinarvand R. Improving the in-vivo biological activity of Fingolimod loaded PHBV nanoparticles by using hydrophobically modified alginate. Drug Dev Ind Pharm 2020;46(2):318–28.

CHAPTER

8

Polysaccharide-based polyelectrolyte complex systems in drug delivery

Gouranga Nandi[a], *Md Saquib Hasnain*[b], *and Amit Kumar Nayak*[c]

[a]Division of Pharmaceutics, Department of Pharmaceutical Technology, University of North Bengal, Raja Rammohunpur, Darjeeling, West Bengal, India, [b]Department of Pharmacy, Palamau Institute of Pharmacy, Daltonganj, Jharkhand, India, [c]Department of Pharmaceutics, Seemanta Institute of Pharmaceutical Sciences, Jharpokharia, Mayurbhanj, Odisha, India

1 Introduction

During the past few years, numerous natural polysaccharides originated from different sources (such as plant, marine, microbiological, etc.) are being explored and exploited for biomedical applications due to their easy availability, low extraction cost, biocompatibility, and biodegradability [1–7]. However, natural polysaccharides fall short to meet up a few vital physicochemical as well as functional properties (such as aqueous solubility, degradability, stability, etc.) as biopolymers for biomedical uses [8,9]. Till date, many research works have already been clearly reported about the modifications of natural polysaccharides, such as cross-linking [7], carboxymethylation [10,11], thiolation [12], esterification [13], interpenetrating polymer networks (IPNs) [14–16], polyelectrolyte complexes (PECs) [17,18], graft copolymerization [19–22], etc., to facilitate the introduction of desired physicochemical as well as functional properties to be used as biopolymers.

Natural polysaccharide-based PECs have been drawing the attention of the biopolymer researchers for their potential and wide biomedical applications, such as drug delivery, enzyme immobilization, tissue engineering,

Tailor-Made Polysaccharides in Drug Delivery
https://doi.org/10.1016/B978-0-12-821286-8.00009-4

DNA binding, biosensor, imaging, diagnostic, etc., with a high level of physiological safety [18,23]. Unlike the complexes obtained from chemical cross-linking using synthetic toxic cross-linker, such as glutaraldehyde, PECs have been found to be physiologically well-tolerated, biocompatible, environment friendly, and biodegradable [24]. Thorough purification of chemically cross-linked complexes is required to remove the toxic cross-linker and to avoid toxicity. PECs have been reported as significantly potential biopolymeric carriers for the peroral delivery of protein and peptide drugs [25,26]. Immunogenicity of most of the synthetic polymers and denaturation of proteins and peptides due to harsh processing conditions for their fabrication make them less preferable for designing protein delivery through peroral as well as parenteral routes [27]. PECs have also been drawing interest in the design of stimuli-responsive drug delivery systems, which can be regulated by different stimuli, such as pH, temperature, ionic strength, light, etc. [28]. However, the physical stability of PECs should be considered carefully as the outcomes of these types of devices greatly depend on it. Various applications with cutting-edge advances of PECs include a wide range of uses, such as medical implants, coatings on films and fibers, microcapsules and microspheres, membranes, cryogels, beads, hydrogels, etc. [18,23–28].

2 What is a polyelectrolyte complex?

Polyelectrolytes can be defined as macromolecules, which have a comparatively large number of charged functional groups in their repeating monomeric units or become charged under a suitable condition [29], and classified as polycations or polyanions according to their charge. A polyelectrolyte complex (PEC) can be defined as a complex of two oppositely charged polyelectrolytes held together by electrostatic interaction(s) [18]. The formation of PECs requires only physical mixing of two oppositely charged polyelectrolytes in solution without any chemical covalent cross-linker [23]. The attractive forces between polyelectrolytes in PECs include reversible strong electrostatic attraction, dipole–dipole interactions, and hydrogen or hydrophobic bonds [30]. The release of low molecular weight counterions results in an increase in entropy, which is considered as the main driving force for the polyelectrolyte complexation [31].

3 Advantages of PECs

Fabrication of various drug delivery devices especially for controlled release as well as biomedical devices with polyelectrolyte complexes offers the following advantages:

(a) Less toxicity and better physiological compatibility of PECs due to the absence of organic precursors, toxic chemical cross-linkers, and catalysts in the formation or fabrication process as compared to that of covalently cross-linked interpenetrating polymeric networks [32].
(b) Greater biodegradability, for example, chitosan gets metabolized by certain human enzymes, such as lysozyme [32].
(c) Drug loading and drug release from PEC-based targeted or sustained release delivery systems can be improved or controlled by modulating the interaction ability of PECs with the drugs or therapeutically significant biomolecules through electrostatic interactions and hydrogen bonding.
(d) PECs are found to be efficient for encapsulation of a wide range of hydrophilic and hydrophobic drugs.
(e) PECs prevent the chemical and enzymatic degradation of the therapeutics in biological fluids.
(f) PECs are capable of responding reversibly to different exogenous stimuli such as light, temperature, electric pulses, etc., or endogenous stimulus, such as enzyme, pH, or redox gradient, which allows the design of PECs for various stimuli-responsive controlled release drug deliveries to improve the bioavailability of drugs by modulating the release of payloads at particular site inside the body.
(g) PECs are more appropriate compared to synthetic complexes for encapsulation of protein or peptide drugs because no denaturation occurs due to the absence of harsh leftover chemical residue in the complex.
(h) In PECs, the ionic groups remain coupled, which reduces the ionic interaction between drug(s) and polymer(s) resulting in compatible carriers for a wide range of drugs.

4 Factors affecting the formation and stability of PECs

Various factors, such as concentration of the polyelectrolytes, mixing ratio, magnitude of the charges, pH of the reaction medium, degree of ionization, molecular weight, distribution of ionic groups, reaction kinetics, drying process, temperature, ionic strength, pH of the medium, etc., affect significantly the formation and physical stability of PECs and, therefore, the pattern of the drug release and other dependent variable characters [33]. PEC formation may result in a concentrated coacervate phase or a more or less compact gel depending on multiple factors, such as the molecular chain length of the two polyanions, their chemical structures, the type of the polyelectrolyte pairs (strong/strong, weak/weak, or strong/weak) along with the distribution of the charged groups along the polymeric backbone [34]. The preparation method of PECs also influences the type of PEC system. For instance, PEC membrane or films require layer-by-layer assembly, whereas the formation of precipitates, compact gels, microparticles, or beads requires direct mixing. The strength of the electrostatic interaction between polyelectrolytes can be modulated by the incorporation of salts, such as sodium chloride and temperature. Mixing of polyelectrolytes having weak charge densities results in the formation of a water-soluble complex. The fabrication of micro- or nanoparticles requires nonstoichiometric mixing of polyelectrolytes having high charge density and/or nearly equal high molecular weights [35]. In disparity, gels often result from the mixing of cationic and anionic polyelectrolytes in equal ratios.

5 Polysaccharides used to fabricate polyelectrolyte complexes (PECs)

A significant number of natural polysaccharides are shown to have excellent polyelectrolyte character and are preferred for the fabrication of PECs due to their less toxicity, physiological compatibility, and intrinsic as well as extrinsic biodegradability [23]. Most of these polysaccharides, such as alginate, pectin, hyaluronic acid, etc., possess anionic functional groups, while very few such as chitosan possess cationic nature [23–28]. Sometimes, neutral nonionic natural polysaccharides, such as konjac glucomannan, are chemically modified to introduce ionic groups through carboxymethylation or sulfonation and then applied to fabricate PECs with counter-polyelectrolytes [36,37]. The commonly used natural polysaccharides are presented in Table 1.

5.1 Chitosan

Chitosan is a cationic polysaccharide having wonderful characteristics and suitable for the fabrication of not only PEC-based drug delivery systems but also for a wide range of novel drug delivery devices, such as multiunit beads, micro- and nanoparticles, stimuli-responsive hydrogel, etc. [30,53]. It is obtained from alkaline *N*-deacetylation of chitin, which is a polysaccharide found in the exoskeleton of insects, crustaceans, and cell walls of fungi and chemically composed of unbranched chains of β-(1-4)-2-acetamido-2-acetamido-2-deoxy-D-glucose [54,55]. Chitosan is a linear chain polysaccharide chemically composed of β-(1-4)-linked D-glucosamine and *N*-acetyl-D-glucosamine units [56]. The deacetylation degree of chitosan is defined as the ratio of glucosamine to *N*-acetyl glucosamine, which determines the magnitude of the net positive charge of chitosan molecules as well as other physicochemical properties. Deacetylation makes chitosan soluble in an acidic medium because of the

TABLE 1 Polysaccharides used to fabricate polyelectrolyte complexes (PECs).

Polysaccharides used in PECs	Chemical composition	Charge/functional group	Biological source	References
Chitosan	Glucosamine and *N*-acetyl glucosamine units via β-(1 → 4) linkages	Cationic/-NH_2	Exoskeleton of crustaceans, insects, and fungi	[38,39]
Alginate	1-4-Linked α-L-guluronic acid (G-block) and β-D-mannuronic acid (M-block) residues	Anionic/-COO^-	Brown seaweeds and marine algae, including *Ascophyllum nodosum*, *Laminaria hyperborea*, and *Macrocystis pyrifera*	[2]
Hyaluronic acid	β-1,4-D-Glucuronic acid-β-1,3-*N*-acetyl-D-glucosamine	Anionic/-COO^-	Extracellular matrix throughout epithelia, connective, and neural tissues	[39,40]
Pectin	1,4-Linked α-D-galactosyluronic acid residues, consisting of acetyl and methyl esterified carboxyl groups	Anionic/-COO^-	Cell walls of all higher plants	[1,41]
Carrageenan	Galactose and anhydrogalactose units covalently linked by glycosidic linkage	Anionic/-OSO_3^{2-}	Red seaweed	[42]
Xanthan gum	Two β-D-glucose units linked at 1 and 4 positions on its main backbone, two mannose units, and one glucuronic acid unit on its side chain	Anionic/-COO^-	Exopolysaccharide secreted from *Xanthomonas campestris*	[43]
Gellan gum	A tetrasaccharide repeating unit of one α-L-rhamnose, one β-D-glucuronic acid, and two β-D-glucose residues	Anionic/-COO^-	Deacylated exocellular polysaccharide obtained from a pure culture of *Pseudomonas elodea*	[20,44]

Continued

TABLE 1 Polysaccharides used to fabricate polyelectrolyte complexes (PECs)—cont'd

Polysaccharides used in PECs	Chemical composition	Charge/functional group	Biological source	References
Cashew gum	β-D-Galactose, α-D-glucose, arabinose, rhamnose, and glucuronic acid monosaccharide unit	Anionic/-COO^-	Gum exudate polysaccharide from the tree, *Anacardium occidentale*	[45,46]
Gum arabic	Mixture of calcium, magnesium, and potassium salt of arabic acid having a backbone of 1,3-linked β-D-galactopyranosyl units; side chains are composed of L-arabinofuranose, L-arabinopyranose, L-rhamnose, and L-glucuronopyranose	Anionic/-COO^-	Gum exudates from stems and branches of two species *Acacia senegal* and *Acacia seyal*	[47,48]
Carboxymethyl cellulose	Cellulose chain having carboxymethyl groups linked to some hydroxyl groups of glucopyranose monomers of the cellulose backbone	Anionic/-COO^-	Semisynthetic cellulose obtained from carboxymethylation of cellulose	[49]
Konjac glucomannan	Polysaccharide chain composed of glucose and mannose unit at 1:1.5–1:1.6 M ratio	–	Polysaccharide extracted from the tuber of the plant *Amorphophallus konjac*	[36,37,50]
Gum kondagogu	Polysaccharide composed of rhamnose, galacturonic acid, glucuronic acid, β-D-galactopyranose, α-D-glucose, β-D-glucose, galactose, arabinose, mannose, and fructose	Anionic/-COO^-	Gum exudate from the plant *Cochlospermum gossypium*	[51]
Gum ghatti	Found as a mixture of sodium, potassium, calcium, and magnesium salts of polysaccharide backbone composed of L-arabinose, D-galactose, D-glucuronic acid, D-mannose, D-xylose, and rhamnose	Anionic/-COO^-	Gum exudates from *Anogeissus latifolia* belonging to the family Combretaceae	[52]

protonation of amino groups on its backbone, and chitosan behaves as a cationic polyelectrolyte in an acidic medium and forms PEC with anionic polyelectrolytes [38]. A significant number of chitosan-based PECs having different applications with various natural polysaccharides, such as alginate, hyaluronic acid, pectin, carrageenan, xanthan gum, gellan, cashew gum, gum arabic, carboxymethyl cellulose, gum kondagogu, etc., have been reported [23,30,31].

5.2 Sodium alginate

Sodium alginate is an anionic natural polysaccharide suitable for the fabrication of PEC with a cationic polyelectrolyte, such as chitosan [18,23]. It is obtained from marine algae and brown seaweeds such as *Laminaria hyperborea*, *Ascophyllum nodosum*, and *Macrocystis pyrifera* [57–59]. It is a hydrophilic linear polysaccharide composed of alternating blocks of 1-4-linked α-L-guluronic acid residue (G-block) and β-D-mannuronic acid residue (M-block), which are found to be arranged in an irregular block-wise pattern of varying proportions of G-G, M-G, and M-M blocks [60]. The carboxylic acid groups of guluronic and mannuronic acid residues attribute anionic site for electrostatic attraction with cationic counterparts and result in the formation of PEC-based hydrogel [18,60]. Sodium alginate also undergoes ionotropic gelation through cross-linking of its carboxylic groups with divalent cations, such as calcium, zinc, and barium [61]. There are two types of ionotropic gelation methods to cross-link alginate with divalent cations, i.e., internal and external gelation [60,62,63]. In internal gelation method, the alginate solution is first mixed with an insoluble calcium salt, such as $CaCO_3$, and the mixture is then dropped into an acidified oil phase which liberates Ca^{2+} ions due to reaction between $CaCO_3$ and acid results in cross-linking between cations and alginate [64]. However, hydrogels obtained from the internal method have been found to be less compact, which results in low drug loading, especially in case of water-soluble drugs [65,66]. In the external method, the alginate solution is dropped directly into an aqueous solution of water-soluble calcium salt, such as $CaCl_2$, which results in the formation of compact hydrogel due to cross-linking of alginate with calcium ions. The hydrogels obtained from the external method have been found to be comparatively compact and yield higher drug loading. A strong electrostatic attractive force between carboxyl groups of alginate and amino groups of chitosan results in the formation of PEC when mixed together in a suitable medium. A wide range of chitosan-alginate PEC-based drug delivery fabrications have been reported, which includes hydrogel beads, microparticles, nanoparticles, nanotubes, filaments, 3D matrix, etc. [18,64].

5.3 Hyaluronic acid (HA)

HA is a naturally derived polysaccharide having a high degree of biocompatible and biodegradable nature, which is also known as hyaluronate or hyaluronan [67]. HA is abundantly found in different tissues of living organisms, such as epithelial, connective, and nerve tissues. It is chemically composed of a unique nonsulfated glycosaminoglycan having the repeating unit of disaccharide, β-1,4-D-glucuronic acid–β-1,3-*N*-acetyl-D-glucosamine [68]. Its average molecular weight has been found to vary from 100 to 8000 kDa. Due to the presence of carboxyl groups on its monosaccharide units, it possesses anionic polyelectrolyte nature and is suitable for PECs with cationic polymers, such as chitosan, etc. [69,70]. PECs of HA with cationic forms of protein collagen and gelatin have also been reported. The combination of HA-chitosan has been studied extensively for the fabrication of PEC-based nanoparticles [70]. HA-based PECs have been reported to be potential for various drug delivery and biomedical applications due to their optimum stability, tunable sizes, protection from enzymatic degradation, low cytotoxicity, etc. [39,40].

5.4 Pectin

Pectin is another highly biocompatible natural polysaccharide found in all higher plants as a cell wall component, which has been explored in a wide range of biomedical applications, including drug delivery [71,72]. It has also been used as food additives, such as a binder, viscosity builder, stabilizer, etc., in food industries [41]. The chemical composition of its polymeric backbone consists of (1-4)-linked α-D-galacturonic acid units repeatedly interspersed by some α-L-rhamnopyranose units and rhamnogalacturonic acid units via α-(1-2) linkage [58,59]. The –COOH groups of the galacturonic acid units remain partially methyl-esterified. The degree of methyl esterification determines the functional properties, especially the magnitude of the total negative charge and therefore ionotropic gelation character as well as the capacity to form PEC. Low-methoxyl pectin is found to form compact hydrogel structures as a result of cross-linking between two –COOH groups via divalent cations such as Ca^{2+}, Zn^{2+}, Mg^{2+}, etc., whereas high-methoxyl pectins with a degree of methyl esterification greater than 50% yield loose hydrogel because of the presence of an inadequate number of –COOH groups in their structure [2,73]. Low-methoxyl pectins are more suitable for the formation of PECs due to the presence of a larger number of free –COOH groups. Since the last three decades, pectin has increasingly been explored for drug delivery, especially colon-specific drug delivery, oral sustained release nanogel, topical wound healing, gastroretentive mucoadhesive, etc., due to its easy availability, low cost, biocompatibility, mechanical strength, and acid stability [2,72–74].

Pectin remains intact in the gastric as well as in the small intestinal environment but gets degraded in the colon by pectinolytic enzymes and other exoenzymes from normal microflora, which makes pectin potential for colon-targeted drug delivery [74]. However, the pectin matrix should be cross-linked by cations, cationic polymers, or coated with a less soluble polymer to prevent drug release in stomach or intestine and successful carrying of the drug in colon [75]. The PECs based on chitosan-pectin have been explored for colon targeting.

5.5 Xanthan gum

Xanthan gum is an exopolysaccharide produced by the bacterium *Xanthomonas campestris* sp. [63]. It is chemically composed of five repeating monosaccharide units: two (1 → 4)-linked β-D-glucose residues on its main chain, two mannose residues, and one glucuronic acid residue on its side chain [76]. On its side chains, a pyruvic acid residue is linked to the terminal D-mannose unit and an acetyl group is linked to the D-mannose unit linked to the main chain. The ratio of the monosaccharide units as well as molecular structure and molar mass vary depending upon the microbial strains and fermentation conditions. Xanthan gum has been widely used for various applications in the food, pharmaceutical, and cosmetic industries [77,78]. Xanthan gum is a natural anionic polyelectrolyte due to the presence of pyruvic and acetic acid residues on its side chains and is capable of forming PEC with cationic polysaccharides like chitosan [79,80]. Xanthan gum has been a safe and biocompatible food and pharmaceutical additive. It has been approved by the United States Food and Drug Administration (USFDA) for its application in pharmaceutical and food industries without specific quantity limitations since 1968 [81].

5.6 Carrageenan

Carrageenan is a member of the natural linear sulfated biopolysaccharides family, which is obtained from red seaweed [82]. Chemically, it is composed of galactose and anhydrogalactose residues linked together by glycosidic linkage [42]. The main chain is composed of an alternative copolymer of 1,4-α- and 1,3-β-D-galactopyranose and 3,6-anhydro-D-galactopyranose [83]. The degree of substitution of the sulfate group depends on the source and the extraction process and determines the physicochemical nature of carrageenan. According to the degree of substitution of a sulfate group, carrageenan has been classified into three categories: kappa (κ), iota (ι), and lambda (λ), among which only the first two categories, i.e., kappa (κ) and iota (ι) carrageenan, show gelling ability [82]. K-carrageenan yields firm, compact, and rigid gel, while the latter produces relatively loose and elastic gel [38]. Carrageenan has been found to have a high magnitude of negative charge due to the presence of ester sulfate groups on its polymeric backbone and to possess the ability to form PEC with cationic polymers [84,85].

5.7 Gellan gum

Gellan gum is an excellent natural polysaccharide produced by a pure culture of an aerobic, gram-negative nonpathogenic bacterium *Pseudomonas elodea* (also known as *Sphingomonas elodea;* family Sphingomonadaceae) as a fermentation product [86,87]. It is an anionic and deacylated exocellular polysaccharide gum having a high molecular weight and is chemically composed of a tetrasaccharide repeating unit with one β-D-glucuronic acid, one α-L-rhamnose, and two β-D-glucose residues in a 1:1:2 ratio [88]. Gellan gum has been used in a wide range of pharmaceutical dosage forms, such as tablets, interpenetrating hydrogel microspheres, stomach-specific controlled release beads, ophthalmic solution, etc. [20]. Being anionic in nature due to the presence of –COOH groups in glucuronic acid residues, gellan gum is a potential candidate for PEC with cationic polymers. Due to greater biocompatibility, gellan gum has also been widely explored for various applications in food and tissue engineering [89].

5.8 Gum acacia/gum arabic

Gum acacia or gum arabic is a natural polysaccharide obtained from the gum exudates from the stems and branches of two species of the acacia tree, i.e., *Acacia seyal* and *Acacia senegal* [90]. It is chemically composed of a mixture of calcium, magnesium, and potassium salt of arabic acid [91]. Arabic acid is a polysaccharide acid having a polymeric backbone composed of 1,3-linked β-D-galactopyranosyl residue with various protein contents [47]. The major composition of gum acacia has been reported as 39%–42% galactose, 24%–27% arabinose, 15%–16% glucuronic acid, 12%–16% rhamnose, and 1.5%–2.6% protein [92]. Gum acacia is therefore considered as a natural glycoprotein having significant water solubility and low viscosity even at high concentrations. It has been used to stabilize pharmaceutical emulsions, especially W/O type, because of the fact that the hydrophobic peptide chains get adsorbed onto the oil–water interface of the dispersed globules and fasten to the oil phase while the polysaccharide chains get oriented toward the water phase and prevent the oil globules from flocculation and coalescence through electrostatic repulsions [93]. Gum acacia has the potential to form PEC with cationic polysaccharides, such as chitosan, due to the presence of a large number of anionic carboxylic groups on its polymeric backbone, and a range of PECs based on gum acacia and chitosan has been reported [94,95]. Gum acacia has also been reported to be used as a polymeric excipient, such as binders and diluents in tablet formulations and as food additives [90].

5.9 Cashew gum

Cashew gum is a natural polysaccharide obtained from gum exudate from the stems of the tree *Anacardium occidentale* [96,97]. It is a complex polysaccharide acid, and the main polymeric backbone is composed of (1 → 3) β-D-galactose residues and the side chains are composed of (1 → 6) β-D-galactose [96]. Its main monosaccharide constituents are glucose, glucuronic acids, rhamnose, and arabinose [98,99]. Cashew gum has been investigated for its various applications, such as antitumor activity, enzyme immobilization capability, antimicrobial activity, suspending and emulsifying agents in different pharmaceutical formulations [100]. Due to the presence of anionic –COOH groups on glucuronic acid residues, cashew gum has been used to develop various types of PEC with cationic polysaccharide chitosan [101]. It has also been reported to have a significant potential as a release retardant in sustained or extended release tablet formulations [5,6,38].

5.10 Sodium carboxymethyl cellulose

Sodium salt of carboxymethyl cellulose is another potential anionic candidate for PECs [102]. It is obtained from the carboxymethylation of cellulose moiety. It possesses excellent aqueous solubility. Carboxymethyl groups ($-CH_2-COOH$) are linked to the hydroxyl groups of the glucopyranose residues of the polymeric backbone of cellulose [103]. Carboxymethyl cellulose is synthesized by the Williamson ether synthesis method consisting of two steps, where the first is alkali treatment of cellulose to form cellulose alkoxide and the second is esterification reaction of cellulose alkoxide with monochloroacetic acid to obtain carboxymethyl cellulose [103,104]. The degree of substitution ranges usually from 0.4 to 1.5, and the molecular weight ranges from 90,000 to 2,000,000 g/mol [105]. The sodium salt of carboxymethyl cellulose dissociates into anionic carboxymethyl cellulose residues and sodium gegenions, when it is dispersed in water, and is therefore capable of forming PEC with chitosan or other cationic polymers [102]. It has been well recognized for its vast applications in drug delivery, food, pharmaceuticals, textile, paper, paint industries, tissue engineering, 3D bioprinting, and antimicrobial and wound dressing applications [49,106].

5.11 Carboxymethyl konjac glucomannan

Konjac glucomannan is a natural hydrophilic polysaccharide obtained from the tubes of the plant, *Amorphophallus konjac*, found in Asia. It is chemically composed of α-mannose units and α-glucose units linked via β-1,4-linkage with a molar ratio of 1.6:1.0 [107]. It has been reported as a potential natural polysaccharide useful in the development of colon-targeted drug delivery systems [108,109]. As there is no anionic functional group in the monosaccharide units of the konjac polymeric backbone, it does not possess the capacity to form PEC with cationic polymers, but carboxymethylation is required to impart negative charge and make it capable of forming PEC. Drug-loaded PEC-based nanoparticles fabricated with carboxymethyl konjac and chitosan have been reported [36,37].

5.12 Gum kondagogu

Gum kondagogu is obtained from the exudate from the stems of the tree-plant, *Cochlospermum gossypium* (family: Bixaceae), mainly originating from India. Its monosaccharide composition includes D-glucuronic acid (19.26 mol%), galactose (18.95 mol%), β-D-galacturonic acid (13.22 mol%), α-D-galacturonic acid (11.22 mol%), mannose (8.30 mol%), arabinose (2.52 mol%), α-D-glucose (2.48 mol%), β-D-glucose (2.52 mol%), and rhamnose (12.85 mol%) [110]. Due to the presence of –COOH groups on glucuronic and galacturonic acid residues of the polymeric backbone of gum kondagogu, it has the capability to form PEC with chitosan. Naidu et al. reported diclofenac-loaded microparticles based on chitosan-gum kondagogu PEC [51]. Carboxymethyl derivative of gum kondagogu has also been tried to improve its gelling property [111]. A significant number of gum kondagogu-based PECs have been reported with various applications in drug delivery [51].

5.13 Gum ghatti

Gum ghatti is obtained from the gummy exudates of the tree, *Anogeissus latifolia*, belonging to the family Combretaceae which is found in the Indian continent. It has been widely used as a viscosity builder, emulsifier, etc., in drug delivery and food preparations [112]. Gum ghatti is an extremely complex polysaccharide that remains as a mixture of calcium and magnesium salts of uronic acid and/or ghattic acids along with approximately 3% protein. It is chemically composed of L-arabinose, D-galactose, D-mannose, D-xylose, and D-glucuronic acid in a molar ratio of 48:29:10:5:10 and less than 1% of rhamnose. The polymeric backbone is composed of 4-O-substituted and 2-O-substituted μ-D-mannopyranose residues and chains of 1 → 6-linked β-D-galactopyranose residues with side chains of

L-arabinose residues [113]. Due to the presence of –COOH groups in the D-glucuronic acid moiety, gum ghatti has been drawing attention in the fabrication of PEC with chitosan or other cationic biopolymers for the development of various drug delivery devices [114,115].

6 Various dosage forms fabricated by polyelectrolyte complexation

A wide range of drug delivery devices as well as biomedical devices have been fabricated with PECs based on natural polysaccharides and their semisynthetic derivatives, which include drug-loaded hydrogel beads, microparticles, nanoparticles, membranes or films, macroporous foams or cryogels, wound dressing scaffolds, etc. [17–26]. Fig. 1 depicts various pharmaceutical dosage forms based on PECs [38].

6.1 PEC-based hydrogel beads

Efficacy of capecitabine-loaded multiple-unit beads of chitosan succinate-alginate PEC was investigated by Sinha and her colleagues for drug targeting to colon cancer [116]. The concentrations of chitosan, sodium alginate, and cross-linker, $CaCl_2$, were optimized using Box-Behnken design in their study to obtain target drug entrapment efficiency and various drug release parameters in colon. The study revealed nonswelling of beads, insignificant drug release in stomach environment, good swelling in pH 7.4, and significant drug release in colonic environment, which ratified the successful delivery of the drug in colon. An inhibition of the proliferation of HT-29 tumor cell to induce apoptosis over a prolonged period of time was revealed in in vitro cytotoxicity assay (MTT) of PEC beads, which indicates sustained drug release in colon as well as enhanced antitumor efficacy.

Piyakulawat and coresearchers studied diclofenac-loaded hydrogel beads of chitosan-carrageenan PEC for peroral controlled release [83]. The optimized composition of the beads with a 2:1 ratio of chitosan and carrageenan and 5% w/v diclofenac sodium was found to show significant sustained release over 8 h. Further cross-linking of the beads with glutaric acid and glutaraldehyde resulted in an increase in the sustained release capacity, and the resulting beads showed to be capable of releasing drugs over even 24 h. The magnitude of the electrostatic interaction between two oppositely charged polymers and degree of cross-linking as well as drug-polymer ratio and pH of the release medium might influence the drug release behavior of the matrix. Chitosan-cashew gum beads loaded with *Lippia sidoides* oil have been reported by Pula et al. for better larvicide activity which might be applied in dengue control [117]. The study

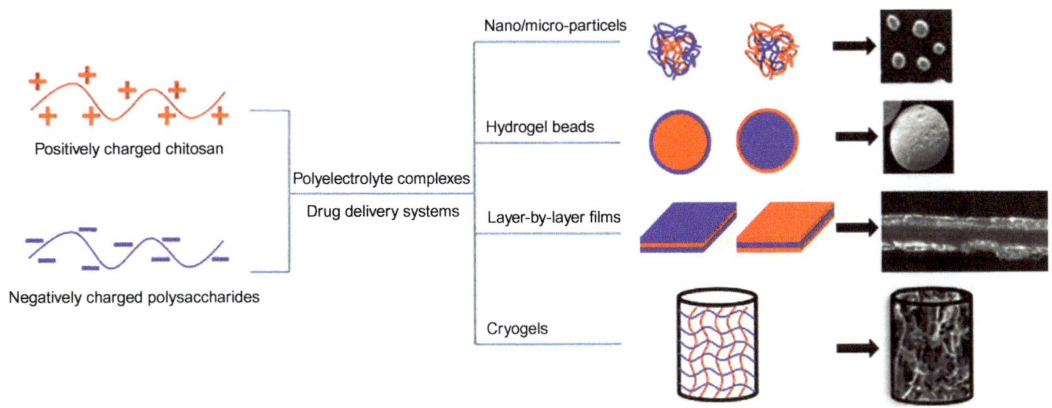

FIG. 1 Various pharmaceutical dosage forms based on PECs. *From Luo Y, Wang Q. Recent development of chitosan-based polyelectrolyte complexes with natural polysaccharides for drug delivery. Int J Biol Macromol 2014; 64: 353–367. Copyright © 2013 with permission from Elsevier B.V.*

revealed the enhanced thermal stability of the PEC beads as well as its capability to sustain the oil release over a prolonged period of time and a prolonged larvicide effect against *Aedes aegypti* larva.

Pectin-trimethyl chitosan chloride beads have been reported by Atyabi et al., for colon delivery of Coomassie Brilliant Blue G-250 as a relatively high molecular weight water-soluble model drug [118]. The influence of various formulation variables such as cross-linker type, cross-linker concentration, curing time, polymer ratio, and pectin concentration on in vitro swelling and drug release was evaluated. They optimized the factors and compositions by factorial design. Various techniques, such as biomineralization or coating of the beads with high-methoxyl pectin or EUDRAGIT L 30 D-55, were employed to modulate the integrity of the beads during gastrointestinal transit as well as drug release.

Yang et al. reported chitosan-gellan PEC beads for controlled delivery of bovine serum albumin [119]. The beads were prepared through a combination of ionotropic gelation and polyelectrolyte complexation techniques. Dense surface, high encapsulation efficiency, and sustained protein release in pH 6.8 with Fickian diffusion mechanism were revealed in the study. A novel carboxymethyl-chitosan-alginate PEC-based hydrogel was described by Lv and coresearchers with the objective of controlled protein delivery by imparting the hygroscopicity modulation ability in it [120]. In vitro cytotoxicity and drug release study revealed the cytocompatibility of the developed hydrogel as well as the sustained release of model protein bovine serum albumin, which indicated potential of the proposed hydrogel for oral protein delivery. Shi and coresearchers also described chitosan-alginate PEC beads for oral delivery of bovine serum albumin [121].

Kulkarni et al. reported a controlled release, floating-cum mucoadhesive PEC beads of glipizide [122]. Chitosan and xanthan gum were used as cationic and anionic polyelectrolyte, respectively, for the preparation of PEC beads. The study showed excellent mucoadhesive as well as sustained drug release over a period of 24 h. A novel hydrogel based on chitosan and chemically modified xanthan gum PEC was described by Malik et al., for sustained delivery of acyclovir over 24 h [123]. Xanthan gum was first grafted with 2-acrylamido-2-methylpropane sulfonic acid using free radical initiator potassium persulfate and mixed with chitosan to obtain PEC-based hydrogel. In vitro drug release showed that the hydrogel was capable of releasing acyclovir over 24 h in a sustained manner. The study demonstrated a potential for developing a pH-sensitive sustained release hydrogel based on PEC using chitosan and modified xanthan gum.

Simple colon-targeted PEC beads based on porous starch-chitosan-pectin were reported by Zhu et al., for colon delivery of doxorubicin [124]. Firstly, they prepared porous maize starch by hydrolysis with a combination of α-amylase and amyloglucosidase, and then porous beads were prepared using the porous starch, chitosan, and pectin. An in vitro simulated digestion method revealed that the designed beads with porous starch-chitosan-pectin released a minimum drug release (13.8%) in the upper part of the gastrointestinal tract, whereas pectin/PS/doxorubicin and pectin/doxorubicin beads showed to release 17.56% and 67.04%, respectively, which substantiated the effectiveness of this delivery design for colon targeting.

6.2 PEC-based microparticles

A dual-layered PEC microbead structure based on alginate, chitosan, and kappa-carrageenan has been described by Sun et al. [125]. The microparticles showed a pH-responsive drug release character and also enhanced stability and swelling in the intestinal environment (pH 7.4). In vitro release study exhibited that the dual layers of the microparticles with chitosan and k-carrageenan successfully resisted drug release in gastric pH and carried most of 5-fluorouracil to the colon. Biodegradable nature, as well as zero hepatotoxicity, was revealed in their investigations. Li and coresearchers developed a bovine serum albumin-loaded chitosan-carrageenan PEC by salt-induced impeding method [126]. PEC formation was reflected in FTIR spectra, and in vitro drug release study was conducted in simulated gastric as well as intestinal fluids, which exhibited pH-responsive drug release character of the PEC matrix with minimum drug release in the gastric environment and controlled release of bovine serum albumin in the intestinal environment.

Chitosan-carboxymethyl cashew gum microspheres were prepared with the objective of oral protein delivery [127]. They used different grades of carboxymethyl cashew gum with different degrees of carboxymethyl substitution and chitosan with high and low molecular weights. The microsphere batch with cashew gum of a higher degree of substitution showed higher swelling but faster drug release rates, whereas those prepared with a low degree of substitution were found to take twice the time for the same drug release. Their investigation showed a non-Fickian kinetic-based release of bovine serum albumin from the PEC-based microspheres.

Curcumin-loaded microcomposites were reported by Samrot et al., where PEC was prepared with chitosan and carboxymethyl cellulose employing the ionic gelation method [128]. In their study, barium chloride and sodium tripolyphosphate were used in different concentrations to make microcomposites. The study revealed significantly higher drug encapsulation efficiency of the microparticles as well as controlled release and antibacterial activity against *Pseudomonas aeruginosa*.

In a report, preparation, characterization, and evaluation of chitosan-gum kondagogu PEC microparticles were presented by Naidu et al. [51]. The total yield of the microparticles was found to be above 80% in the study.

The PEC exhibited a very slow release of diclofenac sodium in 0.1 N HCl acid as compared to phosphate buffer (pH 6.8). An increase in the concentration of gum kondagogu resulted in an increase in drug release. PEC with gum kondagogu/chitosan in a 1:3 ratio showed 98% drug release within 4.5 h, which might be due to a higher degree of swelling of chitosan in acidic medium. A 5.8-fold increase in relative bioavailability in rats was also found in the study.

Lim and coresearchers described the development of mucoadhesive microparticles with the objective of improving the residential time of drugs within the nasal cavity and thereby achieving a better pharmacokinetic profile [129]. They prepared mucoadhesive microparticles with chitosan-hyaluronic acid PEC by a novel emulsification and solvent evaporation method. The in vitro release profiles of the microsphere showed controlled release of gentamicin sulfate. The degree of mucoadhesion was investigated by determining the mucociliary transport rate of the microparticles across an isolated frog palate, where acacia/gelatin microcapsules were used as a positive control. The penetration-enhancing effect of chitosan was combined with the mucoadhesive potential of hyaluronic acid in the study.

Chitosan-xanthan gum microparticles based on PEC were prepared by Caddeo et al. to increase oral bioavailability as well as colonic delivery of natural flavonoid phytoconstituent, quercetin [130]. The microparticles were prepared by mixing two biopolymers in solution form followed by spray drying. Microparticles were then compressed into tablets and further coated with EUDRAGIT to make it gastroresistant, i.e., to prevent quercetin release in the stomach environment. In vitro drug release study revealed the gastroresistant capacity of the tablet as well as complete drug release in the simulated colonic environment, which represents a promising dosage form for quercetin delivery to the colon for better management of inflammatory bowel disease.

6.3 PEC-based nanoparticles

PEC nanoparticles based on chitosan-carrageenan were described by Rodrigues et al., which were prepared by the combination of polyelectrolyte complexation and ionotropic gelation. Tripolyphosphate was used as an ionic cross-linker in their study [131]. Cross-linking by tripolyphosphate exhibited a reduction in particle size and an increase in yield and stability. The smaller size around 150 nm of the nanoparticles having high positive surface charge might be potential tools for mucosal delivery of macromolecules.

In a research work, Abreu et al. described nanogels based on chitosan-cashew gum PEC loaded with *L. sidoides* oil [101]. In vitro oil release and efficacy were investigated using UV–visible spectrophotometer and bioassay method, respectively. The study showed that samples composed of relative ratios of polymer matrix/oil 5:1, gum/chitosan 1:1, and 5% w/v polymer concentration exhibited significantly high loading of 11.8% and encapsulation efficiency of 70%. The average particle size of the nanogels was found to be in the range 335–558 nm. In vitro release study showed sustained oil release from the nanoparticles, and bioassays exhibited oil-loading-dependent better larval mortality compared to pure oil.

Ketoconazole nanoparticles based on chitosan-gellan gum were prepared employing polyelectrolyte complexation by Kumar et al., to improve the antifungal activity against *Aspergillus niger* [132]. Their study revealed that an increase in the concentration of gellan resulted in a significant increase in the size of the particles but a decrease in zeta potential, whereas an increase in the concentration of chitosan resulted in an increase in zeta potential. On relative evaluation, ketoconazole-loaded PEC nanoparticles exhibited significantly enhanced antifungal activity against *A. niger* than placebo nanoparticles and pure drugs.

Fabrication of sustained release and mucoadhesive peroral nanoparticles of quercetin was reported by Kim et al. [133]. The nanoparticles were prepared by polyelectrolyte complexation using chitosan and gum arabic as polyelectrolyte. The PEC nanoparticles were found to exhibit high drug encapsulation efficiency (98.0%), sustained drug release over 8 h, enhanced mucoadhesion and absorption. Cellular antioxidant and in vivo FRAP assays exhibited the antioxidant activities of quercetin absorbed into intestinal cell model and rat blood, respectively.

Another ofloxacin-loaded PEC nanoparticles composed of chitosan-gum ghatti were prepared by Shelly et al. [115]. In their study, a central composite experimental design was employed to analyze the effects of formulation variables, such as concentration of gum ghatti, chitosan, Pluronic F-127, and ofloxacin on particle size and entrapment efficiency. The study also showed that the antibacterial activity of the PEC nanoparticles was comparable to that of the aqueous solution of the drug. In another study, Kumar and Ahuja reported similar work where PEC nanoparticles were prepared with chitosan and carboxymethyl gum kondagogu employing a modified coacervation method [134]. The interaction between carboxymethyl gum kondagogu and chitosan was optimized to prepare PEC nanoparticles using ofloxacin as the model drug. Concentrations of chitosan and carboxymethyl gum kondagogu were optimized by central composite design with two factors and their three levels. The optimized composition of carboxymethyl gum kondagogu (0.031% w/v) and chitosan (0.059% w/v) exhibited an average particle size of 285.9 nm and an entrapment efficiency of 63%. The PEC nanoparticles were found to be capable of sustaining drug release over 24 h with Higuchi kinetic and excellent antibacterial activity.

In another study, Kalam reported hyaluronan-coated chitosan nanoparticles intended for ocular delivery of dexamethasone [135]. In this study, in vitro transcorneal permeation on excised rabbit cornea along with its effect on corneal hydration level, in vivo ocular irritation and drug concentration in tear, and aqueous humor ocular administration of nanoparticles were investigated. The investigation revealed optimum ocular safety of the proposed nanoparticles and about twofold higher bioavailability compared to dexamethasone solution. The enhancement in bioavailability may be due to mucoadhesive nature of the polymers and subsequent increase in residential time for hyaluronan-coated chitosan nanoparticles and accelerated cellular uptake of the nanoparticles by receptor-mediated endocytosis.

A mucoadhesive ocular nanoparticle formulation of an antiglaucoma drug, brinzolamide, was prepared with chitosan and pectin by the PEC coacervation method [136]. The nanoparticles exhibited sustained drug release over 8 h. The pharmacodynamic studies on glaucoma-induced rabbit eye model also exhibited greater intraocular pressure-lowering effect compared to that of a marketed product. Ex vivo corneal permeation study revealed a higher permeation rate also. They described these mucoadhesive and sustained release nanoparticles as a promising approach for improving ocular bioavailability and efficacy of ocular drugs.

6.4 PEC-based films/membranes

In a work, Banerjee and Ganguly demonstrated a trilayered composite using two biopolymer gels with regularly aligned voids in the inner layer with intention of simultaneous incorporation of two drugs and their differential release [137]. The inner layer of the scaffold was composed of calcium alginate, while the outer two layers of chitosan. The investigation was reviewed using bovine serum albumin and vitamin B12 as model drugs. The presence of voids at the inner alginate layer increased the absorptivity to more than 4000%. An excellent adhesive strength was found between layers. This approach showed the potential of the composite film in the sequential release of bioactive substances. Evangelista et al. described supramolecular PECs based on a cyclodextrin-grafted chitosan and carrageenan for controlled release of silver sulfadiazine and improvement in antibacterial activity [138]. In vitro tests showed an obvious bacterial activity toward Gram-positive bacteria *Staphylococcus aureus* and *Enterococcus durans/hirae* and Gram-negative bacteria *Klebsiella pneumoniae* and *Escherichia coli*. In their investigation, cyclodextrin-grafted chitosan-carrageenan supramolecular PEC was found to exhibit potential for controlled drug release.

A PEC film based on chitosan-gum arabic complex was prepared by Sakloetsakun and coresearchers with the objectives of developing mucoadhesive film with significant adhesive strength and less cytotoxicity [95]. The study revealed that an increase in the gum arabic ratio results in an increase in turbidity and a decrease in zeta potential. The developed film was found to have excellent mucoadhesive and adhesive force, which established its potential for use in the coating of various dosage forms and mucoadhesive drug delivery systems.

An environment-friendly pH-responsive film has been demonstrated by Lu et al., which was prepared with chitosan-hyaluronic acid PECs [139]. In this study, chitosan and hyaluronic acid were functionalized with catechol for catechol-based adhesion and fabricated in a layer-by-layer assembly. The film was found to exhibit improved stability compared to the native polymers and reversible pH-dependent swelling and shrinkage. They concluded that this pH-responsive film can be applied as an intelligent smart device in drug delivery and tissue engineering.

A novel chitosan-pectin-gum arabic PEC membrane was described by Tsai et al., as an oral controlled release platform for drug delivery [140]. Insulin was loaded in the membrane as a model drug in their study. The concentrations of the biopolymers used in the membrane were optimized. The addition of gum arabic to the chitosan and pectin solution results in a decrease in the viscosities of the resultant PEC solutions due to the formation of globe-like microstructures. The mechanical strength and hydrophilicity of the PEC membranes were found greater compared to pure chitosan membranes. The optimized PEC membrane was also found to exhibit a steady controlled release of insulin over 6 h.

Aguiar and coresearchers reported a mineralized film composed of chitosan, xanthan gum, and hydroxyapatite for bone tissue engineering [141]. Their work exhibited that the mineralized biofilm possessed improved film stability and controlled swelling degree in different pH buffers. The film was prepared by a layer-by-layer technique. Polyelectrolyte complexation in between cationic chitosan and anionic xanthan gum and Ca^{2+}-induced cross-linking of xanthan moieties impart pH-responsive behavior to the films. The mineralization with in situ hydroxyapatite formation resulted in additional stability in the mineral phase as well as lower crystallinity similar to bone mineral. The films mineralized with calcium phosphate were found to exhibit cellular adhesion in in vitro cell adhesion test using MG63 cells culture. They concluded that the proposed film composed of xanthan and chitosan may be potential candidates for the regeneration of bone tissue.

6.5 PEC-based foams/cryogels

Cryogels may be defined as gel matrices formed in moderately frozen solutions of polymers. These have interconnected macropores that allow unhindered diffusion of solutes of practically any size, as well as mass transport of nano- and even microparticles [142]. Macroporous foams or cryogels have recently been drawing the attention of drug delivery scientists for their wide applications. Fig. 2 depicts five steps to obtain polymeric cryogels, starting with freezing of polymer solution with chemical

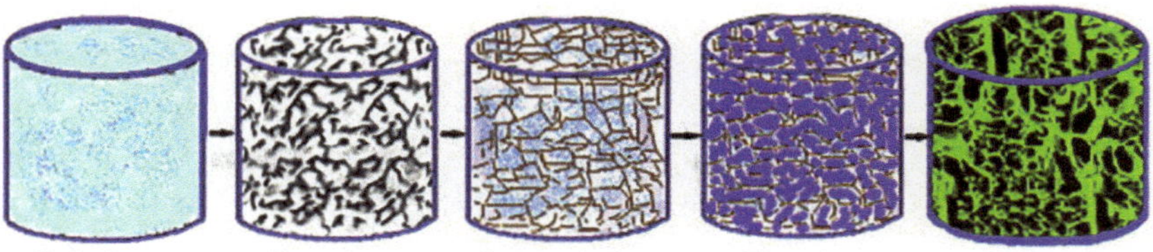

FIG. 2 Cryogel preparation stages: (i) a solution of monomers or polymers with a cross-linker, (ii) frozen, (iii) stored at subzero temperature, and (iv) thawed to form (v) macroporous cryogel in native hydration state (then it can be freeze-dried). *From Gun'ko VM, Savina IN, Mikhalovsky SV. Cryogels: morphological, structural and adsorption characterization. Adv Colloid Interface Sci 2013; 187–188: 1–46. Copyright © 2012 with permission from Elsevier B.V.*

or physical cross-linkers such as polyelectrolytes. In the next step, it is kept in frozen condition for a certain period of time to allow cryogelation and the formation of pores, followed by freeze-drying [142].

Recently, a chitosan-xanthan gum macroporous foam cryogel has been described by Liu et al. [143]. In this method, xanthan gum powder was firstly added into a concentrated solution of chitosan in an aqueous acetic acid solvent, and then it was frozen and subsequently lyophilized. During freezing, the electrostatic attraction between chitosan and xanthan gum gets reinforced, which results in gel formation below freezing point temperature. Nanoclay such as sodium montmorillonite may be added to polymer dispersion before freezing to increase the mechanical strength of chitosan-xanthan cryogel. The freezing method and rate have great influence in physicochemical properties of cryogels. The rapid freezing rate at − 2°C/min resulted in finer pore size about 40 μm, while the slower freezing rate at − 0.25°C/min resulted in bigger pore size about 68 μm, which is depicted in Fig. 3. Furthermore, contact freezing method with a heat exchanger results in aligned macropores, whereas immersion freezing method in a cryobath yields randomly aligned macropores with bamboo-like straight structures [143]. The proposed chitosan-xanthan gum cryogel was evaluated for enzyme encapsulation and its controlled release capacity, which showed significant enzyme encapsulation, its controlled release, and retention of enzyme activity over 30 days.

A biodegradable sponge based on chitosan-sodium alginate PEC was suggested for wound healing [144]. The study exhibited that the swelling capacity of the sponge was found to be proportional to the concentration of chitosan. The study also revealed the biodegradable nature of the sponge as well as its sustained release capacity. The sponge was found to be capable of releasing curcumin over 20 days and better wound healing potential. Various dosage forms fabricated based on the formations of PECs along with the polyelectrolyte combinations, type of methods employed, and applications are presented in Table 2.

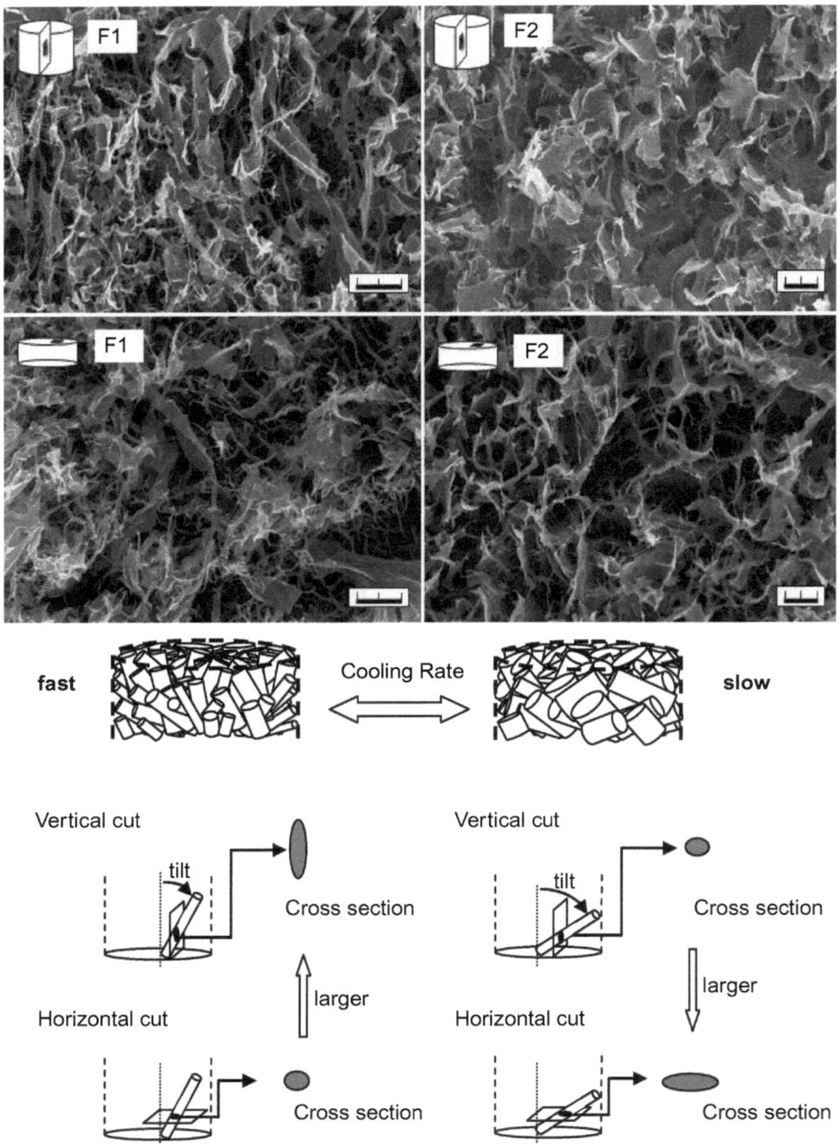

FIG. 3 Comparison of fast freezing (F1) and slow freezing (F2) sample from vertical and horizontally cross section; all scale bars are 100 μm. *From Liu H, Nakagawa K, Chaudhary D, Asakuma Y, Tadé MO. Freeze-dried macroporous foam prepared from chitosan/xanthan gum/montmorillonite nanocomposites. Chem Eng Res Des 2011; 89: 2356–2364. Copyright © 2011 with permission from The Institution of Chemical Engineers, Published by Elsevier B.V.*

TABLE 2 Various dosage forms fabricated based on PECs.

Types of dosage forms	Polymer combinations	Preparation method	Applications	References
Beads/ hydrogel	Chitosan succinate-sodium alginate	Ionotropic gelation and polyelectrolyte complexation; needle extrusion	Colonic drug delivery	[116]
	Chitosan-carrageenan	Ionotropic gelation and polyelectrolyte complexation; needle extrusion	Controlled release of diclofenac sodium	[83]
	Chitosan-cashew gum	Dispersion and cross-linking with glutaraldehyde	Better larvicide activity, useful in dengue control	[117]
	Chitosan-pectin	Ionotropic gelation and polyelectrolyte complexation; needle extrusion	Colon delivery of Coomassie Brilliant Blue G-250	[118]
	Chitosan-gellan	Ionotropic gelation and polyelectrolyte complexation; dispersion method	Controlled protein delivery	[119]
	Chitosan-alginate hydrogels	Mixing method	Controlled protein delivery	[120,121]
	Chitosan-xanthan	Polyelectrolyte complexation; needle extrusion	Gastroretentive sustained release of glipizide	[122]
	Chitosan-xanthan gum hydrogel	Physical mixing in solution forms, molding	pH-sensitive hydrogel for acyclovir delivery	[123]
Microparticles	Chitosan-alginate-kappa carrageenan	Ionotropic gelation (needle extrusion); polyelectrolyte complexation (dispersion method)	Colonic delivery of 5-fluorouracil	[125]
	Chitosan-kappa carrageenan	Polyelectrolyte complexation (dispersion method)	Protein delivery by oral route	[126]
	Chitosan-carboxymethyl cashew gum	Polyelectrolyte complexation (needle extrusion)	Protein delivery by oral route	[127]

Continued

TABLE 2 Various dosage forms fabricated based on PECs—cont'd

Types of dosage forms	Polymer combinations	Preparation method	Applications	References
	Chitosan-carboxymethyl cellulose	Ionotropic cross-linking, polyelectrolyte complexation (dispersion method)	Controlled release of curcumin	[128]
	Chitosan-gum kondagogu	Coacervation phase separation; drying and milling	Enhanced bioavailability	[51]
	Chitosan-hyaluronic acid	Water-in-oil (w/o) emulsification and solvent evaporation technique; complex coacervation	Mucoadhesive; nasal delivery of gentamicin	[129]
	Chitosan-xanthan gum	Mixing in solution, polyelectrolyte complexation and spray drying; compressed into tablet	Gastroresistant matrix; colon targeting of quercetin	[130]
Nanoparticles	Chitosan-carrageenan	Polyelectrolyte complexation, ionic gelation	Mucosal delivery of macromolecules	[131]
	Chitosan-cashew gum	Mixing in solution, polyelectrolyte complexation, and spray drying	Encapsulation of larvicidal essential oil; improved larvicidal activity	[101]
	Chitosan-gellan gum	Dispersion method; polyelectrolyte complexation	Ketoconazole encapsulation for better antifungal activity	[132]
	Chitosan-gum arabic	Dispersion method; polyelectrolyte complexation	Sustained release quercetin, mucoadhesion, enhanced absorption	[133]
	Chitosan-gum ghatti	Dispersion method; polyelectrolyte complexation	Ofloxacin delivery	[115]

TABLE 2 Various dosage forms fabricated based on PECs—cont'd

Types of dosage forms	Polymer combinations	Preparation method	Applications	References
	Chitosan-carboxymethyl gum kondagogu	Coacervation method	Sustained delivery of ofloxacin	[134]
	Chitosan-hyaluronic acid	Polyelectrolyte complexation	Ocular delivery dexamethasone	[135]
	Chitosan-pectin	PEC coacervation	Ocular delivery of brinzolamide	[136]
Films/ membranes	Chitosan-alginate	Ionotropic cross-linking; air bubbling; polyelectrolyte complexation	Sequential release of bovine serum albumin and Vit B_{12}	[137]
	B-cyclodextrin-grafted chitosan-carrageenan	Dispersion; polyelectrolyte complexation	Silver sulfadiazine-mediated silver nanoparticles; antibacterial efficacy	[138]
	Chitosan-gum arabic	Mixing in solution form; casting; solvent evaporation	Mucoadhesive film; coating of drug formulation	[95]
	Chitosan-hyaluronic acid	Polyelectrolyte complexation	pH-responsive drug delivery; tissue engineering	[139]
	Chitosan-pectin-gum arabic	Mixing; polyelectrolyte complexation	Controlled drug release (insulin)	[140]
	Chitosan-xanthan gum	Film-mineralization; dip coating; layer-by-layer deposition	Bone tissue engineering	[141]
Foams/ cryogels	Chitosan-xanthan gum	Cryogelation technique	Enzyme encapsulation and controlled release	[143]
	Chitosan-alginate	Cryogelation	Curcumin topical delivery; wound healing	[144]

7 Conclusion

Natural polysaccharide-based PECs have been investigated as promising biopolymeric carrier matrices for various biomedical applications, including drug delivery, due to their biocompatibility, biodegradability, and green fabricability. They can be tailored as smart polymeric systems in drug targeting in different parts of our body with different intentions. In this chapter, a wide range of novel approaches of drug delivery with PECs have been demonstrated with different dosage forms of PECs, such as hydrogels, beads, microparticles, nanoparticles, films or membranes, foams or cryogels, etc., along with their fabrication process, factors affecting the characters of dosage forms like delivery of various micromolecular and macromolecular drugs, mechanical strength, swelling behavior, etc. More and more novel drug delivery systems will be evolved with PECs upon further understanding of their formation mechanisms. PECs can be tailored as smart devices for delivery of macromolecular drugs, especially proteins and peptides. However, the in vivo evaluation of PEC-based drug delivery systems must be carried out in animal models to fully understand their safety, physiological effects as well as biological fate and obviously in vivo efficacy.

References

[1] Das S, Ghosh A, Changder A, Nandi G, Ghosh LK. Quality-by-design approach for development of sustained-release multiple-unit beads of lamotrigine based on ion-cross-linked composite of pectin and okra mucilage: an in vitro appraisal. Int J Biol Macromol 2020;163:842–53.

[2] Jain D, Sodani A, Ray S, Ghosh P, Nandi G. Formulation of extended-release beads of lamotrigine based on alginate and Cassia fistula seed gum by QbD approach. Curr Drug Deliv 2020;17(5):422–37.

[3] Maity M, Hasnain MS, Nayak AK, Aminabavi TM. In: Nayak AK, Hasnain MS, Aminabhavi TM, editors. Biomedical applications of polysaccharides, tailor-made polysaccharides in biomedical applications. USA: Academic Press, Elsevier Inc; 2021. p. 1–34.

[4] Guru PR, Bera H, Das M, Hasnain MS, Nayak AK. Aceclofenac-loaded Plantago ovata F. husk mucilage-Zn^{+2}-pectinate controlled-release matrices. Starch-Starke 2018;70:1700136.

[5] Hasnain MS, Rishishwar P, Ali S. Use of cashew bark exudate gum in the preparation of 4% lidocaine HCL topical gels. Int J Pharm Pharm Sci 2017;9(8):146–50.

[6] Hasnain MS, Rishishwar P, Ali S. Floating-bioadhesive matrix tablets of hydralazine HCL made of cashew gum and HPMC K4M. Int J Pharm Pharm Sci 2017;9(7):124–9.

[7] Qureshi D, Nayak AK, Kim D, Maji S, Anis A, Mohanty B, Pal K. Polysaccharide-based polymeric gels as drug delivery vehicles. In: Nayak AK, Pal K, Banerjee I, Maji S, Nanda U, editors. Advances and challenges in pharmaceutical technology: materials, process development and drug delivery strategies. USA: Academic Press, Elsevier Inc.; 2021. p. 131–46.

[8] Sarkar D, Nandi G, Changder A, Hudati P, Sarkar S, Ghosh LK. Sustained release gastroretentive tablet of metformin hydrochloride based on poly (acrylic acid)-grafted-gellan. Int J Biol Macromol 2017;96:137–48.

[9] Nayak AK, Pal D. Functionalization of tamarind gum for drug delivery. In: Thakur VK, Thakur MK, editors. Functional biopolymers. Cham: Springer; 2018. p. 35–56.
[10] Patra S, Bala NN, Nandi G. Synthesis, characterization and fabrication of sodium carboxymethyl-okra-gum-grafted-polymethacrylamide into sustained release tablet matrix. Int J Biol Macromol 2020;164:3885–900.
[11] Das B, Dutta S, Nayak AK, Nanda U. Zinc alginate-carboxymethyl cashew gum microbeads for prolonged drug release: development and optimization. Int J Biol Macromol 2014;70:505–15.
[12] Luo Q, Han Q, Wang Y, Zhang H, Fei Z, Wang Y. The thiolated chitosan: synthesis, gelling and antibacterial capability. Int J Biol Macromol 2019;139:521–30.
[13] Jana S, Das A, Nayak AK, Sen KK, Basu SK. Aceclofenac-loaded unsaturated esterified alginate/gellan gum microspheres: in vitro and in vivo assessment. Int J Biol Macromol 2013;57:129–37.
[14] Pal D, Nayak AK. Interpenetrating polymer networks (IPNs): natural polymeric blends for drug delivery. In: Mishra M, editor. Encyclopedia of biomedical polymers and polymeric biomaterials, vol. VI. New York: Taylor and Francis; 2015. p. 4120–30.
[15] Nayak AK, Pal D. Chitosan-based interpenetrating polymeric network systems for sustained drug release. In: Tiwari A, Patra HK, Choi J-W, editors. Advanced theranostics materials. USA: Wiley-Scrivener; 2015. p. 183–208.
[16] Hasnain MS, Ray P, Nayak AK. Alginate-based interpenetrating polymer networks for sustained drug release. In: Nayak AK, Hasnain MS, editors. Alginates in drug delivery. United States: Academic Press, Elsevier Inc.; 2020. p. 101–28.
[17] Malakar J, Nayak AK, Das A. Modified starch (cationized)-alginate beads containing aceclofenac: formulation optimization using central composite design. Starch-Starke 2013;65:603–12.
[18] Mohanta BC, Javed MN, Hasnain MS, Nayak AK. Polyelectrolyte complexes of alginate for controlling drug release. In: Nayak AK, Hasnain MS, editors. Alginates in drug delivery. United States: Academic Press Elsevier Inc.; 2020. p. 297–321.
[19] Priyadarshini R, Nandi G, Changder A, Chowdhury S, Chakraborty S, Ghosh LK. Gastroretentive extended release of metformin from methacrylamide-g-gellan and tamarind seed gum composite matrix. Carbohydr Polym 2016;137:100–10.
[20] Nandi G, Patra P, Priyadarshini R, Kaity S, Ghosh LK. Synthesis, characterization and evaluation of methacrylamide grafted gellan as sustained release tablet matrix. Int J Biol Macromol 2015;72:965–74.
[21] Nayak AK, Bera H, Hasnain MS, Pal D. Synthesis and characterization of graft-copolymers of plant polysaccharides. In: Thakur VK, editor. Biopolymer grafting, synthesis and properties. Netherlands: Elsevier Inc.; 2018. p. 1–62.
[22] Dey S, Roy S, Hasnain MS, Nayak AK. Grafted alginates in drug delivery. In: Nayak AK, Hasnain MS, editors. Alginates in drug delivery. United States: Academic Press, Elsevier Inc.; 2020. p. 71–100.
[23] Alkahtani S, Hasnain MS, Nayak AK, Aminabhavi TM. Polysaccharide-based polyelectrolyte complex systems for biomedical uses. In: Nayak AK, Hasnain MS, Aminabhavi TM, editors. Tailor-made polysaccharides in biomedical applications. USA: Academic Press, Elsevier Inc.; 2021. p. 151–74.
[24] Ishihara M, Kishimoto S, Nakamura S, Sato Y, Hattori H. Polyelectrolyte complexes of natural polymers and their biomedical applications. Polymers (Basel) 2019;11(4):672.
[25] Liu C, Xu H, Sun Y, Zhang X, Cheng H, Mao S. Design of virus-mimicking polyelectrolyte complexes for Enhanced oral Insulin Delivery. J Pharm Sci 2019;108(10):3408–15.
[26] Thompson C, Ibie C. The oral delivery of proteins using interpolymer polyelectrolyte complexes. Ther Deliv 2011;2(12):1611–31.
[27] Muheem A, Shakeel F, Jahangir MA, Anwar M, Mallick N, Jain GK, Warsi MH, Ahmad FJ. A review on the strategies for oral delivery of proteins and peptides and their clinical perspectives. Saudi Pharm J 2016;24(4):413–28.

[28] Bourganis V, Karamanidou T, Kammona O, Kiparissides C. Polyelectrolyte complexes as prospective carriers for the oral delivery of protein therapeutics. Eur J Pharm Biopharm 2017;111:44–60.
[29] Du J, Dai J, Liu JL, Dankovich T. Novel pH-sensitive polyelectrolyte carboxymethyl Konjac glucomannan-chitosan beads as drug carriers. React Funct Polym 2006;66:1055–61.
[30] Il'ina AV, Varlamov VP. Chitosan-based polyelectrolyte complexes: a review. Appl Biochem Microbiol 2005;41:9–16.
[31] Fu J, Schlenoff JB. Driving forces for oppositely charged polyion association in aqueous solutions: enthalpic, entropic, but not electrostatic. J Am Chem Soc 2016;138(3):980–90.
[32] Berger J, Reist M, Mayer JM, Felt O, Gurny R. Structure and interactions in chitosan hydrogels formed by complexation or aggregation for biomedical applications. Eur J Pharm Biopharm 2004;57(1):35–52.
[33] Hamman JH. Chitosan based polyelectrolyte complexes as potential carrier materials in drug delivery systems. Mar Drugs 2010;8(4):1305–22.
[34] Lounis FM, Chamieh J, Gonzalez P, Cottet H, Leclercq L. Prediction of polyelectrolyte complex stoichiometry for highly hydrophilic polyelectrolytes. Macromolecules 2016;49(10):3881–8.
[35] Drogoz A, David L, Rochas C, Domard A, Delair T. Polyelectrolyte complexes from polysaccharides: formation and stoichiometry monitoring. Langmuir 2007;23(22):10950–8.
[36] Du J, Sun R, Zhang S, Zhang LF, Xiong CD, Peng YX. Novel polyelectrolyte carboxymethyl konjac glucomannan-chitosan nanoparticles for drug delivery. I. Physicochemical characterization of the carboxymethyl konjac glucomannan-chitosan nanoparticles. Biopolymers 2005;78(1):1–8.
[37] Du J, Zhang S, Sun R, Zhang LF, Xiong CD, Peng YX. Novel polyelectrolyte carboxymethyl konjac glucomannan-chitosan nanoparticles for drug delivery. II. Release of albumin in vitro. J Biomed Mater Res B Appl Biomater 2005;72(2):299–304.
[38] Luo Y, Wang Q. Recent development of chitosan-based polyelectrolyte complexes with natural polysaccharides for drug delivery. Int J Biol Macromol 2014;64:353–67.
[39] Prestwich GD. Hyaluronic acid-based clinical biomaterials derived for cell and molecule delivery in regenerative medicine. J Control Release 2011;155:193–9.
[40] Xu X, Jha AK, Harrington DA, Farach-Carson MC, Jia X. Hyaluronic acid-based hydrogels: from a natural polysaccharide to complex networks. Soft Matter 2012;8:3280–94.
[41] Ridley BL, O'Neill MA, Mohnen D. Pectins: structure, biosynthesis, and oligogalacturonide-related signaling. Phytochemistry 2001;57:929–67.
[42] Jaiswal L, Shankar S, Rhim J, HyunHahm W. Lignin-mediated green synthesis of AgNPs in carrageenan matrix for wound dressing applications. Int J Biol Macromol 2020;159:859–69.
[43] Hajikhani M, Khanghahi MM, Shahrousvand M, Mohammadi-Rovshandeh J, Babaei A, Khademi SMH. Intelligent super absorbents based on a xanthan gum/poly (acrylic acid) semi-interpenetrating polymer network for application in drug delivery systems. Int J Biol Macromol 2019;139:509–20.
[44] Nayak AK, Bera H, Hasnain MS, De A, Pal D, Samanta A. Gellan gum-based nanomaterials in drug delivery applications. In: Bera H, Hossain CM, Saha S, editors. Biopolymer-based nanomaterials in drug delivery and biomedical applications. United States: Academic Press, Elsevier Inc.; 2021. p. 313–31.
[45] Kim S, Biswas A, Boddu V, Hwang HS, Adkins J. Solubilization of cashew gum from *Anacardium occidentale* in aqueous medium. Carbohydr Polym 2018;199:205–9.
[46] Nayak AK, Ansari MT, Sami F, Bera H, Hasnain MS. Cashew gum in drug delivery applications. In: Hasnain MS, Nayak AK, editors. Natural polysaccharides in drug delivery and biomedical applications. United States: Academic Press, Elsevier Inc.; 2019. p. 263–83.

[47] Ali BH, Ziada A, Blunden G. Biological effects of gum arabic: a review of some recent research. Food Chem Toxicol 2009;47:1–8.

[48] De A, Nayak AK, Kundu A, Das B, Samanta A. Gum arabic-based nanomaterials in drug delivery and biomedical applications. In: Bera H, Hossain CM, Saha S, editors. Biopolymer-based nanomaterials in drug delivery and biomedical applications. United States: Academic Press, Elsevier Inc.; 2021. p. 165–77.

[49] Bayarri S, González-Tomás L, Costell E. Viscoelastic properties of aqueous and milk systems with carboxymethyl cellulose. Food Hydrocoll 2009;23:441–50.

[50] Jian W, Siu K, Wu J. Effects of pH and temperature on colloidal properties and molecular characteristics of Konjac glucomannan. Carbohydr Polym 2015;134:285–92.

[51] Naidu VGM, Madhusudhana K, Sashidhar RB, Ramakrishna S, Khar RK, Ahmed FJ, Diwan PV. Polyelectrolyte complexes of gum kondagogu and chitosan, as diclofenac carriers. Carbohydr Polym 2009;76:464–71.

[52] Pal P, Singh SK, Mishra S, Pandey JP, Sen G. Gum ghatti based hydrogel: microwave synthesis, characterization, 5-fluorouracil encapsulation and 'in vitro' drug release evaluation. Carbohydr Polym 2019;222:114979.

[53] Hasnain MS, Nayak AK. Chitosan as responsive polymer for drug delivery applications. In: ASH M, Abu-Thabit NY, editors. Stimuli responsive polymeric nanocarriers for drug delivery applications, volume 1, types and triggers. Woodhead publishing series in biomaterials. United States: Elsevier Ltd.; 2018. p. 581–605.

[54] Verma A, Dubey J, Verma N, Nayak AK. Chitosan-hydroxypropyl methylcellulose matrices as carriers for hydrodynamically balanced capsules of moxifloxacin HCl. Curr Drug Deliv 2017;14:83–90.

[55] Pal D, Saha S, Nayak AK, Hasnain MS. Marine-derived polysaccharides: Pharmaceutical applications. In: Nayak AK, Hasnain MS, Pal D, editors. Natural polymers for pharmaceutical applications, Vol. II: Marine and microbiologically derived polymers. USA: Apple Academic Press; 2019. p. 1–36.

[56] Kumar D, Gihar S, Shrivash MK, Kumar P, Kundu PP. A review on the synthesis of graft copolymers of chitosan and their potential applications. Int J Biol Macromol 2020;163:2097–112.

[57] Hasnain MS, Jameel E, Mohanta B, Dhara AK, Alkahtani S, Nayak AK. Alginates: Sources, structure, and properties. In: Nayak AK, Hasnain MS, editors. Alginates in drug delivery. United States: Academic Press, Elsevier Inc.; 2020. p. 1–17.

[58] Kandar CC, Hasnain MS, Nayak AK. Natural polymers as useful pharmaceutical excipients. In: Nayak AK, Pal K, Banerjee I, Maji S, Nanda U, editors. Advances and challenges in pharmaceutical technology: materials, process development and drug delivery strategies. USA: Academic Press, Elsevier Inc.; 2021. p. 1–44.

[59] Hasnain MS, Ahmed SA, Alkahtani S, Milivojevic M, Kandar CC, Dhara AK, Nayak AK. Biopolymers for drug delivery. In: Nayak AK, Hasnain MS, editors. Advanced biopolymeric systems for drug delivery. Switzerland: Springer; 2020. p. 1–29.

[60] Ray P, Maity M, Barik H, Sahoo GS, Hasnain MS, Hoda MN, Nayak AK. Alginate-based hydrogels for drug delivery applications. In: Nayak AK, Hasnain MS, editors. Alginates in drug delivery. United States: Academic Press, Elsevier Inc.; 2020. p. 41–70.

[61] Nayak AK, Hasnain MS. Ionotropically gelled alginate particles in sustained drug release. In: Nayak AK, Hasnain MS, editors. Alginates in drug delivery. United States: Academic Press, Elsevier Inc.; 2020. p. 203–30.

[62] Kurakula M, Rao GSNK, Kiran V, Hasnain MS, Nayak AK. Alginate-based hydrogel systems for drug releasing in wound healing. In: Nayak AK, Hasnain MS, editors. Alginates in drug delivery. United States: Academic Press, Elsevier Inc.; 2020. p. 323–58.

[63] Nayak AK, Hasnain MS, Pal K, Banerjee I, Pal D. Gum-based hydrogels in drug delivery. In: Pal K, Banerjee I, Sarkar P, Kim D, Deng W-P, Dubey NK, Majumder K, editors. Biopolymer-based formulations, biomedical and food applications. United States: Elsevier Inc.; 2020. p. 605–45.

[64] George M, Abraham TE. Polyionic hydrocolloids for the intestinal delivery of protein drugs: alginate and chitosan—a review. J Control Release 2006;114:1–14.
[65] Chan LW, Lee HY, Heng PWS. Mechanisms of external and internal gelation and their impact on the functions of alginate as a coat and delivery system. Carbohydr Polym 2006;63:176–87.
[66] Wong TW, Chan LW, Kho SB, Heng PWS. Design of controlled-release solid dosage forms of alginate and chitosan using microwave. J Control Release 2002;84:99–114.
[67] Nayak AK, Ansari MT, Pal D, Hasnain MS. Hyaluronic acid (hyaluronan): pharmaceutical applications. In: Nayak AK, Hasnain MS, Pal D, editors. Natural polymers for pharmaceutical applications, vol. III: animal derived polymers. USA: Apple Academic Press; 2019. p. 1–32.
[68] Souza ABD, Chaud MV, Santana MHA. Hyaluronic acid behavior in oral administration and perspectives for nanotechnology-based formulations: a review. Carbohydr Polym 2019;222:115001.
[69] Nath SD, Abueva C, Kim B, Lee BT. Chitosan-hyaluronic acid polyelectrolyte complex scaffold crosslinked with genipin for immobilization and controlled release of BMP-2. Carbohydr Polym 2015;115:160–9.
[70] Yang L, Gao S, Asghar S, Liu G, Song J, Wang X, Ping Q, Zhang C, Xiao Y. Hyaluronic acid/chitosan nanoparticles for delivery of curcuminoid and its in vitro evaluation in glioma cells. Int J Biol Macromol 2015;72:1391–401.
[71] Nayak AK, Kalia S, Hasnain MS. Optimization of aceclofenac-loaded pectinate-poly (vinyl pyrrolidone) beads by response surface methodology. Int J Biol Macromol 2013;62:194–202.
[72] Nayak AK, Pal D. Blends of jackfruit seed starch-pectin in the development of mucoadhesive beads containing metformin HCl. Int J Biol Macromol 2013;62:137–45.
[73] Nayak AK, Pal D, Santra K. Development of pectinate-ispagula mucilage mucoadhesive beads of metformin HCl by central composite design. Int J Biol Macromol 2014;66:203–21.
[74] Sinha VR, Kumria R. Polysaccharides in colon-specific drug delivery. Int J Pharm 2001;224(1–2):19–38.
[75] Sriamornsak P. Application of pectin in oral drug delivery. Expert Opin Drug Deliv 2011;8:1009–23.
[76] Maji B, Maiti S. Chemical modification of xanthan gum through graft copolymerization: tailored properties and potential applications in drug delivery and wastewater treatment. Carbohydr Polym 2021;251:117095.
[77] Rosalam S, England R. Review of xanthan gum production from unmodified starches by *Xanthomonas campestris* sp. Enzyme Microb Technol 2006;39:197–207.
[78] Kumar A, Deepak Sharma S, Srivastava A, Kumar R. Synthesis of xanthan gum graft copolymer and its application for controlled release of highly water soluble Levofloxacin drug in aqueous medium. Carbohydr Polym 2017;171:211–9.
[79] Ćirić A, Medarević Đ, Čalija B, Dobričić V, Mitrić M, Djekic L. Study of chitosan/xanthan gum polyelectrolyte complexes formation, solid state and influence on ibuprofen release kinetics. Int J Biol Macromol 2020;148:942–55.
[80] Ćirić A, Medarević Đ, Čalija B, Dobričić V, Rmandić M, Barudžija T, Malenović A, Djekic L. Effect of ibuprofen entrapment procedure on physicochemical and controlled drug release performances of chitosan/xanthan gum polyelectrolyte complexes. Int J Biol Macromol 2021;167:547–58.
[81] Kennedy J, Bradshaw I. Production, properties and applications of xanthan. Prog Ind Microbiol 1984;19:319–71.
[82] Qureshi D, Nayak SK, Maji S, Kim D, Banerjee I, Pal K. Carrageenan: a wonder polymer from marine algae for potential drug delivery applications. Curr Pharm Des 2019;25(11):1172–86.
[83] Piyakulawat P, Praphairaksit N, Chantarasiri N, Muangsin N. Preparation and evaluation of chitosan/carrageenan beads for controlled release of sodium diclofenac. AAPS PharmSciTech 2007;8(4):97.

[84] Jianlong W, Yi Q. Microbial degradation of 4-chlorophenol by microorganisms entrapped in carrageenan-chitosan gels. Chemosphere 1999;38:3109–17.
[85] Hugerth A, Caram-Lelham N, Sundelöf L-O. The effect of charge density and conformation on the polyelectrolyte complex formation between carrageenan and chitosan. Carbohydr Polym 1997;34:149–56.
[86] Giavasis I, Harvey LM, McNeil B. Gellan gum. Crit Rev Biotechnol 2000;20:177–211.
[87] Nayak AK, Pal D. Trigonella foenum-graecum L. seed mucilage-gellan mucoadhesive beads for controlled release of metformin HCl. Carbohydr Polym 2014;107:31–40.
[88] Nitta Y, Nishinari K. Gelation and gel properties of polysaccharides gellan gum and tamarind xyloglucan. Int J Biol Macromol 2005;5:47–52.
[89] Silva-Correia J, Oliveira J, Caridade S, Oliveira J, Sousa R, Mano J, Reis R. Gellan gum-based hydrogels for intervertebral disc tissue-engineering applications. J Tissue Eng Regen Med 2011;5:e97–e107.
[90] Nayak AK, Hasnain MS. Gum Arabic based multiple units for oral drug delivery. In: Nayak AK, Hasnain MS, editors. Plant polysaccharides-based multiple-unit systems for oral drug delivery. Singapore: Springer; 2019. p. 25–30.
[91] Nayak AK, Das B, Maji R. Calcium alginate/gum Arabic beads containing glibenclamide: development and in vitro characterization. Int J Biol Macromol 2012;51:1070–8.
[92] Idris OHM, Williams PA, Phillips GO. Characterisation of gum from Acacia senegal trees of different age and location using multidetection gel permeation chromatography. Food Hydrocoll 1998;12:379–88.
[93] McNamee BF, O'Riorda ED, O'Sullivan M. Emulsification and microencapsulation properties of gum Arabic. J Agric Food Chem 1998;46(11):4551–5.
[94] Xu T, Gao C, Feng X, Huang M, Yang Y, Shen X, Tang X. Cinnamon and clove essential oils to improve physical, thermal and antimicrobial properties of chitosan-gum arabic polyelectrolyte complexed films. Carbohydr Polym 2019;217:116–25.
[95] Sakloetsakun D, Preechagoon D, Bernkop-Schnürch A, Pongjanyakul T. Chitosan-gum Arabic polyelectrolyte complex films: physicochemical, mechanical and mucoadhesive properties. Pharm Dev Technol 2016;21(5):590–9.
[96] Hasnain MS, Rishishwar P, Rishishwar S, Ali S, Nayak AK. Extraction and characterization of cashew tree (*Anacardium occidentale*) gum; use in aceclofenac dental pastes. Int J Biol Macromol 2018;116:1074–81.
[97] Paula RCMD, Rodrigues JF. Composition and rheological properties of cashew tree gum, the exudate polysaccharide from *Anacardium occidentale* L. Carbohydr Polym 1995;26:177–81.
[98] Paula RD, Heatley F, Budd PM. Characterization of Anacardium occidentale exudate polysaccharide. Polym Int 1998;45:27–35.
[99] Lima MR, Paula HCB, Abreu F, Silva R, Sombra FM, Paula RCM. Hydrophobization of cashew gum by acetylation mechanism and amphotericin B encapsulation. Int J Biol Macromol 2018;108:523–30.
[100] Ribeiro AJ, de Souza FRL, Bezerra JMNA, Oliveira C, Nadvorny D, de La Roca Soares MF, Nunes LCC, Silva-Filho EC, Veiga F, Soares Sobrinho JL. Gums based delivery systems: review on cashew gum and its derivatives. Carbohydr Polym 2016;147:188–200.
[101] Abreu FO, Oliveira EF, Paula HC, de Paula RC. Chitosan/cashew gum nanogels for essential oil encapsulation. Carbohydr Polym 2012;89(4):1277–82.
[102] Liuyun J, Yubao L, Chengdong X. A novel composite membrane of chitosan-carboxymethyl cellulose polyelectrolyte complex membrane filled with nano-hydroxyapatite I. Preparation and properties. J Mater Sci Mater Med 2009;20(8):1645–52.
[103] Javanbakht S, Shaabani A. Carboxymethyl cellulose-based oral delivery systems. Int J Biol Macromol 2019;133:21–9.
[104] Arca HC, Mosquera-Giraldo LI, Bi V, Xu D, Taylor LS, Edgar KJ. Pharmaceutical applications of cellulose ethers and cellulose ether esters. Biomacromolecules 2018;19(7):2351–76.

[105] Kanikireddy V, Varaprasad K, Jayaramudu T, Karthikeyan C, Sadiku R. Carboxymethyl cellulose-based materials for infection control and wound healing: a review. Int J Biol Macromol 2020;164:963–75.
[106] Maver T, Hribernik S, Mohan T, Smrke DM, Maver U, Stana-Kleinschek K. Functional wound dressing materials with highly tunable drug release properties. RSC Adv 2015;5:77873–84.
[107] Nie H, Shen X, Zhou Z, Jiang Q, Chen Y, Xie A, Wang W, Han CC. Electrospinning and characterization of konjac glucomannan/chitosan nanofibrous scaffolds favoring the growth of bone mesenchymal stem cells. Carbohydr Polym 2011;85:681–6.
[108] Alvarez-Manceñido F, Landin M, Lacik I, Martínez-Pacheco R. Konjac glucomannan and konjac glucomannan/xanthan gum mixtures as excipients for controlled drug delivery systems. Diffusion of small drugs. Int J Pharm 2008;349:11–8.
[109] Liu J, Zhang L, Hu W, Tian R, Teng Y, Wang C. Preparation of konjac glucomannan-based pulsatile capsule for colonic drug delivery system and its evaluation in vitro and in vivo. Carbohydr Polym 2012;87:377–82.
[110] Vinod VTP, Sashidhar RP, Sarma VUM, Saradhi UVRV. Compositional analysis and rheological properties of gum kondagogu (*Cochlospermum gossypium*): a tree gum from India. J Agric Food Chem 2008;56:2199–207.
[111] Kumar A, Ahuja M. Carboxymethyl gum kondagogu: synthesis, characterization and evaluation as mucoadhesive polymer. Carbohydr Polym 2012;90:637–43.
[112] Deshmukh AS, Setty CM, Badiger AM, Muralikrishna KS. Gum ghatti: a promising polysaccharide for pharmaceutical applications. Carbohydr Polym 2012;87:980–6.
[113] Kaur L, Singh J, Singh H. Characterization of gum ghatti (*Anogeissus latifolia*): a structural and rheological approach. J Food Sci 2009;74(6):E328–32.
[114] Lal N, Dubey J, Gaur P, Verma N, Verma A. Chitosan based in situ forming polyelectrolyte complexes: a potential sustained drug delivery polymeric carrier for high dose drugs. Korean J Couns Psychother 2017;79:491–8.
[115] Shelly Ahuja M, Kumar A. Gum ghatti-chitosan polyelectrolyte nanoparticles: preparation and characterization. Int J Biol Macromol 2013;61:411–5.
[116] Sinha P, Udhumansha U, Rathnam G, Ganesh M, Jang HT. Capecitabine encapsulated chitosan succinate-sodium alginate macromolecular complex beads for colon cancer targeted delivery: in vitro evaluation. Int J Biol Macromol 2018;117:840–50.
[117] Paula HCB, Sombra FM, Cavalcante RDF, Abreu FOMS, Paula RCM. Preparation and characterization of chitosan/cashew gum beads loaded with *Lippia sidoides* essential oil. Mater Sci Eng C 2011;31:173–8.
[118] Atyabi F, Majzoob S, Iman M, Salehi M, Dorkoosh F. In vitro evaluation and modification of pectinate gel beads containing trimethyl chitosan, as a multi-particulate system for delivery of water-soluble macromolecules to colon. Carbohydr Polym 2005;61:39–51.
[119] Yang F, Xia S, Tan C, Zhang X. Preparation and evaluation of chitosan-calcium-gellan gum beads for controlled release of protein. Eur Food Res Technol 2013;237:467–79.
[120] Lv X, Zhang W, Liu Y, Zhao Y, Zhang J, Hou M. Hygroscopicity modulation of hydrogels based on carboxymethyl chitosan/alginate polyelectrolyte complexes and its application as pH-sensitive delivery system. Carbohydr Polym 2018;198:86–93.
[121] Shi X, Du Y, Sun L, Zhang B, Dou A. Polyelectrolyte complex beads composed of water-soluble chitosan/alginate: characterization and their protein release behavior. J Appl Polym Sci 2006;100:4614–22.
[122] Kulkarni N, Wakte P, Naik J. Development of floating chitosan-xanthan beads for oral controlled release of glipizide. Int J Pharm Invest 2015;5(2):73–80.
[123] Malik NS, Ahmad M, Minhas MU, Tulain R, Barkat K, Khalid I, Khalid Q. Chitosan/xanthan gum based hydrogels as potential carrier for an antiviral drug: fabrication, characterization and safety evaluation. Front Chem 2020;8:50.
[124] Zhu J, Zhong L, Chen W, Song Y, Qian Z, Cao X, Huang Q, Zhang B, Chen H, Chen W. Preparation and characterization of pectin/chitosan beads containing porous starch

embedded with doxorubicin hydrochloride: a novel and simple colon targeted drug delivery system. Food Hydrocoll 2019;95:562–70.

[125] Sun X, Liu C, Omer AM, Yang L-Y, Ouyang X-K. Dual-layered pH-sensitive alginate/chitosan/kappa-carrageenan microbeads for colon-targeted release of 5-fluorouracil. Int J Biol Macromol 2019;132:487–94.

[126] Li C, Hein S, Wang K. Chitosan-carrageenan polyelectrolyte complex for the delivery of protein drugs. ISRN Biomater 2013;, 629807.

[127] Magalhães GA, Santos CMW, Silva DA, Maciel JS, Feitosa JPA, Paula HCB, Paula RCM. Microspheres of chitosan/carboxymethyl cashew gum (CH/CMCG): effect of chitosan molar mass and CMCG degree of substitution on the swelling and BSA release. Carbohydr Polym 2009;77(2):217–22.

[128] Samrot AV, Akanksha Jahnavi T, Padmanaban S, Philip S-A, Burman U, Rabel AM. Chelators influenced synthesis of chitosan–carboxymethyl cellulose microparticles for controlled drug delivery. Appl Nanosci 2016;6:1219–31.

[129] Lim ST, Martin GP, Berry DJ, Brown MB. Preparation and evaluation of the in vitro drug release properties and mucoadhesion of novel microspheres of hyaluronic acid and chitosan. J Control Release 2000;66:281–92.

[130] Caddeo C, Nácher A, Díez-Sales O, Merino-Sanjuán M, Fadda AM, Manconi M. Chitosan–xanthan gum microparticle-based oral tablet for colon-targeted and sustained delivery of quercetin. J Microencapsul 2014;31(7):694–9.

[131] Rodrigues S, Costa AMRD, Grenha A. Chitosan/carrageenan nanoparticles: effect of cross-linking with tripolyphosphate and charge ratios. Carbohydr Polym 2012;89:282–9.

[132] Kumar S, Kaur P, Bernela M, Rani R, Thakur R. Ketoconazole encapsulated in chitosan-gellan gum nanocomplexes exhibits prolonged antifungal activity. Int J Biol Macromol 2016;93(Part A):988–94.

[133] Kim ES, Kim DY, Lee J-S, Lee HG. Mucoadhesive chitosan-gum arabic nanoparticles enhance the absorption and antioxidant activity of quercetin in the intestinal cellular environment. J Agric Food Chem 2019;67(31):8609–16.

[134] Kumar A, Ahuja M. Carboxymethyl gum kondagogu–chitosan polyelectrolyte complex nanoparticles: preparation and characterization. Int J Biol Macromol 2013;62:80–4.

[135] Kalam MA. The potential application of hyaluronic acid coated chitosan nanoparticles in ocular delivery of dexamethasone. Int J Biol Macromol 2016;89:559–68.

[136] Dubey V, Mohan P, Dangi JS, Kesavan K. Brinzolamide loaded chitosan-pectin mucoadhesive nanocapsules for management of glaucoma: formulation, characterization and pharmacodynamic study. Int J Biol Macromol 2020;152:1224–32.

[137] Banerjee A, Ganguly S. Alginate–chitosan composite hydrogel film with macrovoids in the inner layer for biomedical applications. J Appl Polym Sci 2019;136:47599.

[138] Evangelista TFS, Andrade GRS, Nascimento KNS, Santos SB, Santos FMC, D'Oca CDRM, Estevam CS, Gimenez IF, Almeida LE. Supramolecular polyelectrolyte complexes based on cyclodextrin-grafted chitosan and carrageenan for controlled drug release. Carbohydr Polym 2020;245:116592.

[139] Lu B, Luo D, Zhao A, Wang H, Zhao Y, Maitz MF, Yang P, Huang N. pH responsive chitosan and hyaluronic acid layer by layer film for drug delivery applications. Prog Org Coat 2019;135:240–7.

[140] Tsai R-Y, Chen P-W, Kuo T-Y, Lin C-M, Wang D-M, Hsien T-Y, Hsieh H-J. Chitosan/pectin/gum Arabic polyelectrolyte complex: process-dependent appearance, microstructure analysis and its application. Carbohydr Polym 2014;101:752–9.

[141] Aguiar AE, Silva MO, Rodas ACD, Bertran CA. Mineralized layered films of xanthan and chitosan stabilized by polysaccharide interactions: a promising material for bone tissue repair. Carbohydr Polym 2019;207:480–91.

[142] Gun'ko VM, Savina IN, Mikhalovsky SV. Cryogels: morphological, structural and adsorption characterization. Adv Colloid Interface Sci 2013;187–188:1–46.

[143] Liu H, Nakagawa K, Chaudhary D, Asakuma Y, Tadé MO. Freeze-dried macroporous foam prepared from chitosan/xanthan gum/montmorillonite nanocomposites. Chem Eng Res Des 2011;89:2356–64.
[144] Dai M, Zheng X, Xu X, Kong XY, Li XY, Guo G, Luo F, Zhao X, QuanWei Y, Qian Z. Chitosan-alginate sponge: preparation and application in curcumin delivery for dermal wound healing in rat. J Biomed Biotechnol 2009;595126.

CHAPTER

9

Polysaccharide-based interpenetrating polymeric network systems in drug delivery

Sudipta Das[a], *Arnab Samanta*[a], *Md Saquib Hasnain*[b], *and Amit Kumar Nayak*[c]

[a]Department of Pharmaceutics, Netaji Subhas Chandra Bose Institute of Pharmacy, Nadia, West Bengal, India, [b]Department of Pharmacy, Palamau Institute of Pharmacy, Daltonganj, Jharkhand, India, [c]Department of Pharmaceutics, Seemanta Institute of Pharmaceutical Sciences, Jharpokharia, Mayurbhanj, Odisha, India

1 Introduction

Recently, numerous varieties of polymer-made drug releasing matrix-carrier systems have extensively been researched and developed by the pharmaceutical formulators and scientists for controlling drug releasing to treat/manage various diseases [1–6]. Over the year, the controlling of release rate of small molecular weight drug candidates from the biopolymer-based drug carriers has still treated as a great interest to the pharmaceutical formulators and scientists [6–9]. In particular, the drugs embedded within the carrier matrices exhibit a quicker rate of drug releasing by means of the diffusion process through the matrix pores [10]. For the drug candidates having shorter half-lives (biological), the faster drug releasing rate cannot achieve the prolonged actions of drugs. Therefore, the drug candidates of low molecular weight and higher aqueous solubility necessitate the extensive attention to reduce the frequency dosing of the dosage and also the dose associated side effects via controlling the rate of drug releasing from dosage forms [11]. Such a challenge related to the drug releasing can be solved by employing a suitable biopolymer-based drug delivery carrier matrix system [6,11]. The biopolymeric matrices in

Tailor-Made Polysaccharides in Drug Delivery
https://doi.org/10.1016/B978-0-12-821286-8.00015-X

forms of gels, hydrogels, beads, microparticles, films, pellets, and so on have been commonly researched for controlling drug releases of numerous low molecular drugs [12–27]. A range of synthetic, semisynthetic, and natural-originated biopolymers have been explored and widely utilized in the formulation of these biopolymeric matrix-carrier systems used for controlling the drug releasing [28–33].

As because of the fact that the naturally occurring biopolymers are inexpensive, nontoxic, and biodegradable, these are always being favored in the formula of biopolymeric-based dosage systems over the synthetic polymers [34–42]. In addition, the versatility of chemically structural features facilitates the chemical functionalization of various naturally occurring polymer-candidates to modify functional characters [43,44]. In recent years, the usage of polysaccharides as naturally occurring polymeric-based excipient materials for various pharmaceutical dosage forms has been increased [26,27,41,42]. Polysaccharides are mainly made of many monosaccharides, which are joined to each other via *O*-glycosidic linkages [39,41]. These also possess several numbers of reactive functional moieties varying in chemical compositions and with varied molecular weight-ranges. Though having several advantages, polysaccharides exert some potential limitations such as uncontrolled hydration, lower mechanical features, uncertain chemical stability, viscosity fall during storage, and so on [44,45]. These previously mentioned limitations of polysaccharides can be managed by employing physical blending of polysaccharides with second or multiple biomaterials like another polysaccharides [46–48], synthetic polymers [33,49], bioceramics [50], and so on, and by employing chemical modifications such as carboxymethylation [51,52], thiolation [53,54], esterification [55,56], crosslinking [57,58], graft copolymerization [44,59,60], polyelectrolyte complexation [45,61], interpenetrating polymeric networks (IPNs), semi-IPNs [22,62], and so on. In view of the fact that the homopolymers cannot only fulfill the potential requirement of functional characters as well as performances of native polysaccharides, the development of IPNs materializes as a functional and easiest approach for the improvement of the desirable functional characteristics of polysaccharides [62,63]. The current chapter presents an inclusive discussion on IPN/semi-*IPN*-based drug delivery carriers prepared using different polysaccharides, especially chitosan, pectin, alginate, locust bean gum, cashew gum, xanthan gum, gellan gum, carrageenan, and so on, and toward their utilization in drug delivery.

2 IPNs: Definition, properties, and classifications

In 1914, Jonas Aylsworth and Thomas Edison manufactured the first IPN when they mixed sulfur and natural rubber with crosslinked phenol-formaldehyde resin leading to a tougher quality material [64]. IPNs are formed when at least one polymer-network composed and/or crosslinked in the instantaneous occurrence of other polymer(s) [63,65]. The IUPAC definition of IPN is: "A polymer comprising two or more networks, which are at least partially interlaced on a molecular scale; but not covalently bonded to each other and cannot be separated unless chemical bonds are broken."

There are three key conditions for the development of IPN-structures by the uses of two constituent polymers. These are the following [22,65]:

(i) Component polymer candidates form a polymer network and/or crosslinked in the immediately presence of other polymer(s).
(ii) Component polymer candidates show comparable kinetic features.
(iii) Component polymer candidates are not phase separated, significantly.

The ideal properties of IPN structures are the following [22,63]:

(i) IPN structures present an outstanding accessibility made of two or more polymer candidates with diverse natured characteristics.
(ii) IPN-structures made of two or more polymer networks are slightly interlaced, molecularly. In addition, they cannot be separated without splitting of the chemical bondings.
(iii) The materials designed by using IPNs contribute to the characteristic properties of each network (present in IPN structure). In general, IPN-based materials are capable of meeting up diversified functional properties, and therefore, it is advantageous to synthesize IPN-based materials using two or more different polymers.
(iv) Characteristically, IPN structures are different from the polymer blending and copolymers (block or graft).
(v) Occasionally, IPN structures differ depending on number of crosslinking and types of crosslinks.
(vi) Usually, the ideal IPNs are capable of showing suppress creep and flow.
(vii) IPNs are able to swell in solvents, easily, without any kinds of rapid degradation or quick dissolution.

According to the chemical bonding in-between the constituent polymers, IPNs are usually classified as covalent and noncovalent IPNs [22,63]:

(a) Covalent IPNs: these IPNs are composed of two polymers and existed as covalently crosslinked to single polymer network.
(b) Noncovalent IPNs:
  (i) Noncovalent full-IPNs: These IPNs are composed of two polymers, where they are separately crosslinked devoid of any kinds of covalent interaction(s).

(ii) Noncovalent semi-IPNs: These IPNs are composed of two polymers, where one of these two polymers is crosslinked devoid of any covalent interaction(s).

According to the arrangement patterns of the constituent polymers, IPNs are usually categorized as sequential, novel, semi-, and simultaneous IPNs [22,63]:

(a) Sequential IPNs: The second polymer network is synthesized following the polymerization of network of first constituent polymer candidate.
(b) Novel IPNs: The networks of two or more constituent polymers are formed, which are at least interlocked molecularly, in part, but not joined covalently to each other and cannot be separated from each other unless the splitting of chemical bondings.
(c) Semi-IPNs: Only one polymer is crosslinked, while the second constituent polymer or other polymer(s) is/are present linearly (i.e., not crosslinked).
(d) Simultaneously IPNs: These are synthesized by means of a process wherein polymers are simultaneously polymerized.

Various kinds of IPNs are schematically presented in Fig. 1 [66].

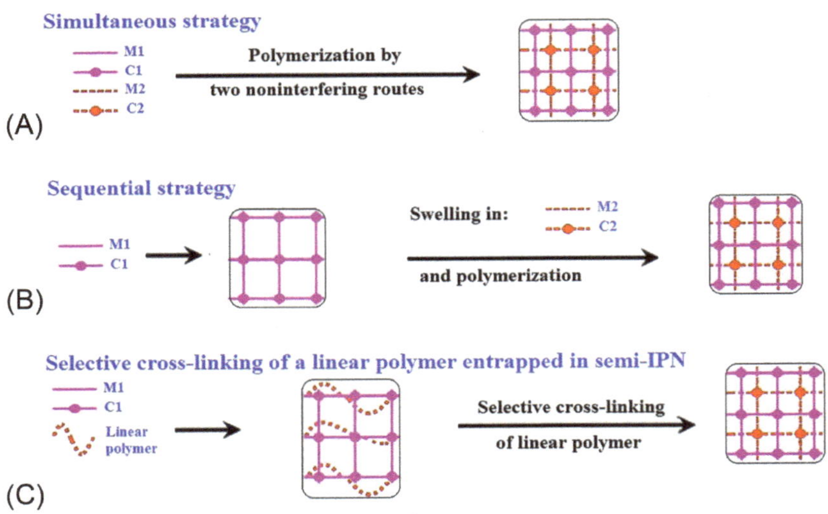

FIG. 1 Schematic representations of different IPN formations: (A) simultaneous strategy, (B) sequential strategy, and (C) selective cross-linking of a linear polymer entrapped in semi-IPN. *Adapted from Dragan ES. Design and applications of interpenetrating polymer network hydrogels. A review. Chem Eng J 2014;243: 572–590, Copyright@ 2014, with permission from Elsevier B.V.*

3 Chitosan-based IPN systems in drug delivery

Chitosan is a cationic marine polysaccharide [67]. Chitosan molecules are composed of β-(1 → 4)-2-amino-2-deoxy D-glucopyranose and β-(1 → 4)-2-acetamido-2-deoxy-D-glucopyranose units [68]. The wide acceptance of chitosan in pharmaceuticals and agriculture is owing to its excellent physicochemical as well as biological characteristics like gel forming ability, acid resistant capability, biodegradability, biocompatibility, and antibacterial activity [31,63]. The functional groups present in the chitosan molecules (hydroxyl groups and amino groups) are usually chemically modified in the formulations of sustained drug releasing matrix-based carrier systems [63,69–72]. During the past few decades, chitosan has found wide biomedical uses like food technology, drug delivery, tissue regeneration, bioprinting, bioimaging, and so on [39,67,71–76].

In a research, novel chitosan-tamarind polysaccharide IPN microparticles for sustained aceclofenac releasing were synthesized and evaluated [76]. The sizing of these microparticles were measured within the range of 490.55 ± 23.24 to 621.60 ± 53.57 μm, whereas the aceclofenac entrapment efficiency was measured within the range of $85.84 \pm 1.75\%$ to $91.97 \pm 1.30\%$. The obtained scanning electron microscopy (SEM) images designated the formation of almost spherical-shaped microparticles (Fig. 2). The exterior surface analysis of the microparticles was found as rough-natured surface and wrinkles. The results of in vitro aceclofenac releasing from the synthesized microparticles exhibited sustained releasing of loaded aceclofenac

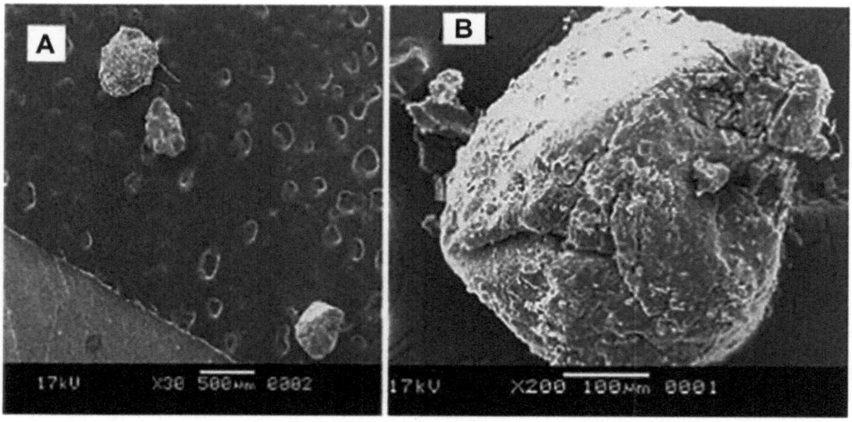

FIG. 2 SEM images of chitosan-tamarind polysaccharide IPN-based microparticles of aceclofenac at 30× (A) and 200× (B) magnifications. *Adapted from Jana S, Saha A, Nayak AK, Sen KK, Basu SK. Aceclofenac-loaded chitosan-tamarind seed polysaccharide interpenetrating polymeric network microparticles. Colloids Surf B: Biointerfaces 2013;105:303–309, Copyright@ 2013, with permission from Elsevier B.V.*

over 8h (Fig. 3). The antiinflammatory (in vivo) activities of those prepared IPN-based microparticles were tested by the carrageenan-induced rat paw edema model, which illustrated a sustained antiinflammatory action, in vivo. In another communication, the same research group further compressed these chitosan-tamarind polysaccharide IPN microparticles to prepare aceclofenac releasing matrix-based tablets, which also exhibited the sustained releasing of loaded aceclofenac over 8h [77].

Rokhade et al. (2009) developed chitosan-hydroxypropyl cellulose semi-IPNs hydrogel-based microparticles of chlorothiazide [78]. These chlorothiazide-loaded semi-IPNs hydrogel-based microparticles were prepared using glutaraldehyde-induced crosslinked emulsification technique. The microparticle-size ranged within 199–359 μm (estimated by using laser light scattering). The drug release (in vitro) pattern was studied using 0.1N hydrochloric acid as medium up to 12h. From the results of different formulations, it was observed that the release rate was varied. It was also found to be dependent upon the amount of hydroxypropyl cellulose, amount of glutaraldehyde, and the extent of chlorothiazide loading within these microparticles. The drug releasing data also indicated that the chlorothiazide releasing from the semi-IPNs hydrogel-based microparticles followed the non-Fickian mechanism. Angadi et al. (2010) prepared and evaluated isoniazid-loaded hydroxyethyl cellulose-chitosan IPN hydrogel microspheres by the glutaraldehyde-induced emulsion crosslink method [79]. The isoniazid encapsulation efficiency was reported to be 50%–66%. SEM images revealed spherically shaped microspheres with smooth surface morphological characteristics. The drug

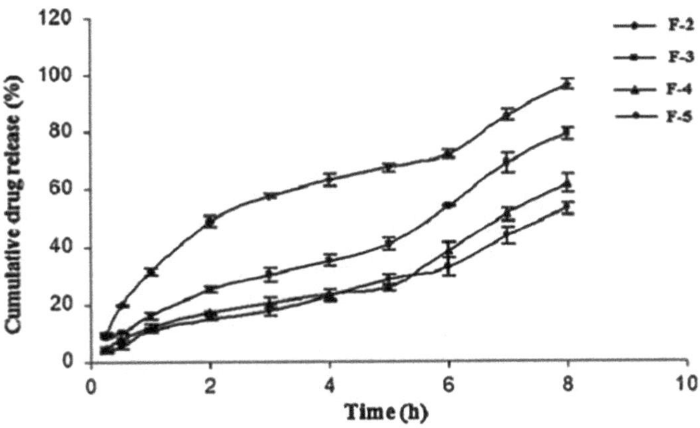

FIG. 3 In vitro aceclofenac release from various chitosan-tamarind polysaccharide IPN-based microparticles of aceclofenac. *Adapted from Jana S, Saha A, Nayak AK, Sen KK, Basu SK. Aceclofenac-loaded chitosan-tamarind seed polysaccharide interpenetrating polymeric network microparticles. Colloids Surf B: Biointerfaces 2013; 105: 303–309, Copyright@ 2013, with permission from Elsevier B.V.*

release (in vitro) results exhibited a sustained isoniazid release profile over a longer time. The maximum release pattern was shown to be 75% over 16h. The drug release (in vitro) indicated the non-Fickian mechanism. The isoniazid release (in vitro) patterns of hydroxyethyl cellulose-chitosan IPN hydrogel microspheres containing isoniazid were found to be influenced by the loading of isoniazid within these microspheres, compositions of microspheres, and crosslinking extents by glutaraldehyde (as covalent crosslinker).

Cefadroxil-loaded IPN-based microgels were developed using chitosan, acrylamide-grafted-poly(vinyl alcohol), and hydrolyzed acrylamide-grafted-poly(vinyl alcohol) [80]. In this research, glutaraldehyde was used as crosslinker (covalent type) to formulate these cefadroxil-loaded pH-sensitive IPN-based microgels. The cefadroxil encapsulation efficiency of IPN-based microgels was increased with increasing of cefadroxil loading from 25% to 100% for all the microgel formulations. The sizing of these cefadroxil-loaded IPN-based microgels size ranged from 42 to 182 μm. The morphology of formulated cefadroxil-loaded pH-sensitive IPN microgels was observed by SEM analysis. The SEM photography of the microgels indicated their spherical shape and smooth surface. These cefadroxil-loaded IPN-based microgels extended the cefadroxil releasing rates more than 10h, which was more promising for controlled release formulations. The media used for dissolution studies were both acidic and basic medium.

In another work, temperature-sensitive IPN-systems made of chitosan (two different grades) and poly(*N*-isopropylacrylamide) were synthesized [81]. The quantity of chitosan used in the temperature-sensitive IPN system after complete washing was found as proportional to the concentration of crosslinker (here glutaraldehyde, which was employed in the post crosslinking). The temperature-enhancement phase transitions of this chitosan-based IPN system were found to be controlled by the changes in the swelling degrees of matrices as well as various thermodynamic factors. In addition, the chitosan-based IPN system exhibited a sustained diclofenac releasing pattern for over 8h in sodium chloride (0.9%) solutions or phosphate buffer (pH 8). IPNs made of lower chitosan post crosslinking degree demonstrated elevated temperature-sensitive diclofenac releasing patterns. It was also noticed that poly(*N*-isopropylacrylamide) played a very important role in this chitosan-poly(*N*-isopropylacrylamide) IPN system. Agnihotri and Aminabhavi (2006) developed semi-IPN-based chitosan-poly(ethylene oxide-*graft*-acrylamide) microparticles, where glutaraldehyde was used as a crosslinker [82]. Poly(ethylene oxide) was grafted copolymerized with acrylamide, and the grafted material was used in this study to prepare microparticles. These prepared semi-IPN based chitosan-poly(ethylene oxide-*graft*-acrylamide) microparticles were loaded with capecitabine (an anticancer drug). The prepared microparticles were found within the mean particle size-range of 82–168 μm. SEM analysis suggested that the capecitabine-loaded semi-IPN hydrogel-based chitosan-poly(ethylene oxide-*graft*-acrylamide) microparticles were spherically shaped. The capecitabine encapsulation efficiencies of these semi-IPN microparticles were ranged in-between 79%–87%. In vitro capecitabine releases from semi-IPN hydrogel-based microparticles were performed in acidic milieu the preliminary 2h, followed by alkaline milieu until completion of dissolution study. The releasing (in vitro) of capecitabine from these semi-IPN chitosan-based microparticles of capecitabine was found to be sustained over 10h. In a work, semi-IPN based microspheres made of chitosan and acrylamide-*graft*-hydroxyethylcellulose were developed via the emulsion crosslinking procedure, where glutaraldehyde was employed as a crosslinker [83]. These semi-IPN microspheres were loaded with diclofenac sodium. Average particle sizing and drug encapsulation efficiency of diclofenac sodium-loaded semi-IPN microspheres were found within the range of 188–310 μm and up to 83%, respectively. The drug releasing (in vitro) from these semi-IPN-based microspheres of diclofenac sodium was studied in acidic milieu for the preliminary 2h and, after that, alkaline milieu for remaining 10h. The drug-releasing rate was found initially faster, but it gradually became slower and sustained up to about 12h (approximately) of drug releasing.

4 Alginate-based IPN systems in drug delivery

Alginate is a marine algal polysaccharide [84,85]. Alginate molecules are composed of 1-4-linked β-D-mannuronic acid (M) and α-L-guluronic acid (G), which are arranged in a blockwise trend as homopolymer blocks (M-M and G-G) or alternating polymeric blocks of M and G with varied M/G ratios [19,84]. It is an aqueous soluble, gel-forming, and anionic natured biopolysaccharide. It is biocompatible and biodegradable [86]. Being an anionic polysaccharide, sodium alginate produces hydrogels by the ionotropic crosslinking gelation by a number of di-/trivalent cations (e.g., Ba^{2+}, Zn^{2+}, Ca^{2+}, Al^{3+}, Fe^{3+}, etc.) [87]. For the formation of gelled alginate matrices, the previously mentioned cations are located within the electronegative natured cavities of alginate molecules like eggs arranged within the "egg-box" on account of the intermolecular interaction by ionotropic crosslinking [87,88]. Since long, these ionotropically gelled alginate hydrogels are being investigated by the different researchers for the encapsulation/loading of different kinds of drugs, proteins, and other bioactive agents [87–89]. Due to this ionotropically gelation ability, alginate has extensively been employed as one of the useful biopolymer to prepare IPNs in combination(s) with other natural originated or synthetic polymer(s) [86,90–95].

In a study, alginate-tamarind polysaccharide IPN-based microbeads were formulated via dual crosslinking (ionotropically crosslinking and covalent crosslinking) gelation method [90]. In this work, diltiazem HCl-Indion 254® resin complex was synthesized and loaded within these *IPN*-based polymeric microbeads. The drug entrapments in the IPN microbeads prepared by the dual crosslinking gelation method were observed lesser in comparison with those of the IPN-based microbeads prepared by the ionotropically cross-linking gelation method. The particle sizing range for these IPN-based microbeads was measured as 986–1257 mm. The drug release (in vitro) from alginate-tamarind polysaccharide IPN-based microbeads encapsulated with diltiazem HCl (pure and uncomplexed) indicated a slower and sustained trend of diltiazem releasing up to 4 h. The IPN-based microbeads encapsulated with diltiazem-Indion 254® resin-complex exhibited diltiazem releasing up to a release period of 9 h. Pharmacokinetic evaluation (in vivo) of IPN-based microbeads loaded with diltiazem-Indion 254® resin complex was performed in the Wister rats, which indicated a comparatively augmented AUC after administration of these IPN-based microbeads loaded with diltiazem-Indion 254® resin complex. This has been noticed as improved bioavailability of diltiazem from these IPN microbead systems in comparison with that of diltiazem HCl (pure and uncomplexed). In another research, sterculia gum-alginate IPN-based microparticles of repaglinide were synthesized via ionotropically cross-linking gelation and the emulsion crosslinking method [91]. To prepare these IPN-based microparticles loaded with repaglinide, aqueous solutions of $AlCl_3$, $CaCl_2$, and $BaCl_2$ were exploited as ionotropic crosslinking agents. The repaglinide encapsulation efficiency of sterculia gum-alginate IPN-based microparticles was calculated within the range, 81.10%–91.70%. Al^{3+} ion-induced IPN-based microparticles exhibited highest repaglinide encapsulation in comparison to that of others (Ba^{2+} and Ca^{2+} ions). The average sizes of prepared microparticles of repaglinide were ranged, 49.75–61.52 μm. The release pattern of repaglinide exhibited sustained pattern of delivery over 24 h, in vitro. The optimized repaglinide-loaded microparticles showed very good antidiabetic activity against streptozotocin-induced diabetic rats, in vivo. From the in vivo results, it was clear that the fall of blood glucose level controlled over a prolonged period with repaglinide-loaded microparticles in comparison with that of pristine repaglinide within a period of 3 h.

Das et al. (2014) formulated isoxsuprine HCl-loaded carboxymethylated cashew gum-alginate IPN-based microbeads for prolonged sustained drug release, where these IPN-based microbeads were produced via ionotropically crosslinking gelation using zinc sulfate as a ionotropic crosslinking agent [92]. The efficiency of drug encapsulation and mean sizing of these IPN-based microbeads ranged within $35.24 \pm 1.18\%$ to $79.92 \pm 2.51\%$ and 603.33 ± 22.28 to 836.67 ± 32.19 μm, respectively. The optimized formulation of alginate-based IPN-based microbeads exhibited 79.92±2.51% efficiency of drug encapsulation with 58.67±2.26% drug release over 7h. The releasing of drug from IPN microbeads was tested in phosphate buffer of pH 6.8 and analyzed, which displayed a prolonged pattern of loaded drug over 7h (Fig. 4). The morphology of formulated optimized formulation of isoxsuprine HCl-loaded alginate-based IPN microbeads was observed by using SEM analysis, and the obtained SEM images revealed spherically shaped particles with no sign of agglomeration (Fig. 5). The surface analysis of these IPN microbeads, on the observation of SEM images, was found as rough surfaces with some wrinkles, cracks. and drug crystals.

Boppana et al. (2015) developed ketoprofen-loaded pH-sensitive IPN microbeads for the sustained drug release prepared employing polyacrylamide-*grafted*-gum ghatti with sodium alginate as excipient polymers [93]. By using microwave irradiation with ceric ammonium nitrate, the grafted-gum ghatti was chemically synthesized and the synthesized polymeric material was made pH-sensitive. Then, it was used for the preparation of ketoprofen-loaded IPN microbeads. These ketoprofen-loaded alginate-based IPN microbeads were prepared via a dual (ionotropic and covalent) crosslinking gelation procedure using calcium ions (ionotropic crosslinking agent) along with glutaraldehyde (covalent crosslinking agent). Ketoprofen-loaded pH-sensitive IPN-based microbeads were

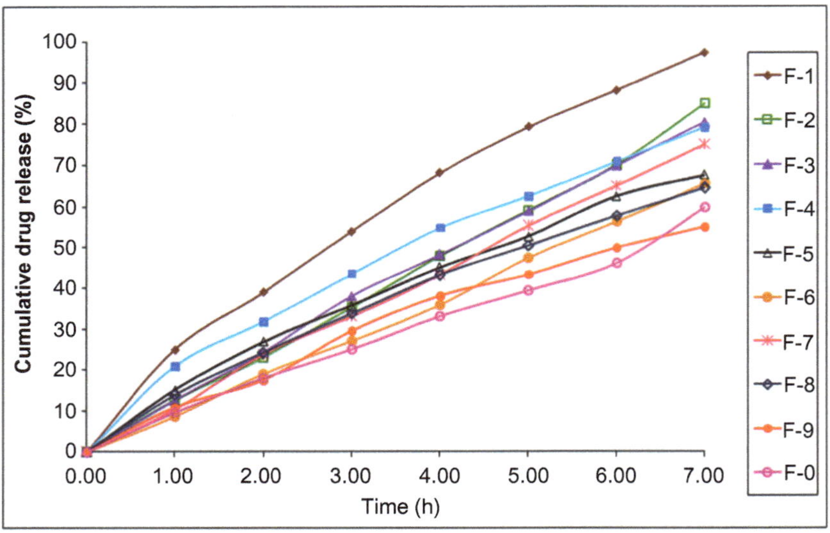

FIG. 4 In vitro drug release from various isoxsuprine HCl-loaded carboxymethylated cashew gum-alginate IPN microbeads. *Adapted from Das B, Dutta S, Nayak AK, Nanda U. Zinc alginate-carboxymethyl cashew gum microbeads for prolonged drug release: development and optimization. Int J Biol Macromol 2014; 70: 505–515, Copyright@ 2014, with permission from Elsevier B.V.*

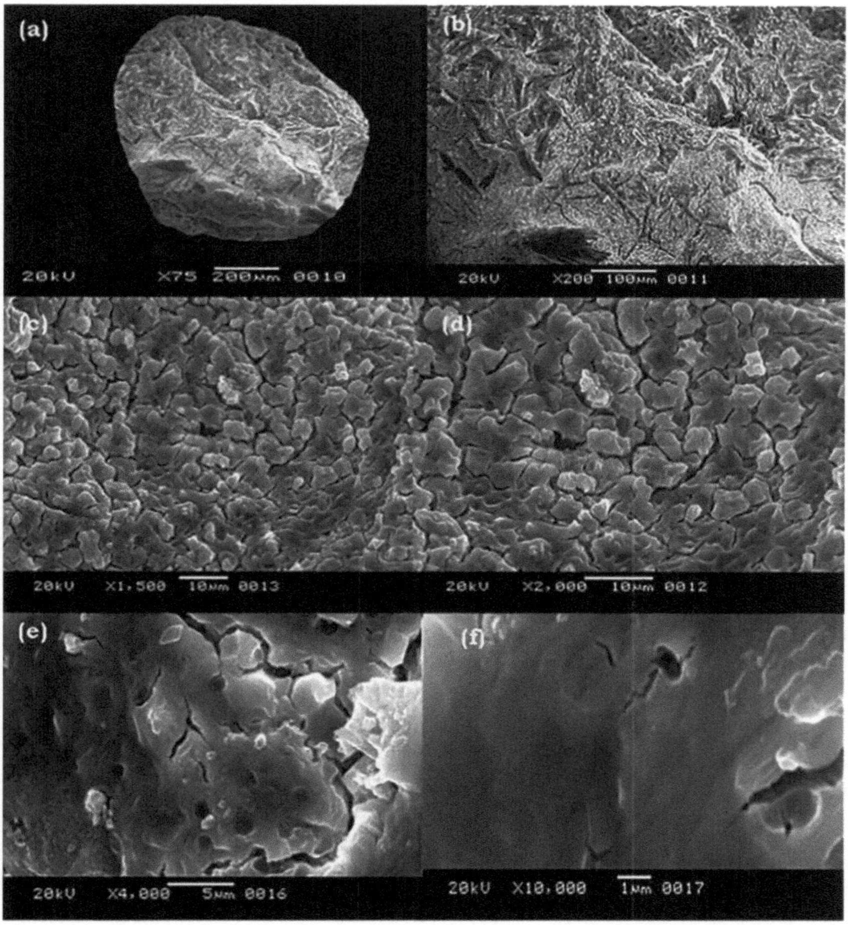

FIG. 5 SEM images of the surface of optimized isoxsuprine HCl-loaded carboxymethylated cashew gum-alginate IPN microbeads at different magnifications (75×, 200×, 1500×, 2000×, 4000×, and 10,000×). *Adapted from Das B, Dutta S, Nayak AK, Nanda U. Zinc alginate-carboxymethyl cashew gum microbeads for prolonged drug release: development and optimization. Int J Biol Macromol 2014; 70: 505–515, Copyright@ 2014, with permission from Elsevier B.V.*

spherical observed by using SEM analysis. The ionotropically cross-linked ketoprofen-loaded IPN microbeads were found with denser and rough morphological features, while dual crosslinked (ionotropic and covalent) IPN-based microbeads were found with relatively smoother morphological features. These ketoprofen-loaded alginate-based IPN-based microbeads demonstrated a prolonged and sustained profile of loaded drug releasing over 12h. The pharmacokinetic (in vivo) study results demonstrated the attainment of comparatively augmented elimination half-life ($t_{1/2}$) within

4.40h for alginate-based IPN microbeads loaded with ketoprofen in comparison to that of pristine ketoprofen (4.20h). The elevated AUC by the administration of ketoprofen-loaded alginate-based IPN microbeads in comparison to that of ketoprofen (pristine) was measured, indicating the better bioavailability of ketoprofen. In addition, the pharmacokinetic results noticeably indicated that these IPN-based microbeads were capable of producing slower elimination of ketoprofen, in vivo. The ketoprofen-loaded pH-sensitive IPN microbeads exhibited a significant antiinflammatory activity (in vivo), when tested with the carrageenan-induced rat paw edema model in the Wister rats. From the in vivo pharmacokinetics and stomach histopathological analyses, it has been seen that ketoprofen-loaded pH-sensitive IPN-based microbeads demonstrated a decreased ulceration and hemorrhage with mucosal erosion due to the slower releasing of drug by IPN-based microbeads in stomach.

In another research, zidovudine-loaded IPN-based microbeads were synthesized using sodium alginate and chemically functionalized (grafted) guar gum [94]. The chemical modification of guar gum was done by means of the grafting copolymerization reaction with *N*-vinyl caprolactam. The *graft*-modified material was then mixed with another polymer-sodium alginate to synthesize IPN-based microbeads by means of the emulsion crosslinking gelation procedure. In the preparation of microbeads, glutaraldehyde was applied as a crosslinker (covalent type). Maximum zidovudine encapsulation efficiency of IPN-based microbeads was measured 68%, where the microbead size was measured $100 \pm 10\,\mu m$. SEM analysis of these IPN hydrogel microbeads suggested semispherical-shaped microparticles with rough surfaces in nature, where a few porous morphological structures were visible. The drug release (in vitro) results revealed a modest variability in overall zidovudine releasing percentage in both pHs (acidic and alkaline). The maximum percentage of zidovudine release from these IPN-based microbeads was measured 96% up to 34h and followed the diffusion controlled non-Fickian mechanism.

Kulkarni et al. (2001) prepared two kinds of cefadroxil-loaded alginate-based IPN beads for the sustained pattern of drug release [86]. Spherically shaped cefadroxil-loaded alginate-based IPN beads were synthesized by utilizing sodium alginate with gelatin and egg albumin. The encapsulation efficiency of cefadroxil was measured as 88%. The cefadroxil releasing (in vitro) study presented a sustained trending of cefadroxil releasing over 400min by cefadroxil-loaded egg albumin-alginate IPN-based beads. In addition, cefadroxil releasing (in vitro) from gelatin-alginate IPN-based beads was experienced more slowly as compared to that of egg albumin-alginate IPN-based beads. Reddy et al. (2008) formulated 5-fluorouracil-loaded alginate/*N*-isopropyl acrylamide semi-IPN-based microspheres via the w/o emulsification technique [95]. The sizing of 5-fluorouracil-loaded semi-IPN microspheres were estimated using laser light diffraction. From the results, it was noticed that as the extent of crosslinking was augmented, the volume mean diameter of semi-IPN-based microspheres was decreased. The 5-fluorouracil releasing (in vitro) results presented a controlled pattern of 5-fluorouracil releasing over 12h.

5 Pectin-based IPN systems in drug delivery

Pectin is an aqueous soluble plant-derived polysaccharide [7]. It is commercially available as low-cost polymeric material, which is being extracted/produced from apple pomaces, citrous peels, beet roots, and so on [96]. The pectin molecules consist of linearly attached (1-4)-linked α-D-galacturonic acid residues interrupted via rhamno-galacturonic acid residue and α-L-rhamnopyranose by α-1-2 linkage [97]. The galacturonic acid residues present in pectin molecules are esterified, partially. Industrially used pectins are classified on the basis of the degree of methylation: (i) high methoxyl pectin (over 50%) and (ii) low methoxyl pectin (between 5% and 50%) [97,98]. In the majority cases, low methoxyl pectin usually experience the ionotropically crosslinking gelation by different divalent metal cations, and these ionotropically crosslinked pectinate-based systems have extensively been researched as biopolymer-made sustained drug release matrix materials [98]. The ionotropically crosslinking gelation of carboxyl groups occurred in low methoxyl pectin molecules by cations like Ca^{2+}, Zn^{2+}, and so on is reported to be related to the "egg-box" model structure. This type of ionotropically crosslinking gelation of low methoxyl pectin differs slightly from the "egg-box" modeling elucidated for ionotropically crosslinking gelation process of sodium alginate [7]. A number of ionotropically crosslinked pectinate-based hydrogels as drug releasing carrier systems have already been researched by the researchers [7,97,98]. Even, pectin has been investigated as a natural polymer type excipient in the formulation of sustained drug releasing IPNs in combination(s) with other naturally originated or synthetic polymeric candidates [99,100].

In a research, trivalent aluminum ion and glutaraldehyde crosslinked pectin-sodium carboxymethyl xanthan gum IPN-based hydrogel beads were prepared for sustained releasing of diltiazem HCl [99]. The morphological features of formulated IPN-based beads were observed by the SEM study, which suggested that these beads were more or less spherically shaped and did not have any rough-natured surface. The diltiazem entrapment efficiency of IPN hydrogel beads was reduced with increment of $AlCl_3$ (concentration). The pectin-sodium carboxymethyl xanthan gum IPN beads were found less swelled and less percentage of loaded diltiazem releasing in the stomach pH (1.2). In addition, the prolonged releasing of loaded diltiazem in the intestinal pH (6.8) was found dependent on the exposure time of crosslinkers used in preparation, polymer concentrations, strength, and drug contents. Bera et al. (2015) formulated dual crosslinked pectinate-sterculia gum IPN-based gastroretentive beads encapsulated with ziprasidone HCl [100]. These IPN-based gastroretentive beads were prepared via the simultaneous ionotropically crosslinking and covalent cross-linking gelation processes. The electrostatic interactions as well as hydrogen bonding among the chains of both the biopolysaccharides might have formed the IPN-based gel matrix. In addition, an IPN-based gel was led by the configuration of acetal linkage by chemical interaction in-between hydroxyl groups of both biopolysaccharides (pectin and sterculia gum) and aldehyde group present in glutaraldehyde molecules. The efficiency of drug encapsulations and average diameters of IPN-based beads were measured 87.98 ± 1.15% and 2.17 ± 0.13 mm, respectively. The morphology of formulated optimized IPN-based beads was observed using SEM analysis, and the obtained SEM images indicated that almost spherically shaped beads were synthesized in this research. In addition, characteristic cracks as well as wrinkles on the bead surface was noticed (resembling to the orange-peel like look) in the obtained SEM images (Fig. 6A and B). The optimized formulation of IPN-based beads of ziprasidone HCl displayed in vitro buoyancy of 63% at 8 h (low lag time) and in vitro sustained pattern of drug releasing in the simulated gastric fluid over duration of 8 h. In maximum cases, the drug release followed Higuchi kinetics and the anomalous transport mechanism. In ex vivo mucoadhesivity study using the goat stomach mucosal membrane, these IPN beads adhered to the mucosal membrane over a prolonged period (8 h), suggesting good ex vivo mucoadhesivity potential.

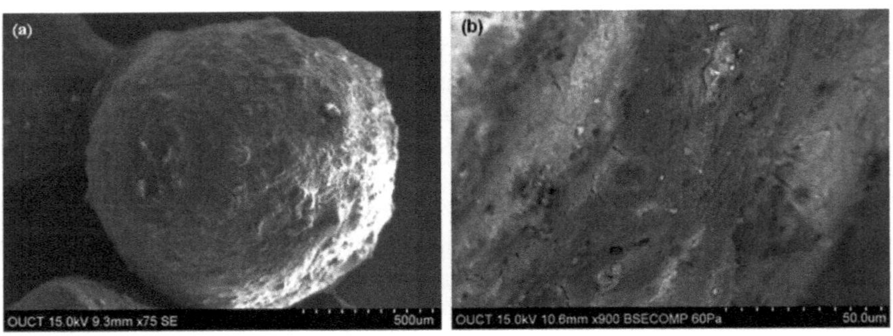

FIG. 6 SEM images of pectinate-sterculia gum IPN mucoadhesive-floating gastroretentive beads of ziprasidone HCl showing rough surface with less zoom (75×) (A) and presence of pores and channels with high zoom (900×) (B). *From Bera H, Boddupalli S, Nayak AK. Mucoadhesive-floating zinc-pectinate-sterculia gum interpenetrating polymer network beads encapsulating ziprasidone HCl. Carbohydr Polym 2015; 131: 108–118, Copyright@ 2015, with permission from Elsevier Ltd.*

6 Gellan gum-based IPN systems in drug delivery

Gellan gum is water soluble linear, exopolysaccharide possessing negatively charge, which is produced via the microbial fermentation technique using *Pseudomonas elodea* [9,101]. It is a tetrasaccharide molecule, which contains glucose, rhamnose, and glucuronic acid (2:1:1) and arranged as repeating units [13]. It is able to produce gels and the gelation of gellan gum can be explained by the occurrence of double-helical structured junctional zones, and subsequently, aggregations of double-helical segments to form a 3-D structural networking by means of complexation due to the ionotropically crosslinking by di- and/or trivalent cations and the formation of hydrogen bondings with the water molecules [29,35].

In a research, gellan gum-egg albumin IPN-based microcapsules were formulated, wherein diltiazem-resin complex was encapsulated [102]. Using ionotropically crosslinking gelation (by $CaCl_2$) and covalent crosslinking gelation (by glutaraldehyde), these IPN-based microcapsules containing diltiazem-resin complex were produced. SEM analysis suggested that the prepared microcapsules were of spherically shaped. The diltiazem-resin complex clearly extended the diltiazem releasing only within 3h. In contrast, encapsulation of the diltiazem-resin complex within these gellan gum-egg albumin IPN-based microcapsules furtherly sustained the diltiazem releasing. The dual crosslinking of IPN-based microcapsules containing a diltiazem-resin complex extended the diltiazem releasing up to 15h in comparison with that of the ionotropically crosslinked IPN microcapsules, which was found to control the diltiazem releasing up to 9h in in vitro study. In a research, carvedilol (a beta blocker) was encapsulated within gellan gum-poly(vinylalcohol) IPN-based microspheres via the emulsion crosslinking process [103]. The particle size was measured, which ranged 230–346 μm. The encapsulation efficiency of carvedilol was found up to 87%. The release (in vitro) of carvedilol in simulated gastrointestinal fluid was sustained up to 12h.

7 Locust bean gum-based IPN systems in drug delivery

Locust bean gum is produced from *Ceratonia siliqua* seeds [104]. Its molecular structure comprises of α-(1,4)-linked β-D-mannopyranose, which is connected to (1,6) α-D-galactose. Locust bean gum is a nonstarch biopolysaccharide of galactomannan type, where galactose as well as mannose is present as 1:4 [105]. It is biocompatible and biodegradable, which is being exploited as drug delivery excipient materials in different dosage forms [105,106].

In a research, capecitabine-encapsulated locust bean gum-alginate IPN-based microbeads were synthesized [107]. Using the ionotropically crosslinking gelation method, capecitabine-encapsulated IPN-based microbeads were prepared, where Ca^{2+} cation acted as ionotropically crosslinking ions. The capecitabine drug entrapment and particle sizing of the optimized formulation of IPN-based microbeads were 81.39±2.9% and 494.37±1.4 μm, respectively. In addition, the optimized formulation showed capecitabine releasing of 92% (in vitro) within 12 h, which followed anomalous mechanism for releasing of capecitabine. In addition, IPN microbeads also showed enhanced pharmacokinetics in comparison with capecitabine (pure). Dey et al. (2010) prepared glipizide-encapsulated carboxymethyl locust bean gum-alginate IPN-based beads using Al^{3+} ions induced ionotropically crosslinking gelation [108]. SEM analysis suggested spherical-shaped beads. These IPN-based beads swelled slowly in gastric pH than that of the observed in intestinal pH. Comparing the in vitro glipizide release pattern, it was revealed that these beads treated with 5% trivalent aluminum exhibited slow glipizide releasing up to 10 h in the alkaline medium.

In a study, chitosan-locust bean gum IPN nanocomposites loaded with aceclofenac were synthesized [109]. In these nanocomposite preparations, glutaraldehyde was applied as a crosslinker (covalent type). Enhanced amount of locust bean gum in these IPN-based nanocomposites reduced the aceclofenac entrapment from 72% to 40%. Even, this condition formed comparatively larger-size particles of nanocomposites. Locust bean gum to chitosan mass ratio of 1:5 in preparation of IPN-based nanocomposites containing aceclofenac provided maximum aceclofenac entrapment efficiency (78.92%), smallest size of nanocomposites (318 nm), and slowest aceclofenac release (8 h) in alkaline solution (pH 6.8). The formulated IPN-based nanocomposites of aceclofenac decreased the releasing of aceclofenac in medium of acidic pH (1.2), in vitro. In another research work, Kaity and Ghosh (2015) prepared buflomedil HCl-loaded locust bean gum-poly(vinylalcohol), carboxymethyl locust bean gum-poly(vinylalcohol), and polyacrylamide-*grafted*-locust bean gum-poly(vinylalcohol) IPN-based microspheres [110]. In this work, they evaluated the pharmacokinetic studies (in vivo). Among all these prepared microspheres, carboxymethyl locust bean gum-poly(vinylalcohol) IPN-based microspheres exhibited a comparable T_{max} with buflomedil HCl oral suspension in the rabbit model. On the other hand, buflomedil HCl-loaded IPN-based microspheres exhibited a controlled releasing pattern of buflomedil HCl (in vivo) than that of buflomedil HCl-loaded IPN-based microspheres.

8 Xanthan gum-based IPN systems in drug delivery

Xanthan gum is obtained from *Xanthomonas campestris* [111]. It is reported as water soluble, hydrophilic, biocompatible, and biodegradable. Xanthan gum also possesses gel-forming properties. Since long, it is being widely exploited in the pharmaceutical field [112–114].

In a research, theophylline-loaded sodium carboxymethyl xanthan gum-casein IPN-based beads as controlled release multiple-unit drug delivery system was formulated [115]. The IPN-based beads were found spherically shaped in appearance and within the size, 602.50 ± 2.42 to 1075.45 ± 6.54 μm. The IPN beads displayed a slower trend of drug releasing in acidic milieu, in vitro. In addition, a maximum theophylline releasing (approximately 20%) was measured within 2h. The increments of casein and glutaraldehyde concentrations used in IPN-based beads preparation influenced the drug loading. Even, the drug loading was found to be suppressed the theophylline releasing from the IPN-based beads in release medium of pH 6.8. In another work, diclofenac sodium-loaded IPN beads of sodium carboxymethyl xanthan gum and sodium carboxymethyl cellulose were synthesized via emulsion ionotropically crosslinking gelation using $AlCl_3$ [116]. The drug (diclofenac sodium) encapsulation efficiencies of IPN-based beads were found rational with intestinal releasing of diclofenac in sustained manner.

Kulkarni and Sa (2008) formulated ketoprofen-loaded pH-responsive IPN-based beads of sodium carboxymethyl cellulose and polyacrylamide-*grafted*-xanthan gum [117]. The SEM study suggested that the IPN-based hydrogel beads of ketoprofen possessed the porous natured matrix in the intestinal pH, while the nonporous natured matrix was noticed in the stomach pH. The in vitro swelling as well as drug releasing performance of xanthan gum-based IPN beads was found as a function of medium pH. As the pHs of swelling medium was changed to the intestinal pH, a substantial increment of the in vitro swelling behavior of IPN beads was noticed. In another research, pH-responsive xanthan gum-poly(vinylalcohol) IPN-based microspheres of diclofenac sodium were formulated [118]. In this research, IPN microspheres were formulated via the emulsion crosslinking process. The loaded drug within the formulated microspheres was found stable and molecularly dispersed. The particle sizing was measured as 310–477 μm. The morphology of IPN-based microspheres was observed by using SEM, which indicated that these microspheres were of almost spherical shaped with smooth surfaces. Drug encapsulation within these IPN-based microspheres was found up to 82.94%. The drug release (in vitro) from IPN-based microspheres was found dependent on the degree of crosslinking as well as the polymer ratio used in the preparation of these IPN-based microspheres.

Bhattacharya et al. (2013) formulated ciprofloxacin HCl-loaded IPN-based microspheres using xanthan gum and poly(vinylalcohol) [119]. Despite the consequences of polymer ratios and crosslinking density, all the ciprofloxacin HCl-loaded xanthan gum-based IPN-based microspheres displayed satisfactory in vitro releasing of loaded ciprofloxacin HCl.

9 Carrageenan-based IPN systems in drug delivery

Carrageenan is a marine-derived anionic natured or no sulfated polysaccharide [120,121]. Carrageenan molecules contain alternating linear chains of α-1,3-D-galactose, and β-1,4 glycosidic linkages in 3,6-anhydro-galactose with ester sulfates (15%–40%) [120]. Based on the sources, solubility, and sulfate content, carrageenan is categorized as Kappa (κ)-, Iota (ι)-, Lambda (λ)-, Mu (μ)-, Nu (ν)-, and Theta (θ). Among these, Kappa-carrageenan (κ-carrageenan) is used as a carrier material in many dosage forms [121–124].

In a work, Swain and Bal (2018) reported the formulation of microwave made IPN-based of guar gum and carrageenan loaded with metronidazole [125]. The release of metronidazole (in vitro) from the optimized beads revealed metronidazole release of 72% within a period of 12 h. Kulkarni et al. (2009) formulated ketoprofen-loaded pH-responsive polyacrylamide-*grafted*-κ-carrageenan/sodium alginate IPN-based beads for intestinal drug delivery [126]. Polyacrylamide-*grafted*-κ-carrageenan was chemically synthesized via the free radical polymerization and, afterward, alkaline hydrolysis in the presence of nitrogen. The ketoprofen-loaded IPN-based beads were synthesized via ionotropic crosslinking and covalent crosslinking gelation. The ketoprofen release (in vitro) was found to be remarkably raised when the medium pH was altered from gastric (acidic) pH to intestine (alkaline) pH. The results of stomach histopathology analysis using albino rats indicated that the ketoprofen releasing from these carrageenan-based IPN beads did not present any indication of gastric mucosal erosion, sign for hemorrhage, and occurrence of ulcer. In another research, ibuprofen-loaded IPN-based beads made of κ-carrageenan-sodium carboxymethyl cellulose were developed [127]. They investigated the influence of polymers ratio, $AlCl_3$ (ionotropic crosslinker) concentration, and gelation period on the drug releasing (in vitro) from these IPN beads in various pHs. The results revealed that the ibuprofen-loaded IPN beads produced pH-sensitive and sustained drug releasing in an acidic pH and also controlled pattern of drug releasing in alkaline pH.

10 Conclusion

In the current chapter, the reports on the formulation and evaluation of different polysaccharide-based IPN-systems for sustained release of drugs were broadly and critically analyzed. The versatile properties of various polysaccharides, such as cost effectiveness, controlled sustained drug releasing pattern at the target sites, biocompatibility, biodegradability, and so on, are recognized as the key factors to develop polysaccharide-based IPN-based drug delivery carrier systems. The various studies suggested that almost all these IPN systems exhibited significant mechanical behavior. This attribute could monitor the swelling as well as drug releasing behavior in a pH-dependent mode, though in vivo performances and safety issues of polysaccharide-based IPN-based drug releasing systems need to be critically evaluated prior to their clinical uses.

References

[1] Shah SA, Sohail M, Khan S, Minhas MU, de Matas M, Sikstone V, Hussain Z, Abbasi M, Kousar M. Biopolymer-based biomaterials for accelerated diabetic wound healing: a critical review. Int J Biol Macromol 2019;139:975–93.

[2] Hasnain MS, Ahmed SA, Alkahtani S, Milivojevic M, Kandar CC, Dhara AK, Nayak AK. Biopolymers for drug delivery. In: Nayak AK, Hasnain MS, editors. Advanced biopolymeric systems for drug delivery. Switzerland: Springer; 2020. p. 1–29.

[3] Hajdu I, Bodnár M, Trencsényi G, Márián T, Vámosi G, Kollár J, Borbély J. Cancer cell targeting and imaging with biopolymer-based nanodevices. Int J Pharm 2013;441(1–2):234–41.

[4] Padhi S, Behera A, Hasnain MS, Nayak AK. Chitosan in colon-targeted drug delivery. In: Hasnain MS, Beg S, Nayak AK, editors. Chitosan in drug delivery. United States: Academic Press, Elsevier Inc.; 2022. p. 107–32.

[5] Kundu A, Padhi S, Behera A, Hasnain MS, Nayak AK. Tumor targeting strategies by chitosan-based nanocarriers. In: Hasnain MS, Beg S, Nayak AK, editors. Chitosan in biomedical application. United States: Academic Press, Elsevier Inc.; 2022. p. 163–88.

[6] Neffe AT, Wischke C, Racheva M, Lendlein A. Progress in biopolymer-based biomaterials and their application in controlled drug delivery. Expert Rev Med Devices 2013;10(6):813–33.

[7] Guru PR, Bera H, Das M, Hasnain MS, Nayak AK. Aceclofenac-loaded *Plantago ovata* F. husk mucilage-Zn^{+2}-pectinate controlled-release matrices. Starch-Starke 2018;70:1700136.

[8] Sinha P, Ubaidulla U, Nayak AK. Okra (*Hibiscus esculentus*) gum-alginate blend mucoadhesive beads for controlled glibenclamide release. Int J Biol Macromol 2015;72:1069–75.

[9] Nayak AK, Pal D. *Trigonella foenum-graecum* L. seed mucilage-gellan mucoadhesive beads for controlled release of metformin HCl. Carbohydr Polym 2014;107:31–40.

[10] Nayak AK, Ahmad SA, Beg S, Ara TJ, Hasnain MS. Drug delivery: present, past and future of medicine. In: Inamuddin, Asiri AM, Mohammad A, editors. Applications of nanocomposite materials in drug delivery. Woodhead publishing series in biomaterials. United States: Elsevier Inc.; 2018. p. 255–82.

[11] Wen H, Jung H, Li X. Drug delivery approaches in addressing clinical pharmacology-related issues: opportunities and challenges. AAPS J 2015;17(6):1327–40.

[12] Nayak AK, Hasnain MS, Pal K, Banerjee I, Pal D. Gum-based hydrogels in drug delivery. In: Pal K, Banerjee I, Sarkar P, Kim D, Deng W-P, Dubey NK, Majumder K, editors. Biopolymer-based formulations, biomedical and food applications. United States: Elsevier Inc.; 2020. p. 605–45.

[13] Nayak AK, Bera H, Hasnain MS, De A, Pal D, Samanta A. Gellan gum-based nanomaterials in drug delivery applications. In: Bera H, Hossain CM, Saha S, editors. Biopolymer-based nanomaterials in drug delivery and biomedical applications. United States: Academic Press, Elsevier Inc.; 2021. p. 313–31.

[14] Nayak AK, Hasnain MS. Plant polysaccharides in drug delivery applications. In: Nayak AK, Hasnain MS, editors. Plant polysaccharides-based multiple-unit systems for oral drug delivery. Singapore: Springer; 2019. p. 19–23.
[15] Nayak AK, Hasnain MS. Some other plant polysaccharide based multiple units for oral drug delivery. In: Nayak AK, Hasnain MS, editors. Plant polysaccharides-based multiple-unit systems for oral drug delivery. Singapore: Springer; 2019. p. 123–1128.
[16] Nayak AK, Das B. Introduction to polymeric gels. In: Pal K, Bannerjee I, editors. Polymeric gels, characterization, properties and biomedical applications. Woodhead publishing series in biomaterials. United States: Elsevier Ltd.; 2018. p. 3–27.
[17] Nayak AK, Hasnain MS, Pal D. Gelled microparticles/beads of sterculia gum and tamarind gum for sustained drug release. In: Thakur VK, Thakur MK, editors. Handbook of springer on polymeric gel. Singapore: Springer Nature; 2018. p. 361–414.
[18] Nayak AK, Pal D. Natural starches-blended ionotropically-gelled micrparticles/beads for sustained drug release. In: Thakur VK, Thakur MK, Kessler MR, editors. Handbook of composites from renewable materials, volume 8, nanocomposites: advanced applications. USA: Wiley-Scrivener; 2017. p. 527–60.
[19] Pal D, Nayak AK. Plant polysaccharides-blended ionotropically-gelled alginate multiple-unit systems for sustained drug release. In: Thakur VK, Thakur MK, Kessler MR, editors. Handbook of composites from renewable materials, volume 6, polymeric composites. USA: Wiley-Scrivener; 2017. p. 399–400.
[20] Nayak AK, Pal D. Sterculia gum-based hydrogels for drug delivery applications. In: Kalia S, editor. Polymeric hydrogels as smart biomaterials. Springer series on polymer and composite materials. Switzerland: Springer International Publishing; 2016. p. 105–51.
[21] Nayak AK. Tamarind seed polysaccharide-based multiple-unit systems for sustained drug release. In: Kalia S, Averous L, editors. Biodegradable and bio-based polymers: environmental and biomedical applications. USA: Wiley-Scrivener; 2016. p. 471–94.
[22] Nayak AK, Hasnain MS, Aminbhavi TM. Drug delivery using interpenetrating polymeric networks of natural polymers: a recent update. J Drug Deliv Sci Technol 2021;66, 102915.
[23] Mohapatra S, Bose S, Bindhani S, Kar RK, Pani NR, Nayak AK. Effect of hydrophilic polymer on solubility and taste masking of linezolid in multi-component cyclodextrin inclusion complex: physicochemical characterization and molecular docking. J Drug Deliv Sci Technol 2021;66, 102876.
[24] Hasnain MS, Guru PR, Rishishwar P, Ali S, Ansari MT, Nayak AK. Atenolol-releasing buccal patches made of *Dillenia indica* L. fruit gum: preparation and *ex vivo* evaluations. SN Appl Sci 2020;2:57.
[25] Hasnain MS, Rishishwar P, Rishishwar S, Ali S, Nayak AK. Isolation and characterization of *Linum usitatisimum* polysaccharide to prepare mucoadhesive beads of diclofenac sodium. Int J Biol Macromol 2018;116:162–72.
[26] Nayak AK, Hasnain MS, Dhara AK, Mandal SC. Herbal biopolysaccharides in drug delivery. In: Mandal SC, Nayak AK, Dhara AK, editors. Herbal biomolecules in healthcare applications. United States: Academic Press, Elsevier Inc.; 2022. p. 613–42.
[27] Kandar CC, Hasnain MS, Nayak AK. Natural polymers as useful pharmaceutical excipients. In: Nayak AK, Pal K, Banerjee I, Maji S, Nanda U, editors. Advances and challenges in pharmaceutical technology: materials, process development and drug delivery strategies. USA: Academic Press, Elsevier Inc.; 2021. p. 1–44.
[28] Ray P, Hasnain MS, Koley A, Nayak AK. Bone-implantable devices for drug delivery applications. In: Pal K, Kraatz H-H, Li C, Khasnobish A, Bag S, Banerjee I, Kuruganti U, editors. Bioelectronics and medical devices, from materials to devices—fabrication, applications and reliability. Woodhead publishing series in electronic and optical materials. United States: Elsevier Inc.; 2019. p. 333–92.

[29] Milivojevic M, Pajic-Lijakovic I, Bugarski B, Nayak AK, Hasnain MS. Gellan gum in drug delivery applications. In: Hasnain MS, Nayak AK, editors. Natural polysaccharides in drug delivery and biomedical applications. United States: Academic Press, Elsevier Inc.; 2019. p. 145–86.
[30] Hasnain MS, Nayak AK. Recent progress in responsive polymer-based drug delivery systems. In: Makhlouf ASH, Abu-Thabit NY, editors. Stimuli responsive polymeric nanocarriers for drug delivery applications: vol. 2: advanced nanocarriers for therapeutics, woodhead publishing series in biomaterials. United States: Elsevier Ltd.; 2019. p. 569–95.
[31] Hasnain MS, Nayak AK. Chitosan as responsive polymer for drug delivery applications. In: Makhlouf ASH, Abu-Thabit NY, editors. Stimuli responsive polymeric nanocarriers for drug delivery applications, volume 1, types and triggers, Woodhead publishing series in biomaterials. United States: Elsevier Ltd.; 2018. p. 581–605.
[32] Hasnain MS, Rishishwar P, Ali S, Alkahtani S, Tabish M, Milivojevic M, Ansari MT, Nayak AK. Formulation and *ex vivo* skin permeation of lidocaine HCl topical gels using dillenia (*Dillenia indica* L.) fruit gum. Rev Mex Ing Quim 2020;19:1465–76.
[33] Nayak AK, Kalia S, Hasnain MS. Optimization of aceclofenac-loaded pectinate-poly (vinyl pyrrolidone) beads by response surface methodology. Int J Biol Macromol 2013;62:194–202.
[34] Hasnain MS, Rishishwar P, Ali S, Nayak AK. Preparation and evaluation of aceclofenac dental pastes using dillenia fruit gum for periodontitis treatment. SN Appl Sci 2020;2(3):1–8.
[35] Ali SA, Nayak AK, Banerjee S, Sen KK, Prabhakar T. *In silico* molecular docking of vetiver oil and formulation of vetiver oil-encapsulated gellan gum-based microcapsules for antidepressant activity. Res J Pharm Technol 2020;13:3135–42.
[36] Ali SA, Nayak AK, Sen KK, Prabhakar T. Preparation and characterization of vetiver oil encapsulated polymeric microcapsules for sedative and hypnotic activity. Int J Res Pharm Sci 2019;10(4):3616–25.
[37] Nayak AK, Pal D. Ionotropically-gelled mucoadhesive beads for oral metformin HCl delivery: formulation, optimization and antidiabetic evaluation. J Sci Ind Res 2013;72:15–22.
[38] Nayak AK, Pal D, Santra K. Swelling and drug release behavior of metformin HCl-loaded tamarind seed polysaccharide-alginate beads. Int J Biol Macromol 2016;82:1023–7.
[39] Maity M, Hasnain MS, Nayak AK, Aminabavi TM. Biomedical applications of polysaccharides. In: Nayak AK, Hasnain MS, Aminabhavi TM, editors. Tailor-made polysaccharides in biomedical applications. USA: Academic Press, Elsevier Inc.; 2021. p. 1–34.
[40] Hasnain MS, Rishishwar P, Rishishwar S, Ali S, Nayak AK. Extraction and characterization of cashew tree (*Anacardium occidentale*) gum; use in aceclofenac dental pastes. Int J Biol Macromol 2018;116:1074–81.
[41] Nayak AK, Hasnain MS, Dhara AK, Pal D. Plant polysaccharides in pharmaceutical applications. In: Pal D, Nayak AK, editors. Bioactive natural products for pharmaceutical applications, advanced structured materials, vol. 140. Cham: Springer; 2021. p. 93–125.
[42] Nayak AK, Ara TJ, Hasnain MS, Hoda N. Okra gum-alginate composites for controlled releasing drug delivery. In: Inamuddin, Asiri AM, Mohammad A, editors. Applications of nanocomposite materials in drug delivery. Woodhead publishing series in biomaterials. United States: Elsevier Inc.; 2018. p. 761–85.
[43] Nayak AK, Pal D. Functionalization of tamarind gum for drug delivery. In: Thakur VK, Thakur MK, editors. Functional biopolymers. Cham: Springer; 2018. p. 35–56.
[44] Nayak AK, Bera H, Hasnain MS, Pal D. Synthesis and characterization of graft-copolymers of plant polysaccharides. In: Thakur VK, editor. Biopolymer grafting, synthesis and properties. Netherlands: Elsevier Inc.; 2018. p. 1–62.

[45] Alkahtani S, Hasnain MS, Nayak AK, Aminabhavi TM. Polysaccharide-based polyelectrolyte complex systems for biomedical uses. In: Nayak AK, Hasnain MS, Aminabhavi TM, editors. Tailor-made polysaccharides in biomedical applications. USA: Academic Press, Elsevier Inc.; 2021. p. 151–74.

[46] Nayak AK, Pal D, Santra K. Ispaghula mucilage-gellan mucoadhesive beads of metformin HCl: development by response surface methodology. Carbohydr Polym 2014;107:41–50.

[47] Nayak AK, Pal D, Pradhan J, Hasnain MS. Fenugreek seed mucilage-alginate mucoadhesive beads of metformin HCl: design, optimization and evaluation. Int J Biol Macromol 2013;54:144–54.

[48] Nayak AK, Pal D. Formulation optimization of jackfruit seed starch-alginate mucoadhesive beads of metformin HCl. Int J Biol Macromol 2013;59:264–72.

[49] Nayak AK, Khatua S, Hasnain MS, Sen KK. Development of alginate-PVP K 30 microbeads for controlled diclofenac sodium delivery using central composite design. DARU J Pharm Sci 2011;19(5):356–66.

[50] Hasnain MS, Nayak AK, Singh M, Tabish M, Ansari MT, Ara TJ. Alginate-based bipolymeric-nanobioceramic composite matrices for sustained drug release. Int J Biol Macromol 2016;83:71–7.

[51] Dodi G, Pala A, Barbu E, Peptanariu D, Hritcu D, Popa MI, Tamba BI. Carboxymethyl guar gum nanoparticles for drug delivery applications: preparation and preliminary in-vitro investigations. Korean J Couns Psychother 2016;63:628–36.

[52] Maity S, Sa B. Ca-carboxymethyl xanthan gum mini-matrices: swelling, erosion and their impact on drug release mechanism. Int J Biol Macromol 2014;68:78–85.

[53] Jalil A, Asim MH, Le NN, Laffleur F, Matuszczak B, Tribus M, Bernkop-Schnürch A. S-protected gellan gum: decisive approach towards mucoadhesive antimicrobial vaginal films. Int J Biol Macromol 2019;130:148–57.

[54] Bahulkar SS, Munot NM, Surwase SS. Synthesis, characterization of thiolated karaya gum and evaluation of effect of pH on its mucoadhesive and sustained release properties. Carbohydr Polym 2015;130:183–90.

[55] Kono H, Otaka F, Ozaki M. Preparation and characterization of guar gum hydrogels as carrier materials for controlled protein drug delivery. Carbohydr Polym 2014;111:830–40.

[56] Lemos PVF, Marcelino HR, Cardoso LG, Souza CO, Druzian JI. Starch chemical modifications applied to drug delivery systems: from fundamentals to FDA-approved raw materials. Int J Biol Macromol 2021;184:218–34.

[57] Majumdar S, Hasnain MS, Nayak AK. Cross-linking of chitosan in drug delivery. In: Hasnain MS, Beg S, Nayak AK, editors. Chitosan in drug delivery. United States: Academic Press, Elsevier Inc.; 2022. p. 277–99.

[58] Ray S, Sinha P, Laha B, Maiti S, Bhattacharyya UK, Nayak AK. Polysorbate 80 coated crosslinked chitosan nanoparticles of ropinirole hydrochloride for brain targeting. J Drug Deliv Sci Technol 2018;48:21–9.

[59] Hasnain MS, Dey S, Nayak AK. Graft copolymers of chitosan in drug delivery applications. In: Hasnain MS, Beg S, Nayak AK, editors. Chitosan in drug delivery. United States: Academic Press, Elsevier Inc.; 2022. p. 301–22.

[60] Dey S, Roy S, Hasnain MS, Nayak AK. Grafted alginates in drug delivery. In: Nayak AK, Hasnain MS, editors. Alginates in drug delivery. United States: Academic Press, Elsevier Inc.; 2020. p. 71–100.

[61] Mohanta BC, Javed MN, Hasnain MS, Nayak AK. Polyelectrolyte complexes of alginate for controlling drug release. In: Nayak AK, Hasnain MS, editors. Alginates in drug delivery. United States: Academic Press, Elsevier Inc.; 2020. p. 297–321.

[62] Hasnain MS, Ray P, Nayak AK. Alginate-based interpenetrating polymer networks for sustained drug release. In: Nayak AK, Hasnain MS, editors. Alginates in drug delivery. United States: Academic Press, Elsevier Inc.; 2020. p. 101–28.

[63] Nayak AK, Pal D. Chitosan-based interpenetrating polymeric network systems for sustained drug release. In: Tiwari A, Patra HK, Choi J-W, editors. Advanced theranostics materials. USA: Wiley-Scrivener; 2015. p. 183–208.
[64] Aylsworth J. Improvement in nutmeg-graters. U.S. Patent, 1111284, Jan 24; 1914.
[65] Matricardi P, Di Meo C, Coviello T, Hennink WE, Alhaique F. Interpenetrating polymer networks polysaccharide hydrogels for drug delivery and tissue engineering. Adv Drug Deliv Rev 2013;65(9):1172–87.
[66] Dragan ES. Design and applications of interpenetrating polymer network hydrogels. A review. Chem Eng J 2014;243:572–90.
[67] Muxika A, Etxabide A, Uranga J, Guerrero P, de la Caba K. Chitosan as a bioactive polymer: processing, properties and applications. Int J Biol Macromol 2017;105(Pt 2):1358–68.
[68] Chatterjee R, Maity M, Hasnain MS, Nayak AK. Chitosan: source, chemistry, and properties. In: Hasnain MS, Beg S, Nayak AK, editors. Chitosan in drug delivery. United States: Academic Press, Elsevier Inc.; 2022. p. 1–22.
[69] Padhi S, Behera A, Hasnain MS, Nayak AK. Uses of chitosan in drug delivery. In: Hasnain MS, Beg S, Nayak AK, editors. Chitosan in biomedical application. United States: Academic Press, Elsevier Inc.; 2022. p. 139–62.
[70] Roy S, Chakraborty T, Begum J, Hasnain MS, Nayak AK. Chitosan: a versatile biopolymer. In: Hasnain MS, Beg S, Nayak AK, editors. Chitosan in biomedical application. United States: Academic Press, Elsevier Inc.; 2022. p. 1–11.
[71] Nayak AK, Ahmad SA, Hasnain MS. Chitosan-based nanoparticles in drug delivery. In: Hasnain MS, Beg S, Nayak AK, editors. Chitosan in drug delivery. United States: Academic Press, Elsevier Inc.; 2022. p. 55–82.
[72] Ansari MT, Murteza S, Ahsan MN, Hasnain MS, Nayak AK. Chitosan as a responsive biopolymer in drug delivery. In: Hasnain MS, Beg S, Nayak AK, editors. Chitosan in drug delivery. United States: Academic Press, Elsevier Inc.; 2022. p. 389–410.
[73] Dey S, Hasnain MS, Nayak AK. Chitosan nanocomposites for biomedical applications. In: Hasnain MS, Beg S, Nayak AK, editors. Chitosan in biomedical application. United States: Academic Press, Elsevier Inc.; 2022. p. 111–38.
[74] Jagga S, Hasnain MS, Nayak AK. Chitosan-based scaffolds in tissue engineering and regenerative medicine. In: Hasnain MS, Beg S, Nayak AK, editors. Chitosan in biomedical application. United States: Academic Press, Elsevier Inc.; 2022. p. 329–54.
[75] Patrulea V, Ostafe V, Borchard G, Jordan O. Chitosan as a starting material for wound healing applications. Eur J Pharm Biopharm 2015;97(Pt B):417–26.
[76] Jana S, Saha A, Nayak AK, Sen KK, Basu SK. Aceclofenac-loaded chitosan-tamarind seed polysaccharide interpenetrating polymeric network microparticles. Colloids Surf B: Biointerfaces 2013;105:303–9.
[77] Jana S, Sen KK, Basu SK. In vitro aceclofenac release from IPN matrix tablets composed of chitosan-tamarind seed polysaccharide. Int J Biol Macromol 2014;65:241–5.
[78] Rokhade AP, Kulkarni PV, Mallikarjuna NN, Aminabhavi TM. Preparation and characterization of novel semi-interpenetrating polymer network hydrogel microspheres of chitosan and hydroxypropyl cellulose for controlled release of chlorothiazide. J Microencapsul 2009;26:27–36.
[79] Angadi SC, Manjeshwar LS, Aminabhavi TM. Interpenetrating polymer network blend microspheres of chitosan and hydroxyethyl cellulose for controlled release of isoniazid. Int J Biol Macromol 2010;47(2):171–9.
[80] Rao KS, Naidu BV, Subha MC, Sairam M, Aminabhavi TM. Novel chitosan-based pH-sensitive interpenetrating network microgels for the controlled release of cefadroxil. Carbohydr Polym 2006;66:333–44.
[81] Alvarez-Lorenzo C, Concheiro A, Dubovik AS, Grinberg NV, Burova TV, Grinberg VY. Temperature-sensitive chitosan-poly(N-isopropylacrylamide) interpenetrated networks with enhanced loading capacity and controlled release properties. J Control Release 2005;102(3):629–41.

[82] Agnihotri SA, Aminabhavi TM. Novel interpenetrating network chitosan-poly(ethylene oxide-g-acrylamide) hydrogel microspheres for the controlled release of capecitabine. Int J Pharm 2006;324(2):103–15.
[83] Al-Kahtani Ahmed A, Bhojya Naik HS, Sherigara BS. Synthesis and characterization of chitosan-based pH-sensitive semi-interpenetrating network microspheres for controlled release of diclofenac sodium. Carbohydr Res 2009;344(5):699–706.
[84] Hasnain MS, Jameel E, Mohanta B, Dhara AK, Alkahtani S, Nayak AK. Alginates: sources, structure, and properties. In: Nayak AK, Hasnain MS, editors. Alginates in drug delivery. United States: Academic Press, Elsevier Inc.; 2020. p. 1–17.
[85] Nayak AK, Das B, Maji R. Calcium alginate/gum Arabic beads containing glibenclamide: development and *in vitro* characterization. Int J Biol Macromol 2012;51:1070–8.
[86] Kulkarni AR, Soppimath KS, Aminabhavi TM, et al. *In-vitro* release kinetics of cefadroxil-loaded sodium alginate interpenetrating network beads. Eur J Pharm Biopharm 2001;51:127–33.
[87] Ray P, Maity M, Barik H, Sahoo GS, Hasnain MS, Hoda MN, Nayak AK. Alginate-based hydrogels for drug delivery applications. In: Nayak AK, Hasnain MS, editors. Alginates in drug delivery. United States: Academic Press, Elsevier Inc.; 2020. p. 41–70.
[88] Nayak AK, Hasnain MS. Ionotropically gelled alginate particles in sustained drug release. In: Nayak AK, Hasnain MS, editors. Alginates in drug delivery. United States: Academic Press, Elsevier Inc.; 2020. p. 203–30.
[89] Reig-Vano B, Tylkowski B, Montané X, Giamberini M. Alginate-based hydrogels for cancer therapy and research. Int J Biol Macromol 2021;170:424–36.
[90] Kulkarni RV, Mutalik S, Mangond BS, Nayak UY. Novel interpenetrated polymer network microbeads of natural polysaccharides for modified release of water soluble drug: in-vitro and in-vivo evaluation. J Pharm Pharmacol 2012;64(4):530–40.
[91] Kulkarni RV, Patel FS, Nanjappaiah HM, Naikawadi AA. In vitro and in vivo evaluation of novel interpenetrated polymer network microparticles containing repaglinide. Int J Biol Macromol 2014;69:514–22.
[92] Das B, Dutta S, Nayak AK, Nanda U. Zinc alginate-carboxymethyl cashew gum microbeads for prolonged drug release: development and optimization. Int J Biol Macromol 2014;70:505–15.
[93] Boppana R, Mohan GK, Nayak U, Mutalik S, Sa B, Kulkarni RV. Novel pH-sensitive IPNs of polyacrylamide-g-gum ghatti and sodium alginate for gastro-protective drug delivery. Int J Biol Macromol 2015;75:133–43.
[94] Eswaramma S, Krishna Rao KSV. Synthesis of dual responsive carbohydrate polymer based IPN microbeads for controlled release of anti-HIV drug. Carbohydr Polym 2017;156:125–34.
[95] Reddy KM, Ramesh Babu V, Krishna Rao K, Subha M, Chowdoji Rao K, Sairam M, Aminabhavi T. Temperature sensitive semi-IPN microspheres from sodium alginate and N-isopropylacrylamide for controlled release of 5-fluorouracil. J Appl Polym Sci 2008;107:2820–9.
[96] Munarin F, Tanzi MC, Petrini P. Advances in biomedical applications of pectin gels. Int J Biol Macromol 2012;51(4):681–9.
[97] Nayak AK, Pal D, Das S. Calcium pectinate-fenugreek seed mucilage mucoadhesive beads for controlled delivery of metformin HCl. Carbohydr Polym 2013;96:349–57.
[98] Nayak AK, Pal D, Santra K. Development of pectinate-ispagula mucilage mucoadhesive beads of metformin HCl by central composite design. Int J Biol Macromol 2014;66:203–21.
[99] Giri TK, Choudhary C, Alexander A, Ajazuddin A, Badwaik H, Tripathy M, Tripathi DK. Sustained release of diltiazem hydrochloride from cross-linked biodegradable IPN hydrogel beads of pectin and modified xanthan gum. Indian J Pharm Sci 2013;75:619–27.

[100] Bera H, Boddupalli S, Nayak AK. Mucoadhesive-floating zinc-pectinate-sterculia gum interpenetrating polymer network beads encapsulating ziprasidone HCl. Carbohydr Polym 2015;131:108–18.
[101] Palumbo FS, Federico S, Pitarresi G, Fiorica C, Giammona G. Gellan gum-based delivery systems of therapeutic agents and cells. Carbohydr Polym 2020;229, 115430.
[102] Kulkarni RV, Mangod BS, Mutalik S, Sa B. Interpenetrating polymer network microcapsules of gellan gum and egg albumin entrapped with diltiazem-resin complex for controlled release application. Carbohydr Polym 2011;83(2):1001–7.
[103] Agnihotri SA, Aminabhavi TM. Development of novel interpenetrating network gellan gum-poly(vinyl alcohol) hydrogel microspheres for the controlled release of carvedilol. Drug Dev Ind Pharm 2005;31:491–503.
[104] Barak S, Mudgil D. Locust bean gum: processing, properties and food applications—a review. Int J Biol Macromol 2014;66:74–80.
[105] Nayak AK, Hasnain MS. Locust bean gum based multiple units for oral drug delivery. In: Nayak AK, Hasnain MS, editors. Plant polysaccharides-based multiple-unit systems for oral drug delivery. Singapore: Springer; 2019. p. 61–6.
[106] Hasnain MS, Nayak AK, Ansari MT, Pal D. Pharmaceutical applications of locust bean gum. In: Nayak AK, Hasnain MS, Pal D, editors. Natural polymers for pharmaceutical applications, volume I: plant derived polymers. USA: Apple Academic Press; 2019. p. 139–62.
[107] Upadhyay M, Adena SKR, Vardhan H, Pandey S, Mishra B. Development and optimization of locust bean gum and sodium alginate interpenetrating polymeric network of capecitabine. Drug Dev Ind Pharm 2018;44:511–21.
[108] Dey P, Sa B, Maiti S. Impact of gelation period on modified locust bean-alginate interpenetrating beads for oral glipizide delivery. Int J Biol Macromol 2015;76:176–80.
[109] Jana S, Sen KK. Chitosan-locust bean gum interpenetrating polymeric network nanocomposites for delivery of aceclofenac. Int J Biol Macromol 2017;102:878–84.
[110] Kaity S, Ghosh A. Comparative bio-safety and in vivo evaluation of native or modified locust bean gum-PVA IPN microspheres. Int J Biol Macromol 2015;72:883–93.
[111] Kumar A, Rao KM, Han SS. Application of xanthan gum as polysaccharide in tissue engineering: a review. Carbohydr Polym 2018;180:128–44.
[112] Cortes H, Caballero-Florán IH, Mendoza-Muñoz N, Escutia-Guadarrama L, Figueroa-González G, Reyes-Hernández OD, González-Del Carmen M, Varela-Cardoso M, González-Torres M, Florán B, Del Prado-Audelo ML, Leyva-Gómez G. Xanthan gum in drug release. Cell Mol Biol (Noisy-le-Grand) 2020;66(4):199–207.
[113] Zhang D, Jiang F, Ling J, Ouyang XK, Wang YG. Delivery of curcumin using a zein-xanthan gum nanocomplex: fabrication, characterization, and in vitro release properties. Colloids Surf B: Biointerfaces 2021;204, 111827.
[114] Trombino S, Serini S, Cassano R, Calviello G. Xanthan gum-based materials for omega-3 PUFA delivery: preparation, characterization and antineoplastic activity evaluation. Carbohydr Polym 2019;208:431–40.
[115] Giri TK, Thakur A, Tripathi DK. Biodegradable hydrogel bead of casein and modified xanthan gum for controlled delivery of theophylline. Curr Drug Ther 2016;11:150–62.
[116] Bhattacharya SS, Shukla S, Banerjee S, Chowdhury P, Chakraborty P, Ghosh A. Tailored IPN hydrogel bead of sodium carboxymethyl cellulose and sodium carboxymethyl xanthan gum for controlled delivery of diclofenac sodium. Polym-Plast Technol Eng 2013;52:795–805.
[117] Kulkarni RV, Sa B. Evaluation of pH-sensitivity and drug release characteristics of (polyacrylamide-grafted-xanthan)–carboxymethyl cellulose-based pH-sensitive interpenetrating network hydrogel beads. Drug Dev Ind Pharm 2008;34:1406–14.
[118] Ray S, Banerjee S, Maiti S, Laha B, Barik S, Sa B, Bhattacharyya UK. Novel interpenetrating network microspheres of xanthan gum–poly(vinyl alcohol) for the delivery of diclofenac sodium to the intestine-in vitro and in vivo evaluation. Drug Deliv 2010;17:508–19.

[119] Bhattacharya SS, Mazahir F, Banerjee S, Verma A, Ghosh A. Preparation & in-vitro evaluation of xanthan gum facilitated superabsorbent polymeric microspheres. Carbohydr Polym 2013;98:64–72.
[120] Campo VL, Kawano DF, da Silva DB, Carvalho I. Carrageenans: biological properties, chemical modifications and structural analysis—a review. Carbohydr Polym 2009;77:167–80.
[121] Yegappan R, Selvaprithiviraj V, Amirthalingam S, Jayakumar R. Carrageenan based hydrogels for drug delivery, tissue engineering and wound healing. Carbohydr Polym 2018;198:385–400.
[122] Pacheco-Quito EM, Ruiz-Caro R, Veiga MD. Carrageenan: drug delivery systems and other biomedical applications. Mar Drugs 2020;18(11):583.
[123] Li L, Ni R, Shao Y, Mao S. Carrageenan and its applications in drug delivery. Carbohydr Polym 2014;103:1–11.
[124] Qureshi D, Nayak SK, Maji S, Kim D, Banerjee I, Pal K. Carrageenan: a wonder polymer from marine algae for potential drug delivery applications. Curr Pharm Des 2019;25(11):1172–86.
[125] Swain S, Bal T. Carrageenan-guar gum microwave irradiated micro-porous interpenetrating polymer network: a system for drug delivery. Int J Polym Mater Polym Biomater 2018;68:256–65.
[126] Kulkarni RV, Boppana R, Mohan GK, Mutalik S, Kalyane NV. pH-responsive interpenetrating network hydrogel beads of poly(acrylamide)-g-carrageenan and sodium alginate for intestinal targeted drug delivery: synthesis, in vitro and in vivo evaluation. J Colloid Interface Sci 2012;367:509–17.
[127] Lohani A, Singh G, Bhattacharya SS, Hegde RR, Verma A. Tailored-interpenetrating polymer network beads of κ-carrageenan and sodium carboxymethyl cellulose for controlled drug delivery. J Drug Deliv Sci Technol 2016;31:53–64.

CHAPTER

10

Polysaccharide nanoconjugates in drug delivery

Mohammed Tahir Ansari[a], *Farheen Sami*[b], *Md Saquib Hasnain*[c], *Mohd Usman Mohd Siddique*[d], *and Amit Kumar Nayak*[e]

[a]School of Pharmacy, Faculty of Science and Engineering, University of Nottingham Malaysia, Semenyih, Selangor, Malaysia, [b]Department of Pharmaceutics, Hygia Institute of Pharmaceutical Education and Research, Lucknow, India, [c]Department of Pharmacy, Palamau Institute of Pharmacy, Daltonganj, Jharkhand, India, [d]Department of Pharmaceutical Chemistry, Shri Vile Parle Kelavani Mandal's Institute of Pharmacy, Dhule, Maharashtra, India, [e]Department of Pharmaceutics, Seemanta Institute of Pharmaceutical Sciences, Jharpokharia, Mayurbhanj, Odisha, India

1 Introduction

Delivery of various therapeutic agents via oral route may be improved by solubility enhancement using nanoengineered drug carrier systems [1]. The nanosized particles help to deliver drugs and also increase absorption across the biological membrane. Polysaccharide nanoconjugates are becoming popular due to various reasons, including increased water solubility, capability to control the drug release at the target site, and decreased side effects [2,3]. Polysaccharide nanoconjugates-based formulations may be helpful in increasing the bioavailability of Biopharmaceutical Classification System class II drugs. Paclitaxel, due to its insolubility, has low bioavailability. Paclitaxel-trimethyl chitosan nanoconjugates have also been reported [4]. Polysaccharide nanoconjugates may increase the gastrointestinal residence time, protect the drug-metabolizing in the hostile gastrointestinal environments, or increase the permeability of drugs across the biological membranes [2]. This chapter envisages the

https://doi.org/10.1016/B978-0-12-821286-8.00002-1

application of polysaccharides in the development of nanoconjugates for treatment, mitigation, and diagnosis (of disease, disorder, and syndrome).

2 Polysaccharide nanoconjugates

Polymer-drug conjugates consist of active pharmaceutical ingredients (API) encapsulated in biodegradable, nontoxic, nonirritant, and compatible polymers. The conjugates are mostly formed with a help of a linker, which has characteristics of responding to stimuli [5,6]. Solubilizers or targeting ligands are used to increase the therapeutic action of the conjugates [7]. Newer research is mostly producing drug molecules that are potent and hence are hydrophobic [8]. Ligand-mediated polysaccharide-drug conjugates exhibit higher toxicity to targeted cells and tissues [9]. Internalized conjugates are transferred into lysosomes, where the activity of lysosomal enzymes releases the attached therapeutic moieties. This release may also be guided by pH (Fig. 1) [2].

Because of their varied functional groups, polysaccharide nanoconjugates can be used as drug vectors, which can further be modified with markers, antibodies, substrates to improve specificity [10]. Furthermore, these chemical structures facilitate their passage through biological barriers. These formulations possess unique features as they contain more than one API which may attack different targets. This method may be used for selective blockage of multiple pathological pathways and improving cancer prognosis. Some of the vectors used can be surfactant-based vesicles, nanosized particles, etc. [11].

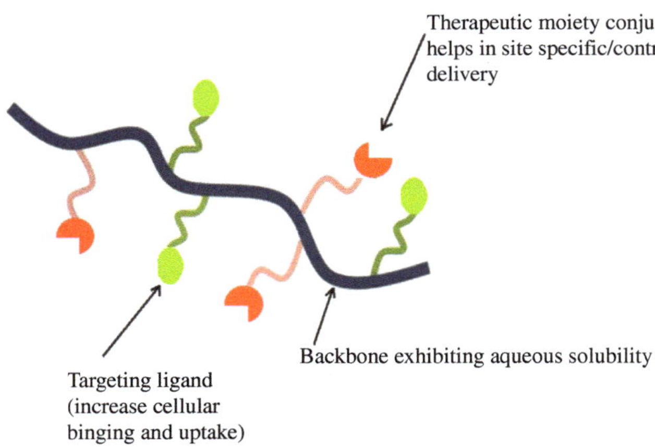

FIG. 1 Applicability of polysaccharide-drug conjugates [2]. *Copyright © 2019 with permission from Elsevier Ltd.*

3 Advantages of polysaccharide nanoconjugates in drug delivery

Since the mid-2000s, nanoconjugates have seen their widespread uses for the delivery of poorly water-soluble and poorly bioavailable drugs. Studies show that nanoconjugates of paclitaxel [4], tamoxifen [12], curcumin [13], etc., improved their activities on the cancer cells. Other specific properties of nanoconjugates are as follows:

(i) Molecules are encapsulated by the nanoconjugates, which protect them.
(ii) They may improve the permeability of drugs and may also increase cellular uptake [2].
(iii) Conjugation improves pharmacokinetics and releases control.
(iv) The formulation can target ABC transporters, such as P-glycoprotein.
(v) Polysaccharides adhere to the mucosal membranes, and may also bind with the cellular receptors [14].
(vi) These are generally biodegradable. These are reduced into small peptides, and may also be utilized in cellular signaling, storage, and even in the formation of new tissue. For example, glycosidase is found in about 1%–3% of the human genome. These enzymes (i.e., glycosidase) break down glycosidic linkages [15]. Few polysaccharides possess inherent bioactivity, and some of these are antiinflammatory and/or antimicrobial. For example, chitosan is an antibacterial compound; whereas, heparin possesses antiinflammatory properties. Polysaccharides work synergistically with drugs when coadministered. Furthermore, ligand-mediated polysaccharide-drug nanoconjugates improve cell specificity and hence, reduce the toxicity on normal cells. Biodegradable excipients show low cytotoxicity, which brings better tolerability to humans [11].

4 Polysaccharide used for nanoconjugation

The nanoconjugates formulated using polysaccharides are intended to have improved pharmacological activity with reduced side effects [3]. The conjugates based on the linker have been able to permeate in the cell either passively or actively [16]. Many different factors come into play with "Enhanced Permeability and Retention" (EPR) responsible for passive targeting. One of the main causes is a defect in tumor vasculature. Targeting may also be guided by spatial and temporal activity. The conjugates may also improve the pharmacokinetic properties of drugs [3]. The cellular mechanism involves targeting specific receptors on cancer and tumor cells. These may also improve diagnosis. The nanoconjugates may also be used in delivering genes.

4.1 Chitosan

Chitin, a natural polysaccharide, is an important part of marine organisms, such as crabs, shrimps, etc. These crustacean parts are first removed, powdered, and processed to prepare chitosan [17,18]. Chitosan is a 66%–95% deacetylated semicrystalline, white solid, having a molecular weight of 3800–20,000 Da [19]. The aqueous solubility has been reported to increase in acidic pH as amino groups can be protonated, 1%–3% of acetic acid solution favors solubility of chitosan [20]. It has been shown that chitosan is safe, nontoxic, nonirritant, mucoadhesive, and compatible with living tissues [21,22]. It can also form complexes with drugs via electrostatic interactions, hydrophobic interactions, and hydrogen bonding [23,24]. Chitosan possesses antimicrobial properties [25,26]. In addition, it is a good adsorbent for cadmium, mercury, and lead [27]. Chitosan has extensively been examined for use in pharmaceutical dosage formulations [28]. Many properties of chitosan have been explored like buccal and mucoadhesive agents, pH-based drug targeting, carrier for proteins and peptides, etc. [16,17,28–30].

Literature reports many methods of formulating chitosan-based nanoconjugates, such as phase separation, spray drying, emulsion-based system, etc. [31,32]. These formulation techniques are maneuvered by numerous factors, such as required kinetic profiles, dispersibility index, stability, and storage issues. Chitosan nanoconjugates may help to overcome solubility and targeting issues during drug development [7]. Popat et al., developed curcumin-cyclodextrin-encapsulated chitosan nanoconjugates with increased drug dispersibility and augmented the cellular uptake [13]. Curcumin-cyclodextrin was synthesized by the spray-drying method. The scanning electron microscopy (SEM) results presented spray-dried hollow microspheres (Fig. 2). Targeted delivery of chitosan-doxorubicin nanoconjugates was synthesized employing succinic anhydride as a crosslinker [33]. A nanoconjugates of trastuzumab was reported with doxorubin using chitosan. These trastuzumab-conjugated self-assembled chitosan-doxorubin nanoconjugates exhibited a prospective effect on ovarian and breast cancer. Studies have proved that a 100 KD had better vector properties in targeting drugs to tumor cells [34]. In research, covalently linked meso-tetraphenylchlorin-chitosan nanoconjugates were developed for photochemical internalization [35]. These nanoconjugates were assessed for their in vivo effectiveness in mice. The results of the in vivo experiment demonstrated that these meso-tetraphenylchlorin-chitosan nanoconjugates could stimulate a strong photochemical internalization and photodynamic therapy in treatment with bleomycin.

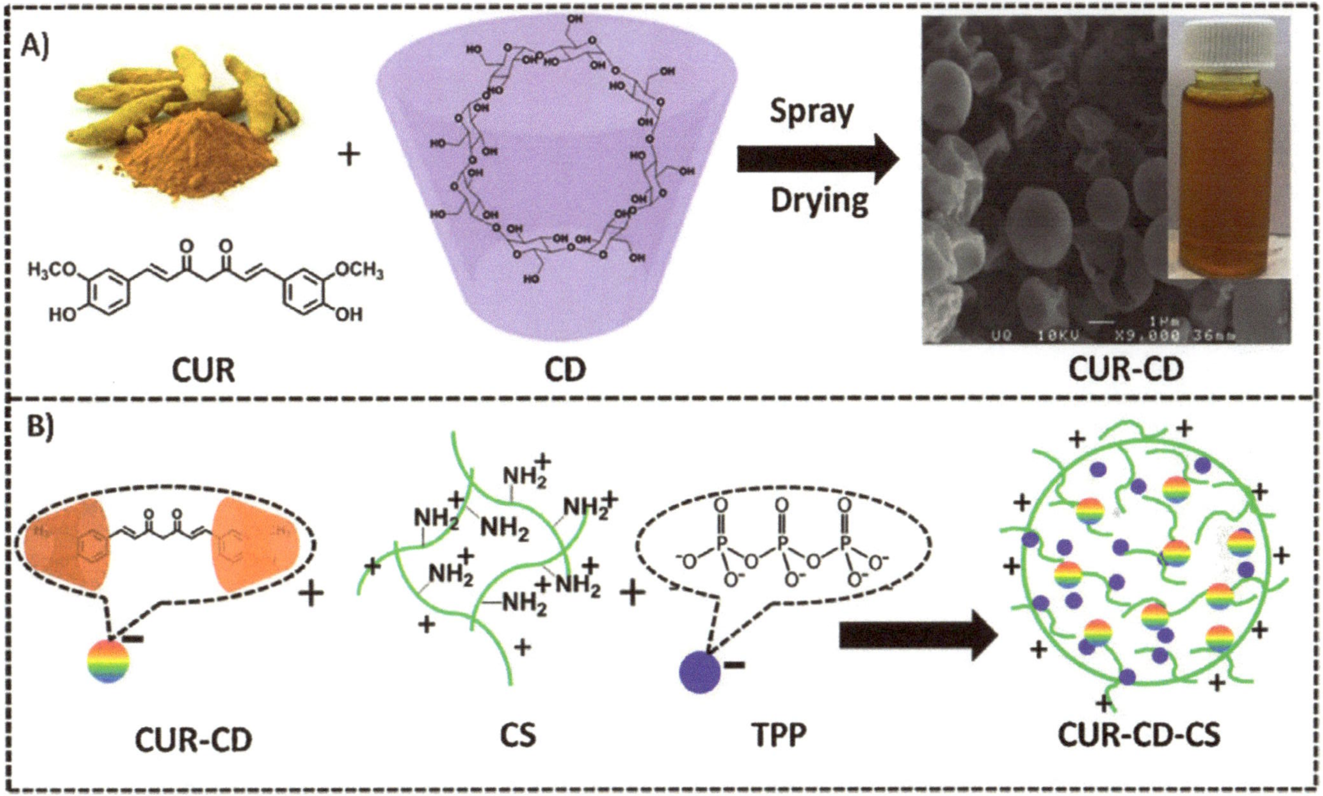

FIG. 2 Schematic representations of (A) synthesis of highly soluble curcumin-cyclodextrin complex by a novel spray drying method. The SEM image represents hollow microspheres after spray drying and inset shows a water solution of curcumin-cyclodextrin; (B) synthesis method of curcumin-cyclodextrin-encapsulated chitosan nanoconjugates [13]. *Copyright © 2014 with permission from Elsevier B.V.*

4.2 Pectin

Pectin is an important component of the plant cell walls [35,36]. Pectin mainly acts as a gelling agent [37]. In general, it is reported to be aqueous soluble but insoluble in nonaqueous and organic solvents. The ester groups have been responsible for its aqueous solubility. It is characterized by a negatively charged chain. The pH and degree of methoxylation both affect charge density. In addition, pectin forms gels through coordination of Ca^{2+} ions (due to ionic gelation), hydrogen bonding, and hydrophobic interactions [38]. Ionic linkage between calcium atoms occurs in low-methoxyl pectin, resulting in ionic gelation [39]. The degree of methoxylation, pH, solutes, etc. has been associated to influence gelation of pectin [38,39]. Due to its good biocompatibility, pectin is an effective vehicle for the delivery of drugs [17,28,40]. The homogalacturonan backbone of pectin is a linear chain of α-(1,4)-linked D-galacturonic acid. α-D-galacturonic acid has plenty of carboxyl and hydroxyl groups. The condensation of carboxyl groups with the amino groups may improve encapsulation efficiency [41]. Calcium salts and L-asparagines may induce gel formation and crosslinking, which eases the formation of nanoconjugates.

Verma et al., reported a novel nanoconjugates system for the effective delivery of cisplatin [41]. Metals possess a positive charge and bind to negatively charged molecules. The ligands present in proteins, and nucleic acids may aid in sustaining the release for up to 12h. It has been reported that these conjugates reduce kidney accumulation and nephrotoxicity. It has a superior affinity for lung tissues and hence can be used for lung cancer treatment. The ability of the conjugate to withstand pectinolytic enzyme degradation was tested by using thiol-derivatives of pectin. The toxicity of the polymer was determined using $CaCO_2$ cells. The pectin-cysteine conjugate showed a fivefold improvement in cohesive properties. The stability of pectin nanoconjugates in acidic and gastric pH was improved by adding zinc [42]. Graphene oxide functionalized conjugates has been used as a carrier for paclitaxel. The conjugates reported improved encapsulation and cellular uptake as evident in in vitro studies using MTT assay using L929 and MCF-7 human cell lines [43]. Methotrexate-conjugated pectin nanoparticles were fabricated by ionotropic gelation. The study demonstrated sustained drug release with methotrexate-conjugated pectin nanoparticles at pH7.4. The study also confirmed that the conjugation to pectin nanoparticles increased the cytotoxicity of methorexate [44]. Lymphatic targeting of pectin-adriamycin conjugates could significantly be affected by the pectin esterification. The drug plasma concentration was significantly improved after the administration of pectin-adriamycin conjugates, locally. It can also be used as a drug matrix for delayed drug delivery to the colon. 5-Flourouracil was successfully delayed, with a latent period of 4h until the matrix reaches the colon [45,46]. The results of in vivo pharmacokinetic evaluation of pectin-based 5-flourouracil tablets in New Zealand white rabbits demonstrated reduced absorption rate constant, which indicated that the drug (here 5-flourouracil) was not released in both stomach as well as small intestine, significantly (Fig. 3). However, drug was significantly released in colonic site, which might be useful for exerting local effects with minor systemic exposure.

4.3 Dextran

Dextran is a polysaccharide composed of repeating units of α-D-glucopyranosyl connected by α-1 to 6 glucopyranosyl bonds [47]. It is commercially produced from sucrose using bacteria, including *Leuconostoc mesenteroids* and *Streptococcus mutans* [48]. It produces a low viscosity solution as compared with other polysaccharides [47]. Dextran is used as a plasma expander. It has wide application in drug delivery systems, such as lubricant in eye drops, cancer-targeting, etc. [48,49].

Dextran-methotrexate conjugation was reported to improve the potency of the drug hence minimizing dose adverse effects [50]. Cisplatin-dextran conjugate improved effective half-life and increased tumor inhibition. Due to its absorbable nature, it has been used to target colon to treat inflammatory bowel disease using a dextran-conjugated prodrug

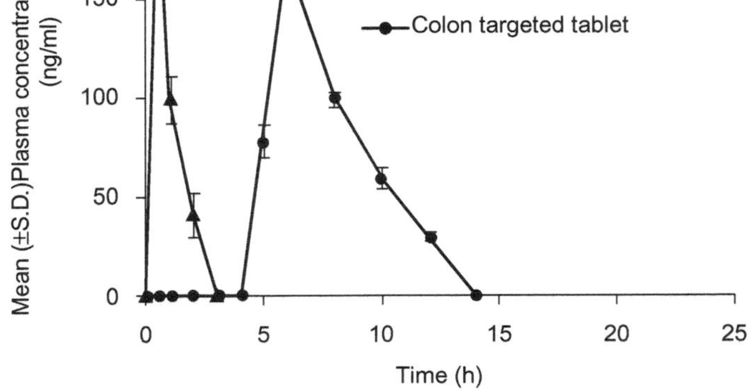

FIG. 3 Plasma concentration of 5-flourouracil in New Zealand white rabbits following oral administration of immediate-release (IR) tablets (dose 7.47 mg) and pectin-based colon-targeted tablets (dose 7.47 mg) (mean ± S.D.; $n = 3$) [46]. *Copyright © 2011 with permission from Elsevier B.V.*

for 5 aminosalicylic acid, and nalidixic acid [51,52]. The conjugates for paclitaxel and doxorubicin showed improved activity against ovarian cancer cells [53]. The dextran-ibuprofen conjugate was reported to improve low-solubility and poor compression characteristics and displayed extended drug release [54]. In recent research, amorphous ibuprofen-diethylaminoethylcellulose dextran nanoconjugate was synthesized using low energy and controlled amphiphile-polyelectrolyte electrostatic self-assembly method [54]. The nanoconjugate produced extended release of poorly aqueous soluble drug ibuprofen dictated by diethylaminoethylcellulose dextran nanoconjugate concentration.

4.4 Cyclodextrins

Cyclodextrins are naturally occurring oligosaccharides consisting of α-1,4 linked D-glucopyranose units [55]. Based on the glucopyranose units, it has been classified as α, β, and γ. Natural cyclodextrins are nonhygroscopic, homogeneous, and crystalline substances [56]. They have a cylindrical shape, the inner cavity is lipophilic. They have the ability to form inclusion complexes of low molecular weight drugs [57]. Because of its biocompatibility is has been found numerous pharmaceutical applications with limitations to its parenteral application [58,59]. Cyclodextrins form inclusion complexes water-insoluble drugs [57,60]. The complexes alter many properties that influence the pharmacokinetics of the drugs [57,58]. The polarity, molecular weight, and structure may affect the degree of complexation. β-Cyclodextrin has been reported to form a stable and a good inclusion complex [61]. Many derivatives of cyclodextrin have also been reported with varying capacities of improving drug properties by forming inclusion complexes [57,58,61]. Some cyclodextrin derivatives include methylated-cyclodextrin, hydroxypropyl β-cyclodextrin, and sulfobutylether β-cyclodextrin. Polymerized β-cyclodextrins, such as anionic-cyclodextrin polymer, soluble γ-cyclodextrin, and epichlorohydrin-cyclodextrin, are of high molecular weight polymers [2]. The drugs for complexation (guest) should have a suitable environment for interaction in the hydrophobic cavity of cyclodextrins [62]. Within the inclusion complexes of cyclodextrins, drugs are partially or completely contained within the cavity of the hosts [56]. Cyclodextrin complexation has been used to increase the aqueous solubility of insoluble drugs in solutions form [61]. Cyclodextrins have been reported to formulate anticancer drug-cyclodextrin nanoconjugates. The cyclodextrin nanoconjugates have been formulated to target drugs. Some studies suggest that it can also address the issue of drug resistance, especially for drugs used in long-term therapy. In a work, Li et al. reported a gold-cyclodextrin-paclitaxel nanoconjugate using [63]. When compared with paclitaxel, nanoconjugate exhibited a 17-fold lower EC50. In another work, magnetically controlled β-cyclodextrin-conjugated dicarbazine was reported by Solanki et al. [64]. In this work, the drug uptake was assayed in a drug-resistant cancer cell line with P-gp overexpression (H460PTX cells). It was evident that the cyclodextrin-based nanoconjugates improved drug uptake in the cancer cells irrespective of any resistance.

4.5 Hyaluronic acid

Hyaluronic acid is a natural-occurring polysaccharide present in mammals [65]. It is found in connective tissues of human body, including the eyes, joints, skin, and umbilical cord, where it aids in tissue lubrication, adhesion, and elasticity [66]. Hyaluronic acid is an anionic, nonsulfated glycosaminoglycan, with alternating β-1,4 and β-1,3 glycosidic linkages [67]. It is highly soluble in water and is capable of producing a highly viscous solution [65,67].

Superior water solubility of docetaxel was reported owing to the conjugation with hyaluronic acid [68]. This conjugation augmented the tumor targeting, pharmacokinetics, and biodistribution when compared with the free drug. Nanoconjugates of hyaluronic acid have been used to treat multiple cancers [69]. The half-life was improved by forming butyric acid-hyaluronic acid nanoconjugates. These conjugates also reduced the side effects as the dose was markedly red hyaluronic reduced [70]. Ethylene diamine-modified hyaluronic acid nanoconjugates exhibited targeted release and promoted programmed cell death with minimal toxicity [71]. Mesoporous silica nanoparticles-based nanoconjugates improved the cell specificity and also sustained the drug release property [72]. Hyaluronic acid-functionalized α-tocopherol polyethylene glycol succinate-hyaluronic acid-cholic acid nanoconjugates were formulated to achieve dual targeting [73]. Doxorubicin was used as the model drug. The nanoconjugates achieved a better-controlled drug release with improved cytotoxic activity as compared with doxorubicin.

4.6 Pullan

Pullulan, is a polysaccharide, composed of $1 \rightarrow 4$ α and $1 \rightarrow 6$ α d-triglucosides linkages [74]. It has been reported to have good water solubility, nontoxic, nonirritant, and is compatible with many drug substances [74,75]. It has also exhibited a good bioadhesive and hence can be used for designing drug delivery systems [74,76,77].

Gene delivery was explored using nanoconjugates synthesized using pullulans [78]. Due to its natural origin, the PEI-pullulan conjugates were nontoxic, nonirritant, and compatible with blood and proteins. The anticancer properties were reported to improve with better cell specificity as the PEI-pullulan mediated the transfection of hepatocytes using asialoglycoprotein receptors. It was evident that the pullulan-based nanoconjugates can be used for gene delivery. Pullulan-deoxycholic acid conjugated doxorubicin self-organized nanogel was developed by Na and coworkers [79]. The study discovered that pullulan-deoxycholic acid conjugated doxorubicin self-organized nanogel has the potential to be used as a carrier for delivering an anticancer drug. The conjugates were reported to improve encapsulation and loading capacity. Circulating chromatin fragments could possibly be removed by pullulan-histone nanoconjugates of adriamycin [80]. The efficacy of the antibody was found to be improved in reducing inflammatory cells and preventing neutropenia as pullulan nanoconjugates.

4.7 Chondroitin sulfate

Chondroitin is found as proteoglycans, found in connective tissue [81,82]. It is composed of sulfated sugars, biodegradable, and biocompatible proteoglycans (having a molecular weight of 20 kDa) [83]. Chondroitin sulfate can be used to inhibit undesirable interactions with plasma proteins and cells while circulating in the body [84].

Chondroitin sulfate has been reported in the synthesis of drug nanoconjugates [85]. Various applications such as improvement insolubility of hydrophobic drugs, inhibition of protein interaction, improved cellular uptake have been reported. Methotrexate-chondroitin sulfate nanoconjugates were reported to have improved drug solubility and efficacy due to improved binding [86]. The antitumor property of methotrexate was reported by formulating nanogels [87]. The nanogels were also reported to have tumor photodynamic therapy due to self-assembled Chorine6 (Ce6)-conjugated chondroitin sulfate nanodrug.

The antiinflammatory activity was analyzed as rat paw edema assay for prednisolone and glycyl prednisolone-chondroitin sulfate conjugate [88]. The experiment revealed that a dose of 5 mg/kg 2d of prednisolone was found to be less effective than 2.5 mg/kg of prednisolone conjugate. The study is expected to improve the outcome of rheumatoid arthritis. The chondroitin sulfate quercetin conjugate exhibited a 24 h of drug-releasing, which was found to be specific to a tumor-relevant condition [89]. **methylthiazol-2-yl)-2,5-diphenyl tetrazolium bromidede (MTT)** MTT assay was conducted on HeLa cells and HSF cells. The histopathological study confirmed the homogeneous distribution of the chondroitin sulfate quercetin conjugate micelles in the tumor cells. The micellar conjugate proved to be effective in low concentration and release the drug as a stimuli-responsive delivery system. The study revealed this micellar conjugate can be an excellent mode of delivery for hydrophobic drug in the selected pathological environment (Fig. 4).

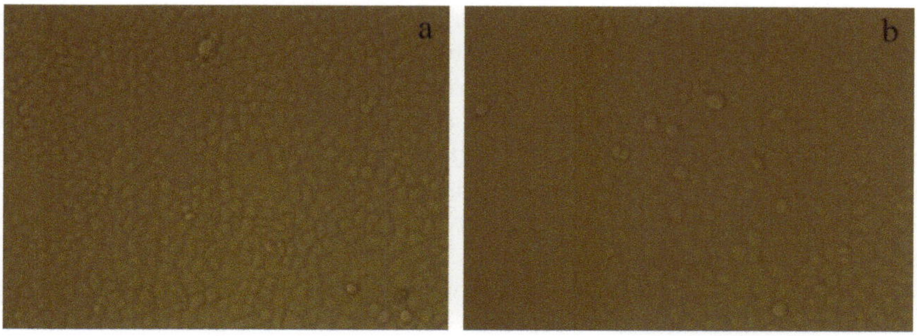

FIG. 4 Morphological features of HeLa cells observed by optical microscope after incubated without (A) or with 200 μg/mL chondroitin sulphatemicelles containing quercetin micelles (B) for 48 h [89]. *Copyright © 2013 with permission from Elsevier B.V.*

4.8 Heparin

Heparin, an anticoagulant and antithrombotic agent containing 1–4 linked pyranosyl uronic acid and 2-amino-deoxyglycopyranose (glucosamine) repeating units, found in human and animal cells is used primarily in wound healing, tumor metastasis, burn injury treatment, and inflammation inhibition [90,91]. The mechanism involves interaction with inflammatory mediators [92,93]. Uronic acid contains molecular chains with lengths ranging from 2000 to 40,000. The chains of heparin depend on the molecular weight, which largely depends on the chemical and enzymatic depolymerization processes of peptidoglycans [94].

Literature suggests that heparin also possesses antitumor activity and hence has been studied extensively in the synthesis of nanoconjugates that can be used for cancer treatment [91]. Ternary heparin-folate-paclitaxel nanoparticles or nanoconjugates were analyzed for their antitumor activity [95]. The synthesized nanoparticles were found primarily concentrated in the tumor cells, which indicated a possible folic acid receptor-mediated endocytosis. The increased concentration of heparin-paclitaxel tumor cells indicated the possible anticancer efficacy. The histopathological study was assisted using fluorescent dye-labeled heparin-paclitaxel nanoparticles for the study.

Heparin- and deoxycholic acid-amphiphilic conjugate were used in treating squamous cell carcinoma. Doxorubicin was encapsulated in the heparin-deoxycholic acid nanoconjugates. High loading efficiency and conjugate release demonstrated enhanced antitumor activity [96]. Another study exhibited anticancer effects of retinoic acid and doxorubicin on epithelial MCF-7 cells [97]. The stability of heparin-doxorubicin nanocomposite could also be improved by pluronic F-68 [98]. The heparin-doxorubicin-pluronic F-68 nanocomposite was formulated to release the drug at a specific tumor site. The activity was assayed in mice cultured with squamous cell carcinoma. The tumor cells were exposed to doxorubicin, which caused apoptosis and caspase-3 activation on a regular basis. Caspases control cell death and reduce apoptosis. In a nanocarriers system, they may amplify apoptosis [40]. The docetaxel-stearylamine-heparin conjugate showed increased half-life, improved encapsulation, and inhibition of growth of the MDAMD 231 cancer cells [73].

Some recently reported polysaccharide nanoconjugates used in drug delivery are summarized in Table 1.

TABLE 1 Some recently reported polysaccharide nanoconjugates used in drug delivery.

Polysaccharide nanoconjugates	Drug(s) delivered	Results	References
Chlorambucil-chitosan nanoconjugate	Chlorambucil	MTT assay showed that this nanoconjugate not only retained its anticancer action against chlorambucil but also presented lesser uncharacteristic toxicity. In addition, in vitro cellular uptake exhibited better uptake of chlorambucil-chitosan nanoconjugate into the MCF-7 cells	[99]
Hyaluronan-cisplatin conjugate nanoparticles	Cisplatin	The hyaluronan-cisplatin conjugated nanoparticles were found pH-responsive guided by Eudragit S100 coating	[100]
Ciprofloxacin-diethylaminoethyl dextran nanoconjugate	Ciprofloxacin	The dissolution efficiency of the ciprofloxacin-diethyl aminoethyl dextran nanoconjugate suspensions was found to be augmented with increasing molar concentration of diethylaminoethyl dextran to a maximum of 100% at 50 μM of diethylaminoethyl dextran followed by a decrease within 3-week	[101]
Diethylaminoethyl dextran-ibuprofen nanoconjugates and diethylaminoethyl dextran-ibuprofen-gellan gum nanoconjugates	Ibuprofen	Ibuprofen nanosized were formed with improved drug performance	[102]

TABLE 1 Some recently reported polysaccharide nanoconjugates used in drug delivery—cont'd

Polysaccharide nanoconjugates	Drug(s) delivered	Results	References
Doxorubicin-loaded nanoconjugates of β-cyclodextrin	Doxorubicin and curcumin	The results of in vitro evaluation indicated the nontoxicity and hemocompatibility of the nanoconjugates. At very low concentrations in cancer cells, Significant cell death was noticed by drug-loaded nanoconjugates	[103]
Porphyrin-β-cyclodextrin conjugate	Tamoxifen	The use of photochemical internalization protocols with 4-hydroxytamoxifen, estrogen-receptor β-positive cell groups showed wide-ranging anticancer effects	[12]
β-Cyclodextrin-ethylenediamine tetra-acetic acid -magnetic iron oxide nanoparticle-conjugated nanocarriers	Camptothecin	The dose-dependent cytotoxicity of camptothecin loaded-β-cyclodextrin-ethylenediamine tetraacetic acid-magnetic iron oxide nanoparticle was confirmed by MTT assay using colon cancer cells and lung cancer cells	[104]

5 Recent progress

The main application of forming nanoconjugates is to improve the drug targeting and drug release. These formulations have allowed realizing the long-term attempt of delivery immunoglobulins, proteins, and peptides to specific target cells [105]. These conjugates have also improved the delivery of antibiotics and addressed the issue of drug resistance [106]. The biodegradable properties have allowed exploring the tissue targeting of drugs [107]. Several monoclonal antibodies are already approved or are in late clinical trials. [107,108]. Some examples include: Lucentis, Adcetris, Avastin, Doxil, Mylotarg and Herceptin. However, due to immunogenicity of antibodies, nonimmunogenic natural polysaccharides may be another attractive option to be used as nanoconjugates platforms [109]. The biocompatible nature may allow the specific cell targeting by tagging the nanoconjugates with specific markers. This will improve cellular uptake in cancer cells and hence cell targeting [110]. With this polysaccharide oral drug, delivery may also be used to target colonic regions by designing a pH sensitive nanoconjugates or microbial activated conjugated system.

The use of siRNA chimeras have further improved the drug targeting as it may inhibit specific cancer related proteins [112]. The research encompasses wide application from tumor targeting to solubility enhancement. Certain polysaccharide has also found application in sustained and delayed drug release formulations.

6 Conclusion

The use of nanoconjugates has been widely discussed in literature. It has been reported to increase solubility, in improved diagnosis, in improved targeting, etc. Most of the studies have used the polysaccharide owing to its nontoxic, nonirritant, compatible, and easy degradable. Through this chapter, various polysaccharides such as chitosan, pectin, cyclodextrins, dextran, etc. have been discussed. Different properties of polysaccharides have been explored and a few methods to develop the nanoconjugates have been discussed. Although there have been numerous studies that shows excellent medical application of polysaccharides but very few have made it to the market. There have been few nanoconjugates that are under clinical trial but still evidence are needed for a successful release of nanoconjugates in the real world Some of the issues that needs to be addressed is the loading capacity, the validation and optimization step, the raw material purity, designing, and production. The derivatives of all these polysaccharides may also prove to be much better and similar studies are required to prove their application. The use of *in-silico* studies can be applied to study the receptor interaction with polysaccharides derivatives. It is envisaged that in near future and looking at the side effects of synthetic excipients, these polysaccharides may find more application in design and development of drug delivery systems. The vastly stable physical and chemical properties of the polysaccharides may pave the future of design and development for a successful product.

References

[1] Chivere VT, Kondiah PPD, Choonara YE, Pillay V. Nanotechnology-based biopolymeric oral delivery platforms for advanced cancer treatment. Cancers (Basel) 2020;12(2):522.

[2] Kumar S, Ali J, Baboota S. Polysaccharide nanoconjugates for drug solubilization and targeted delivery. In: Maiti S, Jana S, editors. Polysaccharide carriers for drug delivery. USA: Woodhead Publishing, Elsevier Inc.; 2019. p. 443–75.

[3] Muinao T, Boruah HPD, Pal M. Current advances on polysaccharide-based nanoconjugates for efficient and targeted drug delivery in cancer treatment. In: Maiti S, Jana S, editors. Polysaccharide carriers for drug delivery. USA: Woodhead Publishing, Elsevier Inc.; 2019. p. 413–41.

[4] He C, Yin C. Trimethyl chitosan based conjugate for oral and intravenous delivery of paclitaxel. Acta Biomater 2017;53:355–66.

[5] Thakor P, Bhavana V, Sharma R, Srivastava S, Singh SB, Mehra NK. Polymer-drug conjugates: recent advances and future perspectives. Drug Discov Today 2020;25(9):1718–26.
[6] Ekladious I, Colson YL, Grinstaff MW. Polymer-drug conjugate therapeutics: advances, insights and prospects. Nat Rev Drug Discov 2019;18(4):273–94.
[7] Tran TTD, Tran PHL. Nanoconjugation and encapsulation strategies for improving drug delivery and therapeutic efficacy of poorly water-soluble drugs. Pharmaceutics 2019;11(7):325.
[8] Lipinski C. Poor aqueous solubility—an industry wide problem in drug discovery. Am Pharm Rev 2002;5:82–5.
[9] Scomparin A, Salmaso S, Bersani S, Satchi-Fainaro R, Caliceti P. Novel folated and non-folated pullulan bioconjugates for anticancer drug delivery. Eur J Pharm Sci 2011;42:547–58.
[10] Patra JK, Das G, Fraceto LF, Campos EVR, Rodriguez-Torres MDP, Acosta-Torres LS, Diaz-Torres LA, Grillo R, Swamy MK, Sharma S, Habtemariam S, Shin HS. Nano based drug delivery systems: recent developments and future prospects. J Nanobiotechnol 2018;16(1):71.
[11] Ljubimova JY, Fujita M, Ljubimov AV, Torchilin VP, Black KL, Holler E. Poly(malic acid) nanoconjugates containing various antibodies and oligonucleotides for multitargeting drug delivery. Nanomedicine 2008;3:247–65.
[12] Theodossiou TA, GonCalves AR, Yannakopoulou K, Skarpen E, Berg K. Photochemical internalization of tamoxifens transported by a "Trojan-horse" nanoconjugate into breast-cancer cell lines. Angew Chem Int Ed Engl 2015;54:4885–9.
[13] Popat A, Karmakar S, Jambhrunkar S, Xu C, Yu C. Curcumin-cyclodextrin encapsulated chitosan nanoconjugates with enhanced solubility and cell cytotoxicity. Colloids Surf B Biointerfaces 2014;117:520–7.
[14] Lemarchand C, Gref R, Couvreur P. Polysaccharide-decorated nanoparticles. Eur J Pharm Biopharm 2004;58:327–41.
[15] Jain A, Gupta Y, Jain SK. Perspectives of biodegradable natural polysaccharides for site specific drug delivery to the colon. J Pharm Pharm Sci 2007;10:86–128.
[16] Valcourt DM, Harris J, Riley RS, Dang M, Wang J, Day ES. Advances in targeted nanotherapeutics: from bioconjugation to biomimicry. Nano Res 2018;11(10):4999–5016.
[17] Hasnain MS, Ahmed SA, Alkahtani S, Milivojevic M, Kandar CC, Dhara AK, Nayak AK. Biopolymers for drug delivery. In: Nayak AK, Hasnain MS, editors. Advanced biopolymeric systems for drug delivery. Switzerland: Springer; 2020. p. 1–29.
[18] Hasnain MS, Nayak AK. Chitosan as responsive polymer for drug delivery applications. In: Makhlouf ASH, Abu-Thabit NY, editors. Stimuli responsive polymeric nanocarriers for drug delivery applications, volume 1, types and triggers. Woodhead publishing series in biomaterials. United States: Elsevier Ltd.; 2018. p. 581–605.
[19] Ahmed T, Aljaeid B. Preparation, characterization, and potential application of chitosan, chitosan derivatives, and chitosan metal nanoparticles in pharmaceutical drug delivery. Drug Des Devel Ther 2016;10:483–507.
[20] Younes I, Rinaudo M. Chitin and chitosan preparation from marine sources: structure, properties and applications. Mar Drugs 2015;13:1133–74.
[21] Rodrigues S, Dionísio M, López CR, Grenha A. Biocompatibility of chitosan carriers with application in drug delivery. J Funct Biomater 2012;3(3):615–41.
[22] Rinaudo M. Chitin and chitosan: properties and applications. Prog Polym Sci 2006;31:603–32.
[23] Shen JW, Li J, Zhao Z, Zhang L, Peng G, Liang L. Molecular dynamics study on the mechanism of polynucleotide encapsulation by chitosan. Sci Rep 2017;7:5050.
[24] Cunha RA, Soares TA, Rusu VH, Pontes FJS, Franca EF, Lins RD. The molecular structure and conformational dynamics of chitosan polymers: an integrated perspective from experiments and computational simulations. In: Karunaratne DN, editor. The complex world of polysaccharides. IntechOpen; 2012. https://doi.org/10.5772/51803.

[25] Abd El-Hack ME, El-Saadony MT, Shafi ME, Zabermawi NM, Arif M, Batiha GE, Khafaga AF, Abd El-Hakim YM, Al-Sagheer AA. Antimicrobial and antioxidant properties of chitosan and its derivatives and their applications: a review. Int J Biol Macromol 2020;164:2726–44.
[26] Qin Y, Li P. Antimicrobial chitosan conjugates: current synthetic strategies and potential applications. Int J Mol Sci 2020;21(2):499.
[27] Upadhyay U, Sreedhar I, Singh SA, Patel CM, Anitha KL. Recent advances in heavy metal removal by chitosan based adsorbents. Carbohydr Polym 2021;251:117000.
[28] Kandar CC, Hasnain MS, Nayak AK. Natural polymers as useful pharmaceutical excipients. In: Nayak AK, Pal K, Banerjee I, Maji S, Nanda U, editors. Advances and challenges in pharmaceutical technology: materials, process development and drug delivery strategies. USA: Academic Press, Elsevier Inc.; 2021. p. 1–44.
[29] Verma A, Dubey J, Verma N, Nayak AK. Chitosan-hydroxypropyl methylcellulose matrices as carriers for hydrodynamically balanced capsules of moxifloxacin HCl. Curr Drug Deliv 2017;14:83–90.
[30] Ray S, Sinha P, Laha B, Maiti S, Bhattacharyya UK, Nayak AK. Polysorbate 80 coated crosslinked chitosan nanoparticles of ropinirole hydrochloride for brain targeting. J Drug Delivery Sci Technol 2018;48:21–9.
[31] Mansur AA, de Carvalho SM, Mansur HS. Bioengineered quantum dot/chitosan-tripeptide nanoconjugates for targeting the receptors of cancer cells. Int J Biol Macromol 2016;82:780–9.
[32] Jolly R, Khan AA, Ahmed SS, Alam S, Kazmi S, Owais M, Farooqi MA, Shakir M. Bioactive *Phoenix dactylifera* seeds incorporated chitosan/hydroxyapatite nanoconjugate for prospective bone tissue engineering applications: a bio-synergistic approach. Korean J Couns Psychother 2020;109:110554.
[33] Yousefpour P, Atyabi F, Vasheghani-Farahani E, Movahedi AA, Dinarvand R. Targeted delivery of doxorubicin-utilizing chitosan nanoparticles surface-functionalized with anti-Her2 trastuzumab. Int J Nanomedicine 2011;6:1977–90.
[34] Agudelo D, Sanyakamdhorn S, Nafisi S, Tajmir-Riahi HA. Transporting antitumor drug tamoxifen and its metabolites, 4-hydroxytamoxifen and endoxifen by chitosan nanoparticles. PLoS ONE 2013;8, e60250.
[35] Gaware VS, Håkerud M, Juzeniene A, Høgset A, Berg K, Másson M. Endosome targeting meso-tetraphenylchlorin-chitosan nanoconjugates for photochemical internalization. Biomacromolecules 2017;18(4):1108–26.
[36] Nayak AK, Pal D, Santra K. Development of calcium pectinate-tamarind seed polysaccharide mucoadhesive beads containing metformin HCl. Carbohydr Polym 2014;101:220–30.
[37] Munarin F, Tanzi MC, Petrini P. Advances in biomedical applications of pectin gels. Int J Biol Macromol 2012;51(4):681–9.
[38] Nayak AK, Hasnain MS, Pal D. Ionically gelled pectinates in drug delivery. In: Nayak AK, Hasnain MS, Pal D, editors. Ionically gelled biopolysaccharide based systems in drug delivery. Gels horizons: from science to smart materials. Singapore: Springer; 2021. https://doi.org/10.1007/978-981-16-2271-7_1.
[39] Nayak AK, Pal D. Plant-derived polymers: Ionically gelled sustained drug release systems. In: Mishra M, editor. Encyclopedia of biomedical polymers and polymeric biomaterials, vol. VIII. New York: Taylor and Francis; 2016. p. 6002–17.
[40] Nayak AK, Hasnain MS, Pal K, Banerjee I, Pal D. Gum-based hydrogels in drug delivery. In: Pal K, Banerjee I, Sarkar P, Kim D, Deng W-P, Dubey NK, Majumder K, editors. Biopolymer-based formulations, biomedical and food applications. United States: Elsevier Inc.; 2020. p. 605–45.
[41] Verma AK, Sachin K. Novel hydrophilic drug polymer nano-conjugates of cisplatin showing long blood retention profile-its release kinetics, cellular uptake and bio-distribution. Curr Drug Deliv 2008;5:120–6.

[42] Majzoob S, Atyabi F, Dorkoosh F, Kafedjiiski K, Loretz B, Bernkop-Schnurch A. Pectincysteine conjugate: synthesis and in-vitro evaluation of its potential for drug delivery. J Pharm Pharmacol 2006;58:1601–10.
[43] Hussien NA, Isıklan N, Turk M. Pectin-conjugated magnetic graphene oxide nanohybrid as a novel drug carrier for paclitaxel delivery. Artif Cells Nanomed Biotechnol 2018;46(suppl 1):1–10.
[44] Chittasupho C, Jaturanpinyo M, Mangmool S. Pectin nanoparticle enhances cytotoxicity of methotrexate against hepG2 cells. Drug Deliv 2013;20:1–9.
[45] Cheng M, Xie P, Tang X, Zhang J, Xie Y, Zheng K, He J. Preparation and lymphatic targeting research of targeting antitumor drug: pectin-adriamycin conjugates. J Biomed Eng 2009;26:569–74.
[46] Dev RK, Bali V, Pathak K. Novel microbially triggered colon specific delivery system of 5-fluorouracil: statistical optimization, in vitro, in vivo, cytotoxic and stability assessment. Int J Pharm 2011;411:142–51.
[47] Varshosaz J. Dextran conjugates in drug delivery. Expert Opin Drug Deliv 2012;9(5):509–23.
[48] Hu Q, Lu Y, Luo Y. Recent advances in dextran-based drug delivery systems: from fabrication strategies to applications. Carbohydr Polym 2021;264:117999.
[49] Huang S, Huang G. The dextrans as vehicles for gene and drug delivery. Future Med Chem 2019;11(13):1659–67.
[50] Dang W, Colvin HB, Saltzman WM. Covalent coupling of methotrexate to dextran enhances the penetration of cytotoxicity into a tissue-like matrix. Cancer Res 1994;54:1729–35.
[51] Vandamme TF, Lenourry C, Charreau M, Chaumeil JC. The use of polysaccharides to target drugs to the colon. Carbohydr Polym 2002;48:219–31.
[52] Lee JS, Jung YJ, Doh M, Kim YM. Synthesis and properties of dextran-nalidixic acid ester as a colonspecific prodrug of nalidixic acid. Drug Dev Ind Pharm 2001;27:331–6.
[53] Abeylath SC, Amiji MM. 'Click' synthesis of dextran macrostructures for combinatorial- designed self-assembled nanoparticles encapsulating diverse anticancer therapeutics. Bioorg Med Chem 2011;19:6167–73.
[54] Abioye A, Kola-Mustapha A. Controlled electrostatic self-assembly of ibuprofen-cationic dextran nanoconjugates prepared by low energy green process—a novel delivery tool for poorly soluble drugs. Pharm Res 2015;32:2110–31.
[55] Uekama K, Hirayama F, Irie T. Cyclodextrin drug carrier systems. Chem Rev 1998;98(5):2045–76.
[56] Luzardo-Alvarez A, Sobarzo-Sánchez E, Blanco-Méndez J, Otero-Espinar FJ. Cyclodextrin-based polysaccharidic polymers: an approach for the drug delivery. Curr Top Med Chem 2014;14(4):542–51.
[57] Carneiro SB, Costa Duarte FÍ, Heimfarth L, Siqueira Quintans JS, Quintans-Júnior LJ, VFD VJ, Neves de Lima ÁA. Cyclodextrin-drug inclusion complexes: in vivo and in vitro approaches. Int J Mol Sci 2019;20(3):642.
[58] Rajewski RA, Traiger G, Bresnahan J, Jaberaboansari P, Stella VJ, Thompson DO. Preliminary safety evaluation of parenterally administered sulfoalkyl ether beta-cyclodextrin derivatives. J Pharm Sci 1995;84(8):927–32.
[59] Szente L, Singhal A, Domokos A, Song B. Cyclodextrins: assessing the impact of cavity size, occupancy, and substitutions on cytotoxicity and cholesterol homeostasis. Molecules 2018;23(5):1228.
[60] Loftsson T, Masson M. Cyclodextrins in topical drug formulations: theory and practice. Int J Pharm 2001;225(1–2):15–30.
[61] Schwarz DH, Engelke A, Wenz G. Solubilizing steroidal drugs by β-cyclodextrin derivatives. Int J Pharm 2017;531(2):559–67.
[62] Denadai AML, Santoro MM, Lopes MTP. A supramolecular complex between proteinases and beta-cyclodextrin that preserves enzymatic activity. BioDrugs 2006;20:283–91.

[63] Li F, Zhou X, Zhou H, Jia J, Li L, Zhai S, Yan B. Reducing both Pgp overexpression and drug efflux with anti-cancer gold-paclitaxel nanoconjugates. PLoS One 2016;11, e0160042.
[64] Solanki A, Sanghvi S, Devkar R. Thakore S β-Cyclodextrin based magnetic nanoconjugates for targeted drug delivery in cancer therapy. RSC Adv 2016;6:98693–707.
[65] Bayer IS. Hyaluronic acid and controlled release: a review. Molecules 2020;25(11):2649.
[66] Toole BP. Hyaluronan: from extracellular glue to pericellular cue. Nat Rev Cancer 2004;4:528–39.
[67] Burdick JA, Prestwich GD. Hyaluronic acid hydrogels for biomedical applications. Adv Mater 2011;23(12):H41–56.
[68] Zhang L, Zhang N. How nanotechnology can enhance docetaxel therapy. Int J Nanomedicine 2013;8:2927–41.
[69] Kemper EM, Van Zandbergen AE, Cleypool C, Mos HA, Boogerd W, Beijnen JH. Increased penetration of paclitaxel into the brain by inhibition of P-glycoprotein. Clin Cancer Res 2003;9:2849–55.
[70] Coradini D, Pellizzaro C, Miglierini G, Daidone MG, Perbellini A. Hyaluronic acid as drug delivery for sodium butyrate: improvement of the anti-proliferative activity on a breast-cancer cell line. Int J Cancer 1999;81:411–6.
[71] Ling X, Zhao C, Huang L, Wang Q, Tu J, Shena Y, Sun C. Synthesis and characterization of hyaluronic acid-platinum (IV) nanoconjugate with enhanced antitumor response and reduced adverse effects. RSC Adv 2015;5:81668–81.
[72] Chen Z, Li Z, Lin Y, Yin M, Ren J, Qu X. Bioresponsive hyaluronic acid-capped mesoporous silica nanoparticles for targeted drug delivery. Chem 2013;19:1778–83.
[73] Arjama M, Mehnath S, Rajan M, Jeyaraj M. Engineered hyaluronic acid-based smart nanoconjugates for enhanced intracellular drug delivery. J Pharm Sci 2021. https://doi.org/10.1016/j.xphs.2021.10.005.
[74] Singh RS, Kaur N, Kennedy JF. Pullulan and pullulan derivatives as promising biomolecules for drug and gene targeting. Carbohydr Polym 2015;123:190–207.
[75] Singh RS, Kaur N, Rana V, Kennedy JF. Pullulan: a novel molecule for biomedical applications. Carbohydr Polym 2017;171:102–21.
[76] Su T, Zhao W, Wu L, Dong W, Qi X. Facile fabrication of functional hydrogels consisting of pullulan and polydopamine fibers for drug delivery. Int J Biol Macromol 2020;163:366–74.
[77] Ding Y, Jiang F, Chen L, Lyu W, Chi Z, Liu C, Chi Z. An alternative hard capsule prepared with the high molecular weight pullulan and gellan: processing, characterization, and in vitro drug release. Carbohydr Polym 2020;237:116172.
[78] Rekha MP, Sharm CP. Hemocompatible pullulan-polyethyleneimine conjugates for liver cell gene delivery: in vitro evaluation of cellular uptake, intracellular trafficking and transfection efficiency. Acta Biomater 2011;7:370–9.
[79] Na K, Park KM, Jo EA, Lee KS. Self organized pullulan/deoxycholic acid nanogel: physicochemial characterization and anticancer drug release behavior. Biotechnol Bioeng 2006;11:262–7.
[80] Rekha MR, Pal K, Bala P, Shetty M, Mittra I, Bhuvaneshwar GS, Sharma CP. Pullulan-histone antibody nanoconjugates for the removal of chromatin fragments from systemic circulation. Biomaterials 2013;34:6328–38.
[81] Amhare AF, Lei J, Deng H, Lv Y, Han J, Zhang L. Biomedical application of chondroitin sulfate with nanoparticles in drug delivery systems: systematic review. J Drug Target 2021;29(3):259–68.
[82] Pal D, Nayak AK, Saha S, Hasnain MS. Pharmaceutical applications of chondroitin. In: Nayak AK, Hasnain MS, Pal D, editors. Natural polymers for pharmaceutical applications, vol. III: animal derived polymers. USA: Apple Academic Press; 2019. p. 117–32.
[83] Zhao L, Liu M, Wang J, Zhai G. Chondroitin sulfate-based nanocarriers for drug/gene delivery. Carbohydr Polym 2015;133:391–9.

[84] Park W, Park SJ, Na K. Potential of self-organizing nanogel with acetylated chondroitin sulfate as an anti-cancer drug carrier. Colloids Surf B Biointerfaces 2010;79:501–8.
[85] Jeong D, Na K. Chondroitin sulfate based nanocomplex for enhancing the stability and activity of anthocyanin. Carbohydr Polym 2012;90(1):507–15.
[86] Wang J, Zhao W, Chen H, Qin A, Zhu P. Anti-tumor study of chondroitin sulfate-methotrexate nanogels. Nanoscale Res Lett 2007;12:572.
[87] Li F, Na K. Self-assembled chlorin e6 conjugated chondroitin sulfate nanodrug for photodynamic therapy. Biomacromolecules 2011;12:1724–30.
[88] Onishi H, Isoda Y, Matsuyama M. In vivo evaluation of chondroitin sulfate-glycyl-prednisolone for anti-arthritic effectiveness and pharmacokinetic characteristics. Int J Pharm 2013;456:113–20.
[89] Yu C, Gao C, Lu S, Chen C, Huang Y, Liu M. Redox-responsive shell-sheddable micelles self-assembled from amphiphilic chondroitin sulfate-cholesterol conjugates for triggered intracellular drug release. Chem Eng J 2013;228:290–9.
[90] He C, Ji H, Qian Y, Wang Q, Liu X, Zhao W, Zhao C. Heparin-based and heparin-inspired hydrogels: size-effect, gelation and biomedical applications. J Mater Chem B 2019;7(8):1186–208.
[91] Rodriguez-Torres MDP, Acosta-Torres LS, Diaz-Torres LA. Heparin-based nanoparticles: an overview of their applications. J Nanomater 2018;2018:9780489.
[92] Linhardt RJ, Dordick JS, Deangelis PL, Liu J. Enzymatic synthesis of glycosaminoglycan heparin. Semin Thromb Hemost 2007;33(5):453–65.
[93] Laremore TN, Zhang F, Dordick JS, Liu J, Linhardt RJ. Recent progress and applications in glycosaminoglycan and heparin research. Curr Opin Chem Biol 2009;13(5–6):633–40.
[94] van Veen JJ, Maclean RM, Hampton KK, Laidlaw S, Kitchen S, Toth P, Makris M. Protamine reversal of low molecular weight heparin: clinically effective? Blood Coagul Fibrinolysis 2011;22:565–70.
[95] Wang X, Li J, Wang Y, Cho KJ, Kim G, Gjyrezi A, Koenig L, Giannakakou P, Shin HJC, Tighiouart M, Nie S. HFT-T, a targeting nanoparticle, enhances specific delivery of paclitaxel to folate receptor-positive tumors. ACS Nano 2009;3:3165–74.
[96] Park K, Lee GY, Kim YS, Yu M, Park RW, Kim IS, Kim SY, Byun Y. Heparin-deoxycholic acid chemical conjugate as an anticancer drug carrier and its antitumor activity. J Control Release 2006;114:300–6.
[97] Zhang T, Xiong H, Dahmani FZ, Sun L, Li Y, Yao L, Zhou J, Yao J. Combination chemotherapy of doxorubicin, all-trans retinoic acid and low molecular weight heparin based on self-assembled multi-functional polymeric nanoparticles. Nanotechnology 2015;26:145101.
[98] Khaliq NU, Sandra FC, Park DY, Lee JY, Oh KS, Kim D, Byun Y, Kim IS, Kwon IC, Kim SY, Yuk SH. Doxorubicin/heparin composite nanoparticles for caspase-activated prodrug chemotherapy. Biomaterials 2016;101:131–42.
[99] Shayegh A, Khalatbari F, Zonoubi N, Zarazvand F, Monavvari F, Hejazinia H, Ebrahimi SES, Hamedani MP, Ali V, Hadadian S, Farzaneh J, Seyedhamzeh M, Ardestani MS. Chlorambucil-chitosan nano-conjugate: an efficient agent against breast cancer targeted therapy. Curr Drug Deliv 2021;18(6):721–8.
[100] Tsai SW, Yu DS, Tsao SW, Hsu FY. Hyaluronan-cisplatin conjugate nanoparticles embedded in Eudragit S100-coated pectin/alginate microbeads for colon drug delivery. Int J Nanomedicine 2013;8:2399–407.
[101] Abioye A, Naqvi M, Pattni D, Adepoju-Bello AA. Non-intuitive behavior of polymer-ciprofloxacin nanoconjugate suspensions: a tool for flexible oral drug delivery. AAPS PharmSciTech 2021;22(7):229.
[102] Kola-Mustapha AT, Armitage D, Abioye AO. Development of aqueous ternary nanomatrix films: a novel 'green' strategy for the delivery of poorly soluble drugs. Int J Pharm 2016;515(1–2):616–31.

[103] Das M, Solanki A, Joshi A, Devkar R, Seshadri S, Thakore S. β-Cyclodextrin based dual-responsive multifunctional nanotheranostics for cancer cell targeting and dual drug delivery. Carbohydr Polym 2019;206:694–705.
[104] Krishnan P, Rajan M, Kumari S, Sakinah S, Priya SP, Amira F, Danjuma L, Pooi Ling M, Fakurazi S, Arulselvan P, Higuchi A, Arumugam R, Alarfaj AA, Munusamy MA, Hamat RA, Benelli G, Murugan K, Kumar SS. Efficiency of newly formulated camptothecin with β-cyclodextrin-EDTA-Fe_3O_4 nanoparticle-conjugated nanocarriers as an anti-colon cancer (HT29) drug. Sci Rep 2017;7(1):10962.
[105] Lingwood D, Ballantyne JS. Alkaline phosphatase-immunoglobulin conjugate binds to lipids *in vitro*, independent of antibody selectivity. J Immunol Methods 2006;311:174–7.
[106] Carter PJ. Potent antibody therapeutics by design. Nat Rev Immunol 2006;6:343–57.
[107] Schrama D, Reisfeld RJ, Becker JC. Antibody targeted drugs as cancer therapeutics. Nat Rev Drug Discov 2006;5:147–59.
[108] Smaglo BG, Aldeghaither D, Weiner LM. The development of immunoconjugates for targeted cancer therapy. Nat Rev Clin Oncol 2014;11:637–48.
[109] Sau S, Alsaab HO, Kashaw SK, Tatiparti K, Iyer AK. Advances in antibody-drug conjugates: a new era of targeted cancer therapy. Drug Discov Today 2017;22:1547–56.
[110] Sugahara S, Okuno S, Yano T, Hamana H, Inoue K. Characteristics of tissue distribution of various polysaccharides as drug carriers: influences of molecular weight and anionic charge on tumor targeting. Biol Pharm Bull 2001;24:535–43.
[112] McNamara 2nd JO, Andrechek ER, Wang Y, Viles KD, Rempel RE, Gilboa E, Sullenger BA, Giangrande PH. Cell type-specific delivery of siRNAs with aptamer-siRNA chimeras. Nat Biotechnol 2006;24(8):1005–15.

CHAPTER

11

Functionalized chitosan in drug delivery

Zahra Shariatinia

Department of Chemistry, Amirkabir University of Technology (Tehran Polytechnic), Tehran, Iran

1 Introduction

Rapid development in the pharmaceutical industry has led to the appearance of numerous targeted, controlled, and stimulus-responsive drug delivery systems that have been achieved to meet clinical requirements [1–5]. For this purpose, diverse drug carriers have been introduced like viruses, polymers, liposomes, peptides, and proteins. Among these materials, natural polymeric hydrogels such as those prepared using alginate, agarose, chitosan (CS), hyaluronic acid, fibrin, and collagen are more attractive because they have shown excellent properties, including good hydrophilicity, biodegradability, colloidal stability, flexible and tunable structures, biocompatibility, facile cellular uptake, resemblance to the natural extracellular matrix, versatile fabrication methods, as well as appropriate physical properties, that are advantageous for the living tissues [6–9].

Advances achieved in the technology of drug nano- and microcarriers have led to obtaining multifunctional compounds that are effective for cancer diagnosis, therapy, as well as treatment monitoring [10–17]. Several benefits of these carriers include bioavailability, particularly for hydrophobic drugs, cell-targeted drug delivery (to decrease the therapeutic dose of the drug), higher mucosal delivery which declines first-pass metabolism, less toxicity of drugs, controlled time in drug transport (stimulus-responsive, pulsatile, sustained, or slow drug release rate), as well as the capability to simultaneously use imaging agents and drugs in one carrier [8,18–22]. In spite of these advantages, there are some challenging issues like cost, security, and scalability that hinder the utilization of such drug carriers in clinics [16,23–26].

Tailor-Made Polysaccharides in Drug Delivery
https://doi.org/10.1016/B978-0-12-821286-8.00001-X

Natural polymers such as polysaccharides, lipoproteins, proteins, and peptides are pharmaceutically significant materials that are widely used to achieve desirable drug delivery vehicles [27–31]. Such polymers can be prepared from renewable resources, i.e., animals and plants, which have much lower immunogenicity and toxicity compared to those of synthetic polymers [32,33]. The physicochemical features of natural polymers including viscoelasticity, dissolution, swelling, hydrophilicity, and biodegradability can be changed by enzymes, pH, ion concentration, temperature, and electrochemical potential, and this can be exploited to design smart drug carriers [3,34–36]. Also, polysaccharides are largely applied as drug delivery systems as they are able to participate in numerous enzymatic and chemical reactions to form novel biomacromolecules.

Natural polymers can be conjugated and functionalized using various substances to obtain suitable materials indicating particular characteristics that are anticipated for the designed drug delivery formulations [37–39]. Most of these bioconjugates exhibit stimulated release, higher stability and solubility, improved mechanical strength, biodegradability, in vivo targeting, and biocompatibility [7,9].

Although chitosan is extensively utilized to enhance permeation in oral drug delivery and reveals exceptional properties, it is not soluble in pure water and is only soluble within acidic solutions like dilute acetic acid and hydrochloric acid solutions [40–42]. Also, it has other drawbacks including low improvement in drugs' bioavailability plus incapability to create micelles. Therefore, various chitosan derivatives have been prepared so far to find materials with enhanced solubility, including quaternized CS, hydroxypropyl CS, and carboxymethyl CS [43]. Furthermore, CS has been chemically functionalized and modified using diverse functional groups to improve its dispersion, binding affinity to metal ions, chemical stability, and selectivity.

Herein, the most important efforts carried out on CS functionalization using polymers, organic molecules, amino acids, peptides, drugs/medication, aptamers, and contrast agents (used in imaging diagnosis) and application of these novel materials as drug delivery platforms are investigated.

2 Functionalized chitosan derivatives as drug delivery systems

It is known that 70% of drug candidates newly introduced and 40% of medications in the pipeline have low water solubilities and this issue delays their clinical applications [44]. Consequently, it is required to develop efficient delivery systems for such drugs. The important problem that is necessary to be solved is enhancing the bioavailability of these poorly water-soluble medicines. There are four steps for the drug transport from the intestinal tract into the circulatory system: (i) dispersion or dissolution inside the intestinal tract, (ii) passage through the intestinal membrane, (iii) entrance to the blood through a vein portal, and (iv) undergoing metabolism in the presence of CYP enzymes and entrance to the blood circulatory system and promoting the therapeutic influences, which is called first-pass effect [45]. Therefore, an effective method to boost the bioavailability of drugs with poor water solubility is the enhancement of the drug performance in one or more steps mentioned previously using drug carriers.

Pectin and chitosan (PEC and CS) can be utilized to design novel biopolymers and bioconjugates. PEC is mainly obtained using skins of citrus fruits that contain D-galacturonic acid repeating units that are suitable for its conjugation with other materials/polymers [46]. PEC is a negatively charged lyophilic colloid that can be stabilized through hydration. The gelling ability of PEC is an important feature that is changed by its esterification degree [47]. Recently, some PEC/CS were synthesized using the dicyclohexylcarbodiimide chemical cross-linker [48]. In fact, carboxyl groups in PEC were conjugated to amino groups on the CS chains to afford *N*-hydroxysuccinimide ester. The PEC/CS conjugate showed an amorphous structure that was not cytotoxic and was more thermostable compared to those of its constituent polymers. Hence, it could be used as a suitable drug delivery vehicle.

A magnetic CS nanobiocatalyst was synthesized using starch oxide to covalently cross-link the CS chains together (Fig. 1) that was then applied in the A^3 coupling catalytic reaction [49]. Then, the aldehyde functional groups were bound to the amino groups in the cysteine structure and Schiff bases were achieved within the cross-linked biopolymer. Next, to avoid the probable hydrolysis of imine bonds, they were then reduced. To obtain the magnetic hybrid nanocomposite, iron oxide nanoparticles were added to the system. Finally, Ag^+ cations were immobilized onto the nanobiocatalyst containing carboxylate and thiol groups that originated from the cysteine amino acid. Various propargylamine compounds were synthesized with excellent to good yields in short reaction periods.

Hybrid superparamagnetic cluster bombs of poly(ethylene glycol), PEG, with CS loaded with doxorubicin, DOX, and drug were developed as tumor-targeted theranostics by the DOX delivery detected using the magnetic resonance imaging [50]. They were simply prepared using co-precipitation of PEG/CS, oleylamine-capped Fe_3O_4 nanoparticles, OA/Fe_3O_4, as well as DOX. The DOX/OA-Fe_3O_4@CS-PEG cluster bombs revealed smaller particle size (~ 80 nm) compared to that of the DOX/CS-PEG nanoparticles (~ 300 nm), large drug loading capacity (24.3%), and saturation magnetization (4.11 emu g^{-1}). Fig. 2 presents the in vitro controlled drug release from the hybrid DOX/OA-Fe_3O_4@CS-PEG cluster bomb and DOX@CS-PEG microspheres in diverse environments. The

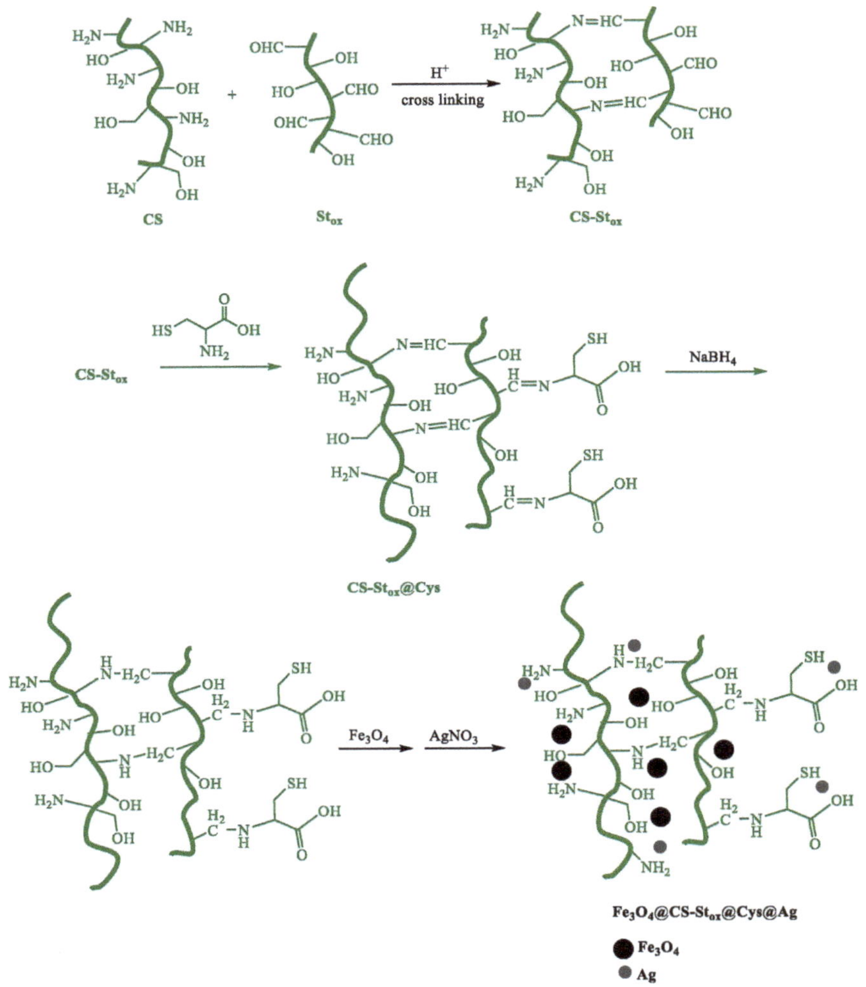

FIG. 1 Preparation of Fe_3O_4@CS-StOX@Cys@Ag^+ nanocomposite. *Reprinted with permission from Rafiee F, Rezaie Karder F. Bio-crosslinking of chitosan with oxidized starch, its functionalization with amino acid and magnetization: as a green magnetic support for silver immobilization and its catalytic activity investigation. Int J Biol Macromol 2020; 146: 1124–1132.*

OA/Fe_3O_4@CS-PEG clusters displayed outstanding in vitro cytocompatibility, but the DOX/OA/Fe_3O_4@CS-PEG clusters were taken up to the HepG2 cells and delivered the DOX drug to the nuclei of cells with improved anticancer efficiency than the native DOX; see Fig. 3. The stimulus-sensitive cluster bombs were disassembled and then self-assembled again to the OA/Fe_3O_4 nanoclusters inside the intracellular

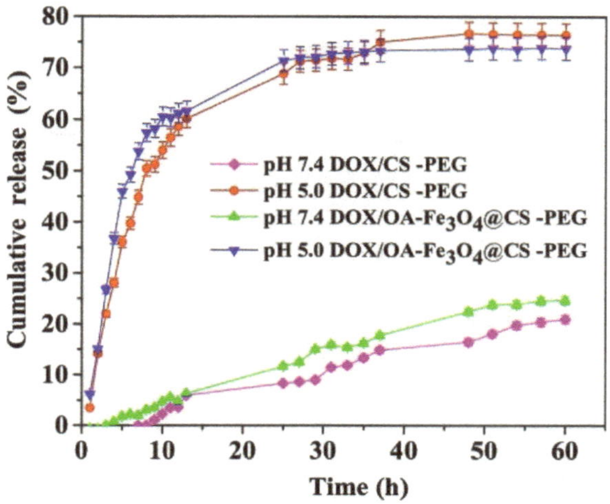

FIG. 2 In vitro controlled release profiles of the DOX/OA-Fe_3O_4@CS-PEG hybrid cluster bombs and the DOX@CS-PEG microspheres at different media. Data are presented as mean ± S.D. (n = 3). *Reprinted with permission from Xie P, Du P, Li J, Liu P. Stimuli-responsive hybrid cluster bombs of PEGylated chitosan encapsulated DOX-loaded superparamagnetic nanoparticles enabling tumor-specific disassembly for on-demand drug delivery and enhanced MR imaging. Carbohydr Polym 2019; 205: 377–384.*

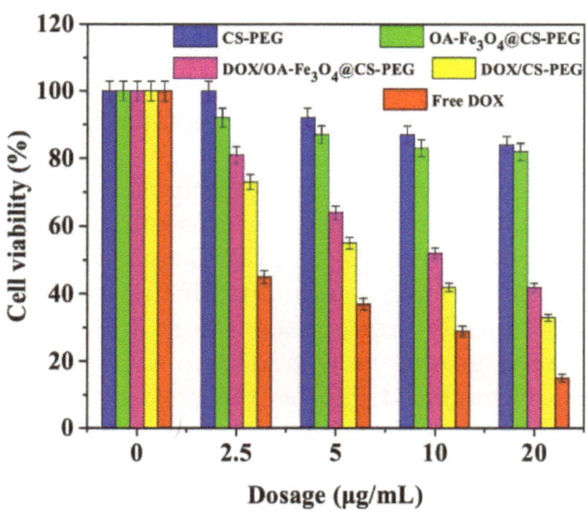

FIG. 3 Cell viability of the CS-PEG, blank OA-Fe_3O_4@CS-PEG hybrid cluster bombs, DOX/OA-Fe_3O_4@CS-PEG hybrid cluster bombs, DOX@CS-PEG microspheres, and free DOX on HepG2 cells after 48 h of incubation. Data are presented as mean ± S.D. (n = 3). *Reprinted with permission from Xie P, Du P, Li J, Liu P. Stimuli-responsive hybrid cluster bombs of PEGylated chitosan encapsulated DOX-loaded superparamagnetic nanoparticles enabling tumor-specific disassembly for on-demand drug delivery and enhanced MR imaging. Carbohydr Polym 2019; 205: 377–384.*

tumor microenvironment with greater saturation magnetization required for the diagnosis by the magnetic resonance imaging because of the tumor-specific release of DOX in addition to the PEG/CS dissolution.

A copolymer of gallic acid/CS/D-α-tocopherol polyethylene glycol 1000 succinate, called GA-CS-TPGS, was prepared (Fig. 4) to construct the paclitaxel, PTX, and micelles that revealed more improved bio-adhesiveness and restricted the P-gp efflux and the drug metabolism within the liver compared to the GA-CS-TPGS [51]. Also, the micelles exhibited higher permeability and solubility that were advantageous for the bioavailability enhancement and the PTX antitumor effect. The PTX micelles altered the pharmacokinetic properties in vivo and the PTX therapeutic activity. The PTX micelles enhanced the PTX bioavailability about 3.80-fold, and a greater antilung tumor effectiveness was perceived for the PTX micelles than the Taxol®. Thus, such micelles enhanced the antitumor efficiency and oral bioavailability of poorly water-soluble medications.

Four CS nanocomposites cross-linked with diverse polyoxalates were achieved to evaluate the release of cisplatin, CDDP, drug in vitro [52]. The reaction of four varied dicarboxylic acids and ethylene glycol, EG, yielded the polyoxalates. The ionic gelation method was employed to encapsulate the CDDP into the CS cross-linked by succinic acid-EG, oxalic acid-EG, tartaric acid-EG, and citric acid-EG. Outstanding drug release kinetics in vitro along with suitable biocompatibility were found for the nanocomposites. The nanocomposites that were not unloaded by the polyoxalates revealed low intrinsic cytotoxicity, but the nanocomposites containing polyoxalates illustrated activities comparable to that of the free CDDP against the MCF-7 cancerous cells. The inhibition of tumor growth by all the CDDP-incorporated nanocomposites was equal to or greater than that of the pristine CDDP.

Some CS hydrogels were fabricated, composed of reactive disulfide bonds to reversibly immobilize thiol functionality; see Fig. 5 [53]. Pure chitosan was chemically conjugated to PEG chains that yielded the hydrogel and then an acryloyl compound, including benzothiazole disulfide group, chemically cross-linked the hydrogel through Michael addition. (CS amine groups were added to the acrylic benzothiazole and the bisacryloyl-modified PEG as the cross-linker.) Several hydrogels were acquired, indicating relatively great gel conversions and containing diverse quantities of benzothiazole disulfide functionality that was thiol-reactive. The UV-Vis spectroscopy was used to determine the amount and presence of reactive disulfide bonds within the hydrogels. A thiol comprising methyl red dye was simply conjugated by the exchange between the thiol and disulfide bonds. The thiol bonds were easily cleaved in the scaffold using dithiothreitol as a disulfide reduction material. Therefore, simple and efficient hydrogels' preparation and reversible/benign thiol immobilization on their chains confirmed

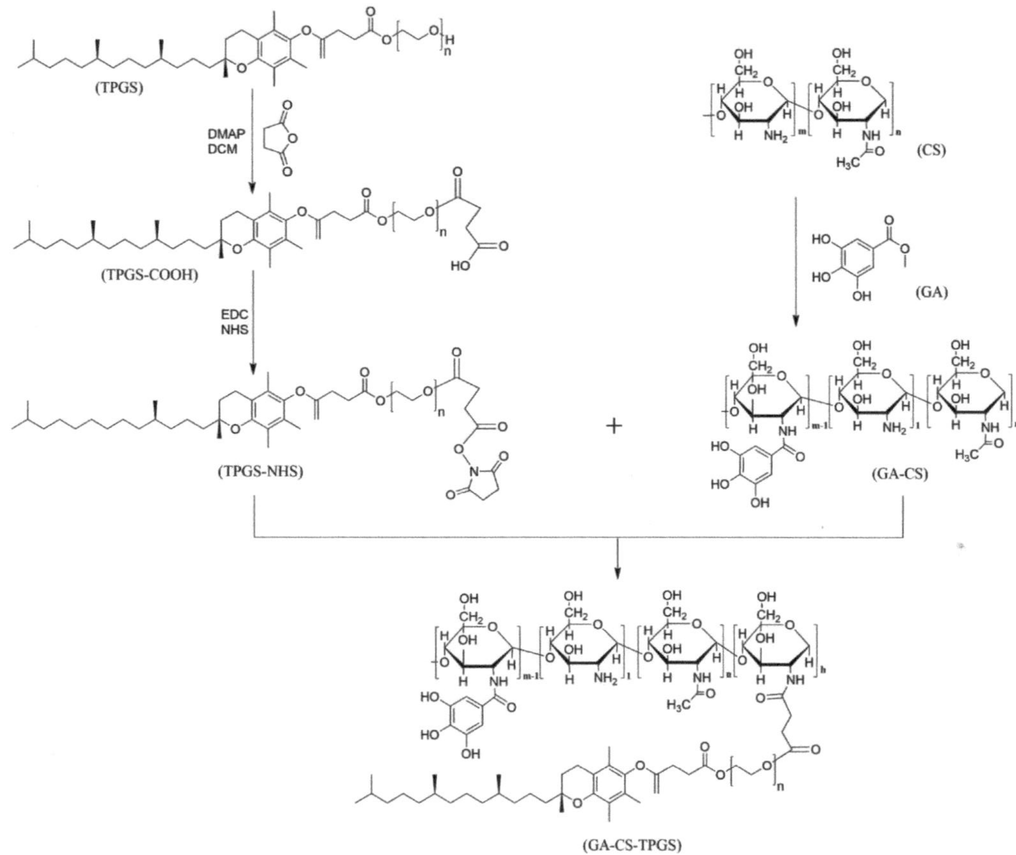

FIG. 4 Synthesis of CS-based GA-CS-TPGS copolymer. *Reprinted with permission from Chen TE, Tu L, Wang G, Qi N, Wu W, Zhang W, Feng J. Multi-functional chitosan polymeric micelles as oral paclitaxel delivery systems for enhanced bioavailability and anti-tumor efficacy. Int J Pharm 2020;578: 119105.*

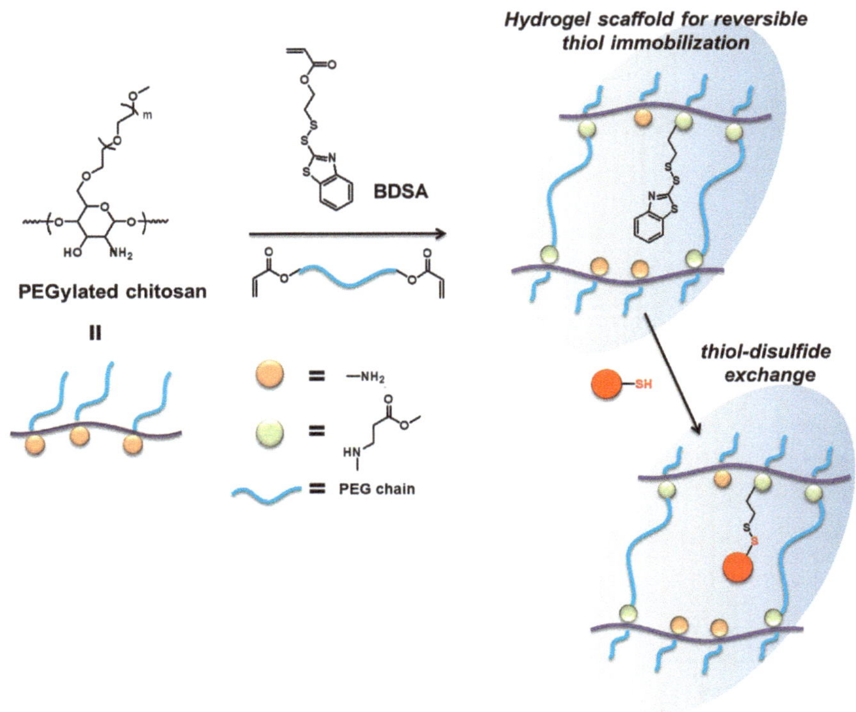

FIG. 5 Formation of hydrogels incorporating thiol-reactive disulfide groups and functionalization of hydrogels by thiol-disulfide exchange reaction (BDSA = benzothiazole disulfide-based acrylic compound). *Reprinted with permission from Arslan M. Fabrication and reversible disulfide functionalization of PEGylated chitosan-based hydrogels: platforms for selective immobilization and release of thiol-containing molecules. Eur Polym J 2020; 126: 109543.*

that such scaffolds could be utilized as excellent platforms in biomedical fields like bioimmobilization, bioconjugation, tissue engineering, and controlled release of proteins and drugs.

An anisamide-bound *N*-octyl-*N*,*O*-maleoyl-*O*-phosphoryl CS, named a-OMPC, was synthesized that formed amphiphilic micelles with the pH-sensitive release feature and great affinity toward sigma-1 receptor-overexpressed tumors by the PTX release (Fig. 6) [54]. The phosphoryl and maleoyl groups cooperatively affect the pH responsiveness of the drug release by transitioning from hydrophilic to hydrophobic nature within the acidic medium of lysosomes and endosomes. The PTX-incorporated a-OMPC micelles, PTX-aM, could increase the cell uptake by the affinity of anisamide to the sigma-1 receptor that led to the quick release of the drug into the lysosomes and endosomes, which raised the toxicity to the PC-3 cells. The in vivo tests proved that the PTX-aM was

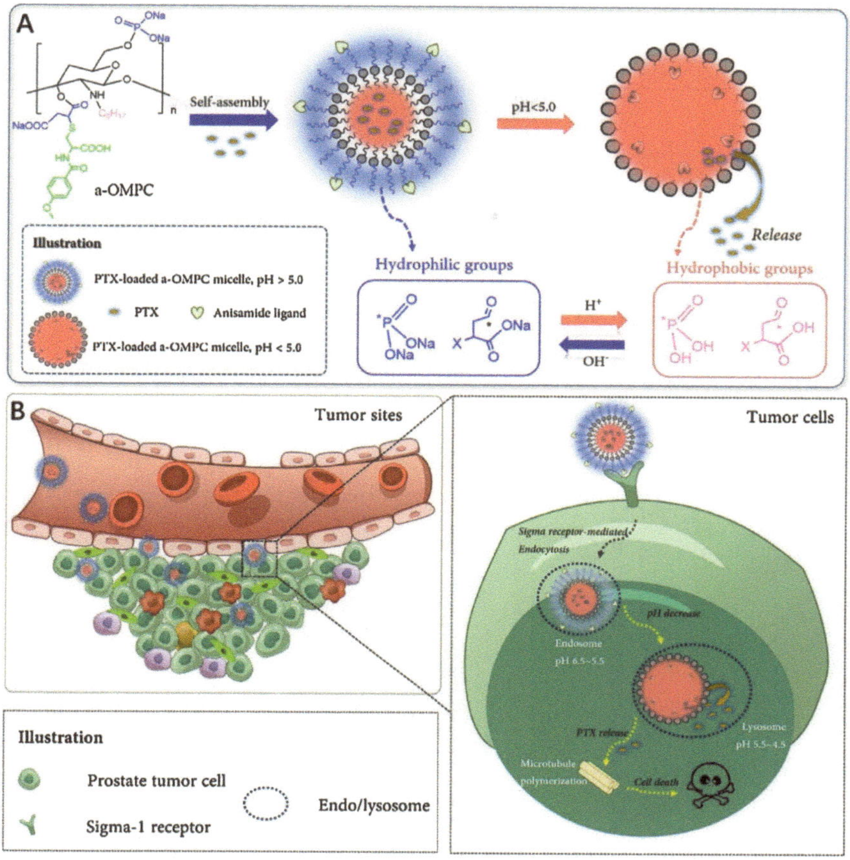

FIG. 6 The pH-responsive amphiphilic CS-based PTX micelles used for sigma-1 receptor-targeted prostate cancer treatment. (A) a-OMPC can self-assemble into hydrophilic PTX-aM loading with PTX in neutral medium, while it can convert from hydrophilic to hydrophobic at pH < 5 due to pH-induced protonation of phosphate and maleate groups, followed by the drug release. (B) PTX-aM can accumulate at the tumor site due to the enhanced permeation and retention effect and then enter the PC-3 cell in a sigma-1 receptor-mediated path. After entrapping by endo-/lysosomes, PTX-aM converts from hydrophilic to hydrophobic due to the acidic milieu, leading to an unstable micellar structure and a fast PTX release, which improves the antitumor efficiency. *Reprinted with permission from Qu D, Jiao M, Lin H, Tian C, Qu G, Xue J, Xue L, Ju C, Zhang C. Anisamide-functionalized pH-responsive amphiphilic chitosan-based paclitaxel micelles for sigma-1 receptor targeted prostate cancer treatment, Carbohydr Polym 2020; 229: 115498.*

highly accumulated in the tumor tissue even 24 h postadministration which caused noticeable inhibition influence and extended survival time for the mice bearing PC-3 tumor xenograft (Fig. 7). Also, the OMPC did not have any apparent acute and hemolytic toxicity, exhibiting that it is a promising material for application as a targeted drug carrier in prostate cancer.

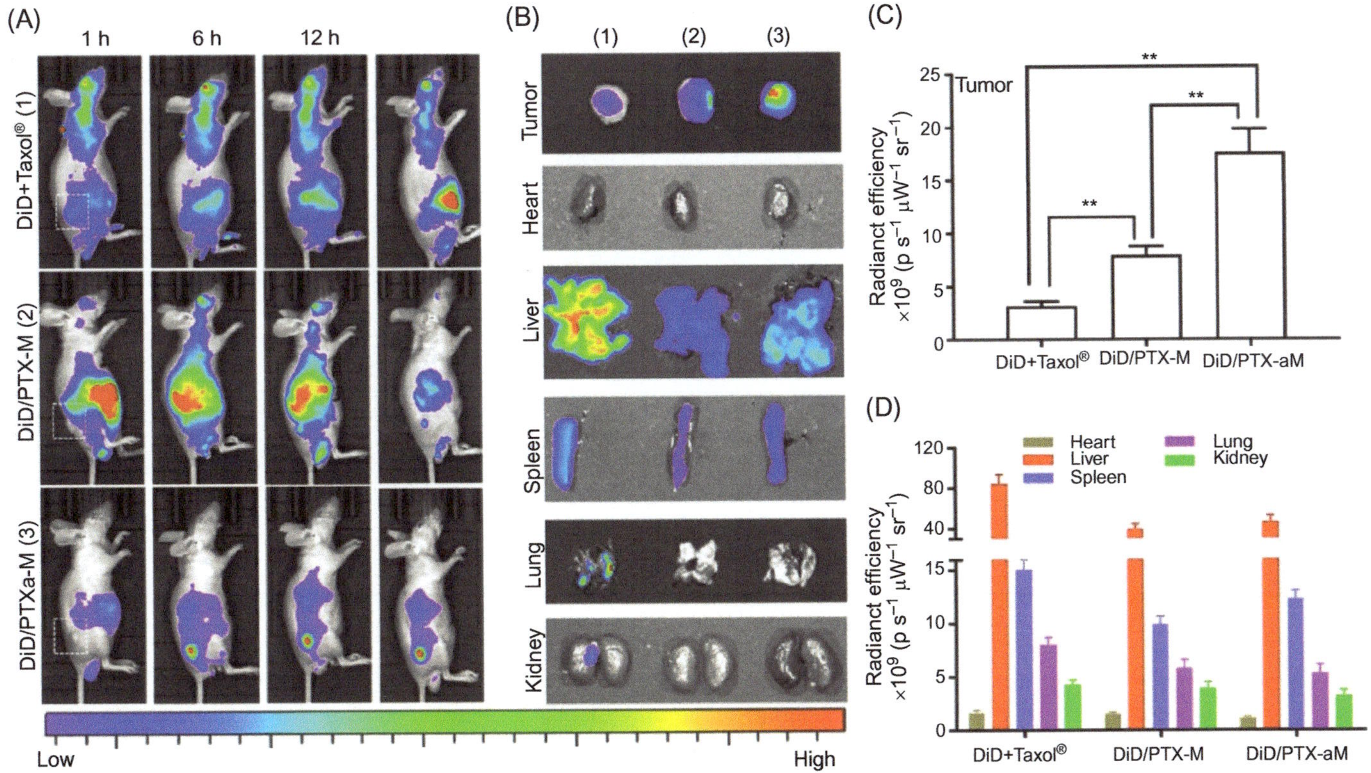

FIG. 7 Investigation of biodistribution. (A) In vivo image of mice treated with various DiD-labeled formulations. (B) Ex vivo image of mice organs after 24-h treatment. (C) Fluorescence intensity of harvested tumors of mice treated with DiD-labeled formulations ($n = 3$). $^{**}P < .01$. (D) Fluorescence intensity of harvested normal organs of mice treated by DiD-labeled formulations ($n = 3$). $^{**}P < .01$; all data are presented as mean ± SD. *Reprinted with permission from Qu D, Jiao M, Lin H, Tian C, Qu G, Xue J, Xue L, Ju C, Zhang C. Anisamide-functionalized pH-responsive amphiphilic chitosan-based paclitaxel micelles for sigma-1 receptor targeted prostate cancer treatment. Carbohydr Polym 2020; 229: 115498.*

Some systems were designed to deliver protein drugs or bioactive substances to damaged tissues to rapidly recover patients [55]. The photo-immobilization technique was utilized for the immobilization of drugs onto the natural polymer because such a method could stabilize growth factors or drugs, which was effective in their sustained release. For this purpose, photo-reactive agents were introduced onto the CS as the natural biocompatible polymer to produce compounds suitable for biomedical applications. Furthermore, the immobilized agent was prepared as micron-sized particles to be used as an injectable compound that could maintain the photo-immobilization stability. When the photo-immobilization was performed on the particles, their exposure to the enzyme within the body was less probable compared to when they were injected into the body without the photo-immobilization. Besides, the photo-immobilized particles could be injected into favorite target sites. Consequently, numerous drugs and growth factors could be used through the photo-immobilization method.

The directly compressed tablets were used as pharmaceutical formulations to deliver drugs using pure CS, CS functionalized with *N*-cinnamyl-substituted *O*-amine, called cinnamyl CS, plus microcrystalline cellulose [56]. Also, acetaminophen was added as the active drug and magnesium stearate (Mg-St) was used as the lubricant within the blend formulations. The control blend contained microcrystalline cellulose, 20wt% acetaminophen, and 0.5wt% Mg-St, which was investigated along with two CS including blends separately fabricated by 20wt% CS and 20wt% cinnamyl CS. All tablets were compacted by a single-punch tablet device. The correlation of compression pressure and tablet hardness was estimated, but the elasticity and plasticity factors were related to the force-displacement plots. The dissolution and disintegration tests were conducted to evaluate the drug carriage capability by the blend formulations. The blends composed of CS and cinnamyl CS revealed appropriate compaction characteristics with great elasticity because they had big particle sizes and showed exceptional dissolution features as they released $> 80\%$ of acetaminophen in 30min. Thus, the cinnamyl CS exhibited good capacity as a costly medicine in directly compressed tablets because of its suitable mechanical strength, improved drug delivery, and greater antioxidative and antibacterial activities compared to the pure CS.

ZnO nanoparticles were functionalized using *N*-succinyl CS and employed as a pH-responsive carrier for the curcumin, CUR, drug [57]. The ZnO nanoparticles were coated with CS through coprecipitation, and then they were chemically modified using succinic anhydride to introduce the –COOH groups that were activated by 1,1′-carbonyldiimidazole to conjugate the CUR. The CUR-conjugated material, CUR-CS-ZnO, showed a spherical morphology and 40nm average size that had very greater water dispersion ability than the free CUR. The CUR release by the carrier was pH responsive that led to the delivery of the drug toward the infected and tumor sites. The Annexin-V FITC/PI and MTT tests proved the greater anticancer potency of CUR-CS-ZnO than that of the free CUR to the MDA-MB-231 breast cancer cells as they induced an apoptotic response without any cytotoxicity to the HEK293 normal cells. Additionally, conjugation of CUR onto the carrier remarkably decreased the MIC by 25–50-folds and MBC values by 10–40-folds against both *Escherichia coli* and *Staphylococcus aureus*, confirming that such formulation was highly suitable as an antimicrobial and anticancer agent.

Several photosensitizers traditionally utilized in photodynamic therapy reveal phototoxic side effects and low targeting to tumors. Stimulus-responsive drug carriers are fabricated to trigger the loaded photosensitizers' release due to their responsiveness to the tumors' acidic microenvironment and intracellular hypoxia by a controlled photoactivity to attain boosted therapeutic activities, as well as minimum side effects [58]. Recently, nitroimidazole-conjugated CS, CS-NA, has been synthesized to prepare nanoparticles of CS-NA complex with rose bengal ω-carboxyheptyl ester that was a rose bengal derivative, RBD, named CS-NA/RBD as a hypoxia and pH double-sensitive delivery system for the RBD [58]. The CS-NA/RBD illustrated ~ 86.9 nm particle size and + 33.4 mV zeta potential, suitable stability in cell culture solution, and higher drug release under hypoxia and acidic conditions (~ 60%) than that measured at neutral pH. The CS-NA/RBD demonstrated > 10 times uptake of nonsmall PC9 lung cancer cells than that of the CS-NA/RB. The reactive oxygen species generation and the antiproliferative activities in the PC9 cells confirmed that the CS-NA/RBD had photodynamic therapeutic properties, reflecting that it was an auspicious nanoplatform for controlled and effective photodynamic cancer treatment.

Multifunctional CS-based nanoparticles, called PY-CS-PLA, were synthesized using CS, cationic L-cysteine, 4-(dimethylamino)pyridine, and polylysine, PL, for the PTX oral delivery (Fig. 8) [59]. The amphiphilic PY-CS-PLA polymer was highly self-assembled to spherical nanoparticles with a 165 nm average size that encapsulated the PTX drug within their hydrophobic cores. The PTX was released in a sustained manner from the modified CS nanoparticles in the pH range of 1.2–7.4. The PY-CS-PLA/PTX efficiently enhanced the PTX uptake by the Caco-2 cells in vitro. The pharmacokinetic tests (Table 1) proved that the PY-CS-PLA/PTX oral bioavailability in rats was 5.63-fold greater than that of the Taxol. Furthermore, the PY-CS-PLA/PTX enhanced the PTX distribution inside the tumor tissue and led to a greater antitumor effect in mice bearing Heps tumor with lower cytotoxicity compared to other prepared systems (Fig. 9). Hence, the PY-CS-PLA/PTX nanomaterial was a favorable vehicle for the hydrophobic antitumor drugs to improve their therapeutic influence and oral bioavailability.

The CS hydrogel was conjugated to L-histidine, HIS, and applied to fabricate a hybrid nanomaterial using ZnO nanoparticles (synthesized

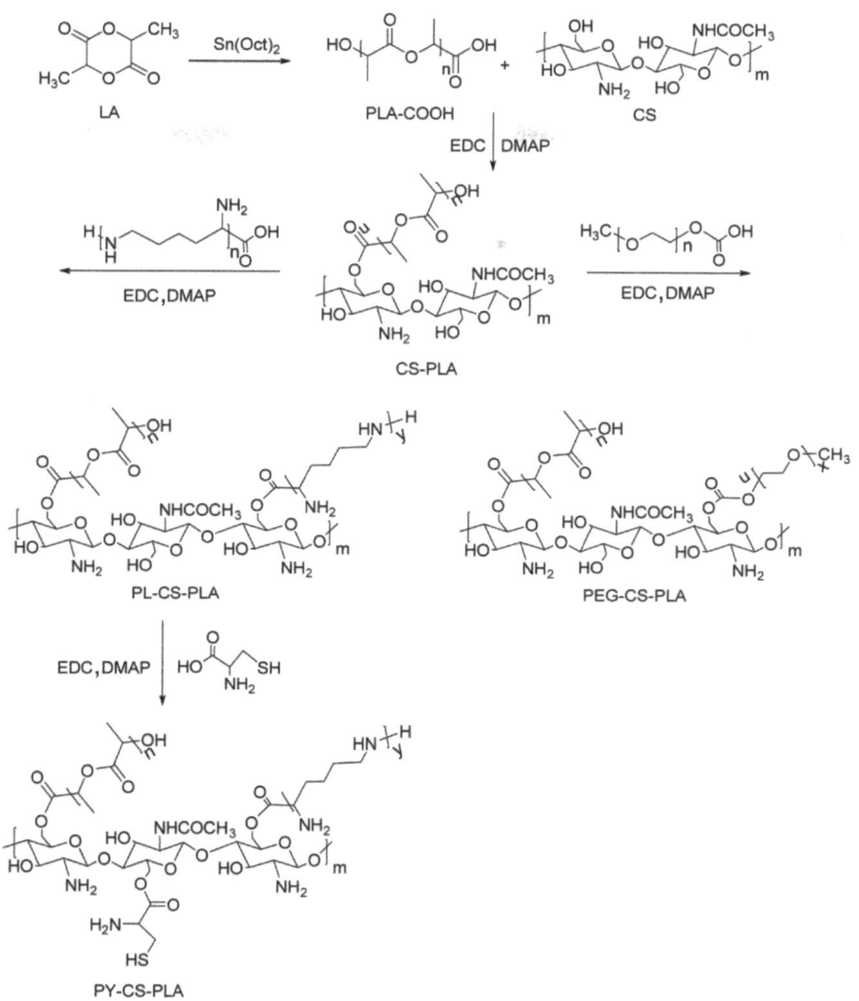

FIG. 8 Synthesis paths of graft copolymers PEG-CS-PLA, PL-CS-PLA, and PY-CS-PLA. *Reprinted with permission from Du X, Yin S, Xu L, Ma J, Yu H, Wang G, Li J, Polylysine and cysteine functionalized chitosan nanoparticle as an efficient platform for oral delivery of paclitaxel. Carbohydr Polym 2020; 229: 115484.*

by the phytochemical method) and dialdehyde cellulose that was employed as a desirable carrier for the polyphenolic drugs, including CUR, quercetin (QE) and naringenin (NRG) [60]. The drug loading efficiencies by the hydrogel were 90.55%, 92.84%, and 89.89%, respectively, for the CUR, QE, and NRG drugs. The optimum drug-loaded carrier revealed the greatest drug release at pH 5. The hydrogel was effectively stabilized

TABLE 1 Pharmacokinetic parameters of PTX in Taxol, PEG-CS-PLA/PTX, PL-CA-PLA/PTX, and PY-CS-PLA/PTX nanoparticles after oral administration in rats (20 mg/kg, mean ± SD, n = 6).

Parameter	Taxol (i.v)[a]	Taxol (p.o)[b]	PEG-CS-PLA/PTX	PL-CA-PLA/PTX	PY-CS-PLA/PTX
$AUC_{0-\infty}$ (μg × h/mL)	5.76 ± 0.43	0.54 ± 0.11	1.37 ± 0.12**	2.27 ± 0.26***	3.04 ± 0.29***
C_{max} (μg/mL)	5.02 ± 0.22	0.11 ± 0.02	0.13 ± 0.03	0.17 ± 0.05	0.22 ± 0.03*
$t_{1/2}$ (h)	1.90 ± 0.32	3.27 ± 0.27	7.69 ± 0.58***	9.48 ± 0.90***	11.26 ± 0.12***
CL (L/h/kg)	1.21 ± 0.12	37.34 ± 2.12	14.56 ± 0.63***	8.81 ± 0.22***	6.58 ± 0.26***
MRT (h)	1.21 ± 0.05	5.11 ± 0.23	11.66 ± 0.88***	14.65 ± 0.79***	15.45 ± 0.83***
F (%)	–	3.28	8.32	13.80	17.47

[a] *i.v = Intravenous injection.*
[b] *p.o = Per os which means oral administration.*
*$P < .05$ vs. Taxol (p.o). **$P < .01$ vs. Taxol (p.o). ***$P < .001$ vs. Taxol (p.o).

by the conjugation of HIS and CS and exhibited sustained release behavior. The drug release mechanism obeyed polymer erosion together with non-Fickian diffusion kinetics. The formulation displayed high antimicrobial activities against *Trichophyton rubrum* and *S. aureus* microorganisms (Table 2). Also, substantial biocompatibility to the L929 cells confirmed that the normal cells could be survived in the presence of the hydrogel. The hybrid system exhibited excellent anticancer activity against A431 cells, which was 15–30-fold greater than that of the pure drugs (Table 3).

The L-cysteine, CYS, was efficiently conjugated to the CS hydrogel by the amidation reaction and then adding ZnO nanoparticles synthesized by the phytochemical method to achieve a nanohybrid delivery vehicle for the NRG drug with improved therapeutic effect [61]. The modified CS was cross-linked through the dialdehyde cellulose that was a green cross-linker obtained from the sugarcane bagasse. The NRG incorporation within the hydrogel was optimized by the Taguchi approach. The hydrogel containing 86.09% NRG was employed for the drug release tests at diverse NRG concentrations and pH values. The highest drug release (72.78%) was acquired at pH 5 using a drug concentration of 1 mg/mL. The conjugation of CYS to the CS enhanced the hydrogel stability and resulted in sustained NRG release. The NRG release happened by polymer erosion accompanied and followed non-Fickian diffusion kinetics. The hydrogel revealed antimicrobial capacity against the *T. rubrum* and *S. aureus* bacteria. The biocompatibility test using the L929 cells proved that the

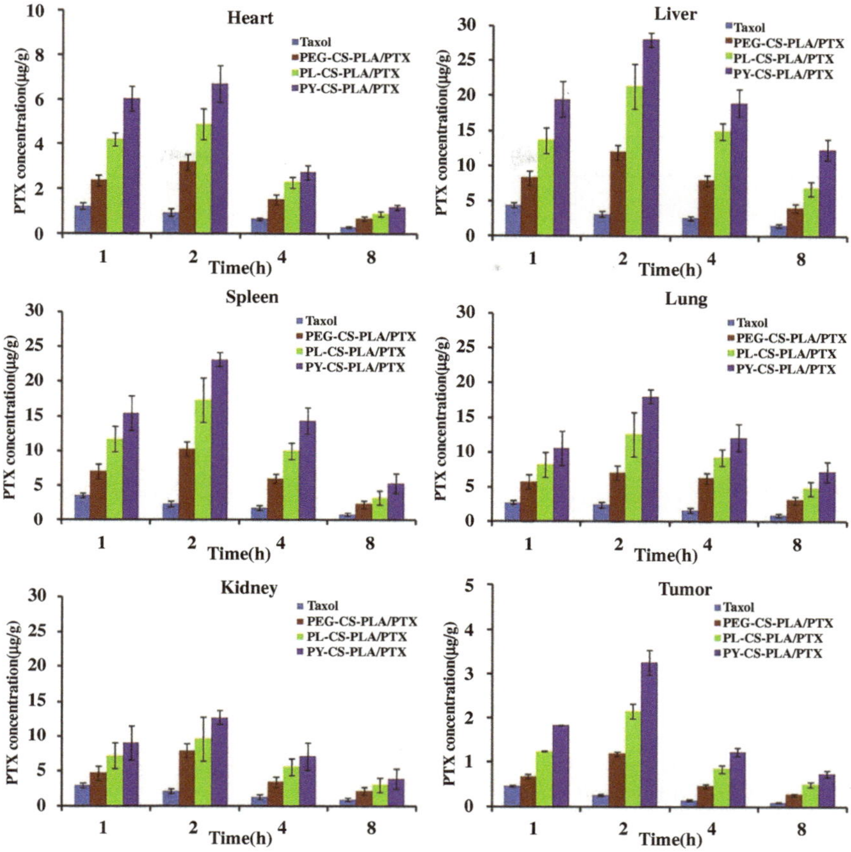

FIG. 9 The PTX biodistribution in Heps tumor-bearing mice after 1, 2, 4, and 8h of oral administration of diverse formulations. Indicated values were mean ± SD (n = 5). *Reprinted with permission from Du X, Yin S, Xu L, Ma J, Yu H, Wang G, Li J. Polylysine and cysteine functionalized chitosan nanoparticle as an efficient platform for oral delivery of paclitaxel. Carbohydr Polym 2020; 229: 115484.*

TABLE 2 The inhibition zones for the hydrogels without/with loaded drugs.

Sample	Antibacterial zone diameter (mm)	Antifungal zone diameter (mm)
CHG	7.20 ± 0.20	5.40 ± 0.30
CHGZ	13.75 ± 1.50	12.00 ± 1.82
HIS-CHGZ	16.00 ± 1.63	14.25 ± 1.89
HIS-CHGZ-QE	20.75 ± 2.06	18.85 ± 0.81
HIS-CHGZ-NRG	17.35 ± 1.60	17.55 ± 1.21
HIS-CHGZ-CUR	22.40 ± 1.91	20.50 ± 1.50

Reprinted with permission from George D, Maheswari PU, Begum KMMS. Chitosan-cellulose hydrogel conjugated with L-histidine and zinc oxide nanoparticles for sustained drug delivery: kinetics and in-vitro biological studies. Carbohydr Polym 2020; 236: 116101.

TABLE 3 IC_{50} concentrations of the samples against A431 human skin carcinoma cells.

Sample	IC_{50} (μg/mL)	Amount of pure drug (μg)
ZNPs	58	–
CHGZ	121	–
HIS	61	–
HIS-CHGZ	52	–
QE	81	40.5
HIS-CHGZ-QE	25	1.33
NRG	83	41.5
HIS-CHGZ-NRG	35	2.57
CUR	23	11.5
HIS-CHGZ-CUR	12	0.80

Reprinted with permission from George D, Maheswari PU, Begum KMMS. Chitosan-cellulose hydrogel conjugated with L-histidine and zinc oxide nanoparticles for sustained drug delivery: kinetics and in-vitro biological studies. Carbohydr Polym 2020; 236: 116101.

hydrogel led to important cell viability. The hydrogel nanohybrid released the NRG and increased the cytotoxicity to A431 human skin cancer cells by twofold than the free NRG.

An ocular carrier was developed using an inclusion complex of hydroxypropyl beta-cyclodextrin, HP-β-CD, modified by a conjugate of CS with *N*-acetyl-L-cysteine, called CS-NAC, which was used to deliver the quercetin hydrophobic drug [62]. The solvent evaporation process was used to achieve the HP-β-CD inclusion complex, and the CS-NAC and HP-β-CD concentrations were optimized through the isolated corneal penetration assessment. The optimized CS-NAC and HP-β-CD concentrations were 0.1 and 20 w/v%, respectively. The CS-NAC/quercetin-HP-β-CD improved the ocular penetration by low ocular irritation and significantly increased the ocular distribution. The CS-NAC/C6-HP-β-CD labeled with coumarin 6, C6, revealed superior fluorescence and was placed deeper in the cornea epithelium than the uncoated material. The CS-NAC/C6-HP-β-CD also transported the drug in the corneal epithelium through intracellular paths but intercellular pathways. Moreover, it delayed the cataract happening for approximately 1 day if administered by the total dosage of quercetin; see Fig. 10. Thus, the HP-β-CD complex modified by the CS-NAC was a green and favorable ocular drug delivery formulation that could improve the corneal penetration and bioavailability of hydrophobic medications such as quercetin.

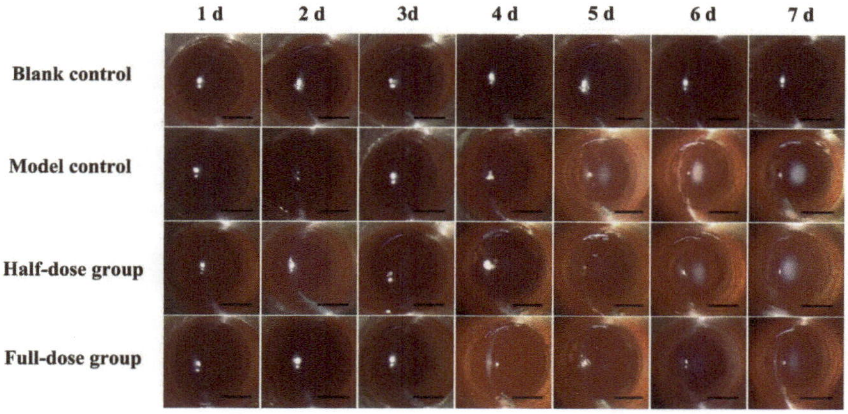

FIG. 10 The slit images of eyes from selenite cataract rats in different groups. (A) Blank control group. (B) Model control group. (C) Half-dose treated group. (D) Full-dose treated group. Scale bar is 2mm. *Reprinted with permission from Lan Q, Di D, Wang S, Zhao Q, Gao Y, Chang D, Jiang T. Chitosan-N-acetylcysteine modified HP-β-CD inclusion complex as a potential ocular delivery system for anti-cataract drug: quercetin. J Drug Delivery Sci Technol 2020; 55: 101407.*

The poly(*N*-isopropylacrylamide)/CS hybrid nanoparticles, NPs, were functionalized by K237 peptide and then encapsulated the PTX anticancer drug to be used as active targeting as well as efficient therapy of human breast carcinoma cells overexpressing KDR/Flk-1 (Figs. 11 and 12) [63]. The NPs functionalized with the peptide exhibited satisfactory temperature and pH sensitivity so that faster drug release was observed at higher temperatures and a little acidic pH in the tumor environment. The K237-functionalized NPs more efficiently inhibited the growth of breast cancer cells compared to their related peptide-free nanoparticles as attested by the MTT assay. The confocal microscopic images displayed that the hybrid nanoparticles exactly targeted the MDA-MB-231 human breast cancer cells that overexpressed the KDR/Flk-1 protein. The boosted effectiveness of the K237-modified nanoparticles to prevent cell proliferation was probably related to the presence of the K237 peptide in the hydrogel that specifically recognized the KDR/Flk-1 existing over the cancer cells. Accordingly, the peptide conjugated hybrid nanoparticles were desirable for application in targeted drug delivery and controlled release of various anticancer pharmaceuticals.

Biopolymer or peptide NPs are widely utilized in encapsulation, targeted transport, and controlled release of drugs, particularly in cancer treatment [64]. Collagen peptide, CP, was employed to prepare CS NPs that revealed stability in physiological environments. Recently, pH-responsive and monodispersed CPCS NPs (~ 100nm) were achieved by the ionic gelation technique through mild facile CP co-precipitation with the CS. The Fourier transform infrared spectra and dynamic light

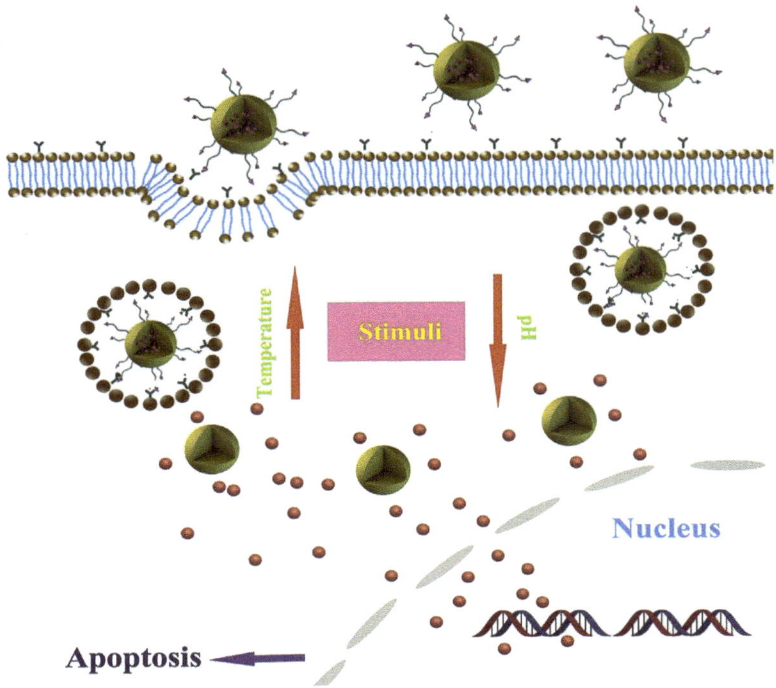

FIG. 11 The strategy underlying the work. *Reprinted with permission from Qian Q, Niu S, Williams GR, Wu J, Zhang X, Zhu L-M. Peptide functionalized dual-responsive chitosan nanoparticles for controlled drug delivery to breast cancer cells, Colloids Surf A Physicochem Eng Asp 2019; 564: 122–130.*

scattering revealed that the electrostatic contacts bond hydrogen formation and were the most significant parameters for the encapsulation of drug and NPs creation, respectively. The scanning electron microscopy images showed that fine and hard CPCS NPs were converted into bigger and soft gel resembling particles by changing the collagen amount. The exceptional polymeric gel NPs displayed great DOX encapsulation plus pH-sensitive drug release. The DOX-encapsulated NPs revealed outstanding antiproliferative features against HeLa cells and satisfactory biocompatibility toward the normal cells; see Fig. 13. Consequently, these NPs were considered smart carriers that could be utilized in clinical cancer treatments.

Some drug carriers were developed for oral mucosa application for the in situ release of biomolecules using CS and poly(lactic-*co*-glycolic acid) (PLGA) biopolymers [65]. These formulations were prepared as nanoparticles to exploit the unique nanomaterials' characteristics and to increase the pharmaceutics' effectiveness. The synthesis of PLGA and CS

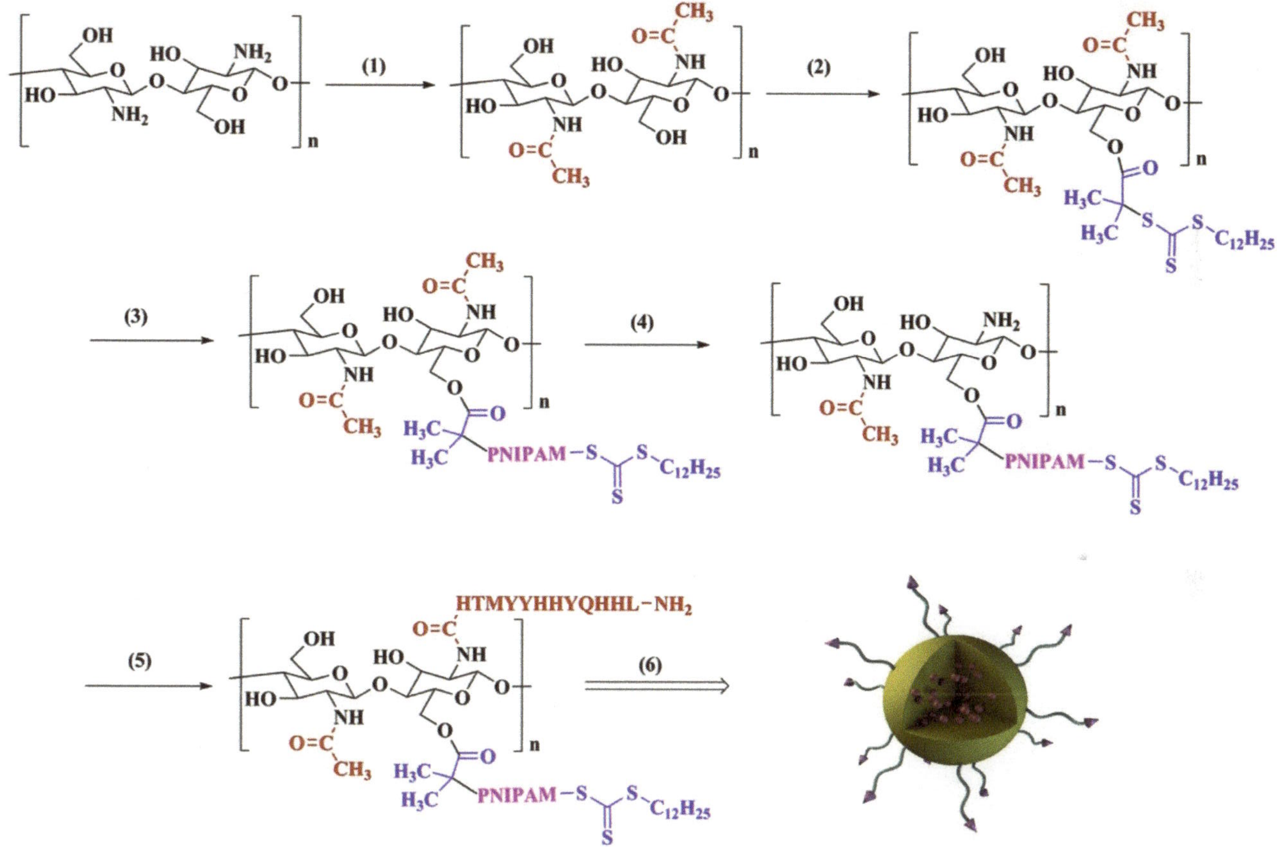

FIG. 12 The synthesis of K237-CS (PTX)-g-PNIPAM NPs. (1) Acetic anhydride, RT, 4h. (2) DDACT, DCC, DMAP, RT, 48h. (3) NIPAM, AIBN, 60°C, 48h. (4) Hydrolysis, RT. (5) K237 peptide, EDC, NHS. (6) PTX, self-assembly. *Reprinted with permission from Qian Q, Niu S, Williams GR, Wu J, Zhang X, Zhu L-M. Peptide functionalized dual-responsive chitosan nanoparticles for controlled drug delivery to breast cancer cells, Colloids Surf A Physicochem Eng Asp 2019; 564: 122–130.*

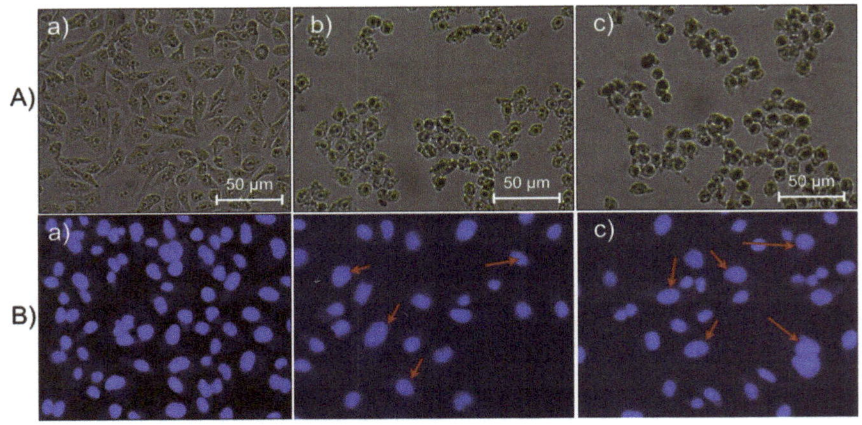

FIG. 13 Microscopic investigation of cytotoxicity of CPCN NPs against HeLa cells. Investigation of morphological changes of cells after addition of DOX-loaded NPs. (A) Optical microscopy images, and (B) fluorescence microscopy images of cells stained with DAPI. (a) Control and (b and c) NP-treated cells at 1.0 and 2.0 µg/mL, respectively. Arrows indicate fragmented DNA in apoptotic cells. *Reprinted with permission from Anandhakumar S, Krishnamoorthy G, Ramkumar KM, Raichur AM. Preparation of collagen peptide functionalized chitosan nanoparticles by ionic gelation method: an effective carrier system for encapsulation and release of doxorubicin for cancer drug delivery. Mater Sci Eng C 2017; 70: 378–385.*

nanoparticles encapsulated by the chlorhexidine dihydrochloride, CHX, was performed using osmosis and ionic gelation methods, respectively. Two diverse approaches were adopted to assist the adhesion of NPs onto the human dental surfaces. The PLGA particles composed of an exterior CS shell were prepared to create positive charges on the surface which allowed the interaction of the CHX-incorporated PLGA nanoparticles with the negative charges existing over the tooth surfaces. However, the CS particles were modified by the glutathione, GSH, which was a peptidomimetic compound. The CHX was released from the CS NPs in a sustained manner. The nanoparticles based on CS were adhered between 20% and 60% onto the human dental surfaces under simulated rinsing and brushing processes, as well as in vitro toxicity assessments onto the human gingival fibroblasts. Appropriate adhesion features and little cytotoxicity of the CS-derived hydrogels made them suitable for treatments and enhanced tooth care in vivo applications such as preparing toothpaste and cosmetics daily utilized in oral care.

A CS-based drug delivery system was fabricated to codeliver both citicoline and simvastatin drugs to tackle the undesirable side effects of simvastatin used by patients with Alzheimer's disorder [66]. The conjugation rate of simvastatin onto the CS was 1.67 times greater compared to that of the citicoline. According to the X-ray diffraction patterns of both drugs, their crystalline characteristic was changed into an amorphous nature upon the synthesis of their conjugates. The scanning electron microscopy micrographs proved that the nanoparticles had a spherical morphology and particle sizes in the range of 100–300 nm. The hemolysis of the red blood cells confirmed that the lowest and the highest values were 6.04% and 89.56%, and it was much lower upon fabrication of the nanoparticles by the ionotropic method. The transmission electron microscopy images revealed that the particles were stabilized by the gelation procedure.

Several magnetic- and reduction-sensitive CS nanocapsules functionalized by folic acid, FA, called FA/RMCNCS, were developed using FA-modified thiolated CS by a facile sono-chemical technique [67]. The FA as the targeting agent, rhodamine B isothiocyanate as the red fluorescent probe, and thiolated Fe_3O_4 magnetic NPs, named SH-Fe_3O_4 MNPs, were immobilized onto and in the nanocapsules' shells. The FA/RMCNCS exhibited a spherical shape and particle sizes in the range of 200–350 nm. The FA/RMCNCS carrier displayed exceptional magnetic-sensitive features. The confocal laser scanning microscopy images proved that the FA/RMCNCS having a core-shell assembly were selectively internalized into HeLa cells by the FA-assisted endocytosis pathway. Furthermore, the reduction-stimulated coumarin 6 release from the FA/RMCNCS confirmed that the drug release was reduction responsive. Overall, the FA/RMCNCS was a reduction and magnetic dual-responsive system so that the FA could mediate targeted drug delivery by the nanocarrier and controllable release of hydrophobic medicines.

A conjugate of quercetin with CS, called QT-CS, was achieved for the DOX oral delivery to enhance the oral bioavailability of DOX (Fig. 14) through raising its water solubility, opening narrow junctions as well as

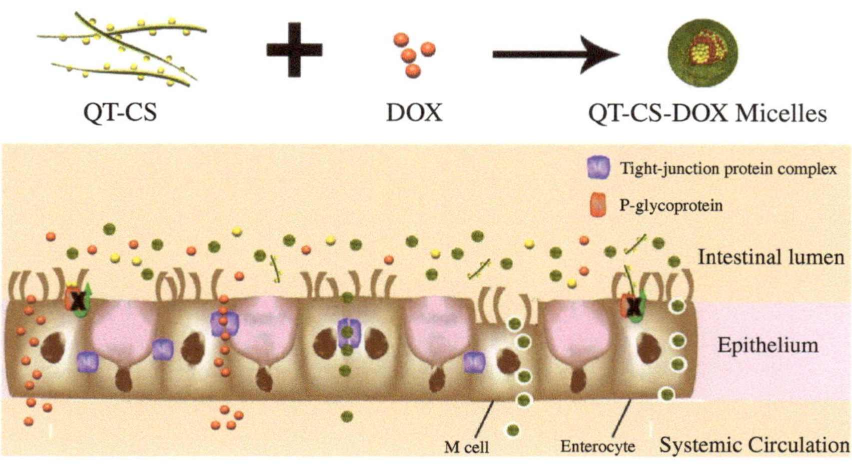

FIG. 14 The influence of QT-CS micelles on increasing the DOX oral absorption. *Reprinted with permission from Mu Y, Fu Y, Li J, Yu X, Li Y, Wang Y, Wu X, Zhang K, Kong M, Feng C, Chen X. Multifunctional quercetin conjugated chitosan nano-micelles with P-gp inhibition and permeation enhancement of anticancer drug, Carbohydr Polym 2019; 203: 10–18.*

P-glycoprotein, P-gp bypassing [68]. The QT-CS was self-assembled as micelles that encapsulated DOX by a great encapsulation rate and displayed a particle size of 136.9 nm and a zeta potential value of + 16.2 mV. The QT-CS-DOX micelles demonstrated sustained drug release within the gastrointestinal simulation fluids with pH values of 7.4 and 1.2. The QT-CS micelles promoted the DOX cellular uptake that was 2.2 times greater compared to that of the free DOX. The DOX-incorporated QT-CS micelles considerably decreased the transepithelial electrical resistance of Caco-2 monolayer cells, ~ 57%. This caused a large obvious permeability coefficient for the DOX that was 10.17 times greater compared to that of free DOX. Hence, the QT-CS micelles were proposed as favorable materials that could orally deliver insoluble anticancer medications.

Methoxy poly(ethylene glycol), MPEG, and linolenic acid, LNA, were conjugated onto the oligochitosan, oCS, chains to afford LNA-functionalized MPEG-oCS compound, named MPEG-oCS-LNA; see Fig. 15 [69]. The amphotericin B (AmB)-encapsulated MPEG-oCS-LNA micelles, called AmB-M, were achieved by the dialysis technique indicating $10.52 \pm 0.22\%$ and drug loading efficiency $82.27 \pm 1.96\%$ drug encapsulation efficacy. The AmB-M increased the water solubility of the AmB ($1.64\,mg\,mL^{-1}$), which was 1640 times greater compared to that of the pure AmB. The AmB-M noticeably decreased the renal cytotoxicity and hemolytic influence of AmB in comparison with the commercial AmB injection, AmB-I. The antifungal capacity of AmB-M against *Candida albicans* was equal to that of the AmB-I though the AmB release from the AmB-M was considerably delayed. The fluorescence spectra proved that the identical antifungal activity was accredited to the boosted AmB-M uptake by the fungal cells due to the combined effects of both oCS and LNA. The AmB-M enhanced the AmB pharmacokinetic factors using the AmB-I control. Finally, the LNA-functionalized MPEG-oCS micelles were considered as an effective and practical drug delivery substitute to the commercially existing more toxic AmB-I.

The targeted colon cancer therapy by the CS-coated transresveratrol, RSV, and FA-conjugated ferulic acid, FER, containing solid lipid nanoparticles, C-RSV-FER-FA-SLNs, was in vitro evaluated [70]. The conjugation of FA was carried out by stearic acid coencapsulation. The SLNs were more stable even in an acidic medium, exhibiting that they were suitable drug carriers. The in vitro anticancer assay against HT-29 cells proved that the C-RSV-FER-FA-SLNs had improved cytotoxicity toward the cancer cells and caused apoptosis relative to the free RSV-FER; see Figs. 16–18. Consequently, the C-RSV-FER-FA-SLNs were considered as an auspicious nanomaterial that could be employed for cancer treatment.

Aptamer-conjugated magnetic CS, Fe_3O_4@CS@Apt, nanoparticles were synthesized to selectively extract and determine ochratoxin A, OTA [71]. It was found that the magnetic CS nanoparticles contained magnetic

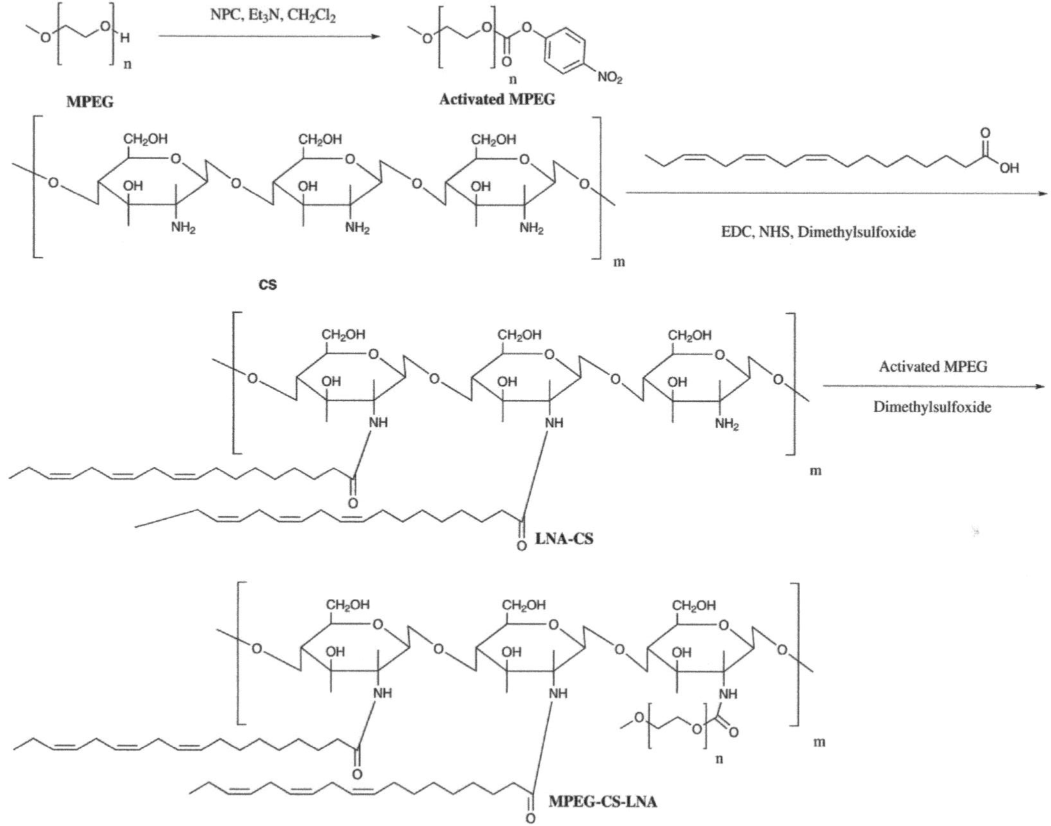

FIG. 15 Synthesis of MPEG-CS-LNA conjugate. *Reprinted with permission from Song Z, Wen Y, Deng P, Teng F, Zhou F, Xu H, Feng S, Zhu L, Feng R. Linolenic acid-modified methoxy poly (ethylene glycol)-oligochitosan conjugate micelles for encapsulation of amphotericin B. Carbohydr Polym 2019; 205: 571–580.*

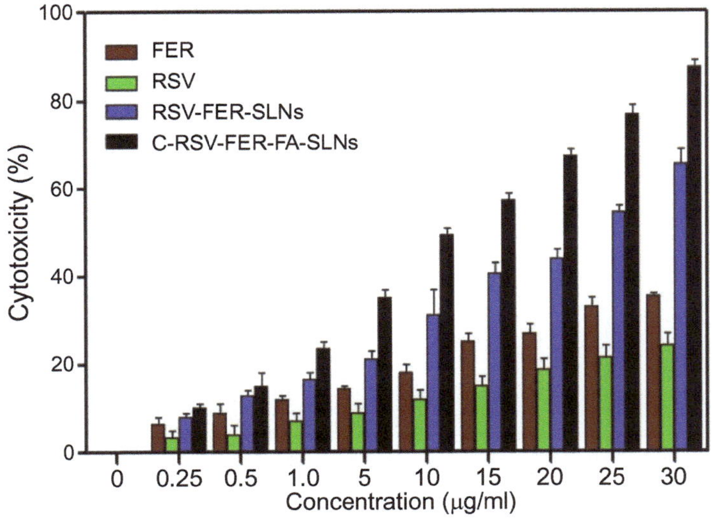

FIG. 16 In vitro cytotoxicity of RSV, FER, RSV-FER-SLNs (uncoated with CS), and C-RSV-FER-FA-SLNs HT-29 cells after 48-h treatment. *Reprinted with permission from Senthil Kumar C, Thangam R, Mary SA, Kannan PR, Arun G, Madhan B. Targeted delivery and apoptosis induction of trans-resveratrol-ferulic acid loaded chitosan coated folic acid conjugate solid lipid nanoparticles in colon cancer cells. Carbohydr Polym 2020; 231: 115682.*

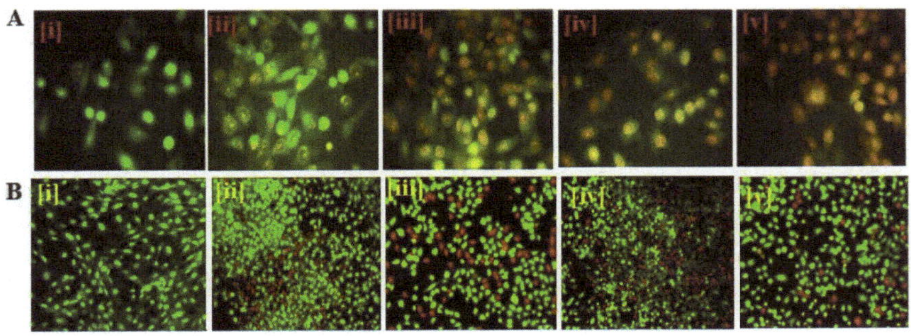

FIG. 17 (A) Fluorescence microscopy images of HT-29 cells stained using AO/EB. [i] Control, [ii] RSV, [iii] FER, [iv] RSV-FER-SLNs (uncoated with CS), [v] C-RSV-FER-FA-SLNs. (magnification = 40 ×). (B) Ao/EB-stained NIH 3T3 cells. [i] Control, [ii] RSV, [iii] FER, [iv] RSV-FER-SLNs (uncoated with CS), [v] C-RSV-FER-FA-SLNs (magnification = 20 ×). *Reprinted with permission from Senthil Kumar C, Thangam R, Mary SA, Kannan PR, Arun G, Madhan B. Targeted delivery and apoptosis induction of trans-resveratrol-ferulic acid loaded chitosan coated folic acid conjugate solid lipid nanoparticles in colon cancer cells. Carbohydr Polym 2020; 231: 115682.*

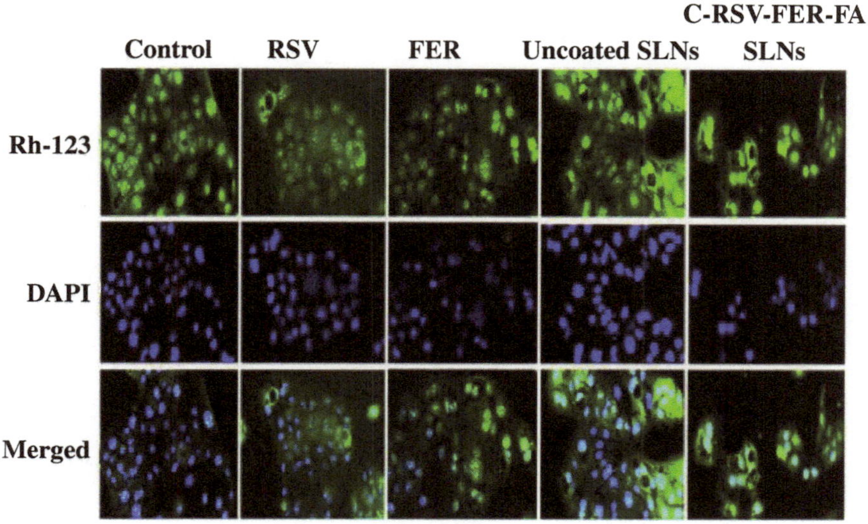

FIG. 18 Fluorescence microscopy (DAPI and Rh-123 staining) images of HT-29 cells treated by RSV, FER, uncoated SLNs (RSV-FER-SLNs (uncoated with CS)), and C-RSV-FER-FA-SLNs for 24 h with respective untreated control cells (magnification = 40 ×). *Reprinted with permission from Senthil Kumar C, Thangam R, Mary SA, Kannan PR, Arun G, Madhan B. Targeted delivery and apoptosis induction of trans-resveratrol-ferulic acid loaded chitosan coated folic acid conjugate solid lipid nanoparticles in colon cancer cells. Carbohydr Polym 2020; 231: 115682.*

cores and CS-coated shells. The OTA-specific aptamers were bound to the magnetic CS nanoparticles. An extraction process was established through optimization. Using food samples that were rich in OTA at 10 and 5 $\mu g\,kg^{-1}$, recovery values were achieved in the range of 91.3%–99.1% with $\leq 4.2\%$ relative standard deviation using magnetic extraction of aptamer-conjugated material. These results were comparable to those attained via immunoaffinity chromatography extraction. Hence, such magnetic adsorbent was an appropriate agent that could be applied for the effective and rapid OTA detection and extraction within the foodstuffs.

Magnetic resonance imaging is commonly applied as a diagnostic method of high positioning precision and dimensional accuracy in clinical trials [72]. To enhance the image contrast, using highly effective magnetic resonance imaging contrast materials is essential as they increase the precision of diagnosis predominantly in precision medicine. Gadolinium, Gd, including complexes, is broadly utilized in the present clinical magnetic resonance imaging processes. Nevertheless, they have shown several side effects in clinics. Such problems must be technically and clinically solved using novel Gd-based compounds. Therefore, an amphiphilic hybrid of gadodiamide-conjugated carboxymethyl-hexanoyl CS, called CHC-Gd, was synthesized (Fig. 19) [72]. The gadodiamide was chosen as it had the smallest size amid other Gd complexes, and it was expected that it had the

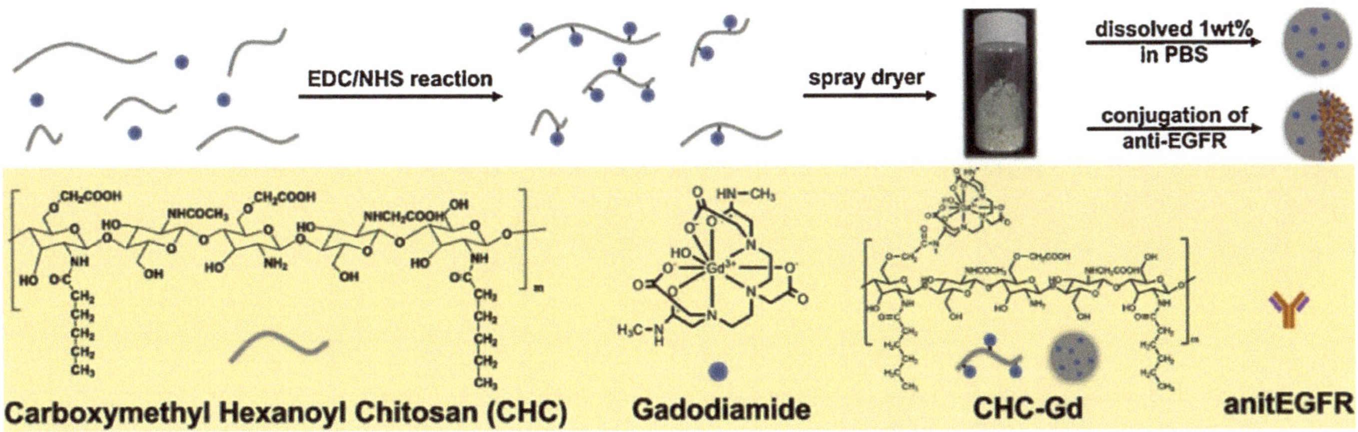

FIG. 19 One-pot synthesis of CHC-Gd hybrid polymer and the one conjugated to antiEGFR for active targeting. *Reprinted with permission from Huang W-T, Ko Y-P, Kuo T-Y, Larsson M, Chang M-C, Jean R-D, Liu D-M. A new type of gadodiamide-conjugated amphiphilic chitosan nanoparticle and its use for MR imaging with significantly enhanced contrastability. Carbohydr Polym 2019; 203: 256–264.*

slightest impact on hybrid physicochemical features (during its practical usage) like colloidal durability, nanostructure formation, cytocompatibility, and especially self-assembling ability. The gadodiamide complexes were conjugated onto the carboxyl functional groups of CHC by the covalent bonds. The native amphiphilic CHC polymer was self-assembled as spherical nanoparticles that had 100–200nm particle size. The hybrid illustrated much enhanced cytocompatibility than that of the free Gd. Thus, the Gd^{3+} ions were highly stabilized inside the nanostructure of CHC. Outstanding in vitro and particularly in vivo contrasting capacity was assessed so that for the in vivo tests, 10–40-fold lower dosages were utilized, relative to the clinical dose of Gd, which resulted in comparable to superior brightness and resolution for the images; see Figs. 20 and 21. Accordingly, the amphiphilic CHC-Gd hybrid could be translated to clinical practices.

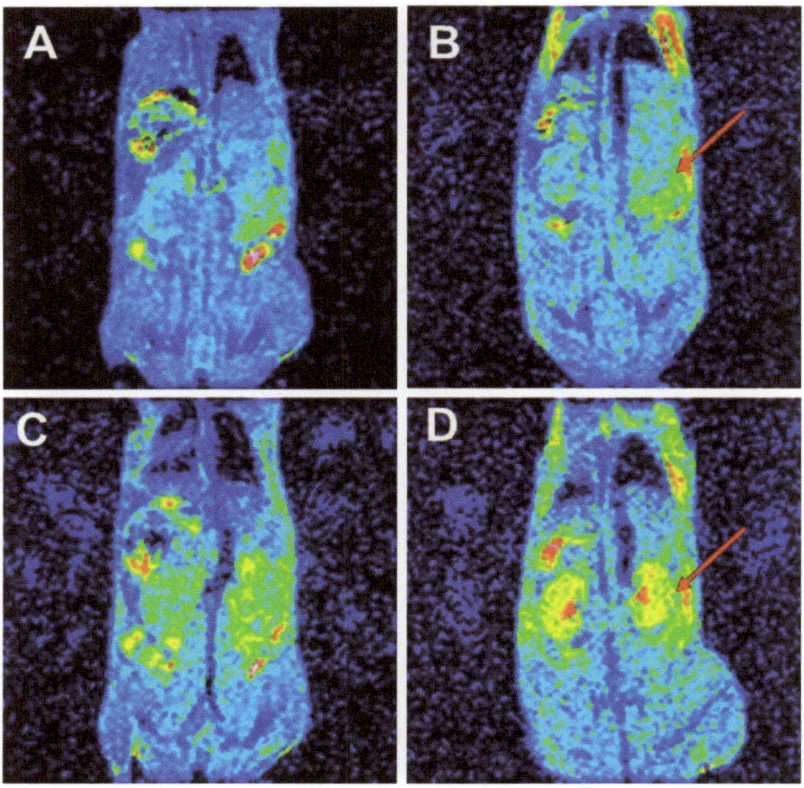

FIG. 20 In vivo MR imaging on ICR mice before (A) (C) and after treated with (B) Gd (0.0085mmol/kg) and (D) CHC-Gd nanoparticles (0.0022mmol/kg) for 40min. The *red* arrows pointed out the kidney labeling by Gd or CHC-Gd. *Reprinted with permission from Huang W-T, Ko Y-P, Kuo T-Y, Larsson M, Chang M-C, Jean R-D, Liu D-M. A new type of gadodiamide-conjugated amphiphilic chitosan nanoparticle and its use for MR imaging with significantly enhanced contrastability. Carbohydr Polym 2019; 203: 256–264.*

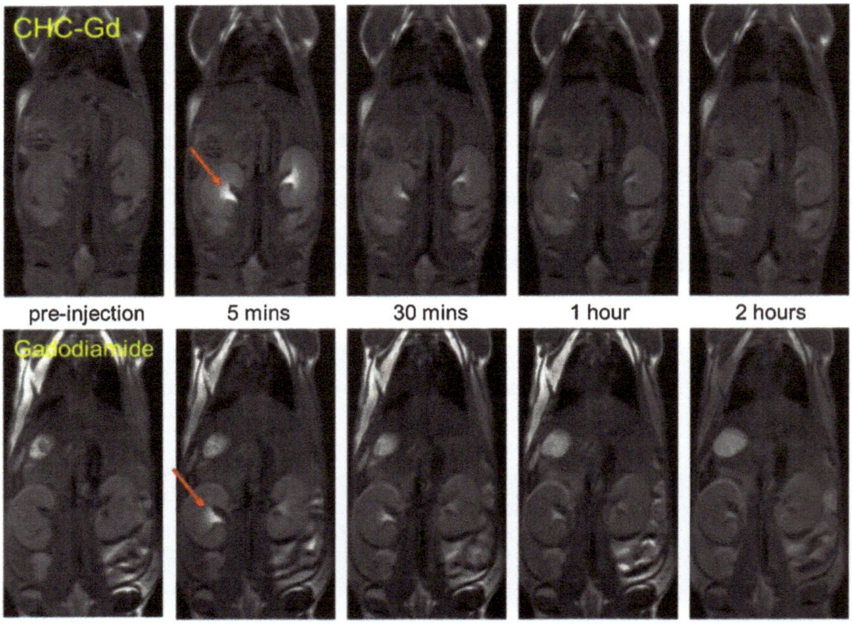

FIG. 21 In vivo MR imaging on ICR mice treated with Gd and CHC-Gd nanoparticles for various time intervals. The *red* arrows pointed out the brightest place labeling by CHC-Gd or Gd. *Reprinted with permission from Huang W-T, Ko Y-P, Kuo T-Y, Larsson M, Chang M-C, Jean R-D, Liu D-M. A new type of gadodiamide-conjugated amphiphilic chitosan nanoparticle and its use for MR imaging with significantly enhanced contrastability. Carbohydr Polym 2019; 203: 256–264.*

3 Conclusion

It has been indicated that CS and its conjugated/functionalized derivatives were exceptional biomaterials that could be used in various biomedical and pharmaceutical applications such as drug delivery systems. However, a few research studies have been carried out on the conjugation of CS as drug vehicles, and most investigations are conducted on the native CS and its composites. Literature review illustrated that the existing conjugated/modified CS derivatives that have so far been synthesized included CS functionalization with polymers, organic molecules, amino acids, peptides, drugs/medication, aptamers, and contrast agents (for imaging/diagnosis). It was interesting that, according to the papers reported, the cytotoxicity and biocompatibility tests, the CS derivatives displayed no apparent cytotoxicity against normal human cells and exhibited good biocompatibility. Therefore, it was found that these materials could be appropriate candidates for clinical applications. Although CS and its derivatives have been well known for a long time, most studies related to them are currently conducted only in laboratories. Thus, more efforts are needed to enter these biomaterials into the clinics and markets.

Acknowledgments

The financial support of this work by the Research Office of Amirkabir University of Technology (Tehran Polytechnic) is gratefully acknowledged.

References

[1] Ali A, Ahmed S. A review on chitosan and its nanocomposites in drug delivery. Int J Biol Macromol 2018;109:273–86.

[2] Ashrafizadeh M, Ahmadi Z, Mohamadi N, Zarrabi A, Abasi S, Dehghannoudeh G, Tamaddondoust RN, Khanbabaei H, Mohammadinejad R, Thakur VK. Chitosan-based advanced materials for docetaxel and paclitaxel delivery: recent advances and future directions in cancer theranostics. Int J Biol Macromol 2020;145:282–300.

[3] Mujtaba M, Khawar KM, Camara MC, Carvalho LB, Fraceto LF, Morsi RE, Elsabee MZ, Kaya M, Labidi J, Ullah H, Wang D. Chitosan-based delivery systems for plants: a brief overview of recent advances and future directions. Int J Biol Macromol 2020;154:683–97.

[4] Shariatinia Z, Jalali AM. Chitosan-based hydrogels: preparation, properties and applications. Int J Biol Macromol 2018;115:194–220.

[5] Shariatinia Z, Mohammadi-Denyani A. Advances in polymers for drug delivery and wound healing applications. In: Advances in polymers for biomedical applications. Nova Science Publisher; 2018.

[6] Shariatinia Z, Mazloom-Jalali A. Chitosan nanocomposite drug delivery systems designed for the ifosfamide anticancer drug using molecular dynamics simulations. J Mol Liq 2019;273:346–67.

[7] Tran PHL, Duan W, Tran TTD. Fucoidan-based nanostructures: a focus on its combination with chitosan and the surface functionalization of metallic nanoparticles for drug delivery. Int J Pharm 2020;575:118956.

[8] Vatanparast M, Shariatinia Z. Revealing the role of different nitrogen functionalities in the drug delivery performance of graphene quantum dots: a combined density functional theory and molecular dynamics approach. J Mater Chem B 2019;7(40):6156–71.

[9] Wei S, Ching YC, Chuah CH. Synthesis of chitosan aerogels as promising carriers for drug delivery: a review. Carbohydr Polym 2020;231:115744.

[10] Kazemi S, Daryani AS, Abdouss M, Shariatinia Z. DFT computations on the hydrogen bonding interactions between methacrylic acid-trimethylolpropane trimethacrylate copolymers and letrozole as drug delivery systems. J Theor Comput Chem 2016;15(02):1650015.

[11] Mazloom-Jalali A, Shariatinia Z. Polycaprolactone nanocomposite systems used to deliver ifosfamide anticancer drug: molecular dynamics simulations. Struct Chem 2019;30(3):863–76.

[12] Mazloom-Jalali A, Shariatinia Z. Molecular dynamics simulations on polymeric nanocomposite membranes designed to deliver pipobromane anticancer drug. J Nanostruct 2020;10(2):279–95.

[13] Mazloom-Jalali A, Shariatinia Z, Tamai IA, Pakzad S-R, Malakootikhah J. Fabrication of chitosan–polyethylene glycol nanocomposite films containing ZIF-8 nanoparticles for application as wound dressing materials. Int J Biol Macromol 2020;153:421–32.

[14] Nikfar Z, Shariatinia Z. Phosphate functionalized (4,4)-armchair CNTs as novel drug delivery systems for alendronate and etidronate anti-osteoporosis drugs. J Mol Graph Model 2017;76:86–105.

[15] Nikfar Z, Shariatinia Z. DFT computational study on the phosphate functionalized SWCNTs as efficient drug delivery systems for anti-osteoporosis zolendronate and risedronate drugs. Physica E 2017;91:41–59.
[16] Shariatinia Z, Erben MF, Della Védova CO. DFT calculations on the hydrogen bonding interactions between adrenaline and trimethoxysilylpropylamine. Main Group Chem 2012;11(4):275–84.
[17] Shariatinia Z, Shahidi S. A DFT study on the physical adsorption of cyclophosphamide derivatives on the surface of fullerene C60 nanocage. J Mol Graph Model 2014;52:71–81.
[18] Fazli Y, Shariatinia Z. Controlled release of cefazolin sodium antibiotic drug from electrospun chitosan-polyethylene oxide nanofibrous mats. Mater Sci Eng C 2017;71:641–52.
[19] Fazli Y, Shariatinia Z, Kohsari I, Azadmehr A, Pourmortazavi SM. A novel chitosan-polyethylene oxide nanofibrous mat designed for controlled co-release of hydrocortisone and imipenem/cilastatin drugs. Int J Pharm 2016;513(1–2):636–47.
[20] Kohsari I, Shariatinia Z, Pourmortazavi SM. Antibacterial electrospun chitosan-polyethylene oxide nanocomposite mats containing ZIF-8 nanoparticles. Int J Biol Macromol 2016;91:778–88.
[21] Kohsari I, Shariatinia Z, Pourmortazavi SM. Antibacterial electrospun chitosan–polyethylene oxide nanocomposite mats containing bioactive silver nanoparticles. Carbohydr Polym 2016;140:287–98.
[22] Vatanparast M, Shariatinia Z. Hexagonal boron nitride nanosheet as novel drug delivery system for anticancer drugs: insights from DFT calculations and molecular dynamics simulations. J Mol Graph Model 2019;89:50–9.
[23] Shariatinia Z, Arabzadeh N, Abdous M. Ab initio calculations on the hydrogen bonding interactions among pseudoephedrinium cation isomers and methacrylic acid. Main Group Chem 2011;10(1):1–16.
[24] Vatanparast M, Shariatinia Z. AlN and AlP doped graphene quantum dots as novel drug delivery systems for 5-fluorouracil drug: theoretical studies. J Fluor Chem 2018;211:81–93.
[25] Vatanparast M, Shariatinia Z. Computational studies on the doped graphene quantum dots as potential carriers in drug delivery systems for isoniazid drug. Struct Chem 2018;29(5):1427–48.
[26] Shariatinia Z, Erben MF, Della Védova CO, Abdous M, Azodi S. Hydrogen bonding interactions between α-, β-glucose, and methacrylic acid. Struct Chem 2011;22(6):1347.
[27] Shariatinia Z. Pharmaceutical applications of chitosan. Adv Colloid Interface Sci 2019;263:131–94.
[28] Shariatinia Z. Pharmaceutical applications of natural polysaccharides. In: Natural polysaccharides in drug delivery and biomedical applications. Elsevier; 2019. p. 15–57.
[29] Shariatinia Z, Barzegari A. Polysaccharide hydrogel films/membranes for transdermal delivery of therapeutics. In: Polysaccharide carriers for drug delivery. Elsevier; 2019. p. 639–84.
[30] Shariatinia Z, Fasihozaman-Langroodi K. Biodegradable polymer nanobiocomposite packaging materials. In: Trends in beverage packaging. Elsevier; 2019. p. 191–241.
[31] Shariatinia Z, Fazli M. Mechanical properties and antibacterial activities of novel nanobiocomposite films of chitosan and starch. Food Hydrocoll 2015;46:112–24.
[32] Hamedi H, Moradi S, Hudson SM, Tonelli AE. Chitosan based hydrogels and their applications for drug delivery in wound dressings: a review. Carbohydr Polym 2018;199:445–60.
[33] Islam N, Dmour I, Taha MO. Degradability of chitosan micro/nanoparticles for pulmonary drug delivery. Heliyon 2019;5(5), e01684.
[34] Lang X, Wang T, Sun M, Chen X, Liu Y. Advances and applications of chitosan-based nanomaterials as oral delivery carriers: a review. Int J Biol Macromol 2020;154:433–45.

[35] Sabourian P, Tavakolian M, Yazdani H, Frounchi M, van de Ven TGM, Maysinger D, Kakkar A. Stimuli-responsive chitosan as an advantageous platform for efficient delivery of bioactive agents. J Control Release 2020;317:216–31.
[36] Safdar R, Omar AA, Arunagiri A, Regupathi I, Thanabalan M. Potential of chitosan and its derivatives for controlled drug release applications—a review. J Drug Delivery Sci Technol 2019;49:642–59.
[37] Shariatinia Z, Nikfar Z. Synthesis and antibacterial activities of novel nanocomposite films of chitosan/phosphoramide/Fe_3O_4 NPs. Int J Biol Macromol 2013;60:226–34.
[38] Shariatinia Z, Nikfar Z, Gholivand K, Abolghasemi Tarei S. Antibacterial activities of novel nanocomposite biofilms of chitosan/phosphoramide/Ag NPs. Polym Compos 2015;36(3):454–66.
[39] Shariatinia Z, Zahraee Z. Controlled release of metformin from chitosan–based nanocomposite films containing mesoporous MCM-41 nanoparticles as novel drug delivery systems. J Colloid Interface Sci 2017;501:60–76.
[40] Abdel-Bary AS, Tolan DA, Nassar MY, Taketsugu T, El-Nahas AM. Chitosan, magnetite, silicon dioxide, and graphene oxide nanocomposites: synthesis, characterization, efficiency as cisplatin drug delivery, and DFT calculations. Int J Biol Macromol 2020;154:621–33.
[41] Wang F, Li J, Tang X, Huang K, Chen L. Polyelectrolyte three layer nanoparticles of chitosan/dextran sulfate/chitosan for dual drug delivery. Colloids Surf B Biointerfaces 2020;190:110925.
[42] Shariatinia Z, et al. Big family of nano- and microscale drug delivery systems ranging from inorganic materials to polymeric and stimuli-responsive carriers as well as drug-conjugates. J Drug Deliv Sci Technol 2021;66:102790.
[43] Zhao J, Li J, Jiang Z, Tong R, Duan X, Bai L, Shi J. Chitosan, N,N,N-trimethyl chitosan (TMC) and 2-hydroxypropyltrimethyl ammonium chloride chitosan (HTCC): the potential immune adjuvants and nano carriers. Int J Biol Macromol 2020;154:339–48.
[44] Tu L, Cheng M, Sun Y, Fang Y, Liu J, Liu W, Feng J, Jin Y. Fabrication of ultra-small nanocrystals by formation of hydrogen bonds: in vitro and in vivo evaluation. Int J Pharm 2020;573:118730.
[45] Brussee JM, Yu H, Krekels EHJ, Palić S, Brill MJE, Barrett JS, Rostami-Hodjegan A, de Wildt SN, Knibbe CAJ. Characterization of intestinal and hepatic CYP3A-mediated metabolism of midazolam in children using a physiological population pharmacokinetic modelling approach. Pharm Res 2018;35(9):182.
[46] Wusigale L, Liang Y. Luo, casein and pectin: structures, interactions, and applications. Trends Food Sci Technol 2020;97:391–403.
[47] Wang S-Y, Meng Y-J, Li J, Liu J-P, Liu Z-Q, Li D-Q. A novel and simple oral colon-specific drug delivery system based on the pectin/modified nano-carbon sphere nanocomposite gel films. Int J Biol Macromol 2020;157:170–6.
[48] Tian L, Singh A, Singh AV. Synthesis and characterization of pectin-chitosan conjugate for biomedical application. Int J Biol Macromol 2020;153:533–8.
[49] Rafiee F, Rezaie Karder F. Bio-crosslinking of chitosan with oxidized starch, its functionalization with amino acid and magnetization: as a green magnetic support for silver immobilization and its catalytic activity investigation. Int J Biol Macromol 2020;146:1124–32.
[50] Xie P, Du P, Li J, Liu P. Stimuli-responsive hybrid cluster bombs of PEGylated chitosan encapsulated DOX-loaded superparamagnetic nanoparticles enabling tumor-specific disassembly for on-demand drug delivery and enhanced MR imaging. Carbohydr Polym 2019;205:377–84.
[51] Chen TE, Tu L, Wang G, Qi N, Wu W, Zhang W, Feng J. Multi-functional chitosan polymeric micelles as oral paclitaxel delivery systems for enhanced bioavailability and anti-tumor efficacy. Int J Pharm 2020;578:119105.

[52] Rajan M, Murugan M, Ponnamma D, Sadasivuni KK, Munusamy MA. Poly-carboxylic acids functionalized chitosan nanocarriers for controlled and targeted anti-cancer drug delivery. Biomed Pharmacother 2016;83:201–11.
[53] Arslan M. Fabrication and reversible disulfide functionalization of PEGylated chitosan-based hydrogels: platforms for selective immobilization and release of thiol-containing molecules. Eur Polym J 2020;126:109543.
[54] Qu D, Jiao M, Lin H, Tian C, Qu G, Xue J, Xue L, Ju C, Zhang C. Anisamide-functionalized pH-responsive amphiphilic chitosan-based paclitaxel micelles for sigma-1 receptor targeted prostate cancer treatment. Carbohydr Polym 2020;229:115498.
[55] Kim S-W, Lee T-H, Lee Y-G, Ito Y, Son T-I. Preparation of azidophenyl-low molecular chitosan derivative micro particles for enhance drug delivery. Int J Biol Macromol 2019;133:875–80.
[56] Ren G, Clancy C, Tamer TM, Schaller B, Walker GM, Collins MN. Cinnamyl O-amine functionalized chitosan as a new excipient in direct compressed tablets with improved drug delivery. Int J Biol Macromol 2019;141:936–46.
[57] Ghaffari S-B, Sarrafzadeh M-H, Salami M, Khorramizadeh MR. A pH-sensitive delivery system based on N-succinyl chitosan-ZnO nanoparticles for improving antibacterial and anticancer activities of curcumin. Int J Biol Macromol 2020;151:428–40.
[58] Li X, Wang J, Cui R, Xu D, Zhu L, Li Z, Chen H, Gao Y, Jia L. Hypoxia/pH dual-responsive nitroimidazole-modified chitosan/rose bengal derivative nanoparticles for enhanced photodynamic anticancer therapy. Dyes Pigments 2020;179:108395.
[59] Du X, Yin S, Xu L, Ma J, Yu H, Wang G, Li J. Polylysine and cysteine functionalized chitosan nanoparticle as an efficient platform for oral delivery of paclitaxel. Carbohydr Polym 2020;229:115484.
[60] George D, Maheswari PU, Begum KMMS. Chitosan-cellulose hydrogel conjugated with L-histidine and zinc oxide nanoparticles for sustained drug delivery: kinetics and in-vitro biological studies. Carbohydr Polym 2020;236:116101.
[61] George D, Maheswari PU, Begum KMMS. Cysteine conjugated chitosan based green nanohybrid hydrogel embedded with zinc oxide nanoparticles towards enhanced therapeutic potential of naringenin. React Funct Polym 2020;148:104480.
[62] Lan Q, Di D, Wang S, Zhao Q, Gao Y, Chang D, Jiang T. Chitosan-N-acetylcysteine modified HP-β-CD inclusion complex as a potential ocular delivery system for anti-cataract drug: quercetin. J Drug Delivery Sci Technol 2020;55:101407.
[63] Qian Q, Niu S, Williams GR, Wu J, Zhang X, Zhu L-M. Peptide functionalized dual-responsive chitosan nanoparticles for controlled drug delivery to breast cancer cells. Colloids Surf A Physicochem Eng Asp 2019;564:122–30.
[64] Anandhakumar S, Krishnamoorthy G, Ramkumar KM, Raichur AM. Preparation of collagen peptide functionalized chitosan nanoparticles by ionic gelation method: an effective carrier system for encapsulation and release of doxorubicin for cancer drug delivery. Mater Sci Eng C 2017;70:378–85.
[65] Chronopoulou L, Nocca G, Castagnola M, Paludetti G, Ortaggi G, Sciubba F, Bevilacqua M, Lupi A, Gambarini G, Palocci C. Chitosan based nanoparticles functionalized with peptidomimetic derivatives for oral drug delivery. N Biotechnol 2016;33(1):23–31.
[66] Mozafari N, Farjadian F, Mohammadi Samani S, Azadi S, Azadi A. Simvastatin-chitosan-citicoline conjugates nanoparticles as the co-delivery system in Alzheimer susceptible patients. Int J Biol Macromol 2019;156:1396–407.
[67] Zhong S, Zhang H, Liu Y, Wang G, Shi C, Li Z, Feng Y, Cui X. Folic acid functionalized reduction-responsive magnetic chitosan nanocapsules for targeted delivery and triggered release of drugs. Carbohydr Polym 2017;168:282–9.
[68] Mu Y, Fu Y, Li J, Yu X, Li Y, Wang Y, Wu X, Zhang K, Kong M, Feng C, Chen X. Multifunctional quercetin conjugated chitosan nano-micelles with P-gp inhibition and permeation enhancement of anticancer drug. Carbohydr Polym 2019;203:10–8.

[69] Song Z, Wen Y, Deng P, Teng F, Zhou F, Xu H, Feng S, Zhu L, Feng R. Linolenic acid-modified methoxy poly (ethylene glycol)-oligochitosan conjugate micelles for encapsulation of amphotericin B. Carbohydr Polym 2019;205:571–80.
[70] Senthil Kumar C, Thangam R, Mary SA, Kannan PR, Arun G, Madhan B. Targeted delivery and apoptosis induction of trans-resveratrol-ferulic acid loaded chitosan coated folic acid conjugate solid lipid nanoparticles in colon cancer cells. Carbohydr Polym 2020;231:115682.
[71] Wang S, Niu R, Yang Y, Zhou X, Luo S, Zhang C, Wang Y. Aptamer-functionalized chitosan magnetic nanoparticles as a novel adsorbent for selective extraction of ochratoxin a. Int J Biol Macromol 2020;153:583–90.
[72] Huang W-T, Ko Y-P, Kuo T-Y, Larsson M, Chang M-C, Jean R-D, Liu D-M. A new type of gadodiamide-conjugated amphiphilic chitosan nanoparticle and its use for MR imaging with significantly enhanced contrastability. Carbohydr Polym 2019;203:256–64.

CHAPTER

12

Modified alginates in drug delivery

Nandan Sarkar[a] *and Arindam Maity*[b]

[a]Department of Pharmaceutical Technology, School of Medical Science, Adamas University, Kolkata, West Bengal, India, [b]Department of Pharmaceutical Technology, JIS University, Kolkata, West Bengal, India

1 Introduction

Drug delivery systems are the pharmaceutical preparations designed to achieve the target-specific or controlled release of therapeutic substances in our body to release the active ingredients. Ideally, it guarantees that the active molecule is administered at the definite site of action and controls the release rate, absorption, and eventually the therapeutic benefits along with adverse effects. Instead of substantial development in the progression of new drug design and discovery, many have undesirable effects due to several factors [1]. The system by which the drug is delivered can also have a significant role in its effectiveness and efficacy. However, though considering the bioavailability of active pharmaceutical ingredients (APIs) remains the main motto of innovations in formulation development, other features are also important. Of late, research on excipient development is receiving more contemplation in the pharmaceutical drug delivery systems because it influences the drug delivery process in innumerable ways [2]. Excipients are the major components of any pharmaceutical preparation and can be of natural or synthetic origin. Synthetic polymers like polythene, polystyrene, polyacrylates, and silicon-based products have savored a long past of use, contributing exclusive properties. But despite the many potential benefits, manufacturers still face several challenges [3].

Since then, lipids, polysaccharides, carbohydrates, proteins, as well as their derivatives, denote a group of natural polymeric substances that are extensively used in the formulation and their presence plays a vital role in the release of drugs from the dosage form. Presently, naturally occurring

Tailor-Made Polysaccharides in Drug Delivery
https://doi.org/10.1016/B978-0-12-821286-8.00010-0

polymers, including collagen, gelatine, chitosan, alginate, and starch, are broadly used [4]. Each of these polymers offers varied advantages, but alginate, a naturally occurring polymer, bargains the utmost versatility due to its physicochemical characteristics, including thickening, gel-forming, stabilizing, and biocompatibility, which makes it a unique biomaterial for different drug delivery systems, including polymeric too.

However, there are several restrictions, primarily stability, which limit the application of alginate in a formulation [5]. Hence, there is a drift to develop "value-added" alginates by modification on the polysaccharide's backbone containing ample free hydroxyl and carbonyl groups. Modifications of alginate can be performed using various approaches such as chemical bonding with synthetic biopolymers, coating the surfaces of alginate with biocompatible artificial micro- or nanosphere polymers, cross-linking with physical or chemical substances, hydrophobization, a variation of guluronic/mannuronic ratio, etc. Further, chemical methods can be united with biochemical techniques that allow for the alteration of alginate properties such as solubility, an affinity for specific proteins, hydrophobicity, etc. [6]. Before selecting any modification, the two key parameters, i.e., solubility and reactivity, should be considered.

Thus, chemically modified alginates significantly expand the versatility of alginate for several types of drug delivery. To date, different categories of alginate-based hydrogels formulations are under investigation and some are available in the market too [7]. The United States Food and Drug Administration (US-FDA) granted the "generally referred to as safe" material grade to alginates. Moreover, foremost regulatory bodies such as Therapeutic Goods Administration, European Medicines Agency, and Health Canada have approved permission for various alginate-based products. At present, commercial alginate-based drug delivery products are utilized in various formulae such as wound dressing sponges, catheters, and microspheres and find application in numerous wound dressing materials, bioink in 3D bioprinting, and drug delivery vehicles for diabetic, ulcer, and chemotherapeutic agents also [8–10].

2 Alginate biopolymer

Alginates are a group of naturally abundant polyanionic polysaccharides isolated from extracellular materials of microorganisms, including the cell wall of brown algae and bacterial species [11]. The main algae sources are *Macrocystis pyrifera*, *Ascophyllum nodosum*, and various types of *Laminaria*, i.e., *L. hyperborea*, *L. digitata, and L. japonica*. It is also produced by two bacterial genera, i.e., *Pseudomonas* and *Azotobacter* [12]. Therefore, the composition, yield, and other structures of alginate depend on (a) species origin from which the alginates are extracted and the method of extraction followed and (b) source of the copolymer used. As a biopolymer, alginate is highly adaptable to a biological system due to its strong non-immunogenic, nontoxic, biocompatible, and biodegradable properties. Alginates are usually referred to as alginic acid, also termed as algin, and with metals such as sodium, calcium, and their salts. However, it can also be used for all types of derivatives of alginic acid.

2.1 Chemistry of alginates

Under natural circumstances, alginate exists in the form of salts of sodium, calcium, or magnesium (Na^+, Ca^{2+}, Mg^{2+}, Sr^{2+}, and Ba^{2+} of alginic acid). Structurally, alginates are unbranched binary linear copolymers. D-Mannuronate unit was considered as the key component of alginate until Fischer and Dorfel et al. recognized the L-guluronate residue instead [13]. Fractional precipitation study with calcium and manganese salts verified that alginates are truly block copolymers and the ratio of mannuronate to guluronate can diverge depending on the source. Alginate comprises homopolymeric blocks consisting of 1,4-β-D-mannuronic acid (M) and 1,4-α-L-guluronic acid (G) residues connected via glycosidic link organized in diverse sequences or blocks like (a) homogenous (poly-G, poly-M) or (b) heterogeneous (MG) block-like design, respectively, covalently bonded together in different arrangements or blocks as represented in Fig. 1. The

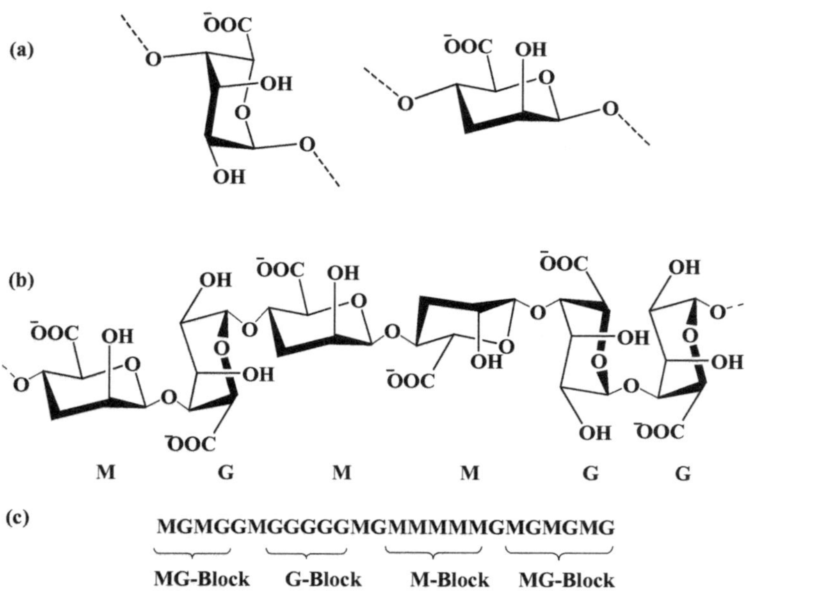

FIG. 1 Schematic representation of the chemical structure of alginate. (A) Unit of guluronate (G) and mannuronate (M), (B) the chair conformation, (C) the distribution of M-block and G-block arrangement.

blocks are composed of repeated M residues (MMMMMM) or G residues (GGGGGG) or alternating G and M residues (GMGMGM) [14].

Alginates from different microorganism origins differ in G and M contents, as well as the extent of each block. The dispersal of the G- and M-blocks relies on several factors such as the category and source of microorganism, the stage, and the constituent of the algae or bacterial strains used. For instance, *L. hyperborea*-derived alginates exhibited the highest G content (60%), while a low G content alginate is derived from *L. japonica*. Bacterial alginates like *Pseudomonas* species-derived alginates are deprived of G-units [15]. Here it is worthy to mention that only the alginates with G-units are supposed to contribute to intermolecular cross-linking with divalent ions (e.g., Ca^{2+}) [16]. The efficient properties of alginates associate strongly with the M/G ratio. The composition (i.e., M/G ratio), sequence, G-block length, and molecular weight are thus perilous parameters influencing the physical properties of alginate. The mechanical strength of alginate hydrogels is characteristically boosted by the increment of G-block length.

2.2 Extraction of alginate from natural origin

Commonly, alginates are extracted from brown algae, which is a simple multistep process. The industrial manufacturing procedure of sodium alginate from brown seaweeds can be categorized as fewer than two: (a) calcium alginate method and (b) alginic acid method [17]. Extraction of alginate from the natural source is typically initiated with the treatment of the dried raw material with mineral acids in a very diluted form. Subsequently purified alginic acid is converted into water-soluble sodium salt in the presence of calcium carbonate. After that, it is malformed back into acid or its anticipated salt. The stepwise procedure is presented in Fig. 2 schematically. The complications of the procedures arise from the physical partings such as the filtration of sycophantic residues from viscous solutions or to separate the gelatinous hastens that hold a hefty amount of liquid within the construct and thereby resist further separation, including filtration and centrifugation.

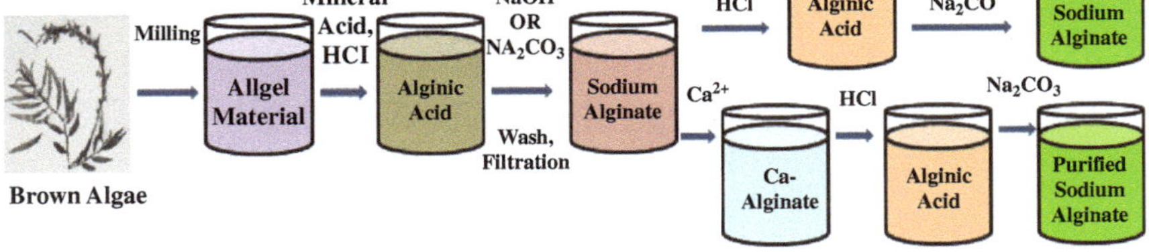

FIG. 2 Stepwise procedure for the extraction of alginate from brown algae.

The alginate contents varied depending on the source of extracted microorganisms. For example, *A. nodosum* gives 22%–30% (on a dry weight basis) alginate contents, whereas *L. digitata* gives 25%–44% [18]. It was observed that bacterial biometabolic synthesis delivers alginate with more distinct chemical assemblies with wide physical properties in comparison with seaweed-derived alginate. The biosynthetic pathway of alginate is commonly divided into the following: (a) initial precursor substrate molecule synthesis, (b) cytoplasmic membrane transference and polymerization, (c) modification and periplasmic transmission, and (d) transfer via outer membrane [19].

Commercial alginates are exclusively derived from brown algae. However, alternative manufacturing through bacterial modification has also been investigated to achieve alginate with more distinct physicochemical properties. The current advancement in the regulation of alginate biosynthesis via microbial fermentation accomplishes alginate with tailor-made assemblies [20] and inclusive applications such as biomedical and drug delivery arrangements compatibility.

3 Physicochemical heterogeneity toward drug delivery

To fulfill the purpose of drug molecule delivery, the physicochemical heterogeneity of alginate is a prime essential criterion. Currently available alginate-based products have a high degree of physicochemical acceptance, which excels their quality and regulates potential applicability for various tenacities, including biomedical to pharmaceutical drug delivery modes or devices. Alginate has been efficaciously used for many ages in a different arena like in food and beverage manufacturing as a thickening or gelling agent and as a colloidal stabilizer. Alginate has well-prized characteristics like biocompatibility, bioadhesion, pH sensitivity, and immunogenicity. Such unique qualities have opened a vast field of magnitude for its usages as a matrix for the entrapment and/or delivery of a variety of molecules such as proteins, drugs, and cells. The comprehensiveness of alginates in drug delivery has been augmented as it delivers: (a) a comparatively inert aqueous atmosphere within the biomatrix; (b) encapsulation process with mild room temperature and removal of organic solvents usages; (c) rich gel porosity of macromolecules with high diffusion rates; (d) the skill to manage this porosity with simple coating method; and (e) dissolution and biodegradation of the system under normal physiological environment.

Alginates are commercially available in various grades of molecular weight, composition, and dispersal pattern of M-block and G-block subunits [21]. The main features accountable for their diverse physicochemical properties remain as solubility, viscosity, stability, sol/gel transition, degradation, water uptake ability, etc. The physical properties meaningfully govern the stability of the prepared alginate-based hydrogels. Thus, the rate of drug release from gels, the phenotype, and the function of cells encapsulated in alginate gels can be considered in a drug delivery system with desired effectiveness and efficacy.

3.1 Molecular weight

The molecular weight of commercially available sodium alginates ranges between 32,000 and 400,000 g/mol [22]. Alginates derived from different natural sources diverge in M and G content, as well as the length of each subunit, and thus molecular weight is also varied. Generally, alginate gels with more solid and inelastic features are conceivable by increasing the molecular weight or G-block content. The increasing molecular weight of alginate can also expand the physical properties of resulting gels. However, an alginate solution prepared from a high molecular weight polymer becomes significantly viscous, which is often unwanted during processing. For instance, proteins or cells mixed with an alginate solution of high viscosity may produce impairment from the high shear forces engendered during the mixing process and administration inside the body. Management of the molecular weight and its manipulation can autonomously regulate the pregel solution viscosity and post gelling stiffness effectively. The flexible modulus of gels can also be improved substantially by keeping the viscosity of the solution marginally raised by using a good amalgamation of high and low molecular weight containing alginate polymers. The mechanical properties of alginate are archetypally enhanced by increasing the molecular weight.

3.2 Solubility

The solubility of alginate in a solvent is measured by the occurrence of its end carboxylic group while being into the solvent and the pH, as well as the ionic strength. For example, if the carboxylic group is protonated, the polymer will not be fully soluble in any of the solvents. Hence, alginic acid is insoluble in water and organic solvents, whereas alginate monovalent salts and alginate esters are water-soluble, forming stable, viscous solutions. Therefore, alginate solubility is limited by several factors such as the solvent pH (a decrease in pH below pK_a 3.38–3.65 may lead to the formation of polymer precipitate), ionic strength, and the gratification of "gelling ions" [23]. Alginate with a more heterogeneous structure like rich MG content is soluble at low pH compared with poly-M or poly-G content alginate molecules that precipitate under these circumstances.

3.3 Viscosity

Sodium alginate aqueous solution (1% w/v) has a dynamic viscosity of 20–400 mPa s at 20°C. The viscosity of alginate biopolymers depends on their concentration, solvent pH (a maximum pH is reached around 3.0–3.5), temperature, and the presence of divalent ions. The parameters of the Mark-Houwink relationship

$$[\eta] = KMv\,a$$

where $[\eta]$ is the intrinsic viscosity (mL/g) and, Mv is the viscosity average molecular weight (g/mol), ($K = 2 \times 10^{-3}$ and $a = 0.97$, for sodium alginate in 0.1 M NaCl solution at 25 °C).

The viscosity of alginate solutions rises as pH diminutions and grasps a maximum around pH of 3–3.5, as carboxylate groups in the alginate backbone become protonated and form hydrogen bonds [24].

3.4 Stability

The stability of a polymer is significantly inclined by the degree of polymerization (DP). The range of depolymerization is commonly determined by the loss of viscosity of a polymer upon different storage conditions. Additionally, the viscosity of alginate is a measure of its stability, where one of low viscosity establishes better stability over time than that of high viscosity. Alginate with low DP displays better stability in contrast to high DP alginates. Thus, it is endorsed that commercial alginates should be stored in rather cold conditions to hold their optimum viscosity.

3.5 Gelation

Alginate can be straightforwardly converted into miscellaneous solid or semisolid constructions beneath mild circumstances because of their inimitable skill of sol/gel transition. Therefore, alginates are frequently used for various purposes like viscosity cumulative agents, thickening agents, and suspension- and emulsion-stabilizing agents in food and pharmaceutical companies. The gelation of alginate can be accomplished under the enormously trifling atmosphere with the assistance of nontoxic reagents. The gels are typically constructed with a reaction between alginate and bivalent ions like Ca^{2+}, Sr^{2+}, and Ba^{2+} [25]. They have a reticulated assembly, which can capture the drugs and be able to release the drugs in a sustained manner. The plain beads have a restriction like a drug forfeiture due to leakage. Hence, now the present trend is to construct more polyelectrolyte complexes of alginate with a combination of other polymers to impart encouragement in network complexity for drug leakage and release.

Alginate gelation can be persuaded in the existence of divalent cations to cross-link with the polymer through the "egg-box" model or by dropping the pH value and lowering the pK_a of monomers using various lactones rings like D-glucono-δ-lactone [26]. It is established from research data that calcium chloride is most frequently used as the vital source of Ca^{2+} cations and is mainly responsible for speedy and irrepressible alginate gelation. The gelation rate is a serious constraint in regulating the gelation process. The slow gelation process delivers uniform gel structures with strong mechanical integrity. One useful tactic for a reduction in the rate of the gel formation process is to use phosphate buffers, i.e., sodium hexametaphosphate. The phosphate groups present in the buffer compete with calcium ions, and as a result gelation process is retarded. In addition, calcium sulfate and calcium carbonate with lower solubility can also prolong the gel-forming process. The gelation rate is also reliant on temperature; at lesser temperatures, the reactivity of Ca^{2+} is also reduced [27].

Alginate structure and proportions of M-, G-, and MG-units greatly influence gelling properties. Additionally, a larger quantity of repeating G-units are responsible for the generation of stiffer, inelastic, and reflexively more stable alginate gels. Alternatively, alginate with rich contents of M-unit forms progressively lenient and more mutable gels. However, MG-blocks in alginate gel regulate its contraction and higher flexibility nature [28]. The datum that alginate may endure in situ gelation makes alginate-based materials promising gears for a wide variety of applications, including injectable vehicles for tissue engineering or topical drug delivery approaches. Alginate capability of hydration and gelling formation supports the greater opportunity to use in the extended release of the active molecule at the desired administration site. Hence, these biopolymers have been widely considered for prolonged or controlled release drug delivery systems.

3.6 Degradation

Degradation of alginate can ensue due to the breaking of the glycosidic bonds between G- and M-units. There are mainly three reasons which are the root cause for this bond cleavage, such as (a) reactions catalyzed by the acidic or alkaline environment, (b) depolymerization caused due to thermal prevalence, and (c) derivatization of alginate by chemical reactions such as oxidation reactions. The alginates with rich G-blocks are less vulnerable to acid and thermal degradation than the alginates with rich M-blocks. Normally, thermal degradation of the polymer takes place at a temperature of more than 80°C [29]. In an acidic condition (where pH stands below 5), alginate usually undertakes hydrolysis at the glycosidic bond. The first step comprises the protonation of the glycosidic oxygen. After that, the reaction proceeds through an intermediate, namely

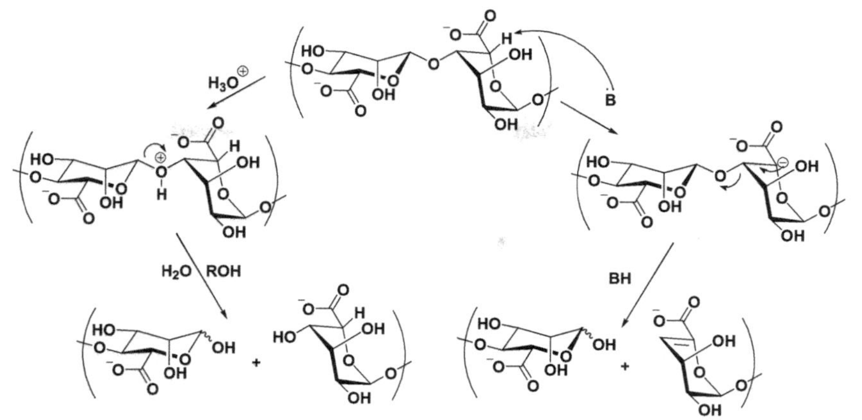

FIG. 3 Mechanism for hydrolysis of alginate in acidic and alkaline medium.

carbonium-oxonium ion to which a water molecule is added [30], whereas, in strong alkaline environments (where pH stands above 10), alginate undertakes degradation via b-elimination reaction. The first step involves the initial proton abstraction from the C5 position, which is facilitated by the electron-withdrawing effects of the carbonyl groups from the adjacent (C6) position. Further, it is followed by the rearrangement of the intermediate formed, which leads to the formation of an aliphatic compound and a protonated anion as represented in Fig. 3 [31].

Alginates are vulnerable to biodegradation in the existence of a group of enzymes commonly termed as alginases, which are usually found in marine algae, mollusks, and microorganisms. However, these enzymes are not present in mammals. A promising research work carried out by Al-Shamkhani and Duncan et al. demonstrated the biodistribution profile of a chemically modified propylene glycol alginate which was radiolabeled with tyrosinamide 125I [32]. The study revealed that the in vivo fate of systemically injected chemically modified alginate depends on the molecular weight. The endorsement is thus encouraged to practice low molecular weight alginates except for the usages through oral delivery of drug molecules where the polymer is supposed to expose to a very acidic environment such as gastrointestinal system.

4 Biological synergistic attributes toward drug delivery

A good biopolymer should hold good bioadhesion, biocompatibility, and immunogenic properties for practice in drug delivery applications so that it can be fully accepted by the biological as well as the physical system itself.

4.1 Bioadhesion

Alginate polymer has very sturdy bioadhesion characteristics, which make it a feasible candidate for mucosal drug delivery approaches. The presence of carboxyl end groups in the alginate skeleton classified it as an anionic mucoadhesive biopolymer. Research studies established that a polymer with charged density remains a strong mucoadhesive agent [33]. The penetration ability of the alginate polymeric chain through a polymer-mucosa interface is the main reason for a great adhesion property. Alginate has been evidenced to have the highest mucoadhesive asset in comparison with other polymers, including chitosan, polystyrene, polylactic acid, and carboxymethyl cellulose. The strong bioadhesive properties of alginate biopolymer potentially improve the overall drug release with mucosal delivery [34] and hence, therefore, serve to boost drug efficacy.

4.2 Biocompatibility

Biocompatibility of alginate is another vital matter of concern regarding the drive of drug delivery and hence extensively investigated in vitro as well as in vivo in the literature by several researchers, though the effect of the alginate composition is still in debate. Mainly, it relates to the variable heights of purity in the alginate studied. For example, it has been testified that alginates with high M-block unit were found to be more promising immunogenic and around 10 times more potent in persuading the production of cytokine when compared with high G-block unit containing alginates [35]. As alginate is mainly derived from natural sources, it potentially contains several impurities such as endotoxins, heavy metals, pyrogens, polyphenolic compounds, and immunogenic materials such as proteins [36]. Contaminant introduction can also arise during the process of gelation reactions when various chemical substances are used to yield the gels. There are mainly three methods by which the raw alginates can be freed from those contaminants. Using free-flow electrophoresis, raw alginate can be purified where the impurities can be separated from the algin using an external electrical field. Alginate can also be purified by involving elution and extraction of impurities from barium cross-linked beads. Alternatively, a third method for purifying native alginate includes a multistep process, involving filtration and precipitation of alginate as alginic acid and consequent extraction of proteins using various organic solvents. However, nowadays different medical-grade alginates are available commercially in the market [37] to meet the advanced requirements of biomedical as well as pharmaceutical applications.

4.3 Immunogenicity

From various research studies, it is verified that the two main reasons for the immunogenicity of alginate biopolymer resulted from the chemical composition and the mitogenic contaminants found in native alginate [38]. Commercially, alginate polymers are available in many different grades, including food, research, and ultra-pure medicinal and medical grade, with much more in pure and free from impurities or contaminants in comparison with raw alginate. The presence of impurities in commercially available alginate exerted various undesired adverse effects such as cytokine release and inflammatory reactions. However, it is also a fact that pure alginate does not hold those contaminants and therefore does not persuade any side effects. Additionally, researchers have found that there is a linear relationship between the level of the mannuronic acid unit and cytokine production [39]. Therefore, it is endorsed that uncontaminated alginate rich in a-L-guluronic acid unit can be utilized for in vivo research to dodge inflammatory responses. When alginate with high a-L-guluronic acid is used as implants, it has proven to produce less of an immunological response than other polymers such as polyvinyl alcohol and agarose gels. Further research on usages of alginate as surgical gauzes and films finds full biodegradability of the polymer in animal tissues with very little response. Investigations involving the implantation of alginate with rich L-guluronic acid content in in vivo model displayed no or little inflammatory reactions, thus making it a very promising drug delivery candidate for mucosal delivery (Table 1) [40].

5 Modification of alginate

Alginate obliges as one of the most multipurpose biopolymers applied in a wide array of abundant applications in drug delivery due to its favorable physiognomies, including thickening, gel formation ability, alleviating application, and biocompatibility. Currently, alginates are used in most industries, typically agri-food, fabrics, cosmetics, medicinal, pharmaceutical, and biomedical. Since it is very apt to formulate alginate biomaterials at low pH and temperature, essential for the encapsulation of delicate biomolecules such as proteins, amino acids, and nucleic acids, there is a high possibility to develop new biomaterials based on alginate products. A necessity for protracted and improved control of drug management has increased the demand for this tailor-made polymer's molecule for several applications.

However, some boundaries limit the application of alginate [41]. It lacks to meet some properties such as enough stability under an

TABLE 1 Various physiological and biological properties of alginate biopolymer apposite for various applications.

Unique physicochemical properties	Divergent applications
Gel formation ability/ gelation	Tissue engineering technology, drug-releasing formulation, taste camouflaging agents, cells immobilization and encapsulation, enhanced biocatalysis, engraved matrices
Hydrophobicity and hydrophilicity	Traditional as well as novel drug delivery system, microencapsulation of drugs and cells
Bioavailability	Food and agriculture industry (such as emulsifier or thickener), wound dressing technology, grafting of cells, resurgence of skin, hydrogel films
Bioadhesion	Medical applications, including devices, surface development, biological reagents, and bio-optoelectronics materials
pH sensitivity/ better pH-responsive biopolymeric nature	Various types of drug delivery approaches like gastrointestinal or mucoadhesive, etc.

aqueous environment, difficulties to regulate the rate of degradation of alginate-based materials, and critical for several medical applications. Hence, there is a drift to construct "value-added" alginate by executing the various types of derivatization methods on the polysaccharide's backbone. Therefore, researchers have modified alginate using various physical or chemical approaches to increase or boost physicochemical properties, biocompatibility, and solubility and to control the biodegradability of alginate-based products for a successful drug delivery strategy.

Alginate can be easily modified in two ways to improve physicochemical properties with reference to biological potential.

A. Physical cross-linking
B. Chemical modification

5.1 Physical cross-linking modification

Among the various physical and chemical derivatizations of alginate, cross-linking has been extensively adopted due to the flexibility, ability to attain desired properties, convenience, and relatively low cost. Fig. 4 depicts the various approaches of alginate cross-linking with respective examples of reagents used. The approaches implemented eased the improvement in the qualities of the alginate. The advantages and restrictions of the various cross-linkers employed to enhance the properties of alginate

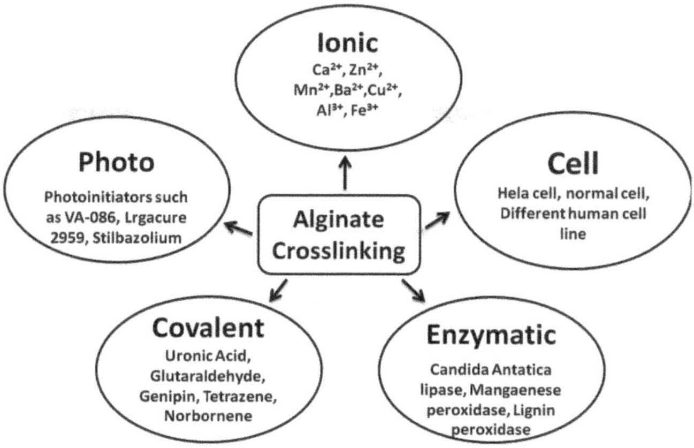

FIG. 4 Schematic representation of various approaches of alginate cross-linking with reagents used, respectively.

have also been discussed. Though there are many methods available for alginate cross-linking, some of them are as follows:

- **I.** Ionic cross-linking
- **II.** Covalent cross-linking
- **III.** Enzymatic epimerization
- **IV.** Photo-cross-linking
- **V.** Cell cross-linking

5.1.1 Ionic cross-linking

One of the simplest and upfront methods of cross-linking alginate to form 3D networks by the diffusion of bivalent ions such as calcium and zinc among the polymer chains is ionic cross-linking [42]. It is extensively used to develop various forms of alginate, like films, beads, fibers, hydrogels, and micro- and nanoparticles. In this crosslinking, ions just exist in the alginate network and may be released in a controlled manner as an import of solubility deviations motivated by pH dissimilarity of the microenvironment in the presence of bivalent cations. Alginates containing rich G content lead to the formation of stronger gels [43]. However, the affinity of alginate also plays a key role in shaping their cross-linking efficacy. The affinity constant for gelling provides us with an outline of the spatial homogeneity of the cross-linking practice together with evidence concerning mechanical stability. Reduction affinity of alginates toward divalent cations was found to be in the following order: Pb > Cu > Cd > Ba > Sr > Ca > Co > Ni > Zn > Mn [44]. Though calcium does not hold the highest affinity, it is the most chosen divalent cation used to cross-link the alginate network.

Alginate cross-linking, including calcium ions, can be achieved employing two tactics: (a) the diffusion method and (b) the internal setting method. The former procedure comprises diffusion of alginate solution from outside the reservoir, whereas the latter embraces the pH, or the solubility of ion source supports in the release of ions. The carboxylate groups of the alginate backbone that are negatively charged generate the largest unit of titratable positions along with the polysaccharide skeleton and are vital to cross-linking and to metal-binding mechanisms. Sections of alginate chains encumbered with G subunits form zigzag structures with cavities of appropriate size having specificity to bivalent ions due to their geometric order [45]. Employing this approach, many complex systems such as interpenetrate or semiinterpenetrate polyelectrolytes may be made up to more precisely control mechanical and swelling properties.

5.1.2 Covalent cross-link

Since ionic cross-linking alginates have very limited stability in vivo due to ion exchange mechanisms occurring at physiological conditions, alginates can also be modified by chemical approaches to obtain polymers with enlightening biological properties. Covalent cross-linking is such a modification technique, which is interceded by the large extent of functional groups along their molecular chain.

Covalent cross-linking alginate can be managed through different chemical routes based on the contribution of chemical groups, i.e., secondary hydroxyl (at C-2-OH and C-3-OH) or carboxylic (at C-6-COOH) groups of alginate skeleton. Diverse categories of cross-linking agents are used for these cross-linking, such as glutaraldehyde, epichlorohydrin, hexamethylene diisocyanate, carbodiimide, and adipic acid dihydrazide. They may variously affect the chemical and mechanical properties of the pure alginates [46]. An alternate method to modify alginates is oxidation reaction on hydroxyl groups at C2 and C3 positions, which leads to the formation of dialdehyde in each oxidized monomer unit by the estrangement of the carbon–carbon bond of vicinal glycols [47]. Reductive amination involving easy addition of substituents or reductive agents results in alginate derivatives with increased degradability and hydrophobicity. For example, dialdehyde and alkyl amine in the presence of a reducing agent like sodium borohydride ($NaBH_4$) or sodium cyanoborohydride ($NaCNBH_4$) can introduce long alkyl chains to the alginates, resulting in novel alginate derivative with polymeric surfactant and amphiphilic properties. All the detailed reactions have been discussed in detail in the chemical modification section later. Alginate solubility also can be enhanced by modification through covalent attachment of long alkyl chains or aromatic groups to the basic polymeric backbone.

5.1.3 Enzymatic epimerization

Enzymatic epimerization process is normally practiced altering M- to G-unit proportion or vice versa and as an amelioration of polymer backbone in M-, G-, or MG-blocks. The type of reactions is catalyzed by mannuronan C5-epimerases which are isolated from the soil bacterium *Escherichia coli* and *Azotobacter vinelandii* [48]. They decipher mannuronic acid residues into guluronic acid residues without breaking the glycosidic bond of the alginate backbone. Additionally, oligosaccharides which are basically polymeric fragments comprising 3–10 simple monosaccharides might be isolated from the alginate backbone.

5.1.4 Photo-cross-linking of alginates

Several potential rewards may be achieved through photo-cross-linking alginate instead of using another type of cross-linking like ionically or covalent. In the case of ironically cross-linked alginate, the resulting material properties of gels significantly depend on calcium. Also, some other essential characteristics such as the paraphernalia of material properties, fixed charge density, and the level of bivalent cations in the respective culture media cannot be explored individualistically in an ionically cross-linked system. The photo-cross-linking method allows the construction of alginate hydrogels without dependency on calcium ions. Apart from that, it is also an appropriate technique for controlling and maintaining gelation timing and kinetics properties.

Previously, researchers used methacrylate as photoinitiators substitution for the secondary alcohols in alginate chemistry. But presently Irgacure 2959 has been established as the primary tool for the generation of viable photo-cross-linked alginate constructs [49]. But the major key limitation of photo-cross-linking techniques remains as follows: (a) during tissue-engineered scaffolds, the photo-cross-linking method revealed the seeded cells toward ultraviolet (UV) light, (b) recent uses of chemical photoinitiators may be cytotoxic in predecessor or in radical form, (c) the necessity of organic solvents to dissolve the photoinitiators in the polymeric precursor solution, and (d) the resulting photogenerated substances can also agitate the construct by generating temperature variance. To overcome the above issues, several approaches are adopted by the researchers. The use of aqueous-soluble photoinitiators, i.e., VA-086 or V-50, provides an advantage for therapeutic cell encapsulation. Alginate modification with methacrylate anhydride trailed by photo-cross-linking with such photoinitiators VA-086 or Irgacure 2959 for chondrocyte scaffolds improves the applicability of these photoinitiators for generating tissue-engineered products [50]. Photoinitiators that can minimize the absorption of UV light, less or no solubility requirements in an organic solvent, and the photoinitiators with no or less cytotoxicity have the immense potential to greatly impact the applicability of photo-cross-linked hydrogel in various medicinally approved scaffolds. Alginate-based hydrogels can also be cross-linked by photoirradiation, a less invasive strategy based on the controlled exposure to ultraviolet (UV) light to rapidly cross-link polymer chains in a physiological environment.

5.1.5 Cell cross-linking

Alginate gels are broadly used as cell carriers in biomedical applications such as tissue engineering and wound dressings, including the delivery of drug molecules to the targeted site of action. The cell encapsulation method involves the initial preparation of a suspension of cells in a sodium or potassium alginate solution. Then the suspension is dribbled with a calcium chloride bath. Once both the reagents are mixed together, calcium ions instantaneously cross-link with the alginate droplet and form a gel bead encapsulating cell [51].

5.2 Chemical modification

To modify the alginate chemically, it is imperative to recognize the precise chemical reaction that occurs during the process. In alginate chemistry, it mainly depends on the presence of the chemical reactivity of the functional groups involved. Two hydroxyl groups at the C2 and C3 positions and one carboxyl group at the C6 position in the main alginate skeleton primarily play the role. Differences in the chemical reactivity between hydroxyl and carboxyl groups hinder the type of reactions. In chemoselective reactions, only one type of reacted functional group is relatively straightforward, whereas, in stereoselective reactions, only one of the two hydroxyl groups (C2 or C3) reacts in a controlled fashion which is much more challenging. The low difference in reactivity between the two hydroxyl groups is responsible for this type of behavior [52]. Another aspect that is precise to alginates is the skill to react to functional groups in an epimer selective fashion. This enables that a specific functional group can be selectively modified on either M or G residues of original alginate. Generally, chemical modification of the alginate biopolymer is employed either to vary the reactivity of alginate by introducing highly reactive functional groups (e.g., aldehyde groups) or to introduce chemical (e.g., phosphate or sulfate) or biochemical (e.g., amino acids) groups which will increase the biointegration and bioaffinity of alginate-based materials. Because the alginate biopolymer itself contains both hydroxyl and acid functional groups, it offers great versatility for chemical modification as are going to be illustrated later. Further, modification of alginates is not only hooked into the solvent but also on the location of the carbon and substituent groups. Two secondary OH positions (C2 and C3) or at the COOH C6 position are often used for modification. Additionally, the reactivity of the alginates is reliant on the sort of functional groups and selective to the sort of chemical modification. Variation in reactivity between the functional groups is often a plus to change alginate selectively for specific applications.

5.2.1 *The chemical modification of alginate hydroxyl groups*

The common chemical modification of alginate hydroxyl groups includes

I. Oxidation
II. Reductive amination
III. Sulfation
IV. Copolymerization
V. Acetylation
VI. Phosphorylation

Oxidation

Oxidized alginate derivatives bear more reactive groups with enhanced derogation properties than innate alginate. Therefore, the recent years' formulation of various oxidized forms of alginate has received much more attention as it provides a high potential to be used in various biomedical applications, including drug delivery. Malaprade et al first described the oxidation of alginate using periodate [53]. It involves alginate oxidation in the presence of sodium periodate that oxidizes the hydroxyl groups on both C3 and C4 positions in the uronic subunits into an open-chain adduct, also known as 2,3-dialdehydic alginate or alginate dialdehyde (ADA) through bond breakage and ring-opening [54]. These aldehyde groups can react spontaneously with hydroxyl groups present on the adjacent uronic acid subunits in the polymer chain to form a hemiacetal. Its formation can prevent complete oxidation of the biopolymer and consumption of sodium periodate. Oxidation of alginate is usually taking place in an aqueous solution at room temperature. The degree of oxidation can be determined via iodometry by titrating any periodate remaining after the reaction. Characterization is carried out using 1H nuclear magnetic resonance (NMR) (aldehyde content) and ^{13}C NMR (to confirm the polymer scissioning that is accompanied by oxidation) [55]. Extensive scissioning of the polymer chain is reflected in the decrease in molecular weight with an increase in the amount of oxidation. Vold et al. and Smidsrod and Painter demonstrated changes in the intrinsic viscosity and chain stiffness in the oxidized alginate samples and concluded that the stiffness and the length of chains were decreased with an increase in the oxidation of alginate samples. The enhanced flexibility of the polymer chains was linked to the open-chain adducts [56]. This open-chain adduct is much more susceptible to hydrolytic scission than unmodified alginate, and while alginates are resistant to biodegradation and are not broken down in mammals, controlled degradation of alginate can be achieved by partially oxidizing the alginate polymer. This property unlocked areas for use of alginate in tissue engineering applications.

Reductive amination

Oxidized alginates are a better candidate than the native alginate due to their varsity of reactivity. However, it further enables chemical modifications, namely reductive amination. It is carried out by introducing an alkyl amine group in the presence of sodium cyanoborohydride ($NaCNBH_3$) which reduces the imine group in the pH (range varies within 6–7) [57]. The resulted alginamine with improved amphiphilic properties proves its potential to be used in many applications, particularly biomedical applications. Amphiphilic alginamine beads are used as a carrier system for controlled release delivery of ibuprofen successfully. The modified alginates which are very rich in amine groups may be used for further derivatization, such as polymer grafting. Alginate polyethylene glycol (PEG)-grafted copolymers were synthesized by the addition of monocarboxyl-terminated PEG to alginates. This grafting process liberated mixed possessions of both alginate and PEG [58]. Kang et al. synthesized a novel series of alginate-derived polymeric surfactants (APSs) with a linear alkyl group containing C8, C12, and C16 chain by oxidation followed by reductive amination with 2,3-dialdehydic alginate [59].

Sulfation

For more than 60 years, sulfated alginate has been extensively used as an anticoagulant due to the structural similarity between sulfated alginate and heparin, which provides high blood comparability. A few diverse methods have been reported for sulfation of alginate with the aid of DCC-H_2SO_4 and $ClSO_3H$/formamide methods [60]. It is one of the most extensively used methods for alginate sulfation. The DCC-H_2SO_4 method is carried out using the tributyl ammonium salt of alginate (TBA-Alg) dissolved in dimethylformamide. NMR analysis confirmed that sulfation takes place at C2 and C3 positions only, and the process resulted in an 80% degree of sulfation with an associated reduction in molecular mass from 10 to 100 kDa [61]. Importantly, the investigation also established that this method of sulfation did not produce any undesired reactions or side products. The DCC-H_2SO_4 and $ClSO_3H$/formamide methods smooth the synthesis of various degrees of substitution ranging from 5% to 120% (each alginate subunit) by fluctuating $ClSO_3H$ concentration. A similar trend was also found for poly-M, poly-G, and poly-MG sulfation. The same method has also been applied to the sulfation of ADA producing sulfated alginates with heightened chain flexibility. Freman et al. prepared a sulfated alginate scaffold with high blood compatibility and anticoagulant action [62].

Copolymerization

Copolymerization techniques of alginate involve the hybridization of other biopotential polymers with alginate. Recently, these processes have been broadly used in many applications, including the release of an active molecule to the specific site of action with a controlled rate either through the addition of another polymer or propagation of monomers, such as sodium acrylate, acrylamide, and vinyl sulfonic acid, onto the hydroxyl group of the alginate backbone [16].

Acetylation

Acetylation of alginates facilitated the treatment of nonaqueous spherical beads of calcium alginate, or alginic acid gel, with acetic anhydride in pyridine without any degradation. At low degrees of acetylation, substitution reactions happened almost exclusively on the mannosyl uronic acid residues, whereas, at high degrees of acetylation, only a trivial proportion of the isolated guluronic acid residues was substituted [63]. The degree and pattern of substitution were studied and investigated using NMR spectroscopy and degradation with specific enzymes. The presence of 0-acetyl groups inhibited depolymerization by alginate lyases. The presence of acetyl groups appears to protect the polymer from degradation by lyases enzymes. Those enzymes are produced by several bacteria, including *A. vinelandii*, and some of the alginate-producing strains of *Pseudomonas* sp. [64]. The acetylation system in alginate-producing bacteria thus seems to promote protection toward their enzymes and degrading enzymes from other microorganisms. A reasonable increase in the degree of acetylation of alginate causes an expansion of the molecular chain, whereas a higher degree of acetylation generates more flexible polymers increasing swelling ability.

Phosphorylation

Phosphorylation of alginate can be accomplished using the urea phosphate method. The reaction is proceeded by the dispersion of alginate polymer in dimethylformamide (DMF). In this way, phosphate groups are introduced at C2 and C3 positions via reactions with the hydroxyl groups. From a detailed NMR study, it was found that the dominant positions of phosphorylation were found as G-2 and M-3 [65]. These are the equatorial functionalities and hence more reactive than their axial counterparts due to condensed steric hindrance. Another useful alternative method of phosphorylation employed using the $H_3PO_4/P_2O_5/Et_3PO_4$/hexanol system yielded a 12.5% degree of phosphorylation. Coleman et al. prepared a series of phosphorylated alginate hydrogels utilizing a heterogeneous urea/phosphate reaction, which boosted the resistance to degradation [66].

5.2.2 Modification of the carboxyl groups

Modification of the carboxyl groups at the C6 position of native alginate skeleton may be achieved, mainly by the following:

I. Ugi reaction
II. Esterification
III. Amidation

Ugi reaction

Ugi reaction is a commonly used multicomponent organic reaction including a variety of components such as a carboxylic acid, an isocyanide, an amine, and an aldehyde or ketone. All the components are mixed with definite practice in certain specific conditions to give a bis-amide molecule. This reaction is employed for alginate biopolymer as a fruitful approach to upsurge the hydrophobic nature [67]. The presence of carboxyl groups in alginate facilitated the Ugi reaction. It is carried out by gradual addition of all the components, such as formaldehyde, *n*-octylamine, and cyclohexyl isocyanide, into alginate and finally form complex derivative, termed as bis-amide alginate that is hydrophobically boosted.

Esterification

A very simple method to chemically modify alginate is the esterification of carboxylic groups, by the reaction of alcohols with alkyl halides in the presence of a catalyst. This type of modification is also preferred particularly to increase the hydrophobicity of alginate, like Ugi reaction. It involves the conjugation of hydrophobic moieties through an ester linkage. The esterification process of alginate is performed by two major approaches [68]. The first method comprises a direct esterification reaction between an alcohol and the alginate carboxyl group in the presence of a catalyst. An excess of alcohol was added for confirming the equilibrium orientation to form the desired product. The other method involves the reaction between alginate and alkyl halide for the formation of expected alginate esters. This approach uses the addition of acidic alginate (algin or alginic acid) with a common base (most commonly tetrabutylammonium hydroxide; TBA-OH is preferred and used) to facilitate the conjugation of alkyl halides. After that, alkyl halide is added to the previous reaction mixture under continuous stirring for an opposite time, which leads to the formation of conjugated alkyl moiety to the alginate through an ester linkage. Mahou et al. have managed to prepare a novel series of alginate-poly(ethylene glycol) hybrid microspheres, by utilizing the esterification reaction of sodium alginate and vinyl sulfone-terminated multiarm PEG (PEG-VS) directly into cell culture medium [69]. They are found to be useful for the transplantation of microencapsulation of cell transport.

Amidation

Amidation of alginate involves an amide bond formation between a primary or secondary amine and a carboxylate-containing alginate molecule in the presence of a water-soluble coupling agent. Normally, 1-ethyl-3-(3-dimethylaminopropyl)carbodiimide hydrochloride (EDC-HCl) is used as a coupling agent [70]. The reaction initiates with the conjugation of EDC-HCl on the alginate carboxyl group. The primary or secondary amine is then added to the mixture to replace the EDC-HCl and amide linkage bind formed. It is found that the efficiency of the reaction can be further increased by using *N*-hydroxysulfosuccinimide (NHS) as a stabilizing agent for EDC intermediates molecule. Amidation of carboxylic groups with amine holding molecules has been alternatively projected to form more hydrophilic derivatives for nucleus pulposus replacement therapy in tissue engineering (Fig. 5).

Some other alginates modifications useful for drug delivery

Alginate coupling with amino acids or peptides Coupling of alginates and amino acids (e.g., cysteine) or peptides (e.g., containing the arginine, glycine, aspartate (RGD) sequence) is also accomplished as the resulting biomaterial displayed enhanced biocompatibility and bioadhesion properties which are important for drug delivery. It involves the reaction between the terminal amine of the amino acid and the carboxylic acid group of alginates through activation of the carboxylic acid group (carbodiimide chemistry). For instance, cysteine has been coupled with alginate (7% substitution of alginate subunits) using stoichiometric quantities of cysteine as confirmed photometrically [71]. Other amino acids, i.e., lysine, aspartic acid, arginine, and phenylalanine, also can be coupled to alginate by a similar process. The aspartate (RGD) sequence is used expansively in biomaterials science due to its very good cell adhesion characteristics. Several RGD-containing peptides have been coupled with alginate via carbodiimide chemistry, including GRGDY, GGGGRGDSP, and GGGGRGDSY. Jindal et al. have managed to prepare a novel series of sodium alginate-cysteine conjugate utilizing carbodiimides with more effective mucoadhesiveness and controlled drug release behavior and cohesivity [72].

Grafting Moreover, there are several studies that describe the production of modified alginate derivatives through grafting approaches with different substances such as polyacrylamide, methacrylate, lectin, galactose, sulfate, cyclodextrins, cysteine, dodecyl amine, and propylene glycol. Yang et al. have managed to graft fatty alcohols like octanol, dodecanol, and hexadecanol with alginates to form novel amphiphilic alginate esters (Alg-C8, Alg-C12, or Alg-C16) [73]. They are beneficial to serve as protein drugs and as a carrier of hydrophobic drug molecules.

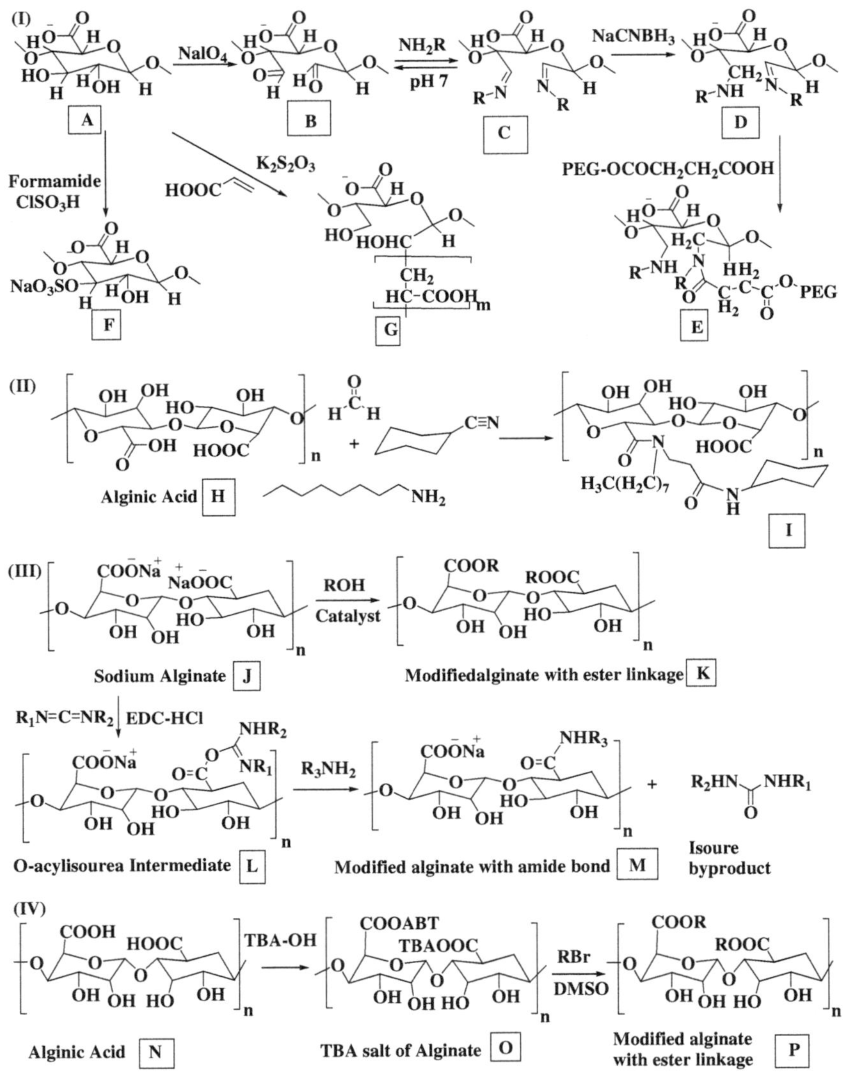

FIG. 5 (I) (A) Conversion of A to B (oxidation reactions of sodium alginate with the aid of sodium periodate). (B) Conversion of B to D via C (reductive amination of oxidized alginate). (C) Conversion of D to E (preparation of alginate-grafted PEG copolymer). (D) Conversion of A to F (sulfation process of sodium alginate using sodium chlorosulfate in formamide). (E) Conversion of A to G (copolymerization of sodium acrylate with alginate). (II) Conversion of H to I (modification of alginate using Ugi reaction). (III) (A) Conversion of J to K (direct esterification reaction of sodium alginate in the presence of excess alcohol and catalyst). (B) Conversion of J to M via L (amidation of alginate using EDC-HCl). (IV) Conversion of N to P (esterification process of alginate using alkyl halides).

Laurienzo et al. have managed to prepare sodium alginate-grafted derivatives using polyethylene glycol (PEG). It is found to be a promising aspirant for an alginate gel with a higher degree of biocompatibility.

6 Application of modified alginate in drug delivery

Modified alginates demonstrated a substantial enhancement in many significant properties that are essential for drug delivery applications, viz. biocompatibility, low toxicity, and gel-forming ability. This is the main cause of immense applications of modified alginates in the controlled or targeted release of active substances in biological systems. Apart from that, these alginate derivatives can be formed in different forms, including gels, beads, hydrogels, fibers, matrices, nano- and microspheres, and membranes of different thicknesses, so that they can be suitable for many varieties of drug delivery schemes. Practically, modified alginates not only can deliver bioactive or pharmaceutical drugs, but they are also skilled to deliver biocargo, such as proteins, DNA, and cells. The nature of cargo delivered depends on the type and specification of derivatization performed on alginates also. Several kinds of chemically modified alginates are successfully applied in numerous biomedical or pharmaceutical applications in various dosage forms (Table 2).

6.1 Pharmaceutical drug delivery

Alginates and their various synthetically modified analogs of physically cross-linked derivatives can boost the pharmacokinetic profile of a pharmaceutical formulation. In general, alginate derivatives have the competence to regulate and endure the release of encapsulated drugs due to their unique gelation ability. Besides, they upsurge the drug concentration in the spot of infection, while lessening its undesired side effects. Furthermore, they can encapsulate a hydrophobic and hydrophilic drug rendering to the nature of alteration performed. Along with the last era, a lot of investigation was performed using alginate and its derivatives in drug delivery applications. The relationship between the drug molecule and the nature of the physicochemical carrier matrix or vice versa affects the nature of the drug release scenario. So, the design of a drug formulation denotes a parallel equilibrium between the carrier matrix environment and drug matrix associations. Thiolated alginate for mucoadhesive drug delivery and sulfated alginate as a heparin mimetic represent the best examples for this type of situation. The use of amphiphilic thiolated alginate derivatives provides the enhancement in protein retention duration and the practice of oxidized alginate for the formation of a covalently cross-linked matrix and covalent add-on of a drug molecule. The practice

TABLE 2 Examples of different chemically modified alginates and their biomedical applications, including various drug delivery systems.

Chemical modification	Material and active constituent	Dosage formulation	Pharmaceutical application
Oxidation	Oxidized sodium alginate and epithelial stem cells	Hydrogel	Enhancement in wound healing therapy of cornea [74]
	Flurbiprofen	Beads	Sustained oral delivery [75]
Reductive amination	Alginate-g-poly (ethylene glycol) and human foreskin fibroblasts	Microspheres	Cell microencapsulation [69]
Sulfation	Sulfated alginate	Microspheres	Reduction rate in secreting cytokines, boosting biocompatibility [76]
Copolymerization	Sodium alginate-polyacrylamide and famotidine	Hydrogel	Gastroretentive sustained delivery [77]
	Starch, sodium alginate, and diclofenac sodium	Hydrogel and beads	Oral drug delivery for pH-dependent matrices [78]
	Alginate methacrylate and human endothelial cell lines (HUVEC and L929)	Injectable hydrogel	Tissue engineering system for myocardial repair [79]
	Galactosylated alginate and hepatocytes	Microcapsules	Cell carrier system with mechanical stability and permeability [80]
	Cyclodextrin, alginate, and *Sphingomonas cloacae*	Beads	Immobilization of bacteria [81]
	Cyclodextrin, alginate, and ondansetron	Gel	Controlled drug delivery [82]
Acetylation	*O*-Acetylated alginate	Biofilms	Efficient biofilm development and protection of microorganism from immune responses [83]

TABLE 2 Examples of different chemically modified alginates and their biomedical applications, including various drug delivery systems—cont'd

Chemical modification	Material and active constituent	Dosage formulation	Pharmaceutical application
Phosphorylation	Phosphorylated alginate	Hydrogel	Mineralization and increasing chelation for tissue engineering [65]
Esterification	Propylene glycol, alginate, and lysozyme	Microparticles	Sustained release of protein encapsulation [84]
Amidation	Amidic derivatized alginate and glibenclamide	Beads	Enhanced dissolution of novel drug delivery system [85]

of chemically modified alginate in the controlled release of drugs is rapidly expanding exclusively sulfated alginate as a heparin mimetic.

6.1.1 *Films*

Ionically cross-linked alginate films were found to be apt for several means of drug delivery. This is one of the most appropriate ways to evenly distribute calcium ions in alginate films to achieve some important criteria, namely enough stability, enough flexibility, and a controlled rate of degradation. Biologically efficient alginate films prepared by either gelation or cross-linking modification improvise biocompatibility, adhesiveness, and mechanically more stability. The films can be further modified with the aid of different plasticizers like glycerol. These types of films were found to be suitable for wound dressing and as secondary barrier films.

Cross-linked alginate films blended with gelatin, using the solvent evaporation technique for drug release applications, have been developed by Dong et al. Ciprofloxacin hydrochloride was used as a model drug, and Ca^{2+} was used as a cross-linking agent. Influence of factors such as the relative amount of alginate to gelatin, the quantity of ciprofloxacin hydrochloride, pH and ionic strength of the release solution, and cross-linking time with Ca^{2+} on release properties of films provides fruitful results [86]. In addition to cross-linking variables, the conditions of the release medium such as pH and ionic strength were found to affect the properties of the films. The longer the cross-linking process, the slower the drug discharge due to the higher level of cross-linking.

6.1.2 Beads

The limited efficiency of alginate as a drug carrier due to its poor mechanical durability and stability can be resolved by cellulose/alginate beads in drug delivery. These types of beads can be prepared by droplet extrusion or precipitation method for drug release. One real example is using the preparation of metformin hydrochloride (MH) drug by using the same method [87]. To evaluate the effects of metformin in different cellulose fibers of alginate matrix on the stability, in vitro drug release properties were evaluated. The results showed that the combination of cellulose with alginate matrix augments the mechanical and thermal stability. The drug release behavior of alginate beads was also improved, and it inhibited the rapid release of alginate in simulated intestinal fluid.

6.1.3 Hydrophobically modified alginate for drug delivery systems

Maiti et al. have developed flurbiprofen delivery using beads of partially oxidized sodium alginate, which is a nonsteroidal antiinflammatory drug [75]. However, at first, it was observed that the release of the drug was very quick; almost all the drug content was consumed within 90 min due to the high rate of diffusion of flurbiprofen molecules from the alginate matrix. To conquer this disadvantage, the researchers included an ionic cross-linker, i.e., calcium ions, and a covalent cross-linker, i.e., adipic acid dihydrazide. The results showed that the release of drugs was extended to approximately 8 h, varying on the cross-linker ratio and thus a decrease in the diffusion rate of the drug and increasing its delivery at higher efficiency.

Choudhary et al. have prepared chemically derivatized alginates by amidation reaction through conjugating lipophilic moiety (C8) [88]. The hydrophobically modified alginate was designed to deliver the lipophilic nonsteroidal antiinflammatory drug, sulindac. The drug release profile also was studied to see the effect of hydrophobic modification on the alginate backbone. The results showed the prolonged drug release profile in the case of modified alginates compared with the case of pure alginate. Thus, the hydrophobic modification was established to boost the release profile of the loaded sulindac drug successfully.

Colinet et al. accomplished a chemically modified amphiphilic alginate on the side chains by polycaprolactone (PCL) conjugation grafts through esterification reaction [89]. These newly modified amphiphilic alginates were used to deliver a poorly soluble and hydrophobic drug, theophylline to a greater extent. Release studies confirmed that conjugation prolonged the release of theophylline to 2 h instead of 1 h in the case of normal alginates.

Mohy Eldin et al. have managed to prepare L-arginine-grafted alginate using p-benzoquinone as an activating agent loaded with a model protein, BSA [90]. The drive of the study was to formulate a pH-responsive system that agrees to a controlled release of BSA in acidic media. The release profile of alginate hydrogels was found to be heightened at acidic conditions for up to 5h. The study also confirmed the fact that the improvement in the release profile is credited to the integration of arginine amine groups, which increases the BSA release to 300% of its original value in pure alginate.

Sahasathian et al. established an advanced gastroretentive delivery vehicle for amoxicillin with the aid of floating and mucoadhesive alginate beads coated with chitosan for high effective abolition of *Helicobacter pylori*, a major contributing mediator of peptic ulcers [91]. These beads displayed better high encapsulation effectiveness, high floating capacity, high drug loading capacity, and a high in vitro mucoadhesion toward the gastric mucosal layer. The release rate of amoxicillin was faster in the simulated gastric fluid than in simulated intestinal fluid and achieved sustained release property of amoxicillin with a high rate of efficiency. Gadad et al. managed to prepare modified alginate floating beads of cefpodoxime proxetil, a third-generation cephalosporin antibiotic by precipitation method incorporating calcium carbonate as a gas-generating agent [92]. The in vitro dissolution study discloses that the concentration of the gas-generating agent and sodium alginate showed good floating time with a good track of release rate.

Murata et al. have succeeded to prepare various types of alginate beads of metronidazole for sustained delivery of drugs [93]. These release profiles of those alginate derivatives were developed not only for the sustained release nature of drugs but also to target the gastric mucosa. Choudhury et al. established alginate floating beads with various kinds of oil entrapped with metformin hydrochloride (HCl) by gelation method without homogenization [94]. The higher the density of the oil used, the larger was the size and improved spherical natured beads were observed. The increase in the concentration of oil triggered an increase in size and the spherical nature of the beads due to their density and volatility. The release profile specifies that the sustaining action of metformin was displayed in the following order: groundnut oil > castor oil > mentha oil > conventional alginate beads. Commercially, several modified alginate-based products are available in the market with a variety of applications, including drug delivery.

6.2 Pharmaceutical biomolecule delivery

Alginate has numerous exclusive properties that have empowered it to be used as a background matrix for the enrichment, entrapment, or delivery of several biomolecules, i.e., DNA, proteins, cells, etc. In general, proteins are vulnerable to denaturation due to the nature of the hostile biological environment like low pH media environment in the stomach.

Thus, alginate or modified alginate derivatized matrices can defend proteins from degradation without affecting their structure and functionality. However, hydrophilicity and the inherent porosity of proteins allow them to diffuse quickly from alginate matrices. Therefore, several approaches were applied efficiently to govern the protein release profile. Chemical modification of alginates through the coupling of hydrophobic moieties in such a manner, which intensifies the loading efficacy and increases the release profile, is one of the most useful and successfully applicable strategies. Different cross-linking approaches like ionic and covalent methods were also found to be useful for further controlling of the protein release in drug delivery [95].

The mild gelation process without using any organic solvents enables biomolecules and cells to be incorporated into the alginate matrices with the retention of full biological activity. Freeze-drying of alginate beads comprising biomolecules is another possible way to maintain their secondary structure and to safeguard their longer stability during storage conditions. Biocompatibility and immunogenicity of alginate are dependable with some important factors like M/G ratio and mitogenic impurities. However, other factors like the form and size of the beads, and smoothness, composition, and viscosity of the membrane can influence alginate immunogenicity. High G content-rich alginates capsules in combination with polylysine are evidenced to induce a severe inflammatory action, though normally the high G content alginates seem to possess higher biocompatibility than the M-rich polymers.

Yao et al. proposed another synthetic derivatization on sodium alginate to expand the stacking productivity and control the release profile by conjugation of a hydrophobic moiety to control the swelling characteristics [96]. The hydrophobic alteration was performed through coupling polybutyl methacrylate (PBMA) onto the sodium alginate backbone through amidation linkage with the use of EDC chemistry. This new framework was utilized in the conveyance of bovine serum albumin (BSA) as a model protein. After synthetic adjustment, the proposed framework was consolidated in a calcium chloride arrangement to shape microspheres. From that point, a similar release profile investigation of BSA was followed between normal sodium alginate and modified alginate microspheres. The outcomes demonstrated a noticeable upgrade in the release profile of BSA from the modified alginates microspheres in comparison with alginate microspheres [97].

6.3 Drug delivery through transplantation of cells

Basic purified alginates with extremely high biocompatible and very low cytotoxic heterogeneity have made it the most widespread biomaterial for xenotransplantation, immunoisolation, and microencapsulation of cells. This is based on meeting systematic scientific and regulatory standards for human application. Drug delivery accomplished via the transplantation of cells or cellular materials has proved to be a feasible therapeutic strategy for the replacement of organs, tissue engineering, and medicinal drug molecule delivery.

This strategy permits the sustained release of drug substances over longer periods through such mechanisms that are not conceivable using traditional therapeutics. Cells are typically obtained either from the allograft (similar species) or more frequently from xenograft (a different species) to the host.

The attribution of this arena can be sketched from the very first research study of Lim and Sun, in 1980. They described the assembly of a microcapsule adjacent to pancreatic islet cells with calcium alginate-poly-L-lysine alginate [98]. Since then, numerous efforts have been attempted to generate a bioartificial pancreas via microencapsulation and immunoisolation techniques of pancreatic islets. In the 20th century, human islets were efficiently implanted into the peritoneal cavity of diabetic humans that persisted viable for almost 2.5 years. And the field has advanced significantly since. Many research assessments contemplate current, historical, and future triumphs along with perceptions in islet encapsulation strategies and technologies till date [99]. The high demand for cellular microencapsulation using alginate-based matrices for drug delivery influences many researchers, and clinical practices addressing a comprehensive range of diseases are also in progress. The complement of required and unwanted properties of alginate-based microcapsules that subsidize their potential achievement is concise in table.

7 Concluding remarks

Alginate is a versatile biomaterial that has numerous applications in biomedical science and engineering due to its favorable characteristics, including biocompatibility and ease of gelation capacity. To date, alginate hydrogels have been chiefly striking in wound healing, tissue engineering, and drug delivery applications as those gels hold structural resemblance to the extracellular environments in tissues and can be easily deployed to play several perilous roles. This book chapter has discussed the detailed chemical structure and the extraction procedure of alginates and, thereafter, the outstanding physicochemical biological properties and their contribution to drug delivery. Then, the chapter pointed out the detailed physical and chemical modification approaches that are performed primarily on both the carboxyl and hydroxyl functional group backbone of alginates. The last part of the chapter had focused on the most advanced biomedical applications of chemically modified alginates. It covered the recent research performed in the biomedical fields and most importantly in drug delivery applications. In the end, it can be concluded that alginate and its modified forms are very promising biomaterials for biomedical fields as they offer advantages in drug delivery materials, such as self-assembled fibers and semiinterpenetrating networks. It is expected that they will have many contributions in the future of drug delivery applications due to their stunning properties.

8 Future directions

In alginate chemistry, the role of the structure of alginate, including M/G ratio, chain extent, and the effect of naturally consequential impurities have been well studied and characterized. Also, the three-dimensional matrix assembling of alginate molecules formed through physical or chemical cross-linking is well stated and fruitfully applied to govern the stability and mechanical properties. A recent study showed that alginate-based three-dimensional (3D) cell culture systems (CCS) and dried alginate macroporous hydrogel scaffolds can yield favorable environments for cellular attachment, proliferation, and differentiation. Presently, two alginate-based 3D products of standard cell culture plates, namely NovaMatrix-3D of NovaMatrix, Norway, and AlgiMatrix of Thermo Fisher Scientific, United States, are available in market in different formats. The enhancement progression of alginate-based devices for drug delivery has empowered consideration in resolving ongoing challenges in clinical practice. Now, many clinical trial experiments are enduring for type 1 diabetes treatment through cell encapsulation-based alginate biomaterials. In another scenario, a big challenge for cancer therapy utilizing alginate-based materials is tuning the size of the capsules that fulfill the criteria of cellular uptake positively. Innovation continues as cell encapsulation with the help of modified alginate polymer is being designed, which may be responsive to external and noninvasive stimuli. It may also introduce desirable pharmacokinetic properties for both drug and cell delivery.

References

[1] Ramsay RR, Popovic-Nikolic MR, Nikolic K, Uliassi E, Bolognesi ML. A perspective on multi-target drug discovery and design for complex diseases. Clin Transl Med 2018;7(1):3.

[2] Wen H, Jung H, Li X. Drug delivery approaches in addressing clinical pharmacology-related issues: opportunities and challenges. AAPS J 2015;17(6):1327–40.

[3] Maitz MF. Applications of synthetic polymers in clinical medicine. Biosurf Biotribol 2015;1(3):161–76.

[4] Bassas-Galia M, Follonier S, Pusnik M, Zinn M. Natural polymers: a source of inspiration. In: Bioresorbable polymers for biomedical applications. Woodhead Publishing; 2017. p. 31–64.

[5] Abasalizadeh F, Moghaddam SV, Alizadeh E, Kashani E, Fazljou SM, Torbati M, Akbarzadeh A. Alginate-based hydrogels as drug delivery vehicles in cancer treatment and their applications in wound dressing and 3D bioprinting. J Biol Eng 2020;14(1):1–22.
[6] Miao T, Wang J, Zeng Y, Liu G, Chen X. Polysaccharide-based controlled release systems for therapeutics delivery and tissue engineering: from bench to bedside. Adv Sci 2018;5(4):1700513.
[7] Zhu J, Marchant RE. Design properties of hydrogel tissue-engineering scaffolds. Expert Rev Med Devices 2011;8(5):607–26.
[8] Song R, Murphy M, Li C, Ting K, Soo C, Zheng Z. Current development of biodegradable polymeric materials for biomedical applications. Drug Des Devel Ther 2018;12:3117.
[9] Tennessean HH, Karlsen J. Alginate in drug delivery systems. Drug Dev Ind Pharm 2002;28(6):621–30.
[10] Bahram M, Mohseni N, Moghtader M. An introduction to hydrogels and some recent applications. In: Emerging concepts in analysis and applications of hydrogels. Intech Open; 2016.
[11] Draget KI, Smidsrod O, Skjak-Braek G. Alginates from algae. In: Biopolym Online, vol. 6. Hoboken, NJ, USA: Wiley; 2005.
[12] Bart HJ, Pilz S, editors. Industrial scale natural products extraction. John Wiley & Sons; 2011.
[13] Rehm BH, Moradali MF, editors. Alginates and their biomedical applications. Singapore: Springer; 2018.
[14] Rinaudo M. Main properties and current applications of some polysaccharides as biomaterials. Polym Int 2008;57(3):397–430.
[15] Lee KY, Mooney DJ. Alginate: properties and biomedical applications. Prog Polym Sci 2012;37(1):106–26.
[16] Sun J, Tan H. Alginate-based biomaterials for regenerative medicine applications. Materials 2013;6(4):1285–309.
[17] McHugh DJ. Production, properties and uses of alginates. In: Production and utilization of products from commercial seaweeds. FAO Fisheries Technical Paper, vol. 288. Campbell, Australia: Food and Drug Administration of the United Nations; 1987. p. 58–115.
[18] Kariduraganavar MY, Kittur AA, Kamble RR. Polymer synthesis and processing. In: Natural and synthetic biomedical polymers. Elsevier; 2014. p. 1–31.
[19] Hay ID, Rehman ZU, Moradali MF, Wang Y, Rehm BH. Microbial alginate production, modification and its applications. J Microbial Biotechnol 2013;6(6):637–50.
[20] Wang Y, Moradali MF, Goudarztalejerdi A, Sims IM, Rehm BH. Biological function of a polysaccharide degrading enzyme in the periplasm. Sci Rep 2016;6:31249.
[21] Imeson AP. Thickening and gelling agents for food. Springer Science & Business Media; 2012.
[22] da Silva TL, Vidart JM, da Silva MG, Gimenes ML, Vieira MG. Alginate and sericin: environmental and pharmaceutical applications. In: Biological activities and application of marine polysaccharides. Rijeka: InTech; 2017. p. 57–86.
[23] Szekalska M, Pucilowska A, Szymanska E, Ciosek P, Winnicka K. Alginate: current use and future perspectives in pharmaceutical and biomedical applications. Int J Polym Sci 2016;2016.
[24] Belalia F, Djelali NE. Rheological properties of sodium alginate solutions. Rev Roum Chim 2014;59:135–45.
[25] Morch YA, Donati I, Strand BL, Skjak-Braek G. Effect of Ca2+, Ba2+, and Sr2+ on alginate microbeads. Biomacromolecules 2006;7(5):1471–80.
[26] Leick S, Henning S, Degen P, Suter D, Rehage H. Deformation of liquid-filled calcium alginate capsules in a spinning drop apparatus. Phys Chem Chem Phys 2010;12(12):2950–8.
[27] Borgogna M, Skjak-Braek G, Paoletti S, Donati I. On the initial binding of alginate by calcium ions. The tilted egg-box hypothesis. J Phys Chem B 2013;117(24):7277–82.

[28] Draget KI, Gaserod O, Aune I, Andersen PO, Storbakken B, Stokke BT, Smidsrod O. Effects of molecular weight and elastic segment flexibility on syneresis in Ca-alginate gels. Food Hydrocoll 2001;15(4–6):485–90.
[29] Holme HK, Lindmo K, Kristiansen A, Smidsrod O. Thermal depolymerization of alginate in the solid state. Carbohydr Polym 2003;54(4):431–8.
[30] Haug A, Larsen B, Smidsrød O. The degradation of alginates at different pH values. Acta Chem Scand 1963;17(5):538.
[31] Haug A, Larsen BJ, Smidsrod O. Alkaline degradation of alginate. Acta Chem Scand 1967;21:2859–70.
[32] Morgan SM, Al-Shamkhani A, Callant D, Schacht E, Woodley JF, Duncan R. Alginates as drug carriers: covalent attachment of alginates to therapeutic agents containing primary amine groups. Int J Pharm 1995;122(1–2):121–8.
[33] Swain S, Behera A, Beg S, Patra CN, Dinda SC, Sruti J, Rao MEB. Modified alginate beads for mucoadhesive drug delivery system: an updated review of patents. Recent Pat Drug Deliv Formul 2012;6(3):259–77.
[34] Verma S. Polymers in designing the mucoadhesive films: a comprehensive review. Int J Green Pharm 2018;12(02).
[35] Otterlei M, Ostgaard K, Skjak-Braek G, Smidsrod O, Soon-Shiong P, Espevik T. Induction of cytokine production from human monocytes stimulated with alginate. J Immunother 1991;10(4):286–91.
[36] Menard M, Dusseault J, Langlois G, Baille WE, Tam SK, Yahia LH, Zhu XX, Hallé JP. Role of protein contaminants in the immunogenicity of alginates. J Biomed Mater Res B Appl Biomater 2010;93(2):333–40.
[37] Calo E, Khutoryanskiy VV. Biomedical applications of hydrogels: a review of patents and commercial products. Eur Polym J 2015;65:252–67.
[38] Tam SK, Dusseault J, Bilodeau S, Langlois G, Halle JP, Yahia LH. Factors influencing alginate gel biocompatibility. J Biomed Mater Res A 2011;98(1):40–52.
[39] Draget KI, Taylor C. Chemical, physical and biological properties of alginates and their biomedical implications. Food Hydrocoll 2011;25(2):251–6.
[40] Shilpa A, Agrawal SS, Ray AR. Controlled delivery of drugs from alginate matrix. J Macromol Sci C Polym Rev J 2003;43(2):187–221.
[41] Paques JP, van der Linden E, van Rijn CJ, Sagis LM. Preparation methods of alginate nanoparticles. Adv Colloid Interface Sci 2014;209:163–71.
[42] Sachan NK, Pushkar S, Jha A, Bhattcharya A. Sodium alginate: the wonder polymer for controlled drug delivery. J Pharm Res 2009;2(8):1191–9.
[43] Gurikov P, Smirnova I. Non-conventional methods for gelation of alginate. Gels 2018;4(1):14.
[44] Haug AR, Smidsrød O. The effect of divalent metals on the properties of alginate solutions. Acta Chem Scand 1965;19(2):341–51.
[45] Yamamoto K, Yuguchi Y, Stokke BT, Sikorski P, Bassett DC. Local structure of Ca2+ alginate hydrogels gelled via competitive ligand exchange and measured by small angle X-ray scattering. Gels 2019;5(1):3.
[46] Reddy N, Reddy R, Jiang Q. Crosslinking biopolymers for biomedical applications. Trends Biotechnol 2015;33(6):362–9.
[47] Matsuhiro B. Organic derivatives of algal polysaccharides. Cah Biol Mar 2001;42(1–2):159–67.
[48] Gimmestad M, Steigedal M, Ertesvag H, Moreno S, Christensen BE, Espin G, Valla S. Identification and characterization of an *Azotobacter vinelandii* type I secretion system responsible for export of the AlgE-type mannuronan C-5-epimerases. J Bacteriol 2006;188(15):5551–60.
[49] Rouillard AD, Berglund CM, Lee JY, Polacheck WJ, Tsui Y, Bonassar LJ, Kirby BJ. Methods for photocrosslinking alginate hydrogel scaffolds with high cell viability. Tissue Eng Part C Methods 2011;17(2):173–9.

[50] Ferreira P, Coelho JF, Almeida JF, Gil MH. Photocrosslinkable polymers for biomedical applications. In: Biomedical engineering-frontiers and challenges, vol. 1. IntechOpen; 2011. p. 55–74.
[51] Andersen T, Auk-Emblem P, Dornish M. 3D cell culture in alginate hydrogels. Microarrays 2015;4(2):133–61.
[52] Wang T, Demchenko AV. Synthesis of carbohydrate building blocks via regioselective uniform protection/deprotection strategies. Org Biomol Chem 2019;17(20):4934–50.
[53] Reakasame S, Boccaccini AR. Oxidized alginate-based hydrogels for tissue engineering applications: a review. Biomacromolecules 2018;19(1):3–21.
[54] Gomez CG, Rinaudo M, Villar MA. Oxidation of sodium alginate and characterization of the oxidized derivatives. Carbohydr Polym 2007;67(3):296–304.
[55] Yang JS, Xie YJ, He W. Research progress on chemical modification of alginate: a review. Carbohydr Polym 2011;84(1):33–9.
[56] He S, Zhang M, Geng Z, Yin Y, Yao K. Preparation and characterization of partially oxidized sodium alginate. Chin J Appl Chem 2005;22(9):1007.
[57] Carre MC, Delestre C, Hubert P, Dellacherie E. Covalent coupling of a short polyether on sodium alginate: synthesis and characterization of the resulting amphiphilic derivative. Carbohydr Polym 1991;16(4):367–79.
[58] Wang HL, Zhang L, Zuo Y, Zou Q, Zhou S, Li YB. Preparation and drug-controlled release of hydrophobically modified alginate. J Funct Mater 2010;9:23.
[59] Kang HA, Jeon GJ, Lee MY, Yang JW. Effectiveness test of alginate-derived polymeric surfactants. J Chem Technol Biotechnol 2002;77(2):205–10.
[60] Arlov O, Skjak-Braek G. Sulfated alginates as heparin analogues: a review of chemical and functional properties. Molecules 2017;22(5):778.
[61] Ronghua H, Yumin D, Jianhong Y. Preparation and in vitro anticoagulant activities of alginate sulfate and its quaterized derivatives. Carbohydr Polym 2003;52(1):19–24.
[62] Freeman I, Kedem A, Cohen S. The effect of sulfation of alginate hydrogels on the specific binding and controlled release of heparin-binding proteins. Biomaterials 2008;29(22):3260–8.
[63] Ertesvag H. Alginate-modifying enzymes: biological roles and biotechnological uses. Front Microbiol 2015;6:523.
[64] Pawar SN, Edgar KJ. Chemical modification of alginates in organic solvent systems. Biomacromolecules 2011;12(11):4095–103.
[65] Coleman RJ, Lawrie G, Lambert LK, Whittaker M, Jack KS, Grondahl L. Phosphorylation of alginate: synthesis, characterization, and evaluation of in vitro mineralization capacity. Biomacromolecules 2011;12(4):889–97.
[66] Rehm BH. Alginates: biology and applications. Springer Science & Business Media; 2009.
[67] Ugi I. The α-addition of immonium ions and anions to isonitriles accompanied by secondary reactions. Angew Chem Int Ed Engl 1962;1(1):8–21.
[68] Hasnain MS, Nayak AK. Alginates: versatile polymers in biomedical applications and therapeutics. CRC Press; 2019.
[69] Mahou R, Meier RP, Bühler LH, Wandrey C. Alginate-poly (ethylene glycol) hybrid microspheres for primary cell microencapsulation. Materials 2014;7(1):275–86.
[70] Jindal AB, Wasnik MN, Nair HA. Synthesis of thiolated alginate and evaluation of mucoadhesiveness, cytotoxicity and release retardant properties. Indian J Pharm Sci 2010;72(6):766.
[71] Madison SA, Carnali JO. PH optimization of amidation via carbodiimides. Ind Eng Chem Res 2013;52(38):13547–55.
[72] Bernkop-Schnürch A, Kast CE, Richter MF. Improvement in the mucoadhesive properties of alginate by the covalent attachment of cysteine. J Control Release 2001;71(3):277–85.
[73] Guarino V, Caputo T, Altobelli R, Ambrosio L. Degradation properties and metabolic activity of alginate and chitosan polyelectrolytes for drug delivery and tissue engineering applications. AIMS Mater Sci 2015;2(4):497–502.

[74] Wright B, De Bank PA, Luetchford KA, Acosta FR, Connon CJ. Oxidized alginate hydrogels as niche environments for corneal epithelial cells. J Biomed Mater Res A 2014;102(10):3393–400.
[75] Maiti S, Singha K, Ray S, Dey P, Sa B. Adipic acid dihydrazide treated partially oxidized alginate beads for sustained oral delivery of flurbiprofen. Pharm Dev Technol 2009;14(5):461–70.
[76] Arlov O, Skjak-Braek G, Rokstad AM. Sulfated alginate microspheres associate with factor H and dampen the inflammatory cytokine response. Acta Biomater 2016;42:180–8.
[77] Tripathi R, Mishra B. Development and evaluation of sodium alginate–polyacrylamide graft–co-polymer-based stomach targeted hydrogels of famotidine. AAPS PharmSciTech 2012;13(4):1091–102.
[78] Chang A. pH-sensitive starch-g-poly (acrylic acid)/sodium alginate hydrogels for controlled release of diclofenac sodium. Iran Polym J 2015;24(2):161–9.
[79] Wang X, Hao T, Qu J, Wang C, Chen H. Synthesis of thermal polymerizable alginate-GMA hydrogel for cell encapsulation. J Nanomater 2015;2015:1–8.
[80] Tian M, Han B, Tan H, You C. Preparation and characterization of galactosylated alginate–chitosan oligomer microcapsule for hepatocytes microencapsulation. Carbohydr Polym 2014;112:502–11.
[81] Pluemsab W, Fukazawa Y, Furuike T, Nodasaka Y, Sakairi N. Cyclodextrin-linked alginate beads as supporting materials for *Sphingomonas cloacae*, a nonylphenol degrading bacteria. Bioresour Technol 2007;98(11):2076–81.
[82] Izawa H, Kawakami K, Sumita M, Tateyama Y, Hill JP, Ariga K. β-Cyclodextrin-crosslinked alginate gel for patient-controlled drug delivery systems: regulation of host–guest interactions with mechanical stimuli. J Mater Chem B 2013;1(16):2155–61.
[83] Nivens DE, Ohman DE, Williams J, Franklin MJ. Role of alginate and its O acetylation in formation of Pseudomonas aeruginosa microcolonies and biofilms. J Bacteriol 2001;183(3):1047–57.
[84] Hurteaux R, Edwards-Leevy F, Laurent-Maquin D, Levy M-C. Coating alginate microspheres with a serum albumin-alginate membrane: application to the encapsulation of a peptide. Eur J Pharm Sci 2005;24(2–3):187–97.
[85] Khames A, Abdelazeem AH, Habash M, Taha MO. Preparation and in vitro characterization of glibenclamide-loaded alginate hexyl-amide beads: a novel drug delivery system to improve the dissolution rate. Pharm Dev Technol 2014;19(7):881–90.
[86] Dong Z, Wang Q, Du Y. Alginate/gelatin blend films and their properties for drug controlled release. J Membr Sci 2006;280(1–2):37–44.
[87] Guo T, Pei Y, Tang K, He X, Huang J, Wang F. Mechanical and drug release properties of alginate beads reinforced with cellulose. J Appl Polym Sci 2017;134(8).
[88] Choudhary S, Bhatia SR. Rheology and nanostructure of hydrophobically modified alginate (HMA) gels and solutions. Carbohydr Polym 2012;87(1):524–30.
[89] Colinet I, Dulong V, Hamaide T, Le Cerf D, Picton L. New amphiphilic modified polysaccharides with original solution behaviour in salt media. Carbohydr Polym 2009;75(3):454–62.
[90] Eldin MS, Kamoun EA, Sofan MA, Elbayomi SM. L-arginine grafted alginate hydrogel beads: a novel pH-sensitive system for specific protein delivery. Arab J Chem 2015;8(3):355–65.
[91] Sahasathian T, Praphairaksit N, Muangsin N. Mucoadhesive and floating chitosan-coated alginate beads for the controlled gastric release of amoxicillin. Arch Pharm Res 2010;33(6):889–99.
[92] Gadad AP, Patil MB, Naduvinamani SN, Mastiholimath VS, Dandagi PM, Kulkarni AR. Sodium alginate polymeric floating beads for the delivery of cefpodoxime proxetil. J Appl Polym Sci 2009;114(3):1921–6.
[93] Murata Y, Sasaki N, Miyamoto E, Kawashima S. Use of floating alginate gel beads for stomach-specific drug delivery. Eur J Pharm Biopharm 2000;50(2):221–6.

[94] Choudhury PK, Kar M. Preparation of alginate gel beads containing metformin hydrochloride using emulsion-gelation method. Trop J Pharm Res 2005;4(2):489–93.
[95] Parhi R. Cross-linked hydrogel for pharmaceutical applications: a review. Adv Pharm Bull 2017;7(4):515–30.
[96] Wong TW. Alginate graft copolymers and alginate–co-excipient physical mixture in oral drug delivery. J Pharm Pharmacol 2011;63(12):1497–512.
[97] Nagpal M, Maheshwari DK, Rakha P, Dureja H, Goyal S, Dhingra G. Formulation development and evaluation of alginate microspheres of ibuprofen. J Young Pharm 2012;4(1):13–6.
[98] de Vos P, Faas MM, Strand B, Calafiore R. Alginate-based microcapsules for immunoisolation of pancreatic islets. Biomaterials 2006;27(32):5603–17.
[99] Murua A, Portero A, Orive G, Hernández RM, de Castro M, Pedraz JL. Cell microencapsulation technology: towards clinical application. J Control Release 2008;132(2):76–83.

CHAPTER

13

Uses of tailor-made plant starches in drug delivery

Md Saquib Hasnain[a], *Mohd Usman Mohd Siddique*[b], *Manoj M. Gadewar*[c], *Mohammed Tahir Ansari*[d], *Mohd Neyaz Ahsan*[e], *Gouranga Nandi*[f], *and Amit Kumar Nayak*[g]

[a]Department of Pharmacy, Palamau Institute of Pharmacy, Daltonganj, Jharkhand, India, [b]Department of Pharmaceutical Chemistry, Shri Vile Parle Kelavani Mandal's Institute of Pharmacy, Dhule, Maharashtra, India, [c]Dept of Pharmacology, School of Medical and Allied Sciences, K.R. Mangalam University, Gurgaon, (Haryana), India, [d]School of Pharmacy, Faculty of Science and Engineering, University of Nottingham Malaysia, Semenyih, Selangor, Malaysia, [e]Department of Medical Laboratory Technology, University Polytechnic, Birla Institute of Technology, Ranchi, Jharkhand, India, [f]Division of Pharmaceutics, Department of Pharmaceutical Technology, University of North Bengal, Raja Rammohunpur, Darjeeling, West Bengal, India, [g]Department of Pharmaceutics, Seemanta Institute of Pharmaceutical Sciences, Jharpokharia, Mayurbhanj, Odisha, India

1 Introduction

Conventionally, in drug delivery formulation systems, excipients serve as bulking agents, disintegrants, sweeteners, adhesives, binders, and so on [1–7]. They are inert in nature and usually do not interfere with the activities of active pharmaceutical ingredients in formulations. Over the decades, the effect of various excipients in the dosage forms has significantly been about augmenting the bioavailability and patient compliance with formulations [8,9]. Different studies revealed that the rate and extent of active drugs in the formulation are affected by excipients, which in turn

Tailor-Made Polysaccharides in Drug Delivery
https://doi.org/10.1016/B978-0-12-821286-8.00004-5

reduces the efficacy and bioavailability of drugs at the site of absorption. Consequently, many plant-based polymers have been used as excipients [10]. Starch is a well-known category of natural polymers being extensively explored in the pharmaceutical industry and mainly obtained from different plant parts and organs [11,12]. Starch molecules comprise amylose and amylopectin, which exist in different proportions depending on the sources from which they are extracted [11,13,14]. Amylose is a linear polysaccharide which accounts for 20%–30% of starch linked with glucose units by ∞-1-4 glycosidic bonds [13]. Amylopectin constitutes around 70%–80% in starch and is linked with ∞-1–6 bond [15].

To maximize the utility of starches as excipients in order to develop various drug delivery dosage forms and other biomedical uses, the physicomechanical and functional properties can be modified [12,16,17]. Basically, four types of starch modifications are carried out—chemical, physical, enzymatic, and genetic—and these modifications involve the incorporation of three hydroxyl groups into the starch copolymer [18]. Chemical modification is the most common form of modification associated with starches, as it increases functionality and is a nondestructive method that helps in both retaining and increasing the efficacy and applicability of the pharmaceutical product [19]. The hydroxyl groups at C2, C3 and C6 positions in starches can be modified by using various chemical approaches like etherification, esterification, and oxidation [18,20]. The extent of modifications at C2, C3, and C6 positions of starches depends on the reaction condition, which may lead to alterations in different functional properties like gelatinization, swelling, solubility, pasting, and retrogradation [15,21]. These newly modified properties make starches more functionalized for various pharmaceutical applications as compared to unmodified starches. The present chapter focuses on the various chemical methods used for tailoring plant starches that enhance their applicability as pharmaceutical excipients in developing different types of dosage forms.

2 Starch: Basic chemistry and properties

Starches are the most abundant, nature-derived plant polysaccharides [22–24]. The word "starch" has Germanic origins and means "strong" in German. Owing to low processing costs, starches are regarded as low-cost biopolymers [25]. Moreover, these are nonirritant as well as biocompatible [26,27]. Starches are biologically degraded by microorganisms and are regarded as biodegradable biomaterials [22,28,29]. Starches are biomacromolecules with high molecular weight encompassing thousands of glucose units connected through glycosidic bonds [30]. Two distinguished structural copolymeric forms constitute the starch molecules: amylose (average content in starch molecules: 20%–25%) and amylopectin (average content in starch molecules: 75%–80%) [11]. Starch copolymer chain with amylase and amylopectin components is presented in Fig. 1 [18]. Among these two, amylose can be seen in a linear structural arrangement with glucose units bounded together by α-(1,4)-linkages and to some extent by α-(1,6)-bonds [11,30]. In the molecular structure of starches, amylose includes a degree of polymerization up to 6000, which is reported to be dependent on the sources [7,11]. On the other hand, the structure of amylopectin is well-branched with α-(1,6)-bonds in the branching points [11]. Within the molecules of natural starches, both the relative ratio of amylose to amylopectin as well as α-(1,6) branch points are dependent on the origin [26]. The molecular mass of amylose is about 105–106 g/M, and for amylopectin it is about 107–109 g/M [7,26]. Many hydroxyl groups are found in starch chains. For example, there are two secondary hydroxyl moieties at the C-2 and C-3 positions of each glucose unit accompanied by one primary hydroxyl moiety at the C-6 position, when this is not connected.

Generally, pure starches are white in color and odorless and tasteless [11,31]. These are almost insoluble in cold water and organic solvents. However, due to leaching out of amylase, starches swell gradually in warm water and lose their crystallinity [31]. In addition, amylose is capable of forming hydrocolloid-type gels as well as stronger films. The crystallization of starches on cooling decreases the consistency in storage (i.e., retrogradation) and the discharge of water molecules (i.e., syneresis) [31–34]. The retrogradation of starch molecules is influenced by several factors—relative amylase/amylopectin concentration ratio in starch molecules, temperature, presence of polar substances, and so on [33,34]. Increased swelling, amplified viscosity, and solubility are some of the required parameters that usually characterize the gelation process of starches [35]. With an increasing concentration of amylose, the gel strength of starches improves, whereas with a higher

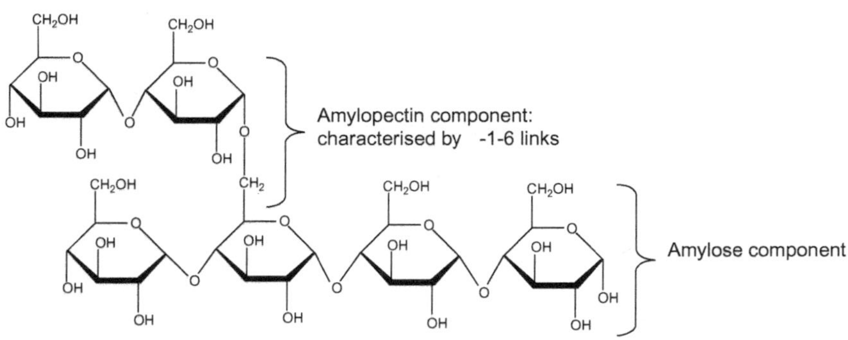

FIG. 1 The molecular structures of amylase and amylopectin [18]. *From Masina N, Choonara YE, Kumar P, du Toit LC, Govender M, Indermun S, Pillay V. A review of the chemical modification techniques of starch. Carbohydr Polym 2017;157:1226–1236. Copyright © 2016 Elsevier Ltd.*

amylopectin concentration, relatively translucent and softer gels are obtained [32,35]. Moreover, it is reported that amylose produces relatively stronger matrices, whereas amylopectin usually leads to the production of brittle and low-mechanical-strength matrices [7,11]. Pure starches are more or less broken down following oral ingestion [11]. Starches are considered a promising candidate for developing numerous sustainable products due to their renewability and low processing costs [14,22,23,29,36]. Over the past decades, numerous research groups have been investigating the industrial applications of a variety of potential nonconventional sources of natural starch [37]. It has been already found that starches have many industrial applications, such as textiles, adhesives, papers, plastics, cosmetics, pharmaceuticals, and other biomedical areas (tissue engineering, wound dressings, adsorption, etc.) [38–47]. Physicochemical as well as functional properties of starches from nonconventional sources should be recognized for their exploitations in many biomedical fields [25,48,49]. However, in some instances, the use of these materials may be challenged by a number of potential constraints like poor processability, lower moisture resistance, incompatibility with some biopolymers (mainly hydrophobic biopolymers), and low stability in acidic milieu [50–54]. Furthermore, because of the poor flow properties, less compressibility, and faster drug releasing in physical pHs, native starches are unsuitable for controlled drug releasing [11]. Because of the presence of hydroxyl groups in the molecular structure, starches are widely researched polymeric materials for both physical and/or chemical modifications [18,53–56]. These modified starch materials are nowadays used in various biomedical applications, including in drug delivery [16,57–60]. Several starch-based composite materials are also being explored as sustained drug-releasing carrier materials in drug delivery [39–42,45,59].

3 Plant-derived starches as pharmaceutical excipients in drug delivery

Natural starches occur as a prime-category constituent of biomacromolecules of storage carbohydrates in many plants, such as corn, rice, wheat, potatoes, peas, beans, tapioca, cassava, and banana [7,16,38,40]. Generally, starches are found in cereals, seeds, rhizomes, tubers, root of vegetables, and corns [11,40]. The native form of natural starches is granular with semicrystalline microscopic structures with specific characteristic shapes as well as sizes [29,37]. The native starch granules extracted from various plant resources possess different characteristics with respect to their shapes, sizes, as well as structures [11,29]. There has been a rapid rise in the annual global production of numerous types of plant-derived starches. Recently, the growing industrial demands of these plant-derived starches have accelerated the industry's and researchers' interest in searching for newer origins of starch and developing novel approaches to natural starch extraction procedures [11,22,38,40]. Majority of plant-derived starches are extracted from cereals (60%–80%; from maize, rice, wheat, oat, barley, etc.), legumes (25%–50%; from pea, bean, chickpea, etc.), tubers (60%–90%; from arrowroot, potato, cassava, cocoyam, etc.), and some green or immature fruits (e.g., banana) [11]. In more recent times, researchers have been exploring methods to extract starches from various plant-based sources that can potentially be used as pharmaceutical excipients in a variety of industrial, food, and medicinal products—such as emulgents, thickening agents, suspending agents, binders, disintegrating agents, matrix-forming materials, sustained-release materials, biomucoadhesives, film-formers, gelling agents, colon-targeting agents, and capsule shell materials—and, in particular, their potential use in developing numerous pharmaceutical dosage forms [60–65]. Some of the plant-derived starches that can be potentially be used as pharmaceutical excipients in various pharmaceutical dosage forms are summarized in Table 1.

4 Synthesis of tailor-made plant starches and their uses in drug delivery

Chemical moieties used for structural modification of starches are classified into two categories—mono-functional reagents and bi-functional reagents—based on their chemical properties [18,101]. Mono-functional reagents are mainly responsible for providing cationic, hydrophobic or covalently reactive groups [102]. These modifications result in gelatinization of starches, which give more stabilized derivatives by forming association in-between amylose and amylopectin [103]. Hydroxypropylation is most commonly method employed for structural modification of starches using mono-functional reagent [104]. Bi-functional reagents react with more than one hydroxyl groups and permit cross-linking between polymers [15,105]. Tri-meta-phosphates and phosphoryl chlorides are commonly used cross-linking agents, which stabilize starches by modification of its solubility, mobility and swelling [106]. Chemical modifications of starches are a widely used method for the synthesis of different modified starches with different chemical properties [18,53–55]. Other methods involve the use of toxic and/or corrosive chemicals, which makes such modified starches unsuitable for various pharmaceutical applications [107]. Some of the methods used for chemical modifications of starches and their variations are summarized in Fig. 2 [18].

TABLE 1 Plant-derived starches utilized as potential pharmaceutical excipients in developing various pharmaceutical dosage forms.

Plant-derived starches	Type of excipients	References
Maize starch	Binder, disintegrant, release-retardant, film-former	[62,66–68]
Potato starch	Binder, disintegrant, release-retardant, film-former release-retardant, gelling agent	[63,69–72]
Tapioca starch	Mucoadhesive, disintegrant, matrix-former, release-retardant	[73,74]
Dioscorea starch	Binder, matrix-former, release-retardant	[75–78]
Rice starch	Disintegrant, film-former	[69–81]
Bora rice starch	Mucoadhesive, disintegrant, matrix-former, release-retardant, colon-targeting agent	[61,82–86]
Sago starch	Binder, matrix-former, release-retardant, capsule shell material	[87–90]
Jackfruit seed starch	Emulsifier, binder, suspending agent, mucoadhesive, matrix-former, release-retardant	[36,40–42,91–93]
Indian palo rhizome starch	Matrix-former, release-retardant	[94]
Mung starch	Disintegrant	[95]
Taro starch	Matrix-former, release-retardant	[96]
Cocoyam starch	Binder	[97]
Tiger nut starch	Matrix-former	[64]
Ginger starch	Binder	[98]
Sorghum starch	Mucoadhesive, disintegrant, matrix-former	[99,100]

4.1 Oxidation

Oxidation of starches results in improved physiochemical properties, which help in the enhancement of adhesivity thereby promoting the release of active ingredients with a controlled-release formulation [108]. Various derivatives of starches are produced by treatment with different oxidizing agents in controlled temperature and pH [109]. To achieve high yield of different starch derivatives, hydroxyl groups are targeted for oxidation. The properties of newly synthesized starches are mainly influenced by the oxidative reagent used in the process of conversion, ensuring better physiochemical properties as compared to native starches [110].

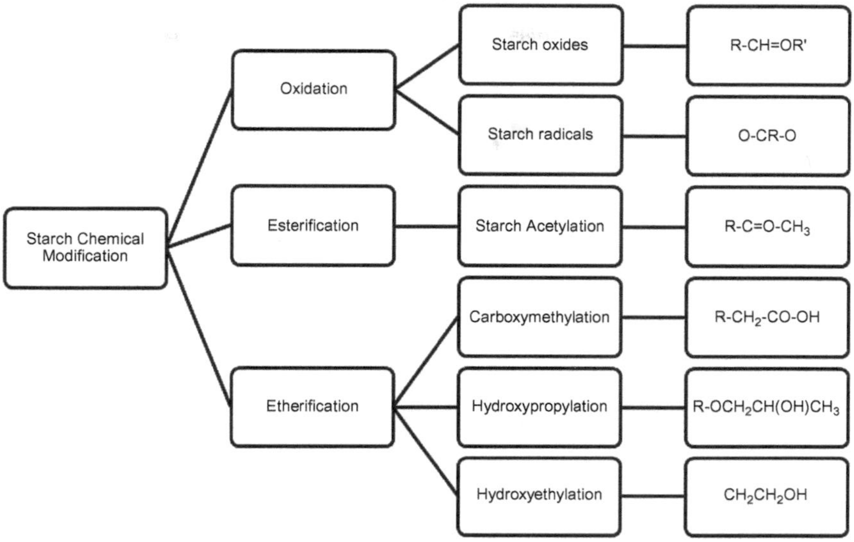

FIG. 2 Various methods used for chemical modifications of starches and their variations [18]. *From Masina N, Choonara YE, Kumar P, du Toit LC, Govender M, Indermun S, Pillay V. A review of the chemical modification techniques of starch. Carbohydr Polym 2017;157:1226–1236. Copyright © 2016 Elsevier Ltd.*

Altered physicochemical properties of oxidized starches typically result in decreased viscosity and increased clarity of starches [9].

Chemical modifications of starches involve the substitution of hydroxyl group at C2, C3, and C6 positions via oxidative mechanism, which consists of a series of reactions [111,112]. The most commonly used oxidative agents for chemical modifications are sodium hypochlorite and hydrogen peroxide. Introducing aldehyde group to native starch involves two chemical reactions [113]. In the first step, oxidation of hydroxyl groups to carbonyl or carboxyl group takes place followed by the depolarization of chains in between the glucopyranose units by the rapture of ∞-(1–4) links in adjucent glucose units [114,115].

Due to ease of availability and its effect on starch properties, sodium hypochlorite is widely used as an oxidizing agent in the commercial production of modified starches. Various factors influencing the process of oxidation are pH [116], temperature and reaction time [117], concentration of sodium hypochlorite [116], and the molecular structure of native starches and their sources [118]. The mechanism of chemical modification involves the oxidation of hydroxyl group in amylose and amylopectin polymer in native starches, which depends on the extent of oxidation and partial depolymerization of amylose and amylopectin [119]. The physicochemical properties of the starches mainly depend on the ratio of carbonyl and/or carboxyl groups present within oxidized starches, thus making

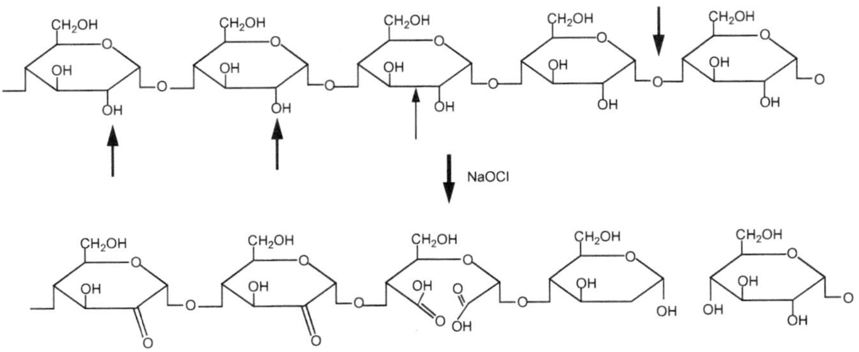

FIG. 3 Sodium hypochlorite oxidation of starch, showing carbonyl and carboxyl group formation in the ∞-(1-4) D-glucose chains of amylose and/or amylopectin polymers [120]. *From Vanier NL, El Halal SLM, Dias ARG, da Rosa Zavareze E. Molecular structure, functionality and applications of oxidized starches: a review. Food Chem 2017; 221:1546–1559. Copyright © 2016 Elsevier Ltd.*

them suitable for various industrial applications. Fig. 3 depicts the oxidation reaction that occurs between starches and sodium hypochlorite, which produces carbonyl and carboxyl groups [119].

Another oxidizing agent used for the modification of starches is hydrogen peroxide (H_2O_2); it is obtained from a variety of sources, and it doesn't form any toxic product as it will degrade in water and oxygen [110]. The oxidation of starch in the presence of H_2O_2 is a complex mechanism, and it mainly occurs via generation of free radical chain reaction. Decomposition of H_2O_2 in the presence of metal ions is faster and results into generation of hydroxyl free radicals, which are highly unstable and react with carbohydrates by extracting hydrogen from C-H groups on sugar rings, thereby forming new radicals. The carbonyl and carboxyl groups are formed during oxidation to a lesser extent in the process of oxidation [110].

Starches are cleaved into 1,2-glycol structures by peroxide oxidation forming two CHO/glucose units. Oxidation of starches by periodates results in the production of di-aldehyde group, which is highly reactive and acts as a cross-linking agent. Periodate reaction is an oxidative diol-scission reaction [120]. Modifications of starches using periodate oxidation are already in use for a wide variety of applications (in pharmaceuticals, papers, textiles, etc.) [120,121]. The major disadvantage of periodate oxidation is that it is an expensive method and, thus, only limited to industrial applications [119]. Another technique used for modification of starches is the use of ozone [122]. Ozone oxidation produces less harmful byproducts like carbon dioxide, water, and inorganic ions.

4.2 Esterification

Esterification of starches results in the formation of alkyl or aryl derivatives from the hydroxyl groups; it alters the retrograde properties of native starches and converts them to intra-amylase chain reaction with amylopectin, which is an outer chain [18,103]. Acylated starches are classified into three categories based on the degree of substitution, such as low, medium, and high. The value of the degree of substitution is 0.01–0.2 for low-acetylated starches and they are easily solubilized in water [123]. These starches are mainly produced by using acetic anhydride and sodium hydroxide as catalysts [124]. The reaction of native starches with sodium hydroxide results in the formation of alkoxide that reacts with hydroxyl to form acetylated starch derivatives [15]. The value of the degree of substitution is 0.3 and 0.1 for medium and low starches, respectively. They are easily solubilized in water as compared to low-acetylated starches [21]. Those starches having a high-degree-substitution value are insoluble in water but soluble in various organic solvents like ether, chloroform, and benzene. Acetylation of starches is mainly influenced by their origin and different reaction conditions [9].

Low amylose starches possess a high degree of substitution value because acetylation is mainly observed in amorphous regions owing to its nonhindrance with amylopectin for the C=O incorporation [125]. This change in native starches improves various physicochemical properties such as hydrophobicity, processability, and flexibility. Physical changes in starches are mainly produced by reacting starches with organic acids having long chains, such as anhydrides, acid chlorides, or their derivatives. These transformations in native starches are useful in sustained-release formulations, controlled biodegradation, and enhanced stability against acid secretion in GIT for some of the oral dosage formulations [18,21,126]. Paulos et al. (2016) synthesized nanoparticles by acetylating *Dioscorea deltoidea* native starch with acetic anhydride [124]. For the fabrication of nanoparticles from native starch, emulsification was carried out under high-pressure homogenization followed by solvent evaporation. The size of nanoparticles was mainly found to be influenced by factors such as solvent, surfactant, concentration of surfactant, and the time required for the process of homogenization by nanoparticles less than 200 nm in size and a polydispersity index (PDI) of < 0.2. Najafi et al. (2016) made an attempt to deliver acetylated corn starch nanoparticles of antibacterial drug—ciprofloxacin [127]. These acetylated corn starch nanoparticles of ciprofloxacin were synthesized by reacting native corn starches with acetic anhydride and acetic acid and with changing the degree of substitution. With this approach, the entrapment efficiency of ciprofloxacin was within the range of 67.7%–89.1%. In another work, Minimol et al. (2013) synthesized amphiphilic PEGylated starch acetate nanoparticles with a particle size of 32 nm; these nanoparticles get self-aggregated when they come into contact with insulin [128]. This approach can be used in protein drug delivery systems.

4.3 Etherification

Etherification reaction involves the substitution of hydroxyl groups on glucose moieties by $COOCH_3$, hydroxypropyl, or any modified group to form a chain [18]. The limitation with the esterification of starches is the need to synthesize cationic starch with hydroxypropyl group [129]. Commonly used etherification processes are hydroxypropylation, carboxymethylation, and hydroxyethylation. Carboxymethylation involves the replacement of hydroxyl group with $-COOCH_3$ group which is less polar in nature [130]. The Williamson ether synthesis is a commonly used method of synthesis of $-COOCH_3$ starch derivatives [131–133]. It involves the incorporation of $-COOCH_3$ group between monochloric acid and starch in the presence of sodium hydroxide in starch backbone [134].

Etherification improves the water solubility of starches due to an increase in the cross-linking and reduced swelling properties [135]. The introduction of carboxymethyl group in starch molecules increases the pH sensitivity [136]. Hydroxypropylation is another method used for the etherification of starches and involves the reaction of starches in the presence of alkaline catalyst with propylene oxide at room temperature [9]. The hydroxyl groups in starches were replaced by the substitution of nucleophilic group with hydroxypropyl group. The starches modified by these methods have similar physicochemical properties like carboxyl-methylated starches. However, because of its larger size the hydroxypropyl group disrupts the forces in starch moieties, resulting in the formation of granular starches (owing to the rupture of hydrogen bond and increasing water solubility along with swelling index) [137]. The synthesized starches are not able to recrystallize due to weak hydrogen bonds and bulky hydroxypropyl groups [104]. Etherification of starches by this approach improves the starches' solubility, swelling index, and viscosity in the presence of the hydroxypropyl group. Starch derivatives prepared by this method are reported to be more stable in low-temperature conditions, such as cold storage, which increases the applicability of etherified starches as excipients in different formulations [104]. Hydroxyethylation targets three hydroxyl groups for replacement with $-OHC_2H_5$ group, and the mechanism involves the oxidation of starches [138]. The esterified starches are widely used in the manufacture of hydrogels.

4.4 Cross-linking

In this method, the degree of hydrogen bond is reinforced by chemical bonds by connecting the polymer chains with three-dimensional networks [139]. In most cases, cross-linkers react with hydroxyl groups of starch molecules, which results in the alteration of some of the physicochemical properties like tensile strength and oil absorption capacity.

For the hydrophobic modification of starches, commonly used cross-linkers are citric acid and di-aldehydes.

4.5 Grafting

In this method, polymers are introduced in the native starch backbone by covalent bonding [38]. The modification of starches by grafting results in the formation of starches with desired functional properties, and grafting can be carried out using the following two methods. In the first method, coupling agents were used [140,141]. Metal catalyzed radical polymerization reaction is widely used in the modification of native starches and involves the transfer of atom. Other grafting techniques are atom transfer radical polymerization (ATRP), copper-mediated polymerization (Cu°-mediated), reversible addition fragmentation chain transfer (RAFT), nitroxide-mediated polymerization (NMP), and so on. Graft modifications of starches are used for preparing thermoplastic biodegradable starches [127,142]. Casas et al. (2010) reported using biosynthesized grafting to modify starches; they used free radical co-polymerization, which involves the reaction of co-polymers of ethyl methacrylate with tapioca starch or hydroxypropyl tapioca starch followed by freeze-drying giving higher yields [143]. The graft technique produced a better yield of $213.50 \pm 3.50\%$ for oven-dried starch-graft-ethyl methacrylate; $229.70 \pm 6.80\%$ for freeze-dried hydroxypropyl tapioca starch as compared to $148.60 \pm 6.20\%$ for oven-dried tapioca starch-graft-ethyl methacrylate; and $170.70 \pm 4.50\%$ for freeze-dried tapioca starch-graft-ethyl methacrylate. These modified starches were used to study the controlled-release profile of the drug theophylline, in which the freeze-dried starches grafted with hydroxypropyl tapioca starch-graft-ethyl methacrylate showed a better release profile via passive diffusion. However, grafted starch with ethyl methacrylate showed enhanced binding properties with reduced drug release property in tapioca starch-graft-ethyl methacrylate-based tablet matrices; this demonstrated better binding properties with decreased drug release performance as compared to hydroxypropyl tapioca starch. The drying process and various breaking forces involved in the modification influenced the dissolution performances of grafted starches. The dissolution characteristics of these starches are mainly based on the matrices of the tablets and the initial amount of drug translation to the dissolution medium. The radial drug release from tapioca starch-graft-ethyl methacrylate- and hydroxypropyl tapioca starch-graft-ethyl methacrylate–based tablet matrices showed the initial amount of area rendering to the dissolution medium as unveiled by the drug release pattern.

5 Clinical potential of tailor-made starches

A few clinical trials were undertaken to evaluate the uses of tailor-made starches as excipients in formulations of many drug delivery dosage forms. Vandenbossche et al. (1992) presented comprehensive information related to the uses of modified starches in drug delivery application by demonstrating the release profile of theophylline and many more commercially available products for the treatment of various diseases [144]. They studied all the possible ratios of combination and found nonimprovement in the release profile as compared to commercially available controlled-release products. Wiedermann (2008) demonstrated the use of $-OHC_2H_5$ starches in the patient suffering from sepsis and discussed the clinical applications of $-OHC_2H_5$ starches in the form of either colloids or gels over the conventional infusion [145]. It was observed that modified starches increased the risk of renal failure; hence, the use of these starches should be restricted in the patient suffering from sepsis. The use of $-OHC_2H_5$ starches may be beneficial, if it is used in intravenous (IV) form. In a recent study carried out by Narayanan et al. (2015), the nanoparticles of modified starches were prepared by cross-linking and precipitation, where the modified starches were used as transporters for delivery of drugs with different hydrophobicity [146]. Furthermore, these nanoparticles served as a platform to determine the release profile of the drug and the chemical nature of modified starches upon administration. Modified starches, especially tapioca, showed prominent results in rats for the treatment of diarrhea when used as an adjuvant [147]. Another study carried out by Correia et al. (2008) demonstrated the use of modified starch for the treatment of type Ia and Ib glycogen storage disorder/disease when compared with native starches; the modified starch was reported to maintain the blood glucose concentration over longer periods, thereby eliminating the need for additional dosing. The applicability of modified starches in clinical use is mainly influenced by the type of modification and the disease state of the patient to be treated.

6 Conclusion

The present chapter provided a discussion on improving the functional properties of starches by various chemical modifications—such as oxidation, esterification, etherification, cross-linking, and grafting—and their use as potential pharmaceutical excipients. In these chemical modifications, different functional groups were introduced into the starch backbone, which has been reported to facilitate significant improvements to starch-based systems. The chemical modifications of starches enable the development of improved-quality starch-based systems in an inexpensive and less time-consuming approach. The chemically modified starch materials have been found capable of meeting the requirements for their use as pharmaceutical excipients in various drug delivery formulations.

References

[1] Nayak AK, Pal D, Pradhan J, Ghorai T. The potential of *Trigonella foenum-graecum* L. seed mucilage as suspending agent. Indian J Pharm Educ Res 2012;46:312–7.

[2] Nayak AK, Hasnain MS. Plant polysaccharides in drug delivery applications. In: Nayak AK, Hasnain MS, editors. Plant polysaccharides-based multiple-unit systems for oral drug delivery. Singapore: Springer; 2019. p. 19–23.

[3] Nayak AK, Pal D, Pany DR, Mohanty B. Evaluation of *Spinacia oleracea* L. leaves mucilage as innovative suspending agent. J Adv Pharm Technol Res 2010;1(3):338–41.

[4] Kandar CC, Hasnain MS, Nayak AK. Natural polymers as useful pharmaceutical excipients. In: Nayak AK, Pal K, Banerjee I, Maji S, Nanda U, editors. Advances and challenges in pharmaceutical technology: materials, process development and drug delivery strategies. USA: Academic Press, Elsevier Inc.; 2021. p. 1–44.

[5] Hasnain MS, Ahmed SA, Alkahtani S, Milivojevic M, Kandar CC, Dhara AK, Nayak AK. Biopolymers for drug delivery. In: Nayak AK, Hasnain MS, editors. Advanced biopolymeric systems for drug delivery. Switzerland: Springer; 2020. p. 1–29.

[6] Nayak AK, Hasnain MS, Pal K, Banerjee I, Pal D. Gum-based hydrogels in drug delivery. In: Pal K, Banerjee I, Sarkar P, Kim D, Deng W-P, Dubey NK, Majumder K, editors. Biopolymer-based formulations, biomedical and food applications. United States: Elsevier Inc.; 2020. p. 605–45.

[7] Nayak AK, Hasnain MS, Dhara AK, Pal D. Plant polysaccharides in pharmaceutical applications. In: Pal D, Nayak AK, editors. Bioactive natural products for pharmaceutical applications, advanced structured materials, vol. 140. Cham: Springer; 2021. p. 93–125.

[8] Averous L. Synthesis, properties, environmental and biomedical applications of polylactic acid. In: Ebnesajjad S, editor. Handbook of biopolymers and biodegradable plastics. Elsevier Inc.; 2013. p. 171–88.

[9] Singh J, Kaur L, McCarthy OJ. Factors influencing the physico-chemical, morphological, thermal and rheological properties of some chemically modified starches for food applications—a review. Food Hydrocoll 2007;21:1–22.

[10] Ražem D, Katušin-Ražem B. The effects of irradiation on controlled drug delivery/controlled drug release systems. Radiat Phys Chem 2008;77(3):288–344.

[11] Nayak AK, Pal D. Natural starches-blended ionotropically-gelled microparticles/beads for sustained drug release. In: Thakur VK, Thakur MK, Kessler MR, editors. Handbook of composites from renewable materials, volume 8, nanocomposites: advanced applications. USA: Wiley-Scrivener; 2017. p. 527–60.

[12] Malakar J, Nayak AK, Das A. Modified starch (cationized)-alginate beads containing aceclofenac: formulation optimization using central composite design. Starch-Starke 2013;65:603–12.

[13] Dimantov A, Greenberg M, Kesselman E, Shimoni E. Study of high amylose corn starch as food grade enteric coating in a microcapsule model system. Innov Food Sci Emerg Technol 2004;5:93–100.

[14] Nayak AK, Pal D, Santra K. *Artocarpus heterophyllus* L. seed starch-blended gellan gum mucoadhesive beads of metformin HCl. Int J Biol Macromol 2014;65:329–39.

[15] Tharanathan RN. Starch-value addition by modification. Crit Rev Food Sci Nutr 2005;45(5):371–84.

[16] Acevedo-Guevara L, Nieto-Suaza L, Sanchez LT, Pinzon MI, Villa CC. Development of native and modified banana starch nanoparticles as vehicles for curcumin. Int J Biol Macromol 2018;111:498–504.
[17] Xiao H, Yang T, Lin Q, Liu GQ, Zhang L, Yu F, Chen Y. Acetylated starch nanocrystals: preparation and antitumor drug delivery study. Int J Biol Macromol 2016;89:456–64.
[18] Masina N, Choonara YE, Kumar P, du Toit LC, Govender M, Indermun S, Pillay V. A review of the chemical modification techniques of starch. Carbohydr Polym 2017;157:1226–36.
[19] Jamzad S, Tutunji L, Fassihi R. Analysis of macromolecular changes and drug release from hydrophilic matrix systems. Int J Pharm 2005;292(1–2):75–85.
[20] Khan F, Ahmad SR. Polysaccharides and their derivatives for versatile tissue engineering application. Macromol Biosci 2013;13(4):395–421.
[21] Pu H, Chen L, Li X, Xie F, Yu L, Li L. An oral colon-targeting controlled release system based on resistant starch acetate: synthesization, characterization, and preparation of film-coating pellets. J Agric Food Chem 2011;59(10):5738–45.
[22] Dereje B. Composition, morphology and physicochemical properties of starches derived from indigenous Ethiopian tuber crops: a review. Int J Biol Macromol 2021;187:911–21.
[23] Vandeputte GE, Delcour JA. From sucrose to starch granule to starch physical behaviour a focus on rice starch. Carbohydr Polym 2004;58:245–66.
[24] Rodrigues A, Emeje M. Recent applications of starch derivatives in nanodrug delivery. Carbohydr Polym 2012;87:987–94.
[25] Daudt RM, Külkamp-Guerreiro IC, Cladera-Olivera F, Thys RCS, Marczak LDF. Determination of properties of pinhão starch: analysis of its applicability as pharmaceutical excipient. Ind Crop Prod 2014;52:420–9.
[26] Thomas HD, Atwell WA. Starches. Practical guides for the food industry. St. Paul Minnesota: Egan Press; 1999.
[27] Alissandratos A, Baudendistel N, Hauer B, Baldenius K, Flitsch S, Halling P. Biocompatible functionalisation of starch. Chem Commun (Camb) 2011;47(2):683–5.
[28] Bendoraitiene J, Lekniute-Kyzike E, Rutkaite R. Biodegradation of cross-linked and cationic starches. Int J Biol Macromol 2018;119:345–51.
[29] Zobel HF. Molecules to granules: a comprehensive starch review. Starch/Stärke 1988;40:44–50.
[30] Sang Y, Bean S, Seib PA, Pedersen J, Shi YC. Structure and functional properties of sorghum starches differing in amylose content. J Agric Food Chem 2008;56:6680–5.
[31] Bashir K, Aggarwal M. Physicochemical, structural and functional properties of native and irradiated starch: a review. J Food Sci Technol 2019;56(2):513–23.
[32] Fredriksson H, Silverio J, Andersson R, Eliasson AC, Aman P. The influence of amylase and amylopectin characteristics on gelatinization and retrogradation properties of different starches. Carbohydr Polym 1998;35:119–34.
[33] Chang Q, Zheng B, Zhang Y, Zeng H. A comprehensive review of the factors influencing the formation of retrograded starch. Int J Biol Macromol 2021;186:163–73.
[34] Lian X, Kang H, Sun H, Liu L, Li L. Identification of the main retrogradation-related properties of rice starch. J Agric Food Chem 2015;63(5):1562–72.
[35] Hu WX, Chen J, Zhao JW, Chen L, Wang YH. Effect of the addition of modified starch on gelatinization and gelation properties of rice flour. Int J Biol Macromol 2020;153:26–35.
[36] Nayak AK, Pal D. Blends of jackfruit seed starch-pectin in the development of mucoadhesive beads containing metformin HCl. Int J Biol Macromol 2013;62:137–45.
[37] Moorthy SN. Physicochemical and functional properties of tropical tuber starches: a review. Starch/Stärke 2002;54:559–92.
[38] Nayak AK, Bera H, Hasnain MS, Pal D. Synthesis and characterization of graft-copolymers of plant polysaccharides. In: Thakur VK, editor. Biopolymer grafting, synthesis and properties. Netherlands: Elsevier Inc.; 2018. p. 1–62.

[39] Hasnain MS, Ahmad SA, Chaudhary N, Hoda MN, Nayak AK. Biodegradable polymer matrix nanocomposites for bone tissue engineering. In: Inamuddin, Asiri AM, Mohammad A, editors. Applications of nanocomposite materials in orthopedics, woodhead publishing series in biomaterials. United States: Elsevier Inc; 2019. p. 1–37.
[40] Nayak AK, Hasnain MS, Alkahtani S. Jackfruit seed starch-based composite beads for controlled drug release. In: Hasnain MS, Nayak AK, Alkahtani S, editors. Polymeric and natural composites—Materials, manufacturing and biomedical applications. Advances in material research and technology (series). Springer Nature Switzerland AG; 2022. p. 213–40.
[41] Nayak AK, Pal D. Formulation optimization of jackfruit seed starch-alginate mucoadhesive beads of metformin HCl. Int J Biol Macromol 2013;59:264–72.
[42] Nayak AK, Pal D, Hasnain MS. Development, optimization and *in vitro-in vivo* evaluation of pioglitazone-loaded jackfruit seed starch-alginate beads. Curr Drug Deliv 2013;10:608–19.
[43] Nayak AK, Pal D. Natural polysaccharides for drug delivery in tissue engineering. Everyman's Sci 2012;XLVI:347–52.
[44] Nayak AK, Hasnain MS, Aminbhavi TM. Drug delivery using interpenetrating polymeric networks of natural polymers: a recent update. J Drug Deliv Sci Technol 2021;66:102915.
[45] Nayak AK, Alkahtani S, Hasnain MS. Biomedical nanocomposites. In: Nayak AK, Hasnain MS, editors. Biomedical composites-perspectives and applications. Springer Nature, Switzerland AG: Springer International Publishing; 2021. p. 35–69.
[46] Maity M, Hasnain MS, Nayak AK, Aminabavi TM. Biomedical applications of polysaccharides. In: Nayak AK, Hasnain MS, Aminabhavi TM, editors. Tailor-made polysaccharides in biomedical applications. USA: Academic Press, Elsevier Inc; 2021. p. 1–34.
[47] Nayak AK, Hasnain MS, Tabis M, Aminabhavi TM. Use of tailored polysaccharides in dentistry. In: Nayak AK, Hasnain MS, Aminabhavi TM, editors. Tailor-made polysaccharides in biomedical applications. USA: Academic Press, Elsevier Inc; 2021. p. 287–304.
[48] Chakraborty R, Kalita P, Sen S. Natural starch in biomedical and food industry: perception and overview. Curr Drug Discov Technol 2019;16(4):355–67.
[49] Singla D, Singh A, Dhull SB, Kumar P, Malik T, Kumar P. Taro starch: isolation, morphology, modification and novel applications concern—A review. Int J Biol Macromol 2020;163:1283–90.
[50] Zarski A, Bajer K, Kapuśniak J. Review of the most important methods of improving the processing properties of starch toward non-food applications. Polymers (Basel) 2021;13(5):832.
[51] BeMiller JN, Huber KC. Physical modification of food starch functionalities. Annu Rev Food Sci Technol 2015;6:19–69.
[52] Nagar CK, Dash SK, Rayaguru K, Pal US, Nedunchezhiyan M. Isolation, characterization, modification and uses of taro starch: a review. Int J Biol Macromol 2021;192:574–89.
[53] Fan Y, Picchioni F. Modification of starch: a review on the application of "green" solvents and controlled functionalization. Carbohydr Polym 2020;241:116350.
[54] Zhou J, Tong J, Su X, Ren L. Hydrophobic starch nanocrystals preparations through crosslinking modification using citric acid. Int J Biol Macromol 2016;91:1186–93.
[55] Tomasik P, Schilling CH. Chemical modification of starch. Adv Carbohydr Chem Biochem 2004;59:175–403.
[56] Wang X, Huang L, Zhang C, Deng Y, Xie P, Liu L, Cheng J. Research advances in chemical modifications of starch for hydrophobicity and its applications: a review. Carbohydr Polym 2020;240:116292.
[57] Santoyo-Aleman D, Sanchez LT, Villa CC. Citric-acid modified banana starch nanoparticles as a novel vehicle for β-carotene delivery. J Sci Food Agric 2019;99(14):6392–9.

[58] Dang X, Yang M, Shan Z, Mansouri S, May BK, Chen X, Chen H, Woo MW. On spray drying of oxidized corn starch cross-linked gelatin microcapsules for drug release. Korean J Couns Psychother 2017;74:493–500.
[59] Soe MT, Pongjanyakul T, Limpongsa E, Jaipakdee N. Modified glutinous rice starch-chitosan composite films for buccal delivery of hydrophilic drug. Carbohydr Polym 2020;245:116556.
[60] Hong Y, Liu G, Gu Z. Recent advances of starch-based excipients used in extended-release tablets: a review. Drug Deliv 2016;23(1):12–20.
[61] Ahmad MZ, Bhattacharya A. Isolation and physicochemical characterization of Bora rice starch from Assam as pharmaceutical excipients. J Pharm Res 2009;2:1299–303.
[62] Akin-Ajani OD, Itiola OA, Odeku OA. Effects of plantain and corn starches on the mechanical and disintegration properties of paracetamol tablets. AAPS PharmSciTech 2005;6(3):E458–63.
[63] Bayor MT, Tuffour E, Lambon PS. Evaluation of starch from new sweet potato genotypes for use as a pharmaceutical diluent, binder or disintegrant. J Appl Pharm Sci 2013;3:S17–23.
[64] Builders PF, Anwunobi PA, Mbah CC, Adikwu MU. New direct compression excipient from tigernut starch: physicochemical and functional properties. AAPS PharmSciTech 2013;14(2):818–27.
[65] Nayak AK, Bera H, Hasnain MS. Particulate matrices of ionotropically gelled alginate- and plant-derived starches for sustained drug release. In: Nayak AK, Hasnain MS, editors. Alginates in drug delivery. United States: Academic Press, Elsevier Inc.; 2020. p. 257–95.
[66] Autamashih M, Isah AB, Allagh TS, Ibrahim MA. Effects of selected diluents and maize starch mucilage binder on the tablets formulation of the crude aqueous extract of *Vernonia galamensis*. Int J Pharm Technol 2011;3:2746–56.
[67] Setty CM, Deshmukh AS, Badiger AM. Hydrolyzed polyacrylamide grafted maize starch based microbeads: application in pH responsive drug delivery. Int J Biol Macromol 2014;70:1–9.
[68] Palviainen P, Heinämäki J, Myllärinen P, Lahtinen R, Yliruusi J, Forssell P. Corn starches as film formers in aqueous-based film coating. Pharm Dev Technol 2001;6(3):353–61.
[69] Nayak AK, Hasnain MS. Potato starch based multiple units for oral drug delivery. In: Nayak AK, Hasnain MS, editors. Plant polysaccharides-based multiple-unit systems for oral drug delivery. Singapore: Springer; 2019. p. 113–6.
[70] Malakar J, Nayak AK, Jana P, Pal D. Potato starch-blended alginate beads for prolonged release of tolbutamide: development by statistical optimization and *in vitro* characterization. Asian J Pharm 2013;7:43–51.
[71] Jha AK, Bhattacharya A. Preparation and *in vitro* evaluation of sweet potato starch blended sodium alginate microbeads. Adv Nat Appl Sci 2008;2:122–8.
[72] Nazim S, Dehghan MHG, Shaikh S, Shaikh A. Studies on hydrotrope potato starch gel as topical carrier for rofecoxib. Der Pharm Sin 2011;2:227–35.
[73] Biswas N, Sahoo RK. Tapioca starch blended alginate mucoadhesive-floating beads for intragastric delivery of metoprolol tartrate. Int J Biol Macromol 2016;83:61–70.
[74] Wannaphatchaiyong S, Heng PWS, Suksaeree J, Boonme P, Pichayakorn W. Lidocaine loaded gelatin/gelatinized tapioca starch films for buccal delivery and the irritancy evaluation using chick chorioallantoic membrane. Saudi Pharm J 2019;27(8):1085–95.
[75] Okunlola A, Odeku OA. Evaluation of starches obtained from four Dioscorea species as binding agent in chloroquine phosphate tablet formulations. Saudi Pharm J 2011;19(2):95–105.
[76] Okunlola A. Design of bilayer tablets using modified Dioscorea starches as novel excipients for immediate and sustained release of aceclofenac sodium. Front Pharmacol 2015;5:294.

[77] Okunlola A, Odeku OA. Compressional characteristics and tableting properties of starches obtained from four dioscorea species. Farmacia 2009;57:756.

[78] Okunlola A, Adebayo AS, Adeyeye MC. Development of repaglinide microspheres using novel acetylated starches of bitter and Chinese yams as polymers. Int J Biol Macromol 2017;94(Pt A):544–53.

[79] Ruangchayajatuporn J, Palanuph S, Sinchaipanid N, Mitrevej A. Evaluation of various starches as tablet disintegrants in direct compression formulation. J Ind Pharm 1999;3:1.

[80] Bourtoom T, Chinnan MS. Preparation and properties of rice starch-chitosan edible blend film. LWT-Food Sci Technol 2008;41:1633–41.

[81] Chan SY, Goh CF, Lau JY, Tiew YC, Balakrishnan T. Rice starch thin films as a potential buccal delivery system: effect of plasticiser and drug loading on drug release profile. Int J Pharm 2019;562:203–11.

[82] Ahmad MZ, Akhter S, Ahmad I, Rahman M, Anwar M, Jain GK, Ahmad FJ, Khar RK. Development of polysaccharide based colon targeted drug delivery system: design and evaluation of Assam Bora rice starch based matrix tablet. Curr Drug Deliv 2011;8(5):575–81.

[83] Sachan NK, Bhattacharya A. Feasibility of Assam bora rice based matrix microdevices for controlled release of water insoluble drug. Int J Pharm Pharm Sci 2009;1:96–102.

[84] Sachan NK, Bhattacharya A. Evaluation of Assam Bora rice starch as a possible natural mucoadhesive polymer in the formulation of microparticulate controlled drug delivery systems. J Assam Sci Soc 2006;47:34–47.

[85] Ahmad MZ, Akhter S, Anwar M, Singh A, Ahmad I, Ain MR, Jain GK, Khar RK, Ahmad FJ. Feasibility of Assam Bora rice starch as a compression coat of 5-fluorouracil core tablet for colorectal cancer. Curr Drug Deliv 2012;9(1):105–10.

[86] Mohapatra S, Siddiqui AA, Anwar M, Bhardwaj N, Akhter S, Ahmad FJ. Synthesis and characterization of novel carboxymethyl Assam Bora rice starch for the controlled release of cationic anticancer drug based on electrostatic interactions. AAPS PharmSciTech 2018;19(1):134–47.

[87] Sinchaipanid N, Ketjinda W, Pongwai S, Mitrevej A. A preliminary study of sago starch as a tablet binder. Mahidol J Pharm Sci 1995;22:101–6.

[88] Singh AV, Nath LK. Evaluation of chemically modified hydrophobic sago starch as a carrier for controlled drug delivery. Saudi Pharm J 2013;21(2):193–200.

[89] Misale BV, Gavali HBM, Katare SD, Yadav AV. Sago starch capsule shell: a suitable alternative to gelatin capsule shells. Indian J Pharm Educ Res 2008;42:48–52.

[90] Murthy KVR, Nyamathulla S, Parveen DT, Ashok Z, Archana M, Mohan EG, Meghana K. Effect of sago starch on controlled release matrix tablets of tramadol HCl. J Chem Pharm Res 2010;2:232–9.

[91] Narkhede SB, Bendale AR, Jadhav AG, Patel K, Vidyasagar G. Isolation and evaluation of starch of *Artocarpus heterophyllus* as a tablet binder. Int J PharmTech Res 2011;3:836–40.

[92] Khunkitti W, Aromdee C, Vorarat S, Chitropas P. The potential of jackfruit starch for use as suspending agent and emulsifying agent. Songklanakarin J Sci Technol 2006;28:145–55.

[93] Sabale V, Patel V, Paranjape A. Isolation and characterization of jackfruit mucilage and its comparative evaluation as a mucoadhesive and controlled release component in buccal tablets. Int J Pharm Investig 2012;2:61–9.

[94] Das D, Jha S, Kumar KJ. Isolation and release characteristics of starch from the rhizome of Indian Palo. Int J Biol Macromol 2015;72:341–6.

[95] Mitrevej A, Sinchaipanid N. Mung starch: preparation and study of tablet disintegration property. Mahidol J Pharm Sci 1990;17:1–8.

[96] Deepika V, Jayaram Kumar K, Anima P. Isolation and partial characterization of delayed releasing starches of Colocasia species from Jharkhand, India. Carbohydr Polym 2013;96(1):253–8.

[97] Nasipuri RN. Evaluation of cocoyam starch as tablet binder and disintegrant. Pharm Acta Helv 1979;54:48.

[98] Ibezim EC, Ofoefule SI, Omeje EO, Onyishi VI, Odoh UE. The role of ginger starch as a binder in acetaminophen tablet. Sci Res Essay 2008;3:46.

[99] Deshpande AV, Panya LB. Evaluation of sorghum starch as a tablet disintegrant and binder. J Pharm Pharmacol 1987;39:495.

[100] Garr GSM, Bangudu AB. Evaluation of sorghum starch as a tablet excipient. Drug Dev Ind Pharm 1991;17:1.

[101] Wolf BW, Bauer LL, Fahey GC. Effects of chemical modification on in vitro rate and extent of food starch digestion: an attempt to discover as lowly digested starch. J Agric Food Chem 1999;47(10):4178–83.

[102] Sui Z, BeMiller JN. Relationship of the channels of normal maize starch to the properties of its modified products. Carbohydr Polym 2013;92(1):894–904.

[103] Jeon Y, Viswanathan A, Gross R. Studies of starch esterification: reactions with alkenyl-succinates in aqueous slurry systems. Star 1999;51(2–3):90–3.

[104] Pal J, Singhal RS, Kulkarni PR. Physicochemical properties of hydroxypropyl derivative from corn and amaranth starch. Carbohydr Polym 2002;48:49–53.

[105] Wang Y-J, Wang L. Physicochemical properties of common and waxy corn starches oxidized by different levels of sodium hypochlorite. Carbohydr Polym 2003;52(3):207–17.

[106] Xiao C. Current advances of chemical and physical starch-based hydrogels. Star 2012;1:1–7.

[107] Chakraborty S, Sahoo B, Teraoka I, Miller LM, Gross RA. Enzyme-catalyzed regioselective modification of starch nanoparticles. Macromolecules 2005;38(1):61–8.

[108] Onofre F, Wang Y-J, Mauromoustakos A. Effects of structure and modification on sustained release properties of starches. Carbohydr Polym 2009;76(4):541–7.

[109] Yaacob B. Optimization of reaction conditions for carboxymethylated sago starch. Iran Polym J 2011;20(3):195–204.

[110] Sangseethong K, Termvejsayanon N, Sriroth K. Characterization of physicochemical properties of hypochlorite- and peroxide-oxidized cassava starches. Carbohydr Polym 2010;82(2):446–53.

[111] Balakrishnan B, Jayakrishnan A. Self-cross-linking biopolymers as injectable *in situ* forming biodegradable scaffolds. Biomaterials 2005;26(18):3941–51.

[112] Li Y, Zhang Z, van Leeuwen HP, Cohen S, Martien A, Norde W. Uptake and release kinetics of lysozyme in and from an oxidized starch polymer microgel. Soft Matter 2011;7(21):10377–85.

[113] Gao C, Liu M, Chen S, Jin S, Chen J. Preparation of oxidized sodium alginate-graft-poly((2-dimethylamino) ethyl methacrylate) gel beads and *in vitro* controlled release behaviour of BSA. Int J Pharm 2009;371(1–2):16–24.

[114] Zhang L, Liu P, Wang Y, Gao W. Study on physico-chemical properties of dialdehyde yam starch with different aldehyde group contents. Thermochim Acta 2011;512(1–2):196–201.

[115] Zhang Y, Wang X, Zhao G, Wang Y. Preparation and properties of oxidized starch with high degree of oxidation. Carbohydr Polym 2012;87(4):2554–62.

[116] Sánchez-Rivera MM, García-Suárez FJL, Velázquez del Valle M, Gutierrez-Meraz F, Bello-Pérez LA. Partial characterization of banana starches oxidized by different levels of sodium hypochlorite. Carbohydr Polym 2005;62(1):50–6.

[117] Dias ARG, Zavareze ER, Elias MC, Helbig E, Silva DO, Ciacco CF. Pasting, expansion and textural properties of fermented cassava starch oxidized with sodium hypochlorite. Carbohydr Polym 2011;84:268–75.

[118] Kuakpetoon D, Wang Y. Characterization of different starches oxidized by hypochlorite. Star 2001;53:211–8.
[119] Vanier NL, El Halal SLM, Dias ARG, da Rosa Zavareze E. Molecular structure, functionality and applications of oxidized starches: a review. Food Chem 2017;221:1546–59.
[120] Veelaert S, Wit D, Tournois H. An improved kinetic model for the periodate oxidation of starch. Polymer 1994;35:5091–7.
[121] Veelaert S, Polling M, Wit D. Structural and physico-chemical changes of potato starch along periodate oxidation. Starch/Starke 1994;46:263–8.
[122] Chan HT, Leh CP, Bhat R, Senan C, Williams PA, Karim AA. Molecular structure, rheological and thermal characteristics of ozone-oxidized starch. Food Chem 2011;126:1019–24.
[123] Elomaa M. Determination of the degree of substitution of acetylated starch by hydrolysis, 1H NMR and TGA/IR. Carbohydr Polym 2004;57(3):261–7.
[124] Paulos G, Mrestani Y, Heyroth F, Gebre-Mariam T, Neubert RH. Fabrication of acetylated dioscorea starch nanoparticles: optimization of formulation and process variables. J Drug Deliv Sci Technol 2016;31:83–92.
[125] Tuovinen L, Peltonen S, Liikola M, Hotakainen M, Lahtela-Kakkonen M, Poso A. Drug release from starch-acetate microparticles and films with and without incorporated alpha-amylase. Biomaterials 2004;25(18):4355–62.
[126] Beneke CE, Viljoen AM, Hamman JH. Polymeric plant-derived excipients in drug delivery. Molecules 2009;14(7):2602–20.
[127] Najafi SHM, Baghaie M, Ashori A. Preparation and characterization of acetylated starch nanoparticles as drug carrier: ciprofloxacin as a model. Int J Biol Macromol 2016;87:48–54.
[128] Minimol PF, Paul W, Sharma CP. PEGylated starch acetate nanoparticles and its potential use for oral insulin delivery. Carbohydr Polym 2013;95(1):1–8.
[129] Xie M, Duan Y, Li F, Wang X, Cui X, Bacha U, et al. Preparation and characterization of modified and functional starch (hexadecyl corboxymethyl starch) ether using reactive extrusion. Starch-Stärke 2017;69(5–6):16000061.
[130] Lawal OS, Storz J, Storz H, Lohmann D, Lechner D, Kulicke W-D. Hydrogels based on carboxymethyl cassava starch cross-linked with di- or polyfunctional carboxylic acids: synthesis, water absorbent behavior and rheological characterizations. Eur Polym J 2009;45(12):3399–408.
[131] Assaad E, Mateescu MA. The influence of protonation ratio on properties of carboxymethyl starch excipient at various substitution degrees: structural insights and drug release kinetics. Int J Pharm 2010;394(1–2):75–84.
[132] Zdanowicz M, Spychaj T. Viscosity changes of aqueous carboxymethyl starch by partial crosslinking and montmorillonite addition. J Appl Polym Sci 2014;131(18).
[133] Zdanowicz M, Spychaj T, Lendzion-Bieluń Z. Crosslinked carboxymethyl starch: one step synthesis and sorption characteristics. Int J Biol Macromol 2014;71:87–93.
[134] Quadrado RF, Fajardo AR. Microparticles based on carboxymethyl starch/chitosan polyelectrolyte complex as vehicles for drug delivery systems. Arab J Chem 2020;13:2183–94.
[135] Chen Y, Wang G. Adsorption properties of oxidized carboxymethyl starch and cross-linked carboxymethyl starch for calcium ion. Colloids Surf A Physicochem Eng Asp 2006;289:75–83.
[136] Lee S, Kim ST, Pant BR, Kwen HD, Song HH, Lee SK, et al. Carboxymethylation of corn starch and characterization using asymmetrical flow field-flow fractionation coupled with multiangle light scattering. J Chromatogr A 2010;1217(27):4623–8.
[137] Ju B, Yan D, Zhang S. Micelles self-assembled from thermoresponsive2-hydroxy-3-butoxypropyl starches for drug delivery. Carbohydr Polym 2012;87(2):1404–9.
[138] Chen R, Hob H, Sheu YM. Development of swelling/floating gastroretentive drug delivery system based on a combination of hydroxyethyl cellulose and sodium

carboxymethyl cellulose for Losartan and its clinical relevance in healthy volunteers with CYP2C9 polymorphism. Eur J Pharm Sci 2010;39:82–9.
[139] Ojogbo E, Ogunsona EO, Mekonnen TH. Chemical and physical modifications of starch for renewable polymeric materials. Mater Today Sustain 2019. https://doi.org/10.1016/j.mtsust.2019.100028.
[140] Mostafa KM, Samarkandy AR, El-Sanabary AA. Grafting onto carbohydrate polymer using novel potassium persulfate/tetramethylethylene diamine redox system for initiating grafting. Adv Polym Technol 2011;30(2):138–49.
[141] Meimoun J, Wiatz V, Saint-Loup R, Parcq J, Favrelle A, Bonnet F, et al. Modification of starch by graft copolymerization. Starch-Starke 2017;70(1–2):1600351.
[142] Liu S, Sun G. Radical graft functional modification of cellulose with allyl monomers: chemistry and structure characterization. Carbohydr Polym 2008;71(4):614–25.
[143] Casas M, Ferrero C, Jiménez-Castellanos MR. Graft tapioca starch copolymers as novel excipients for controlled-release matrix tablets. Carbohydr Polym 2010;80:71–7.
[144] Vandenbossche MR, Lefebvre RA, De Wilde GA, Remon JP. Performance of a modified starch hydrophilic matrix for the sustained release of theophylline in healthy volunteers. J Pharm Sci 1992;81(3):245–8.
[145] Wiedermann CJ. Systematic review of randomized clinical trials on the use of hydroxyethyl starch for fluid management in sepsis. BMC Emerg Med 2008;8(1).
[146] Narayanan D, Nair S, Menon D. A systematic evaluation of hydroxyethyl starch as a potential nanocarrier for parenteral drug delivery. Int J Biol Macromol 2015;74:575–84.
[147] Wingertzahn MA, Teichberg S, Wapnir RA. Modified starch enhances absorption and accelerates recovery in experimental diarrhea in rats. Pediatr Res 1999;45:397–402.

CHAPTER

14

Cancer targeting by tailor-made polysaccharides

Azim Ansari[a], *Abdullah Sheriker*[b], *Mohd Usman Mohd Siddique*[a], *Mrunali Patil*[a], *Sameer N. Goyal*[b], *Sheikh Murtuja*[c], *Mohd Neyaz Ahsan*[d], *Md Saquib Hasnain*[e], *and Amit Kumar Nayak*[f]

[a]Department of Pharmaceutical Chemistry, Shri Vile Parle Kelavani Mandal's Institute of Pharmacy, Dhule, Maharashtra, India, [b]Department of Pharmacology, Shri Vile Parle Kelavani Mandal's Institute of Pharmacy, Dhule, Maharashtra, India, [c]Department of Pharmaceutical Science and Technology, Birla Institute of Technology, Mesra, Jharkhand, India, [d]Department of Medical Laboratory Technology, University Polytechnic, Birla Institute of Technology, Ranchi, Jharkhand, India, [e]Department of Pharmacy, Palamau Institute of Pharmacy, Daltonganj, Jharkhand, India, [f]Department of Pharmaceutics, Seemanta Institute of Pharmaceutical Sciences, Jharpokharia, Mayurbhanj, Odisha, India

1 Introduction

According to a survey conducted in 2020 in the United States, cancer is a global health threat and it was observed that the rate of occurrence of cancer varies from 1.6 to 1.8 million new cases every year and as many as 0.6 million cancer-affected people die every year [1]. The basic approach to cancer management considers the following factors: type of cancer, stages of cancer, potential biotargets, and patients' overall health condition. Routine therapeutic approaches include surgery for removal of tumors, use of chemotherapeutic agents, and radiation-based therapy, as well as the use of immunomodulators and potential targeted treatment methods [2–6]. Surprisingly, it is the chemotherapy-based treatment approach that is regarded as the method with the most potential for success, as it exerts more deleterious toxic effects against cancer cells than normal cells.

Tailor-Made Polysaccharides in Drug Delivery
https://doi.org/10.1016/B978-0-12-821286-8.00011-2

Despite this advantage, conventional chemotherapy practice poses severe disadvantages, such as resistance to anticancer drugs, poor response, fatal toxic effects, low bioavailability, and nonuniform distribution of drugs [6]. Thus, given the rise in the number of cancer-related deaths globally, the need to overcome these disadvantages and improve the efficacy of chemotherapeutic agents to successfully manage cancer has become ever-more important. In this regard, one novel approach is to develop an effective and powerful drug delivery system (DDS) that can overcome the disadvantages in the use of chemotherapeutic agents in cancer management. Being tumor-specific, DDSs offer major advantages, such as enhanced drug removal from systemic circulatory and immune system, altered physicochemical characteristics of drugs, controlled release of drugs, and reduction in drug dosage [7,8].

The pH-sensitive syntheses of nanocarriers using linkers such as disulfide and hydrazone have the ability to deliver drug molecules at potential tumor-specific sites without harming normal cells. This helps improve clinical efficacy and patient compliance. Lipids, polymers, and viruses are used in the formulation of novel DDSs, such as liposomes, micelles, nanoparticles, nanogels, nanofibers, nanocomposites, and nanoconjugates with distinct properties [9]. Among these techniques, polysaccharides-based DDS is the widely approved biomaterial method for the preparation of novel nanoparticle system, and this system has attracted the attention of many researchers given the improvement it has the potential to bring in the clinical formulation, testing, and marketing of drugs to be used in cancer management.

2 Polysaccharides and their importance

Polysaccharides are carbohydrate-based biomacromolecules composed of either monosaccharides or disaccharides, which are joined to one another by glycosidic bond. Naturally, these polysaccharides are extracted from various resources, such as algae (alginate, agar, etc.), plants (pectin, guar gum, tamarind gum, sterculia gum, etc.), microbes (dextran, xanthan gum, gellan gum, etc.), and animals (chitosan, chondroitin, hyaluronic acid, etc.) [10,11]. Polysaccharides are ideal for developing new nanoparticles due to their safety, hydrophilicity, highly stability, biodegradability, and nontoxicity properties (Fig. 1). Polysaccharides contain a wide variety of functional groups, such as hydroxyl, amino, aldehydes, and carboxylic acid [12].

During the past few decades, numerous polymers, including polysaccharides, proteins, and fats, are being used to prepare a variety of nanocarriers for use in cancer therapy [8,10,11]. Currently, due to the potential advantages they provide, such as nontoxicity, aqueous solubility, and

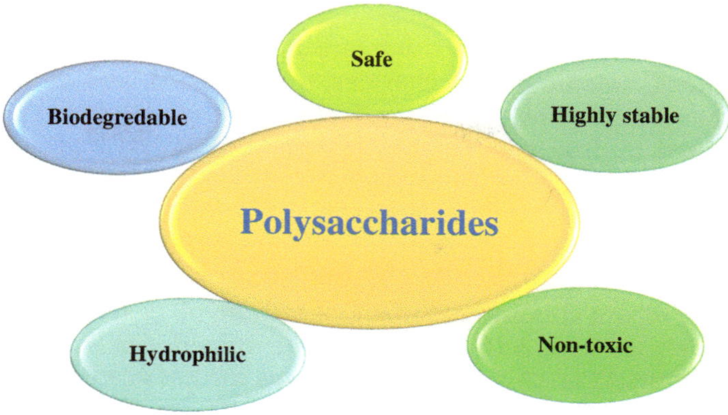

FIG. 1 Importance of polysaccharide for targeted drug therapy.

biodegradability, polysaccharides are frequently used in the preparation of cancer-targeting nanocarriers [10,11]. However, a few disadvantages exist affecting the physicochemical as well as functional properties of polysaccharides and may hinder the effective formulation of cancer-targeting nanocarriers. For this reason, polysaccharides are being tailored via a number of functional modifications—carboxymethylation, thiolation, cross-linking, polyelectrolyte complexation, interpenetrating polymer networkings, and graft copolymerizations [13–23]. Polysaccharides-based nanoparticles have a tendency to bypass ABC transporters such as P-gp and BCRP. Also, these nanoparticles are selectively taken up by M-cells (microfold cells), and some polysaccharides like hyaluronic acid are more targeted toward CD4 overexpressing cells [11,12].

Anticancer drugs, such as cisplatin, 5-fluorouracil (5-FU), and taxanes produce deleterious effects on cancerous cells, but they can also create potential toxic effects, such as liver toxicity, neutropenia, and hypersensitivity reactions. They are also associated with low water solubility, which speeds up the toxic effects of these agents. Therefore, these drawbacks have prompted researchers to pursue the alternative of formulating and administering polysaccharide-based nanoparticles in cancer management [8]. This chapter presents a discussion on the potential use of tailor-made polysaccharides in cancer-targeting applications.

3 Tailor-made chitosan-based systems for cancer-targeting applications

One frequently employed and positively charged natural polysaccharide is chitosan (CS), which is composed of randomly distributed β-(1 → 4)-linked D-glucosamine (deacetylated unit) and

N-acetyl-D-glucosamine (acetylated unit) [23,24]. Due to its positive charge, chitosan has a tendency to interact with anionic substances, such as polyanions, anionic polysaccharides, nucleic acids, and various negatively charged proteins [25,26]. Furthermore, it is a well-accepted biomaterial used in drug and gene delivery due to its advantages such as less toxicity, improved stability, biocompatible nature, and biodegradable profile [26–29]. Since the past few decades, various research works have been carried out focusing on the use of chitosan in cancer treatment and its associated inhibitory effects [26,30]. Sekar et al. used the salification method to prepare chitosan ascorbate, which involves the interaction of chitosan with ascorbic acid [31]. Under the influence of acidic environment, the synthesized chitosan ascorbate was further used for the preparation of nanoparticles having a particle size of 170 nm. The preparation of nanoparticles was carried out using pentasodium tripolyphosphate (as an ionotropic cross-linker) by ionotropic gelation and controlling the concentration of ascorbic acid. The nanoparticles thus prepared exhibited potential antioxidant property and decreased viability of cervical cancer cells, such as HeLa cells, without affecting normal cells, such as human fibroblast WI-38 cells. The overall results of this experimental work suggested that chitosan ascorbate nanoparticles can be used as potential nanocarriers in the delivery of anticancer drugs drug to target the cancer cells.

In other experiments carried out by Nascimento et al., chitosan-based nanoparticles were prepared that targeted epidermal growth factor receptor (EGFR) in order to deliver siRNA for the management of nonsmall-cell lung cancer (NSCLC) [32]. Under the influence of NSCLC, the potential targeted EGFRs were found to be overexpressed. Under this condition, the targeted nanoparticles were prepared by conjugation of EGFR-binding peptides and PEG 2000 with chitosan followed by complexation of the derivatives of chitosan formed with Mad2 siRNA. In this experiment, two types of chitosan with different molecular weights were used. The low-molecular-weight (50 kDa) chitosan produced nanoparticles with smaller particles size than the high-molecular-weight (90 kDa) chitosan. Both nanoparticle formulations showed approximately 100% encapsulation efficiency and increased selective uptake by NSCLC cells (A549 cells). Furthermore, it was observed that both the nanoparticle formulations successfully delivered the encapsulated siRNA and downregulated the expression of Mad2 causing enormous death of cancer cells due to apoptosis [33]. This study also reported that nanoparticles made of low-molecular-weight chitosan exhibited more anticancer activity than high-molecular-weight chitosan nanoparticles. In order to check the efficacy of low-molecular-weight chitosan-based nanoparticles, they were further tested in other different mice models of cancer, such as cisplatin-sensitive model, resistant-mice model, and platinum-resistant model. In these models, targeted nanoparticles exhibited maximum inhibition of tumor growth compared to the nontargeted formulation. In order to deliver small molecules, chitosan nanoparticles were successfully employed in the management of cancer. In this regard, a similar experiment was carried out by Esfandiarpour-Boroujeni et al. in the management of breast cancer with the use of folate-modified chitosan nanoparticles for the encapsulation of curcumin [34]. As breast cancer is associated with increased stimulation of folate receptors and folate has great affinity to bind these receptors, the folate receptors were regarded as potential targets for chitosan-based nanoparticles in the management of breast cancer. Under acidic environment, amino groups present in chitosan undergo protonation, causing the swelling of polymer matrix and sustained release of curcumin over a period of 1 week. Targeted anticancer therapy approaches using tailor-made chitosan-based systems are illustrated in Fig. 2.

4 Tailor-made hyaluronic acid-based systems for cancer-targeting applications

Hyaluronic acid is a nonsulfated glycosaminoglycan and linear polysaccharide that consists of alternate chains of D-glucuronic acid and *N*-acetyl-D-glucosamine residues [35]. It is widely employed in biopharmaceuticals, and, due to its tumor targeting tendency, it is widely used in the delivery of nanoparticles in the pharmacotherapy of cancers. Intracellularly, in various types of cancer, the transmembrane glycoproteins CD44 are overstimulated, and hyaluronic acid has a strong tendency to recognize and bind the receptors present in these cells [35–37]. Moreover, hyaluronic acid has other beneficial and favorable properties, such as biocompatibility, biodegradability, and specific targeting ability, resulting in its increased use in the formulation and development of novel DDSs [37–39]. Furthermore, chemically modified hyaluronic acid-based nanoparticles encapsulate not only small molecules but also other molecules, such as imaging agents and siRNA encapsulation for smooth and easy targeted delivery of therapeutics. To explore the usefulness of hyaluronic acid, Ganesh et al., developed hyaluronic acid-based nanoparticles for the encapsulation of cisplatin, siRNA, and near IR dye indocyanine green (ICG) in order to image tumor cells as well as facilitate combination therapy [40]. Because of its anionic characteristic, hyaluronic acid fails to encapsulate the negatively charged siRNA. Therefore, in order to overcome this limitation, different types of fatty amines or cationic polymers are usually included in the backbone structure of hyaluronic acid and the hyaluronic acid-based conjugates thus formed are used for the encapsulation of siRNA. The selective encapsulated siRNA showed a higher rate of success in destroying different tumor cell models, such as breast cancer MDA-MB468 cells and metastatic tumors in mice. Also, these hyaluronic

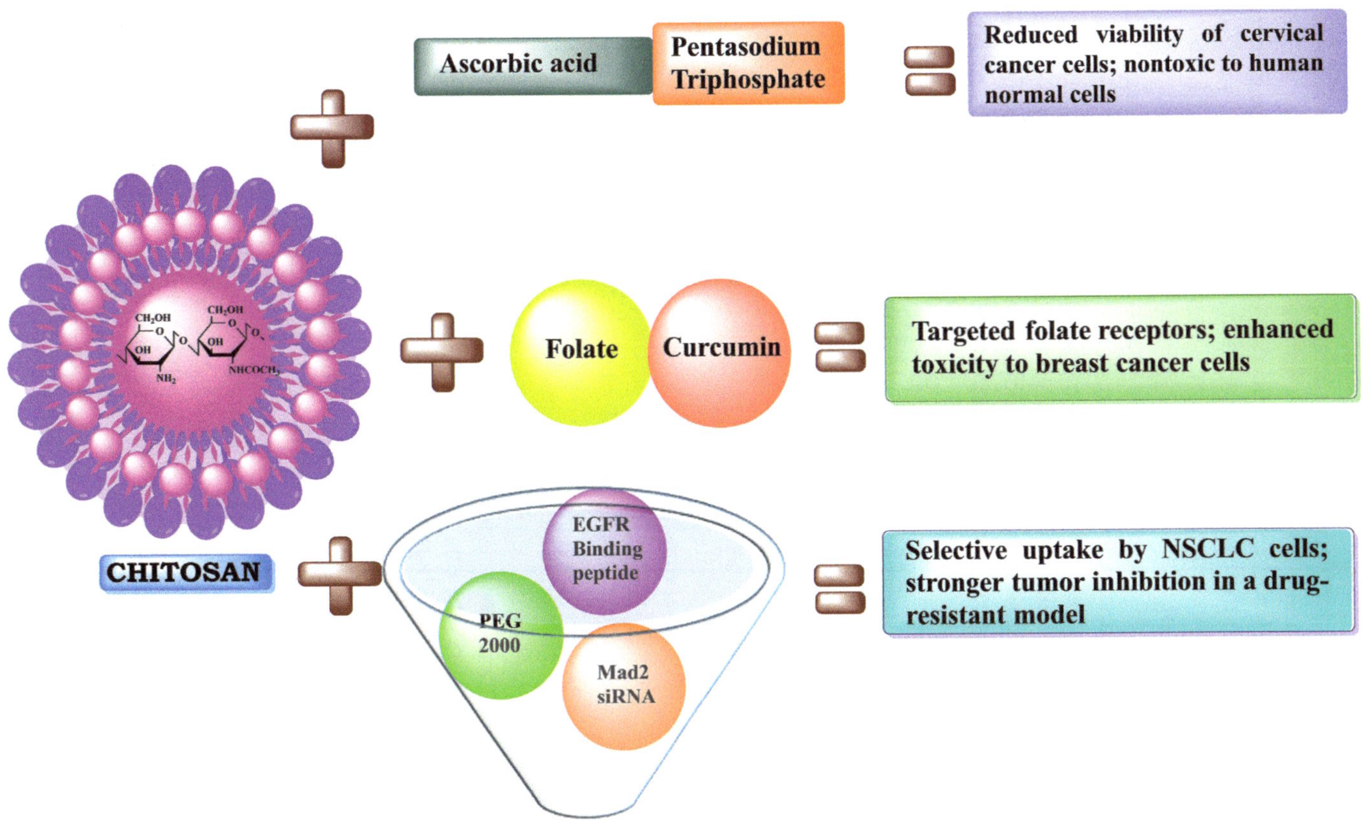

FIG. 2 Tailor-made chitosan-based systems for targeted anticancer therapy.

acid nanoparticles were further modified (tailor-made) and standardized in order to minimize the cisplatin resistance by encapsulation of ICG formulation for imaging of whole body and loading of cisplatin and siRNA into the matrix of targeted CD44 receptors for use in lung cancer treatment [40]. Favorable effects were noticed with the combination therapy in the management of resistant cancer.

In another research by Zhong et al., similar kinds of hyaluronic acid-based nanoparticles were used for the effective delivery of doxorubicin (DOX) into the overstimulated drug-resistant CD44 tumor cells [41]. The hyaluronic acid-based nanoparticles were developed via functionalization with L-lysine methyl ester and lipoic acid and cross-linking of hyaluronic acid. The developed functionalized hyaluronic acid-based nanoparticles significantly release the loaded DOX followed by stimulation of glutathione (GSH) in the cytoplasm of CD44 hyperexcited tumor cells. It was also noticed that the developed nanoparticles exhibited greater antitumor potency, as these nanoparticles were accumulated to greater extent around the CD44 cells in DOX-resistant cancer cells, such as MCF-7/ADR cells and inhibited the growth of tumor cells as well as increased the survival time of mice [41]. Yan et al. also developed hyaluronic acid-based nanoparticles in the delivery of DOX by conjugating the *n*-octyl acrylate backbone of hyaluronic acid with cationic amphiphilic copolymer consisting of PEGylated cationic quaternary amine in order to accelerate the endocytosis process by minimizing the impact of negative charge of the whole system. The developed DDS was associated with the release of DOX from the vehicle in an acidic environment of endosome, exerted potential antibacterial activity, and minimized the risk of bacteria-induced tumor resistance [42]. As an extension of this work, Tian et al. successfully developed the dual functionalized hyaluronic acid nanoparticles after their modification with liver-targeting ligands, such as glycyrrhetinic acid and pH-responsive L-histidine [43]. Under acidic environment, protonation of imidazole backbone of histidine caused an increment in particle size and stimulated the release of DOX. The released DOX from these tailor-made hyaluronic acid-based nanoparticles exerted potential cytotoxicity against human hepatoma cell line HepG2 and H22 tumor-bearing mice [43].

In order to enhance in vitro as well as in vivo therapeutic efficacies of DOX, Han et al. successfully prepared cross-linked hyaluronic acid-based nanoparticles [44]. In this work, the cross-linking of hyaluronic acid was carried out using 2-(pyridyldithio)-ethylamine (PDA) as cross-linker and polycaprolactone (PCL) to target the nucleus of squamous carcinoma cells (SCC7 cells) and to facilitate the controlled release of DOX at the target sites, respectively. Being a disulfide cross-linker, PDA was associated with controlled release of DOX, whereas the hydrophobic nature of PCL helped in the encapsulation of DOX in the influence of GSH [44]. Cadete et al. developed docetaxel-loaded hyaluronic acid nanoparticles by employing the self-emulsification method, in which there were no organic solvents or heat [45]. In order to enhance the safety of delivery system, the amphiphilic hyaluronic acid derivative was synthesized by functionalization and conjugation of sodium hyaluronate with dodecylamine. The developed nanoparticles were found to be stable for 24h in human plasma, which caused the growth inhibition of A549 cells as the nanoparticles enhanced the cancer cell-induced intracellular uptake of docetaxel [45].

Zhang et al. prepared the hyaluronic acid-based nanoparticles using poly(lactic-*co*-glycolic acid) (PLGA) in order to achieve the co-transmission of docetaxel and α-naphtho-flavone [46]. In this setting, initially, the nanoparticle core was modified with polyethyleneimine (PEI) to develop the positive charge followed by coating of nanoparticles with hyaluronic acid enhancing the hyaluronic acid-mediated endocytosis of cellular uptake of payloads. The developed formulation might be advantageous to minimize the risk of multidrug resistance in breast cancer cells, such as MCF-7/1B1 cells, and initiate the apoptosis mechanism. Also, this tailor-made hyaluronic acid-based nanoparticle system was associated with significant enhancement of bioavailability of docetaxel than the free form of docetaxel and docetaxel-loaded PLGA nanoparticles [47]. Some other hyaluronic acid-coated inorganic nanoparticles, including gold nanoparticles (AuNPs), silica nanoparticles (SiNPs), and metal-organic frameworks (MOF), were also used for targeted delivery in cancer treatment [48,49]. The use of hyaluronic acid in the formulation of DDS might help for controlled release, targeted delivery, formulation stabilization, and biocompatibility improvement. Targeted anticancer therapy approaches using tailor-made hyaluronic acid-based systems are illustrated in Fig. 3.

5 Tailor-made pectin-based systems for cancer-targeting applications

Pectin is a nonstarch polysaccharide available in fruits and vegetables. The molecular structure of pectin consists of D-galacturonic acid (GalA) units, which are joined by α-(1,4)-glycosidic linkage forming a chain-like structure [50]. It is obtained from plant cell walls after their extraction, and, characteristically, it is a more complexly branched substance having good aqueous solubility [51–55]. Physiologically, under the environment of gastrointestinal system, it remains intact, but it is absolutely degraded by colonic bacterial enzyme [56]. Therefore, pectin is considered as a useful biodegradable polymer for the delivery of drugs in the management of colon cancer [55,56].

During the past few years, many researchers have tried to use modified citrus pectin (MCP), which is believed to increase the bioavailability of pectin thereby elevating its blood concentration [57]. It is believed that in the management of metastatic cancers, such as melanoma and various organ

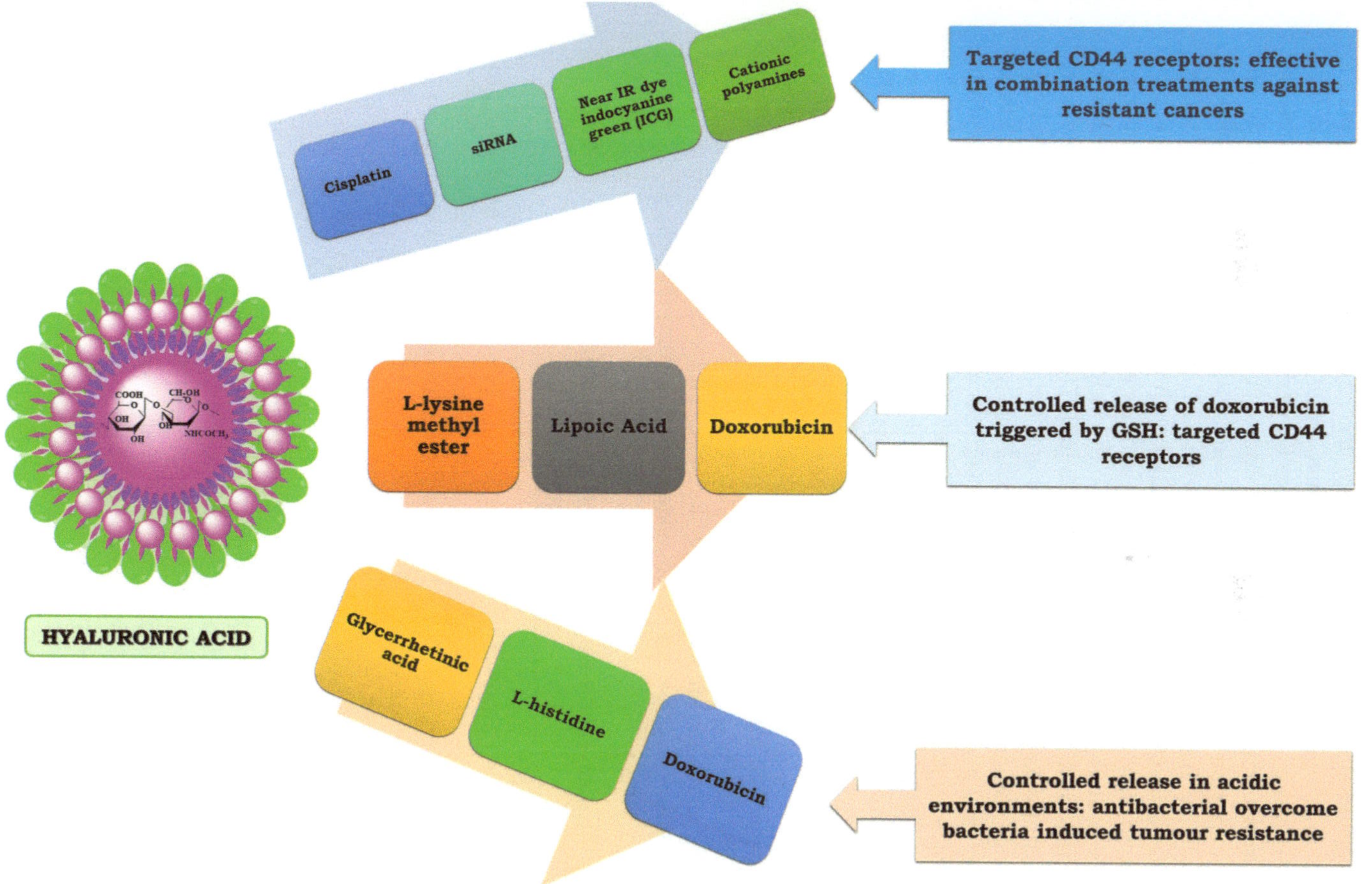

FIG. 3 Tailor-made hyaluronic acid-based systems for targeted anticancer therapy.

cancers like colon, breast, and prostate, the citrus pectin and MCP play a useful and vital role [58]. In this context, these agents have been tested in various rodent models of cancer, where they tend to suppress both the development of secondary tumors and angiogenesis process [59,60]. In the same experiment, cancer cells were treated with noneffective dose of paclitaxel (PTX, 100 nM) in combination with 0.1% pectin-MCP, which exerted the synergistic cytotoxic effect associated with 75% reduction cell viability followed by a 3.9-fold elevation in the activity of caspase-3 [61]. In ovarian cancer rodent model, Chandran et al. developed gemcitabine-loaded fibrin nanoparticles embedded in pectin [62]. The developed nanoparticles were found to be more biocompatible and helpful to increase the half-life of drugs. Also, these nanoparticles exhibited good cytotoxicity effects on cancer cells and were also found to initiate the programmed cell death of cancer cells, such as PA-1 ovarian cell-line culture.

In order to control the drug release profile under a pH-sensitive environment, a number of research works were carried out to study the use of 5-FU in the development of colon-targeting drug delivery system [63,64]. In this context, it was observed that under acidic environment, the rate of drug release was decreased. On the contrary, at pH 7.4 the rate of drug release was enhanced indicating that pectin may interfere with absorption of drug from the upper part of gastrointestinal tract; thereby, it may reduce the toxic effects associated with drug. Targeted anticancer therapy approaches using tailor-made pectin-based systems are illustrated in Fig. 4.

6 Tailor-made heparin-based systems for cancer-targeting applications

Heparin is composed from alternating units of uronic acid and glucosamine residues which are joined by 1,4 disaccharide linkage [65]. It is a well-known negatively charged natural polysaccharide due to its high content of sulfate. The heparin sulfate (HS) is abundantly found in the mucosal tissue of animals and remains attached to core proteins. Its average molecular weight ranges from 3 to 50 kDa [65,66]. HS is widely accepted as heparin communicates with various functional proteins, such as growth factors, extracellular matrix components, and adhesion molecules through the electrostatic mechanism. In addition, heparin shows a greater tendency to interact with serine protease inhibitor and, thereby, increases both selectivity and specificity of drugs against cancer cells [65–67]. The outcome of many researches revealed that low-molecular-weight heparin has a greater potential to increase the rate of survival in cancer patients [68]. The pathophysiology of ovarian cancer is associated with suppressed expression of gene for heparan sulfate 6-*O*-endosulfatase-1 (HSulf-1) and is thought to play a vital role in the development of tumors. Again, it has been observed that due to nonspecific distribution and potential toxic

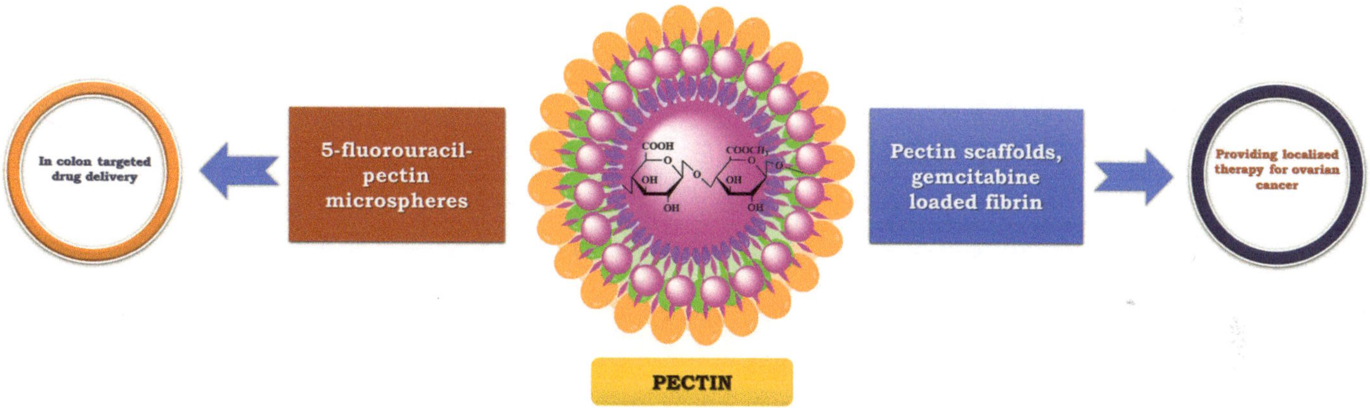

FIG. 4 Tailor-made pectin-based systems for targeted anticancer therapy.

effects, the use of cis-diamminedichloroplatinum (II) (DDP, cisplatin) is decreased. In order to minimize this limitation, the combination of HSulf-1/HPEI complexes with cisplatin (DDP) is employed against monotherapy of HSulf-1 or DDP alone for effective pharmacotherapy of ovarian cancer [69]. In another work, the systemic delivery of epidermal growth factor receptor (EGFR)-targeted heparin DDP (EHDDP) nanoparticles were developed as novel DDP, which elevated the time of blood circulation and modified both the pharmacokinetics and biodistribution of platinum (Pt) against the lung cancer cell lines [70].

Heparin has the potential to act as a harmless carrier for anticancer drugs, and it is useful in the development of multifunctional bioconjugates for targeted delivery systems for anticancer drugs [68]. In this context, heparin has the potential to inhibit the formation of endothelial tubules by preventing the binding of angiogenic factors [71]. The pathophysiology of various organ cancers, such as ovary, brain, lung, breast, and myeloid cells, has revealed the hyperstimulation of folate receptors. The heparin-PEG-folate (H-PEG-F) containing succinylated-heparin conjugated with folate via PEG 1000/3000 spacers with taxol has been developed to stimulate the intracellular target-specific delivery of drugs against folate receptors [72]. These novel conjugate systems were found to entrap a high amount of hydrophobic drugs within the core system, whereas the H-PEG-F conjugate caused both stabilization of nanoparticles and presented the folate functional group on the surface. Similarly, the heparin-polyethyleneimine (HPEI) nanoparticles also successfully delivered the plasmid-expressing mouse survivin-T34A (ms-T34A) and alleviated the C-26 carcinoma in both in vitro and in vivo experimental models of cancers. The results of in vivo experiment exhibited favorable results where HPEI nanoparticles effectively transfected the Lac-Z report gene into C-26 cells. Moreover, HPEI-based ms-T34A nanoparticle administration through intratumoral injection significantly alleviated the growth of C-26 carcinoma cells by stimulating the programmed cell death and inhibited the process of angiogenesis [73].

The use of combination of two or more chemotherapeutic agents has been carried out both clinically and preclinically in the management of various types of human cancers, and results showed promising outcomes with enhanced therapeutic effectiveness. In this regard, the nanogel of heparin-pluronic (Hep-Pr)-based encapsulation of PTX and DNase was developed for effective intracellular drug transportation [74]. The applied combination of Hep-Pr nanogel with PTX and DNase showed a dose-dependent synergistic cytotoxicity compared to single drug or free-drug treatments. Recently, a binary drug delivery system for cancer with PTX and DOX has also been studied for in vitro release profile [75]. The release of DOX was found to be pH-dependent, ensuring more drugs to be released in the tumor cells than in the normal ones. Targeted anticancer therapy approaches using tailor-made heparin-based systems are illustrated in Fig. 5.

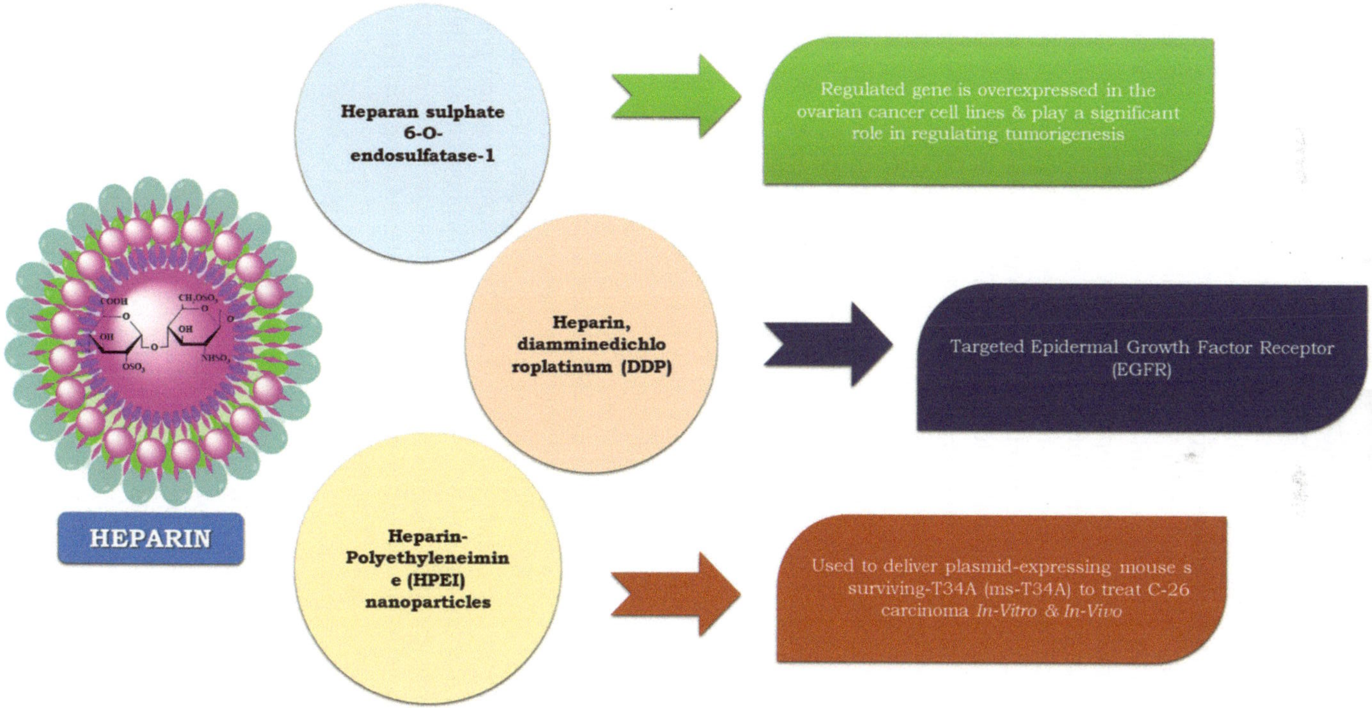

FIG. 5 Tailor-made heparin-based systems for targeted anticancer therapy.

7 Tailor-made dextran-based systems for cancer-targeting applications

Dextran is obtained from the microbial sources such as *Leuconostoc mesenteroides*, and it contains (1-6)-linked glucan with side chain attached to 3 position of the backbone glucose units [76,77]. Naturally, it is available as a colloidal, inert, and polar compound. Since the past few decades, dextran and its tailored (modified) forms are being used as biopolysaccharide excipients in the development of many novel DDSs [76]. It is commonly used in the preparation of a wide range of DDSs, such as hydrogels [77], micelles [78], and core-shell nanoparticles [79]. In a recent research, Thambi et al. successfully investigated the preparation of carboxymethyl dextran nanoparticle for the delivery of DOX by conjugating dextran with lithocholic acid through a disulfide linkage [80]. In the availability of GSH, these nanoparticles effectively released DOX at SCC7 cancer cell targets and exerted maximum cytotoxic effects through enhanced permeation and retention (EPR) mechanism in a tumor-bearing mice model. In addition, this study reported effective therapeutic outcome and excellent biodistribution characteristics as compared to simple DOX-loaded nanoparticles. The therapeutic efficacy of curcumin is well documented in the management of different kinds of cancers, and it is believed that the polyphenolic moiety of curcumin has the tendency to conjugate with different types of polymers [81]. In another research, the self-assembled conjugated nanoparticles of dextran-curcumin were prepared by Curio et al., and these are further utilized for the encapsulation of methotrexate (MTX) in the management of breast cancer [82]. These MTX-loaded nanoparticles showed prominent anticancer activity as these systems released MTX in sustained manner with rapid accumulation of MTX in MCF-7 cells. In addition, MTX in association with curcumin significantly exerted potential anticancer activity against MCF-7 cancer cells. This combination therapy approach has garnered the attention of many researchers and encouraged them to use it along with drug-polymer conjugates as drug carriers to deliver therapeutic agents for cancer treatment [82].

In another research, Lee et al. developed gold-dextran nanoparticles having increased serum stability over a period of 6 days for the image-guided photodynamic treatment of cancers [83]. The in vitro study revealed the efficient uptake of these gold-dextran nanoparticles by SCC7 cells, whereas the in vivo study showed that these nanoparticles produced good antitumor activity because of their good stability profile enabling the smooth delivery of chlorine 6 at the tumor site without causing its leakage. Zhang et al. encapsulated the microRNA into the lipid-modified dextran-based polymeric nanoparticle in which the modification of dextran acrylate was carried out by stearyl amine to obtain self-assembly of nanoparticles [84]. The developed nanoparticles were further loaded with microRNA, which showed greater stability ensuring the efficient delivery of microRNA into cancerous cells. These nanoparticles reduced the growth and proliferation of carcinoma cells. In another research, Foerster et al. successfully developed PEGylated dextran nanoparticles for the efficient delivery of siRNA to the myeloid liver cells [85]. Characteristically, these PEGylated dextran nanoparticles yielded smaller-sized particles with altered biodistribution and cellular uptake properties along with no cytotoxic effects. According to the results of in vitro study, these tailor-made dextran-based nanoparticles were not only protected from uptake by the peripheral blood mononuclear cells and murine cells but also enhanced their accumulation into liver cells. Alternatively, these nanoparticles failed to alter the plasma circulation time and were eliminated within 24 h with potential ability to target liver macrophages [85]. Tang et al. developed self-assembled pH-dependent dextran-based nanoparticles to conjugate folic acid for the enhancement of DOX loading by electrostatic interaction mechanism [86]. These developed nanoparticles exerted maximum antitumor activity and improved the survival time of murine breast carcinoma 4T1 cells. Targeted anticancer therapy approaches using tailor-made dextran-based systems are illustrated in Fig. 6.

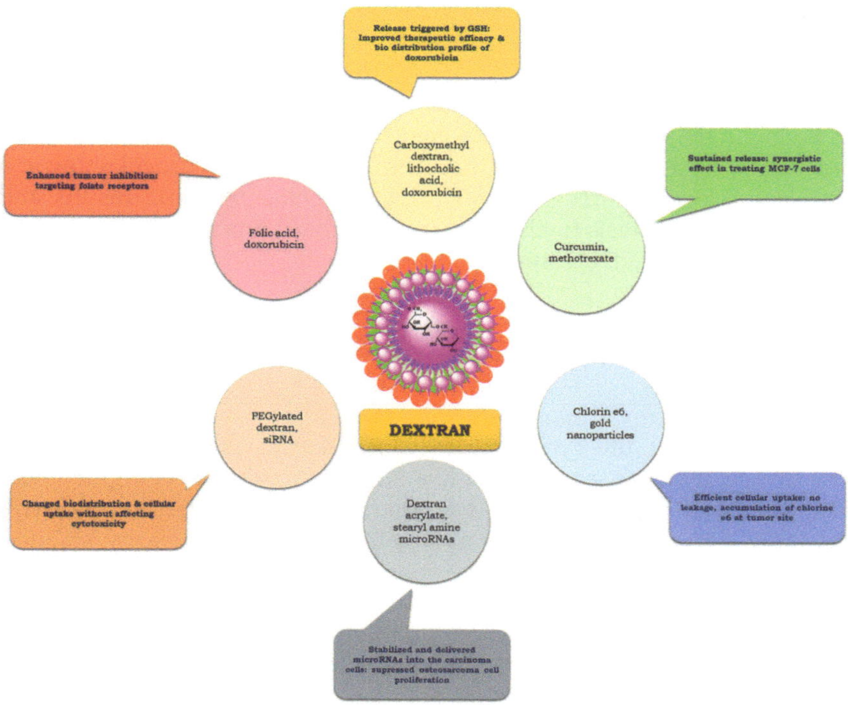

FIG. 6 Tailor-made dextran-based systems for targeted anticancer therapy.

8 Tailor-made chondroitin sulfate-based systems for cancer-targeting applications

The backbone of chondroitin sulfate (CS) consists of an alternate layer of D-glucuronic acid and *N*-acetyl galactosamine unit which is sulfated at either 4 or 6 position [87,88]. Naturally occurring CS has greater water solubility, whereas cross-linked CS has less water solubility ensuring the development of better shield [89]. Therefore, the cross-linked CS is frequently used as a carrier for effective and specific delivery of bioactive compounds into overexpressed receptors on the cancer cells, such as CD44 receptor cells. After recognition and attachment with CD44 cells by CS, these particles further undergo the phagocytosis mechanism and by the action of degrading enzymes, such as hyaluronidase. This degradation facilitates effective drug release at the site of cancer cells. On the basis of reported literature, we found that the conjugation of nanoparticles is responsible for the enhancement of antitumor activity of hydrophobic compounds like curcumin [90].

In a research, a nanogel of DOX was formulated with acetylated CS (AC-CS3) with an improved potential antitumor activity [91]. In another study, the coating of CS-macromer (NMChS) onto functionalized mesoporous silica nanoparticles (MSNs) was carried out by CS-macromer (NMChS) to deliver DOX [92]. It was observed that the developed NMChS-MSNs nanocarriers were pH-dependent with modified-release characteristics. Combination strategy of biopolymers also showed effective results in anticancer drug delivery. One such example showed a hydrogel based on the alginate, where alginates were physically cross-linked by calcium ions (Ca^{2+}) in the presence of CS. These alginate-CS hydrogel showed a good colon-targeted drug delivery potential [93]. Swelling results and morphological analysis further showed that the alginate-CS hydrogel had a clear pH-dependent behavior.

9 Tailor-made cyclodextrin-based systems for cancer-targeting applications

Fundamentally, the cyclodextrin (CD) is cyclic oligosaccharide, and, structurally, it possesses a tunnel-like structure having seven glucopyranose units [94]. Externally, it has a polar and hydrophilic core, whereas internally it has a nonpolar and hydrophobic core. The polarity, stability, and biological activity of small hydrophobic drugs is enhanced partially or completely enhanced by the use of CD-cavity [95]. In a research, Choi et al. used the same principle for the preparation of PTX-loaded CD-based hydrogels in order to enhance the water solubility of PTX after incorporating it into inclusion complex with (2,6-di-*O*-methyl)-β-cyclodextrin (DMbCD) [96]. In another work, the folate receptor-based novel nanoscale drug delivery was explored in order to enhance the tumor-targeting ability of antitumor agents [97]. For the entrapment of hydrophobic drug like Gefitinib, the folic acid-decorated bovine serum albumin (BSA) was formulated followed by its conjugation with carbodiimide coupling with carboxymethyl-β-cyclodextrin (CM-β-CD). In an extension of this work, adamantane (Ada) and conjugation of cytotoxic DOX with folic acid-based CD carriers (FACD) were formulated to form a drug complex which showed an eight-fold capacity to increase DOX uptake; this has also been shown to enhance the targeted delivery of DOX into specific folate receptor-positive tumor cell receptors [97]. According to extensive literature data, CD has better membrane-solubilizing capacity and is responsible for the modification of membrane integrity and absorption process like passive diffusion and carrier-mediated transportation of drug molecules [98]. This principle was effectively used for the preparation of oral drug delivery of nanosponges (NS) of tamoxifen-loaded β-CD against MCF-7 cells, where this formulation exhibited cytotoxic action for a period of 24–48h as compared to that of the tamoxifen formulation [99]. Likewise, to control the intracellular uptake and antitumor activity, CD-curcumin nanoparticle was prepared [100]. This β-CD-curcumin self-assembled drug delivery system was associated with improved release of curcumin, which will be effective in the management of prostate cancer than with the curcumin-only option. This study further proved that β-CD-curcumin exerted a potential effect on the proliferation of C4-2 and DU145 prostate cancer cell lines [100].

The surface of AuNP carriers was modified by CD for the encapsulation of β-lapachone [101]. In the presence of low and high concentration of glutathione cancer cells (MCF-7 and A549 cells, respectively), the release rate of β-lapachone from the surface of AuNP-1 was standardized. In the pathophysiology of cancer, the transferrin receptors (TfR) are upregulated. On the basis of this mechanism, Davis et al. studied the clinically targeted use of CD-containing polymer (CDP) and human transferrin (Tf) as a potential binding site in order to enhance the therapeutic outcome of RNA interference (RNAi) [102]. For the development of pH-dependent nanoparticles for the bio-imaging applications, conjugated nanocarriers of PTX with the β-CD were developed [103]. In the context of porphyrin receptors, numerous researches were carried out to explore their potential role in their binding with the CD backbone as well as to analyze their photosensitizing efficacy of porphyrin functional group against the targeted area of cancer cells [104].

10 Tailor-made pullulan-based systems for cancer-targeting applications

Pullulan, a natural hydrophilic polysaccharide, is extracted from dimorphic fungi, namely, *Aureobasidium pullulans* [105]. It contains alternating subunits of α-1,6-linked maltotriose which are joined by α-1,4-glucosidic bonds [105,106]. It is widely used in the area of engineering and system of targeted drug delivery because of its safety profile. Pullulan is more specific to liver for the biological applications. Also, it is free from toxicity, immunogenic reactions, mutagenic ability, and carcinogenicity [106,107]. Therefore, it is widely used in the optimization of various forms of DDSs. The previous reports showed that curcumin in association with glycyrrhetinic acid (GA)-modified pullulan nanoparticles (GAP NPs) improved curcumin's water solubility and stability and its release at target sites [108]. These tailor-made pullulan nanoparticles are released in a sustained manner against different pH environments. To speed up the drug penetration capacity of PTX in heterogenic tumor condition, it was embedded in the cationic biodegradable nanogel (DpNG) along with acetylated pullulan and low-molecular-weight polyethyleneimine (1.8 kDa) [109]. In order to develop vaccines against cancer, cholesteryl pullulan (CHP) antigen delivery system was optimized for its safety, immune reactions, and clinical benefits [110]. For the localized specific vaccine delivery, CHP was targeted for its delivery in the medulla region of medullary macrophage of the core of lymph node [111]. It was found that with the help of hydrophobic bond, CHP formed a stable polypeptide complex through solubilization and stabilization processes.

Amphiphilic drug delivery system is one of the most frequently used systems as it allows polymers like pullulan to self-assemble in nanomicelles after dialysis, and amphiphilic α-tocopherol pullulan polymers (PUTC1, PUTC2, and PUTC3) are considered as most important [112]. Also, the amphiphilic biotin-modified cholesteryl pullulan (Bio-CHSP) conjugates were efficiently prepared after an interaction of biotin with the cholesterol moiety in aqueous media and were evaluated for their role as a carrier for mitoxantrone, and their ability to self-aggregate was studied using the fluorescence technique [113]. The partial carboxymethylation of pullulan and further development of its hydrazine hydrate derivative was used for the delivery of pH-based nanoparticles of DOX [114]. This system of drug delivery released the loaded DOX at a faster rate at pH 5 (75% within 2 h) than pH 7 (15% within 12 h), in vitro. In another research, Li et al. developed pH-sensitive DOX-pullulan conjugates using hydrazone bonds, which enabled the immediate diffusion of DOX from acidic endosomal/lysosomal climate to nucleus [115]. For the purpose of combination therapy against hepatocellular carcinoma cells (HCC), pH-dependent MTX nanoparticles were prepared by using combretastatin A4 (CA4) based on pullulan as a carrier drug delivery system [116]. In context of gene therapy, polyethyleneimine (PEI; 25 kDa)-conjugated pullulans (PPE1, PPE2, and PPE3) were prepared for the transportation of gene to the target site [117].

In one research, a faster rate of DOX release (in vitro) from folate-decorated maleilated pullulan-doxorubicin (FA-MP-DOX) conjugation under acidic environment against active tumor was studied [118]. Scomparin et al. prepared activated pullulan by periodic oxidation and functionalization of reduced cysteamine and 1.9 kDa of $PEG(NH_2)_2$ [119]. In this study, they carried out a cysteamine thiol-induced conjugation of DOX under pH-dependent hydrazone spacer followed by conjugation of folic acid with derivatized $PEG\text{-}NH_2$. According to the in vitro study, it was observed that both free DOX and (FA-PEG)-Pull-(Cyst-DOX) were speedily taken up by upregulated KB tumor cells in which the folate receptors were overexpressed [119]. Bae et al. synthesized self-quenching pullulan/folate-pheophorbide-A (Pheo-A) conjugates-based nanogels and investigated their potential to reduce photosensitizer (PS) phototoxicity in normal tissues [120]. This enhanced the efficacy of tumor treatment.

11 Tailor-made alginate-based systems for cancer-targeting applications

Alginate is a natural water-soluble polysaccharide and is obtained from algae like kelp and various bacteria, including *Pseudomonas aeruginosa* [121–125]. Alginate-based hydrogels have a greater tendency to form cross-linked networks under aqueous media with divalent ions [126–132]. These hydrogels of mitoxantrone were effectively used by Huebsch et al. in the management of xenograft tumors. They showed that the ultrasound-stimulated drug release effectively inhibited tumor growth as compared with the option of using only sustained drug release [133]. The underlying possible antitumor activity of alginate-based hydrogels was due to the formation of tight junction through interaction of (guluronic acid) G-blocks in the availability of divalent cations like Ca^{2+}, Zn^{2+} as compared to the weakly formed junctions in MG-blocks [134].

For improved therapeutic outcomes of many antitumor drugs, the uses of alginate-based nanoparticles have been investigated; for example, DOX-loaded alginate-based hydrogels for liver cancer liberated DOX in sustained manner [135,136]. Likewise, Ma et al. developed targeted nanoparticles of superparamagnetic iron oxide with alginate (SPIO-alginate), and the magnetic resonance imaging (MRI) showed that SPIO-alginate was associated with higher rate of identification of hepatic carcinoma (HCC) in the cirrhotic liver as compared to MRI contrast agents [137]. Recently, Boekhoven et al. prepared targeted amphiphilic alginate cross-shell nanoparticles for DOX release, and these nanoparticles exhibited a 60-fold greater tendency to exert cytotoxic effects against MDA-MB 231 breast carcinoma cells [138]. Goren et al. targeted human mesenchymal stem cells (hMSCs) by synthesizing alginate-poly-L-lysine microcapsules and further evaluated them through fluorescence and H3-thymidine assay techniques [139]. The results of this study revealed that encapsulated hMSCs produced a lower amount of immunogenic reactions, a threefold reduction of cytokine expression, compared to the entrapped cell lines. Fundamentally, chitosan-based alginate nanoparticles are frequently used in the delivery of hydrophobic drugs to cancer cells with improved biocompatibility and reduced toxicity [140,141]. The prepared PTX-loaded hydroxyapatite (HAp)-alginate beads significantly delayed the precipitation of breast cancer with minimal adverse effects [142]. For the oral delivery of antitumor nutraceuticals, alginate and chitosan were used for the preparation of polymeric-ceramic nanocarriers [143]. Furthermore, the prepared nanocarriers showed better permeation ability and also efficiently transported the iron-saturated bovine lactoferrin protein (Fe-bLf) at the targeted sites of the tumor and prevented the progression of cancer. Moreover, for the sustained release of the combination of cyclophosphamide and 5-FU, alginate-based microparticles were prepared using the ionic gelation technique [144,145]. Clinical reports showed that these alginate-based microparticles enhanced anticancer activity by 5–8-folds compared to the free drug situation. In the context of local heat generation (hyperthermia)-induced cancer treatment strategy, alginate-based microparticles showed promising anticancer capacity [145]. The targeted, biocompatible, and biodegradable magnetic nanoparticles of alginate were synthesized using the emulsion/reticulation method, which overcame the impact of biological barriers and caused the physical degradation of tumor cells [146]. Targeted anticancer therapy approaches using tailor-made alginate-based systems are illustrated in Fig. 7.

12 Tailor-made amylose-based systems for cancer-targeting applications

The plant-derived linear polysaccharide like amylose consists of 15%–30% unbranched starch with many glucopyranose subunits (α-1,4-D-glucose), which are joined through α (1 → 4) bonds [147]. The α-glycosidic bonds of α-amylose is responsible for the formation of its left-handed helical structure. It is widely used as a drug carrier for the controlled drug release of hydrogels and also as a solubility enhancer because of its safety and nontoxicity profiles [148,149]. Dried amylose is also used for the preparation of colon-specific drug delivery system. Although the amylase film is potentially resistant to the action of pancreatic amylases, it is digested by colonic microflora, i.e., bacteroides, bifidobacterium, and so on. The porous coating on amylose promotes the release of drugs under the harsh environment of gastrointestinal tract, which destroys its target specificity. To minimize this limitation, water-insoluble polymers like ethyl-cellulose are frequently incorporated in the amylose films to control the swelling of amylose in targeting

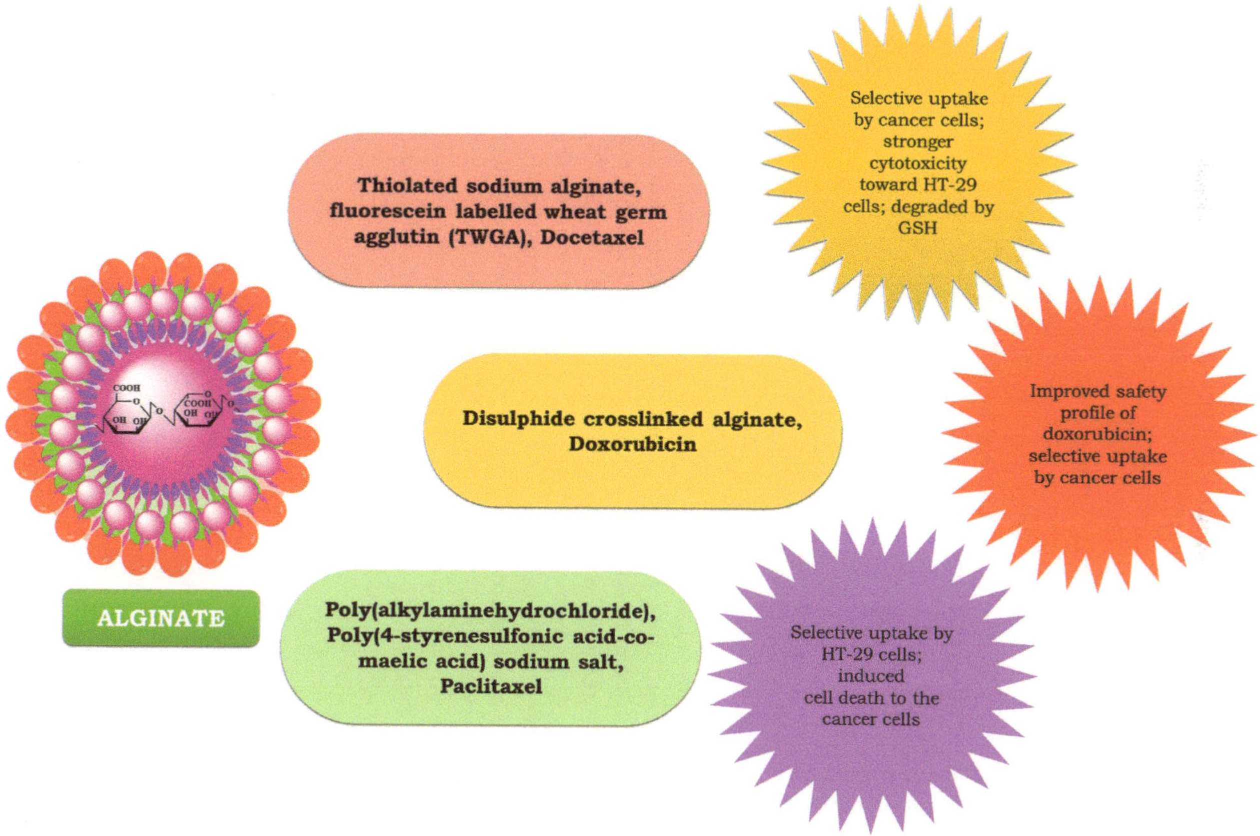

FIG. 7 Tailor-made alginate-based systems for targeted anticancer therapy.

the colon [150,151]. Also, one in vitro dissolution study showed that the use of amylase-ethylcellulose coat (1:4) reduced this limitation under stimulated gastrointestinal environment for a period of 12h. Fujii et al. proposed the application of cycloamylose nanogel as a DDS for siRNA-based cancer therapy [152]. Cholesterol-bearing cycloamylose nanogel with spermine group (CH-CA-Spe) was used to deliver vascular endothelial growth factor (VEGF)-specific short interfering RNA (siVEGF) into tumor cells. Intra-tumor injections of the complex significantly suppressed neovascularization and tumor growth of RCC in mice. The treatment also inhibited the induction of myeloid-derived suppressor cells, while it decreased interleukin-17A production leading to a positive impact on systemic immune responses against malignancies [152].

13 Conclusion

The rising occurrence of cancer cases and deaths related to cancer lead to increased economic burden of the global population and debilitating effects on their physical and emotional well-being. The effective and safe delivery of anticancer drugs is always a major concern for pharmaceutical chemist and drug delivery formulators. Various molecules and their chemical derivatives are being tried for targeted drug therapy to lessen the severe toxicities associated with anticancer drugs. Phytochemicals and biological macromolecules are considered to be promising candidates owing to their safety, biocompatibility, and biodegradability. This chapter presented a discussion on the various tailor-made polysaccharide-based targeted cancer drug therapies and their effectiveness. The various tailor-made polysaccharides are an effective means of targeted drug delivery, and their effectiveness in anticancer therapeutics has been demonstrated well in past studies.

References

[1] Siegel RL, Miller KD, Fedewa SA, Ahnen DJ, Meester RG, Barzi A, et al. Colorectal cancer statistics, 2017. CA Cancer J Clin 2017;67(3):177–93.

[2] Gianfaldoni S, Gianfaldoni R, Wollina U, Lotti J, Tchernev G, Lotti T. An overview on radiotherapy: from its history to its current applications in dermatology. Open Access Maced J Med Sci 2017;5(4):521.

[3] Sullivan R, Alatise OI, Anderson BO, Audisio R, Autier P, Aggarwal A, et al. Global cancer surgery: delivering safe, affordable, and timely cancer surgery. Lancet Oncol 2015;16(11):1193–224.

[4] Christofi T, Baritaki S, Falzone L, Libra M, Zaravinos A. Current perspectives in cancer immunotherapy. Cancer 2019;11(10):1472.

[5] Baudino TA. Targeted cancer therapy: the next generation of cancer treatment. Curr Drug Discov Technol 2015;12(1):3–20.

[6] Nurgali K, Jagoe RT, Abalo R. Adverse effects of cancer chemotherapy: anything new to improve tolerance and reduce sequelae? Front Pharmacol 2018;9:245.
[7] Hossen S, Hossain MK, Basher M, Mia M, Rahman M, Uddin MJ. Smart nanocarrier-based drug delivery systems for cancer therapy and toxicity studies: a review. J Adv Res 2019;15:1–18.
[8] Peer D, Karp JM, Hong S, Farokhzad OC, Margalit R, Langer R. Nanocarriers as an emerging platform for cancer therapy. Nat Nanotechnol 2007;2(12):751–60.
[9] Shankar R, Samykutty A, Riggin C, Kannan S, Wenzel U, Kolhatkar R. Cathepsin B degradable star-shaped peptidic macromolecules for delivery of 2-methoxyestradiol. Mol Pharm 2013;10(10):3776–88.
[10] Liu Z, Jiao Y, Wang Y, Zhou C, Zhang Z. Polysaccharides-based nanoparticles as drug delivery systems. Adv Drug Deliv Rev 2008;60(15):1650–62.
[11] Zheng Y, Monty J, Linhardt RJ. Polysaccharide-based nanocomposites and their applications. Carbohydr Res 2015;405:23–32.
[12] Dumitriu S. Polysaccharides: structural diversity and functional versatility. CRC Press; 2004.
[13] Nayak AK, Pal D. Functionalization of tamarind gum for drug delivery. In: Thakur VK, Thakur MK, editors. Functional biopolymers. Cham: Springer; 2018. p. 35–56.
[14] Nayak AK, Bera H, Hasnain MS, Pal D. Synthesis and characterization of graft-copolymers of plant polysaccharides. In: Thakur VK, editor. Biopolymer grafting, synthesis and properties. Netherlands: Elsevier Inc.; 2018. p. 1–62.
[15] Alkahtani S, Hasnain MS, Nayak AK, Aminabhavi TM. Polysaccharide-based polyelectrolyte complex systems for biomedical uses. In: Nayak AK, Hasnain MS, Aminabhavi TM, editors. Tailor-made polysaccharides in biomedical applications. USA: Academic Press, Elsevier Inc.; 2021. p. 151–74.
[16] Nayak AK, Hasnain MS, Tabis M, Aminabhavi TM. In: Nayak AK, Hasnain MS, Aminabhavi TM, editors. Use of tailored polysaccharides in dentistry. USA: Academic Press, Elsevier Inc.; 2021. p. 287–304.
[17] Das B, Dutta S, Nayak AK, Nanda U. Zinc alginate-carboxymethyl cashew gum microbeads for prolonged drug release: development and optimization. Int J Biol Macromol 2014;70:505–15.
[18] Nayak AK, Pal D. Chitosan-based interpenetrating polymeric network systems for sustained drug release. In: Tiwari A, Patra HK, Choi J-W, editors. Advanced theranostics materials. USA: Wiley-Scrivener; 2015. p. 183–208.
[19] Pal D, Nayak AK. Interpenetrating polymer networks (IPNs): Natural polymeric blends for drug delivery. In: Mishra M, editor. Encyclopedia of biomedical polymers and polymeric biomaterials, vol. VI. New York: Taylor and Francis; 2015. p. 4120–30.
[20] Ray S, Sinha P, Laha B, Maiti S, Bhattacharyya UK, Nayak AK. Polysorbate 80 coated crosslinked chitosan nanoparticles of ropinirole hydrochloride for brain targeting. J Drug Delivery Sci Technol 2018;48:21–9.
[21] Nayak AK, Kalia S, Hasnain MS. Optimization of aceclofenac-loaded pectinate-poly (vinyl pyrrolidone) beads by response surface methodology. Int J Biol Macromol 2013;62:194–202.
[22] Nayak AK, Pal D. Ionotropically-gelled mucoadhesive beads for oral metformin HCl delivery: formulation, optimization and antidiabetic evaluation. J Sci Ind Res 2013;72:15–22.
[23] Malakar J, Nayak AK, Das A. Modified starch (cationized)-alginate beads containing aceclofenac: formulation optimization using central composite design. Starch-Starke 2013;65:603–12.
[24] Hasnain MS, Nayak AK. Chitosan as responsive polymer for drug delivery applications. In: Makhlouf ASH, Abu-Thabit NY, editors. Stimuli responsive polymeric nanocarriers for drug delivery applications, volume 1, types and triggers. Woodhead Publishing series in biomaterials. United States: Elsevier Ltd.; 2018. p. 581–605.

[25] Nayak AK, Hasnain MS, Pal K, Banerjee I, Pal D. Gum-based hydrogels in drug delivery. In: Pal K, Banerjee I, Sarkar P, Kim D, Deng W-P, Dubey NK, Majumder K, editors. Biopolymer-based formulations, biomedical and food applications. United States: Elsevier Inc.; 2020. p. 605–45.
[26] Yong SK, Shrivastava M, Srivastava P, Kunhikrishnan A, Bolan N. Environmental applications of chitosan and its derivatives. In: Reviews of environmental contamination and toxicology, vol. 233; 2015. p. 1–43.
[27] Hasnain MS, Ahmed SA, Alkahtani S, Milivojevic M, Kandar CC, Dhara AK, Nayak AK. Biopolymers for drug delivery. In: Nayak AK, Hasnain MS, editors. Advanced biopolymeric systems for drug delivery. Switzerland: Springer; 2020. p. 1–29.
[28] Kandar CC, Hasnain MS, Nayak AK. Natural polymers as useful pharmaceutical excipients. In: Nayak AK, Pal K, Banerjee I, Maji S, Nanda U, editors. Advances and challenges in pharmaceutical technology: materials, process development and drug delivery strategies. USA: Academic Press, Elsevier Inc.; 2021. p. 1–44.
[29] Verma A, Dubey J, Verma N, Nayak AK. Chitosan-hydroxypropyl methylcellulose matrices as carriers for hydrodynamically balanced capsules of moxifloxacin HCl. Curr Drug Deliv 2017;14:83–90.
[30] Bhattarai N, Gunn J, Zhang M. Chitosan-based hydrogels for controlled, localized drug delivery. Adv Drug Deliv Rev 2010;62(1):83–99.
[31] Sekar V, Rajendran K, Vallinayagam S, Deepak V, Mahadevan S. Synthesis and characterization of chitosan ascorbate nanoparticles for therapeutic inhibition for cervical cancer and their in silico modeling. J Ind Eng Chem 2018;62:239–49.
[32] Nascimento AV, Singh A, Bousbaa H, Ferreira D, Sarmento B, Amiji MM. Mad2 checkpoint gene silencing using epidermal growth factor receptor-targeted chitosan nanoparticles in non-small cell lung cancer model. Mol Pharm 2014;11(10):3515–27.
[33] Nascimento AV, Singh A, Bousbaa H, Ferreira D, Sarmento B, Amiji MM. Overcoming cisplatin resistance in non-small cell lung cancer with Mad2 silencing siRNA delivered systemically using EGFR-targeted chitosan nanoparticles. Acta Biomater 2017;47:71–80.
[34] Esfandiarpour-Boroujeni S, Bagheri-Khoulenjani S, Mirzadeh H, Amanpour S. Fabrication and study of curcumin loaded nanoparticles based on folate-chitosan for breast cancer therapy application. Carbohydr Polym 2017;168:14–21.
[35] Nayak AK, Ansari MT, Pal D, Hasnain MS. Hyaluronic acid (hyaluronan): pharmaceutical applications. In: Nayak AK, Hasnain MS, Pal D, editors. Natural polymers for pharmaceutical applications, vol. III: animal derived polymers. USA: Apple Academic Press; 2019. p. 1–32.
[36] Toole BP. Hyaluronan-CD44 interactions in cancer: paradoxes and possibilities. Clin Cancer Res 2009;15(24):7462–8.
[37] Oh EJ, Park K, Kim KS, Kim J, Yang J-A, Kong J-H, et al. Target specific and long-acting delivery of protein, peptide, and nucleotide therapeutics using hyaluronic acid derivatives. J Control Release 2010;141(1):2–12.
[38] Hoffmann S, Vystrčilová L, Ulbrich K, Etrych TS, Caysa H, Mueller T, et al. Dual fluorescent HPMA copolymers for passive tumor targeting with pH-sensitive drug release: synthesis and characterization of distribution and tumor accumulation in mice by noninvasive multispectral optical imaging. Biomacromolecules 2012;13(3):652–63.
[39] Goodarzi N, Ghahremani MH, Dinarvand R. Targeting CD44 by hyaluronic acid-based nano drug delivery systems may eradicate cancer stem cells in human breast cancer. J Med Hypotheses Ideas 2011;5:26.
[40] Ganesh S, Iyer AK, Gattacceca F, Morrissey DV, Amiji MM. In vivo biodistribution of siRNA and cisplatin administered using CD44-targeted hyaluronic acid nanoparticles. J Control Release 2013;172(3):699–706.
[41] Zhong Y, Zhang J, Cheng R, Deng C, Meng F, Xie F, et al. Reversibly crosslinked hyaluronic acid nanoparticles for active targeting and intelligent delivery of doxorubicin to drug resistant CD44+ human breast tumor xenografts. J Control Release 2015;205:144–54.

[42] Yan X, Chen Q, An J, Liu D-E, Huang Y, Yang R, et al. Hyaluronic acid/PEGylated amphiphilic nanoparticles for pursuit of selective intracellular doxorubicin release. J Mater Chem B 2019;7(1):95–102.
[43] Tian G, Sun X, Bai J, Dong J, Zhang B, Gao Z, et al. Doxorubicin-loaded dual-functional hyaluronic acid nanoparticles: Preparation, characterization and antitumor efficacy in vitro and in vivo. Mol Med Rep 2019;19(1):133–42.
[44] Han HS, Thambi T, Choi KY, Son S, Ko H, Lee MC, et al. Bioreducible shell-cross-linked hyaluronic acid nanoparticles for tumor-targeted drug delivery. Biomacromolecules 2015;16(2):447–56.
[45] Cadete A, Olivera A, Besev M, Dhal PK, Gonçalves L, Almeida AJ, et al. Self-assembled hyaluronan nanocapsules for the intracellular delivery of anticancer drugs. Sci Rep 2019;9(1):1–11.
[46] Zhang J, Song J, Liang X, Yin Y, Zuo T, Chen D, et al. Hyaluronic acid-modified cationic nanoparticles overcome enzyme CYP1B1-mediated breast cancer multidrug resistance. Nanomedicine 2019;14(4):447–64.
[47] Lee D, Beack S, Yoo J, Kim SK, Lee C, Kwon W, et al. In vivo photoacoustic imaging of livers using biodegradable hyaluronic acid-conjugated silica nanoparticles. Adv Funct Mater 2018;28(22):1800941.
[48] Cao F, Yan M, Liu Y, Liu L, Ma G. Photothermally controlled MHC class I restricted CD8+ T-cell responses elicited by hyaluronic acid decorated gold nanoparticles as a vaccine for cancer immunotherapy. Adv Healthc Mater 2018;7(10):1701439.
[49] Zhao Q, Liu J, Zhu W, Sun C, Di D, Zhang Y, et al. Dual-stimuli responsive hyaluronic acid-conjugated mesoporous silica for targeted delivery to CD44-overexpressing cancer cells. Acta Biomater 2015;23:147–56.
[50] Nayak AK, Pal D. Plant-derived polymers: ionically gelled sustained drug release systems. In: Mishra M, editor. Encyclopedia of biomedical polymers and polymeric biomaterials, vol. VIII. New York: Taylor and Francis; 2016. p. 6002–17.
[51] Nayak AK, Pal D, Santra K. Development of pectinate-ispagula mucilage mucoadhesive beads of metformin HCl by central composite design. Int J Biol Macromol 2014;66:203–21.
[52] Nayak AK, Pal D, Santra K. Development of calcium pectinate-tamarind seed polysaccharide mucoadhesive beads containing metformin HCl. Carbohydr Polym 2014;101:220–30.
[53] Nayak AK, Pal D, Das S. Calcium pectinate-fenugreek seed mucilage mucoadhesive beads for controlled delivery of metformin HCl. Carbohydr Polym 2013;96:349–57.
[54] Nayak AK, Pal D. Blends of jackfruit seed starch-pectin in the development of mucoadhesive beads containing metformin HCl. Int J Biol Macromol 2013;62:137–45.
[55] Mukhiddinov Z, Khalikov DK, Abdusamiev F, Avloev CC. Isolation and structural characterization of a pectin homo and ramnogalacturonan. Talanta 2000;53(1):171–6.
[56] Chourasia M, Jain S. Polysaccharides for colon targeted drug delivery. Drug Deliv 2004;11(2):129–48.
[57] Jun Y, Katz A. PectaSol-C modified citrus pectin induces apoptosis and inhibition of proliferation in human and mouse androgen-dependent and- independent prostate cancer cells. Integr Cancer Ther 2010;9(2):197–203.
[58] Nicholas J. Fighting cancer metastasis and heavy metal toxicities with modified citrus pectin. Life Extention 2009;9:40–6.
[59] Johnson KD, Glinskii OV, Mossine VV, Turk JR, Mawhinney TP, Anthony DC, et al. Galectin-3 as a potential therapeutic target in tumors arising from malignant endothelia. Neoplasia 2007;9(8):662–70.
[60] Niture SK, Refai L. Plant pectin: a potential source for cancer suppression. Am J Pharmacol Toxicol 2013;8(1):9.
[61] Hossein G, Keshavarz M, Ahmadi S, Naderi N. Synergistic effects of PectaSol-C modified citrus pectin an inhibitor of Galectin-3 and paclitaxel on apoptosis of human SKOV-3 ovarian cancer cells. Asian Pac J Cancer Prev 2013;14(12):7561–8.

[62] Chandran S, Praveen G, Snima K, Nair SV, Pavithran K, Chennazhi K, et al. Potential use of drug loaded nano composite pectin scaffolds for the treatment of ovarian cancer. Curr Drug Deliv 2013;10(3):326–35.
[63] Paharia A, Yadav AK, Rai G, Jain SK, Pancholi SS, Agrawal GP. Eudragit-coated pectin microspheres of 5-fluorouracil for colon targeting. AAPS PharmSciTech 2007;8(1):E87–93.
[64] Leclere L, Van Cutsem P, Michiels C. Anti-cancer activities of pH-or heat-modified pectin. Front Pharmacol 2013;4:128.
[65] Paliwal R, Paliwal SR, Agrawal GP, Vyas SP. Recent advances in search of oral heparin therapeutics. Med Res Rev 2012;32(2):388–409.
[66] Li Y, Rodrigues J, Tomás H. Injectable and biodegradable hydrogels: gelation, biodegradation and biomedical applications. Chem Soc Rev 2012;41(6):2193–221.
[67] Szczubiałka K, Kamiński K, Zasada K, Karewicz A, Nowakowska M. Heparin—a key drug in the treatment of the circulatory degenerative diseases: controlling its action with polymers. Curr Pharm Des 2012;18(18):2591–606.
[68] Lazo-Langner A, Goss G, Spaans J, Rodger M. The effect of low-molecular-weight heparin on cancer survival. A systematic review and meta-analysis of randomized trials. J Thromb Haemost 2007;5(4):729–37.
[69] Liu P, Gou M, Yi T, Qi X, Xie C, Zhou S, et al. The enhanced antitumor effects of biodegradable cationic heparin-polyethyleneimine nanogels delivering HSulf-1 gene combined with cisplatin on ovarian cancer. Int J Oncol 2012;41(4):1504–12.
[70] Peng X-H, Wang Y, Huang D, Wang Y, Shin HJ, Chen Z, et al. Targeted delivery of cisplatin to lung cancer using ScFvEGFR-heparin-cisplatin nanoparticles. ACS Nano 2011;5(12):9480–93.
[71] Cho KJ, Moon HT, Park G-E, Jeon OC, Byun Y, Lee Y-K. Preparation of sodium deoxycholate (DOC) conjugated heparin derivatives for inhibition of angiogenesis and cancer cell growth. Bioconjug Chem 2008;19(7):1346–51.
[72] Wang Y, Wang Y, Xiang J, Yao K. Target-specific cellular uptake of taxol-loaded heparin-PEG-folate nanoparticles. Biomacromolecules 2010;11(12):3531–8.
[73] Zhang L, Gao X, Men K, Wang B, Zhang S, Qiu J, et al. Gene therapy for C-26 colon cancer using heparin-polyethyleneimine nanoparticle-mediated survivin T34A. Int J Nanomedicine 2011;6:2419.
[74] Joung YK, Jang JY, Choi JH, Han DK, Park KD. Heparin-conjugated pluronic nanogels as multi-drug nanocarriers for combination chemotherapy. Mol Pharm 2013;10(2):685–93.
[75] Ye L, Gao Z, Zhou Y, Yin X, Zhang X, Zhang A, et al. A pH-sensitive binary drug delivery system based on poly (caprolactone)–heparin conjugates. J Biomed Mater Res A 2014;102(3):880–9.
[76] Varshosaz J. Dextran conjugates in drug delivery. Expert Opin Drug Deliv 2012;9(5):509–23.
[77] Hennink WE, De Jong S, Bos GW, Veldhuis T, Van Nostrum C. Biodegradable dextran hydrogels crosslinked by stereocomplex formation for the controlled release of pharmaceutical proteins. Int J Pharm 2004;277(1–2):99–104.
[78] Jeong Y-I, Do Hyung Kim C-WC, Yoo J-J, Choi KH, Kim CH, Ha SH, et al. Doxorubicin-incorporated polymeric micelles composed of dextran-b-poly (DL-lactide-co-glycolide) copolymer. Int J Nanomedicine 2011;6:1415.
[79] Jeong Y-I, Chung K-D, Choi KC. Doxorubicin release from self-assembled nanoparticles of deoxycholic acid-conjugated dextran. Arch Pharm Res 2011;34(1):159–67.
[80] Thambi T, You DG, Han HS, Deepagan V, Jeon SM, Suh YD, et al. Bioreducible carboxymethyl dextran nanoparticles for tumor-targeted drug delivery. Adv Healthc Mater 2014;3(11):1829–38.
[81] Giordano A, Tommonaro G. Curcumin and cancer. Nutrients 2019;11(10):2376.

[82] Curcio M, Cirillo G, Tucci P, Farfalla A, Bevacqua E, Vittorio O, et al. Dextran-curcumin nanoparticles as a methotrexate delivery vehicle: a step forward in breast cancer combination therapy. Pharmaceuticals 2020;13(1):2.
[83] Lee M, Lee H, Rao NV, Han HS, Jeon S, Jeon J, et al. Gold-stabilized carboxymethyl dextran nanoparticles for image-guided photodynamic therapy of cancer. J Mater Chem B 2017;5(35):7319–27.
[84] Zhang L. Polymeric nanoparticle-based delivery of microRNA-199a-3p inhibits proliferation and growth of osteosarcoma cells. Int J Nanomedicine 2015;10:2913.
[85] Foerster F, Bamberger D, Schupp J, Weilbächer M, Kaps L, Strobl S, et al. Dextran-based therapeutic nanoparticles for hepatic drug delivery. Nanomedicine 2016;11(20):2663–77.
[86] Tang Y, Li Y, Xu R, Li S, Hu H, Xiao C, et al. Self-assembly of folic acid dextran conjugates for cancer chemotherapy. Nanoscale 2018;10(36):17265–74.
[87] Lee J-Y, Chung S-J, Cho H-J, Kim D-D. Bile acid-conjugated chondroitin sulfate A-based nanoparticles for tumor-targeted anticancer drug delivery. Eur J Pharm Biopharm 2015;94:532–41.
[88] Pal D, Nayak AK, Saha S, Hasnain MS. Pharmaceutical applications of chondroitin. In: Nayak AK, Hasnain MS, Pal D, editors. Natural polymers for pharmaceutical applications, vol. III: animal derived polymers. USA: Apple Academic Press; 2019. p. 117–32.
[89] Rubinstein A, Nakar D, Sintov A. Colonic drug delivery: enhanced release of indomethacin from cross-linked chondroitin matrix in rat cecal content. Pharm Res 1992;9(2):276–8.
[90] Radhakrishnan K, Tripathy J, Datey A, Chakravortty D, Raichur AM. Mesoporous silica–chondroitin sulphate hybrid nanoparticles for targeted and bio-responsive drug delivery. New J Chem 2015;39(3):1754–60.
[91] Park W, Park S-J, Na K. Potential of self-organizing nanogel with acetylated chondroitin sulfate as an anti-cancer drug carrier. Colloids Surf B Biointerfaces 2010;79(2):501–8.
[92] Xi J, Qin J, Fan L. Chondroitin sulfate functionalized mesostructured silica nanoparticles as biocompatible carriers for drug delivery. Int J Nanomedicine 2012;7:5235.
[93] Fajardo AR, Silva MB, Lopes LC, Piai JF, Rubira AF, Muniz EC. Hydrogel based on an alginate–Ca 2+/chondroitin sulfate matrix as a potential colon-specific drug delivery system. RSC Adv 2012;2(29):11095–103.
[94] Kakuta T, Takashima Y, Nakahata M, Otsubo M, Yamaguchi H, Harada A. Preorganized hydrogel: self-healing properties of supramolecular hydrogels formed by polymerization of host–guest-monomers that contain cyclodextrins and hydrophobic guest groups. Adv Mater 2013;25(20):2849–53.
[95] Szente L, Szemán J. Cyclodextrins in analytical chemistry: host–guest type molecular recognition. ACS Publications; 2013.
[96] Choi SG, Lee S-E, Kang B-S, Ng CL, Davaa E, Park J-S. Thermosensitive and mucoadhesive sol-gel composites of paclitaxel/dimethyl-β-cyclodextrin for buccal delivery. PLoS One 2014;9(10), e109090.
[97] Morabito A, Costanzo R, Rachiglio AM, Pasquale R, Sandomenico C, Franco R, et al. Activity of gefitinib in a non–small-cell lung cancer patient with both activating and resistance EGFR mutations. J Thorac Oncol 2013;8(7):e59–60.
[98] Oda M, Saitoh H, Kobayashi M, Aungst BJ. β-Cyclodextrin as a suitable solubilizing agent for in situ absorption study of poorly water-soluble drugs. Int J Pharm 2004;280(1–2):95–102.
[99] Torne S, Darandale S, Vavia P, Trotta F, Cavalli R. Cyclodextrin-based nanosponges: effective nanocarrier for tamoxifen delivery. Pharm Dev Technol 2013;18(3):619–25.
[100] Yallapu MM, Jaggi M, Chauhan SC. β-Cyclodextrin-curcumin self-assembly enhances curcumin delivery in prostate cancer cells. Colloids Surf B Biointerfaces 2010;79(1):113–25.

[101] Park C, Youn H, Kim H, Noh T, Kook YH, Oh ET, et al. Cyclodextrin-covered gold nanoparticles for targeted delivery of an anti-cancer drug. J Mater Chem 2009;19(16):2310–5.
[102] Davis ME. The first targeted delivery of siRNA in humans via a self-assembling, cyclodextrin polymer-based nanoparticle: from concept to clinic. Mol Pharm 2009;6(3):659–68.
[103] Sharker SM, Kim SM, Kim SH, In I, Lee H, Park SY. Target delivery of β-cyclodextrin/paclitaxel complexed fluorescent carbon nanoparticles: externally NIR light and internally pH sensitive-mediated release of paclitaxel with bio-imaging. J Mater Chem B 2015;3(28):5833–41.
[104] Králová J, Kejik Z, Briza T, Poucková P, Kral A, Martásek P, et al. Porphyrin–cyclodextrin conjugates as a nanosystem for versatile drug delivery and multimodal cancer therapy. J Med Chem 2010;53(1):128–38.
[105] Prajapati VD, Jani GK, Khanda SM. Pullulan: an exopolysaccharide and its various applications. Carbohydr Polym 2013;95(1):540–9.
[106] Wang J, Dou B, Bao Y. Efficient targeted pDNA/siRNA delivery with folate–low-molecular-weight polyethyleneimine–modified pullulan as non-viral carrier. Mater Sci Eng C 2014;34:98–109.
[107] Vijayendra S, Shamala T. Film forming microbial biopolymers for commercial applications—a review. Crit Rev Biotechnol 2014;34(4):338–57.
[108] Yuan R, Zheng F, Zhong S, Tao X, Zhang Y, Gao F, et al. Self-assembled nanoparticles of glycyrrhetic acid-modified pullulan as a novel carrier of curcumin. Molecules 2014;19(9):13305–18.
[109] Yim H, Park S-J, Bae YH, Na K. Biodegradable cationic nanoparticles loaded with an anticancer drug for deep penetration of heterogeneous tumours. Biomaterials 2013;34(31):7674–82.
[110] Kageyama S, Wada H, Muro K, Niwa Y, Ueda S, Miyata H, et al. Dose-dependent effects of NY-ESO-1 protein vaccine complexed with cholesteryl pullulan (CHP-NY-ESO-1) on immune responses and survival benefits of esophageal cancer patients. J Transl Med 2013;11(1):1–10.
[111] Muraoka D, Harada N, Hayashi T, Tahara Y, Momose F, Sawada S-I, et al. Nanogel-based immunologically stealth vaccine targets macrophages in the medulla of lymph node and induces potent antitumor immunity. ACS Nano 2014;8(9):9209–18.
[112] Wang J, Cui S, Bao Y, Xing J, Hao W. Tocopheryl pullulan-based self assembling nanomicelles for anti-cancer drug delivery. Mater Sci Eng C 2014;43:614–21.
[113] Yang W, Wang M, Ma L, Li H, Huang L. Synthesis and characterization of biotin modified cholesteryl pullulan as a novel anticancer drug carrier. Carbohydr Polym 2014;99:720–7.
[114] Lu D, Wen X, Liang J, Gu Z, Zhang X, Fan Y. A pH-sensitive nano drug delivery system derived from pullulan/doxorubicin conjugate. J Biomed Mater Res B Appl Biomater 2009;89(1):177–83.
[115] Li H, Bian S, Huang Y, Liang J, Fan Y, Zhang X. High drug loading pH-sensitive pullulan-DOX conjugate nanoparticles for hepatic targeting. J Biomed Mater Res A 2014;102(1):150–9.
[116] Wang Y, Chen H, Liu Y, Wu J, Zhou P, Wang Y, et al. pH-sensitive pullulan-based nanoparticle carrier of methotrexate and combretastatin A4 for the combination therapy against hepatocellular carcinoma. Biomaterials 2013;34(29):7181–90.
[117] Rekha M, Sharma CP. Hemocompatible pullulan–polyethyleneimine conjugates for liver cell gene delivery: in vitro evaluation of cellular uptake, intracellular trafficking and transfection efficiency. Acta Biomater 2011;7(1):370–9.
[118] Zhang H, Li F, Yi J, Gu C, Fan L, Qiao Y, et al. Folate-decorated maleilated pullulan–doxorubicin conjugate for active tumor-targeted drug delivery. Eur J Pharm Sci 2011;42(5):517–26.

[119] Scomparin A, Salmaso S, Bersani S, Satchi-Fainaro R, Caliceti P. Novel folated and non-folated pullulan bioconjugates for anticancer drug delivery. Eur J Pharm Sci 2011;42(5):547–58.
[120] Bae B-C, Na K. Self-quenching polysaccharide-based nanogels of pullulan/folate-photosensitizer conjugates for photodynamic therapy. Biomaterials 2010;31(24):6325–35.
[121] Pawar SN, Edgar KJ. Alginate derivatization: a review of chemistry, properties and applications. Biomaterials 2012;33(11):3279–305.
[122] Hasnain MS, Jameel E, Mohanta B, Dhara AK, Alkahtani S, Nayak AK. Alginates: sources, structure, and properties. In: Nayak AK, Hasnain MS, editors. Alginates in drug delivery. United States: Academic Press, Elsevier Inc.; 2020. p. 1–17.
[123] Nayak AK, Ansari MT, Sami F, Balvir Singh HK, Hasnain MS. Alginates as drug delivery excipients. In: Nayak AK, Hasnain MS, editors. Alginates in drug delivery. United States: Academic Press, Elsevier Inc.; 2020. p. 19–39.
[124] Ray P, Maity M, Barik H, Sahoo GS, Hasnain MS, Hoda MN, Nayak AK. Alginate-based hydrogels for drug delivery applications. In: Nayak AK, Hasnain MS, editors. Alginates in drug delivery. United States: Academic Press, Elsevier Inc.; 2020. p. 41–70.
[125] Hasnain MS, Ray P, Nayak AK. Alginate-based interpenetrating polymer networks for sustained drug release. In: Nayak AK, Hasnain MS, editors. Alginates in drug delivery. United States: Academic Press, Elsevier Inc.; 2020. p. 101–28.
[126] Hasnain MS, Nayak AK, Kurakula M, Hoda MN. Alginate nanoparticles in drug delivery. In: Nayak AK, Hasnain MS, editors. Alginates in drug delivery. United States: Academic Press, Elsevier Inc.; 2020. p. 129–52.
[127] Chowdhury S, Chakraborty S, Maity M, Hasnain MS, Nayak AK. Biocomposites of alginates in drug delivery. In: Nayak AK, Hasnain MS, editors. Alginates in drug delivery. United States: Academic Press, Elsevier Inc.; 2020. p. 153–85.
[128] Das S, Pattanayak D, Nayak AK, Yi DK, Nanda SS, Ansari MT, Hasnain MS. Alginate–montmorillonite composite systems as sustained drug delivery carriers. In: Nayak AK, Hasnain MS, editors. Alginates in drug delivery. United States: Academic Press, Elsevier Inc.; 2020. p. 187–201.
[129] Nayak AK, Hasnain MS. Ionotropically gelled alginate particles in sustained drug release. In: Nayak AK, Hasnain MS, editors. Alginates in drug delivery. United States: Academic Press, Elsevier Inc.; 2020. p. 203–30.
[130] Hasnain MS, Ahmed SA, Behera A, Alkahtani S, Nayak AK. Inorganic materials–alginate composites in drug delivery. In: Nayak AK, Hasnain MS, editors. Alginates in drug delivery. United States: Academic Press, Elsevier Inc.; 2020. p. 231–56.
[131] Mohanta BC, Javed MN, Hasnain MS, Nayak AK. Polyelectrolyte complexes of alginate for controlling drug release. In: Nayak AK, Hasnain MS, editors. Alginates in drug delivery. United States: Academic Press, Elsevier Inc.; 2020. p. 297–321.
[132] Sosnik A. Alginate particles as platform for drug delivery by the oral route: state-of-the-art. Int Sch Res Notices 2014;2014, 926157.
[133] Huebsch N, Kearney CJ, Zhao X, Kim J, Cezar CA, Suo Z, et al. Ultrasound-triggered disruption and self-healing of reversibly cross-linked hydrogels for drug delivery and enhanced chemotherapy. Proc Natl Acad Sci 2014;111(27):9762–7.
[134] Sikorski P, Mo F, Skjåk-Bræk G, Stokke BT. Evidence for egg-box-compatible interactions in calcium– alginate gels from fiber X-ray diffraction. Biomacromolecules 2007;8(7):2098–103.
[135] Abou Taleb MF, Alkahtani A, Mohamed SK. Radiation synthesis and characterization of sodium alginate/chitosan/hydroxyapatite nanocomposite hydrogels: a drug delivery system for liver cancer. Polym Bull 2015;72(4):725–42.
[136] Liao Y-T, Liu C-H, Yu J, Wu KC. Liver cancer cells: targeting and prolonged-release drug carriers consisting of mesoporous silica nanoparticles and alginate microspheres. Int J Nanomedicine 2014;9:2767.

[137] Ma HL, Xu YF, Qi XR, Maitani Y, Nagai T. Superparamagnetic iron oxide nanoparticles stabilized by alginate: pharmacokinetics, tissue distribution, and applications in detecting liver cancers. Int J Pharm 2008;354(1–2):217–26.

[138] Boekhoven J, Zha RH, Tantakitti F, Zhuang E, Zandi R, Newcomb CJ, et al. Alginate–peptide amphiphile core–shell microparticles as a targeted drug delivery system. RSC Adv 2015;5(12):8753–6.

[139] Goren A, Dahan N, Goren E, Baruch L, Machluf M. Encapsulated human mesenchymal stem cells: a unique hypoimmunogenic platform for long-term cellular therapy. FASEB J 2010;24(1):22–31.

[140] Das RK, Kasoju N, Bora U. Encapsulation of curcumin in alginate-chitosan-pluronic composite nanoparticles for delivery to cancer cells. Nanomed Nanotechnol Biol Med 2010;6(1):153–60.

[141] Bhunchu S, Rojsitthisak P. Biopolymeric alginate-chitosan nanoparticles as drug delivery carriers for cancer therapy. Pharmazie 2014;69(8):563–70.

[142] Kobayashi M, Sakane M, Abe T, Ikoma T, Ochiai N. Anti-tumor effect of a local delivery system; hydroxyapatite-alginate beads of paclitaxel. Bioceram Dev Appl 2012;2:D110193.

[143] Kanwar JR, Mahidhara G, Kanwar RK. Novel alginate-enclosed chitosan–calcium phosphate-loaded iron-saturated bovine lactoferrin nanocarriers for oral delivery in colon cancer therapy. Nanomedicine 2012;7(10):1521–50.

[144] Batyrbekov YO, Rakhimbaeva D, Musabekov K, Zhubanov B. Alginate based microparticle drug delivery systems for the treatment of eye cancer. MRS Online Proc Libr 2009;1209(1):1–6.

[145] Brulé S, Levy M, Wilhelm C, Letourneur D, Gazeau F, Ménager C, et al. Doxorubicin release triggered by alginate embedded magnetic nanoheaters: a combined therapy. Adv Mater 2011;23(6):787–90.

[146] Ciofani G, Riggio C, Raffa V, Menciassi A, Cuschieri A. A bi-modal approach against cancer: magnetic alginate nanoparticles for combined chemotherapy and hyperthermia. Med Hypotheses 2009;73(1):80–2.

[147] Cohen R, Orlova Y, Kovalev M, Ungar Y, Shimoni E. Structural and functional properties of amylose complexes with genistein. J Agric Food Chem 2008;56(11):4212–8.

[148] Malafaya PB, Silva GA, Reis RL. Natural–origin polymers as carriers and scaffolds for biomolecules and cell delivery in tissue engineering applications. Adv Drug Deliv Rev 2007;59(4–5):207–33.

[149] Arora D, Sharma N, Sharma V, Abrol V, Shankar R, Jaglan S. An update on polysaccharide-based nanomaterials for antimicrobial applications. Appl Microbiol Biotechnol 2016;100(6):2603–15.

[150] Wilson PJ, Basit AW. Exploiting gastrointestinal bacteria to target drugs to the colon: an in vitro study using amylose coated tablets. Int J Pharm 2005;300(1–2):89–94.

[151] Siew LF, Basit AW, Newton JM. The potential of organic-based amylose-ethylcellulose film coatings as oral colon-specific drug delivery systems. AAPS PharmSciTech 2000;1(3):53–61.

[152] Fujii H, Shin-Ya M, Takeda S, Hashimoto Y, Mukai SA, Sawada SI, et al. Cycloamylose-nanogel drug delivery system-mediated intratumor silencing of the vascular endothelial growth factor regulates neovascularization in tumor microenvironment. Cancer Sci 2014;105(12):1616–25.

CHAPTER

15

Delivery of genes and growth factors using tailor-made polysaccharides

Mrunali Patil[a], *Mohd Usman Mohd Siddique*[a], *Abdullah Sheriker*[b], *Azim Ansari*[a], *Sameer N. Goyal*[b], *Md Saquib Hasnain*[c], *and Amit Kumar Nayak*[d]

[a]Department of Pharmaceutical Chemistry, Shri Vile Parle Kelavani Mandal's Institute of Pharmacy, Dhule, Maharashtra, India, [b]Department of Pharmacology, Shri Vile Parle Kelavani Mandal's Institute of Pharmacy, Dhule, Maharashtra, India, [c]Department of Pharmacy, Palamau Institute of Pharmacy, Daltonganj, Jharkhand, India, [d]Department of Pharmaceutics, Seemanta Institute of Pharmaceutical Sciences, Jharpokharia, Mayurbhanj, Odisha, India

1 Introduction

Therapeutic management of cancers using gene therapy offers many advantages related to its greater effectiveness along with fewer potential adverse events. Unfortunately, due to limited knowledge of the gene-delivery vectors, this system of therapy is not widely used [1–3]. Different naturally occurring polysaccharide macromolecules contain monosaccharides, joined together by O-glycosidic bonds. These polysaccharides are widely obtained from sources such as plants, animals, microbes, and marine sources, and are frequently used as carrier biomaterials for effective optimization of gene delivery systems in pharmacotherapy for various diseases like cancers [4–7]. Furthermore, nanomedicines have been successfully developed using these polysaccharides. These polysaccharide-based nanocarriers are beneficial in the transportation of a wide variety of medicines like proteins, peptides, antibiotics, anticancer agents, and nucleic

Tailor-Made Polysaccharides in Drug Delivery
https://doi.org/10.1016/B978-0-12-821286-8.00014-8

acids, via different routes of administration. As compared to synthetic polymers, these natural polysaccharides exhibit more compatible properties for the delivery of therapeutic agents [5,8–12]. Surprisingly, the present research is more directed on the polysaccharide-based nanoformulations as delivery systems for drugs, genes, and other biologicals to treat a number of diseases.

2 Polysaccharides

As a naturally available biopolymer, the molecular structure of polysaccharides is generally composed of linear or branched structures, containing many monosaccharides joined together by O-glycosidic bonds [13]. The structural formula for a naturally available polysaccharide is $Cx(H_2O)y$, where x is 200–2500. Humans, animals, plants, microbes, and algae are regarded as sources of polysaccharides, as shown in Fig. 1. Therapeutically, polysaccharides have excellent efficacy, as they play a vital role in the development of structure, cellular recognition, inter- and intracellular communication, injury protection, cell adhesion, and modulation of the stimulus response. Currently, polysaccharides are widely used as potential drug delivery carrier materials, biologically active ingredients, and excipients to accelerate drug delivery [13,14]. The other semisynthetic products, like starch acetate, methylcellulose, chitosan sulfate, carboxymethylcellulose, ethyl pullulan, etc., are also being obtained from polysaccharides via tailoring of polysaccharide structures using a chemical modification process. Furthermore, polysaccharides also modulate immunogenic, hemostasis, fertilization, and pathological responses and play a vital role in growth and

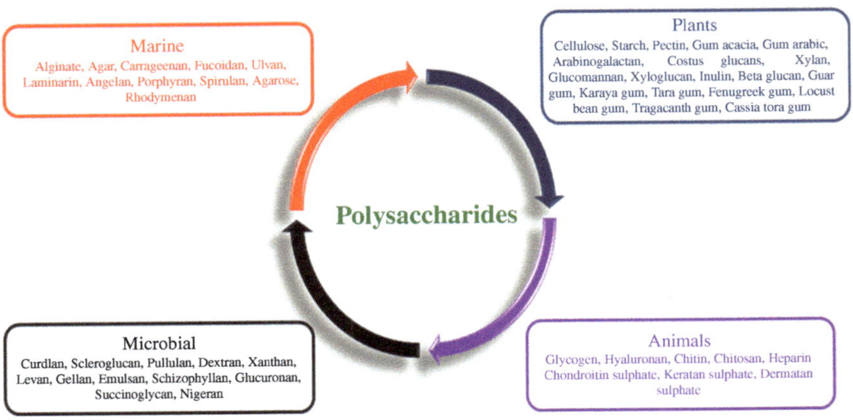

FIG. 1 Various sources of polysaccharides, including plants, animals, marine sources, and microbials, with examples.

development. Principally, polysaccharides are commercially available in natural, synthetic, and modified forms [15,16].

The most important advantages of certain polysaccharides as biopolymers for biomedical applications are: biodegradability, biocompatibility, ease of chemical modification and processibility, abundant availability from natural resources, and low production/extraction cost (Fig. 2). The natural polysaccharides, obtained from several natural resources, are frequently used in drug delivery because of their safe and biocompatible profile [17]. Chemically, polysaccharides possess different molecular structures. Therefore they are easily subjected to chemical modifications (tailoring of the structure) due to the presence of a wide variety of functional groups in their backbone structure [18–20].

2.1 Chitosan

Chitosan (CS) is usually obtained from chitin, which is a deacetylated cationic linear polymer of chitin [21]. Structurally, the CS backbone consists of two types of principal copolymers, such as β-(1–4)-glucosamine with a randomly located *N*-acetyl-D-glucosamine unit. These copolymers are 2-amino-2-deoxy-D-glucopyranose (GlcN or D units) and 2-acetamido-2-deoxy-D-glucopyranose units (GlcAc or A units) linked by a β(1 → 4) glycosidic bond [17]. An extensive study revealed that CS has potential beneficial drug delivery ability, as it is regarded as biodegradable, biocompatible, nonantigenic, harmless, and biofunctional. The chemical solubility of CS is different, as it is readily soluble in acidic solvents with pH less than 6.0, whereas it is insoluble in polar solvents like water. Also, it

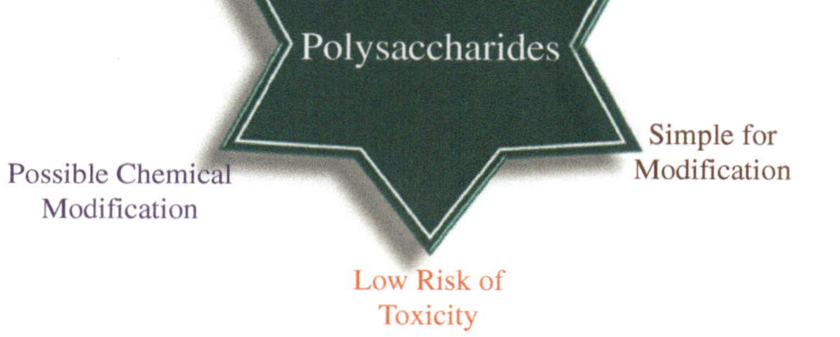

FIG. 2 Advantages of polysaccharides as biopolymers for biomedical applications.

shows different solubility characteristics among different inorganic acid solvents. CS is completely soluble in 1% hydrochloric acid, aqueous, and several organic solvents, but it is insoluble in solvents like sulfuric acid and phosphoric acid, creating tremendous scope for its chemical modification [21–23].

2.2 Dextran

The glucose unit with α-(1,6)-glucan in its 3 position results in the development of the high molecular weight compound dextran. Culture of lactic acid-producing bacteria like *Leuconostoc mesenteroides* NRRL B-512 is being used for dextran synthesis [24,25]. Dextran is soluble in a variety of organic solvents like water. In order to target the colon for drug delivery, an anaerobic gram-negative intestinal bacteria synthesized dextran-degrading enzymes, which could play a potential role in the preparation of dextran-derived nanoparticles [26,27].

2.3 Cellulose

The cell wall of plants, algae, fungi, and bacteria is derived from cellulose, which is regarded as a primary structural unit. The molecular structure of cellulose is made from glucose units that are joined together by β-glycosidic bond linkage, forming a highly organized fibrillar backbone [28]. It has greater rigidity due to the presence of inter- and intramolecular hydrogen bonding between the hydroxyl groups [28,29].

2.4 Alginates

Alginate, a linear chain anionic polysaccharide, is alternatively arranged residues of 1,4-linked β-D-mannuronic acid (M) and α-L-guluronic acid (G) [30,31]. Alginate is principally obtained from brown algae and bacteria such as *Pseudomonas* and *Azotobacter*, which are widely used for the synthesis of acetylated alginate. Factors such as composition, sequence, and molecular weight determine the physical characteristics of alginate [32]. Because of its biocompatibility, biodegradability, and hydrophilic and greater mucoadhesive nature, alginate is widely employed as a biopolymeric excipient in the development of many dosage forms for delivery of numerous drugs [33–36].

2.5 Hyaluronic acid

Hyaluronic acid or hyaluronate (HA) is a natural polymer available in various biological fluids. The backbone of HA is composed of *N*-acetyl-D-glucosamine and glucuronic acid subunits, which help in encapsulation of cells with sustained-release potential [37]. The potential unit of HA, hyaluronan, is responsible for the hydrodynamic properties of HA, like viscosity and water-absorbing ability. Also, it is a water miscible, biodegradable, biocompatible, and anti-antigenic polymer and it can be chemically modified. Because of its excellent viscoelastic characteristics, it is widely employed in the preparation of viscoelastic gels, soft/stiff hydrogels, porous sponges, etc. [38,39].

2.6 Fucoidan

Structurally, fucoidan is a sulfated polysaccharide. Usually, it is found in brown algae in the fucose and sulfate forms [40]. Fucoidan possesses a potential antioxidant property, as it causes the elevation of glutathione, superoxide dismutase, and glutathione peroxidase, which significantly alleviate acetaminophen-induced lung damage. Therapeutically, wound care products containing fucoidan have a greater tendency to interact with several macromolecules present in biological systems, where they cause cell adhesion, migration, and proliferation [40]. In the research carried out by Aisa et al. with cell lines of human lymphoma HS-sultan, it was observed that fucoidan significantly attenuated cell proliferation and also facilitated the mitochondrial pathway of apoptosis, exhibiting a potential anticancer property [41]. Similarly, Purnima et al. explored a fucoidan-based 3D scaffold in combination with VEGF in the management of ischemia, where it was significantly associated with acceleration of neovascularization in mice and enhancement of the process of angiogenesis [38,42,43].

2.7 Cyclodextrin

The enzymatic conversion of starch produces natural cyclodextrins (CDs), which contain α-(1,4) linked-glucopyranosyl cyclic oligomeric derivatives [20,24]. There are three types of CD, namely α, β, and γ CDs, which are derived from six, seven, and eight glucose units, respectively. The extracellular surface of CD is hydrophilic in nature and its hydrophobic cavity allows the movement of lipophilic substances across the membrane. This unique feature of CD plays a vital role in the enhancement of the bioavailability of poorly soluble or biodegradable drugs by facilitating their transportation across the biological membrane [20,24].

2.8 Pullulan

The neutral homopolysaccharide pullulan is obtained from starch with the help of the fungal strain of *Aureobasidium pullulans*, and it contains maltriose subunits, which are joined together by an α-(1, 6) bond. It is widely used in the food and pharmaceutical industries because it has extraordinary physicochemical properties, such as enhanced aqueous solubility and adhesiveness with minimal viscosity in water [44].

2.9 Arabinogalactan

Structurally, the backbone of arabinogalactan contains galactose and arabinose subunits, and it is a highly branched neutral polysaccharide. Usually, arabinogalactan is obtained from the larix tree and it is 99.9% pure with additional enhanced physicochemical properties. It is widely employed as a potential drug carrier because it shows 70% aqueous solubility with improved biocompatibility, biodegradability, and conjugation characteristics [45,46].

3 Gene therapy and applications of tailor-made polysaccharides for gene delivery

Useful peptides or proteins are synthesized for gene therapy, where genetic materials are usually introduced into the cell. Fundamentally, gene therapy is dependent on effective transportation of genetic material along with its efficient expression and production of the desired proteins within the cell [47]. The majority of defective gene-induced diseases are successfully treated with the help of gene therapy [1,4]. The specific cell target approach of gene therapy involves various underlying mechanisms, including activation, silencing, and in vivo/in vitro presentation of gene knockup or knockdown [2]. Gene therapy is regarded as a promising alternative therapeutic system of medicine for the effective management of different clinical abnormalities, to replace conventional drugs [3]. The various physical methods or specific carrier systems like vectors are developed for the introduction of desired genetic material into the cell nucleus. The various methods are of interest, such as direct cell electroporation, injection of DNA, and gene vector systems [1,4]. Both viral and nonviral carrier systems for drug delivery are generally used in gene therapy. Despite an efficient gene delivery ability, viral vectors are not as frequently used, as they cause inflammatory and immunogenic reactions [45,46]. On the other hand, nonviral vectors are easily prepared, can deliver high molecular weight genes, and have a lesser tendency to cause immunogenic reactions [48,49]. Despite the greater efficacy and lesser clinical toxicity, the general practice of gene therapy is restricted because of the failure to develop efficient gene delivery vector systems. Apart from this, the cationic polymers and lipid-derived nonviral gene vectors are alternatively employed in cancer pharmacotherapy. However, the clinical utility of these polymer systems is limited because of their reduced gene expression ability, creating a tremendous opportunity to develop potential carrier material systems with improved gene expression ability. The free nucleic acids are administered by intratumoral and intramuscular routes of drug administration in order to prevent their plasma enzyme-induced degradation. The unmasked nucleic acids are not suitable candidates for gene therapy, as they undergo rapid degradation and clearance phenomena, follow a wide distribution pattern, and are not effectively taken up by cells. Hence, there is tremendous scope for the development of nontoxic and efficient gene delivery systems, which creates major opportunities for researchers to produce target-specific gene delivery systems for the management of different diseases [11].

Gene delivery systems are promising therapeutic systems for the eradication of many inherited genetic abnormalities and acquired diseases that modulate the cellular function. Among the highlighted disorders successfully treated with the use of gene therapy are cystic fibrosis, emphysema, retinitis pigmentosa, sickle cell anemia, phenylketonuria, hemophilia, Duchenne muscular dystrophy, various types of cancers, vascular disease, neurodegenerative disorders, and inflammatory conditions [50]. Polysaccharide-derived tissue-specific gene delivery systems have good compatibility with human body systems and can play an important role in the eradication of different types of diseases with minimal clinical toxicity. For the efficient delivery of genes, a wide variety of polysaccharides such as dextran, pullulan, hyaluronan, chitosan, etc., are used. For the target-specific delivery of genes, an emulsion of HA microspheres was prepared by a cross-linking method. The conjugated HA microspheres were derivatized with HuEP5C7.g2, a humanized monoclonal antibody for E- and P-selectin with the help of protein A, and the developed system demonstrated facilitation of adhesion and expression of E- and P-selectin receptors. The adipicdihydrazide-based cross-linked HA caused a controlled-release pattern of DNA over a period of 60 days. Initially, microsphere injection caused the rapid release of DNA, followed by a greater degree of transfection of DNA after 14 days [50].

The nucleic acids readily undergo a degradation process, so are delivered with the help of nonviral gene vectors for their greater penetration into cancer cells. The nonviral gene vectors are generally classified as polyplex, lipoplex, hybrids of lipid-based polymer (lipopolyplex), and both organic and inorganic hybrid vectors. Fundamentally, organic hybrid vectors are biodegradable, exhibit good compatibility with biological systems, and have efficient functional ability. Likewise, the inorganic hybrid vectors are also considered to be promising delivery systems, as they are both chemically and thermally stable, and exhibit the desired size, shape, and structure. The delivery of cancer genes by using nonviral vectors is described in Fig. 3. Generally, examples of nonviral vectors employed

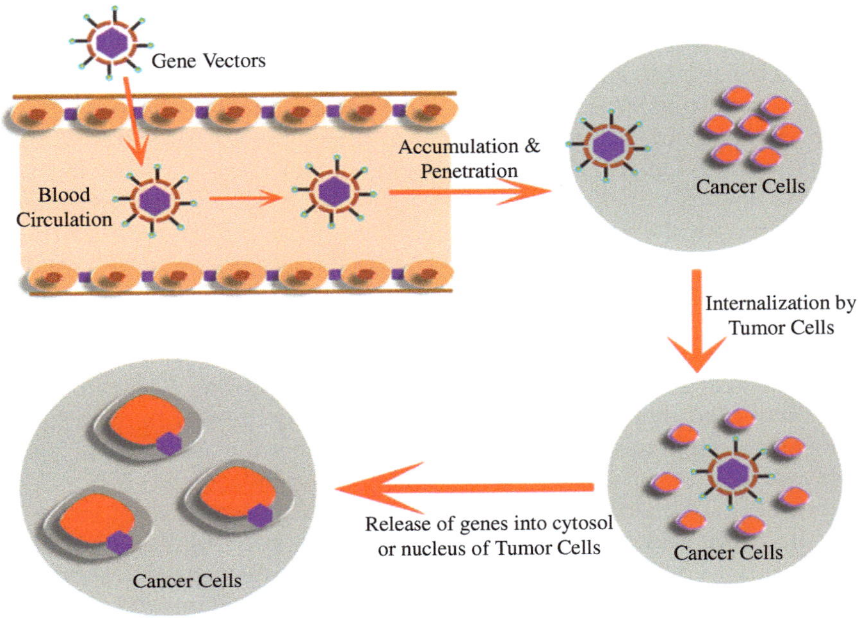

FIG. 3 Delivery of cancer gene using nonviral vectors.

for tumor gene delivery are cationic polymers, cationic lipids, and inorganic nanoparticles [51–53]. Important applications of polysaccharides in gene therapy include polysaccharide composites and nanomaterials, nanocomplexes, nanogels, polymeric biomaterials for cartilage repair, polysaccharide vectors, proteins, and peptides, among others (Fig. 4). Polysaccharide-mediated gene delivery and growth factor delivery are illustrated in Fig. 5.

The physicochemical properties of polysaccharides can be easily modified; hence, these agents are considered as having potential for delivery on nonviral genes [38,54]. Also, polysaccharides have a greater tendency to modify the large genes into compact subunits and to cover the influence of the negative charge of DNA [55]. An electrostatic interaction between ionic polysaccharides and DNA results in the formation of a polymer-DNA complex, which is also called a polyplex. Polysaccharide nanoparticles are being prepared by a molecular condensation process in which positively charged nonviral vectors interact with polyplexes in order to reduce the molecular size of pDNA. The formed condensed DNA-vector nanoparticles have little positive charge, which helps in their electrostatic interaction and internalization with the cell membrane. Followed by their entry into the cell, these polyplexes escape the mechanism of endosomes and undergo a

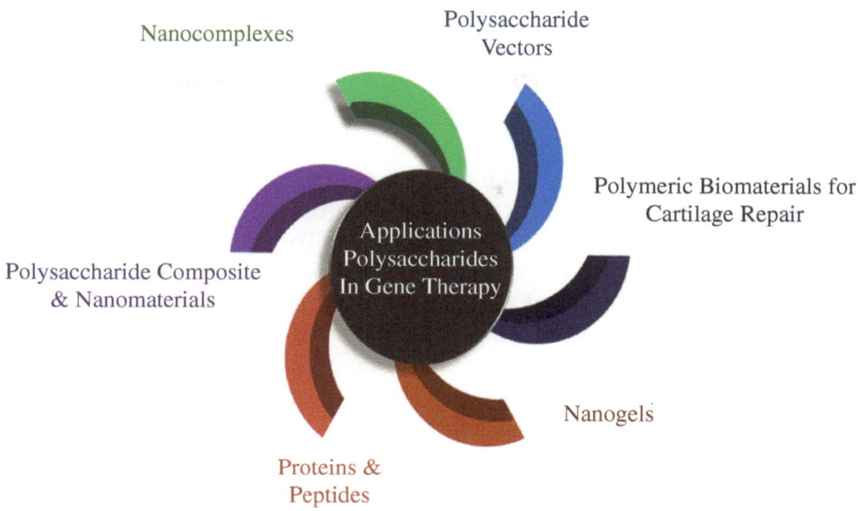

FIG. 4 Various applications of polysaccharides in gene therapy.

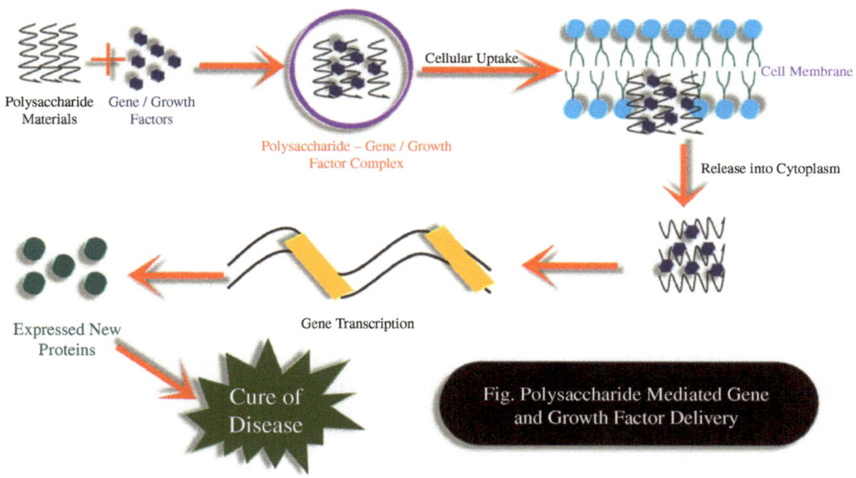

FIG. 5 Polysaccharide-mediated gene and growth delivery factor.

dissociation process in order to release the nucleic acid content into the nucleus for gene expression [56]. Furthermore, polysaccharides such as chitosan allow electrostatic interaction with negatively charged DNA, thereby preventing their degradation by nuclease [4]. Both natural (e.g., chitosan, cyclodextrin, and dextran) and semisynthetic derivatives (e.g., dextran spermine) of cationic polysaccharides are principally used as polymers in gene delivery [3].

4 Growth factors and applications of tailor-made polysaccharides for growth delivery

Therapeutic regimens involving the use of growth factor (GF) are now becoming a potential fast-growing field in biomedical science. Pharmacotherapy with GF, such as epidermal growth factor (EGF), provides efficient and immediate relief from chronic pain conditions by facilitating the quick healing of wounds [57]. The underlying protective mechanism induced by EGF involves a series of events such as facilitation of regeneration of epidermal and mesenchymal membrane, activation of cell multiplication cascade, and induction of cell motility. Also, it stimulates the repair of damaged epithelial tissue, reduces the risk of infection, and minimizes the period of hospitalization. Despite this, EGF has limited therapeutical utility, as it is associated with certain drawbacks such as having a short half-life period and undergoing quick dilution in body fluids. Furthermore, a hallmark of certain types of cancers such as squamous carcinoma, brain gliomas, and breast cancer is upregulation of EGF receptors. Taking this into consideration, for effective and safe treatment with EGF, there is a need to develop more localized and sustained drug delivery systems [58,59]. In this context, encapsulated liposomes of EGF have been developed to promote their stability and prevent their enzymatic degradation [10]. Growth factor plays a key role in the overall development of the cell through a series of events including cell proliferation and differentiation followed by cell migration. Fundamentally, the growth factors are obtained from tissue, such as platelets in higher concentrations, and act as key factors in the modulation of physiological responses like angiogenesis, wound repair, and immune responses. In this regard, growth factors are successfully encapsulated within α-granules of platelets; however, the exact underlying mechanism is unclear. At any rate, encapsulated growth factors in granules of platelets bring about useful therapeutic benefits characterized by cell proliferation, cell migration, cell signaling and adhesion, and angiogenesis, among others [58,59].

5 Conclusion

The severe and unwanted side effects of traditional anticancer medication are of major concern because they require increased supportive care. This additional cost of treatment increases the financial burden on the patient's family, which finally leads to noncompliance by the cancer patient. Newer medications and methods are always under development, which can overcome this major drawback of cancer therapy. Various newer technologies or procedures are being proposed, accepted, and implemented for cancer management. Among these, gene therapy has major advantages related to its greater effectiveness along with minimal potential adverse events. The tailor-made polysaccharides are widely used carriers for effective delivery of genes in a number of diseases like cancers, immune reactions, and others. This chapter summarizes the use of tailor-made polysaccharides as a gene carrier in cancer. The various tailor-made polysaccharides provide an effective means for delivery of genes, showing their effectiveness in anticancer drug therapy.

References

[1] Zhou Z, Liu X, Zhu D, Wang Y, Zhang Z, Zhou X, Qiu N, Chen X, Shen Y. Nonviral cancer gene therapy: delivery cascade and vector nanoproperty integration. Adv Drug Deliv Rev 2017;115:115–54.

[2] Ngwuluka NC. Responsive polysaccharides and polysaccharides-based nanoparticles for drug delivery. In: Stimuli responsive polymeric nanocarriers for drug delivery applications, vol. 1. Elsevier; 2018. p. 531–54.

[3] Khan W, Hosseinkhani H, Ickowicz D, Hong PD, Yu DS, Domb AJ. Polysaccharide gene transfection agents. Acta Biomater 2012;8(12):4224–32.

[4] Zheng Y, Xie Q, Wang H, Hu Y, Ren B, Li X. Recent advances in plant polysaccharide-mediated nano drug delivery systems. Int J Biol Macromol 2020;165(Pt B):2668–83.

[5] Wang Y, Wang PG. Polysaccharide-based systems in drug and gene delivery. Adv Drug Deliv Rev 2013;9(65):1121–2.

[6] Liu L, Yan Y, Ni D, Wu S, Chen Y, Chen X, Xiong X, Liu G. TAT-functionalized PEI-grafting rice bran polysaccharides for safe and efficient gene delivery. Int J Biol Macromol 2020;146:1076–86.

[7] Barclay TG, Day CM, Petrovsky N, Garg S. Review of polysaccharide particle-based functional drug delivery. Carbohydr Polym 2019;221:94–112.

[8] Deng WW, Cao X, Wang M, Qu R, Su WY, Yang Y, Wei YW, Xu XM, Yu JN. Delivery of a transforming growth factor β-1 plasmid to mesenchymal stem cells via cationized *Pleurotus eryngii* polysaccharide nanoparticles. Int J Nanomedicine 2012;7:1297–311.

[9] Kumari L, Badwaik HR. Polysaccharide-based nanogels for drug and gene delivery. In: Polysaccharide carriers for drug delivery. Elsevier; 2019. p. 497–557.

[10] Kaminski GA, Sierakowski MR, Pontarolo R, Santos LA, de Freitas RA. Layer-by-layer polysaccharide-coated liposomes for sustained delivery of epidermal growth factor. Carbohydr Polym 2016;140:129–35.

[11] Takakura Y, Nishikawa M, Yamashita F, Hashida M. Development of gene drug delivery systems based on pharmacokinetic studies. Eur J Pharm Sci 2001;13(1):71–6.

[12] Yang R, Chen F, Guo J, Zhou D, Luan S. Recent advances in polymeric biomaterials-based gene delivery for cartilage repair. Bioact Mater 2020;5(4):990–1003.

[13] Maity M, Hasnain MS, Nayak AK, Aminabavi TM. Biomedical applications of polysaccharides. In: Nayak AK, Hasnain MS, Aminabhavi TM, editors. Tailor-made polysaccharides in biomedical applications. USA: Academic Press, Elsevier Inc.; 2021. p. 1–34.

[14] Nayak AK, Hasnain MS, Dhara AK, Pal D. Plant polysaccharides in pharmaceutical applications. In: Pal D, Nayak AK, editors. Bioactive natural products for pharmaceutical applications. Advanced structured materials, vol. 140. Cham: Springer; 2021. p. 93–125.

[15] Muhamad II, Lazim NAM, Selvakumaran S. Natural polysaccharide-based composites for drug delivery and biomedical applications. In: Hasnain MS, Nayak AK, editors. Natural polysaccharides in drug delivery and biomedical applications. United States: Academic Press, Elsevier Inc.; 2019. p. 419–40.

[16] Nayak AK, Ahmed SA, Tabish M, Hasnain MS. Natural polysaccharides in tissue engineering application. In: Hasnain MS, Nayak AK, editors. Natural polysaccharides in drug delivery and biomedical applications. United States: Academic Press, Elsevier Inc.; 2019. p. 531–48.
[17] Ng JY, Obuobi S, Chua ML, Zhang C, Hong S, Kumar Y, Gokhale R, Ee PLR. Biomimicry of microbial polysaccharide hydrogels for tissue engineering and regenerative medicine—a review. Carbohydr Polym 2020;241:116345.
[18] Alkahtani S, Hasnain MS, Nayak AK, Aminabhavi TM. Polysaccharide-based polyelectrolyte complex systems for biomedical uses. In: Nayak AK, Hasnain MS, Aminabhavi TM, editors. Tailor-made polysaccharides in biomedical applications. USA: Academic Press, Elsevier Inc.; 2021. p. 151–74.
[19] Nayak AK, Hasnain MS, Tabis M, Aminabhavi TM. Use of tailored polysaccharides in dentistry. In: Nayak AK, Hasnain MS, Aminabhavi TM, editors. Tailor-made polysaccharides in biomedical applications. USA: Academic Press, Elsevier Inc.; 2021. p. 287–304.
[20] Mizrahy S, Peer D. Polysaccharides as building blocks for nanotherapeutics. Chem Soc Rev 2012;41(7):2623–40.
[21] Pal D, Nayak AK, Saha S. Interpenetrating polymer network hydrogels of chitosan: applications in controlling drug release. In: Mondal MIH, editor. Cellulose-based superabsorbent hydrogels. Switzerland: Springer Nature; 2019. p. 1727–68.
[22] Hasnain MS, Nayak AK. Chitosan as responsive polymer for drug delivery applications. In: Makhlouf ASH, Abu-Thabit NY, editors. Stimuli responsive polymeric nanocarriers for drug delivery applications, vol. 1, types and triggers. Woodhead publishing series in biomaterials. United States: Elsevier Ltd.; 2018. p. 581–605.
[23] Ray S, Sinha P, Laha B, Maiti S, Bhattacharyya UK, Nayak AK. Polysorbate 80 coated crosslinked chitosan nanoparticles of ropinirole hydrochloride for brain targeting. J Drug Deliv Sci Technol 2018;48:21–9.
[24] Sinha VR, Kumria R. Polysaccharides in colon-specific drug delivery. Int J Pharm 2001;224(1–2):19–38.
[25] Liu Z, Jiao Y, Wang Y, Zhou C, Zhang Z. Polysaccharides-based nanoparticles as drug delivery systems. Adv Drug Deliv Rev 2008;60(15):1650–62.
[26] Joshy KS, George A, Snigdha S, Joseph B, Kalarikkal N, Pothen LA, Thomas S. Novel core-shell dextran hybrid nanosystem for anti-viral drug delivery. Korean J Couns Psychother 2018;93:864–72.
[27] Huang G, Huang H. Application of dextran as nanoscale drug carriers. Nanomedicine (Lond) 2018;13(24):3149–58.
[28] Abeer MM, Mohd Amin MC, Martin C. A review of bacterial cellulose-based drug delivery systems: their biochemistry, current approaches and future prospects. J Pharm Pharmacol 2014;66(8):1047–61.
[29] Ullah H, Santos HA, Khan T. Applications of bacterial cellulose in food, cosmetics and drug delivery. Cellulose 2016;23(4):2291–314.
[30] Malakar J, Nayak AK, Das A. Modified starch (cationized)-alginate beads containing aceclofenac: formulation optimization using central composite design. Starch-Starke 2013;65:603–12.
[31] Nayak AK, Pal D, Hasnain MS. Development, optimization and *in vitro-in vivo* evaluation of pioglitazone-loaded jackfruit seed starch-alginate beads. Curr Drug Deliv 2013;10:608–19.
[32] Hasnain MS, Jameel E, Mohanta B, Dhara AK, Alkahtani S, Nayak AK. Alginates: sources, structure, and properties. In: Nayak AK, Hasnain MS, editors. Alginates in drug delivery. United States: Academic Press, Elsevier Inc.; 2020. p. 1–17.
[33] George M, Abraham TE. Polyionic hydrocolloids for the intestinal delivery of protein drugs: alginate and chitosan—a review. J Control Release 2006;114(1):1–14.
[34] Gacesa P. Alginates. Carbohydr Polym 1988;8(3):161–82.

[35] Draget KI, Smidsrød O, Skjåk-Bræk G. Alginates from algae. In: Steinbuchel A, Rhee SK, editors. Polysaccharides and polyamides in the food industry: properties, production, and patents. Berlin, Heidelberg: Springer; 2005. p. 1–30.
[36] Hasnain MS, Nayak AK. Alginate-inorganic composite particles as sustained drug delivery matrices. In: Inamuddin, Asiri AM, Mohammad A, editors. Applications of nanocomposite materials in drug delivery. Woodhead publishing series in biomaterials. United States: Elsevier Inc.; 2018. p. 39–74.
[37] Nayak AK, Ansari MT, Pal D, Hasnain MS. Hyaluronic acid (hyaluronan): pharmaceutical applications. In: Nayak AK, Hasnain MS, Pal D, editors. Natural polymers for pharmaceutical applications, vol. III: animal derived polymers. USA: Apple Academic Press; 2019. p. 1–32.
[38] Platt VM, Szoka Jr FC. Anticancer therapeutics: targeting macromolecules and nanocarriers to hyaluronan or CD44, a hyaluronan receptor. Mol Pharm 2008;5(4):474–86.
[39] Vasvani S, Kulkarni P, Rawtani D. Hyaluronic acid: a review on its biology, aspects of drug delivery, route of administrations and a special emphasis on its approved marketed products and recent clinical studies. Int J Biol Macromol 2020;151:1012–29.
[40] Hong SW, Lee HS, Jung KH, Lee H, Hong SS. Protective effect of fucoidan against acetaminophen-induced liver injury. Arch Pharm Res 2012;35(6):1099–105.
[41] Purnama A, Aid-Launais R, Haddad O, Maire M, Mantovani D, Letourneur D, Hlawaty H, Le Visage C. Fucoidan in a 3D scaffold interacts with vascular endothelial growth factor and promotes neovascularization in mice. Drug Deliv Transl Res 2015;5(2):187–97.
[42] Kimura R, Rokkaku T, Takeda S, Senba M, Mori N. Cytotoxic effects of fucoidan nanoparticles against osteosarcoma. Mar Drugs 2013;11(11):4267–78.
[43] Huang Y, Chen J, Lam U, Chen S. Preparing, characterizing, and evaluating chitosan/fucoidan nanoparticles as oral delivery carriers. J Polym Res 2014;21:1–9.
[44] Leathers TD. Biotechnological production and applications of pullulan. Appl Microbiol Biotechnol 2003;62(5):468–73.
[45] Seifert GJ, Roberts K. The biology of arabinogalactan proteins. Annu Rev Plant Biol 2007;58:137–61.
[46] Pinhassi RI, Assaraf YG, Farber S, Stark M, Ickowicz D, Drori S, Domb AJ, Livney YD. Arabinogalactan-folic acid-drug conjugate for targeted delivery and target-activated release of anticancer drugs to folate receptor-overexpressing cells. Biomacromolecules 2010;11(1):294–303.
[47] Azzam T, Raskin A, Makovitzki A, Brem H, Vierling P, Lineal M, Domb AJ. Cationic polysaccharides for gene delivery. Macromolecules 2002;35:9947–53.
[48] Baghdan E, Pinnapireddy SR, Strehlow B, Engelhardt KH, Schäfer J, Bakowsky U. Lipid coated chitosan-DNA nanoparticles for enhanced gene delivery. Int J Pharm 2018;535(1–2):473–9.
[49] Wu S, Ni D, Yan Y, Pan X, Chen X, Guan J, Xiong X, Liu L. Safe and efficient gene delivery based on rice bran polysaccharide. Int J Biol Macromol 2019;137:1041–9.
[50] Nayerossadat N, Maedeh T, Ali PA. Viral and nonviral delivery systems for gene delivery. Adv Biomed Res 2012;1:27.
[51] Schatzlein A. Non-viral vectors in cancer gene therapy: principles and progress. Anticancer Drugs 2001;12(4):275–304.
[52] Mintzer MA, Simanek EE. Nonviral vectors for gene delivery. Chem Rev 2009;109(2):259–302.
[53] Kaneda Y, Tabata Y. Non-viral vectors for cancer therapy. Cancer Sci 2006;97(5):348–54.
[54] Mellet CO, Fernández JMG, Benito JM. Cyclodextrin-based gene delivery systems. Chem Soc Rev 2011;40(3):1586–608.
[55] Dragan ES, Dinu MV. Polysaccharides constructed hydrogels as vehicles for proteins and peptides. A review. Carbohydr Polym 2019;225:115210.
[56] Efthimiadou EK, Metaxa A-F, Kordas G. Modified polysaccharides for drug delivery. Polysacch Bioact Biotechnol 2015;1805–35.

[57] Behm B, Babilas P, Landthaler M, Schreml S. Cytokines, chemokines and growth factors in wound healing. J Eur Acad Dermatol Venereol 2012;26(7):812–20.
[58] Gedda L, Olsson P, Pontén J, Carlsson J. Development and in vitro studies of epidermal growth factor-dextran conjugates for boron neutron capture therapy. Bioconjug Chem 1996;7(5):584–91.
[59] Chen RR, Mooney DJ. Polymeric growth factor delivery strategies for tissue engineering. Pharm Res 2003;20(8):1103–12.

Index

Note: Page numbers followed by *f* indicate figures and *t* indicate tables.

Q

R

S

T

U

V

X

Z

Papier | Fördert gute Waldnutzung
FSC® C083411

Kolibri 360 GmbH
Ferdinand-Jühlke-Straße 7
99095 Erfurt, Deutschland
produktsicherheit@kolibri360.de